The
BOOK *of* KNOWLEDGE
The Children's Encyclopedia

EDITORS-IN-CHIEF

HOLLAND THOMPSON, Ph.D.
The College of the City of New York

ARTHUR MEE
Temple Chambers, London

WITH AN INTRODUCTION BY

JOHN H. FINLEY, LL.D.
Late President of the College of the City of New York
and Commissioner of Education State of New York

DEPARTMENTS

The Earth	The United States
Stories and Legends	Familiar Things
All Countries	Our Own Life
Golden Deeds	The Fine Arts
Helps to Learning	Men and Women
Literature	Poetry and Rhymes
Animal Life	Plant Life
Famous Books	Things to Make
Dominion of Canada	and Things to Do

Book of Wonder

VOLUME XI

New York
THE GROLIER SOCIETY
LONDON: THE EDUCATIONAL BOOK COMPANY

D 11

CONTENTS OF THIS VOLUME

This is a short guide to the principal contents of this volume. It is not possible to give all of the questions in The Book of Wonder, or the titles of all of the Little Verses and Problems, but in all cases the pages are given where such sections of the book begin. In the big Index, Volume 20, you will find every title and every subject, including the pictures.

PAGE

THE BOOK OF THE EARTH
The Stars in Their Brightness . . 3783
What We Know about the Stars . 3921
What Is Happening in the Sky . . 4037

THE BOOK OF PLANT LIFE
Mushrooms, Edible and Poisonous . 3905
Wild Fruits of the Countryside . 4019
The Life of a Tree . . . 4093

THE BOOK OF ANIMAL LIFE
Ducks and Geese . . . 3881
Herons, Storks and Cranes . . 4005
Sea Birds and Their Inland Kin . 4121

THE BOOK OF OUR OWN LIFE
The Eye's Wonderful Curtain . . 3801
Smell and Taste . . . 3955
The Real Master of the Body . . 4065

THE BOOK OF WONDER
Why does the fire go out? . . 3839
What are our eyebrows for? . . 3840
What makes the wind whistle? . 3841
Why have we lines on our hands? . 3842
Why does a bee sting? . . 3843
Where does an apple come from? . 3975
How do fish live in a frozen pond? . 3976
Why are there more stars some nights than others? . . . 3977
Why do we not laugh when we tickle ourselves? . . . 3978
What is smoke made of? . . 3979
Who arranged the days? . . 4131
Why does the whistle change as the train comes nearer? . 4132
Why is it difficult to write on glass? . 4133
Why does the kettle sing? . 4134
Do any people have blue blood? . 4135

THE BOOK OF FAMILIAR THINGS
A Piece of Rope . . . 3791
The Reign of Wooden Ships . 3909
How Fish and Oysters Are Taken . 4051

THE BOOK OF LITERATURE
Great Fiction in Its Full Tide . . 3891
Prose Writers of Our Time . . 3999

PAGE

THE STORY OF THE FINE ARTS
The First Sculptors . . . 3873
The Early Days of Greece . . 3987

THE BOOK OF ALL COUNTRIES
France in Modern Times . . . 3813
Tne Beginnings of Germany . . 3959

THE BOOK OF THE UNITED STATES
The Northeastern States: II . . 3773
Administrations of the Presidents . 3937

THE BOOK OF MEN AND WOMEN
Cromwell and His Men . . . 3845
Two Spies of the Revolution . . 3995
The Story of Frederick the Great . 4043

FAMOUS BOOKS
Les Misérables . . . 3861
The Waverley Novels . . . 4069

THE BOOK OF GOLDEN DEEDS
How Grotius Left the Castle . . 3805
The Brave French Maid of Noyon . 3806
The Devotion of a Roman . . 3806
The Sacrifice of Iphigenia . . 3808
The Mother of the Gracchi . . 3811
A Lithuanian Girl's Quick Wit . 3811
The Girl Who Held the Fort . . 4089
The Man Who Saved St. Helier . 4092

THE BOOK OF STORIES
The Old Couple at the Mill . . 3829
The Princess Who Became a Goose Girl 3830
The Fruit of Happiness . . . 3832
A Fairy Funeral . . . 3836
The Cat and the Parrot . . . 3837
The Story of Faithful John . . 3901
The Shepherd-Maid and the Sweep . 3903
Rum-Pel-Stilt-Skin . . . 3981
The Geese Who Kept Guard of Rome 3982
The Magic Boy Fiddler of Sicily . 3983
Three Nights in the Enchanted Castle 3984
The Story of Fairyfoot . . . 4137
The Dog That Knew His Master . 4139
Undine, the Story of a Water Nymph 4141
La Plus Sage Fille du Wessex . . 4143
Fables of Æsop . . . 3986, 4144
Le Roi, le Noble et le Paysan . . 4144

THE BOOK OF POETRY

SPEECHES FROM SHAKESPEARE

Scenes from Hamlet	3927
The Fall of Cardinal Wolsey	3928
The Great Speech of Mark Antony	3929
The Shepherd's Happy Life	3930
A Great Day for England	3931
The Noblest Roman	3931
The Lesson of the Honey Bees	3931
In Praise of England	3931
A Father's Advice to His Son	3932
Man's Greatest Treasure	3932
The Wayward Daughter's Fate	3932
A Man's Good Name	3932
The Quality of Mercy	3932
Friends and Flatterers	3932
The Light of Our Virtues	3932
The Seven Ages of Man	3933

Wise Sayings from Shakespeare	3933
Songs from Shakespeare	3934–3936
On Sir Philip Sidney	4029
Only a Boy	4030
The Bailiff's Daughter	4030
Time	4030
Envoy	4030
The Coming of Spring	4032
A Parable	4032
Song of Marion's Men	4032
Concord Hymn	4032
A Dedication	4032
Love's Reasonings	4033
Two Men	4033
Why It Was Cold in May	4033
The Poet and the Bird	4033
What Does It Matter?	4033
To a Skylark	4034
Rain on the Roof	4034
Now the Day Is Over	4034
Teeny-Weeny	4036
Henry Hudson's Last Voyage	4109
The Fly-away Horse	4111
Slave and Emperor	4111
Foot Soldiers	4111
The Douglas Tragedy	4112
La Belle Dame sans Merci	4112
Ode to the West Wind	4113
On the Road	4114
At Twilight	4114
Rencontre	4114
In Absence	4114
Fidelity	4115

PAGE

She Is Far from the Land	4115
The Old Familiar Faces	4115
Cuddle Doon	4116
Common Natures	4116
Dispute between Nose and Eyes	4116
Little Verses	4035, 4117–4120

THINGS TO MAKE AND THINGS TO DO

How to preserve flowers	3853
How to make a concrete walk	3854
Outdoor games for boys and girls	3855
Drawing a cat with the aid of two coins	3855
How to make candy at home	3856
How to make old clothes new	3857
How to make your own fire-screen	3858
The game of stickerchief	3859
What is wrong in these pictures?	3860
How to make a useful workbench	4013
Preparing a picnic lunch basket	4015
How to speak by signs	4016
The boy's home museum	4018
How to prevent nails and screws from rusting quickly	4079
The coin and the handkerchief	4080
Dolls of many nations	4081
What to do in trouble	4082
A fleet of little boats	4083
How to keep fruit fresh	4084
A little toy cannon	4085
A whistle that a boy can make	4085
How to know sailing ships	4086
Ices made without a freezer	4088
How to apply paint to wood	4088

FRENCH

Little Picture-Stories	3838, 3998, 4064

COLORED PLATES

Pictures of Beautiful Paris	3825–3828
Sculptures of Egypt and Assyria	3877–3880
Edible American Mushrooms	3904
Poisonous American Fungi	3905
The Light that Explains the Stars	3920
How the Starlight Tells Us of What the Stars Are Made	3921
Executives of the United States	3945–3948
Wild Fruits of the Countryside	4021–4028
The Life of a Tree	4093–4108
Pussy-cat, Where Have You Been?	4117
Old King Cole	4118
Ding Dong Bell, Pussy's in the Well	4120

Photo, Leonard Schwartz, Dover.
The Capitol of Delaware at Dover.

THE NORTHEASTERN STATES
PART II

IN our first story of the Northeastern states we told you something of the geology, the agriculture and the forests of the section. However, only a small part of the population is engaged either in agriculture or lumbering. We come now to mining and manufacturing, which employ a much larger proportion of the people.

CONTINUED FROM 3596

Pennsylvania leads all states in the United States in the value of mineral products, producing 26 per cent of the total output. No other state in this group can be considered as a mining area, since no one of them produces as much as one per cent of the total value of mineral products.

All the anthracite, or hard coal, produced in the United States is found in the Ridge and Valley section of Pennsylvania, with Scranton and Wilkes-Barre as the main centres. Bituminous, or soft, coal is more widely distributed, yet Pennsylvania produces 32 per cent of the total value. Many of the pictures in our story of Coal beginning on page 785 were made in Pennsylvania. Originally this state was the chief petroleum and natural-gas area also, but the wells have been yielding less and less, until to-day the

state stands sixth in this respect. It was the discovery of petroleum in Pennsylvania that put an end to a romantic industry of the Northeast, namely, whaling. Kerosene became so cheap that it was no longer profitable to fit out ships to seek the whale. Limestone is mined in Pennsylvania and New York in quantities, where it is used in part to mix with iron-ore as a flux in the process of separating the iron from the ore.

Although not large in value compared with some other minerals, the marble and the granite quarries of Vermont and the granite of the New England states have a wide reputation. Vermont furnishes nearly half of all the marble produced in the United States. Most of New England is granite; one hears of the "granite hills"; and New Hampshire is called the "Granite State." All of this granite is not of the same value. Most granites that will break into blocks will do for paving-stones, curbstones, and building foundations, but if a stone for a monument or a statue is desired, the rock must have certain definite characteristics. There must be an even texture; that is, all the constituent min-

3773

erals must be of about the same size and preferably of small size. There should be also a uniform color throughout. Again, all granites do not polish with equal ease, and all do not carry lettering with the same degree of clearness. Some of the New England granites are suitable for monuments, statues and inscriptions, and these stones are shipped to distant places. A number of these valuable quarries dot the Northeast. Vermont is the first state, Massachusetts is second, New Hampshire fifth and Maine sixth.

We have seen that the section is not the most important from the standpoint of agriculture and that, except for Pennsylvania, the mineral resources are not large. When we come to manufactures, however, the story is different.

The last Census of the United States tabulates sections of the United States according to the value of their manufactured products. First place is given to the Middle Atlantic states (New York, New Jersey and Pennsylvania), second place to the East North Central states (Wisconsin, Michigan, Illinois, Indiana and Ohio), and third place to New England. This does not tell the whole story. The "value added by manufacture" is even more favorable to this section. Let us see what we mean.

In some goods the factory adds little to the value of the raw material. For example, flour is not worth so very much more than wheat. On the other hand, the cost of the raw material used in making the works of a watch is much less than the price for which the movement sells. We say that the "value added by manufacture" is greater in the second case, and in much of the manufacturing in this section the value of the raw materials is greatly increased by the skilled labor used upon them.

In ranking the states of the United States on this basis it is found that New York leads, Pennsylvania is second, Massachusetts fifth, New Jersey sixth, Connecticut eleventh, and Rhode Island sixteenth. But states differ much in size. A better way to find out how important the manufactures are in the life of a state is to divide the total value added by manufacture by the number of square miles in the state. If we do this we find that Rhode Island leads all the other states. A square mile of this state averages more than any other state.

THE VALUE OF POWER IN MANUFACTURING GOODS

Manufacturing demands power. The hilly character of the land in this section makes possible the artificial damming of streams at short intervals. The glacial invasion, by dumping débris in the valleys, turned many streams from their original courses. These streams, in cutting down their new valleys, found ledges that were not easily worn away and appear now as falls and rapids. Niagara River is a stream which was diverted and now falls over a cliff. These falls and rapids are common in the glaciated area, and early manufacturing concerns found them advantageous as power sites. Some manufacturing villages are named because of falls or rapids, as, for example, Little Falls, New York, and Chicopee Falls, Massachusetts. Later the falls did not furnish enough power for increasing manufacturing, and steam power was substituted in part. Since a large part of the coal of the United States is in this Northeastern section, it continued to hold the advantage. Now the tendency is toward electric power generated by water. But as this type of power can be transported, the factory site may be located at a place which meets other demands of manufacturing.

There is now being considered a plan to unite all the power plants in the Northeast into one big unit. The project is called the Super-power Plan for the area from Boston to Washington. If it should be completed, manufacturing plants will no longer develop their own power. All the water power of the section will be converted into electric power and will be fed into the main and auxiliary lines which will cover most of the Northeast. If any plant needs power, it will only be necessary to tap the main lines and be served with power, somewhat as residences throughout the land are now served with electricity for lighting purposes. By this Super-power Plan there will be developed enough power to run all the factories, all the steam and electric railroads, and to light all places, at a cost considerably under the total spent to-day. If all our railroads and factories were run by electricity we should get rid of the smoke nuisance. But in addition to this comfort, in New England alone it is estimated that such a plan will save many millions of dollars in coal.

MINE AND QUARRY

A coal-mine in the Lykens Valley district of the anthracite region which is in northeastern Pennsylvania. Almost all of the anthracite coal contained in the United States is found in this region, Pennsylvania's entire anthracite field covering an area of almost 470 square miles.

Vermont produces more granite than any other state, and has some noted quarries. This is the "Rock of Ages" quarry near Montpelier, from which great blocks are broken out to be sent over the United States. The state has also much excellent marble.   Photo, Ewing Galloway.

An air view of the heart of Philadelphia, looking east toward the Delaware River. The inset shows the Elverson Building, the home of the Philadelphia Inquirer.　　　© Aero Service Corporation.

The Baldwin Locomotive Works is not only one of the largest but also one of the oldest establishments in the United States. This is the assembling shop at the Eddystone plant, where the monsters are put together. Locomotives in every stage of construction may be seen.

THE CITY OF IRON AND STEEL

This part of Pittsburgh, where the Allegheny (to the right) and the Monongahela rivers come together to form the Ohio, is called the "Golden Triangle" because the leading financial and commercial buildings are here. The resulting congestion of traffic is a great problem. © Aero Service Corporation.

Pittsburgh is the steel centre of America, and the Carnegie Steel Works with the forest of tall chimneys is only one of the many industrial establishments which have made the city famous. © Ewing Galloway.

SOME OF THE OTHER DEMANDS OF MANUFACTURING

Another necessity of manufacturing is raw materials. Very curiously, this area is lacking in this respect. Most of the materials for manufacturing come from distant places. New Jersey, for example, leads the states in three things—dyeing and finishing textiles, smelting copper and refining petroleum. Of these, only the first obtains its materials for manufacture within the borders of the state. Massachusetts leads the states in the manufacture of boots and shoes, rubber boots, cotton and woolen goods. There is another side to the story, however. If raw materials—rubber, for instance—cannot be manufactured in the locality where they grow, then places on regular transportation lines have a distinct advantage. Since the East is one of the gateways of the country, and since practically all the harbors of the East are in the Northeastern section, the other sections of the country are at a disadvantage so far as foreign raw materials are concerned. New York City is the greatest port in the land, and goods of all varieties pass through it. Therefore that city is well located for much raw material of manufacturing.

On the other hand, in an article like cotton, grown in this country, there is a question about the advantages of manufacturing. The cotton-growing states have built many mills, and now they are threatening the supremacy of the Northeast in cotton-manufacturing. The rank by states in 1920 for cotton goods was: Massachusetts, North Carolina, South Carolina, Georgia, Rhode Island and Connecticut. Will the advantage of having the raw material on the spot offset other advantages?

There is another type of raw material that is manufactured at the sources—those of a perishable nature. Canning and preserving, in order of rank by states, is given as follows: California, New Jersey, Maryland, New York and Pennsylvania. Can you tell what is the article handled in each case? Can you tell why?

THE NEED OF MARKETS MUST BE CONSIDERED

A third demand of manufacturing is the market. This is important in some cases. Thus, agricultural implements are manufactured largely in the agricultural section of the country. The order of states is: Illinois, Wisconsin, Indiana, Ohio and New York. But textile-mill machinery is manufactured in mill areas, and the outstanding area for this type is the Northeast. In general, however, the greatest demand for most products is in the area of densest population, and in the United States the belt from Boston to Washington is, above all others, the most densely settled area. This area, then, is the nation's greatest market.

A fourth necessity is a supply of labor. One would not build a cotton-mill in the middle of a desert where there are no people, but in a locality where there are plenty of people to work. If one watches the people pouring out of a large factory at noon it is easy to realize that the workers must be crowded into a limited area, especially if they can go home for dinner. The Northeastern section, then, has three of the four great demands for manufacturing, and these have given the people the opportunity which the poor conditions for agriculture denied them.

THE CONCENTRATION OF INDUSTRIES IN DIFFERENT LOCALITIES

This means that very frequently a single product is manufactured in a single locality, and it is interesting to note how some of the useful things are made almost entirely in this great manufacturing section. Most of the cotton cloth was made here until the Southern states began manufacturing on a large scale. So perhaps in time some of these other products will be made in quantities elsewhere.

Over 75 per cent of the boots and shoes are made in four states—Massachusetts, New York, New Hampshire and Pennsylvania. Massachusetts alone makes 45 per cent of them; 33 per cent of all the boots and shoes are made in six cities—Brockton, Lynn, Haverhill and Boston, all in Massachusetts; New York City; and Manchester, New Hampshire.

Over 90 per cent of the jewelry is made in two centres, one about New York City and the other about Providence, Rhode Island. About 90 per cent of the silk goods of the country is made in Pennsylvania, New Jersey, New York and Connecticut. Paterson, New Jersey, produces 25 per cent of the entire product; 75 per cent of the woolen and worsted goods are made in Massachusetts, Rhode Island, Pennsylvania and New York.

There are many such products which are listed in the Census reports, and they give a very good understanding of the

SOME IMPRESSIVE PUBLIC BUILDINGS

Springfield, Massachusetts, is one of the most attractive cities in New England. The larger picture is the Municipal Group, and the insets are the Public Library and the Memorial Bridge.

The State Capitol of New York at Albany is regarded as one of the most important works of H. H. Richardson, of whom we tell you more in the story of American Architecture. Several years ago it was much damaged by fire.

SCENES IN TWO STATES

Baltimore, Maryland, is called the "monumental city." The War Memorial, recently completed at the joint expense of state and city, contains a memorial hall, an auditorium and meeting-rooms for patriotic societies. The tall column is the Washington Monument, with the Lafayette Statue in front.

This air view of Trenton, the capital of New Jersey, shows a part of the city on the Delaware. The city leads in the manufacture of pottery and has other important industries.

Baltimore photos, J. H. Schaefer & Son; photo of Trenton, copyright, Aero Service Corporation.

FACTORIES IN THREE STATES

Photo, courtesy Canadian National Railways.

Berlin, in the New Hampshire Hills; Mount Westminster in the distance.

Brockton is noted for its manufacture of shoes. The falls of the Merrimac at Lawrence, seen at the left, have been an important source of power for a century.

The Colfax Plant of the Duquesne Light and Power Company at Pittsburgh is said to be the largest in the world. Both rivers in the city are lined with manufacturing plants of immense size.

Photo of Falls, copyright, Ewing Galloway; that of Brockton by Fairchild Aerial Survey, by courtesy of Brockton Chamber of Commerce; that of Pittsburgh, copyright, Aero Service Company.

various sections of the country. There are also many products which, for some good reason, are not manufactured at all in this area.

The New England states, according to the last Census, are 79.2 per cent urban and 20.8 per cent rural; the Middle Atlantic states are 74.9 per cent urban and 25.1 rural; Delaware is about 45 per cent urban, and Maryland about 40 per cent. Individual states in this group range from Rhode Island, 97.5 per cent urban, to Vermont, 31.2 per cent urban. This means, according to the Census definition, that in Vermont, for example, only 31.2 per cent of the people are living in towns with a population of 2,500

Massachusetts, with 27, New York, with 22, and New Jersey, with 21, equal or exceed any other state. Ohio, next in line, has 21. Vermont has no city of this size. Delaware has 1; New Hampshire, 2; Maine and Maryland, 3 each; Rhode Island, 5; Connecticut, 9; and Pennsylvania, 20.

Most of the cities in the group of fifty largest cities have a number of important activities. Few are given over to one industry. New York is listed as leading all cities in the United States in the manufacture of clothing, fur goods, ink, jewelry, millinery, pens, tobacco-pipes, soap and cigars. It is a wide variety, but if one lists the items in which

The central portion of the State House in Boston with its gilded dome was built in 1795 according to the plans of Charles Bulfinch, the celebrated architect, but the building has been much enlarged and extended since. In the foreground is Boston Common, important as a meeting-place from colonial times to the present.   Photo, George Brayton.

people or more. Compare either of the two groups of states mentioned above with the South Atlantic states, which have 31 per cent of their population urban and 69 rural.

Out of the fifty largest cities listed for the United States, eighteen are in this Northeastern area. They are with their rank: New York (1), Philadelphia (3), Boston (7), Baltimore (8), Pittsburgh (9), Buffalo (11), Washington (14), Newark (15), Jersey City (22), Rochester (23), Providence (27), Worcester (35), Syracuse (37), New Haven (39), Bridgeport (44), Hartford (46), Scranton (47) and Paterson (49). In addition to the fifty largest cities, eighteen other cities in the Union had more than 100,000 inhabitants in 1920, and eleven of them are in the section.

Again, of the cities of the United States having 25,000 inhabitants or more,

the city stands in second and third places, the numbers of them become confusing. Other Eastern cities are similar in character, but have a smaller number of leading industries. Many of these cities are, in addition, business centres for extensive manufacturing enterprises in the surrounding cities and towns. Thus, Boston, while it does not excel in any industry, gets much of its business on adjacent manufacturing centres. The city, for this reason, is the country's greatest wool market. Some of the smaller cities are notable because their industry is almost the sole producer of certain products. Thus, Troy, New York, produces over 90 per cent of all the collars and cuffs; Waterbury, Connecticut, 25 per cent of the needles, pins, and hooks and eyes; and Gloversville, New York, 35 per cent of the gloves and mittens.

THE NEXT STORY OF THE UNITED STATES IS ON PAGE 3937.

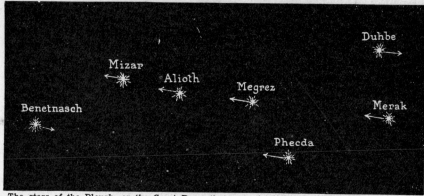

The stars of the Plough, or the Great Bear, that move in different directions, as shown by the arrows.

THE STARS IN THEIR BRIGHTNESS

IF an astronomer could mount the back of a comet and fly unhurt through the sun's family of planets, what mysteries of the earth's neighbors he might solve! He would see the other side of the moon, he might scan the deserts of Mars, or peer between the cloud rifts of Venus to the snow mountains beneath. Countless meteorites would pass him soundlessly by.

He might see little Eros tumble headlong past. If, while still a young man, he had caught the mane of Halley's Comet just at the right moment, Saturn and Jupiter would have unfolded their secrets to him before he was middle-aged. He would be an old, old man before he returned to the earth's neighborhood with tidings of green Uranus or distant Neptune, and he would scarcely be able to breathe out the truth about the "Unknown Planet" before death overtook him.

But that would be all. He could learn no more in his miraculous lifetime. If he set out to search the depths of space, his flying horse would be all too slow. A star has been found which moves two hundred miles a second. Suppose we change our seat on a comet for this. Even on a steed like that he would never reach the nearest star, for it would take

CONTINUED FROM 3672

4,000 years to get there.

The nearest star is Alpha Centauri, a very bright star, the third brightest in the heavens, though it cannot be seen in our northern skies, but only from the southern hemisphere. It is so bright because it is so near, a mere stone's throw away compared with the distances of other stars innumerable.

The two stars next to Alpha Centauri are invisible to the naked eye. They have been given no names, but are known to the astronomers only by numbers. Then comes great Sirius, the flaming Dog Star; but to reach him on the same steed would take 8,000 years. Five more very faint stars, still not to be seen by the eye, are within a 10,000-year journey; but before our Runaway Star—for that was the odd name first found by astronomers for the swiftly flying horse of our fable—could reach the Pole Star, 40,000 years would have gone by. Space is, we perceive, a little crowded near our sun; it empties farther out.

Crowded, we said, yet think of the loneliness of stars. What would it be like if, when traveling at that incredible speed of two hundred miles a second, we left the populous solar system to seek out the nearest star? The light from the sun would have dwindled to a mere speck: in all the

3783

sky would be nothing brighter than a star. Blackness would wrap one round about, and cold so terrible that the lightest gas would be solid. But no gas could ever be met on that journey, nor anything solid—nothing at all but frozen emptiness. Then, after thousands of years, Alpha Centauri would draw near, and it would be seen that it was not a single sun but two suns, one very like ours but brighter, the other yellower and giving only a quarter of its bright companion's light.

Recently a very faint red star has been discovered revolving about the twin stars which make up Alpha Centauri. It is now between us and them, and since it is actually the nearest star, it has been named Proxima Centauri.

Now let us draw another picture. Astronomers never speak of the distances of the stars in miles, but in light-years—the number of years a ray of light, the fastest traveling thing possible, would take to reach them. Alpha Centauri is four and a third light-years away, and a light-year is six million million miles—a figure the mind can hardly grasp. Astronomers have even a greater measure. This is a parsec, which is about three and a third light-years.

But around Alpha Centauri and its companion that black gulf

THE DISTANCE OF THE STARS
This picture is not drawn to scale but it helps us to understand the enormous distance of some of the stars from the earth. A wireless message takes a fraction of a second to reach Australia, but the message would take thousands of years to reach some of the stars.

stretches; and round every star in the heavens is a gulf of emptiness as great or greater. Imagine a box-room of 600 cubic feet, rather bigger than 8 feet by 8 feet by 8 feet, with a speck of dust floating in it. That speck of dust represents the lonely star. All the stars have, on the average, 600 cubic light-years surrounding them. A speck of dust did we say? The speck would be too small for any mortal eye to see with the finest microscope that mortal hands have made. If you thought of it as an atom you would not be far wrong, yet from each of these mighty atoms light is forever reaching distances a thousand times as great as the billion-mile sides of their box-room.

Some stars are more solitary than others, as some regions of the universe of stars are more crowded than others. Our sun lives cosily among a number of near neighbors. Sirius and its morning herald Procyon are but two out of ten within ten light-years. But you need seek the skies no farther than the stars of the Plough to come on a far more desolate space. Seven are the stars of the Plough, and those at the end, Benetnasch, the point of the handle, and Dubhe, the top of the ploughshare, move apart from the rest of the company.

The five middle suns of this great group

A WONDERFUL SIGHT IN THE HEAVENS

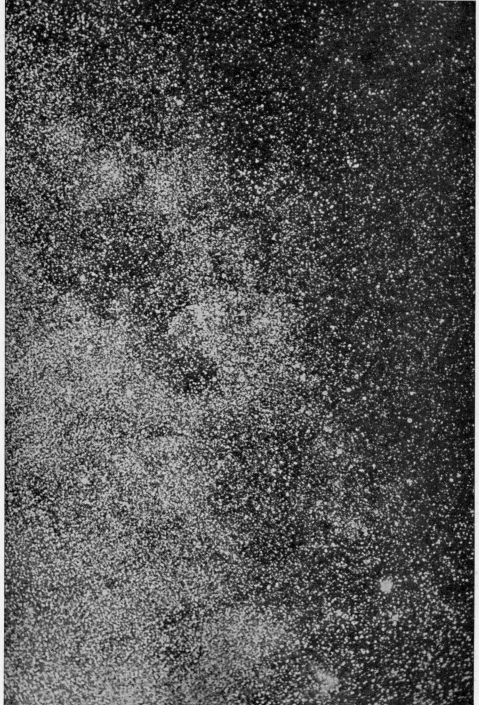

A GREAT BELT OF STARS THAT SWEEPS ACROSS THE HEAVENS—A PART OF THE MILKY WAY
From a photograph by Mr. E. E. Barnard.

—Mizar, Alioth, Megrez, Phecda and Merak—are all moving together like a flight of silvery arrows. Their distance from us is forty times as great as that of Alpha Centauri; but these five companions live in a block of space, a wilderness, a void, by the side of which our sun's domain is crowded. Sixty light-years separate Mizar from Merak, and though, in looking upward to them, other fainter stars seem to mingle with them, they are either much nearer to us, or else sunk unmeasurable distances in far-off space. The five stars travel alone.

They are migrating stars, the vanguard of a flock which numbers others that are far more distant from them. Sirius may be a lagging member of the flock, and so is the brightest star in the Corona Borealis, and there are five others so widely scattered in the sky that only many years' watching have shown to astronomers their association.

THE STREAMS OF STARS THAT TRAVEL OUT INTO LIMITLESS SPACE

The sun, traveling at enormous speed toward a point in the constellation of Hercules at thirteen miles a second, seems also to belong to a star squadron. The star Algol may be going our way, so is one of the stars in the constellation of Perseus, and so are two of the stars of the Swan; but not the other three. Such flocks go on and on among the other stars, following some unknown law peculiar to themselves; and when seen in far perspective they cease to look like single stars but appear to cluster together, and so are called star-clusters.

Something of the distances of those star-clusters has been learned, and something is known of the distances of many stars the eye cannot see. But very few of all the stars are near enough to have their distances calculated within a billion miles, though they are measured in light-years. Their brightness is no test. Rigel, the seventh brightest star, is so far away that it is possible that when the light we now see left it, Queen Elizabeth sat on the throne of England. Of all that we can see, no more than seventy have told the secret of their distance within the limits of accuracy of a light-year. Seventy out of how many?

THE WONDERFUL SIGHT THE TELESCOPE REVEALS IN THE HEAVENS

Putting aside the Milky Way, the very framework and substance of the stellar universe, there are fewer than 10,000 stars visible in the heavens, even to the sharpest eyes; and not more than about one-third of these can be seen at any one time. But when a telescope is turned to the skies the tale is vastly different. Let us first say what is meant by the magnitude of stars.

The brightest stars, like Sirius, Aldebaran, Canopus, Vega, Capella and Arcturus, which the ancients knew, used all to be called first-magnitude stars, though Sirius is eleven times brighter than Aldebaran, and Canopus twice as bright. But taking Aldebaran as a star of the first magnitude, it is said to be about two and a half times as bright as a star of the second magnitude; and a star of the second magnitude is about two and a half times as bright as one of the third magnitude. Thus a star of the first magnitude is about a hundred times as bright as a star of the sixth magnitude, and stars a little fainter than the sixth magnitude are the faintest that most human eyes can see.

When we turn on the telescope, more and more magnitudes come into sight—stars of the seventh, eighth, ninth, tenth, right up to the eighteenth magnitude in the greatest telescopes of all. All the great telescopes of the world are now turned on to the skies to count the stars in order to make the Great Star Map for the use of the next century. Till these labors are ended we shall not know how many stars have been counted and their places found, but of stars up to the tenth magnitude about 373,000 have been counted.

THE BOUNDLESS UNIVERSE AND ITS THOUSAND MILLION STARS

But that is far from being the limit of their number. The eye tires in looking through a telescope for stars which appear only as the merest points of light, never large or shining. But the photographic plate does not tire. The longer it is turned through a telescope on to the skies the more light it grasps, the more stars it takes in—stars very much fainter than the tenth magnitude, and fainter even than that. The stars on the Great Star Map will be counted and numbered.

The number cannot yet be told, but astronomers believe that all the stars together will be at least a hundred millions, perhaps many more.

THE NEXT STORY OF THE EARTH IS ON PAGE 3921.

FINDING OUR WAY BY THE STARS

The pictures on these pages will help us to find our way at night without a compass. The top picture on each page shows the stars in front of us when we face the north, and the bottom picture shows the stars seen in the south. The northern stars are the best guide because their apparent movement is less than that of the southern stars, this being due to the fact that the whole of the heavens appear to revolve round the Pole Star, the only fixed point we see.

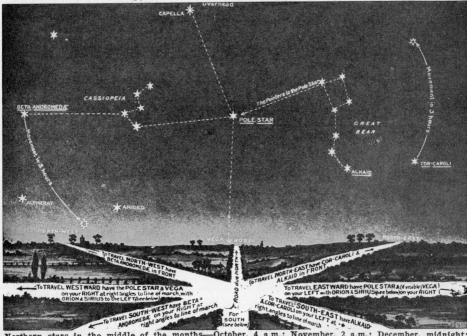

Northern stars in the middle of the months—October, 4 a.m.; November, 2 a.m.; December, midnight; January, 10 p.m.; February, 8 p.m.; March, 6 p.m.

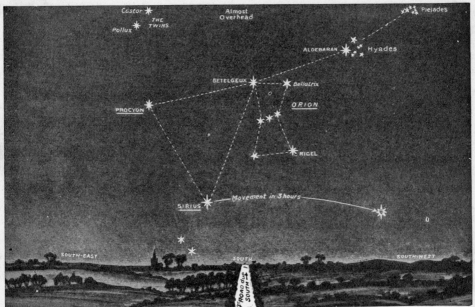

Southern stars in the middle of the months—October, 4 a.m.; November, 2 a.m.; December, midnight; January, 10 p.m.; February, 8 p.m.; March, 6 p.m.

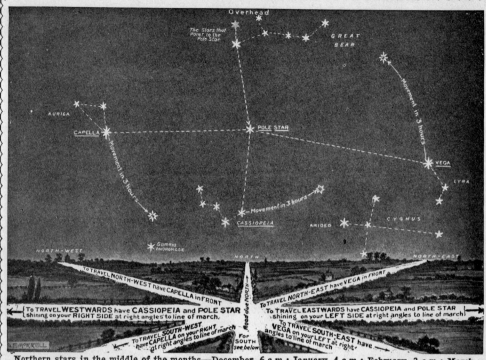

Northern stars in the middle of the months—December, 6 a.m.; January, 4 a.m.; February, 2 a.m.; March, midnight; April, 10 a.m.

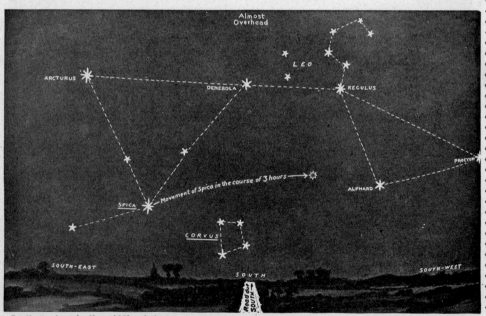

Southern stars in the middle of the months—December, 6 a.m.; January, 4 a.m.; February, 2 a.m.; March, midnight; April, 10 a.m.

In taking the stars as finger-posts we have to allow for their general movement from hour to hour, and examples are given in each of these pictures to show the movement of some leading stars. In the southern sky the movement that applies to one applies generally to all, but in the north the nearer a star is to the Pole Star the less is its change of position in a given time. It is not always the brightest stars that are the best guides, since everything depends on their position in relation to the horizon.

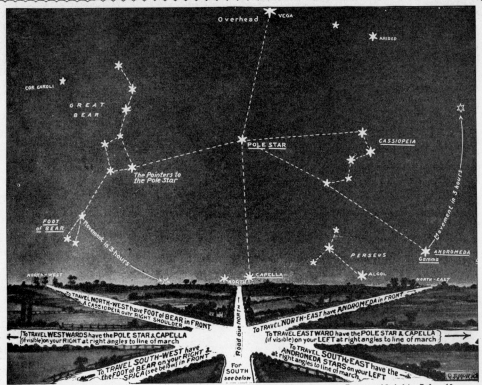

Northern stars in the middle of the months—April, 4 a.m.; May, 2 a.m.; June, midnight; July, 10 p.m.

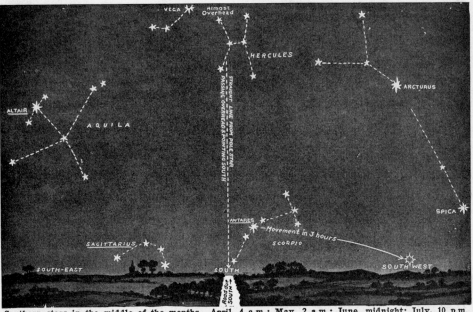

Southern stars in the middle of the months—April, 4 a.m.; May, 2 a.m.; June, midnight; July, 10 p.m.
The object of these star pictures is to link up the leading stars with the horizon and the points of the compass, and to show them as they appear near the times stated to an observer in the northern hemisphere about the latitude of Labrador. Toward the south the northern stars will be slightly lower in the sky and the southern stars slightly higher. Our artist has shown imaginary crossroads radiating to different points of the compass, and also the guiding stars.

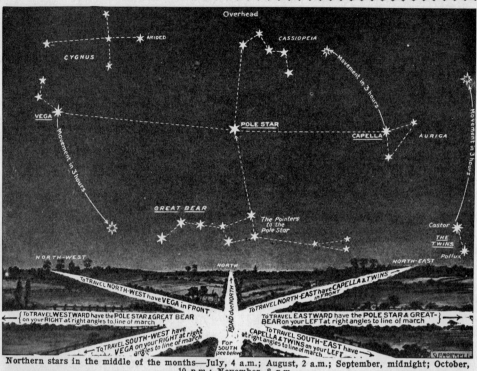

Northern stars in the middle of the months—July, 4 a.m.; August, 2 a.m.; September, midnight; October, 10 p.m.; November, 8 p.m.

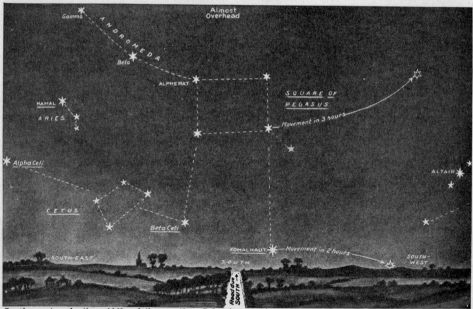

Southern stars in the middle of the months—July, 4 a.m.; August, 2 a.m.; September, midnight; October, 10 p.m.; November, 8 p.m.

In the eastern, southern and western skies planets have often to be taken into account. All the stars in the course of six hours will travel from their position on the first pair of pictures on page 3787 to those of the second on page 3788 and soon to the third on page 3789, and then to the positions shown in these pictures, the movement being in the direction of the arrows. Therefore their positions can be easily estimated for any hour between, the movement for half-time (three hours) being indicated in the case of the principal stars by an outline star. The positions of the northern guiding stars hold good for about two hours before and after the time stated. The relative brightness of stars is shown by the number of rays.

You may not see a connection between this picture and a rope; yet the leaves of the Agave yield Sisal hemp, so called because it grows around Sisal in Yucatan. 21,000 leaves yield about 1,300 pounds of fibre. There are plantations like this in Mexico, and in India and South Africa.

A PIECE OF ROPE

THERE is a baby rope in the cages of most song birds. It is in the seed pot. If we look we shall find only seed: canary seed, rape seed, mustard seed, perhaps, and hempseed. It is the hempseed that is the baby rope. If we were to sow some of those seeds, we should find that they would grow, in rich, damp soil, fed by the hot sun, into great plants. The true hemp is a native of Asia, but it has been naturalized in Europe and America. It sometimes reaches a height of twenty feet, but is generally much lower. The numerous flowers are yellowish green, and the whole plant is so handsome that it is occasionally grown for ornament. Hemp is grown to some extent in nearly all European countries, but Russia furnishes the most. To see the best American hemp we must go to some parts of Kentucky or to California, but Wisconsin furnishes most. Not so much is grown in the United States as formerly, on account of the greater use of Manila hemp, of which we shall speak presently.

It is the stalk of the plant that we need for our ropes and strings and twines. Upon it grows a bark made up of fibres. If we want fine fibre

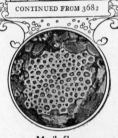

CONTINUED FROM 3682

Manila fibre.

to make cloth, we pluck up the plant as soon as it has flowered. If we want coarser fibre for the making of sails, we let it grow a little longer. If we want the coarsest of all—for strings and cords and ropes—we let the hemp grow as long as it will. The plant is prepared for use in much the same way as flax. It is "retted," or allowed to rot on the ground, until the fibres separate easily. Then the fibres are removed from the remainder of the stalks by beating and combing, and are then packed into bales.

So much for the baby rope which we see in the seed pot of the bird cage. But there are various other things which make rope. In the Sisal hemp, shown at the top of the page, the fibres of the leaves are used, and the rope made from them is excellent. Though grown chiefly in Mexico, it also grows in Cuba, Africa and Asia. Those brown ropes which are never tarred, and are so much lighter than hempen ropes, are made from the husk of the coconut and are called coir ropes. They are not common and are used chiefly in the East. Then there is a fine rope, used in the driving of machinery, which is made of cotton.

3791

Such ropes are often used in place of leather belting, and for some purposes they are much more satisfactory. Jute, coming from India, makes an inferior kind of rope. But the most wonderful rope is made from a plant named abaca, a relative of the banana, and more generally called Manila hemp, though it is not really hemp at all. It grows chiefly in the Philippine Islands, and the islanders receive about $50,000,000 a year for it. On the whole it is the most satisfactory material for rope.

Abaca grows best on the slopes of volcanic mountains, and the plants are three or four years of age before they are of use. The plant is cut just before flowering, and the layers of fibre are stripped from the core and dried. Two natives working together will cut and scrape about twenty-five pounds of the fibre in a day. A machine has been invented to do this work, but hand labor is so cheap in the Philippines that it has not yet come into common use.

HOW THE ROPE IS MADE FROM THE SHORT FIBRES

Formerly ropes were made almost entirely by hand, but machinery has been introduced, as in so many other industries. The making of rope is now an elaborate process in which wonderful machines are used. The fibre enters the factory in bales. After being combed out so that all the fibres lie one way, some of these are twisted tightly into yarn, and then several yarns make a single strand. Then as many strands as are necessary are twisted together to form rope. The thickness of a strand depends entirely on the number of threads that are twisted together. Usually a rope is made of three strands, and any cordage over an inch in circumference is called a rope, or a hawser. Anything smaller is called cord, twine or line. When three or more ropes are twisted into one, the result is known as a cable. We show you some pictures of rope-making in the following pages.

THE GREAT STRENGTH OF A FIBRE ROPE

It is wonderful to think that short pieces of fibre twisted together can be made to cling so tenaciously that a cable made up of them will keep in check such a ship as the Leviathan, the Majestic or the Mauretania, and prevent it from breaking away from the quay where it is moored. A Manila rope only an inch thick needs a pull equal to about four tons to break it.

We have told you something of most or all of these fibres in the story beginning on page 2783. More rope is made of Manila fibre than all others combined, since it is stronger, more durable and resists salt water better. Sisal fibre is injured by salt water, but much of the rope used on farms is made from it. The principal use of Sisal, however, is for binding twine, used by the self-binding reapers in the grain-fields. Some of the fibre of the Phormium, or New Zealand flax, is used in this country. Though it is not so strong as Manila, its appearance is something like it, and sometimes it is mixed with Manila by unscrupulous manufacturers. Rope made from the true hemp is still used on shipboard to some extent, but is almost always impregnated with tar, to prevent injury from water. The fibre is also used to fill seams.

Eastern monarchs, when they wanted a particularly strong rope in days gone by, would have one made of human hair, and such a rope is extraordinarily tenacious. There is one in a London museum, several inches thick and several thousand feet long, that was made for a mikado of Japan, and it weighs two tons.

ROPES MADE FROM STEEL AS WELL AS FROM FIBRE

About a hundred years ago the manufacture of ropes from wire began in a small way, and now this is a flourishing industry in Great Britain and the United States, though of course much more rope is manufactured from vegetable fibre. These wire ropes are generally made from the finest steel wire. Several wires are twisted together to make a strand, and several strands are twisted into a rope. Generally there are more strands in a wire rope than in one made from hemp. Sometimes several hundred wires are used in making one rope. These wires are often wound around a core of fibre. Such ropes are very strong and are used for hoisting and for bracing. Flagpoles and other tall spars are often braced with wire ropes, and masts on ships also. A wire rope a little less than one inch in diameter has about the same strength as a Manila rope two and three-quarters inches in diameter.

THE NEXT STORY OF FAMILIAR THINGS IS ON PAGE 3909.

PICTURE STORY OF A PIECE OF ROPE

Manila hemp, from the Philippine Islands, is the finest fibre for rope-making. It has great strength and flexibility, and when tarred does not deteriorate in sea-water.

The tree is cut down and the leaves are cut off. Then the workman strips the fibrous coat off the stem, splitting it into lengths about three inches wide.

These strips are scraped until only the fibre remains. This is then washed, dried and picked over before being taken to the baling press to be packed for export. Two men prepare 25 pounds of hemp in a day.

COCONUT FIBRE FOR MAKING A ROPE

Another vegetable fibre known as coir, obtained from the husk of the coconut, is also largely used for rope-making. The fibre is short. Coir is from an Indian word meaning "rope."

Coir rope is spun in India and Ceylon in a very simple way. Each native holds under his left arm a bundle of prepared coir. The ends are fastened to a wheel which another native turns, and so the rope grows longer. A coir rope will stretch nearly half its length, so that it is admirable for taking sudden strains. It is rarely seen in this part of the world.

THE OLD-TIME WAY OF SPINNING ROPE

The old-fashioned way of making rope has almost died out. Men used to comb out the hemp by drawing it through a series of long spikes fixed into boards like inverted rakes; but this process is now done very rapidly by a special machine.

The rope-walk, where hand-spinning of rope was carried out by men who walked up and down twisting the strands as they went, used to be a familiar sight in all our seaports. But the introduction of machinery for making fibre ropes and the use of wire rope have caused their disappearance.

THE RAW FIBRE AND THE FIRST PROCESS

The fibre comes to the warehouses packed in bales. Here we see a corner of the warehouse. The portable electric elevator can be run to any part of the room and will lift the bales so that they can be stored compactly. Bales of Manila weigh about 275 pounds, and Sisal about 400 pounds.

Here we see the bales opened, and the fibre is being fed into the breaker. This untangles the matted fibres and renders them roughly parallel. Very often jets of oil are sprayed on the fibre to make it more pliable. The fibres issue in loose untwisted roping called a sliver.

THE FIBRE IS SPUN INTO YARN

On the left you see a sliver issuing from the breaker. On the right several slivers are being fed into a drawing frame, which combs and draws them out into a single sliver no larger than one of the parts. This process may be repeated several times in order that the sliver may be even in thickness.

On the right you see finished sliver issuing from the tall cans and being fed into the jennies, or spinning frames, which pull out the fibres still farther and impart a twist. The product is yarn, which you see winding on the reels at the left.

THE YARN IS BECOMING ROPE

Small rope is sometimes made directly from the yarn. On the left of this Thread Rope machine reels of yarn are being twisted into strands. In the centre three strands are being twisted into the rope which you see wound on the drum at the right.

Oftener, however, the yarn is twisted into strands on one machine, and then these strands are made into rope on another. On each of these machines you see many yarns from the reels on the right being twisted into single strands, which are wound on the drums you see at the left.

MAKING ROPE AND TARRING YARN

Three strands wound on the large drums you saw on the preceding page are brought to this machine, which rapidly twists them into a rope. Generally a rope consists of only three strands, but more may be used to make a rope for some special purpose.

When rope is to be exposed to the weather it is often tarred. Small ropes may be tarred when completed, but usually the yarn is passed through a long vat of heated pine tar. At the end the surplus tar is squeezed out and the yarn is again wound upon reels.

A ROPE-WALK OVER A MILE LONG

Here we see the upper end of a modern rope-walk. Elaborate rope-making machinery takes the place of the men who walked up the alley. This rope-walk has six alleys, each 1,200 feet long—or over a mile in all.

The interior of a great rope warehouse.

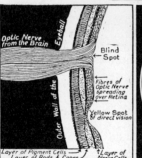
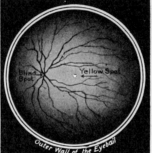
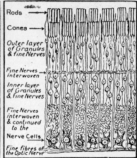

In the first picture we see a section of the eyeball between the blind spot and the optic nerve. The middle picture shows the interior of the eyeball, with the nerve-fibres. In the right-hand picture a portion of the retina is highly magnified, showing the various layers and the rods and cones.

THE EYE'S WONDERFUL CURTAIN

NOW let us turn to one of the most wondrous parts of ourselves— the retina of the eye, the curtain at the back which actually is a part of the brain. It is indeed a complicated structure, made up chiefly of delicate nerve-fibres and nerve-cells. There is also in it, as in every other part of the body, a certain amount of supporting tissue to hold the rest together. It is very interesting to discover that this supporting tissue of the retina is made of a special kind of cell which we find forming the supporting tissue of the brain itself.

CONTINUED FROM 3686

The various parts of the retina are usually described as being arranged in ten layers, some consisting of cells and others of nerve-fibres. It is the ninth layer from the front that we must carefully look at, because here we find the cells which are most deeply concerned with seeing. We might expect these cells to be in the very front of the retina, immediately behind the glassy jelly (called the *vitreous humor*) of the eyeball. They are not, and the light must pass through eight layers of structure before it finally reaches the true vision cells. All these layers are extremely thin and delicate, and are to be seen only under a microscope of very high power.

The inside of the brain is hollow and is lined with cells. The brain part of the eye is formed by a hollow outgrowth from the brain, and that outgrowth is indented to form the retina. The vision cells are not on the front of the retina, but close to the back. They are really the same as the cells that line the cavity of the brain, and when the brain sends out its little bulb on the way to make the eye, these cells line the bulb.

The vision cells are of two kinds, called rods and cones from their shape. They form altogether a regular palisade of cells on which the light strikes, and if the refracting materials in front are just right, the light is sharply focused at the point where it reaches the retina. There are far more rods than cones in the eye, but the cones are more important.

In every retina there are two spots which differ from the rest of it. One is the place where the great optic nerve spreads out to form the retina. At that point there are no rods or cones, and so it is blind. Light falling on that point is not seen.

Close beside this blind spot is another spot, called the yellow spot, and this part of the retina is where all the best seeing is really done. It is packed with cones and nothing else. That is why we say the cones are more important than the rods. This spot is called yellow because there is a certain

3801

amount of yellow material lying in the supporting tissue between the cells there. The spot is less pigmented than the surrounding area.

THE YELLOW SPOT IN OUR EYE THAT DOES ALL OUR BEST SEEING

When we study the yellow spot we notice that every kind of arrangement has been made to promote good seeing there. The layers that lie in front of the cones—they lie in front of the vision cells everywhere in the retina—are at their very thinnest in this particular place. Some of them, indeed, are practically not to be found. Also, there are no large blood-vessels to get in the way of the light, but only extremely small capillaries.

All our best seeing is done by means of this spot. Whenever we wish to see a thing precisely we turn our eyes so that the light from it shall fall on the yellow spot. The business of the muscles that move the eyeballs is to move them together in such a way that the light of any particular thing we want to see shall fall on our two yellow spots—one in each of our eyes.

It seems that the gathering of cones in one place, without any rods, so as to form a yellow spot occurs only in the highest kinds of backboned animals—birds and mammals. There is also good reason to believe that throughout the whole retina, but especially in the neighborhood of the yellow spot, there has been a gradual development in the seeing of colors, and it is these wonderful cones that are responsible for this.

WHY WE SEE TWO STARS AS IF THEY WERE ONE

It seems to be proved that if two things are to be seen as two, the light from them must fall on two cones in the retina. If the two things are so small, or if they are so far away and so close to each other that the light from them falls on only one cone in the retina, they are seen as only one thing. This is the case with the double stars which are so extremely common in the sky. Every advance in the structure of the telescope shows us that more and more stars which we called single are really double stars.

When the eye is unaided, the light from the two stars falls on only one cone, and so to us it is only one star. Every time an astronomer resolves a star into two, as we say, what happens is that the telescope has spread the light out sufficiently for it to strike two cones in the retina. Evidently the fineness of vision will depend on the nearness of the cones to each other. That means that it is greatly to our advantage to see with the part of the eye where the cones are tightly packed against one another without rods or anything else separating them. That, of course, is what the yellow spot does for those of the higher animals in which it has been developed.

Careful study of these facts makes it certain that for every cone in the retina there must be a special path in the optic nerve, and at least one special cell, perhaps as many as a thousand, in the vision centre of the brain.

THE LITTLE RODS OF THE EYE THAT HELP US TO SEE IN A DIM LIGHT

It has been shown that the rods have the business of helping us to see in dim light, which the cones do not notice. Ordinary daylight is so bright that the rods are exhausted by it and made useless. Therefore in such light we see by the cones only. But the case is different if the rods are shielded from bright light for a little. When this happens they get time to remake the chemical substances necessary for their work, and then they can act.

Let us see how this works out. When we go into a dimly lighted room, or out of doors from a brightly lighted room, at first we see practically nothing, and then afterward we begin to see. The principal reason is that the rods of the retina are exhausted by the bright light to which they have been exposed, and the cones cannot see in a dim light. After a few minutes the rods regain their power. The blood is always flowing rapidly through the retina, and is rich in materials from which the rods can make the special substances on which light acts when we see. So, after a little while, we begin to see again, but we see no colors. The rods are unable to distinguish one color from another; if they see at all, they see a sort of bluish gray.

There is another interesting point we may notice. Suppose we have gone out of doors on a starlit night and notice a star, not too bright a star. As long as we do not look straight at it, we shall see it; but as soon as we look straight at it, so as to see it as well as possible, it disappears. The reason is that when we look straight at anything we place our eyeballs so that the light shall fall directly upon the yellow spot. But there are no rods, only cones, at the yellow spot, and as the cones do not take any notice of very faint light, the star disappears.

THE IMPORTANT CELLS THAT MAKE UP THE TENTH LAYER OF THE RETINA

All our new discoveries teach us how valuable and important the cones are, and what a great advance in the history of vision it was when the cones were gathered together to form the yellow spot. We have said that the rods and cones form the ninth layer of the retina. Still deeper is the tenth and last layer of the retina, composed of cells which are filled with a dark brown material.

These cells seem to be very important and useful. For one thing, under the influence of light we find that the pigment in the cells seems to run into the ninth layer, so as to form a dark sheath round each rod and cone. This may be very important in enabling each of the vision cells to act without getting muddled with the others. Further, the pigment in these pigment cells makes a great store of material, on which the vision cells themselves can draw. Unless the vision cells, the rods and cones, are properly supplied with materials, they lose their power.

A LAW OF THE RETINA THAT IS TRUE OF ALL LIFE

It is a law about the action of the retina that what we feel is not in simple proportion to the intensity or strength of what excites us. We might suppose that what would happen is this: add so much to the brightness of the light, and we should feel accordingly; do it again and again, and the result will always correspond. But that is not the case, as we all know when we think of it. Add one candle to one candle, and we know the difference; add one to ten, and we scarcely know the difference; add one to fifty, and no one would notice the difference. Add one voice to four voices, and we all know the difference; add one to forty, and no one could tell.

If this were the right place for it, it might be shown that this law is true of all our lives. It means that the higher the pitch of our talking or of our writing, of our newspapers, the more difficult is it to increase the impression made by them.

The man who is always shouting must shout very much louder if he is to excite our attention; but the person who speaks in a gentle voice has only to raise it the least bit and we at once give him our attention.

This law is true of all sensations and feelings, and of all our responses. It is probably true of every kind of living matter, and its discovery was one of the great feats of the nineteenth century. We mention it here because it can be very beautifully studied in the retina.

THE CHEMICAL CHANGES THAT SEND A MESSAGE TO THE BRAIN

The question of time is very important in regard to the action of the retina. Do we see as soon as the light strikes us? Do we stop seeing as soon as the light ceases? The answer is No to both these questions. It takes a little time for the light to act before we see. During that time we have little doubt that the light is breaking up the special chemical substances which are lying ready for it in the vision cells, and it is these chemical changes that excite the fibres of the nerve of vision and send a message to the brain.

It is probable that people vary in regard to the period between the coming of the light and the sensation of its presence. We notice a similar thing in other cases as well as sensation. We find that there is always a period, perhaps about the hundredth of a second, between the moment at which a nerve says to a muscle, "Contract!" and the moment at which the muscle obeys. In this case, also, we suppose that chemical changes are going on in the muscle-cell which require a little time.

It has been proved also that the different parts of the retina are not the same in this respect. The cones are of a higher type than the rods. They are affected by light more quickly than the rods are, and it is possible to prove that first of all we see by the cones only, and then by the rods, too. This makes a difference to what we see, because when the rods come into action they contribute a sort of uniform gray light to everything equally; whereas the moment before we were seeing by the cones only, and they see colors. Also, we find that the retina goes on seeing for a little while after the light has ceased. If the light is moderate, the average length of the after-sensation is probably about one-fortieth of a second.

VIBRATIONS OF THE ETHER GIVE US AN IMPRESSION OF COLOR

In some ways the most wonderful of all the feats the eye performs is the seeing and distinguishing of colors. We believe that certain wave motions, when they fall on an eye, give rise to light. Apart from eyes to see, all nature is in darkness. We can count the number of vibrations of the ether that affect the eye in a single second. The smallest number per second that we can see is roughly about 400,000 billions. When we see these we get an impression of red. The highest number we can see is roughly about 800,000 billions, and when such vibrations affect our eyes we see a sort of violet.

Now, in music, a note that is an octave higher than another has exactly twice the number of vibrations in a second. We may say that the amount of light that our eyes can see corresponds to one octave, as the number of vibrations of the violet is about twice the number of the red vibrations.

Our ability to distinguish colors depends on the cones in the retina. We do not see the color of objects whose light falls on the outermost parts of the retina, where there are practically no cones. Also our eyes vary in sensitiveness at different parts of the color scale. At the actual extremes, such as red and blue, we do not notice slight differences in color so sharply as we do in between the extremes, as in the yellow and green.

Colors vary in several ways. For instance, they vary in brightness, as we all know. The brightness of a color depends simply on the extent to which it excites the brain.

THE SEVEN COLORS OF WHICH WHITE LIGHT IS MADE

Quite apart from any question of the eyes, the question of color is simple, because it is exactly the same as the question of the pitch of sounds. Ten vibrations a second means one sound, eleven means another, twelve another, and so on. In the same way, between light made of waves running 400,000 billions to the second and light made up of waves running 800,000 billions to the second there are hundreds of billions of colors.

If we take white light and pass it through a prism we get a band of colors called the spectrum. When we look at it quite clearly we get the impression, not of a regular, even change of color from one end to the other, but of comparatively few colors to which we give definite names. Of these various colors, which are commonly described as seven, some give us the impression of being mixed and others of being pure. For instance, the color we call purple is mixed, because, when we come to consider it, we see that what we call purple is really the result of our seeing a blue and a red together. What we call orange is mixed; what we are really seeing is a red and a yellow together. Then, again, Prussian blue is not a pure blue, but a mixture of blue and green.

HOW THE EYE SEES ALL THE COLORS OF THE RAINBOW

Now contrast with these colors such a color as crimson red. Nothing will persuade us that that is a mixture of other colors: it is simply red itself. There is also a tone of green which we cannot imagine to be made up of anything else, and the same is true of violet. Probably these are the only three colors of which this can be said. So we call red, green and violet primary colors.

When we call red, green and violet primary colors we are talking about the way in which the eye sees. In paints we are taught to call red, blue and yellow the primary colors, but this is not quite the same thing as the spectral colors. When two paints are mixed we get a result different from that which we get when two rays of colored light are thrown upon an object.

Light consists of waves of every rate of vibration, and any one of these rates is as good as another. But the eye, instead of being able to see each of these, has only means for seeing three of them directly, and these three are red, green and violet. All the other colors it sees by mixing in various proportions these three kinds of sensation.

Of course we now want to know what are the things in the eye which correspond to these various kinds of color sensation. This can be clearly answered as regards the gray color, for we know that that is due to the rods. We know also that the cones are responsible for the other kinds of color sensation, but unfortunately we can go no farther than this, except by guessing.

THE NEXT STORY OF OUR OWN LIFE IS ON PAGE 3955.

HOW GROTIUS LEFT THE CASTLE

GROTIUS, or Hugo van Groot, to give him his Dutch name, was a famous scholar, writer and politician, born in the reign of the great Queen Elizabeth. He spoke and wrote boldly what he thought to be right in politics and religion and so offended the Dutch Government that they condemned him to imprisonment for life and took away all his property. They shut him up in the castle of Louvestein, but allowed his wife to stay with him.

Now, the wife of Grotius was a clever woman and devoted to her husband, and she set her wits working to try to find a way of escape for him. But it was not till eighteen months had passed by that a way was found which promised anything like success.

Grotius spent his time in writing and often needed to borrow books from outside the prison to help him in his work. He got permission to borrow what books he wanted, and they were sent to him in a large trunk. As he finished with the books, he returned them to a friend outside the castle and took the opportunity of putting into the trunk clothes which needed to be washed. The guards of the castle used to open the trunk and search it, but they never found anything more dangerous than the books and linen of the prisoner.

This went on until the guards grew

CONTINUED FROM 3468

tired of searching the trunk, and the keen eyes of Madame Grotius noticed how they were wearying of their duty. In a flash she saw a possibility of escape for her husband. If she could only get *him* into the trunk! First of all she made some holes in it to admit air. This being done, she persuaded her husband to sit by the fire and pretend to be ill.

On the day that the trunk had to be sent away, she helped Grotius into it, and fastened down the lid. Then, when the man came to carry away the trunk, he found the bed curtains drawn, and the wife with finger to her lips urging quiet for the sake of the invalid. The man hoisted the trunk on his shoulders, exclaiming at its weight; but he carried it away.

And so Grotius was taken to the house of a friend, and then, dressed like a miller, he got away to Antwerp.

But what of his wife, who had risked so much for her husband? At first she thought to delay discovery by dressing in her husband's clothes, and sitting crouched over the fire. But no jailer appeared; so, allowing time for her husband to get away, she went to the guards, told them their prisoner had escaped, and scolded them for failing to do their duty. Taken aback, they let her walk out of the castle. Soon after she joined her husband.

THE BRAVE FRENCH MAID OF NOYON

AT a house in the little town of Noyon, in France, something had gone wrong with the drains, and workmen had to be sent down to open the drain and clean out the sewer. That is a dangerous thing to do, because of the poisonous gases that are in a sewer.

In this case, four men were busily at work when they were overcome by the sewer-gas, and were unable to give the signal to be drawn up out of the sewer.

The people in the house wondered what was the matter, and grew alarmed, but no one dared venture down.

Then a brave servant maid, a girl of seventeen, in pity for the poor men, begged to be tied to the rope and let down into the sewer.

This was done, and she reached the group of men lying helpless down below. As quickly as her trembling hands would allow her, she tied one man to the rope, and jerked it as a signal for drawing him up. Willing hands hauled up the burden, and when he reached the surface the unconscious man was still alive.

A second time the girl tied a man to the rope, and he was drawn into safety.

But the next time the girl found the dangling rope come down for her to catch, she was gasping for breath. She struggled against the feeling of suffocation, and tried to fasten the third man to the rope.

This she just managed to do, but she herself would soon have been unconscious, so, with a desperate effort, she wound her long hair round the rope and tied it tightly. Then she lost consciousness; but the watchers above carefully, very carefully, pulled the double burden up into safety, just in time.

The fresh air soon revived the girl, and then she thought of the fourth man down in the dangerous sewer. It was hardly likely that he would still be alive; but there was a slight chance, and so again, the fourth time, this noble girl risked her life. But this time her effort was in vain, for when the poor man was drawn up, he was already lifeless.

The French nation loves to reward a brave action, and some handsome gifts found their way to the unselfish maid who so cheerfully and readily risked her own life for the sake of others.

THE DEVOTION OF A ROMAN

IN ancient days the city of Rome was only one among several states in the middle of Italy, though at the time of which we are telling she was already the most powerful among them all. And because the other cities feared her power, having no mind to be made, one by one, the subjects of Rome, many of them, who were all called Latins, made a league against her. They gathered an army together and went up against the Romans, and the Roman army went out to meet them.

The Romans were under the command of two consuls, both of them known as valiant men. One was Titus Manlius, surnamed Torquatus, because in his youth he had overcome in single combat a gigantic warrior of the Gauls who wore about his neck a collar of gold called a torque, which torque belonged to Manlius after he had slain the Gaul. And the other was Publius Decius Mus, who, when he was not yet in chief command, had saved the consul from defeat by his skill and valor. So these two men led their forces to the neighborhood of Mount Vesuvius.

Now, the old Romans believed that when men died their souls were borne away to the underworld, where the gods ruled who were called Dei Manes; and they thought that the entrance to the underworld was hard by Mount Vesuvius, where the army was now encamped. Moreover, the two consuls, Manlius and Decius, dreamed each of them the same dream, in which they beheld a mighty form veiled, which spoke to them, saying: "If the leader of the Romans shall devote himself to the Dei Manes, the Romans will vanquish the Latins; but if the Latin leader shall devote himself, then the Latins will vanquish the Romans." Now, to devote themselves meant to die willingly for the sake of their country.

So when Manlius and Decius met on the morrow to hold counsel, they learned how each had dreamed the same dream; and each was ready to devote himself to the gods for the sake of Rome, according to the vision. Thereupon the two agreed

THE BRAVE ROMAN CONSUL, DECIUS MUS, GOING TO DIE FOR THE SAKE OF ROME

that when they came to battle with the Latins, each leading a wing of the army, and the Latins should get the better of one wing, then the one who commanded there should devote himself to the Dei Manes, and hurling himself upon the foe, should give up his own life, thus insuring the victory to Rome.

Now, when the Romans and the Latins were set over against each other in battle array, and the armies met in the shock of combat, it befell that, on the wing where Decius commanded, the Latins made so fierce an onset that the front ranks of the Romans were driven back upon the second line. Then Decius knew that the hour had come. Thereupon he summoned the chief of the priesthood, who was called the Pontifex Maximus, and solemnly dedicated himself for a sacrifice to the Dei Manes, according to the sacred rites of the Romans. Having girded his robes in the manner of one about to offer a victim on the altars of the gods, he rushed upon the ranks of the Latins. The Roman historian Livy tells

us that he appeared in the view of both armies as a being much more majestic than a mere man, and as one sent from heaven to help his friends and bring destruction upon their enemies. Wherever he was carried by his horse there the Latins were seized with panic, and though Decius fell, pierced by darts, the Romans fought with fresh ardor and the Latins fled in terror all along that wing. A messenger was sent post-haste to Manlius, on the other wing, to tell him how the bidding of the vision had been accomplished, and that Decius was slain.

Men said that Manlius was sorely grieved, because, but for the compact between them, it might have been granted to him to perform the act of self-sacrifice instead of Decius. But when the Latins, as well as the Romans, understood what had befallen, both Romans and Latins believed that the gods were on the Roman side, giving to them the assurance of victory, and to the Latins the assurance of defeat; and so the promise was fulfilled, and the Romans were victorious.

A RECORD IN MARBLE OF LIFE IN IPHIGENIA'S LAND

THE SACRIFICE OF IPHIGENIA

THE Greeks were ready to embark for Troy, but no favoring wind came to swell their sails which, as the days passed, hung limp and motionless against the tall masts of the fleet. In order to learn how they might obtain favor with the gods they consulted Calchas the soothsayer, only to be told that no favoring wind would blow until a supreme sacrifice should be made; that Iphigenia, fair daughter of Agamemnon, must be slain upon the altar to appease the immortal gods.

King Agamemnon was as one distraught, so fierce in his heart was the conflict between his honor as a warrior and his love for his child. At last, urged by his companions, he sent for Iphigenia, feigning that before his departure he would give her in marriage to Achilles, whose virtues and merits he highly extolled. Iphigenia was secretly pleased to be the chosen bride of so great a warrior, and regal preparations for the journey were speedily made.

But the decision by no means ended the struggle in the mind of the wretched king. As days passed his gloom deepened, until one night at midnight he sat down in his tent at Aulis and, with head bowed in sorrow over the pine tablet in his lap, wrote to his queen words blotted with hot tears. When at last he fastened it with his seal, he called to his aged attendant and said: "Old man, thou knowest how Calchas bade me offer my daughter Iphigenia that the fleet might have a prosperous voyage to Troy; how, when I heard the words, I bade the herald go throughout the army and bid them depart every man to his own country, for I would not do this thing; how my comrades, even my brother Menelaus, persuaded me until I consented; how then I wrote a letter to my queen that she should send our daughter to this place to be married to King Achilles. Now I have changed my mind, and write, 'Send not the child to this land, for I will give her in marriage at another time.' So hasten. Sit down in the wood which overlooks the road, and suffer not thine eyes to sleep. Beware lest any chariot with my queen and daughter pass, and see well to it that thou keep this seal unbroken."

Scarcely had the old man left the tent when Menelaus, suspecting what the king might do, laid violent hands on him, wrested the letter from him and broke the seal.

"Help! my lord!" cried the old man. "Here is one who hath taken the letter and broken the seal!"

As the king, greatly alarmed by the old man's cries, rushed from his tent he was halted by a messenger, who said with due courtesy: "Greetings, great King, I am come as thou commandedst, bringing thy fair daughter with thy queen Clytæmnestra; with them is thy little son Orestes. They pause by the spring to rest the horses after a long journey. All the army is gathered around them asking many questions as to why they have come; one altogether comely seems already quite enamored of thy fair daughter, and the queen is impatient for thy faithful embrace. The child Orestes clings to his sister's hand and begs to be taken to his father. Make haste to join them lest some ill betide, for I would prove myself thy faithful steward over so great a keeping. I fear lest one steal the heart, another the jewels, and yet another the wedding finery with which the escorts are laden, while I come to tell thee."

Now was the king tormented as to madness. What should he say to the trusting queen, bringing at his command his daughter whose husband was to be Death? She must return to the maidens left at home. To Iphigenia he would say that she must deck herself in bridal robes and jewels. What could he say to little Orestes, who would cry with anguish if his sister ceased to lead him by the hand?

While he was still in torment with such thoughts the royal chariot drew up before the tent; attendants helped the queen and her daughter to alight. Tenderly they greeted the king, after which the queen busied herself giving orders to her servants; to one she committed the care of the boy Orestes, to others the unloading and safe-keeping of the caskets she had brought for her daughter's marriage.

But Iphigenia, seeing the troubled countenance of her father, began to ask him many questions. "Art thou not glad to see me, my father? Why art thou so sad?"

"He that commands an army has many cares."

"Perish these wars and all thy troubles! Suffer thyself to return to us in peace. My father, if thou art truly glad to see me, as thou sayest, why dost thou weep?"

"I weep because thou hast a journey to make, far from me."

"And must I make it alone or with my mother?"

"Alone, my child, for none may go with thee."

"Sendest thou me to dwell elsewhere?"

"Hold thy peace, child. Questioning ill becomes thee."

"I go, dear father, on whatever journey thou biddest. Only order the army, win all battles, and come back as thou ever dost, victorious."

"But I must first make sacrifice to the gods."

"That is well, for due honor must ever be paid the immortal gods. Shall I lead in the dances, my father?"

"O my child, how do I envy thy sweet innocence! And now go into the tent. But first kiss me, for long shall we be parted." When she was gone, he cried aloud: "O city of Priam, what woes thou bringest!"

Then came to him the queen, not noticing his distress, so occupied was her mind with the marriage of her daughter. With many questions did she torment him; about the estate of the bridegroom, his lineage, and where he dwelt; the time and place of the marriage, and what part was it the king's pleasure that she should take? Should she not hold the torch for the bride? To which the imperious king replied that his pleasure it was that she return at once to the maidens left at home, for he himself would attend to everything needful. Nor could all the murmurings of the queen avail, for the king said sternly: "Be persuaded, lady. Both that which is within and that which is without the house do I order."

Thus dismissing her, he left to arrange her departure. Scarcely was he gone when there came a herald announcing Achilles with a message from the army for the king, which message was that the men were wearied with waiting, and unless they might speedily sail, would return each man to his own land.

As soon as the queen heard his name, she advanced to Achilles, and making it known to him who she was, greeted him as her daughter's bridegroom. And when the young man seemed much abashed, the more amazed did he look when she said to him: "I know that men are often abashed with strangers when the talk is of their marriage."

"What sayest thou, lady? I cannot speak for wonder at thy words," replied the young man. "I was never suitor for thy daughter."

Then the queen herself was beyond measure astonished, and cried in wrath: "Is it not shameful indeed that I, a queen, bring my daughter to an unwilling bridegroom?"

And as Achilles would depart to make questionings as to what it all meant there came the old man who had carried the letter and bade him stay; and when he had been assured that no harm should befall him for telling, he told the whole truth.

Then indeed was the queen undone. "Alas, what treachery is this that I suffer!

O son of Thetis, help me now in this extremity, for wrong has been done under thy name. It is thy name that has undone us, both me and my child. Suffer her not to die for the wrongs which are not hers nor yet mine. Would there were an altar to which I might flee, or any friend but thee in the whole army."

"Lady, I learned from the most righteous of men to be true and honest. Know then that since thy daughter has been given me in word, my sword shall soon see whether any take her from me!"

Even as he spoke these words to the anguished queen came King Agamemnon to say that all was ready for the departure of the queen.

"Tell me," she cried, "wouldst thou slay thy daughter and mine? Have I not long been a loving and faithful wife to thee, and is this my recompense that thou slayest my innocent child, having caused me with false promises to bring her here?"

Then was the king bowed in silence, not knowing what to say. Nor did the queen cease her reproaches, which continued with such piteous cries as caused her daughter to hear. Running from the tent with the child Orestes, Iphigenia cast herself on her knees before her father, saying: "O my father, slay me not! I am thy child. I was the first to call thee 'father' and the first to whom thou didst say 'my child.' And thou wouldst say to me: 'Some day I see thee a happy wife like thy mother in the home of a noble husband.' And I would answer: 'For all thy benefits I shall reward thee, for when thou art old and perhaps broken, I shall receive thee and care for thee with the tenderest love.' All this I remember, though thou forgettest. Listen, I pray thee, to the entreaties of my mother and to the cries of the child my brother. Though he be but a babe too young for words, yet weeping, he implores thy mercy. For their sake, if not for mine own, have pity and slay me not."

While still the distracted king stood bowed in doubt came Achilles running from the camp to say there was terrible tumult among the men, who were crying out that the maiden must be sacrificed without delay, and that when he would have stayed them from their purpose, they had hunted him with stones, so that he had barely escaped with his life. Nevertheless he would fight for the maiden, and trusted there might be faithful men and true who would stand by him and help him to save her life.

When the maiden heard his words, she stood forth and said: "Hearken, my mother, be not angry with my father. It is idle to fight against Fate. This young man must not suffer, for his help will avail nought, and he will only perish. All Greece looks to me. Without me the ships cannot make their voyage, nor the city of Troy be taken. Wherefore I give myself a willing offering for the people. Let the Greeks take the city of Troy and it shall be my memorial."

Nor could the maiden be turned from her resolve, though they besought her with tears and entreaties. So they that were appointed led her to the grove of Artemis, where was erected an altar. The whole army of Greece gathered around. "I pray the gods that ye prosper," said the maiden. "Win victory in this war, and come back in safety to your homes. To this end with good heart do I offer my neck to the sword." Then did the king cover his face with his mantle. All the host marveled at her good courage. The herald commanded silence, and the soothsayer put a garland upon her head and drew the sharp knife from his sheath.

Then there befell a marvelous thing. Calchas struck with his knife, and the sound of the stroke was plainly heard by all. But the maiden was not there. In her stead lay a great hind, and the altar was red with the blood thereof.

For Artemis was merciful, and caught
The victim away in darkness, and the Greeks
Slaughtered a hind, esteeming it the maid.
But she was rapt to Tauris, there became
The priestess of the sanctuary. . . .

When Orestes grew up he went in search of his dear sister and came at length to Tauris. To this city had Iphigenia been carried by Artemis to serve as a priestess in the temple. It was her duty to sacrifice all strangers to the goddess, and she was about to perform this gruesome task when she recognized Orestes. Then, indeed, were they joyful. They fled the city, taking the image of Artemis with them.

The story of Iphigenia has been told with slight variations by many writers, in particular Euripides and Æschylus, who were two of the greatest dramatists of all time.

THE MOTHER OF THE GRACCHI

THERE was once a very gracious and beautiful lady in Rome named Cornelia. She might have married a king, but she preferred to be the wife of a Roman citizen. Her husband's name was Gracchus, and her two sons were called the Gracchi. She loved them devotedly, educated them in virtue and manliness, and trained them to be noble citizens of Rome.

One day there came to her home a fashionable lady, who is thus described by old Robert Burton: "Some light housewife belike, that was dressed like a May lady, and, as most of our gentlewomen are, was more solicitous of her head-tire than of her health, that spent her time between a comb and a glass, and had rather be fair than honest (as Cato said), and have the commonwealth turned topsy-turvy than her tires marred."

This fashionable companion lady "did nought but brag of her fine robes and jewels." The noble Cornelia listened with patience, because she was hostess to the other, and showed nothing of the disdain she felt for the vain, frivolous creature.

But presently the grand lady said to Cornelia: "You must have jewels, too. Pray show me your most precious things, for I love to look upon jewels." Then Cornelia rose and went out of the chamber, and presently returned, leading by the hand her two manly sons. "These," said she, "are the only jewels of which I can boast."

Those sons grew to be heroic men, and all Rome knew that the mother had helped to make them valiant and upright. In her own lifetime, a statue was raised to Cornelia, and on it was written: CORNELIA MATER GRACCHORUM, a Latin inscription meaning CORNELIA, MOTHER OF THE GRACCHI.

Cornelia showing her "jewels."

To be the mother of heroic men is a great destiny. The name of Cornelia will live forever, and her famous sons are now remembered chiefly because they had so great and good a mother, and did credit to her training.

A LITHUANIAN GIRL'S QUICK WIT

DURING the World War a village in Lithuania, which was a part of Russia, had been captured by the Germans. A group of German soldiers entered one of the farmhouses, leaving sentries on guard outside. Calling the farmer's daughter, a girl of seventeen, the commander ordered her to serve his men with wine, and threatened that if she did not, the house should be burned and its occupants killed or captured.

When the girl had reached the cellar where the wine was stored, a bold plan came into her mind. Before carrying the wine to the soldiers she would drop into it a powder made of bluebells, which would drug the men. Quickly this was done.

The men drank deeply of the berry wine, and in a little while they had fallen into a stupor. Then, carrying some of the wine to the sentries, the girl explained that the commander had sent it to them. They, too, drank and were overpowered.

After she and her father had disarmed and firmly tied the stupefied men, the young heroine made her way to the Russian commanding officer, who sent a detachment of soldiers back with her.

Restored to consciousness by a dash of cold water, the Germans were amazed at their predicament. Later their young captor was rewarded with St. George's Cross, a decoration rarely given.

THE NEXT STORY OF GOLDEN DEEDS IS ON PAGE 4089.

THE PLEASANT LAND OF FRANCE, WITH ITS CHIEF RIVERS AND TOWNS

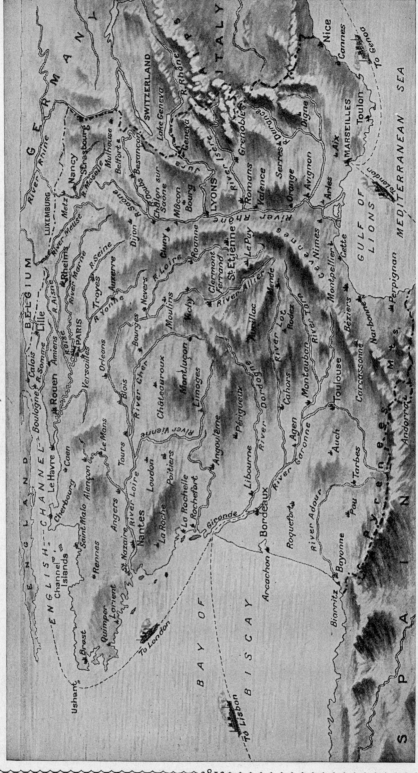

If you look carefully at this map you will see that France possesses great natural highways between the Mediterranean and the Atlantic Ocean. The first follows the valleys of the Rhone and the Saône and across the Côte d'Or hills into the valley of the Seine. The second, skirting the Cevennes hills, gains the Atlantic by way of the valley of the Garonne. France has noticeably good inland waterways with its principal rivers and their tributaries all connected by a series of canals.

© Ewing Galloway.

This is, perhaps, the most famous square in Europe. In the days of the Terror it was called the Place de la Révolution; but it has now been named the Place de la Concorde, or the Place of Peace.

FRANCE IN MODERN TIMES

CONTINUED FROM 3576

THERE are many famous sayings about that beautiful country, "La Belle France," that have come down to us from the lips of those who knew her in the far past. Let us take two of them, that all French children know well, as a guide to our picture of France of modern days.

There was a learned and brave Dutchman named Grotius, who spent much time in France during the reign of the good King Henry IV and his son—about the time of Queen Elizabeth. When Grotius was asked what he thought of France, he answered earnestly: "France is the most beautiful kingdom there is—after the Kingdom of Heaven."

Then, again, hundreds of years before Grotius said this, there was an old traveler and geographer named Strabo—the first, as far as we know, who tried to give an interesting account of countries, not a mere list of names—who wrote with enthusiasm, when France was still Gaul, about the grand mountain masses in the south and southeast, about the fine spreading rivers, about the seas brought near by a protecting God. "Gaul," said Strabo, "must one day be the most flourishing place on earth." Now let us try to find out what was in the mind of Strabo when he spoke of the bounding seas, the mountain masses, the spreading rivers, and their influence on the future greatness of the country.

It is a wonderful point in the position of France that, though part of a great continent, it has many of the advantages of an island. It can send ships direct across four seas. By way of the North Sea it can trade easily with Germany and the Baltic countries; across the narrow Channel, which the French call La Manche—meaning "the sleeve," from its shape—it has constant and quick communication with England. France is so near to England that more than once the possibility of making a tunnel under the sea from Dover to Calais has been discussed. If this were done, trains could carry passengers and goods from either side as easily and quickly as from London to Dorking, or any other journey of twenty miles.

At present one must face a sea voyage, often very rough and unpleasant, lasting about an hour, for they still depend on the service of the various steamer routes which act as links to bind not only England and France closely together, but England to the whole continent of Europe, and to the great

3813

Eastern world beyond. But this communication with the narrow seas is not all. The ports on the west of France face the great Atlantic highway to the New World; and the blue Mediterranean on the south carries not only the commerce of all southern Europe and northern Africa, but also the fleets of ships taking the direct line to the East by way of the Suez Canal—that first wonderful ship canal, built by a Frenchman.

THE BOUNDARIES OF FRANCE BY LAND AND BY SEA

But France has land frontiers as well as the ever-restless, hungry seas. There are the snow-tipped Pyrenees, stretching from the Atlantic to the Mediterranean, still keeping guard between France and Spain. It was in vain that Louis XIV cried out so triumphantly when his grandson came to the throne of Spain: "The Pyrenees are no more," for the white peaks still look down over the grand passes and green slopes, where shepherds tend their flocks, to France on the north, to Spain on the south.

Thousands and thousands of valuable and heroic French lives have been spent through the centuries in guarding or in trying to extend the land frontiers on the east of France, from the days of Charlemagne to the present day. In many parts, especially in the lowlands of Belgium and on the wooded sides of the Vosges Mountains in Germany, the battlefields lie too thick to count. The Jura Mountains separate France from Switzerland, and the great mass of mountainous land south of Lake Geneva lies between France and Italy. This grand country is the western end of the highest land in Europe, which stretches right across Switzerland and the Tyrol to the Danube. The highest peak, Mont Blanc, the white mountain, is in France, and is three and a half times as high as Ben Nevis.

THE FOUR COUNTRIES THAT FRANCE TOUCHES ON HER EASTERN BORDERS

Here, then, are the four countries which France touches on her eastern borders—Belgium, Germany, Switzerland, Italy. On these frontiers were forts and strong towns, and thousands of soldiers were massed in silent watchfulness, even in the days before the Great War broke out. But these frontier barriers were in truth the great outlets by which France was connected with the

very heart of Europe. All day and all night trains pass uninterruptedly over the frontiers, from Paris, Lyons, Marseilles and other great junctions, carrying passengers and goods to every capital and every centre of industry in the wide continent. Lines run down into Spain, by each end of the Pyrenees, near the seashore, and even the massive Alps are now no barrier, as they were of old; for French skill has pierced the tunnel of Mont Cenis, and the train quickly passes from the land of dazzling snow and glaciers to the land of dazzling sunshine, gay flowers and blue lakes.

Now, the size of this country thus bounded by sea and land is nearly twice as large as that of Great Britain. The whole of France lies in the middle of the temperate zone, halfway between the icy cold of the North Pole and the burning heat of the Equator. Added to the advantage of the moderate climate that this position gives it, it is also neither too damp nor too dry, for the west winds—like those that help England's dairy farming and cotton industry—bring plenty of rain, which in turn is dried up by the land winds from the northeast.

THE GREAT GROUP OF HIGHLANDS IN THE CENTRE OF FRANCE

But we have spoken only of one of the mountain masses mentioned by Strabo. The other is the great central group of highlands which the French call the "Massif Central." This is the most prominent feature in the country, and goes far to make the face of France what it is. The valley of the Rhone separates the Massif Central from the Massif of the Alps, and a narrow plain separates it from the great chain of the Pyrenees. The Massif Central is not nearly so lofty as the Alps and the Pyrenees, being more nearly the height of the Jura and the Vosges; but it extends over nearly a fifth part of France, forming a most wonderful and beautifully varied country in the old province of lovely Auvergne. The chain of the Cevennes, rising from the Rhone valley, forms part of this central plateau of high land.

In the mountains of Auvergne we see the fantastic shapes of the old volcanic peaks, which ages ago poured out streams of fiery lava and clouds of stones and ashes. To-day their "mouths" hold dark lakes, or cattle feeding on soft,

HERE AND THERE IN BEAUTIFUL FRANCE

Mont Saint Michel in Normandy.

A street in Cauterets in the Pyrenees.

The Napoleon Monument at Ajaccio, his birthplace.

The little town of Ajaccio, capital of the island of Corsica.

A lock on St. Martin's Canal, Paris.

The docks at Calais.

rich, green grass. The bare, bold granite heights, and deep rifts in which the rivers run 1,500 feet below, make a fine contrast with the fertile lower slopes and valleys. It was in the quiet, smiling valleys of the Cevennes that some of the bitterest persecutions of the Albigensian Protestants took place in the bad days of Louis XV.

THE GREAT SPREADING RIVERS THAT RUN THROUGH THE VALLEYS OF FRANCE

And now we come to the "spreading rivers." From the great and varied Massif Central, the face of France slopes gently toward the Channel and the Atlantic, forming the vast plains of the northwest and the southwest. Toward the Mediterranean the slope is steeper. In the large plains lie three out of the four great river-systems of France, which spread over it like the veins of leaves; they are the Seine, the Loire and the Garonne. The hills that rise on the immense plains serve but to give a gentle rise to the otherwise flat country, and to guide the courses of the numerous streams and rivers.

We have already glanced at the Rhone, the most rapid of French rivers, in the part of its course between the Alps and the Cevennes. It rises in the snows of Switzerland, passes through Lake Geneva, and soon after turns sharply south, as it receives the slow Saône from the Vosges. In the angle formed by the meeting of the two rivers lies the great city of Lyons. The Rhone valley has always been the chief highway between the north and south, from the days when the Roman traders and soldiers pushed their way through the forests and swamps to the time when the Marseilles battalion marched to Paris, singing their song, and the Paris and Marseilles coach lumbered along from town to town, after the fashion of our own coaches in the beginning of the last century.

THE LONG RIVER LOIRE AND THE SEINE THAT WINDS SLOWLY TO PARIS

The Rhone forms a marshy delta where it joins the Mediterranean, and there are sand-bars across its mouths. Marseilles, the greatest port in France, lies to the east of the delta on the stormy Gulf of Lions—so named after the violence of the storms, not after the city of Lyons. The Garonne is the other great river of the south, rising in the Pyrenees and collecting on its right bank numbers of streams from the mountains of Auvergne in the great central highlands. Its waters pour into the Atlantic through a wide and long mouth, called the Gironde, below Bordeaux.

The Loire, the longest of French rivers, three times as long as the Thames, flows in a great semicircle from the Central Mountains, joined on its way by many tributaries; its waters also pour into the Atlantic. Both the Garonne and the Loire are subject to great floods, and dikes are built in many places to prevent the waters from bursting over the plains. It is a sad calamity when the flood proves too strong. The fields then all lie under water, and in towns people have to go about in boats; often many are drowned, and their homes destroyed.

The slow, winding Seine—its name means the Tranquil—rises in the hills on the right bank of the Saône, and, joined by the Marne at Paris, flows through Rouen to the chief port of North France, Le Havre, on the English Channel. It carries more merchandise than any of the other great rivers. Along its banks lies much beautiful scenery.

THE WATERWAYS THAT BEAR GOODS FROM ONE END OF FRANCE TO THE OTHER

It is reckoned that France has 150 rivers on which boats of various sizes can carry goods a long way inland, which is a great advantage, as so much of this solid-shaped country is far from the sea. But there are, besides these rivers, hundreds of miles of canals, some connecting or improving the different river-systems, some joining the Atlantic and the Mediterranean by the valley of the Garonne, some joining the Rhone, above its delta, with the sea. And so it is that many kinds of heavy goods, for which there is no hurry in transport, can be carried by water from one end of the country to another.

Sometimes the canals go through tunnels in the hills, sometimes they are carried by aqueducts across valleys. It is a strange sight to see a barge with sails crossing by an aqueduct high up in the air. On and on these barges go, on their "inland voyage," day after day, generally drawn by a horse, sometimes taken in tow by a launch, past the banks of blue forget-me-nots; past the groups of laughing children in blue smocks and

HIGHWAYS AND BY-WAYS IN FRANCE

An old lady of the Landes country.

A girl of Alsace.

A laborer in the Pyrenees.

A water cart drawn by oxen, near Biarritz.

Comrades in harness—an odd sight on the road.

A lady of Provence.

Breton mother and child.

A maid of Brittany.

pinafores, looking like large forget-me-nots themselves; through the cornfields and the orchards and the vineyards and the fine farms so carefully tended; past the villages and the castles, the towns and the great cathedrals.

WHAT THE CHILDREN SEE FROM THE BOATS AS THEY SAIL ALONG

Truly, the families of the bargees can learn what is grown in France, what the people do in France, without looking in books. They see that wheat is grown nearly everywhere, for France generally produces in her great plains more than any other country, except North America and Russia, and many thousands of men and women work in the fields to raise it, in the mills to grind it, in the barges and trains to carry it where it is needed. Still, there is not enough to feed all the people, and more must be brought from other countries.

The bargees, too, see much of the vineyards all along the courses of the Loire and the Garonne, and in the district east of Paris, called La Champagne. There are also great numbers of vineyards all along the Saône and the Rhone, and on the Mediterranean coast. France not only uses a great quantity of wine at home, for it is much cheaper than with us, but sends away all over the world many different kinds. Thousands of workers gather and press the grapes, make casks and bottles, and attend to all the various processes necessary before the wine is ready.

In the valley of the Rhone also grow mulberry trees, which feed great numbers of silkworms, and at Lyons and in the neighborhood are factories, which send out their famous silks, satins, ribbons, velvets, to every country where fine materials for clothes and furnishing are needed. The factories also get supplies of raw silk from Italy and from the East.

THE COAL-FIELDS AND THE FACTORIES THAT THEY FEED WITH POWER

Round the edge of the central highlands are coal-fields, of which the largest, St. Etienne, near Lyons, supplies the silk factories. As some iron and other metals are also found here and there about the same districts, there are various industries carried on, such as the making of tools and machinery. But the canals, and railway lines, too, lie thickest in the northeast of France, and many barges used to pass to and from the largest coal-fields of the country, situated on the borders of Belgium. France produces only two-thirds of the coal needed in the country; the rest she buys from Great Britain and the United States. She also had to buy iron and other metals needed at Lille, the chief town of a large district of tall chimneys and black smoke, with a deafening whiz and whir of machinery, and crowds of workers, all reminding us of manufacturing centres at home. Here were iron and steel works, and linen and cotton factories. These industries are carried on all along the northeastern frontier, Nancy and Belfort being particularly famed for cotton and metal works. Many factories were destroyed during the World War.

The raw cotton from America and other places comes to Le Havre, at the mouth of the Seine, which is often called the Liverpool of France, and from it are supplied Rouen, the Manchester of France, where there are many cotton factories, and also the rest of the cotton towns in the north and east.

THE MAKING OF THE THINGS THAT FILL THE SHOP WINDOWS IN PARIS

The linen from these districts is made chiefly from flax grown in the fields of the north. Great quantities of the blue cotton and linen materials worn so much in France are made in these mills. To supplement the wool of the sheep grown on the Ardennes and in French pastures, supplies come by way of England from Australia and New Zealand, and from South America, to feed the various woolen factories of the north and east.

From the old decaying granite of the Massif Central come kaolin, from which the finest china is made, though sometimes it is found easier to bring this special white clay up the Seine from the granite of Cornwall and Norway. At Sèvres, near Paris, and at Limoges, near Auvergne, most beautiful china is made. The French are particularly skillful in painting the shining surface. They also make very pretty peasant pottery, which costs about as many cents as the fine china does dollars.

But to see samples of the numberless things made in France, we must look into the shop windows of Paris. Thousands of other nations go to Paris—it takes only seven and a half hours from London—and everyone can find something of interest and delight in this

TWO DIFFERENT KINDS OF RIVERS

The Saône, a river of eastern France, rises in the Faucilles mountains in the department of Vosges and flows into the Rhone at Lyons. Its course is very winding and therefore not very rapid. Upon its banks are the important towns of Chalon-sur-Saône and Mâcon. For about two-thirds of its length (301 miles) the Saône is canalized. Itself a feeder of the Rhone, its most important tributaries are the Doubs and Seille.

This wonderful Alpine glacier, near Chamonix, is known as the Mer-de-glace, or "sea of ice." We know that when sufficient weight of snow accumulates in a region above snow-line the mass yields to pressure and flows outward and downward. Thus in mountain regions we have rivers of ice, or glaciers, and in polar regions icebergs. Glaciers move slowly, faster in the centre and on top than at the sides and bottom.

splendid city. There are less than half as many people in Paris as in London; the river running through the city is clean, and there are scarcely any fogs.

THE TREASURES OF PARIS AND THE PLEASURES OF ITS STREETS

Visitors who love history can find endless pleasure in wandering about the streets and squares, the bridges and palaces, where great events moved so quickly a hundred years ago. Those who love art can find splendid treasures in the museums and galleries. And as for the shops, besides the china, there is the wonderful and costly lace made in various parts of the country, the finest muslins and cambrics, the brocades and velvets from Lyons, the cloths from Amiens, the clocks and jewelry, of which a good deal is made in the neighborhood of Paris, as well as the thousands of things that people buy for presents. Paris fashions in clothes are famed all the world over, and dressmakers and milliners come from other countries to find out what is going to be worn, and to copy the latest and smartest styles for their customers at home.

From this rich and beautiful city of Paris—one is apt to forget the great lines of fortifications round it, making it the largest fortified camp in the world—radiate not only the great roads of France, but nearly all the chief railway lines; for Paris is the very centre of the trade and industry of France, a sort of living heart, whose pulse-beats are felt to the farthest frontiers by means of the great arteries of roads, waterways and railways. A railway train requires only about five hours to reach Lille and the district of which it is the centre, from Paris, and the lines pass on through Belgium and Germany to Holland, Austria, Russia. Another branch of the railway passes through Amiens, where we may see the most perfect cathedral in France, to Boulogne and Calais.

THE RAILWAY FROM PARIS TO THE SEA, AND THE SHIPS AT MARSEILLES

The east of France down to the Mediterranean is served by the Paris-Lyons-Mediterranean Railway. The main line follows the old route through the Rhone valley, passing Lyons and Avignon, where the splendid palace of the pope still speaks of the times when this city and its neighborhood belonged to the Roman Church. Marseilles itself, the queen of the south, is a great world-port; every language is heard in its streets, from the sailors who bring ships there. Marseilles is one of the chief markets in France, and has factories for tile-making, soap and oil. Through Marseilles passes French trade with the Far East, with the New World, with Africa, and, nearer still, steamers link it to the island of Corsica, about half the size of Wales, which passed to France from Italy the year before the birth of its greatest son, Napoleon Bonaparte.

Thousands of Americans pass through Paris and Marseilles, not only on their way to Egypt and the East, but to spend the winter in the beautiful coast district between Marseilles and Italy—the Riviera. They leave fogs, snow and cold winds behind in their own country, and in the course of a few days—fourteen hours from Paris to Marseilles—pass to warm sunshine in a bright, clear air, under a blue sky, and can sit out of doors, facing the blue sea, enjoying the scent of roses and the sight of brilliant patches of geraniums, as well as the beauty of orange and lemon orchards and olive groves.

THE SPLENDOR OF THE OLD TOWNS OF SOUTHERN FRANCE

Nice is one of the largest and most fashionable of the Riviera towns, and all nations of Europe gather here to find health and to amuse themselves. Fine scents and soaps come from this part of France and the best salad oil from olives.

The line of the south does not run to Paris, but connects the Atlantic with the Mediterranean, along the valley of the Garonne and its canals. There are towns in this part of France of surpassing interest. Toulouse is a splendid city of churches and mansions, with a museum and a fine library. It is at the meeting of the ways for commerce and industry of all kinds. Carcassonne is also on this line, and on the canal of the south; its strong walls still tell of its importance in the old days when it was the key to the narrow passage between the Massif Central and the Pyrenees. The wonderful cathedral of Albi, so lofty and grand, is but one among the great number of cathedrals found all over France, the undying glory of those who built them in the Middle Ages, and the delight of all who in later days love art and architecture.

To go from Cette, on the Mediterranean, to Bordeaux, the great wine port of the west, takes eleven hours of railway traveling, and lines branch off to many health resorts in the Pyrenees, and to Spain. Bordeaux is reached from Paris in about ten hours, passing Orleans, Tours—the garden of France—and Poitiers on the way.

Normandy and Brittany are served by the railway of the west. Cherbourg, the great naval and military port of the Channel, on the bold Cotentin peninsula, is reached in eight hours from Paris. Many German and English liners touch here on their way to and from America. Like Plymouth, it has a great breakwater to protect its harbor. Another naval and military port, Brest, on this line, at the extreme west of France, is five hours farther from Paris.

NORMANDY AND BRITTANY, AND THE GREAT SEAPORTS OF FRANCE

Le Havre, the second port in France, is about six hours from Paris by rail. The tall lighthouse above the town looks down on a busy scene of ships and docks, for the Seine is the great northern door into the country, and by it goods are taken to Rouen and to distant Paris. We can see the cotton for the factories unloaded on the wharves of Rouen, under the shadow of the great churches for which it is so famous. And on the heights overlooking the windings of the "tranquil" river, in the fine, wide valley, stands the statue of Joan of Arc.

English people travel much in Normandy, which is so close to England; the seaside places are charming, and the long, tree-bordered roads are good for cycling. The cathedrals and churches are full of interest, and the apple orchards are a beautiful sight in their white spring dress. It is most interesting to watch the cider being made in the presses by the roadside in autumn. Over the wide-spreading valleys, in both Normandy and Picardy, grow fields of beet-root, so much used to make sugar; also great quantities of potatoes, largely sent to England. From Le Havre pass out millions of eggs and tons of butter and cheese from the dairy farms of the north. A gay sight it is on market days in Normandy and Brittany when the country folk crowd into the towns to buy and sell. Such pretty white caps and shining ornaments there are, such red and blue umbrellas,

glowing brass pots full of milk, and such loud, animated talking. The serious-looking babies in close white caps seem the only quiet people.

THE CLATTER OF THE CHILDREN'S SHOES, AND THE BLUE SMOCKS AND BLOUSES

Perhaps the first morning you wake up in France you will wonder what causes that clatter, clatter, clatter over the stones. You look out and see merry little crowds of children, boys and girls, in blue smocks and blouses, the girls with hair very neatly plaited, all hastening to school, with their satchels on their backs. The clatter is from the wooden shoes, or sabots, that many of them wear. They are like the clogs of the Lancashire mill-workers, whose ancestors, it is said, got the pattern of the clogs from the French Huguenots, who did so much to help on the spinning and weaving in England when they left their native land for that country.

The French care a great deal about education, and have built fine schools all over the country. There are all sorts of schools, and all have an equal chance of getting the teaching their brains are best fitted to grasp. Every Frenchman over twenty-one shares in the government of the country.

So the greatest trouble is taken to teach the children to be good citizens, and to know their mother country well, her resources and her needs, and to understand what their brothers and sisters are doing in the ninety departments of France. Those departments were formed at the Revolution from the old provinces, so that the same fair laws and government should prevail equally all over the country.

DIFFERENCES IN LANGUAGE AND CUSTOMS IN FRANCE

You see, therefore, that the French people are descended from almost as many races as there are now represented in the United States and Canada. Their descendants have of course mingled together and become one people; but they have many different characteristics in the different parts of the country. If we were to travel down the coast of France, we should find that the inhabitants of Normandy, which was peopled by the Northmen, are not at all like the people of Brittany, which was settled by the ancient Britons; and the Gascons, who live on the shore of the Bay of Biscay, at the foot of the

Pyrenees, which made the last stronghold of the Iberians, have a special character of their own. In the matter of language there are still great differences. Originally all these people spoke different languages, and the dialect, or patois, of one part of the country is still quite distinct from that of other parts. Although French is, of course, taught in the schools, the people of Brittany still speak their old language, which is the same as that of the Welsh, and indeed if a Welshman and a Breton were to speak to one another in their native languages they could understand each other. The people in the north, near the Belgian frontier, are very like the Belgians, and are quite different from the people of Marseilles and Avignon, and the people of these towns differ from the peasants of the "Landes," near Bordeaux, where the herdsmen walk about on stilts in the damp, heavy sands of the plain on which they pasture their flocks and herds and their geese.

It is natural that all these people should have had different ways of living, and many quaint superstitions and customs still survive. These customs are slowly dying out, however, and before long most of them will have disappeared.

But in spite of all their differences, there is one point on which there is no lack of unity among the French people, and that is their intensely passionate love of their beautiful country. The instant she is attacked, from north and south, east and west, they rise as one man to defend her. They will bear any privation, and are ready at any moment to sacrifice themselves and all they have for her sake. In time of peace every man who reaches the age of twenty, unless he is unfit either because he is not strong enough or because there is something wrong with his mind, must serve in the army. The term of service is two years, and from this full term there is no way of escape.

MANY PEASANT OWNERS OF THE LAND IN FRANCE

Though there are many large cities in France, the people do not readily take to town life, and nearly half the population is engaged in agriculture. Much of the land is owned by the peasantry, who hold farms of from five to fifty acres, and the man who owns fifty acres of good land is very well off indeed. On these small farms a good deal of work is done by hand, and in some places agriculture is still very primitive. The people are slow to give up their old ways, but of late years new machinery has been introduced, the state supports agricultural schools and colleges, and improved ways of farming are taking the place of the old.

Even in the manufacturing parts of the country the people are not prone to gather into the large factories. Many of the beautiful textiles that come to us from France are made by cottage workers, some of whom, since the introduction of electricity, have been able to increase the amount of their business by using the new power looms.

The people, as a rule, live simply, and, as the French are as a general thing very thrifty, most of them are able to save. Their thriftiness sometimes becomes miserliness, but there are few, even among very poor people, who are not able to lay something away for their old age. It is because of the thrifty habits of the whole people that France has again and again in her history been able to turn disaster into prosperity.

We must not let ourselves think, however, that the French devote themselves only to farming and manufacturing. Among this great people there are not only some of the greatest painters and sculptors, architects and writers, in the world, but France has also given to the world some of the greatest scientists and philosophers of all time and of our own day. You will find some of their names mentioned with honor in the Book of Men and Women.

HOW THE PEOPLE OF FRANCE ARE GOVERNED

Although France is a republic, the government is not quite like the government of the United States. In some ways it is more like the government of England. The president is elected for seven years, and he may be re-elected for a second term, but he has not very much real power. He sends his messages to the legislature in writing, although every recent president has been a member either of the Senate or of the Chamber of Deputies, and does not lose his seat on his election to the presidency. He has the power to negotiate treaties, and even in some cases to ratify them, but they must in all cases be reported to the legislature as soon as possible, and he cannot declare war without the consent of both the houses. He has the power to dissolve the Chamber of Deputies, but only on the advice of the Senate, and every one of his acts must be signed by a minister. He also has the power of pardoning offenders against the law.

You see, the power of the president is well hedged round. The real ruler is the Prime Minister. Since the date of the Constitution, however, no prime minister has ever stayed in office during the four years for which the Chamber of Deputies is elected.

The Constitution does not decree that the members of the Cabinet must be members of the legislature; but, as a matter of practice, the majority of them are. The Minister of War is usually an officer in the army, and the Minister of Marine an officer in the navy. Sometimes the Minister of Foreign Affairs is called in from the outside, but the rule is that the other Cabinet ministers are either senators or deputies, and under the Constitution they are responsible to the legislature for their acts. If the majority of the Chamber of Deputies does not uphold the Cabinet on any question, the Prime Minister is expected to resign. The President then appoints a new prime minister, who proceeds to form a new cabinet. Each appointment must be signed by a minister as well as by the president, and when the ministry changes, a member of the old cabinet stays in office long enough to sign the appointment of the new prime minister.

Changes of ministry have happened so often that a government sometimes goes out of power before a year has passed, but the president cannot be put out of office before his term has expired unless he is impeached by the Lower House, tried by the Senate and found guilty. One president, however, who became very unpopular, was forced to resign because he could find no one to serve in his cabinet.

The legislature is composed of two houses, the Chamber of Deputies and the Senate. The deputies must be twenty-five years old, are elected by manhood-suffrage vote and serve for four years. Members of the Senate are elected by the deputies of the department that they are to represent, the members of the council of the department, the members of the local councils, and a delegate from each commune, which corresponds somewhat to our township. Each senator serves for a term of nine years, but one third of the Senate is elected every three years, so that the whole body never goes out of office at one time. For the election of the president, the two houses sit together in what is called the National Assembly, and the candidate who receives the majority of their votes is elected. He receives about $240,000 a year as salary, and as much more for expenses. He is also provided with an official residence by the state. The senators and deputies are each paid the same salary of about $5,400 a year.

There is nothing in France that corresponds to the state or provincial government of the United States and Canada. The councils of the departments are appointed by the government, and so are the governors, who are called prefects. Each department is subdivided into arrondissements. The councils of the arrondissements are elected; but these councils are presided over by sub-prefects, who are appointed by the government; and the council has to do with little except local taxation. The councils of the commune, which transact local affairs, are also elected, and these local councils are presided over by the *maires*, who are also the local police officers and are directly responsible to the central government for the maintenance of the laws by the people.

THE GREAT COLONIAL EMPIRE OF THE FRENCH

France has a great colonial empire. In Africa, as we read in the story of that continent, Algiers and Tunis, the Desert of Sahara, and a great part of the fruitful western coast are under her rule, and part of Morocco is under her protection. She has large possessions in the Congo, Madagascar belongs to her, and she owns part of Somaliland on the western coast of the Red Sea.

In Asia she has large possessions to the south of China: Annam, Cambodia, Cochin-China and Tonking; and in America she still holds part of Guiana on the northern coast of South America, a few of the West Indian Islands, and the small islands of St. Pierre and Miquelon off the coast of Newfoundland.

FRENCH PEOPLE ARE NOT GOOD COLONISTS

But the love of country is so intense among the French that they do not willingly go abroad even to their own colonies, and consequently the colonies are not prosperous. They do a good deal for the education of the native people of the colonies, but they do not go to live there. This is true of even Algiers and Tunis, which lie across the Mediterranean, almost at the door of southern France. These two colonies, however, come nearer to being prosperous than any of the others. The climate of both is delightful. They can be made true garden spots, and already they provide quantities of early fruit, flowers and vegetables for the markets of northern France and England.

Perhaps one of the reasons why the French are not enthusiastic about going to live in their colonies is that they have not been forced out by the necessity of earning a living. The population of France has been at a standstill for many years, and until her people increase in number, she cannot send out many strong young men to make her colonies prosperous children of the motherland.

Since the time of the Franco-Prussian War France has gained steadily in importance, and has become a great power in the councils of the world. Since the time of Napoleon III France and England, who had for so long been enemies, have been friends, and the agreement between them has helped both. Once it seemed as though they might quarrel over Africa. As we read in the story of Africa, a French captain named Marchand tried to establish French possession in the Sudan and cut communication between Egypt and the Upper Nile. For a while it looked as though the French legislature would uphold him, in which case there would have been war, but happily for the world, wiser counsels prevailed. Later all the old sources of contention between the two nations were removed, and the friendship between them became stronger as time went on.

Twice within a few years afterward there was danger of a quarrel with Germany over Morocco, part of which had been drawn under French influence; but in each case the other powers took the part of France, Germany was forced to give way, and the trouble passed over.

At home, there were many quarrels. Education, which had always been in the hands of the religious orders, was taken over by the state, most of the orders were dispersed, and the care of the church buildings was taken from the clergy, and all this created much bad feeling. There were many political difficulties and some bad strikes; but on the whole the country was peaceful and prosperous. Commerce and manufactures increased, great dominions were gained in Africa, science and education advanced, and friendship with other nations was cultivated. The friendship between France, England and Russia became so close that it was called an *entente cordiale*, and the alliance which had been signed between France and Russia provided that if either nation were attacked the other would come to its rescue. There had been disputes with Spain over Morocco, but these had been settled, and good feeling between Italy and France, which had had several disputes over territory in Africa, grew up.

THE BEGINNING OF THE WORLD WAR

In 1914 France presented the picture of a civilized, cultured nation, at peace with all the world. But in that year Germany, which was about to go to war with Russia, invaded France (knowing that France would support Russia), and the World War which plunged the whole world into war began.

After the Belgian forts had been taken, the German armies swept on and almost reached Paris. There, on the Marne River, they were defeated in September by the French armies under General Joffre, aided by a small English army, which had been sent over, but it was impossible then to drive them entirely out of France. During the next four years some of the bloodiest fighting the world has ever seen took place on French soil. Finally, when British, Portuguese, Italians, and, at last, Americans as well, were arrayed alongside the French, the strong German lines were broken, and their discouraged leaders asked for peace, which was finally signed June 28, 1919. By the terms of peace France received back her old territory of Alsace-Lorraine, which had been torn away in 1871, and also partial compensation for the destruction of the war. The northeastern part of France, where were most of the great factories, had been under German control for four years, and the sufferings of the people can never be told.

THE NEXT STORY OF ALL COUNTRIES IS ON PAGE 3959.

PICTURES OF BEAUTIFUL PARIS

SEVEN BRIDGES OF PARIS

THE CHAMPS ELYSEES, THE MOST FAMOUS AVENUE IN PARIS, SEEN FROM
THE ARC DE TRIOMPHE

THE MOST MAGNIFICENT PLEASURE HOUSE IN EUROPE—THE PARIS OPERA

NAPOLEON'S TOMB—THE DOME
DES INVALIDES

THE ALEXANDER III BRIDGE
ACROSS THE SEINE

THE LOUVRE

IN THE GARDENS OF VERSAILLES

THE HOTEL DE VILLE—THE TOWN HALL OF PARIS

THE GREAT ARC DE TRIOMPHE, UNDER WHICH
THE UNKNOWN WARRIOR LIES

THE PANTHEON, IN WHICH THE
GREAT DEAD LIE

THE LITTLE ARC DE TRIOMPHE
NEAR THE LOUVRE

THE BOULEVARD MONTMARTRE, A
CHARACTERISTIC STREET OF PARIS

THE GREAT COLUMN ON THE SITE
OF THE BASTILLE

THE VENDOME COLUMN IN THE HEART
OF PARIS

THE MADELEINE, PARIS, IS BUILT IN THE STYLE OF A ROMAN TEMPLE; IT IS NOT
MODELED ON THE GREEK PARTHENON

THE OLD COUPLE AT THE MILL

CONTINUED FROM 3719

AN old man and his wife, who lived in a little cottage on a hillside, seemed unable ever to agree. They were always quarreling and jangling, and they became the talk of the villagers.

If the old man said a rook was black, his wife declared that it was white; if the woman said a cow was brown, the man would insist that it was black; and so it went on day after day.

At last their jangling was heard in Fairyland, and one of the little old men of the wood determined to put a stop to the quarreling. If the couple did not cease of their own accord, he said, then they should have a lesson which would make them agree.

But the cottager and his wife did not stop their silly quarrels.

At last one day, when they wanted some corn ground, they put the sack in an old-fashioned hand-cart and started to wheel this to the mill.

"You are not pulling at all, husband," said the woman, as she pushed the cart behind.

"What do you mean, wife?" shouted the husband from the front. "Why, it is I who am getting the cart uphill. You are not pushing at all, and I believe that you are hanging on the cart into the bargain."

So they went on, and their jangling did not lighten the load. At last they managed to get the cart up the hill, and wheeling it to the door of the mill, unloaded the sack and carried it in.

Then they went outside to look at the sails going round, and the man stood in front of the mill, while his wife went round to the back.

"Look at the sails!" shouted the husband. "They are going round in the opposite direction to the sun!"

"What do you mean?" cried his wife. "They are going with the sun!"

"You obstinate woman!" said the man. "Anyone can see that the sails are going against the sun."

Of course, both were right, for while one was looking at the top of the sails, the other was looking at the bottom.

"Ah," thought the little man of the woods, "now is my time to teach them a lesson." So when the man cried out angrily for the tenth time, "Cannot you see that the wings are going against the sun?" the little gnome prompted him to seize hold of a sail.

Of course, the woman answered back, and the sly gnome prompted her also to catch hold of one of the sails.

The man and woman were unable to stop the sails, but after they had gone up a little way they could hold on no longer, and fell to the ground.

"Oh," said the man, rubbing his poor head, "didn't that hurt!"

"Yes," said the wife, also rubbing her bruises, "that it did."

Then they limped into the mill, got their flour, and trundled it off home in the cart, agreeing together for the first time—that the fall from the mill had hurt them. But as they had agreed once, they found it easier to agree again, and then again, until at last a more loving couple could not be found.

3829

THE PRINCESS WHO BECAME A GOOSE GIRL

A BEAUTIFUL Princess was to be married to a Prince whom she had never seen.

All preparations were made for the wedding, and the time came when the Princess had to bid farewell to her mother. The Queen was very sad at this parting, for the Prince's kingdom was so far away that she might never see her daughter again.

As they were saying good-bye the Queen remembered a charm and pricked her finger so that three drops of blood fell on her handkerchief. Giving it to her daughter, she said: "Carry this with you wherever you go, and no harm can ever befall you. Lose it: you are in danger."

The Princess spent her days tending the geese.

The Princess thought this strange, but she obeyed, and soon set out with her maid to the land where the Prince lived.

They were both riding, and before they had gone far, the Princess began to feel very thirsty.

"Please fetch me some water from the brook," she said to the maid.

But the maid answered rudely: "I shall not. Get it yourself."

The Princess made no reply, but alighted from her horse, drew the water, and rode on again.

And the handkerchief said: "If your mother knew, it would break her heart."

By-and-by the Princess said again: "I am thirsty again with the dust. Please fetch me some water."

But the maid answered: "You may fetch it yourself. I am not going to be your maid any longer."

Again the Princess made no reply, but alighted from her horse and drew the water.

And the handkerchief said: "If your mother knew, it would break her heart."

The Princess wept, and the handkerchief fell from her hand into the brook.

Then the maid, who knew that the handkerchief could no longer protect her mistress, said: "Give me your dress, and take mine. We will change places. Take my horse, and I shall take your horse Falada. I shall marry the Prince, and everyone must think that I am the Princess. If you refuse, I shall kill you."

The Princess was so terrified that, to save her life, she consented, and they rode on. Presently they came to the palace, and the maid was treated as the Princess, and the Princess as the maid. As the poor Princess stood, sad and alone, in the courtyard, the King looked out of the window and saw her.

"Do you want work?" he asked kindly, feeling for her loneliness.

"Yes, please," answered the Princess.

"I want a girl to help my lad Kurdchen to tend the geese," said the kindly King, "and if you would like to stay here, you may be my little goose girl."

And so the Princess became a goose girl, and spent her days with Kurdchen, tending the geese.

Now, the wicked maid was afraid that the horse Falada might tell the King all that had happened, so she ordered his head to be cut off. But the Princess loved Falada, and she persuaded Kurdchen to hang its head over the kitchen door, and every day as she went out she would say to it: "Do you know who I am, Falada?"

And the head would answer her: "You are the Princess. If your mother knew, it would break her heart."

One day the Princess let down her golden hair while Kurdchen was by. The lad was so struck with its beauty that he wanted to cut off a lock for himself. But the Princess refused, and this made him so angry that he ran to the King and told him that she was a witch.

When the King heard the story of the talking head that hung over the door and the goose girl's beautiful golden hair, he wondered what it all meant. The next day he sent for her, to discover.

The Princess entered the palace and appeared before the King, who was so impressed with her beauty and grace that he said: "You are no goose girl. Tell me who you are."

"Alas! I dare not say," she replied. "I have sworn to tell no one, and if I break my word I shall be killed."

Then the King said: "I am the King of all this land. No one shall hurt you. Tell me all, and I will protect you."

The Princess burst into tears.

"I am the real Princess who was to marry your son, the Prince," she said; "but my maid took away my dress and my horse because she wished to marry

him herself, and she threatened to kill me if I told anyone. If my mother knew, it would break her heart."

"Do not be afraid," said the King, who

Kurdchen ran to tell that the Princess was a witch.

had long suspected the maid and knew at once that this was really the Princess who ought to marry his son.

The King comforted her, had her dressed in royal robes, and sent for the Prince. She looked so beautiful and happy that the Prince immediately fell in love with her, and they were married that very day. A great feast was prepared, to which all the people of the Court were invited, and there was much rejoicing and merry-making because the true Princess had married the Prince. The wicked maid was severely punished, as she well deserved, and banished from the country, and the Prince and Princess lived happily ever after.

THE FRUIT OF HAPPINESS

By Howard Pyle

ONCE upon a time there was a servant who served a wise man, and cooked for him his cabbage and his onions and his pot-herbs and his broth, day after day, time in and time out, for seven years.

In those years the servant was well enough contented, but no one likes to abide in the same place forever, and so one day he took it into his head that he would like to go out into the world to see what kind of a fortune a man might make there for himself. "Very well," says the wise man, the servant's master; "you have served me faithfully these seven years gone, and now that you ask leave to go you shall go. But it is little or nothing in the way of money that I can give you, and so you will have to be content with what I can afford. See, here is a little pebble, and its like is not to be found in the seven kingdoms, for whoever holds it in his mouth can hear while he does so all that the birds and the beasts say to one another. Take it—it is yours, and, if you use it wisely, it may bring you a fortune."

The servant would rather have had the money in hand than the magic pebble, but, as nothing better was to be had, he took the little stone, and, bidding his master good-bye, trudged out into the world to seek his fortune. Well, he jogged on and on, paying his way with the few pennies he had saved in his seven years of service, but for all of his traveling nothing of good happened to him until, one morning, he came to a lonely place where stood a gallows, and there he sat him down to rest, and it is just in such an unlikely place as this that a man's best chance of fortune comes to him sometimes.

As the servant sat there, there came two ravens flying, and lit upon the crossbeam overhead. There they began talking to one another, and the servant popped the pebble into his mouth to hear what they might say.

"Yonder is a traveler in the world," said the first raven.

"Yes," said the second, "and if he only knew how to set about it, his fortune is as good as made."

"How is that so?" said the first raven.

"Why, thus," said the second. "If he only knew enough to follow yonder road over the hill, he would come by-and-by to a stone cross where two roads meet, and there he would find a man sitting. If he would ask it of him, that man would lead him to the garden where the fruit of happiness grows."

"The fruit of happiness!" said the first raven, "and of what use would the fruit of happiness be to him?"

"What use? I tell you, friend, there is no fruit in the world like that, for one has only to hold it in one's hand and wish, and whatever one asks for one shall have."

You may guess that when the servant understood the talk of the ravens he was not slow in making use of what he heard. Up he scrambled and away he went as fast as his legs could carry him. On and on he traveled, until he came to the crossroads and the stone cross of which the raven spoke, and there, sure enough, sat the traveler. He was clad in a weather-stained coat, and he wore dusty boots, and the servant bade him good-morning.

How should the servant know that it was an angel whom he beheld, and not a common wayfarer?

"Whither away, comrade?" asked the traveler.

"Out in the world," said the servant, "to seek my fortune. And what I want to know is this—will you guide me to where I can find the fruit of happiness?"

"You ask a great thing of me," said the other; "nevertheless, since you do ask it, it is not for me to refuse, though I may tell you that many a man has sought for that fruit, and few indeed have found it. But if I guide you to the garden where the fruit grows, there is one condition you must fulfil: many strange things will happen upon our journey between here and there, but concerning all you see you must not ask a question and say not a word. Do you agree to that?"

"Yes," said the servant, "I do."

"Very well," said his new comrade; "then let us be jogging, for I have business in the town to-night, and the time is none too long to get there."

So all the rest of that day they journeyed onward together, until, toward evening, they came to a town with high towers and steep roofs and tall spires. The servant's companion entered the gate as though he knew the place right well, and led the way up one street and down another, until, by-and-by, they came to a noble house that stood a little apart by itself, with gardens of flowers and fruit-trees all around it. There the traveling companion stopped, and, drawing out a little pipe from under his jacket, began playing so sweetly upon it that it made one's heart stand still to listen to the music.

Well, he played and played until, by-and-by, the door opened, and out came a serving-man. "Ho, piper!" said he, "would you like to earn good wages for your playing?"

"Yes," said the traveling companion, "I would, for that is why I came hither."

"Then follow me," said the servant, and thereupon the traveling companion tucked away his pipe and entered, with the other at his heels.

The house-servant led the way from one room to another, each grander than the one they left behind, until at last he came to a great hall where dozens of servants were serving a fine feast. But only one man sat at table—a young man with a face so sorrowful that it made a body's heart ache to look at him. "Can you play good music, piper?" said he.

"Yes," said the piper, "that I can, for I know a tune that can cure sorrow. But before I blow my pipe I and my friend here must have something to eat and drink, for one cannot play well with an empty stomach."

"So be it," said the young man; "sit down with me and eat and drink."

So the two did without second bidding, and such food and drink the serving-man had never tasted in his life before. And while they were feasting together the young man told them his story, and why it was he was so sad. A year before he had married a young lady, the most beautiful in all that kingdom, and had friends and comrades and all things that a man could desire in the world. But suddenly everything went wrong; his wife and he fell out and quarreled until there was no living together, and she had to go back to her old home. Then his companions deserted him, and now he lived all alone.

"Yours is a hard case," said the traveling companion, "but it is not past curing." Thereupon he drew out his pipes and began to play, and it was such a tune as no man ever listened to before. He played and he played, and, after a while, one after another of those who listened to him began to get drowsy. First they winked, then they shut their eyes, and then they nodded until all were as dumb as logs, and as sound asleep as though they would never waken again. Only the servant and the piper stayed awake, for the music did not make them drowsy as it did the rest. Then, when all but they two were tight and fast asleep, the traveling companion arose, tucked away his pipe, and, stepping up to the young man, took from off his finger a splendid ruby ring, as red as blood and as bright as fire, and popped the same into his pocket. And all the while the serving-man stood gaping like a fish to see what his comrade was about. "Come," said the traveling companion, "it is time we were going," and off they went, shutting the door behind them.

As for the serving-man, though he remembered his promise and said nothing concerning what he had beheld, his wits buzzed in his head like a hive of bees, for he thought that of all the ugly tricks he had seen, none was more ugly than this—to bewitch the poor sorrowful young man into a sleep, and then to rob him of his ruby ring after he had fed them so well and had treated them so kindly.

But the next day they jogged on together again until by-and-by they came to a great forest. There they wandered up and down till night came upon them and found them still stumbling onward through the darkness, while the poor serving-man's flesh quaked to hear the wild beasts and the wolves growling and howling around them.

But all the while the angel—his traveling companion—said never a word; he seemed to doubt nothing nor fear nothing, but trudged straight ahead until, by-and-by, they saw a light twinkling far away, and, when they came to it, they found a gloomy stone house, as ugly as eyes ever looked upon. Up stepped the servant's comrade and knocked upon the door—rap! tap! tap! By-and-by it was opened a crack, and there stood an ugly old woman, blear-eyed and crooked and gnarled as a winter twig. But the heart within her was good for all that. "Alas, poor folk!" she cried, "why do you come here? This is a den where lives a band of wicked thieves. Every day they go out to rob and murder poor travelers like yourselves. By-and-by they will come back, and when they find you here they will certainly kill you."

"No matter for that," said the traveling companion; "we can go no farther to-night, so you must let us in and hide us as best you may."

And in he went, as he said, with the servant at his heels trembling like a leaf at what he had heard. The old woman gave them some bread and meat to eat, and then hid them away in the great empty meal-chest in the corner, and there they lay as still as mice.

By-and-by in came the gang of thieves with a great noise and uproar, and down they sat to their supper. The poor servant lay in the chest listening to all they said of the dreadful things they had done that day—how they had cruelly robbed and murdered poor people. Every word that they said he heard, and he trembled until his teeth chattered in his head. But all the same the robbers knew nothing of the two being there, and there they lay until near the dawning of the day. Then the traveling companion bade the servant be stirring, and up they got, and out of the chest they came, and found all the robbers sound asleep and snoring so that the dust flew.

"Stop a bit," said the angel—the traveling companion—"we must pay them for our lodging."

As he spoke he drew from his pocket the ruby ring which he had stolen from the sorrowful young man's finger, and dropped it into the cup from which the robber captain drank. Then he led the way out of the house, and, if the serving-man had wondered the day before at that which his comrade did, he wondered ten times more to see him give so beautiful a ring to such wicked and bloody thieves.

The third evening of their journey the two travelers came to a little hut, neat enough, but as poor as poverty, and there the comrade knocked upon the door and asked for lodging. In the house lived a poor man and his wife; and, though the two were as honest as the palm of your hand, and as good and kind as rain in spring-time, they could hardly scrape enough of a living to keep body and soul

together. Nevertheless, they made the travelers welcome, and set before them the very best that was to be had in the house; and, after both had eaten and drunk, they showed them to bed in a corner as clean as snow, and there they slept the night through.

But the next morning, before the dawning of the day, the traveling companion was stirring again. "Come," said he; "rouse yourself, for I have a bit of work to do before I leave this place."

And strange work it was! When they had come outside of the house, he gathered together a great heap of straw and sticks of wood, and stuffed all under the corner of the house. Then he struck a light and set fire to it, and, as the two walked away through the gray dawn, all was a red blaze behind them.

Still, the servant remembered his promise to his traveling companion, and said never a word or asked never a question, though all that day he walked on the other side of the road, and would have nothing to say or to do with the other. But never a whit did his comrade seem to think of or to care for that. On they jogged, and, by the time evening was at hand, they had come to a neat cottage with apple and pear trees around it, all as pleasant as the eye could desire to see. In this cottage lived a widow and her only son, and they also made the travelers welcome, and set before them a good supper and showed them to a clean bed.

This time the traveling comrade did neither good nor ill to those of the house, but in the morning he told the widow whither they were going, and asked if she and her son knew the way to the garden where grew the fruit of happiness.

"Yes," said she, "that we do, for the garden is not a day's journey from here, and my son himself shall go with you to show you the way."

"That is good," said the servant's comrade, "and if he will do so I will pay him well for his trouble."

So the young man put on his hat, and took up his stick, and off went the three, up hill and down dale, until by-and-by they came over the top of the last hill, and there below them lay the garden.

And what a sight it was, with the leaves shining and glistening like so many jewels in the sunlight! I only wish that I could tell you how beautiful that garden was. And in the middle of it grew a golden tree, and on it golden fruit. The servant who had traveled so long and so far, could see it plainly from where he stood, and he did not need to be told that it was the fruit of happiness. But, after all, all he could do was to stand and look, for in front of them was a great raging torrent, without a bridge for a body to cross over.

"Yonder is what you seek," said the young man, pointing with his finger, "and there you can see for yourself the fruit of happiness."

The traveling companion said never a word, good or bad, but, suddenly catching the widow's son by the collar, he lifted him and flung him into the black, rushing water. Splash! went the young man, and then away he went whirling over rocks and water-falls. "There!" cried the comrade, "that is your reward for your service."

When the servant saw this cruel, wicked deed, he found his tongue at last, and all that he had bottled up for the seven days came frothing out of him like hot beer. Such abuse as he showered upon his traveling companion no man ever listened to before. But to all the servant said the other answered never a word until he had stopped for sheer want of breath. Then—

"Poor fool," said the traveling companion, "if you had only held your tongue a minute longer, you, too, would have had the fruit of happiness in your hand. Now it will be many a day before you have a sight of it again."

Thereupon, as he ended speaking, he struck his staff upon the ground. Instantly the earth trembled, and the sky darkened overhead until it grew as black as night. Then came a great flash of fire from up in the sky, which wrapped the traveling companion about until he was hidden from sight. Then the flaming fire flew away to heaven again, carrying him along with it. After that the sky cleared once more, and, lo and behold! the garden and the torrent and all were gone, and nothing was left but a naked plain covered over with the bones of those who had come that way before, seeking the fruit which the traveling servant had sought.

It was a long time before the servant found his way back into the world again, and the first house he came to, weak and hungry, was the widow's.

But what a change he beheld! It was a poor cottage no longer, but a splendid palace, fit for a queen to dwell in. The widow herself met him at the door, and she was dressed in clothes fit for a queen to wear, shining with gold and silver and precious stones.

The servant stood and stared like one bereft of wits. "How comes all this change?" said he, "and how did you get all these grand things?"

"My son," said the widow woman, "has just been to the garden, and has brought home from there the fruit of happiness. Many a day did we search, but never could we find how to enter into the garden, until, the other day, an angel came and showed the way to my son, and he was able not only to gather of the fruit for himself, but to bring an apple for me also."

Then the poor traveling servant began to thump his head. He saw well enough through the millstone now, and that he, too, might have had one of the fruit if he had but held his tongue a little longer.

Yes, he saw what a fool he had made of himself, when he learned that it was an angel with whom he had been traveling the five days gone.

But, then, we are all of us like the servant for the matter of that; I, too, have traveled with an angel many a day, I dare say, and never knew it.

That night the servant lodged with the widow and her son, and the next day he started back home again upon the way he had traveled before. By evening he had reached the place where the house of the poor couple stood—the house that he had seen the angel set fire to. There he beheld masons and carpenters hard at work hacking and hewing, and building a fine new house. And there he saw the poor man himself standing by giving them orders. "How is this," said the traveling servant; "I thought that your house was burned down?"

"So it was, and that is how I came to be rich now," said the one-time poor man. "I and my wife had lived in our old house for many a long day, and never knew that a great treasure of silver and gold was hidden beneath it, until a few days ago there came an angel and burned it down over our heads, and in the morning we found the treasure. So now we are rich for as long as we may live."

The next morning the poor servant

jogged along on his homeward way more sad and downcast than ever, and by evening he had come to the robbers' den in the thick woods, and there the old woman came running to the door to meet him. "Come in!" cried she; "come in and welcome! The robbers are all dead and gone now, and I use the treasure that they left behind to entertain poor travelers like yourself. The other day there came an angel hither, and with him he brought the ring of discord that breeds spite and rage and quarreling. He gave it to the captain of the band, and after he had gone the robbers fought for it with one another until they were all killed. So now the world is rid of them, and travelers can come and go as they please."

Back jogged the traveling servant, and the next day came to the town and to the house of the sorrowful young man. There, lo and behold! instead of being dark and silent, as it was before, all was ablaze with light and noisy with the sound of rejoicing and merriment. There happened to be one of the household standing at the door, and he knew the servant as the companion of that one who had stolen the ruby ring. Up he came and laid hold of the servant by the collar, calling to his companions that he had caught one of the thieves. Into the house they hauled the poor servant, and into the same room where he had been before, and there sat the young man at a grand feast, with his wife and all his friends around him. But when the young man saw the poor serving-man he came to him and took him by the hand, and set him beside himself at the table. "Nobody except your comrade could be so welcome as you," said he, "and this is why. An enemy of mine one time gave me a ruby ring, and, though I knew nothing of it, it was the ring of discord that bred strife wherever it came. So, as soon as it was brought into the house, my wife and all my friends fell out with me, and we quarreled so that they all left me. But, though I knew it not at that time, your comrade was an angel, and took the ring away with him, and now I am as happy as I was sorrowful before."

By the next night the servant had come back to his home again. Rap! tap! tap! he knocked at the door, and the wise man who had been his master opened to him. "What do you want?" said he.

"I want to take service with you again," said the traveling servant.

"Very well," said the wise man; "come in and shut the door."

And for all I know the traveling servant is there to this day. For he is not the only one in the world who has come in sight of the fruit of happiness, and then jogged all the way back home again to cook cabbage and onions and pot-herbs, and to make broth for wiser men than himself to sup.

That is the end of this story.

A FAIRY FUNERAL

WILLIAM BLAKE lived to be seventy years of age, yet he never ceased to be a child; though he rose to the full stature of manhood, the elves could always reach to whisper in his ear. Throughout his life he was cheered by visions. Walking on the sands by the sea, he would meet great men of the past, patriarchs, prophets and poets; many a time he conversed with Moses, Homer, Dante and Milton. His faithful wife Katherine, walking by his side, could not see them, yet never doubted they were there. When Blake was questioned as to the appearance of these great men he saw and conversed with, he replied, "All, all majestic shadows, gray but luminous, and superior to the common height of men." Not only by the sea, but in the pretty slip of garden which lay before his modest cottage, many a fanciful sight appeared to him.

"Did you ever see a fairy's funeral, madam?" he once said to a lady who happened to be in his good company.

"Never, sir," was the answer.

"I have," said Blake, "but not before last night. I was walking alone in my garden; there was great stillness among the branches and flowers, and more than common sweetness in the air; I heard a low and pleasant sound, and I knew not whence it came. At last I saw the broad leaf of a flower move, and underneath I saw a procession of creatures, of the size and color of green and gray grass-hoppers, bearing a body laid out on a rose-leaf, which they buried with songs, and then disappeared. It was a fairy funeral."

THE CAT AND THE PARROT

MADAME THEOPHILE was a sandy cat of whom a French writer, Théophile Gautier, tells us this charming story:

She had a white chest, a pink nose, and blue eyes; she was called Madame Théophile because she dwelt with me on the most friendly terms, sleeping at the foot of my bed, dreaming on the arm of my chair while I wrote, descending to the garden to follow me in my walks, assisting at my meals, sometimes even intercepting a morsel of food which I might be carrying on my fork to my mouth.

One day a friend of mine, who was going away for a few days, confided to my care his parrot. The bird, feeling himself transported to a strange land, climbed by means of his beak to the top of his perch, and sitting there silent and trembling, rolled around him eyes full of alarm.

Madame Théophile had never seen a parrot, and this creature, so new to her, evidently caused her immense surprise. As motionless as an embalmed cat from Egypt, she regarded the bird with an air of profound meditation, putting together all the notions of natural history which she had been able to gather on the tiles, in the courtyard and in the garden. The shadow of her thoughts passed across her blinking eyes, and I could read there, quite as well as if she had spoken out with her voice, this summing up of her examination: "Decidedly this strange creature cannot be a green fowl."

Arrived at this decision, the cat got down from the table where she had established her observatory, and went and crouched in a corner of the room, stomach on the ground, the elbows protruded, the head low, the spring of the spine extended —like a cunning panther watching gazelles that have come from their homes to quench their thirst at a lake.

The parrot followed these movements with feverish anxiety; he bristled his feathers, rattled his chain, lifted an agitated foot, and sharpened his beak on the edge of his feeding-tin. Instinct told him that an enemy was contemplating some kind of wickedness.

As for the eyes of the cat, fixed upon the bird with fascinated intensity, they said, in a language which the parrot perfectly well understood, and which had nothing in the least uncertain about it: "Although green, this chicken ought to be good eating."

I followed this scene with interest, ready to interfere when occasion called. Madame Théophile had drawn nearer to the parrot; her pink nose quivered, she half closed her eyes, opened and shut her claws. Little thrills ran up and down her spine; like a greedy man sitting down before a delicious truffled pullet, she delighted herself with the thought of the succulent and rare meal which she was about to make. This foreign dish, so new to her and yet so tempting, tickled her appetite.

Suddenly her back bent like a stretched bow, and one elastic jump took her to the foot of the perch. The parrot, realizing his danger, with a voice low and solemn, said suddenly: "Have you breakfasted, James?"

This phrase caused the cat an indescribable terror, and she sprang back. A flourish of trumpets, a smash of plates and dishes, a pistol fired at the ear could not have given her a more frantic terror. All her ideas of birds were reversed. All her instincts were at fault. Her face expressed clearly the staggering thought that had suddenly come to her: "This is not a bird: this is a gentleman. He speaks!"

Then the parrot began to sing, with a great shout in his voice which was perfectly deafening, for he had realized that the fright caused by his speech was his best means of defense.

The cat threw toward me a hurried glance of interrogation, and, my reply not satisfying her, she buried herself under the bed, from which it was impossible to make her move an inch all the day long.

Next day, a little more courageous, Madame Théophile ventured to make another timid attack, but with precisely the same fortune as had met her the last time.

From that moment she threw up the sponge and accepted the green bird as a man who must be treated with respect. Though she watched him attentively, she never again made the slightest attack upon him.

THE NEXT STORIES ARE ON PAGE 3901.

FRENCH—A LITTLE PICTURE-STORY

YOU will not be able to learn to speak French from these lessons. There are some sounds in French which cannot be made clear on paper, and you will be able to understand these only by hearing them spoken. But this page will help if you are learning French at school, or if there is someone at home who can help you to understand how the words should be said. These lessons tell us the story of a short visit to England and of a longer stay among the French. The first line in each case is in French; the second line gives the English word for the French word above it. But the French people do not put their words together as we do, and the third line shows how we make up the words into English.

Pierre—Peter.

Jeannette—Jenny.

La bonne—The nurserymaid.

Je m'appelle Pierre, et j'ai dix ans.
I myself call Peter, and I have ten years.
My name is Peter, and I am ten years old.

Ma sœur Jeannette a huit ans.
My sister Jenny has eight years.
My sister Jenny is eight years old.

Mon petit frère a deux ans.
My little brother has two years.
My little brother is two years old.

On l'appelle Bébé.
One him calls Baby.
He is called Baby.

Bébé va venir et la bonne aussi.
Baby is going to come and the nurse also.
Baby is coming and nurse also.

Nos malles—Our trunks.

Notre bonne a fait toutes nos malles.
Our nurse has made all our trunks.
Our nurse has packed all our trunks.

Nos jouets sont dans la grande malle.
Our toys are in the large trunk.
Our toys are in the large trunk.

L'école—The school.

Jeannette et moi nous allons à l'école.
Jenny and I we go to the school.
Jenny and I go to school.

Maintenant nous sommes en vacances.
Now we are in holidays.
Now we are on our vacation.

Nous allons en France.
We are going in France.
We are going to France.

Nous allons avec papa et maman.
We go with Papa and Mamma.
We are going with Papa and Mamma.

Nos jouets—Our toys.

Nous avons beaucoup de jouets.
We have many of toys.
We have many toys.

Bébé emporte son bateau à voiles.
Baby is taking his boat with sails.
Baby is taking his sailing boat.

THE NEXT FRENCH STORY IS ON PAGE 3998.

The fire dies down in the cottage.—From the painting by Walter Langley, R.I.

WHY DOES THE FIRE GO OUT?

A FIRE, or anything else that is burning, will go out if the supply of air or oxygen to it is stopped, or if that supply is made so scanty that the burning goes on very slowly. In this case not enough heat is produced to keep the coal, or whatever is burning, at the temperature at which it is capable of combining with oxygen. A fire, or anything else, will also go out when there is nothing more left to burn.

When a fire goes out in the ordinary way there is still plenty of burnable stuff left in the grate; and there is still plenty of air in the room, of course; but there is not a good enough draft up the chimney, and the air of the room is not getting to the coal of the fire quickly enough. The air enters the fire almost entirely from below; but perhaps there are many ashes in the grate, choking up the spaces between the bars, and the air cannot get to the coal. So the fire dies of suffocation; it cannot get air. If we clear away the ashes the fire goes on burning.

Almost everyone is puzzled by the two different ways in which a thing may give out heat and light. A thing does this when it is hot; but it may be hot either because it is burning or for some other reason. The fire is hot *because* it is burning, and that is

CONTINUED FROM 3734

why it gives out heat and light. The thread in an electric lamp gives out heat and light *because* it is hot, but it is hot, not because it is burning, but because it is made hot by electricity passing through it. The sun gives out heat and light because it is hot, but the sun is not burning. The sun is actually so hot that oxygen cannot combine with the other elements in it. The heat that comes from the sun across nearly a hundred million miles of space is entirely due to other causes.

Similarly, the centre of the earth is like a fire. It gives out a great quantity of heat; but it is unlike a fire in that it is not burning any more than the sun is, or the thread in an electric lamp.

We should use the word glowing, and then we can say that the sun and the inside of the earth are glowing, though they are not burning. The current through an electric lamp makes the thread glow, though it does not burn. A fire and many other things glow when they burn because the burning makes the things so hot that they glow. Any kind of matter that is made hot enough will glow, that is to say, will give out light and heat. The way to describe this condition of matter is to say that it will radiate, or give off, rays of light and heat. 3839

WHAT IS PAIN, AND WHY DOES IT HURT?

Not the wisest man can answer this question, but we know some things about it. We know that certain nerves run to the skin, and that when they are excited the result is pain—just as when the eye nerve is excited the result is sight. We know that when these nerves are damaged and cannot work, the skin cannot feel pain. Also, we know that when any other nerves are excited too intensely, the result is painful. Loud music may be very pleasant, but there is a point beyond which it quite suddenly becomes painful. Similarly, a bright light may be beautiful and pleasant, but beyond a certain point it suddenly becomes painful.

No one, however, has any idea what happens in the nerve or in the nerve-cells when this change comes, though it has lately been thought that when a nerve is very highly excited it changes in shape. This, however, does not tell us in the least why pain should go with it. No one could explain what pain was to a person who had never felt it, except by causing him pain. Similarly, you cannot describe sight to a person born blind. Words cannot describe these things, except to people who know them by experience.

WHAT ARE OUR EYEBROWS FOR?

This is an easy question we ought all to be able to answer, yet many grown-up people could not tell you.

There are two good reasons why we have eyebrows. One is a reason of use, and the other of beauty. In the first place, if we had none, the drops of sweat that form on our foreheads when we get warm would run into our eyes; and this would be bad, not only because it would blur our seeing, but also because sweat is really poisonous, and a thing to get rid of, which is one of the best reasons for washing.

Now, our eyebrows catch the drops of sweat and turn them aside. That is quite a good enough reason in itself, but there is another. The eyes are the most beautiful and interesting part of our faces, not only from their form, but also because they and the eyelids move so quickly, and so give the idea of life. That is why a face looks so different when the eyes are shut.

Now, the eyebrows are not only beautiful in themselves, but have the special purpose of calling attention to the eyes, just as we draw attention to a specially important word in a letter by underlining it. That is why some foolish people make their eyebrows darker than they really are; but if you have a bright and healthy mind your eyes will look nice enough without any silly help of that kind.

HOW DO WE KNOW THE HEIGHT OF A MOUNTAIN?

It is not very easy to measure a mountain, but there are various ways of doing so. One of them is too difficult to explain here, or to anyone who has not learned a good deal about angles, and so on, already. But there is a much less difficult way of measuring the height of a mountain, though it is not such an exact way. In order to use this way you must go up the mountain yourself, and it will, at any rate, tell you how high you have gone. People use this way when they want to know how high they have gone in a balloon. They take up a barometer, or a weather-glass, with them.

Now, a barometer is simply a measurer of heaviness; it measures how heavy the air is above it. The higher you go the less air there is above you, and so, as you ascend, the mercury in the barometer moves in a little tube according as a less weight of air presses upon it from above. If you know already how much difference it makes in a barometer to go to a certain height, then you can tell how high you are on a mountain or in a balloon. But you must use the other way, with measurements of angles and special instruments, if you want to measure the height of a mountain without climbing it.

WHY DOES A PIN GET HOT IF RUBBED AGAINST A STONE?

All rubbing, or friction, produces heat. If you had a really delicate thermometer you could easily prove that paper and india-rubber and the air around them all get hotter when you rub out something you have written. The motion that starts the rubbing is changed into the special kind of invisible motion called heat. In the case of a pin rubbed against a stone, we notice the heat-effect of friction particularly well. This is, in the first place, because the pin has a sharp point, which hinders the easy movement on the uneven surface of the stone; and, second, because the pin is made of metal, and all metals are very good conductors of heat. So the heat runs up the pin very easily and quickly, just as it runs up a poker held in the fire, and that is why we feel it so distinctly and quickly.

WHAT MAKES THE WIND WHISTLE?

The howling and whistling and all the other noises made by the wind are not so easily noticed by us when we are out of doors as when we are in a house. As the moving air forces itself through chinks of doors and windows, or perhaps even down the chimney, and so on, it sets all sorts of things that it meets vibrating, or trembling, and so produces all kinds of sounds, and these are often almost musical. Often people are very much frightened by these noises, yet if they went out of doors into the wind itself they would not hear them so well. The wind passing through the air—that is to say, the current of air passing through the air—does not make itself known to us because what our ears can hear is not a current, but a wave in the air. You cannot hear a draft.

IS THERE ANY COLOR IN THE SEA?

Land animals and land plants are of all the colors of the rainbow, from the red plant of Arctic snow to the peacock's gorgeous tail, from the yellow buttercup to the golden humming-bird.

In the sea, too, life decks itself in rainbow colors. There we find meadows of green and blue and red algæ; there we find blue flying-fish, rosy sea-anemones, and red coral, and iridescent mackerel. In fact, there is hardly a color on land that cannot be matched in the sea.

But down into the deepest depths of the sea the color of life goes, as the sunlight goes. More than 3,000 feet deep photographic plates bring back impressions, and so violet and ultra-violet rays must penetrate there, though most of the rays of light do not penetrate to half that depth. The Swiss naturalist Hermann Fol, making investigations in a diving-suit near Nice, noticed that even at a depth of thirty feet red things looked black, showing that the red rays did not reach so far. It is pretty certain that below 1,500 or 1,700 feet no color—unless violet—can be seen by the light of the sun; and below that depth all fishes are brown, or black, or violet-black. The last bright color to disappear is red, and where the red ceases violet-black begins.

Even in the depth of the sea, however, there is light of a kind, for many of the deep-sea fishes carry lanterns; at least, they have phosphorescent spots and organs that light up the darkness. One fish of this kind is named the midshipman, because it has a row of luminous spots on it like the gilt buttons of a midshipman.

If a man could go down to the depth of the ocean and look around, he would find himself in a darkness lighted only as by stars, and by the light of the stars he would see only violet and black fishes. Besides fishes, there are numerous sea creatures, such as squids and bacteria, which are luminous, so that the depths of the sea are never without some light.

WHY CANNOT FISHES LIVE ON LAND?

The answer to this is curious. Every living thing must have air or die. The fish comes out of the water, where there is very little air, into the air itself, and there it dies for lack of air. It is drowned on land for lack of air, and dies of what is called suffocation, just as you or I would be drowned in the water.

But why cannot the fish help itself to the air around it when it is put on earth? Why should it starve in the midst of plenty? The reason is that in order to breathe air you must have lungs, or something like lungs, and the fish has none; while in order to get the air which is dissolved in water, which the fish does, you must have something quite different from lungs, which are called gills. The fish has no lungs, but only gills. We have no gills, but only lungs. Therefore we die in the water and the fish dies out of it. If an animal had both gills and lungs, then it would be able to get air from the air or to get the air which is in the water, as it pleased; and it could live both on the land and in the sea.

CAN A FISH SEE AND HEAR US?

If we go to an aquarium or to a pond, we shall see for ourselves that fishes can see us, and see very well and quickly, too. Every fisherman knows this. He knows, too, that fish are very particular about color, and that they catch things by sight as well as by smell; for a fisherman's flies are not scented, but colored, and the fish come to them very readily if they are of the right kind. Then we all know that fishes have eyes, for we have all seen them, and they are quite highly developed eyes. But fishes are decidedly inferior to us in hearing; though they are by no means deaf, they do not respond to music as they seem to respond to color.

WHY ARE PLANTS WHITE WHEN GROWN IN THE DARK?

The green stuff that we know so well in plants is made by sunlight. Without it the plant can do little. If the plant is grown in the dark the green stuff is not made, and without it the plant is white. The green stuff in plants is like the red stuff in our blood; though these two things differ in color and in the work they do, their use is very similar. They both contain iron, which gives color to almost anything it is found in. They both demand sun for their making, and if plants grown in the dark are white, so also are children grown in the dark, because their blood has not enough red stuff in it. It is cruel to permit children to spend their lives in dark, sunless dwellings, but there are millions who grow up in this way, and whose lives are spoiled for want of the red stuff, just as the plant is spoiled for want of the green stuff.

WHY DO NOT WE FEEL THE EARTH GOING ROUND?

The answer to this is that we are going round with the earth, and as we move round with it at exactly the same rate, we notice nothing. If you were in a train and did not look out, and the train moved at a constant speed in a straight line, and gave no jolts, you would not know whether it was moving or not.

The real lesson we learn from this question is that the only kind of movement we can feel is *relative* movement—that is to say, movement of one thing as compared with another. If the earth or a train moved more slowly or more quickly than our bodies, then we should feel the movement. If we could imagine our bodies moving alone in space with no stars for mile-posts, then we should not know they were moving, for there would be nothing with which to compare the motion. We can feel relative motion simply because there is something to compare it with.

WHY HAVE WE LINES ON OUR HANDS?

Some people have said that the use of these lines is to give us a better hold on things, but probably that is not their real use. If it were so, we should really have to say that they were scarcely worth having. It is much more likely that the use of these lines is to help the sense of touch in our hands and fingers, where touch is so very important. By making little valleys and ridges they increase the surface of the skin, and by going in different directions they help us to feel the kind of surface that anything has which we touch. The little endings of the nerves of touch are placed to the greatest advantage by means of these lines, and that seems to be the reason why they are so very well marked on just those parts of the skin where delicacy of touch is most important. From very earliest times there have been those who have tried to show that character and destiny can be read from these lines—according to their different length, position and appearance.

WHY DOES NOT OIL MIX WITH WATER?

When two kinds of liquid, added together, mix perfectly, it is because the molecules that make up the one liquid are just as ready to link on with the molecules of the other liquid as with one another. The most perfect case is, of course, when the two liquids are the same, as when water is added to water, and the next most perfect case is where the liquids are very similar, so far as the linkage of their molecules is concerned, as when water and alcohol are mixed. But when oil and water are added to each other, we have two liquids which are made of very different kinds of molecules. The molecules of water are very small, and those of oil are enormous—made of great numbers of atoms, instead of only three apiece, as water is. And the large molecules of oil find it more natural and easy to link with each other than with the molecules of water, and the molecules of water find it more natural and easy to link with one another than with the molecules of oil, so that, as a visible result of these invisible causes, the oil and the water keep apart.

WHAT DOES THE WORD EUREKA MEAN?

This famous word means "I have found it," and the story goes that it was used by one of the greatest philosophers of antiquity, Archimedes, who lived in the city of Syracuse in Sicily. The king's crown had been in the hands of the goldsmith, who was suspected of having replaced some of the gold by some other metal; and Archimedes was set the task of finding whether this was so. He did it by putting the crown into his bath, and noticing how much the water rose; and he is said to have run out into the streets shouting "Eureka! Eureka!"

And now, when we have found out something we have been searching for, we sometimes repeat this famous exclamation.

WHY IS THE SHAPE OF A RAINDROP ROUND?

Why does the rain form drops at all? We know now that there is always something which we may call a speck of solid stuff in the inside of a raindrop, and when the drop was made it was made by the water-gas, or water-vapor, in the air turning liquid upon this solid speck, as steam from boiling water turns liquid on a cold plate held above it.

But you want to know why, when it is formed, a raindrop is so nearly round. The answer is the same as the answer to the question why water forms in round drops on a plate, and the question why it runs in drops down the window-pane when it rains. When water turns liquid it really consists of a kind of crowd of tiny parts, each of which is itself a part, or particle, as we say, of water, just as a human crowd is made of men and women.

Now, these little particles of water behave rather as a crowd might behave if all the men and women making it were to catch hold of each other's hands, so that they were all joined together. If they all held on to each other as tightly as they could, and especially if all the people on the outside of the crowd held each other's hands so as to make a ring, then that crowd would be something like the crowd of particles of water that make up a drop of water. They all prefer to hold on to each other, and stick together, and that is why the drop is formed.

WHY DOES A BEE STING?

The use of the bee's sting is exactly the same, in its own way, as the use of the nettle's stinging hairs. The sting is really a fine, sharp, barbed tube, through which a drop of poisonous stuff can be sent when the bee stings. It is the worker-bees that sting—those that do the work of the hive. A bee can sting only once, as a general rule; for when the sting is driven in deeply, the barb may prevent it from being withdrawn. It is torn away from the bee's body, and the bee is so injured that it soon dies. Thus a bee stings only when its position is desperate.

The lesson is that when we are stung *we* usually begin the quarrel. *We* make ourselves offensive to the bee. If we do not, it will seldom dream of stinging us. Many people make friends with bees, will let them crawl on their hands and faces, and never get stung. But, if you get out your handkerchief and attack the bee, it is bound to do its duty, even at the cost of its life, and you have to pay a painful price, too.

WHAT HOLDS THE STARS IN THEIR PLACES?

This is a question that thinking people have been asking for many ages, and you are quite right to ask it, but the answer is that the question is not really a correct one. The stars are not kept in position, but are all in motion, and sometimes the stars *do* fall on to one another, we now believe. Astronomers now think that they can find in the heavens two great streams, to one or other of which all the stars belong, and these two streams of stars are moving through and past each other in opposite directions.

No one has any idea at all how this process started, nor what the results of it will be, but at any rate we are quite certain that there is no such thing as what for so long has been called a fixed star, anywhere. Some people have thought that there may be a centre somewhere, which all the stars move round, but we cannot find any proof that this is really so.

WHERE DOES THE WATER GO AT LOW TIDE?

The shortest answer to this would be that, at low tide, the water goes to the places where it is high tide. As the earth spins, under the pull of the moon and the sun, the water is always being moved about. Of course it is always somewhere, and if it is not in one place, it must be in another. When it is pulled to one part of the earth and heaped up there, that makes high tide.

As we watch the tide rising, what we see is the water being heaped up in our neighborhood, mainly under the influence of the moon. But if it is heaped up there, it is being drawn away from somewhere else, and that somewhere else is the place where the tide is ebbing. No tide rises but some other tide falls.

THE NEXT WONDER QUESTIONS ARE ON PAGE 3975.

OLIVER CROMWELL, LEADER OF THE IRONSIDES, RIDING THROUGH YORK
From the painting by Ernest Crofts, R.A.

ARCHBISHOP LAUD FROM HIS PRISON WINDOW GIVES STRAFFORD A LAST BLESSING
The Earl of Strafford and Archbishop Laud were great friends in private, and colleagues in the government; they ruled the people as with an iron hand. When the voice of the people began to be heard, Charles I suffered them both to be charged with treason and put to death, although they had been his devoted supporters. Strafford died first, and this picture shows him on his way to execution, passing by the window of Laud's prison, kneeling down to receive the old archbishop's blessing.

John Pym.

Thomas, Lord Fairfax.

Prince Rupert.

Admiral Blake.

John Hampden.

Sir John Eliot.

General Ireton.

John Bradshaw.

CROMWELL AND HIS MEN

CONTINUED FROM 3612

THERE was a great painter called Van Dyck who made many portraits of King Charles I. If you have ever seen one of them, it is easy for you to understand why, with all his faults and his follies, he was loved with a passionate devotion, and how he still casts a spell over the minds of men.

There is a dignity, a majesty, in the grave, delicate face; a charm in the haunting, melancholy eyes; a kingly air in the pose, which makes you feel that this was a man for whose sake many would die gladly. And yet we can see that it is not the face of a man wise in counsel or strong in action.

Now, if you look on the face of Cromwell, it is as though it had been hewn roughly out of solid granite, grim and massive and hard; there is power in every line, but of grace or graciousness no whit. This man is a born fighter and a born leader. The other is born for defeat.

From his youth Charles had evil counselors. His father, King James I, was so learned but so narrow-minded that a king of France described him as the "wisest fool in Christendom." Never was a monarch so undignified as he; perhaps that is one reason why Charles bore himself always with such dignity. James gave the prince for a companion a young gentleman who was handsome, brave, proud and worthless. Him he made a lord, and he became famous as the Duke of Buckingham.

Buckingham utterly won the heart of Charles, and taught him to think that princes and their favorites are altogether above the law. Moreover, it was due to Buckingham that Charles married the pretty French princess Henrietta Maria, who proved a counselor fully as bad as Buckingham himself after the duke was slain by a crazed assassin. So that the two people whom Charles loved best in the world were the worst advisers he could have found; yet it was their advice he always followed.

But of all the ill counsel he got from these two, or from his father, the worst was their teaching that the word of a king may be lightly given and lightly broken. This, more than aught else, brought Charles to his final ruin. For, though the people were wroth with him before he signed the promises in the Petition of Right, they were far more angry afterward, because they felt he had played them false. Again, when he gave up Strafford to his doom, all knew that he had broken his word; and when the Parliament resolved to fight, it was because they would not trust him. When at last Cromwell and his party resolved that the king must die, it was

3845

because they had lost all hope that he would keep his promises if he were allowed to live.

Yet Charles really believed he was in the right, except when he surrendered Strafford, for he held that the king is appointed by God, and should rule his people, not as the people think good for themselves, but as the king thinks good for them, and that, whether he rules ill or well, none can call him to account save the King of kings. Besides that, he saw that the Parliament was now demanding rights which it had never claimed before, and he thought that if he gave way, there might remain to the king no power at all.

After the king had most openly broken the law by entering the House of Commons, seeking there to arrest the five men who were the chiefs of the party that opposed him, he went away from London, and there was little hope that war could be avoided. Some months later Charles unfurled his standard at Nottingham, and this was the beginning of the great Civil War.

OLIVER CROMWELL, THE MAN WHO WAS TO CONQUER THE KING

Let us see, now, what manner of life had been lived by the man who was to conquer the king. Oliver Cromwell had farmed his lands in Huntingdonshire without seeking to make a stir in the world. Once, indeed, he had come forward in his own part of the country as champion of the people's rights in the matter of certain lands of which they were being robbed, but for the rest he was known chiefly as a very religious man who for his religion's sake had been willing to leave his own home and seek a new one in America. But he and his company were stayed by the king's orders when they were about to cross the sea.

In Parliament at first Cromwell was a rough, uncouth figure, unskilled and confused of speech, yet a man of mark by reason of his deadly earnestness.

When the war broke out and the tide of battle ran against the Parliament, it was Cromwell who saw how the tide must be turned. He saw that what made Rupert's soldiers so irresistible was the proud sense of honor which made them fear nothing but disgrace, and that these men must win unless they were fought by soldiers who for love of a great cause feared death as little as they.

Cromwell went down to the eastern counties and gathered troops of men picked out for their zeal in religion, but also for their strength and valor and horsemanship. These men he trained in utter obedience, so that when they came to the shock of battle, these Ironsides swept all before them, yet were ready to rally to their chief's command and hold back from needless pursuit and plunder.

THE BATTLE OF NASEBY, AFTER WHICH CHARLES GAVE HIMSELF UP

So, at Marston Moor and Naseby, under Cromwell and Lord Fairfax, the Ironsides smote the gallants whom none had been able to resist. But after the rout of Naseby the king's cause was lost, and Charles gave himself up to the Scots, who were in arms to aid the English Parliament; and after some time the Scots handed him over to the Parliament.

But now Cromwell and the soldiers grew ill content with the Parliament, because it was willing to make terms with the king without having secured the liberty of religion, which was the thing they most cared about. Therefore they sent a troop of soldiers to bring the king from Holmby House and keep him under charge of the Army itself. And then, because the Army and the Parliament were in disagreement, the king tried privately to treat with each of them and to make them the more obstinate in their disagreements with each other, hoping he might yet win the day.

But when he tried to escape from the country, and was stopped in the Isle of Wight and held prisoner at Carisbrooke Castle, the Royalists rose in insurrection, and Cromwell saw that the king had been only making pretenses. He saw that when the insurrection was put down, there could be no peace in the land unless the king's life was ended and the will of the Army was made to prevail.

THE STRANGE SPECTACLE THAT ENGLAND SHOWED THE WORLD

Then England showed the world a strange spectacle. They who had risen in arms against the king in the name of the law now set up a tribunal to judge the king which was itself without rights from any law. So that now it was the king who stood for the law, and his judges who stood for arbitrary power, or the power that is not restrained by law. And the Army, having this power, cut off the head of the king in the name of the people of England, though all knew that the chief part of the people of England shrank in horror from the deed.

Thus, in the last days of his life the false king who had wrought so much ill to the land became a martyr, and throughout those days he acted with a most royal dignity and showed great tenderness and courage. He would make no defense before judges who had no right to try him. In his prison he remained calm and collected, mindful of his friends and his children, but with his thoughts bent on eternity. And when the last hour came, and he stepped through the window of Whitehall on to the scaffold and looked on the crowds that had gathered to see how a king can die,

> He nothing common did or mean
> Upon that memorable scene,
> But bowed his comely head
> Down as upon a bed.

When the executioner struck off his head and raised it, with the words, "This is the head of a traitor," the crowd answered with groans and tears.

THE MANNER OF MAN THAT OLIVER CROMWELL WAS

Let us turn now to the man who, more than any other, had brought about this just and necessary, but terrible, deed. Cromwell had striven his hardest to make terms with Charles and to restrain the Army, which would willingly have made away with him long before; but at last he had judged that there was no way left but the way he took. When his mind was made up, he never faltered. On the king's death-warrant there is no signature written more firmly than Oliver Cromwell's.

For no man could be more utterly merciless than he if it seemed to him that the need had arisen for firmness, as he showed when he slew and spared not at the pitiless taking of Drogheda and Wexford in Ireland. Yet he had no love for bloodshed; his mercilessness was the more terrible because he loved mercy. He made himself king of England in all but the name, just as he slew King Charles—because he could see no other way of restoring order in the land.

He established order and made the country prosperous. The foreign nations which at first treated England as an outcast state when she had put her king to death became eager for Cromwell's friendship and feared his hostility. At his bidding the French stopped persecuting Protestants. Since the days of Eliza-

beth the foreign nations had cared nothing for England's will or wishes, till Cromwell trained his army and Blake proved himself a match for Van Tromp on the seas. And Cromwell did this when the country had just been rent with a great civil war, and when one-half of it was thirsting to overthrow his government.

OLIVER'S STORMY LIFE ENDS IN A STORM ON HIS GREAT DAY OF TRIUMPH

Perhaps it is not easy to love a man so rugged and ungainly; it was easy to hate him. His enemies hated him so much that during the last years of his life he always wore mail under his dress lest he should be slain by an assassin.

With all his massive, uncouth force, Cromwell was tender of heart. It is pleasant to think how, when the grim soldier had become the greatest man in the land, he brought his old mother up to live in his house; and because she, in her fondness for him, lived ever in fear that his foes would kill him, he made it a rule to show himself to her every evening, so that she might go to sleep knowing he was safe.

Cromwell had taken up the task of fighting the king, of killing the king, and of ruling the country because he saw things that must be done, and no other was fit or able to do them.

"God knows," he said, speaking sober truth, "I would have been glad to have lived under my woodside, and to have kept a flock of sheep, rather than to have undertaken this government."

He was willing enough to lay the task down. "My work is done," he said as he lay on his deathbed; "yet God will be with His people."

HOW THEY SNATCHED CROMWELL'S BODY FROM THE ABBEY

He lived a stormy life; it was fitting that a great storm should be raging in the very last hour of his life. On the anniversary of two of his great victories, Dunbar and Worcester, the spirit of the great Protector passed away.

No Englishman has been more abused than Oliver Cromwell. The Royalist historian of the period, the Earl of Clarendon, summed him up as a "brave, bad man," and that estimate was passed on into several school histories, and has warped the judgment of generations.

The bitterness of the supporters of the Stuarts was such that after Charles II had succeeded to the throne of his father, Cromwell's body was torn out of its

CHARLES STUART, THE FAITHLESS KING

It is easy, in looking at this picture by Van Dyck, to see why, with all his faults, men loved King Charles with a passionate devotion. There is a dignity in the delicate face, a charm in the haunting, melancholy eye, a kingly ease in the pose, which makes us feel that this was a man for whose sake men would die. Yet he was a faithless king.

grave in Westminster Abbey, hanged on a gallows at Tyburn, and then beheaded; the head being placed on a pole on the top of Westminster Hall, and the body buried at the gallows. This vengeful course was timed to take place exactly twelve years after the beheading of Charles I.

But the judgment of later times is shown in the fact that a tablet to his memory has been placed in the Abbey by the authorities of that venerable pile; his statue stands between the Abbey and the Houses of Parliament, one of the finest statues, in one of the finest positions, in London; and the sober mind of history declares him to be not only one of the greatest but one of the most honest of Englishmen. It is remembered in his favor that at the height of his power he remained true to his principles and refused the English crown; that he was tolerant toward all forms of religion in an intolerant age; and that his piety was attested by the purest minds of his generation, those who knew him best.

It was the Life of Cromwell written by Thomas Carlyle, with evidence clear as noonday from Cromwell's own letters, that brought justice to his memory and almost silenced the voices of hatred and ignorance. Faults he had, of course, but the final verdict of history is that he was a great, good man.

Now let us look at some of the leaders that gathered about Cromwell in those great and stirring days.

At first there were three men who stood up in Parliament against the king—Sir John Eliot, John Pym and Thomas Wentworth. Of these three the first died, as men say, a martyr to his cause.

The Parliament, headed by these three, made the king sign a declaration, which was called the Petition of Right, that it was not lawful for him to make the people pay taxes without consent of Parliament, or to put people in prison unless they were brought to trial and it was proved that they had broken the law. But he had hardly signed it before he began to demand certain taxes and put people in prison if they refused to pay. When Parliament came together, Eliot made a great speech which stirred everyone to be more resolute in resisting the king's unlawful demands. This made Charles so angry that he had Eliot thrown into prison and kept in close confinement so that he became very ill; and, as Charles would not make the imprisonment any less severe, Sir John died. Men loved his memory, for he had been a very noble gentleman, caring nothing for his own ease, but ready to endure all things if so he might help to keep England a free nation.

Very different was Wentworth, who had been Eliot's friend; for, just after Charles had signed the declaration, Wentworth went over to the king's side, so that the other side, of which he had been a chief, called him the "Apostate," a name which means a man who has deserted a great and worthy cause.

From that time there was no man who wrought so shrewdly or so sternly to make the king all-powerful as Thomas Wentworth; either because, having seen that there was no hope of agreement, he thought the rule of the king would be better than the rule of Parliament;

OLIVER CROMWELL, THE MAN OF IRON

This picture by Ford Madox Brown shows Oliver Cromwell on his farm, and we see in his face, calm and hard, the power that is missing from the face of Charles, as we see in Charles's face the grace that is missing from the face of Cromwell. In the whole story of England there has not been a stronger, braver, truer man than Cromwell.

or because he loved the king and hoped thus to save him.

At any rate, this Wentworth, with the grim face and the fathomless, unsmiling eyes, was sent first to rule the North of England and then Ireland. With an iron hand he ruled, careless of law, but careless, too, whether the foes he crushed were strong or weak; and all had to obey his will while for eleven years he ruled without the help of any Parliament.

But a time came when Charles needed more money than he dared demand without Parliament's consent; and when the Parliament met, seeing how strong and clever a servant Charles had in Wentworth, who was now Lord Strafford, and that if Strafford lived he might make the king too strong for Parliament, they charged him with treason and passed an act declaring that he was dangerous to the state and must be beheaded. Fearing the wrath of the people, and that if Strafford were not slain they would clamor for the life of the queen, whom they hated no less, Charles yielded his consent, even though he had promised Strafford that not a hair of his head should be harmed. Can we wonder at Strafford's bitter exclamation when he heard of the betrayal: "Put not your trust in princes!" This man who had served both parties was now slain, for the king had given up to death his most faithful servant. Now there was none left who could save him from his own doom.

JOHN PYM, WHO ROSE AGAINST THE MAN WHO HAD BEEN HIS FRIEND

The third great opponent of King Charles was John Pym, a country gentleman who was also a lawyer. When the Parliament met again, it was John Pym who first ventured to attack the king and who did everything in his power to bring about the destruction of Wentworth, who had once been his friend. It was Pym who most roused the people in the country and whose words carried most weight in Parliament. He was the boldest as well as the shrewdest of all the Parliament men. Beside him stood one who was not so skilled an orator, but was no less honored for nobility of character—John Hampden, the champion of the people.

These two had some ado both to give heart to those who feared the evils of a civil war more than they hated tyranny, and to restrain those who were too hasty to take thought how best liberty might be secured.

But so great was Pym's influence that he came to be called King Pym, by his opponents in mockery, but by his friends in admiration. And those two, more than any others, the king himself sought to overthrow, so that one day he came suddenly down to the House of Parliament, where the Commons was sitting, having with him a band of soldiers, and willing there to arrest them with three others even in the Parliament itself. But they, having warning, had gone down the Thames by boat into the city of London, where they were too well loved for the king to dare attempt their capture. So Charles retired in wrath, and after that it was but a few months before there was open warfare between the king and the Parliament.

BRAVE JOHN HAMPDEN IS STRUCK DOWN BY A BULLET IN BATTLE

When the war began, John Pym remained in London to direct the counsels of the Parliament, and this he did with great wisdom until he died, about a year and a half later. But John Hampden went at the head of a troop of horse which he had raised at his own cost, to be one of the leaders of the army of the Parliament in battle.

It was Hampden who, when the king, ruling without Parliament, put an unlawful tax upon the people, refused to pay it and was punished by the judges who were afraid to give judgment against the king.

He was a man who tried always to do what he counted right, at whatever cost, so that even his foes honored him; and once it was said that it was only his coolness and wisdom that had restrained the king's party and the Parliament party within the House of Commons from falling upon each other even in the House itself. Therefore all men were grieved, even the king's men, when John Hampden was struck down by a bullet in the fight of Chalgrove Field; for they knew that when he died, the chance was less than it had been that the two sides might yet find some way of agreement.

PRINCE RUPERT—CAVALRY-LEADER, SEA-ROVER AND MAN OF SCIENCE

The most active leader on the king's side when war broke out was Prince Rupert of the Rhine, a son of Charles's sister. His courage was much greater than his discretion, for his impetuosity lost more than his bravery won.

Mrs. Cromwell wrote beautiful letters to Oliver, who wrote from Dunbar telling her of his victory, and adding, "Thou art dearer to me than any other creature."

When the war was lost to the king on land, Rupert tried to keep an opening for new attempts by maintaining himself at sea as the leader of a Royalist fleet. The Scilly Isles and the Channel Islands were his bases for a time, but he was finally driven out of the seas around England by the bravery and skill of Admiral Blake, who left him no rallying-place, but declared that any country that gave Rupert's ships a place of refuge was forthwith by that act an enemy of England.

But Rupert was more than a dashing cavalry-leader on land and a daring rover on the seas: he was a keen student of science, and the discovery of the process of printing pictures known as mezzotint stands to his lasting credit.

Also on the king's side was that fine character Lucius Carey, Lord Falkland. When the Parliament which was called the Long Parliament first met, he stood on the same side as Pym and Hampden, hoping the king and the Parliament might both learn wisdom and come to agreement; but when he saw them growing more bitterly at enmity, till the Parliament seemed to be grasping at the whole power, he went over to the king's side, fearing the tyranny of the Parliament more than the tyranny of the king. For this reason, in sadness of soul, Falkland chose loyalty before liberty; and when he was slain in battle, men said that he had died willingly.

CROMWELL'S CLOSEST FRIEND IN THE ARMY THAT WON THE WAR

Henry Ireton was Cromwell's most intimate friend in the army that won the war. He was a Nottinghamshire gentleman who had been educated at Oxford and trained for the bar, and quite early he saw that Cromwell was a military genius. Cromwell, on his part, knew the value of Ireton's superior education, knowledge of the law, and force of character, so he made him his cavalry-leader and took him as his intimate adviser, and presently Ireton married Bridget Cromwell and was his leader's son-in-law.

At first Ireton's views of the king were quite moderate. He believed in giving Charles every chance of winning back the people's favor. When, however, he found that Charles could not be trusted, he became sternly bent on punishing him for what he thought was treason to the nation, and he signed the warrant for his execution. When the war passed over to Ireland, Ireton acted there as Cromwell's second in command, and there he died in active service. His body was brought to England and buried with honor in Westminster Abbey, but after the Restoration of the Stuart family to the throne the grave was opened and the body of Ireton was hanged aloft at Tyburn, near the place where the Marble Arch now stands, then buried at the foot of the gallows.

John Bradshaw, a Cheshire lawyer who had removed to London, was chosen to preside over the council that tried the king in Westminster Hall. Bradshaw was not present at the meeting that elected him president of the council, and at first he wished to be excused from taking the office; but as he was urged to consent, he gave way, and he conducted the trial with great sternness. As a convinced republican, Bradshaw was outspoken in opposing Cromwell when he feared the Protector might allow himself to accept the kingship. He died before the Restoration and was buried in the great Abbey; but his body also was brutally dug up, carted away to Tyburn, and exposed there.

Another body—that of Admiral Robert Blake, General of the Sea in the Commonwealth period—was taken from the Abbey and buried in St. Margaret's churchyard.

Yet Blake had not taken any part in the trial and execution of the king. His offense, in the eyes of the people who were wreaking their revenge on the dead, was that he had been the man who chased Prince Rupert off the seas when the prince tried to continue the Civil War there. That Blake had defended England against attacks from abroad and had gained the command of the seas, was not counted as patriotism, though again and again the country had offered him enthusiastic thanks for gallant exploits.

THE MOST FAMOUS SEAMAN OF HIS TIME IN THE WORLD

Blake was a Somersetshire man who, after an education at Oxford, became a sea-trading merchant, and then a member of Parliament. When the war began, he helped to defend Bristol for the Parliament and was the last to surrender. Later he made successful defenses of Lyme and Taunton, and then was transferred to a command at sea. Against the Dutch, in many desperate battles, the Spaniards, the Portuguese, and against Algerian and Tunisian pirates he won great victories that made the open sea a safe highway for British ships. Worn out by incessant toil, he died outside Plymouth Sound as he came homeward, the most famous seaman in the world.

Any fair review of Cromwell and the men who gathered about him must admit that, after great patience, they took up arms reluctantly, though the cause they defended was just, for it was resistance to forms of oppression which the laws and traditions of the nation did not allow to kings. They developed in England a sturdy public spirit, and individually they were men of a rare strength of character who in a time of turmoil and chaos raised the nation to a high level.

THE NEXT STORY OF MEN AND WOMEN IS ON PAGE 3995.

HOW TO PRESERVE FLOWERS

WHEN you look at all the gay flowers in the garden during the summer you CONTINUED FROM 3772 feel sorry that they last such a short time. A clever German has discovered a way by means of which real flowers may be preserved in their natural colors, and these will last a good many months without fading. It is not very difficult to deal with flowers in this way, and if the directions are carefully followed you are almost certain to meet with success.

In order to preserve the flowers a large and rather shallow box should be obtained. You will not need the lid, and even the bottom must be knocked out, so that you have a kind of frame. Across the inside of the frame nail a piece of wire-netting with the mesh about the same as that used for rabbit-hutches. This is fixed in its place instead of the bottom of the box in order to give a support to the flowers, which you will put in presently, and yet to allow the air, which will dry the blossoms, to come freely through. You next get a board which is quite flat and large enough for the frame to stand on, leaving a little space all round. The only thing that is now required is a quantity of silver sand, and this can be bought at any store.

When you get the sand it will have a lot of dirt mixed with it, however clean it may look, and this must be removed. The best way to get rid of the dirt is to put some of the sand into a large pie-dish, and then pour some water on to it. A great deal of the dirt will float upon the surface of the water, and if the liquid is poured away many of the bits will go also. But you will have to repeat this process several times with each lot of sand until it is quite clean. The best way to judge as to whether it is ready or not is to take a little in the palm of the hand, and see whether you can find any black pieces among the white mineral grains.

When all the sand has been washed in this way, it should be spread out on a tray and allowed to become perfectly dry. Great care must be taken that it does not get dirty again. The time has now come when the flowers may be gathered in the garden. Some kinds are much more easily preserved than others, and it will be found that roses, asters, and chrysanthemums are especially good. In a general way white flowers are not so successful, as the petals are apt to turn rather a dirty yellow in color. Pinks and crimsons are perhaps the best colors of all, though you cannot well discover those which will answer the purpose without trying them. The flowers must be quite dry.

Place the frame on its stand of wood with the wire-netting downward. First of all put a thin layer of the clean sand inside, and after this place the flowers on the wire-netting, spreading the petals with your fingers. It is now time to cover in the flowers with a layer of sand, and this should be put on very evenly. In the case of some flowers it is a good plan to turn the heads upward before covering in with sand. Supposing the flower is bell-shaped, such as a tulip, the inside must be filled with the sand. When the flowers are quite covered in, if the box should be deep enough, one more lot of blooms may be arranged.

The frame containing the drying flowers may now be removed, and it should be placed in a warm, dry place. Of course, the bottom part must be taken with it, or all the sand will fall out. A good position for the frame is on a shelf in a sunny greenhouse, where the drying process can go on quickly; or, failing this, somewhere in the kitchen. After about ten days you may take a peep at your flowers by just pushing away a little of the sand; if the blossoms feel crisp and dry the time has come to take them out. Supposing, however, that they are still moist, they must be left in the sand a little longer. When the specimens are quite finished they may be taken out from the frame, care being exercised in handling them, as at this stage the petals are very brittle. It will be found that the blooms are nicely preserved, and in such a condition that they will last without any water being put into the vase or bowl which contains them.

HOW TO MAKE A CONCRETE WALK

HOW would you like to help father make a concrete walk? The ordinary concrete sidewalk is composed of slabs 4 feet square. These slabs are made by cutting deep lines to make joints across the walk at regular intervals. Ordinarily it is not found advisable for sidewalk slabs to have a greater surface area than 36 square feet. The necessity for constructing walks in slabs is that unless the stretch of concrete is broken by having joints made in it, the walk will eventually crack from expansion and contraction caused by temperature changes.

However, if a walk has been properly jointed and if the foundation, concrete mixtures, workmanship, and other details have been done correctly, it should not crack. The cracked sidewalk which you have seen is usually thin slabs, poor foundations, poor drainage beneath the walks, and mixtures that are weak or lean in cement.

The materials required for such a concrete-water, it is usually advisable to dig out the area and make a 6-inch or 8-inch fill of clean gravel or cinders. This is made as compact as possible and is used as a foundation for the concrete. Lengths of tile should be connected to this foundation or sub-base at sufficiently frequent intervals and made to lead to free outlets so that water will be conducted from beneath the pavement. If this is not done, the foundation merely becomes a water hole to collect and retain water. Having prepared the foundation and set up the side forms, the next thing to do is to set cross forms at intervals corresponding to the length of slabs, as shown.

The concrete walks are either of one- or two-course construction. Two-course construction means that a leaner concrete, such as 1:3:5 or a 1:2½:4 mixture (this means 1 part cement, 3 or 2½ parts clean sand, and 5 or 4 parts pebbles) may be used for the base, and the finished surface consists of a ½-inch or ¾-

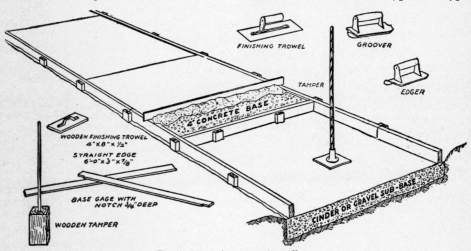

The making of a concrete walk.

walk construction are cement, sand, pebbles or broken stone and water. In addition, the tools used in making a concrete walk are a square pointed shovel, a mixing-board or platform, a sharp-pointed stick, a straightedge, a tamper and a wood float to smooth the surface of the concrete. These tools are seen in the picture on this page.

The picture also shows a lay-out for concrete-walk construction. The side forms are first staked in place as shown. They should be 2 inches by 4 inches, and are set on edge and staked to line and grade so that they will not bulge out of place while the concrete is being tamped.

All loose earth, vegetation and soft spots must be dug out, and the area on which the walk is to be laid must be made thoroughly compact by tamping. If the soil where the concrete is to be placed is of a nature that would drain readily and thoroughly after rains, no sub-base will be necessary. If, however, the ground seems to be of a nature that retains inch layer of rich sand-cement mortar, such as a 1:2 mixture. It is best to use one-course construction, which means that the same mixture, preferably a 1:2:3, is used throughout and placed at one operation. One advantage of one-course construction is that there is no trouble like separation of top course and base, as often happens, due to poor workmanship, when two-course construction is used.

First the concrete should be mixed to a jelly-like consistency. It should then be placed in the forms, lightly tamped and spaded into place, then struck off by running the straightedge along the top of forms to remove concrete in excess of that required to fill them. Finishing should be done by using a wood float, smoothing the surface firmly but not excessively, as overtroweling brings too much fine cement to the surface and makes it less wear-resisting. In placing the concrete, forms for alternate slabs are filled first. When these slabs have hardened sufficiently to permit removing the cross-pieces, concrete is placed for the remaining slabs. Finishing tools known as groovers and edgers are used to properly finish joints between slabs and to give a neat, rounded corner to the outer edges of the walk.

One of the most important details of walk construction is to protect against too rapid drying-out. From the nature of the work, a large surface area is exposed to the air. Sun and drying wind will spoil the best of concrete if left unprotected until it has hardened enough to be proof against the action of drying influences. Immediately after the concrete has hardened so that a covering of moist earth would not mar the surface, two inches at least of such a covering should be applied. This should be kept in place and moist for about a week to permit the concrete to harden properly.

These principles for concrete-walk construc-

tion have many possibilities of application. A series of these walks laid side by side would form a floor. If one of the concrete-walk slabs were set on edge, we would have a thin section of a wall. However, walks are usually made 4 inches or 5 inches thick, while most walls are made 6 inches o 8 inches thick. Still, the principle of construction is similar, with the exception that in walls it is usually necessary to insert reinforcement of steel, such as rods or wire, because walls are subjected to different loads and stresses than those to be met by floors and walks which are laid on the ground. The concrete-highway pavement which you now see so often may be regarded as another extension of the concrete walk.

In later volumes we shall learn how to make steps and other conveniences from concrete.

OUTDOOR GAMES FOR BOYS AND GIRLS

BUTTERCUPS AND BEES

THIS is a new game, but may prove good fun. There should be an even number of players, say, twelve—six girls and six boys: that is, six buttercups and six bees. The buttercups sit or stand on the lawn in a row, each holding a cup made of a piece of paper, twisted into the shape of a fool's cap. A number is penciled on the inside of each —1, 2, 3, 4, 5, 6—according to how many buttercups there are. The bees then stand a short distance away, each with a little ball of crumpled paper. These are numbered as the cups are; but before beginning the game, the boys should exchange balls with one another, so that the buttercups cannot possibly tell the number of any boy's "bee." For the same reason the girls should exchange cups. This being done, and the lines formed again, the paper balls, or bees, are tossed all at once into the air toward the buttercups, the higher the better, and the buttercups do their best to catch them. Any player whose cup number is the same as that on the bee it has caught changes places with the boy who threw it, and the last couple to do this ends the game. The winners are the couple who have become buttercups or bees in turn the greatest number of times during the game. As some may find

it difficult now and then to catch the bee in the cup, it is quite allowable to pick it up from the grass where it has fallen, and drop it in. The exchanges of the cups and the balls should take place every time the bees are returned, as there would be very little fun to any of the players if their side knew the numbers of the others.

BATTLEDORE AND SHUTTLECOCK

THIS game is about six hundred years old, and is still popular. The battledore is made of stretched parchment like a little drum, with a long light handle. The shuttlecock should not have too many feathers, or it will not fly quickly enough. At first it may seem difficult to keep it in the air with the battledore, but with a little practice this will soon become easy. Although one player can play alone, it is much better when two players play together, striking alternately at the shuttlecock and keeping it in the air as long as possible. The player who misses loses, and the other player counts a point. If there are several players, they stand in a ring, and pass the shuttlecock from one to the other, the first who fails to strike it being out. The last player left is, of course, the winner.

DRAWING A CAT WITH THE AID OF TWO COINS

THE four little pictures shown here prove to us how very simple a thing it is to make amusing drawings. We need a ten-cent

our five-cent piece to the right, overlapping slightly, and run our pencil around its edge, being careful not to cut into the first circle.

and a five-cent piece, a pencil and a piece of paper. We first put our ten-cent piece on the paper and draw around it; then we place

The ears, eyes, nose, mouth, tail, and two curves for hip and elbow, are then inserted, and a few more strokes complete our pussy.

HOW TO MAKE CANDY AT HOME

WE are all fond of candy, but perhaps some of you have never tried to make your own. Many kinds of candy are so simple to make, and give such little trouble, that you may like to try some of these recipes.

PEPPERMINT CREAMS

Mix in a bowl 3 ounces of arrowroot with 3 gills of cold water until smooth. Put this into a lined saucepan with 1 pound of white sifted sugar, and keep stirring it. Let it boil for 10 minutes; then move the saucepan off the fire, but stir the contents till cool. Flavor with a few drops of peppermint extract. Take up lumps of the mixture, roll them into little balls, and put them on a slab of marble that has been buttered slightly to prevent sticking. When cold, roll the creams in icing sugar. These candies are also made by flavoring fondant mixture with peppermint.

CREAM FONDANTS

Put into a pan on the fire 2 pounds of granulated sugar, and pour on to it 1 small teacupful of hot water. Allow this to boil about 8 minutes, or till it thickens, but on no account stir it. To test it, take up a little on a new wooden skewer. If a thread forms on taking a drop between the thumb and first finger and separating them, pour the mixture into a bowl and, while warm, beat it with a wooden spoon till creamy. As it cools flavor it with vanilla, raspberry, or some other extract, and color half of it pink with cochineal. The candy is then ready.

CHOCOLATE CREAMS

Take some of the fondant mixture and roll it into balls with the hands. Place the balls on a sheet of oiled paper and leave it for 24 hours. Cut up about ¼ pound of some unsweetened chocolate and soften it in a pan standing in another one of boiling water. Add to the chocolate 2 tablespoonfuls of water and 2 ounces of confectioner's sugar, and stir until smooth. A tiny lump of butter and a few drops of cream improve the chocolate. Drop the fondant balls into it, get them out with the aid of a fork, and lay them on paper to cool and dry.

COCONUT BALLS

Put into a pan and boil, unstirred, ½ pound of white sugar and ¾ of a small teacupful of water until a few drops crackle when dropped into cold water from the end of a wooden skewer. Now stir in 1 ounce of desiccated coconut. Take lumps of the mixture and roll them into little balls.

VANILLA CARAMELS

Boil over the fire in an aluminum or tin-lined saucepan, stirring frequently, 1 pound of loaf sugar, 3 dessert-spoonfuls of glucose, and 1 small teacupful of water. Test it by dropping a little into cold water. If it hardens, add 1 gill of cream and ½ ounce of butter. Boil again, stirring frequently, till a little turns brittle on being dropped into cold water; then flavor with vanilla extract and pour the caramel on to a tin or oiled marble slab. Cut it into convenient squares and wrap them neatly in oiled paper.

NOUGAT

Blanch and chop coarse ½ pound of almonds and dry them in the oven. Put ¾ pound of castor sugar with 1 dessert-spoonful of lemon-juice into a pan, and stir it with a wooden spoon till it colors slightly. Drop in the almonds. Pour the nougat on to a marble slab, press it into cubes or mark it in squares with a knife dipped in hot water, and break them up when cold.

TURKISH DELIGHT

Melt 1 ounce of gelatine in 1 teacupful of cold water, and put this into a saucepan with 1 pound of fine sugar and the juice of an orange and a lemon. Boil it up three times and then simmer it about 20 minutes till sticky. Butter a soup-plate and pour half the mixture into it. Color the remainder with a few drops of cochineal, pour it on to the rest, and set it to stiffen. Then warm the plate slightly to loosen it, turn it on to paper dusted with confectioner's sugar, cut it into squares, and sugar these also. Store it in a tin.

MARZIPAN POTATOES

Prepare some marzipan as described in making Easter eggs, page 3505, or mix ½ pound each of castor sugar and ground almonds with the white of egg, beaten stiff and flavored with almond extract. Shape pieces into the form of new potatoes, punching dents for the "eyes" with a skewer. Roll the potatoes in cocoa in order to coat them brown.

MARZIPAN FRUITS AND NUTS

Strawberries, cherries, mushrooms, dates and walnuts can be made with marzipan. The hulls of the strawberries are cut out of green crinkled paper, the stalks of the cherries of twists of paper or green-covered wire. The marzipan is shaped and rolled in sugar colored with cochineal and placed on paper to harden.

Real fruit may be halved and marzipan placed between the halves.

A mushroom is shaped by flattening a lump of marzipan in the hand and hollowing a centre for the stalk. Dust the under-side with cocoa. Roll some marzipan for the stalk, and dip one end in white of egg to make it stick in the hole. If the white part looks too yellow, moisten the surface with white of egg and dust it with sifted sugar.

A flattened lump of marzipan can be inserted between the two halves of a dried walnut or replace the stone of a date.

Acorns in cups and numbers of delicious bonbons can be devised out of marzipan.

MARSHMALLOWS

Dissolve 2 ounces of gum arabic in 1 gill of cold water. Warm and strain it into a pan over a fire, with 4 ounces of confectioner's sugar, stirring constantly till a little forms a ball when dropped into cold water. Remove the pan, add 1½ whites of eggs previously beaten stiff. Flavor with caramel flavoring. Stir and turn mixture on to a tin sprinkled with confectioner's sugar to set for 12 hours. Cut into cubes and dust these with confectioner's sugar.

HOW TO MAKE OLD CLOTHES NEW

A LESSON IN DARNING, PATCHING AND MENDING

EVERY girl should know how to repair the inevitable damage done to her clothes by constant wear and tear, and there can be no comparison between a hasty, bungled mend and a neat patch or a smooth, even darn. Let us first consider darning, work which incompetent needlewomen often dislike very much. We are going to see how, with a little patience, we may obtain quite beautiful results.

DARNING

The darning cotton should be fairly soft, not too coarse for the material, and as like it in color and texture as possible. When about to darn a stocking we thread the long-eyed darning needle by holding it in our left hand, point downward, loop the end of the darning cotton over it and draw the needle out of the stretched loop so formed. With the finger and thumb of our right hand we press the looped cotton through the eye. No knot is needed.

We start darning on the wrong side at the left bottom corner of the hole—not close up to it but outside the part wearing thin, for if the darn is not begun beyond it, this worn part will give, through the increased strain, directly the stocking is put on. The stitch is really a weaving of the darning cotton with the worn and broken threads of the stocking. The needle takes up as many stitches as it can conveniently hold, picking up a thread, then leaving one, first in a row away from us, then in a row toward us. We must then take care, before

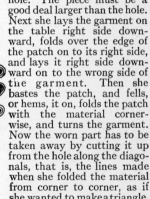

1. A darn.

drawing the thread up loosely with our right hand, after taking the needleful, to hold down with our left thumb the loop forming at the end of the thread, and leave it there to allow for shrinkage in washing. We should also be careful not to pucker the material when pulling the thread. The stitches are repeated in the same direction, backward and forward, and the thread crossed over the hole when we arrive at it. It is better not to let the row of loops at the ends be in line, but in steps up to the longest stitches made across the hole, then down again beyond it. This prevents too great a strain on the two threads at the ends of the darn; but of course the shape of the darn must depend on that of the hole.

Having finished this warp darning, we cut the darning cotton, turn the stocking round to the left and cross the previous threads as shown in picture 1, in a kind of lattice-work, taking care not to pierce the darning already done, but passing the needle over and under the strands alternately. The crossing is done in a regular oblong. Careful darners always put a hard wooden ball in the foot of the stocking and mend over that.

PATCHING

When a garment becomes worn and ragged in one part, and the possibility of darning it is hopeless, we have to patch it. For the patch we need a piece of material to match the garment. This is a matter of importance, for it would not do to use a thinner, more flimsy piece of material, and equally it would not do to apply a thicker, more coarsely woven one. If the color of the garment has faded, and we have a piece of unused cloth in which the color is still bright, we can usually make the color fade by exposing it to the sun or washing it in water with a little soda dissolved in it.

We will suppose a little girl has worn a hole in an under-garment, and she is going to sew on a patch. She lays the piece of calico over the garment with the hole in the centre, and cuts out of it a square or a four-sided piece, according to the shape of the hole. The piece must be a good deal larger than the hole. Next she lays the garment on the table right side downward, folds over the edge of the patch on to its right side, and lays it right side downward on to the wrong side of the garment. Then she bastes the patch, and fells, or hems, it on, folds the patch with the material corner-wise, and turns the garment. Now the worn part has to be taken away by cutting it up from the hole along the diagonals, that is, the lines made when she folded the material from corner to corner, as if she wanted to make a triangle, until a point is reached clear of the worn part, and enough material is left to turn under and sew on to the patch, as shown at B in picture 2; A, of course, shows the outer edge of the patch, and C is the original hole. In sewing round this inside square, care must be given to the corners. She snips these up a little way and turns the edge under with her needle. The patch should lie flat; it will do so if the width between the fell and the sewing is ⅜-inch wide.

A flannel patch is whipstitched on to a garment as shown on page 338, for the patch would not lie flat if it were filled and sewn on exactly like a calico patch. For a patch at the elbow or near a seam, rip up the seam and make a new one for one side of the patch. Be careful to see that the patch and the material have their threads running in the same direction.

REPAIRING A SLIT

Slits will sometimes spoil the nicest frocks. A straight, clean-edged slit is easy to repair, for we can place the two edges together and darn or fine draw it—that is, draw it together with fine warp darning stitches; but a three-cornered or jagged slit is more difficult to treat. The method depends on the nature of the tear; sometimes a patch may be necessary. If the material be striped, the edges can be placed together and run on the wrong side. In doing this we slope the running to a point at both ends. Such a little seam is only possible when the stripes are narrow and close together. In the case of a three-cornered tear, we may darn the edges together, using either No. 60 cotton or fine silk, according to the material. No loops are left at the ends as in stocking darning, and the darn is fine drawn with very fine stitches placed close together, so that they are hardly visible to the eye.

A three-cornered tear is often successfully treated by hemming a patch on the back of the material with very fine stitches, and tucking in the frayed edge of the tear with the needle just enough to allow the edge to be hemmed down with fine stitches on the right side. The hems must be quite close together. A clean tear in a woolen garment may be mended in fishbone stitch.

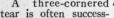

2. Patching.

GLOVE MENDING

How long gloves would last if those dreadful holes did not come as it were by magic!

A common fault in glove mending is the use of too coarse a cotton or silk. We should choose quite a fine kind and use a small needle. Then, when the seam of a kid glove splits, it is easy to make the same little stitches as the glove-maker did before. In mending holes in cotton or silk materials, it is best to put the finger of the glove with the hole in it upon the first finger of the left hand, and fine draw the hole. As the hole is usually close to the seam at the tip, we can use the material turned under at the seam to make a foundation for the tiny darn. We must fasten off the thread on the wrong side, or we shall get that unsightly thread popping out of the finger-ends like a jack-in-the-box. A tear is more troublesome to repair, and this usually comes in a new pair of kid gloves, the skin of which has become rotten, or has a thin, weak spot. If the glove is longer than is really necessary, it is a good idea to cut off a little strip at the sleeve end, shape a piece to fit in the tear exactly, and stitch in the patch in the same way as the seams are sewed.

3. Fishbone stitch.

The fewer the punctures of the kid with the needle, the better. Drawing the two edges close together usually makes matters worse, for the kid is likely to tear in a fresh place.

HOW TO MAKE YOUR OWN FIRE-SCREENS

FIRE-SCREENS can be made so that they are both serviceable and decorative in the household. The foundation framework is easily constructed by a boy or girl who has some skill in using tools and materials. The most useful screen is made in three panels, each 4½ feet high and 1½ feet wide. The frames are made preferably of thoroughly seasoned white pine, to avoid warping. They are usually mitred at the corners and braced in the middle. Strips of 1-inch pine cut 2 inches wide will secure the proper strength and weight.

The frames should be covered either with brown sheeting or with unbleached muslin, which is stretched as tight as possible. It is held in place by very small tacks, which are driven into the edges of the frames. After doing this, carefully cut away all the surplus material. Then prepare a sizing of thin flour paste, and with it wet thoroughly every portion of the muslin. In stretching, the cloth may pull unevenly and cause slight roughness of the surface. However, this can be smoothed down while wet and held in place by the paste when it dries. The drying takes only a short time. When it is accomplished the result will be a working surface which is quite tight and satisfactory.

In selecting the paper covering individual taste may be exercised. The beautiful varieties of paper-hangings render it almost impossible to make a real poor selection. If it is to be used in the nursery the little ones will be most interested in both bright colors and quaint figures. The background of the screen should ordinarily be of somewhat dark wallpaper of indefinite pattern. In cutting the paper for the front of a panel a margin of about 1½ inches should be allowed on all sides, while the back piece should be the exact size of the frame. The paste should contain a little starch, but it must be free from lumps and not very thick. It needs to be applied as evenly as possible. Care is needed to see that every part of the paper is covered by it. Place the paper upon the frame, beginning at the top and allowing the surplus 1½-inch margin to lap over. Put a piece of wrapping-paper under the hand and slowly smooth the pasted part for about 6 inches down from the upper edge, thus pressing out all air bubbles and wrinkles. When this is successfully done, continue the same process, always smoothing downward.

Should any creases or other irregularities fail to disappear during the slow rubbing, take the paper by the two lower corners, lift it from the muslin until past the roughness, and then press again. In this way you are certain to remove any imperfections and to secure a perfectly plain surface. The margin is next to be pasted and will lap perhaps ¼ inch on the back. This will, however, be covered by the paper for the back of the panel, which is to be applied in the same way as the front piece.

The hardest part of the work is now over. Next secure an illustrated book of nursery rhymes or children's stories. Cut out every figure in the book, large and small alike. Select three of the largest and handsomest for the centre pieces, and about these arrange the others attractively without regard to the stories which they illustrate. The result will be cer-tain to be admired. The back may be either ornamented in a similar manner or left plain. Four brass hinges are needed to fasten the frame together. A line of brass-headed nails might well be added all around the edges, both to serve as a protection of the paper and as a finish. Finally two small brass handles placed on top of the outer panels, to avoid soiling by frequent handling of the screen, complete one of the most attractive and serviceable furniture decorations in the house.

THE GAME OF STICKERCHIEF

A SPLENDID game that can be played by any number of children is stickerchief. It is quite as exciting as hockey or tennis and it has the advantage of not requiring expensive balls, racquets or sticks.

Stickerchief is played with a handkerchief and some short pieces of bamboo, of the sort used by gardeners to hold up tall flowers. A dozen of these bamboos can be bought at any florist's for a small sum.

The game can be played on a lawn of any size, and the grass will not be injured, as it is not necessary to make any white lines on it. Two goals, one at each end of the lawn, are required and these will merely be formed by the flower-sticks stuck into the grass about four feet apart. When two sticks have been placed at each end of the lawn in this way you can begin.

It is best to make the first attempt with only two players. Each must have one of the light bamboo sticks, and they must stand the handkerchief. Then they have a fine struggle for it. Sometimes the handkerchief flies off the stick while the player is running with it, and then the other player can often catch it before it reaches the ground. Some-times it is skillfully knocked off, and some-times neatly lifted off. Any way is considered fair; the game is simply to get the handkerchief through the opponent's goal and to prevent him from scoring. A game is finished when a goal is scored. A match consists of five games, and the player who wins the larger number of games is the victor.

After a little practice any number of children can play together. Two captains are chosen, and these captains pick the players who are to form the teams. Four, six, or even ten players may be in each team; in fact, the only limit is the size of the lawn.

When all are ready, and have been provided with the sticks, the captains tell the players where they are to stand—some close to the

The game of stickerchief as played by a boy and girl.

in the centre of the lawn between the two goals. Now they must place a handkerchief on the ground, and stand on opposite sides of it with the ends of the sticks just touching the ground, about a foot away from the hand-kerchief, as you see in the picture.

Then one player must count "One—two —three—go!" and at the word "go" both must try to pick up the handkerchief on the sticks. This is much more difficult than it looks. Each player tries to knock his op-ponent's stick away.

Presently one manages to pick up the handkerchief, and then runs as fast as he can toward the opponent's goal. Of course, the other player follows, and tries to get the handkerchief off the stick. If he manages to get it on to his own stick he rushes with it to the other goal.

In a few minutes both players become tremendously excited, for often they get within a few feet of the goal before they drop goal, and others near the middle of the lawn. Then the captains take their places by the handkerchief, and start the game at the word "go." Of course, it becomes ever so much more exciting when a number are playing, and often it is quite a long time before either side can score a goal.

If there are many players on each side they ought to be distinguished in some way, so that they can be recognized at once as friends or foes. It is a good plan to tie little bows of ribbon in the middle of each stick. One side can have green bows and the other red. These look pretty, and are very easily seen.

The game is a splendid one for a children's party, as boys and girls can play together. It has all the fascinations and excitement of hockey, without the danger of bruises that are too often caused by hard balls and heavy sticks. The light bamboos used for sticker-chief cannot hurt anybody.

THE NEXT THINGS TO MAKE AND TO DO ARE ON PAGE 4013.

WHAT IS WRONG IN THESE PICTURES?

There is something wrong in each of these pictures. It will help us to cultivate our powers of observation to try to discover the mistakes the artist has purposely made. They are pointed out on page 4014.

A STORY OF FRANCE

VICTOR HUGO, one of the greatest of French writers, was born at Besançon in 1802. His father was a distinguished general in Napoleon's army. Hugo began to write poetry when he was not yet twenty. But he became famous, not only through his poetry, but through his plays and his novels. Les Misérables is his masterpiece. Because of it many authorities claim that he is the greatest writer since Shakespeare. This is the story of a soul purified by heroism and glorified through suffering. Valjean, the ex-convict hero, is one of the most splendid characters in fiction. Hugo died in 1885.

LES MISERABLES

CONTINUED FROM 3752

EARLY in October, 1815, a tramp entered Digne, a little French town. It was near sunset. The man went into the Mayor's office, and then set out to find a place where he could spend the night. His appearance was against him, for his clothes were ragged, his beard was ragged, and his hair was uncombed. Added to these signs of poverty was a thick coating of dust from the highway. He went into the best inn that the town boasted, and asked for a meal and a bed for the night. The landlord looked at him sharply, and secretly sent a servant to the Mayor's office. The answer from the Mayor was sufficient to make him send the stranger away. When the tramp protested, the innkeeper said: "Your name is Jean Valjean. I know what you have been. Make yourself scarce!"

Valjean went out into the cold night and tried another and cheaper hotel. But there he met with a similar reception. In the whole town of Digne he could find no one to take him in. He tried to creep into a kennel, but the dog drove him out. Hungry, cold, and with very bitter feelings, he took to the road again. But finding no refuge, he returned to the town and sat down on some stone steps. A kindly passer-by advised him to knock at a house beside the bishop's palace.

He was admitted and was invited to supper and offered a bed. The stranger thought he was the guest of the parish priest, but in reality his host was the beloved Bishop of Digne, a man who spent his life doing good deeds and looking after the poor. Valjean was a rough-looking man of about forty-eight, and his appearance terrified the bishop's sister and servant; but the good old priest ignored their fear. The stranger at once said he was Jean Valjean, a released convict who had served nineteen years in the hulks. He had been freed four days and was walking from Toulon to Pontarlier. He had had to show his yellow passport to the Mayor, and as a result he had been refused shelter.

Early in the morning Valjean rose, stole the silver plate from the cupboard, and departed. He was brought back by the police, who said he had claimed that the priest had given him the silver. The good bishop bade the officers free the man. Then he handed Valjean two silver candlesticks, telling the ex-convict that he had forgotten them. Dazed and wondering, the man left the house.

More than two years later a Parisian girl, Fantine, started to walk from Paris to Montreuil. With her was her little girl. The father had deserted them, and Fantine was going to her home to look for work. But passing through Montfermeil, Fantine was attracted by two little girls whose parents, the Thénardiers, kept an inn. She made an arrangement whereby Madame Thénardier agreed to keep her little girl Cosette, for whose support Fantine would pay a certain number of francs each month.

At Montreuil, Fantine secured work in the factory in which black glass jewelry was made. The owner of this factory was Father Madeleine. No one knew anything of Father Madeleine except that, coming to the town a stranger, he had saved two children of the police captain from a fire. That was two and a half years before Fantine arrived. Madeleine had brains, and he had built up his factory and brought prosperity to the whole district. Many men were jealous of the fortune he was making, but they could find nothing against him. Inspector Javert of the police, however, watched him carefully, for he felt that he had seen Madeleine on some other occasion.

Fantine was given a position in the factory, and sent money regularly to the Thénardiers. Little did she know that she was dealing with a pair of rogues and that her beloved Cosette was treated worse than a dog. At five years of age Fantine's child was made to do the work of a servant, and she was beaten and kicked without mercy. On every possible occasion the Thénardiers made more demands for money from poor Fantine. Finally she lost her position. She did not appeal to Father Madeleine, who had become Mayor, and she was penniless. To get money for her child she went from bad to worse, until at last she was arrested. Inspector Javert ordered her to jail for six months, but in the nick of time Father Madeleine appeared and freed the girl. Fantine, who was seriously ill, was sent to a hospital.

Just at this time an accident occurred near Montreuil. An old man named Fauchelevent was caught under a heavy cart which had been overturned. Father Madeleine saw the accident, and, through his enormous strength, although at the risk of his life, he lifted the cart singlehanded and saved the old man's life. Javert saw the deed and recognized Father Madeleine as Jean Valjean. His strength had betrayed him.

Fantine, who was dying, pleaded to have her child with her, and Madeleine promised to have Cosette brought. But at that moment he heard that an innocent man was in danger of being sent to the hulks as the notorious Jean Valjean. He took part of his enormous fortune from the bank and buried it. Then he gave himself up to free the innocent man. Javert made the arrest, and Valjean was sent to jail for life. In the meantime Fantine died. Valjean was transferred to a ship as a convict sailor, but after making a heroic rescue of a shipmate, he disappeared in a raging sea; and the Government announced that he was dead.

But the Government was wrong. Valjean had escaped. He went at once to the spot in which he had hidden his fortune, and then started for Montfermeil. The name of the Thénardier inn was "The Sergeant of Waterloo." Thénardier pretended that he had been a sergeant in Napoleon's army and that at the battle of Waterloo had saved the life of a Colonel Pontmercy. The truth was that he was only a rogue who was stealing from the bodies of the dead. Colonel Pontmercy had recovered consciousness as Thénardier bent over to rob him, and had assumed that the man had saved his life.

Valjean reached the inn after meeting poor little Cosette, who was running away from the cruel treatment she had received. On payment of a large sum he took possession of the little girl. Thénardier immediately repented his bargain and raised an alarm that Cosette had been kidnaped. Javert heard this report and became suspicious that Valjean was not dead. The Inspector tracked the former convict and the little girl to Paris. Luckily Valjean saw his pursuer. His escape was very narrow. He scaled a high wall and found himself in a convent garden. The gardener proved to be old Fauchelevent who, out of gratitude, told the head of the convent that Valjean was his brother. For several years Cosette was a pupil in the convent, and Valjean was safe as a gardener.

In the meantime events were taking place at the little town of Vernon which were to have a profound influence on Valjean and Cosette. A youth, Marius Pontmercy, was living with his grandfather Gillenormand, a Royalist. Marius had never seen his father, Colonel Pontmercy, because his grandfather would not allow it. But at the Colonel's death he learned all about his father's distinguished career, and became an ardent Republican. This led to a quarrel with his grandfather. Marius left for Paris to study law. At times he nearly starved, but he managed to pass his examinations. His father had left a letter in which he asked Marius to bear the title of Baron, which had been conferred by Napoleon, and to do his best to befriend a sergeant Thénardier, who had saved his life at Waterloo.

When Cosette had been a few years in the convent, Valjean decided that she must be taken away so that she would know life outside its walls. He took a house, and they lived very quietly. One of their diversions was walking or sitting in the Luxembourg Gardens. There Marius saw Cosette and, without knowing her name, fell in love with her.

At that period Marius was living in the Gorbeau House, a poverty-stricken lodging-house. A family called Jondrette also lived there, but they were very poor. Marius had helped them with money until he discovered that they lived on what they could get from sending out begging letters.

One of these letters was sent to Valjean, who lived under the name of Urbain Fabre. Valjean came to help the Jondrettes, but was recognized as Valjean by Jondrette, who was really Thénardier. Thénardier and his wife entered into a vile plot to rob, and even kill, Valjean. Marius, in the next room, overheard the plan and reported it to the police.

Valjean was decoyed to Gorbeau House and was set upon by Thénardier and his gang of ruffians. At a critical moment Inspector Javert appeared on the scene and arrested the ruffianly crew, but Valjean made his escape in the confusion. Marius had seen everything from a hole in the wall, and he was overwhelmed at the thought that it was this villain of a Thénardier to whom his father had owed his life. But Eponine, one of Thénardier's daughters, had an affection for Marius, and, unknown to her father, she found out Cosette's address for the young man. Cosette and Marius met and fell in love.

Thénardier escaped from prison, and would have robbed Valjean's house, but Eponine would not allow it. Her threats to call the police prevented the attempt. Valjean was making plans for going to England. When Cosette told Marius, the young man became almost mad.

The revolution of 1832 broke out, and Marius joined the Revolutionists. Barricades were thrown up in the streets, and behind them Marius was fighting. At his side was Gavroche, a *gamin*—that is, a street urchin of Paris. This little street arab was the son of Thénardier. Marius sent him with a letter to Cosette, and Gavroche gave it to Valjean. Valjean immediately went to the barricade to Marius. He found that Inspector Javert was held prisoner by the Revolutionists and was condemned to death. The ex-convict asked permission to be the executioner, but instead of killing his enemy, he let him escape. Gavroche was killed heroically. So, too, was Eponine, who was fighting in the garb of a man. The Revolutionists were overcome, and Marius was wounded. Valjean seized the young man and disappeared.

How he managed to do this, is told in the words of the book.

THE RESCUE OF MARIUS

IT was in the sewers that Valjean had descended.

A great city is like the ocean, the diver may go from sight beneath it.

The transition was incredible. In the heart itself of the metropolis, Valjean had stepped out of life, and in a twinkling, the time to lift a trap-door and slam it behind him, he had passed from broad day into utter obscurity, from midday to midnight, from turbulence to stillness, from the uproar of thunder to the stagnation of the mausoleum; and by a prodigious change beyond any he had met in an eventful career, from extreme peril to most perfect security.

It was a fall abruptly into a cave, a disappearance into the dungeons of the capital; the strange period of quitting the street, where death was everywhere, for this sepulcher sheltering his life. Safety had opened a panel to rescue him. Celestial bounty had taken him by treachery, in a measure. To think of Providence plotting an ambuscade!

The wounded man did not stir, and the bearer did not know whether he was carrying one living or dead.

His first sensation was blindness, for all at once he saw nothing. He also seemed deafened, hearing no sounds at all.

The frenzied, murderous storm unchained a few feet overhead sent no waves to him, thanks due to the space of earth between; nearly lost and indistinct, it came merely as a murmur in a depth. All he felt was that he had a firm foothold, and that sufficed him.

Stretching out one arm, and then the other, he touched two sides of a passage, and learned that it was narrow; he slipped, and was sure that it was wet. He thrust out a foot warily, dreading a hole, a fissure, or gulf, but the flagging was prolonged; a rank fetidness notified him where he was.

In a few instants he recovered his sight. A little light fell through the grating by which he had come, and he began to make out the objects. The tunnel in which he was earthed up, a word suiting the situation, was walled up in his rear. This was one of the drifts called, in the language of sanitary engineers, branches. Before him rose another wall—blackness itself. The gleam from the manhole died away ten or twelve feet from where Valjean stood, and made just a feeble mist on the damp borders of the drain for a few yards square. Beyond that the opaqueness was massy; it appeared horrible to have to plunge into it, and entrance was like ingulfing one's self. But still this wall of dense fog could be invaded.

Valjean had to make haste. As he had spied the sewer-grating, the soldiers might do the same, and all depended on this chance. They might likewise descend into the subterraneans, and search here. There was not a moment to lose. He had laid Marius on the ground, and picking him up and settling him on his shoulders, he marched onward. It was resolutely that he trod the darkened way.

In reality they were less safe than he imagined. Perhaps perils, no less dread, and of another kind, awaited him. After the fulgent cyclone of battle, the cavern of pit-holes and miasma—after chaos, the pestilence. Valjean had only fallen from one hell to a lower one.

When he had gone fifty steps he had to stop. A question arose. The corridor struck another closed-in gulley transversely. Which was he to take of the two ways—the right or the left? How

find any way in this black labyrinth? It had but one clew—its trend; to follow its incline must bring one out at the river.

Valjean had divined this at the outset. He reckoned that he was in the sewer of the Main Markets. Selecting the left run, and keeping to the slope, he ought, in a quarter of an hour, arrive at some outlet on the Seine, between two bridges; but this would be the appearance, in daylight, on the most crowded part of the town. Perhaps he would come up into some cross-road culvert. What stupor would be in the passengers to see two men, one bearing the other, emerging from the ground at their feet. Up would run the policemen and the guards from the next watch-house. He would be arrested immediately on coming forth. Better to turn deeper into this abode of plague and trust to its blackness—leave Providence to point out the safer issue.

He went up the incline, taking the turn to the right hand.

When he had gone round the corner, the faint light from the air-hole vanished, the curtain of gloom fell anew, and he was blind once more. Yet he advanced, and as rapidly as possible.

Both of Marius's arms were drawn round in front, so that, holding them in one hand, he was able to use his other to grope his way. Marius's feet dangled down behind him. His cheek touched his and stuck to it, for it was bleeding. He felt, streaming and soaking his clothes, a warm fluid from the wounded one; it was blood. But a warm feeling on his face, where Marius's mouth was near, indicated breathing, and, consequently, life.

This arched way was less narrow than the first, but the explorer moved painfully.

Recent rains had not wholly run off, and made a little torrent in the center of the gully, so that he was forced to hug the wall not to walk in the water. Thus he went on, befogged. He resembled some nocturnal creature groping in the Unseen World, and astray in the shady subterraneans.

Gradually, however, whether the light through ventilating shafts did lessen the murkiness to some degree, or his sight became accustomed to it, he had dim perception return to him, and could faintly get an idea of the walls beside him and the vault over his head. The pupil dilates in night and finally sees day, as the soul dilates in misfortune and finds Heaven.

But to steer wisely was difficult.

In a measure, the lines of the drains agree with those of the streets. In Paris, at that time, were twenty-two hundred public ways. Imagine the tangle of branches which the sewers represented. Put end to end, they would have stretched over a line of twenty odd miles.

Valjean made a mistake at the start. He thought he was under St. Denis Street, and it was a pity he was not. Under that thoroughfare is an old stone sewer, dating from 164–, running straight to the main sewer, with only one turn and one branch. But the gut of Truanderie Street, with an outlet by Corinth Tavern, never communicated with this; it ended in the Montmartre Street sewer, and here Valjean was involved. Opportunities to get lost abounded. The Montmartre sewers are the most entangled of all the old system.

Happily, he had left behind him the maze by the Markets, but he had more than one embarrassing riddle, and more than one street-corner—for they are streets, in their kind—offering notes of interrogation.

If Valjean had had the plans in his head, he would have soon perceived, by merely touching the wall, that he was not in the ancient St. Denis Street sewer; instead of the noble old architecture, high and royal even here, in costly cut stone base and the best mortar, he would have found the modern economical expedient, cement and rubble filling; but he did not know anything on this head.

He went straight ahead, with anxiety, and yet steadily, seeing and knowing nothing, buried in chances—or, rather, ingulfed in Providence.

Some feeling of horror by degrees stole over him. The shades in which he blundered sunk into him. He strode in an enigma. This aqueduct of mud is dreadful; the criss-crossing is dizzying. It was lugubrious to be caught in this city of dreadful night. Valjean was obliged to find—almost to invent—his route without seeing the region. Every step in such a blank might be destruction.

How could he get clear of it? Where meet an outlet? Would he meet it in time? Would this colossal granite sponge let him bore and pierce through it? Would he not be strangled in some inextricable knot of duskiness? Would he not arrive at a chasm not to be crossed or fathomed? Might not Marius die of loss of blood or of hunger? Would not the end be that both would perish and become two skeletons in some corner of the foul den? He was unaware. He asked without finding an answer. The bowels of Paris were a precipice. Like the Prophet Jonah, he was in the intestines of Leviathan.

Suddenly he encountered a surprise.

At the most unexpected period, though he had not ceased to move straightforward, he discovered that he was no longer tending upward; the water in the gutter slapped against his heels, instead of washing his toes. Therefore, the sewer was on the decline. How was this? Was he going suddenly to come out upon the river? This was a great danger, but to recede was a greater one. He pressed on.

He was not going toward the Seine. The water-shed of Paris at this part on the right bank throws the wet down one steep into the river, but off the other into the main sewer. He was at the ridge summit, and took the outer drain, which was right, though he did not know it.

Every time he came to a fork, he felt the angles, and if he found the fresh opening wider than that he was traveling, he chose it, reasoning that the narrower ones were secondary, and would end in no way out and only divert him from his aim, the principal issue. Thus he avoided the plot of the Dædalus.

At a certain time he guessed that he was leaving the part of the city where traffic was suspended by the barricades, and petrified, and entering under Paris lively and normal, for suddenly rumbled overhead the far but continuous roll of thunder. It was the turning of wheels.

He had been walking for upward of half an hour, as he computed, without any thought of resting; but he had shifted the hand which held Marius's. The darkness was thick as ever, but it cheered him.

All at once he saw his shadow before him. It was defined in a dim, reddish glimmer, vaguely impurpling the paving at his feet and the arch above, and gliding on both sides along the slimy walls of the passage. Stupefied, he turned round.

Behind him, in the part of the tunnel which he had passed through, at a distance which seemed immense, a sort of dread star flashed across the gloom, as if watching him.

It was the eye of the Police rising in the drains. Behind its rays confusedly moved eight or ten black, upright, indistinct but alarming forms.

The explanation is easy for us. On the 6th of June, a hunt in the sewers was ordered. It was feared that the vanquished would take to them for escape, and Prefect Gisquet was to sweep occult Paris as Marshal Bugeaud was the upper town. Three platoons of police and sewer-men explored the subterranean ways, both river-banks, and the Old City islands. The police were armed with rifles, life-preservers, swords, and daggers.

The right bank squad had their lantern now directed to the part where Valjean was fleeing. It had investigated the parts under Cadran Street. While searching there with the light, Valjean had passed a curved gallery, where he would have been caught. But on themselves coming out of it, the policemen thought they heard steps, and they were the fugitives', indeed. The sergeant lifted his lantern on high, and all stared in the fog whence had come the sound.

It was a moment of inexpressible tribulation for the man.

Luckily, though he saw the bull's-eye well, it did not see him; it was light, but he the shadow. He was afar, and mingled with the mist. He stood up against the wall and waited. He did not clearly understand what it was about. Want of sleep and food, the smells, emotions, all had lifted him into the visionary state. He saw the flare and black creatures around it, but he did not comprehend what they were.

On his stopping, all sound ceased. The watch listened, and heard nothing more; they looked with the same non-result. They consulted. The man at bay saw them gather, and they whispered. They concluded that they had been mistaken, that there was no person, and consequently no noise, and that it was useless to march into this trench. Instead of so losing time, they had better hasten toward St. Merry's, where there would be work and some rebel to track, if any, in that district.

The sergeant ordered his platoon to take the left toward the incline to the Seine. If he had broken them into two squads, and sent them both ways in the outer belt, Valjean would be taken. This hung by a thread. It is likely that the headquarters' instructions, from foreseeing a meeting with the fugitive rebels in force, commanded no scattering of the police. The rounds went on the march, leaving the missed one behind. Valjean perceived nothing of this movement, save the eclipse of the lantern which suddenly turned.

Before going, the sergeant, to relieve his conscience, fired off his rifle in the direction of Valjean. The report echoed over and over again under the crypt, and a bit of mortar falling with a splash into the water warned Valjean that the bullet had struck the vault above him.

Slow and measured paces resounded for awhile on the pave, deadened more and more by distance, the group of dark forms faded as the light waved and floated, reddening the arched roof, but all disappeared. The silence recovered rule over the shadows, and Valjean, not daring yet to move, stayed a long while leaning against the wall, with ears stretched and eyes dilated, watching the vanishing of this phantom patrol.

It is only fair to state that the police coolly fulfilled their duties of keeping the ways clear in these grave public disturbances. A riot was no excuse, in their eyes, for letting the malefactors take the bit in their teeth, and for society to be neglected because the ruling powers were in peril. The ordinary service went on together with the extra, and was not ruffled.

In the midst of an incalculable political event in progress, under the pressure of possible revolution, without allowing insurrection and its barricades to hinder him, a detective was "shadowing" a suspicious character.

This was occurring on the Seine right bank, a little this side of the Invalides Bridge. The two men were watching each other, and one avoiding his pursuer. The leader tried to increase the distance between, the other to approach. It was like a quiet game of "tag." Neither wanted to hurry on matters, and both moved slowly, as though fearing that too much haste would spoil his chances. It was a wild creature following its prey without seeming to have run it down expressly. The prey was on its guard, and went warily.

The proper interval between the weasel dogged and the canine trailer was observed. The fugitive had little substance and a sickly look; the would-be captor was a tall man of rough appearance, whose charge would be overpowering. Feeling himself the weaker, the first avoided any encounter; but he did so with an enraged manner; in his eyes were all the somber hostility of enforced flight and the menace in fear driven to bay.

The strand was lonely, with not only no passenger, but neither boatman nor longshoreman from the barges moored hard by.

From the quay the pair could be viewed, and for those examining them from that distance the runaway would appear a tatterdemalion, hairy and sneaking, restless and shivering under a ragged blouse; the other was an old-school police officer, wearing the official long-skirted coat buttoned up to the chin.

What was the latter's aim? Probably to overtake the leader and provide him with warmer clothes.

When a police officer dogs a man in rags, it is to put him in the state livery. But the color comes into play. Clothe the capture in military uniform, and he becomes glorious; in convict suit, and he is disagreeable. This one was doomed to wear the felon's garb.

This is what he was endeavoring to elude.

If he let him run free without overhauling him, it was because he hoped to drive him into some haven for his kindred cruisers, or at a meeting with some dangerous criminals. This timing of a capture is called "shadowing," as formerly it was "dogging."

What made the supposition more likely was that the pursuer, catching sight of an empty cab on the embankment, made a sign to the driver. He understood, evidently recognized what sort of fare he was engaged for, wheeled round, and followed the couple. This was not noticed by the ragged rascal, who was on a lower level. The hack rolled along under the Champs Elysées trees with only the hack-driver's bust and the upheld whip seen over the parapet.

One of the secret instructions to the police contains this article:

"Always have a hackney-carriage at hand in case of an arrest."

While each was maneuvering with irreproachable strategy, the two men neared a sloping ledge which allowed the hackmen to drive down to the water's edge and water their horses; this has been done away with, as it spoiled the symmetry of the embankment, but if the eye is gratified, the horses suffer with thirst.

It was likely that the hunted man was going to try by this rise to escape among the trees of the pleasure-ground, though it would be sprinkled with police who would lend their brother-officer a willing hand. This point is not far from the "Francis I House," and a soldiers' guard-house stands close.

To his watcher's high astonishment, the chased man did not go up the incline of the watering-place, but kept right along the river-edge. His position became critical.

Unless he meant to walk into the river, what did he mean to do?

There was no further means to get upon the bank, no slope, and no steps; and they were near the mark where the river, by an elbow at Jena Bridge, was entered by the strand finishing with a slender tongue. Here the fugitive would inevitably be blocked between the straight up and down wall on his right, the water in front and left, and the policeman in the rear.

The actual end of the walk was hidden by a heap of rubbish some seven or eight feet high, dumped there after some house pulling down. But the man could never think of hiding himself there after simply turning it. The expedient would be puerile. Certainly he would not think of it. The simplicity of the thieving class does not go to that degree.

The pursued one reached and doubled this petty cape, so that he was lost to the other's sight. Not seeing, he judged, ostrich-like, that he was no longer seen; he snatched at the advantage by throwing off all dissimulation and stepped out rapidly. In a few instants he was at the rubbish pile, and went round it, where he stopped, stupor-stricken; the hunted man had disappeared.

The strand only ran thirty paces further, where it dived under the water, plashing the quay wall. The fugitive could not have climbed here or swum the stream without being seen.

What had become of him?

The man in the buttoned-up coat

strode to the end of the shore, where he stood thoughtful for awhile, with his eyes searching and his hands clinched convulsively. Suddenly he beat his brow. He had descried, where the land ended and the water begun, a broad, low iron grating under an arched way, garnished with a heavy lock, and on three enormous hinges. This opened on the water as well as on the foreshore. An inky flow rolled out of this orifice, and proved it was meant to disgorge into the river. Inside the rusted and clumsy bars a dark arched passage could be discerned.

The man folded his arms and looked at the grate with a reproachful manner. The look not satisfying him, he tried to push it, but it resisted solidly as well as his shaking. It was probable that it had been opened, although he had heard no noise, singular in so rusty a gate. But it was certain that it was fastened up now. This betrayed that the man who had gone through had a key rather than a "lock-pick." This belief burst upon his mind so forcibly that he tried to shake the grate open, which drew from him this indignant exclamation:

"This is going too far! The sneaks are carrying the Government's own keys now!"

But speedily calming down, he expressed his throng of ideas by syllables accented almost ironically:

"Whew! this is where the Break-o'-day Boys dwell when they say, 'Under *Pantin* (Paris)!'"

This spoken, hoping one knows not what, either to see that man come forth or others arrive to join him, he posted himself concealed behind the heap of trash, with the fretful patience of a dog in the leash.

On his side, the hack-driver, who had regulated his movements by the detective's, halted on the upper roadway; foreseeing a long spell of waiting, he hung a moist bag of fodder to his horses' heads respectively. The scarce passengers on the bridge, before going away, turned their heads briefly to regard the two features of the still-life scene, the watcher on the strand and the driver by the parapet.

During this incident, Valjean had resumed his walk without stopping any more.

It became more and more laborious. The level of the gullies varied; the medium height is five feet six, calculated for the average man, so that Valjean was forced to stoop not to knock Marius's head against the key-stones. At every instant he had to bend, rise, and feel the wall. The moisture on the sides and the viscousness on the floor gave bad rest for hand and foot. He stumbled over this dung-heap of the great city.

The intermittent glimmer of the ventilator holes appeared but at very long spaces, and so dull that the brightest sunbeam was but like the moon's ray; all the rest was dark, fog, miasma, opacity. Valjean felt hunger and thirst, the latter particularly; it was as bad as being on the sea, for there was "water, water, everywhere, but not a drop to drink." His prodigious strength began to flag, though little lessened by age, thanks to his chaste and sober life. Fatigue burdened him, and his failing powers increased the weight of his load. Marius, perhaps dead, weighed like a lifeless body.

Valjean sustained him in such a way that his chest was not squeezed in and his respiration went on regularly.

Between his legs he felt the rats scamper; one was so frightened that he bit him in passing.

From time to time, through air-holes, a whiff of pure wind came to revive him.

It might be three o'clock in the afternoon that he arrived at the main drain.

He was amazed by the sudden enlargement. He was unexpectedly in a hall where his hands could not touch the walls and his head went nowhere near the roof. The grand sewer is eight by seven feet.

Here was a cross-road where a wiser man would be puzzled. Valjean went for the largest, the circuit drain. But the question arose: to go up or down? He thought that the circumstances were pressing now, and that he must reach the river, that is to say, go down the general incline.

He turned to the left.

This was good again.

If he had gone the other way, he must have met a wall and would be lost, exhausted after a thousand exertions in the gloom. There was, indeed, another way, which would have brought him out *via* the Bastille, on the Seine, near the Arsenal; but he never could have got through such ramifications; it would have required profound knowledge.

He knew nothing at all about this underground and frightful medley of passages, and if he had been asked where he was, he must have replied:

"In night!"

His instinct served him to the point; to follow the slope was possible safety.

At the crossing of the branch from the Madeleine Church Ward he came to a halt from weariness. A rather large air-hole, probably Anjou Street, gave quite a vivid light. With gentleness befitting a brother handling another wounded, he set Marius on the ledge of the drain-side. The bleeding countenance appeared in that glare as if in a grave. His eyes were closed, his hair glued to his temples, like paint-brushes dipped in varnish and dried, his dead hands dangled, his limbs were cold, and blood had coagulated at the corners of the mouth. A clot of gore filled up the knot of his neck-cloth, the shirt was sucked into the gashes, and the coat chafed the raw lips of the wounds.

With his finger-tips thrusting back the garments, Valjean laid his hand on his bosom, where the heart still throbbed.

Valjean tore his shirt, stanched the blood as well as he could, and bound up the wounds; then, bending over the scarce breathing and wholly unconscious man, he regarded him with inexpressible hate.

In disarranging his clothes he had found two objects in his pockets—a small loaf of bread, bought by Marius in hurrying to the barricade, and his note-book. He opened the latter while eating the bread. On the first leaf he found these lines, written by the young man:

"My name is Marius Pontmercy. Carry my remains to my grandfather's, Monsieur Gillenormand, No. 6 Filles-du-Calvaire Street, in the Swamp."

Valjean read, and stood for a second self-absorbed, repeating the directions. He replaced the book in Marius's pocket, and as strength returned to him from having eaten, he took him up, as before, on his back, carefully settled his head down on the hollow over his left shoulder, and resumed the descent of the drain.

The main drain, following the Menil-montant water-shed, is nearly four miles long; it is pretty well all paved.

Nothing enlightened the wanderer on the parts of Paris he traversed, or on what he accomplished. But the growing pallor of the gleams through the venti-lator shafts, met now and again, told him that the day was waning, and the rolling of vehicles, from continuous, had become broken, and finally ceased. He concluded that he was no longer under busy Paris at its core.

Where there are less streets, the sewers have less openings, so that the gloom deepened around him. But he continued to progress, though he had to grope his way.

This shade became suddenly terrible.

The refugee felt that he was wading, and that, instead of being muddy water, it was mud.

He was confronting a sink-hole. The old style of sewers was subject to crevasses and sinking spots. The water soaked in where the surrounding ground was very sandy; the paving, of small stones, gave way where undermined. The bottom, for a distance, sunk, but the floor remained, floated on the fluid, and submerged in the sand. It is the quick-sand of the sea-shore suddenly met on dry land. The saturated soil is in fusion, the molecules are held in suspension in a shifting medium, neither earth nor water. The depth is sometimes so great that to walk into one is most disastrous. If the water dominates, death comes promptly —it is swallowing up; if the earth is the stronger element, the death is slower, and it is stifling.

Imagine such a death! If such a drawing down into the depth is awful on the sea strand, what must it be in a sewer? Instead of the full air and light, the clear horizon, the vast surge, the free clouds from which rain life itself—the hopes under every form, probable way-farers, boats landing, possible rescue up to the latest time, it is blindness and bewilderment, a black roof as of a tomb already begun, death in a witches' caldron with the lid on; suffocation in a pool, a stone box, where asphyxia opens its claw in the mire and clutches you by the throat; fetidity mingles with the death-rattle; mud instead of sand, sul-phureted hydrogen instead of tempest, ordure instead of ocean! Here he can call, gnash teeth, writhe, and go down in agony with that immense city over-head knowing nothing!

The inexpressible horror of such a fate!

Sometimes death redeems its atrocity by a dread dignity. On the funeral pyre of shipwreck it may be grand; in flame or foam a proud attitude is possible; one is transfigured. But not so here. Death is uncleanly; it is humiliating to expire. Filth is synonymous with shame; it is paltry, ugly, and loathsome. To die in a butt of malmsey, like Clarence, may pass; but in the ditch, like Jane Shore, is horrible. It is hideous to battle in it; it is floundering while dying. It is shady enough to be hell, but so nasty as to be a swinish wallow, and the dying one can not tell whether he will be a ghost or a toad.

Elsewhere the sepulcher is sinister, but here it is nameless.

The depth of these sinks varies, as well as the widths and degree of turbidity, according to the density of the soil. One may be three or four feet, or eight or ten, or again bottomless. Here the mess is almost solid, there nearly liquid. In one a man goes under in a day, in the next it takes but minutes. A child might walk over where a man would sink. The first rule for safety is to lighten one's self as much as possible. The scavenger tosses away his scoop-shovel, lamp, or wading-boots when he feels his footing melt away from under him.

This species of defect was frequent about the Champs Elysées, hard to treat with hydraulic works and tender under buildings subterraneous on account of excessive inconstancy. When the part was rebuilt, in 1836, where Valjean was now inmeshed, the quicksand gave the men six months' work.

The previous day's rain had caused this subsidence. The water had filtered under the flooring and dislocated it so that it settled down. It was impossible to say how far, as the darkness was thicker here than elsewhere. It was a pit of mud in a cavern by night.

Jean Valjean felt the flooring fail him, and he was walking in mire. Over the silt was water, but he had to cross somehow. To retrace his steps was out of the question. He was tired, and Marius expiring. Where else had he to go?

He dashed on. Besides, the depression did not seem bad at the start; but, as he proceeded, the mud deepened. He was soon up to mid-leg in it, and in water to the knees. Still he waded, holding up his burden as high as he could out of the water. The mud came up to his hams now, and the water to the girdle. He could not retire, and yet was sinking more

and more. The hodge-podge which might have buoyed up one man could not uphold two.

Either of them might struggle through alone, but Valjean continued, though, perhaps, he was carrying no better than a dead man.

The water laved his armpits, and he felt still sinking; he could hardly move, on account of the clogging of the stuff he forged slowly through. The density which was sustenance to him was also the hindrance. Still he held up Marius, and gained a little, though at a tremendous outlay of vitality; but he sunk and sunk. Only his head was above water, and his arms upholding Marius. In the old paintings of the deluge you may remember the mother holding up her child in this same way.

Still going down, he had to lean his head back to keep the sludge out of his mouth and get a breath. Seen in this gloom, he would have presented but a mask floating on the surface to the eye. He himself dimly saw Marius held over him with livid face. He made a desperate effort with a thrust of the foot forward, met something solid, and had a foothold.

It was time.

He rose and stiffened himself, taking root with a kind of madness. This limit had the effect of the first step of the stairs leading up into life.

This firm mass met in the mud in the critical instant was the other side of the bottom, sagged down without parting into pieces, as a net might do. Well built pavements will form an inverted arch and hold together thus. This portion of the floor was a ladder on which one was saved.

Valjean had but to climb up it, and find himself on the further side of the sink-hole.

On leaving the water he stumbled over a stone, and was thrown on his knees. He thought this a warning, and stayed there for a spell, with his spirit departed in a prayer of thanksgiving.

He arose, shivering with cold, infected, bent under the corpse he was ever bearing, streaming with filth, but his soul clarified with a strange luster.

Once more he took up the road.

Though he had not left his life in the quicksand, his strength seemed there. That mighty effort had exhausted him.

Such was his lassitude that he was obliged to stop and lean against the wall every few steps and recover his breath. Once, having sat on the ledge to shift Marius's position on him, he feared that he could never rise again. But if his vigor was dead, not so his spirit. He did rise.

He trudged on desperately, almost swiftly, for a hundred strides, without raising his head, and scarcely breathing, till he suddenly knocked his head against a wall. Lifting his eyes, he saw a light low down and afar at the end of the underground passage. This time it was not artificial and threatening light, but the good, white light of day.

Valjean saw the outlet.

What he felt would be experienced by a damned soul amid the furnace, who suddenly disclosed to him the gates of Gehenna. Toward that radiant doorway it would fly with its stumps of scorched wings. Valjean no longer felt fatigue or the weight of Marius, and he recovered the steel muscles of his legs. He ran rather than walked.

As he drew nigh, the issue became more and more defined. It was a flat arch, not so high as the vaulted way leading thither, and less wide than the gallery which narrowed as it neared it. The tunnel finished like a funnel, a vicious shrinking, logical in a prison-hall, but unreasonable in a gully, and since corrected.

Arriving there, he came to a halt, for it was an exit through which he could not depart.

The archway was filled up with a strong grated door, not often turned apparently on its oxidized hinges; it was fastened to its stone sockets by a thick, heavy lock, which seemed an enormous brick from its rusted color. The keyhole could be seen, as well as the massive bolt which it moved, deeply shot into its socket of iron. This had been pushed forward two nicks, it was plain—that is, double-locked. It was one of those old-fashioned locks relying on bulk with which old times abounded.

Outside this barrier was the open air, the river, day, the narrow strand, but enough to walk upon—Paris! that gulf where a hunted man so easily can hide, the broad horizon—freedom! On the right was Jena Bridge, on the left the Invalides Bridge, a spot propitious for waiting for night and making off. This shore facing Gros-Caillou was one of the loneliest places in the town. Flies were buzzing in and out through these bars.

Day was declining; it was about half past eight.

Valjean laid Marius alongside the wall in the dry part of the gutter-way, marched up to the grating, and grasped the bars with both hands; the shock was maniacal, but not a quiver responded. The grating did not budge. Valjean tried the bars one after another, hoping to be able to wrench out one and use it for a lever to break the rest or prize off the lock. Not one moved. A tiger's teeth are not set firmer in their sockets. There was no lever here, and no forcing was possible.

The barrier was invincible; he had no means to open that door.

Was he doomed to finish here? What was he to do? What would befall him? Was he to retrace his steps, recommence the dreadful journey already barely struggled through? He had not the strength. Besides, how could he again cross that quicksand from which nothing but a miracle had extricated him? After that, what about that company of police who would be continuing their search? Were they to be twice eluded?

And then, how go? What direction should he take? To follow the incline was not to arrive at any goal. Would he arrive at an opening, or a dead wall, or an outlet sealed up like this? All the issues might be fastened up thus. Chance had left open the man-trap by which he had entered, but the others had been looked to, evidently.

He had succeeded in escaping—into a prison.

All was over. His toil had been useless. Exhaustion had eventuated in failure.

Young man and old were taken in the somber, immense toils of death, and Valjean felt that the horrid spider was running over the vibrating threads in the dark.

He turned his back to the grate, and fell rather than sat on the ground near Marius, ever unmoving, and his head sunk on his knees.

No way out! It was the last drop of woe.

Of whom did he think in his profound depression? Not of himself or of Marius, but of the young woman whom both loved—of Cosette.

In the midst of this disheartenment, a hand was laid on his shoulder, and a voice spoke low:

"Halves!"

Somebody in this darkness? Nothing is so like despair as dreaminess, and Valjean might believe he was dreaming. He had not heard any steps. Was it possible? He raised his eyes.

A man stood before him.

He was clad in a smock; his feet were naked; he carried his shoes in one hand, evidently having taken them off, that he might creep up to the stranger without being heard.

Valjean had not a moment's hesitation. Unforeseen as was such a meeting, he recognized this man as Thénardier.

They had met under peculiar circumstances every time. The first was when Valjean, fleeing from justice, came to Thénardier's inn at Montfermeil to take away the child, Cosette, of an unfortunate woman, named Fantine. She had left her little daughter in the keeping of the Thénardiers, who had extorted more and more money from her, on various pretexts, so as to drive her into a life of shame to acquit herself of the debts. Valjean had paid all demands and removed the ill-treated child.

After eight years, he and Cosette, a grown girl, in their rounds of alms-giving, had been decoyed by a begging letter into Thénardier's garret in Paris. Here the ingrates, after benefiting by their kindness, had entrapped Valjean into returning alone; their project was to make him sign a check for a large sum, while they held his supposititious daughter as hostage. Luckily, the captive had only pretended to agree to their designs to gain time to sever his bonds. Released by his own hands, he had shown that they could not daunt him, but when, with Christian resignation, he let them wreak their worst, the police rushed in, led by Inspector Javert, and foiled the villains. In the scuffle Valjean disappeared.

Thénardier had been sent to prison, but he had escaped.

Although startled by his appearance here, Valjean was so inured to surprises and alarms that he instantly recovered his presence of mind. Besides, the state of affairs could not be made worse; a certain degree of distress can not rise on the crescendo, and even a Thénardier can not add to the blackness of such a night.

There was an instant of expectancy.

. . . .

We must leave Hugo's words to tell the rest of the story briefly.

With relief Valjean saw that Thénardier did not recognize him. The pretended sergeant of Waterloo offered to let Valjean out of the sewer for half of what he had received from his victim, as he supposed Valjean had murdered Marius. Valjean gave him all he had in his pocket and was let out. But he ran into the arms of Inspector Javert. Javert, who was very silent, accompanied him to the home of the Gillenormands, where Marius was left with his grandfather. Valjean asked then to be permitted to call at his home. Javert agreed and waited downstairs. But when Valjean came down, the Inspector had disappeared. The hard-hearted police inspector had failed in his duty because Valjean had saved his life at the barricade. But because he felt his failure he drowned himself in the Seine.

Gillenormand had forgiven his grandson and consented to the marriage with Cosette. Valjean immediately settled the whole of his fortune on the pair. After the wedding he told Marius the truth about himself. He as a young man had stolen a loaf of bread to feed his sister's family. For that he had been thrown into prison. When he was freed, the action of the Bishop of Digne had made him want a better life.

Marius was dismayed and angry. He did not want Cosette to have anything more to do with Valjean, but he relented to the extent of allowing his wife to see the old man once a day. Gradually that dropped off. One day Thénardier appeared and threatened to expose Valjean. He told Marius that Valjean had committed a murder, and in proof he produced a piece of cloth torn from the supposed victim's coat. Marius recognized the material as that from his own coat, and he knew then—what he had never been able to discover—that Valjean had rescued him from the barricade.

With his heart full of grief at his own conduct he took Cosette at once to Valjean's lodging. He was just in time, for the old man was dying. But it was with joy that Valjean gave them his blessing.

THE NEXT STORY OF FAMOUS BOOKS IS ON PAGE 4069.

Nile gods uniting Upper and Lower Egypt; relief from temple of Rameses I at Abydos.

THE FIRST SCULPTORS

ONCE, when the world was young and strange, a world of unfamiliar lands and seas, there lived a man who was more watchful of Nature's ways than his fellow-men were. One day he discovered a kind of clay that would bake in the sun's heat, and he made a rough bowl, shaping the clay with his hands. His fellow-men may have considered him great beyond compare; they may have killed him for daring to apply natural forces and to make something new.

CONTINUED FROM 3710

Be that as it may, in the process of time other baked pots were made; and there came a day when one man had an impulse to make some marks on his bowl—a pattern. That was probably some seven or eight thousand years before Christ. In that first rough bowl, patterned with marks made by the potter's thumb, we can read the first chapter of one of Time's fairy tales that tell of the wonder of imagination and development. We may ask how the matchless vases of the Greek potters could ever have been formed had not that earliest of all potters, perhaps a bit afraid at his own daring, made the first clay pot.

The sense of shape and line, the instinct for what we call art, was not developed as an æsthetic gift; it grew out of usefulness. To be of any use at all a bowl must needs be of a certain shape and proportion. Its decoration was an afterthought; but slowly and unconsciously, as centuries went by, the sense of the beautiful developed. In a general way, the forms that were kept were those most free from unnecessary curves; and the ornamentation of pottery went through the same processes, working toward simplicity.

The earliest ornaments on the earliest bowls and stone pillars were Nature's ornaments, in spirit if not in shape. They were lines, curves, and forms which potters had learned by studying either the sea with its repeating wave lines, or the forest trunks and leaf masses, or the subtle repetition of curve in mountain ranges. From the day of the earliest potter to the present, such forms—man's puny and mechanical attempt to reproduce Nature's majestic lines—have been the basis of ornament. A student in an art school to-day struggling to work out a "repeat" for a wall-paper or floor-covering design, is not so far as one might suppose from the untutored savage making groups of rhythmical marks on his clay dish, in spite of the several thousand years that lie between, with their accumulation of civilization's habits and problems. The old mysterious beat and throb of natural life, with line after line strangely alike, yet differing one from another, is the beginning of rhythm. This is the force which stirs in the consciousness of poets and musicians.

EARLY SCULPTURES THAT EXPRESSED THE THOUGHTS OF THE ARTISTS

This decoration by ornament which does not use the forms of men and animals was the second chapter of the wonderful story of design. Of the first we know something already; it told us about the cave-men of Europe and their marvelous drawings on rock, bone and ivory—drawings executed thousands of years before the first potter made his first bowl.

The earliest history which tells us of art, history gathered from records and inscriptions, is that of Egypt, Babylonia and Assyria. It begins more than four thousand years before Christ. At first— for centuries, that is to say—Egyptian art was the laborious expression of the instinct and religion of the race; the sculptors were "thinking aloud," and were not conscious of their work as art. Only in later times did this expression of themselves become an art, when they gave special thought and skill to this kind of work as a craft. Their early statuary, then, was an attempt to give shape to their imaginations. Besides, they thought that they could gain favor and protection from the gods, whom they considered the rulers of the world, by creating magnificent forms to represent them. Thus we see that the sculpture of ancient Egypt was concerned with something that only a strong imagination helps us to understand. Starting with the consciousness of life, the certainty and mystery of death, and the fear of the unknown, they built up out of these a definite religion which was to govern their lives and help them to face death with calmness and courage.

THE LIFE OF OTHER DAYS PRESERVED IN THE TOMBS OF EGYPT

Next in importance after the gods came the kings. The bulk of the statuary which the marvelous climate of Egypt has preserved for us represents the imaginary life of the gods and the glorified doings of rulers. The representations of both deities and heroes centred, for the Egyptians, in temples and tombs stately in their massiveness.

No relics of domestic art in any other country can equal the magnificence of sculpture, pottery and jewels found in the tombs of Egyptian kings and queens. And we do not yet know how many treasures may lie buried from our view. The discovery of Tutankhamen's tomb late in the year 1922 amazed the world by the splendors revealed—stores of objects showing skill in modeling and color.

The labor in the tombs was done for the most part by unknown sculptors and craftsmen who had no idea they were working upon something which six thousand years later would be described as Egyptian art; they were merely doing what they had been commanded to do, and its purpose was duty to the dead.

From this scheme of thought were brought forth the magnificent statues of the gods and kings of Egypt which stand apart, in their largeness of spirit and grandeur of symbolism, in the art of the world. If we had only two words to describe Egyptian statuary, we should say that it was huge and it was calm; it expressed that central idea of "enduringness" round which, like a husk round a kernel, the creed of the race was wrapped.

HOW WE CAN TRACE THE PROGRESS OF EGYPTIAN ART

And so we get statues like those colossal figures of kings, rulers and gods which make the most casual and ignorant visitor to our great museums stand in amazement, and feel that, after all, his or her understanding of life and destiny is very narrow and changing. In the Egyptian rooms of the Metropolitan Museum objects belonging to widely separated periods are brought together; but imagination helps us to see them as they stood in the vastness of great temples, in sealed tomb-chambers or out upon the "lone and level sand."

At first thought it would seem that this statuary had not changed at all in its four thousand years of making; when we study it more closely we see the impress of successive epochs. The sturdy, broad figures of the earlier centuries gave place to more slim, more elongated forms; presently the time of falling-off comes, followed by a brief period of striving after older ideals. Then Egyptian art ceases to be, dies before the country itself falls apart in the grip of successive conquering nations. It has been said that for sheer technique in their art the sculptors of Egypt have never been surpassed. In spite of their excellence in this respect they were strangely unable to get away from certain curious conventions. We have already learned something of these in connection with painting in ancient Egypt.

One convention decreed that the body of a standing figure must be quite vertical; this stiffness, this absence of all bending and curving attitudes, is all the more peculiar to us because no other race since has even remotely imitated the convention. Another law of Egyptian art, painting and sculpture alike decreed that in all cases both feet—always depicted as huge—should rest flatly and firmly on the ground. The most extraordinary convention of all has been described as the *law of frontality*. This meant that in all cases the shoulders must squarely confront the spectator, and the eye must always be drawn in full, no matter what the position of the face. So that a man who is represented as walking—say, along a frieze—has his head, legs and feet drawn in profile, and his shoulders swung round in full view, and the eye drawn in the large and perfect almond shape which was the Egyptian type of beauty.

THE SCULPTURE OF ANCIENT EGYPT AND THE SCULPTURE OF TO-DAY

Another curious racial characteristic is shown in the exaggerated stillness of the sculptured figures. A great many of them are rigidly seated and appear clamped to their stone benches. The Egyptian sculptor seemed to represent moving figures under protest; it was abhorrent to him to show zest and energy of motion, and powerful muscles in play. He smooths down the figures of his great kings and gods, and is happiest when the faces seem like a mask.

When we think of our fluid and changing forms of art to-day we find it hard to believe that for four thousand years these several conventions should have been firmly held. Of all schools of art, that of Egypt has deserved to live on.

As the religion of the Egyptians was largely animal- and nature-worship, a great deal of brute life in varying forms is shown in their sculptured reliefs and statuary. The artists made a convention of their animal subjects, often blending the human and brute or bird forms in one body. This constant repetition of animal shapes has a great deal to do with the magnificent decorative power of their reliefs. Shapes so forceful and restrained, planned on such noble lines with all unnecessary detail refined away, could not help making wonderful decoration. The world has never since seen the like, and artists of later centuries have often turned to Egyptian decoration for models or inspiration.

The most remarkable of the many kinds of animal convention that the sculptors of Egypt created was the sphinx—a human-headed lion. The origin of this type is unknown, and about it many legends have clustered.

THE SPHINXES OF EGYPT AND THE WINGED BULLS OF ASSYRIA

Sphinxes were often set in pairs at the entrances to temples; one such hall, built by Queen Hatshepsut, was approached by an avenue of sphinxes. The most famous portrayal of this type of animal is that colossal sculpture near the Great Pyramid at Gizeh—a sphinx 150 feet long and 70 feet high.

The Assyrians, near neighbors of the Egyptians, also had a conventionalized animal form—a man-headed and winged bull, which decorated their halls and palaces, and was sometimes carved in the round but more often in relief. The marked difference between the Egyptian rendering of the sphinx and the Assyrian rendering of the bull shows, in itself, the whole difference between the art of the two nations. Where the Egyptians smoothed down the actual form, the Assyrians and Babylonians insisted on, and rather exaggerated, it; the one ideal was repose, the other brute activity. And so we get the wonderful monuments in the Louvre and the British Museum where each part of animal form is "hammered out," and it would seem that with a little encouragement the muscles would slip the leash of granite, marble or bronze and become alive before our eyes.

THE CRUEL STORY TOLD IN THE ART OF ASSYRIA AND BABYLONIA

The tale that we find in the reliefs, monuments and bronzes that have been preserved of the Babylonian and Assyrian empires is very much like the tale of any Eastern tribe—plunder, battle, triumph, long lines of prisoners, and acres of spoil. In Egypt, as we know, the doings and glories of the gods and the honors of death were the chief themes of the national art. Assyrian art centred, instead, about ideas of cruelty and tyranny. We shudder with horror over the story in Assyrian reliefs. Those ranks of men so finely sculptured, with their strange angular beards and pointed head-dresses, were either in the act of torturing and killing enemies or marching on to the scene of bloodshed.

Although the Babylonians and Assyrians did not accept the Egyptian law of frontality, they shared the convention of the full-drawn eye in a profile face. And you will notice in the pictures of the winged bull and the winged lion that each one has five legs. This is because the figure stood as a guardian at a gateway, and was to be seen both at front-face and in side view. But, as the form was in raised relief against a wall, one of the two feet of the front view did not show in the side view; so, an extra foot must be represented. This was an Assyrian convention. But the Assyrians surpassed their neighbors in portraying animals. There are few more wonderful things in the whole story of art than the Assyrian reliefs of the wounded lion and lioness in the British Museum. And in other instances we can see how beautifully the Assyrian craftsmen could draw horses.

SWEEP AND INFLUENCE OF EGYPT, ASSYRIA AND BABYLONIA

Although they differ so greatly in foundation feeling, Egyptian and Assyrian sculpture are somewhat akin in hugeness and grandeur. In each case, we may say, their works of art are all that is left of long-enduring and mighty nations whose activities were the heart-beats of the ancient world. In each case their art kept its unity for some four thousand years. Those far-away ages are reckoned in great sweeps of time; but as the centre of civilization moved westward, epochs of art covered periods less and less broad. They fitted into centuries; later, into generations; and in our own times it is generally accepted that ten years will include the life period of a style of art.

The art of Babylonia and Assyria had an even greater effect on the outlying countries than Egyptian art had. We know that it dominated the art of the Israelites, of the Hittites and of the Phœnicians. For example, we have only to read the description of Solomon's Temple to recognize Assyrian influence. The cherubim upon the Ark of the Covenant were unquestionably related to the Assyrian man-headed winged bulls.

The Hittites, neighbors and often foes of both Egypt and Assyria, drew more upon the latter country than the former in the matter of art influence, as we can perceive when we look at their sculpture and note how they represented the lion and the human form.

PERSIAN SCULPTURE, SHORT OF LIFE BUT SPLENDID

As for Persian sculpture, brilliant and short-lived, it owed a large debt to both Egypt and Assyria. In the ruins of the gray marble palaces built by Darius and other Persian kings, on the great terrace platform at Persepolis, the heavy columns have something of the hugeness belonging to Egypt's pillared temples, while the details reflect the ornamental characteristics of Assyria. With these elements the Persians combined other ideas caught from neighboring peoples, and the result was a very ornate scheme of decoration. It included the human-headed bulls of the Assyrians and the same magnificent arrangement of reliefs upon the walls. Some of the finest of these, as we read on page 297, were in the palace of Darius at Susa. Now, parts of the enameled brick friezes from that same ancient capital—"Shushan the palace," where Queen Esther probably once walked about—are to be seen in the Louvre in Paris.

AND AFTER ALL THESE OTHERS CAME GREECE

About three hundred years before the birth of Jesus there came to Susa and Persepolis, Alexander, the conqueror from the west—from Europe. In the halls of the Persian monarchs he paused to feast and to revel in his young glory; and at Persepolis, in token of his newly won supremacy, he set fire to the famous palace of Darius. We shall soon see how, in the two centuries which lie between the conquests of Darius of Persia and the conquests of Alexander of Greece, a few sculptors upon the little peninsula of Greece had had opened to them the door where Beauty lives and had learned more of her secrets than ever have been revealed to anyone else in all the world. Their statues and reliefs, even when marred by time, are the finest expression of man's conception of form. So, after Egypt's display of calm enduring splendor, and Assyria's presentation of vigorous strength came the fine realization of beauty among the hills of Greece.

THE NEXT STORY OF THE FINE ARTS IS ON PAGE 3987.

SCULPTURES OF EGYPT AND ASSYRIA

SETI II

KING KHAFRA

THE SHEIK EL BELED

SETI I

A SCRIBE

MAHU, DIRECTOR OF WORKS, AND HIS WIFE

AN EGYPTIAN OFFICIAL

HAPI, THE NILE GOD

A HUSBAND AND HIS WIFE

A STATUE 6,500 YEARS OLD

A SPHINX INSCRIBED WITH THE NAME OF THOTHMES III

RAMESES THE GREAT

AMENHOTEP III

SHRINE OF THE GOD OSIRIS

A HEAD 5,000 YEARS OLD   GUDEA, KING OF BABYLON   AN ASSYRIAN OFFICER

THE WINGED LION FROM THE PLACE OF
ASHUR-NASIR-PAL

THE WINGED BULL FROM A DOORWAY IN
THE PALACE OF SARGON

HUNTING SCENES FROM THE ASSYRIAN SCULPTURES, NOW IN THE BRITISH MUSEUM

THE ASSYRIAN GOD
NEBO

ASHUR-BANI-PAL LEADING HIS HORSES—A
MARBLE SLAB FROM NINEVEH

A BOUNDARY STONE
FROM ANCIENT BABYLON

ASHUR-NASIR-PAL AND A COURTIER

ASSHUR, THE CHIEF ASSYRIAN GOD

AN ASSYRIAN LION HUNT. FROM THE MARBLE SLABS OF NINEVEH

Swans on a European lake.

DUCKS AND GEESE

POETRY and rhythm of movement have power to charm us. It is a source of delight to watch a swift drop, like a dark bolt from the sky, to the bosom of some quiet lake, straighten at the right moment, skim the unruffled surface, drink as he goes, then rise again into the air.

CONTINUED FROM 3764

But there is infinite variety in nature—variety of form, of method, of habit—and we never need feel that we have exhausted all material for wonder and admiration. We find among birds as complete perfection for water life as we find among the swallows, the swifts, the humming-birds and the hawks for life on the wing.

In many of the birds we have been studying we noted that feet and legs were of smaller consequence than wings, but we reach now a company of birds in which feet have a new importance. We are now to consider briefly birds which, while developing extraordinary feet for swimming, have retained their wings, and with them the mastery of the air.

Nature has done for the web-footed birds what man has done for himself with sails, oars and screw-propellers. Man first hung a skin on a pole to catch the breeze that should move his log. He broadened and flattened the end of another pole and used it as a scull. He applied another device in metal to form a screw which should worm its way through the water and drive his steamship. But Nature was before man with this plan, though we are so familiar with the appearance of the feet of ducks and geese that we may miss the wonder of it. Nature has a way of accomplishing marvels with great simplicity, and the foot of a water bird is one of her crowning examples.

A domestic hen must keep to the land or die; a duck may exhaust the food on the land, and then boldly take to the water and pillage a new world. The essential difference between the two is that the duck has grown a tough skin which connects its toes with elastic muscular web. This simple device does for the water bird what sails and oars and screw-propellers do for our ships and boats.

Its feet are the water bird's fortune. These living paddles give a bird the keys of stream and lake and river, and open each ocean to some kind of the Order. The birds can fly to every sea, and navigate them all. They are superior to fish and mammals, for they tread the earth, swim the waves and currents, and sail the air with power and endurance beyond challenge.

One or more of the thirty species of Cormorants are to be found in every part of the world where there are large bodies of water. Even in Greenland they find abundant food. The Common Cormorant and the Double-crested are best known in our waters, though the smaller Florida Cormorant and the Mexico Cormorant live in the South and occasionally wander northward. Both of the first two named are called Shag in different sections.

The great black bird is three feet in length, measuring from tip to tip of beak and tail, and all that great force of energy needs support.

Perhaps there is something of the vulture in a cormorant's appetite, for the bird will eat when its body is packed with food— eat till its meal is returned, impossible of digestion through excessive stuffing of the stomach. It is then that we see it ashore, listless, inelegant, with the great wings hung out to dry, as it seems, widespread in order to catch the breeze that shall make those damp pinions fit for further service.

The Gannet alighting at its nest.

To get into the air is not easy for the cormorant, but when once launched, how graceful, how strong and unwearying it is! Down on the water it has something of the submarine's qualities. It can swim with its back awash, it can swim under the water, it can lower its long head and neck beneath the surface, like an inverted periscope, and fish as it travels. It can dive from a height and snatch up prey with speed and precision.

There is intelligence in these water birds, and great aptitude for human society. From times before history cormorants have fished for their Chinese masters. At first the bird has a ring slipped over its neck to prevent it from swallowing its catch till it has filled its owner's creel; but trained birds need no such restraint: they retrieve fish for their friends with the fidelity of well-broken dogs.

The same practice was once pursued with these birds in England. When we hear a cormorant named it is generally as a symbol of greed and a pest to fishermen. The truth of one of these statements was tested in Australia, where cormorants were ruthlessly butchered on the charge of ruining important fisheries.

In vain was it pointed out that they existed largely on crabs, crayfish, shrimps and eels. The birds went, but the good fish went faster, for the friends of the cormorants were right and the persecutors wrong. The cormorants had actually been policing the waters by eating the enemies of the coveted fish, and when the birds were killed devourers of trout and other delicacies were left to work their will.

In Africa, Australia, South America and in many parts of Asia, there is the chance of confusion between cormorants and darters, for there is considerable resemblance. Darters are birds of river, lake and swamp, perching, in spite of their webbed feet, on rocks and trees by day, and flying in great flocks, toward sundown, to fish the waters of their desire. Only one of the four species of this tropical bird is found in the United States—the Anhinga, often called the Snake-bird or Water-turkey. It is found in the Gulf states.

If they were creatures of the sea, we might imagine that darters, with the cormorants, were in part responsible for sea-serpent legends, so long and sinuous are their necks. As it is, darters do suggest snakes in the inland waters when, with bodies deeply submerged and necks writhing and darting, they swim with only this part visible.

PELICANS AND THEIR COUSINS

The Frigate Bird.

The Gannet, or Solan Goose.

Black Cormorant.

The Darter.

The Crested Pelican.

European Pelican.

Australian Pelicans.

Crested Cormorants.

Tropic Birds guarding their egg.

The pictures on these pages are reproduced by courtesy of Mrs. M. H. Crawford and Messrs. Mortimer Batten, R. Chislett, S. Crook, Seton Gordon, F. Pitt, C. Reid, and York & Son.

A LIVING AIRPLANE THAT CAN DROP LIKE A DART TO THE SEA

There can be no such doubt about the Gannet, or Solan Goose, the connecting link between the darters, cormorants and pelicans. It is found over both shores of the North Atlantic. The almost white plumage here serves to distinguish it, but that is not conclusive at all times; it takes a gannet six years to grow to maturity. Only then does it get the entirely white coat of feathers, varied only by the black flight feathers and the buff of head and neck.

The manner of the bird is, however, quite distinctive. We see it flying, thirty-six inches of it, high in the air, watching with keen yellow eyes the wrinkled sea beneath. It espies its prey—a shoal of mackerel or herring. Then a lovely living airplane is converted into a sort of projectile. Suddenly, as you watch, the bird, changing from a level keel, seems to stand on its head in the air, then down like a great white dart it flashes into the midst of the shoal.

Though this bird is sometimes called the Booby, that name really belongs to a smaller species which seldom comes farther north than Georgia. It is dark brown above, white below, and is a little smaller. It does seem stupid, and may be knocked down with a stick.

THE FLIGHT OF THE GANNETS LIKE A SNOWSTORM UPSIDE DOWN

Countless thousands of gannets may be found on Bass Rock in Scotland, or on Bird Rock in Canada. One of them stays by its eggs till a hand pushes it from its nest. Then it will fall over the cliffs into the air, and emit a half-digested fish or two in the process. In the young, however, the habit appears to be a defense. The young birds writhe, ugly, repulsive, in their filthy nests, and, casting up their oily meals, make themselves so offensive that the invader retreats.

Yet there is a wonder of loveliness in a gannet rookery. The birds nest so thickly together that their home, seen from afar, suggests a great white sail on the horizon. When thousands rise from their roosting-places into the air all together, then it is as if the island were snowing upward!

Pelicans are another family found in all parts of the world. On the land they are among the most comic-looking of birds. They have an ungainly, waddling gait; they have beaks of which the lower half is a huge flexible bag net, and the upper half a sort of lid to the lower. The feathers are loose and harsh, and, wet as these seem, they give to the birds a farcical, bedraggled appearance.

Nevertheless, beauty is in that pink flush on the plumes of most pelicans; there is great grace and charm in their powerful measured flight from one feeding-place to another. Intelligence of a high order brings about a most effective co-operation between them.

THE CUNNING OF THE PELICANS IN THEIR HUNT FOR FOOD

Though crabs and lobsters find their way into the interior of the great white pelicans, fish form the staple diet. To catch these the birds combine in a half-circle, or crescent, each bird in its proper station, a yard from its fellows. Thus deployed, they swim from deep water into shallow, driving the terrified shoals before them. Then, when escape is impossible, the birds lower their great bills and gobble.

They finish their feast as they march ashore, doze, digest and depart, either into the same water, or to another part, perhaps a good flight away. Both white and brown pelicans are numerous in the United States and in some warmer countries. The White Pelican is more common on the Pacific coast and in the interior; the Brown is confined to the South Atlantic coast. They teem in such multitudes that unbroken flights of them have been seen to extend for miles.

Probably no reader of this day needs to be assured that the ancient legend as to mother pelicans feeding little ones on their own flesh and blood is false. What they do is to open their great beaks and let the little ones feast on the fish within their throats.

Very conspicuous are the webs on the feet of the pelicans; very slight on the feet of the next group—those great flying robbers, the Frigate, or Man-of-war, birds, the greater of which is confined to the warmer parts of the Atlantic, and the Pacific and Indian oceans, the lesser species being peculiar to the Indo-Pacific. They are birds that prey on other birds such as the boobies and the peaceful terns. Since they are less dependent on swimming, they have their toes much less webbed than others of the family, but are feathered to the extremities.

THE LIGHT-WINGED PIRATES THAT COME FROM THE CENTRAL BLUE

They are simply lovely parasites, superb fliers, as pirate birds must be. They do little work on their own account, but loaf about the trees while honest birds go out to fish. Then they sally forth from their retreats as their victims sail home. Terns and boobies are heavy with good feeding. They cannot escape these marauders, which chase and buffet them without remorse till they eject some of their fish, and fly for safety. The frigate birds need nothing better, for, fast as the fish falls from on high, still faster is their downward swoop to catch it. In midair they snap up their booty as surely as a dog catches a biscuit.

SOME SWIFT-FLYING BIRDS OF TROPICAL CLIMES

The frigate birds are beauties, but not so exquisite as the Tropic Birds. They are white, with black on the wings and tail, and the legs are a bright yellow. Both the Red-billed and the Yellow-billed occasionally venture into the United States, but their home is in the tropics. They are particularly abundant in the South Seas. They can outfly our swiftest steamers, circling round them, and keeping them company for miles.

Still, there is something to be said for the possibilities of a temperate land, for we possess many of the next fascinating assembly—the ducks, geese and swans. Some of them are seen only in the aviaries and sheltered houses of the zoo, but we have our natives, and we have our millions of winter visitors, coming down each autumn from the shrill, tempestuous North.

With many of them the student may become familiar if he will diligently search the wilds. Many of these birds suffer the disadvantage of temporarily losing all power of flight. When they molt they lose the primary feathers of their wings and cannot fly for a time. Until new flight feathers rush through their growth these great-winged creatures must skulk. For the time being they are as helpless as crabs which have shed their shells. Like the crabs, they must hide. However, Nature has made them superbly fit for the life they lead—powerful of wing, strong of leg for driving through the water, and so shaped that they offer a minimum of resistance to water as they thrust their way forward.

WINTER VISITORS FROM THE FROZEN ARCTIC REALMS

Their king, the Swan, lends us its name as our symbol for grace and beauty. On land it is awkward, but on the water it rides with exquisite ease, with the wings slightly raised in pride or anger, the neck arched in harmony. The swan is the ideal for which we strive when we build a yacht to excel all others for beauty and speed. Seven species are generally recognized. The Tame, or Mute, Swan is the common European species which has been imported for our parks and lakes. Europe has two other swans—the Whooper and Bewick's Swan—which breed in the Far North, but come south in winter. The Black Swan of Australia has also been introduced into Europe and America.

In North America we have two wild swans. The Whistling Swan breeds in the Far North and winters along the South Atlantic. The Trumpeter also breeds in the North, but winters in the interior of the continent. There is also a Black-necked Swan in South America.

It is a long journey that these great white beauties take each spring and autumn, but they fly fast. The trumpeter swan is said to cleave the air at the rate of over a hundred miles an hour! Probably the so-called mute swans are as fast, but we know less of their speed, as they are not compelled to make migrations; they remain with us all the year, as they have lost the fear of man. They are called mute because they utter no cry, but the wild mutes have as clear a clarion as the true whoopers.

In breeding-time they are savage. Not only do they resent approach to their nests, but they furiously repel intrusion in the stretch of water which they consider their own. You set them at liberty on a certain reach of the river, and then they turn on you at nesting-time as fiercely as some great dog to which you have given a bone.

THE WONDERFUL VARIETY OF THE GREAT FAMILY OF GEESE

Let us pass beyond the borderland into the company of undoubted Geese. In doing so we are not to indulge in any smile of derision. How it came to be believed that geese are foolish birds we do not know, unless the great display of importance which the tame varieties make suggested the idea. The truth is that geese are bold, intelligent, admirable

The Shoveler.

A fine Swan.

The Pintail.

A group of Aylesbury Ducks.

Wild Ducks after food.

Pink-footed Goose.

The Goosander.

Australian Brent Goose.

Long-tailed Duck.

Indian Runner Duck.

Whistling Swan, or Whooper.

GREAT TRIBE OF DUCKS AND GEESE

Gray Lag Goose.

The Black Swan on its nest.

The Pochard.

A family of geese.

Wild geese in a meadow.

Hooded Merganser.

Bewick's Swan.

Golden-eye Duck.

Sheldrakes on a lake.

The Muscovy Duck.

birds. The fact that they once saved Rome from invasion need not be attributed to their wisdom. What happened was that their quick senses detected the sounds of movements made by advancing enemies when faithless sentries slept. Their wakefulness was characteristic of the high vitality and general alertness of the tribe.

Practically everywhere in the world there are geese of some sort, for there are perhaps forty species. Generally they come between the swans and the ducks in size, but some are smaller than some ducks. Some of the forms are surprising. The Pied Goose, for example, is but a half-webbed Australian, with the claws long and sharp for perching. The Spur-winged Geese of Africa are long-legged, high-built, quick walkers and runners, and make keen, clever pets; but they fight like gamecocks, a matter rendered formidable by the presence on each leg of a long, sharp spur—the so-called spur wing. The Tree Ducks of South America are really geese which often make their nests in hollow trees far from the water. Some of them visit the United States. Australia has a curious bird in the Cape Barron Goose, whose beak is as remarkably short as that of the spur-winged is long.

Generally geese prefer temperate and cold lands to the tropics. They are usually splendid fliers and swimmers, but they depend chiefly upon a vegetable diet. A flock of geese will crop the grass of a pasture closer than cattle. It is believed that the domestic geese of Europe which were brought to this country were derived from a wild species—the Gray Lag. It is found in Europe, Asia and Africa. Some of the larger varieties of domestic geese come from China to Europe. Selection has done wonders with them.

THE WILD GEESE, FOUND IN NORTH AMERICA

North America has ten or twelve species of wild geese, most of which breed in Canada or Alaska and spend their winters in the United States. The Canada Goose is the most common species. It is grayish brown, with black tail and neck and a white patch under the throat. The Greater Snow Goose is found in the East, while the Lesser Snow Goose breeds in Alaska and is rarely seen east of the Mississippi.

The Brant is a large blackish brown goose found both in Europe and Eastern America, while the Black Brant, a smaller species, is seldom seen except in the West. Other American species are the Blue, the White-fronted and the Barnacle. In migrating, geese generally fly in the shape of a great V, with an old gander in the lead.

DUCKS OF THE SEAS AND RIVERS

There are many more species of Ducks than of swans and geese together. About 150 species are recognized, and about fifty are found in North America. Most of them are included in the sub-families of river ducks and sea ducks, but there is another group of the mergansers, often called fish ducks. In spite of the names, however, river ducks are often found in salt water, and many of the sea ducks frequent the rivers.

The best-known river duck is the Mallard, common over the northern hemisphere. The domestic ducks of Europe and America came from this wild ancestor, and probably the Chinese ducks also. The Black, or Dusky, Duck is common along the Atlantic coast of North America, but is not found in the Old World. Like the mallard, it is much sought by hunters. The Gadwall, or Gray Duck, is common on both continents, but is so shy that it is seldom seen. It feeds only in the twilight or at night.

The Teals are interesting ducks found in both hemispheres, though the American teals differ slightly from the European. The Green-winged is found all over North America and can with difficulty be distinguished from the European teal. The Blue-winged is confined to America. The Cinnamon Teal belongs to the Pacific slope.

Other interesting river ducks are the Shoveler, found in both hemispheres, and the Widgeon, a European bird, which sometimes straggles to this continent. Our Baldpate resembles it closely. Another duck found on both shores of the Atlantic is the Pintail, so-called from the shape of the feathers of its tail. The most beautiful of all the river ducks is the Wood Duck, of which we say more in the chapter on Birds of the South.

SOME OF THE MOST IMPORTANT SEA DUCKS

Though they sometimes enter rivers, the sea ducks usually prefer the salt water of bays and marshes. The most valued by the hunter are the Canvasback, the Redhead, or Pochard, and the Ruddy. The first and third are found only on this continent, but the Redhead is found in Europe as well. The American Scaup Duck, or Blue-billed, is a large duck which breeds only in the Far North. Though somewhat resembling the canvasback, it is much inferior in flavor.

Others that may be mentioned are: the Golden-eye, the Old Squaw, the Scoters, the Bufflehead and the Harlequin. This latter is the most beautiful of the sea ducks, and is surpassed only by the wood duck. It is slaty blue, with white and chestnut stripes and chestnut sides. It is not common, but is sometimes kept in captivity.

On farms in districts not too crowded with human society the wild ducks drop down among the tame, stay, feed, fatten, and

The European Flamingo.

A group of Flamingoes.

A family of Crested Screamers.

grow ready for migration. But they try to take the tame ducks with them when they leave. They waddle about in front of the home-keeping kind, flapping their wings and rising short distances into the air in front of their domestic cousins, anxious, solicitous, puzzled as to why the white plump sluggards do not soar on high and bear them company.

The wild duck is small compared with domestic breeds. An Aylesbury duckling at two months weighs between four and six pounds. It is the most popular breed in England. The Rouens, which were developed in France, closely resemble the plumage of the mallard, but take all summer to feed up to the ten or eleven pounds to which they finally run. The most popular breed in America is the Peking. These birds are white, with a canary-yellow tinge in their plumage. Though smaller than the Aylesbury, they are prolific in eggs, but here they do not compare favorably with the Indian Runner Ducks.

These Oriental birds first came to us late in the nineteenth century from India, and have become great favorites, chiefly because of their wonderful powers as producers of eggs. Other domestic ducks raised for market are the Cayuga, Muscovy, and the Gray and the White Call. Raising ducks for market has become an important industry, and many farms sell more than ten thousand a year.

Other ducks which we welcome to ornamental waters are the East Indian; the Mandarin, a real child of China; the Crested White; and others. Several species of wild ducks are sometimes kept in captivity by clipping their wings.

THE CURIOUS HABIT OF THE EIDER DUCK

All of the ducks yield a downy feathering, but none to equal that of the Eider Duck, which surrenders its covering to clothe our beds in winter. There are several species of eider ducks. All make their home on rocky coasts, where their colonies embrace astonishing numbers of nests.

Three species of eider ducks are found in America, but only in the Far North. They are so thickly covered with soft down that they seem to be unable to live in temperate climates, though a few come as far south as Massachusetts in winter. All three, the American Eider, the King and the Northern have the same habits. When the eggs are laid the female plucks the down from her breast to cover them. If this be taken away, she bares her breast still further; and if this be removed, the male strips his breast.

The fish ducks are represented in America by the Mergansers, the American, the Red-breasted and the Hooded. All are often called Sheldrakes, though that name properly belongs to a bird of the Old World. The American is often called the Goosander, and is also found in Europe. The hooded merganser is eaten, but the flesh of the other two is too fishy to be palatable.

The list of ducks is not yet complete, but we must hasten to what the Persians call the Red Goose, and what we know as the Flamingo. Flamingoes are something like storks and herons, but either the old Persians were wiser than we knew or they made a brilliant guess, for the flamingo is decidedly cousin to both geese and ducks, and to the next group which follows, the screamers. Long of leg, with a swan-like neck, the flamingo is remarkable for an extraordinary beak, as curious in its way as that of the pelican. When feeding with the head at the bottom of the water, the birds turn up the beak so as to make it form a scoop, and so shovel up their food, which consists, in the main, of shellfish.

Where snowy white and rosy red commingle with tips of black to wing feathers, no bird in the world can be more lovely in coloring than these strange creatures. The effect at a distance is magical in its charm. A flight of flamingoes is likened to the travel of rosy islands through the skies.

Flamingoes are found in southern Spain, Africa, the West India Islands, South America and the southern world generally, though not in Australia. Formerly many flamingoes were found in Florida and other southern states, but they have become rare. Mother Nature has developed nothing more remarkable as a blend of the beautiful with the bizarre.

THE SWIMMING BIRD WITH HORNY SPURS ON ITS WINGS

After all, we shall have to leave the webbed feet in order to bring in one family where the feet are not really webbed. These are the Screamers of South America. The toes, with only a fragment of web, are long and powerful as are the legs; the skin is curious, indeed unique, through its yielding and crackling to the touch, owing to the presence immediately beneath of air-cells. The bird is about the size of a swan, yet it has an insignificant beak, but is formidable through the presence of two powerful and forbidding horny spurs on each wing. One variety has a curious curved horn five or six inches long, upon the head; the other has none.

So we end in the water as we began, and leave these delightful birds in possession. They are all mariners of no mean standard. The earth is at their feet, the waters are a perpetual source of harvest from which to win for them the stuff of life, and the air is to them a place of passage as the sea to sailors. They are like hydroplanes with power to run on land, in the water and in the air.

THE NEXT STORY OF ANIMAL LIFE IS ON PAGE 4005.

Anthony Trollope.

Mrs. Gaskell.

Lord Lytton.

Mary Mitford.

Thomas Hardy.

Charles Reade.

W. Harrison Ainsworth.

George Eliot.

George Meredith.

Benjamin Disraeli.

GREAT FICTION IN ITS FULL TIDE

WE have traced the rise of English fiction in the eighteenth and early nineteenth centuries to its peak in the great romances of Sir Walter Scott, followed quickly by the mid-Victorian wave, crested by Dickens. That wave was of extraordinary volume. It reached its greatest height between 1845 and 1865, when British fiction had a range and power never attained before or since.

CONTINUED FROM 3691

Dickens and Thackeray, whose striking personalities and works we have already read about, cannot be taken as sufficient for an age which also included Lytton, Disraeli, Charles Reade, and Charles Kingsley, Charlotte Brontë, George Eliot and Anthony Trollope; George Meredith and the beginnings of Thomas Hardy, besides such individual stories as Cranford and Lorna Doone. In the quarter of a century between 1845 and 1870 all these writers were writing, together with Dickens and Thackeray. It was an age resplendent in fiction, as in other forms of literature.

There was a fine period of fiction from 1810 to 1830, made memorable by Scott and Jane Austen; then a remarkable tidal wave thirty years later which, apart from Dickens and Thackeray, was largely a study of country life. Between these two several novelists were writing in the veins of history and romance suggested by the example of Scott, and the sea was introduced into fiction. Also what may be called the novel of public life made its appearance.

The chief story-tellers of this between-stage were Lord Lytton (Edward Bulwer) and Benjamin Disraeli. Mention may also be made of William Harrison Ainsworth. The sea, which had provided subjects for Defoe and Smollett, was once for all taken by Captain Frederick Marryat. After eighty years or more all these novelists are being read, and eighty years of life suggests that they have some substantial worth.

Lytton, Disraeli and Ainsworth had all begun to write romances before the death of Scott. Disraeli and Lytton were men with a considerable social standing and political ambition, and their early stories, especially Disraeli's, picture life as it appealed to men who studied the structure of society in their day.

A peculiar feature in the early Thirties was that, as order prevailed in the land and such law-breaking as highway robbery became a thing of the past, writers were inclined to make it a subject of romance. Both Lytton and Ainsworth—Lytton in Paul Clif-

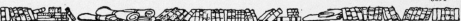

ford and Eugene Aram, and Ainsworth in Rookwood and Jack Sheppard—worked up studies in criminality. To this day crime has been brought into fiction more freely than is either wise or harmless, for the criminal almost always is a scamp, and often a bully, and there is rarely anything heroic in him.

THE PAGES OF FICTION THAT TELL THE FACTS OF HISTORY

Lytton had begun, in Pelham, by making himself (slightly disguised) the hero of the story. He soon branched out usefully into historic fiction, and many of us get our ideas of Roman history from his Last Days of Pompeii and Rienzi, and of periods of English history from his stories Harold and The Last of the Barons. Under Lytton's historical stories is sound fact, but as tales they somewhat lack swiftness and directness.

Later Lytton moved with the times, making studies of family life in the country. In the Fifties he wrote cleverly and more naturally in such tales as The Caxtons, My Novel, and What Will He Do with It? Later still, he published, in The Coming Race, one of the most suggestive forecasts of what may be in the future; and his studies of the changes that have come about are impressive.

As a writer of fiction Lytton was busy for forty-five years, and kept changing his point of view all the while. His ability was many-sided. He attained a good deal of success as a novelist, a dramatist, an orator and a poet, but failed to reach the front rank along any of the avenues to fame that he successively trod. His weakness was the touch of artificiality which appeared in all his work. He was rarely quite at ease, but he left work in fiction that deserves study.

DISRAELI, HARRISON AINSWORTH AND CAPTAIN MARRYAT

Lord Beaconsfield (Benjamin Disraeli) used fiction first as a means of winning men's attention and of showing his cleverness. Then, when he had become known as a man who must be reckoned with, in his best novels, Coningsby and Sybil, he wrote to advance the ideas he regarded as needed in public life. Later, in Tancred, he showed the luxuriance of his Oriental mind; and in his old age he amused himself by writing stories in which real people appeared under thin disguises. The Disraeli novels are interesting chiefly for the light they throw on the character of their strange author, except that Coningsby and Sybil have a place in the social and political story of England in the Forties of the nineteenth century. They will be read by those who combine an interest in politics with an interest in literature, but the story-telling power in them is not great.

Harrison Ainsworth's stories, such as The Tower of London, Old St. Paul's, and Windsor Castle, are written with spirit and a dramatic sense that we like, but their historical foundation is less firm than Lytton's tales from the past, and their literary coloring tends to gaudiness. Ainsworth was an energetic Lancashire man who had a busy life in London, and wrote Lancashire stories truer to life than his more widely read romances.

No man ever had a better right to describe life at sea than Captain Marryat, for he saw all sides of it for twenty-four years, in war and peace, before he began to tell his experiences in the form of tales. Peter Simple, Jacob Faithful, Masterman Ready, and Midshipman Easy, are known, we may suppose, to all boys, sooner or later, and, though sometimes rough in the telling, they are manly and honest. His story of Frank Mildmay is largely his own life. Life at sea has furnished many stories since Marryat, but none have been more faithfully descriptive, though some may have had a more stirring plot.

CHARLES KINGSLEY AND HIS NOVELS WITH A PURPOSE

Two men of very independent character, who wrote novels with a special purpose during the Fifties and Sixties of the nineteenth century, and also historical romance, were Charles Kingsley and Charles Reade.

Kingsley, a fine type of Devonshire character, was much more than a novelist, though it is by his novels that he is best remembered. He was a popular social reformer of a mild kind, a preacher who crowded Westminster Abbey when he was a canon there, a poet, a writer of popular science, and a professor of modern history at Cambridge. He was, too, a singularly healthy-minded, breezy man. Some of his novels were written for the purpose of calling attention to the needs of the working class in the country and in the towns. These were Alton Locke, Yeast, and Two Years Ago. Of these three Alton Locke is much the most real to-day; but Kings-

Charles Kingsley loved the English hills, and was happy in the open-air life which fills so much of his books.

ley's social novels do not rank with his enthusiastic historical romances, Hypatia, Westward Ho! and Hereward the Wake. The last two, with scenes laid in Devonshire and in the Lincolnshire Fens, which Kingsley knew intimately, are fine pictures of past times.

CHARLES READE, WHO TRIED TO CORRECT SOCIAL EVILS

Charles Reade was a writer of most irregular quality. At his best he wrote with a vividness that contrasts strongly with much crude commonplace and excited denunciation that is not artistic. He set out to attack certain evils, such as the harshness of prison life, the scandals of private lunatic asylums, and the violence of labor organizations. Reform does not fit itself naturally to fiction. The novel is not suitable for spreading a sense of horror.

Charles Reade thought differently, however. Most of the evils he denounced have passed away, and his reforming novels seem unreal now. What he might have been as a novelist if he had kept away from violent controversy and had lived in the quieting atmosphere of the distant past is shown by the success of The Cloister and the Hearth. This is one of the best English historical stories, though toward its close it is overshadowed by an almost intolerable sadness. Reade was a writer of much power, with many faults.

The special feature of English fiction when it reached its high-water mark, between 1845 and 1870, was the extraordinary comprehensiveness of its scope. Dickens was at the height of his popularity and skill, and Thackeray was welcomed as the satirist of aspiring society.

THE NEW KIND OF NOVEL THAT TOOK A FOREMOST PLACE IN FICTION

David Copperfield and Vanity Fair were both published in 1849. Disraeli published Tancred in 1847. Kingsley's Alton Locke came out in 1850, and Lytton's Caxtons belonged to the same year. It was into this world of varied fiction that the novel of country life and character came, and took a foremost place which it has never lost since.

Country life had had its place in English fiction from the first, in the best work of Fielding and Smollett, and also of Jane Austen, who had taken her readers into the country almost exclusively. There, however, the reader lived with people of only one class, and never reached the mass of country folk. But there had been close studies of country life in Ireland by Maria Edgeworth; in Scotland by John Galt, whose Annals of the Parish, a Scottish minister's story of his people, had appeared in 1821; and in England Mary Russell Mitford had published sketches of Our Village for twenty years—1812 to 1832—enough to fill four volumes, and containing the best pictures yet produced of the kind of people who form the backbone of English manhood. These were the country writings which led up to the works of the Brontë sisters, George Eliot, Mrs. Gaskell, Anthony Trollope and Thomas Hardy.

THE THREE SISTERS WHO WROTE AS IF THEY LIVED THEIR STORIES

The Brontë sisters brought into fiction a note of personal intensity more real than anything that had gone before. What they wrote seemed to come direct out of the individual feeling of the writer. It does not read as if the writer were describing somebody else who had been observed, but as if the narrative had been actually lived. Indeed, to a very large extent the novels by Charlotte Brontë, the eldest of the three sisters, were scarcely disguised pages from her life.

The sisters were the daughters of a grimly intellectual Irish father, who was the clergyman of Haworth, on the edge of the Yorkshire moors. Their mother died when they were young, and they were brought up in isolation, with their father's books for reading, and their own thoughts for furtive tale-telling as an amusement, varied by walks on the dark and lonely moors. All of them found expression to some extent in poetry; Anne, the youngest, in religious verse; Charlotte as a literary exercise taken on her way to a splendid mastery of prose; and Emily as a poet capable of a loftier flight than any woman in the English tongue. All of them, too, wrote fiction.

They were poor and had to earn their living. All served as governesses, Charlotte being the most successful, first in Yorkshire, among the kind of people described in her novel Shirley, and later in Brussels, as described in her Villette. Then, in 1847, Charlotte captured the best judgment of the literary world of her day by her tale Jane Eyre, which ever since has remained in the foremost rank of fiction.

In the same year Emily Brontë published her Wuthering Heights, with her sister Anne's Agnes Grey; and the next year Anne's Tenant of Wildfell Hall was published. The three sisters, writing anonymously under pen-names, preserved their initials as Currer Bell, Ellis Bell and Acton Bell. Emily died of tuberculosis in 1848, and Anne died of the same disease in 1849, the year in which Charlotte published her second novel, Shirley, with her sister Emily as its heroine. In 1853 she published Villette. Next year

Heights, and the profound and moving poem beginning "No coward soul is mine," written just before her death, to be sure of that. Anne had less originality.

No novelist has established more firmly than Charlotte Brontë the sacredness and dignity of the individual soul. In Jane Eyre she took as her subject a small, plain, insignificant-looking woman like herself, and made of her a heroine who passed unscathed through the fiercest trials of suffering and passion to triumph

The Brontë sisters writing their stories in the rectory at Haworth, in Yorkshire.

she married her father's curate, the Reverend A. B. Nicholls, and died in 1855.

Thus, in eight years from the issue of Charlotte Brontë's first tale, all three tragic sisters had died, and the family, which originally had consisted of five girls and a ne'er-do-well brother, Branwell, was extinct. The sadness of the lives of these clever women, two of them unquestionably possessed of genius, may have had some influence in concentrating attention on them, but Charlotte Brontë fairly won all the fame that is hers, and Emily had in her the promise of absolute greatness, if her life could have been prolonged through years of happiness and prosperity. One has only to read her weirdly powerful story, Wuthering

with unfaltering strength and tenderness. Villette is a book of equal strength. Shirley, in which she tried to avoid the minor key, was written amid distressing surroundings when her sister Emily and her brother Branwell were far spent on their journey to death. Her own success as a novelist failed to sweeten the draft of sadness.

Charlotte Brontë had the power of filling in her background with an atmosphere that had a weird kind of suitability. Emily had the same rare gift in perhaps even greater measure. It is this gift which in part gives Wuthering Heights its sombre impressiveness. Both sisters could draw the rugged Northern character as faithfully as they could suggest the stern Northern scenery. It was the independent soul they loved to sketch, and they loved it because they had it, though they were frail and slight women.

Here we must mention the biographer of the Brontë family, Mrs. Gaskell, who, besides giving us one of the most interesting biographies in the English language, wrote herself, in Cranford, exquisite sketches of rural England midway through the nineteenth century. In Mary Barton and in North and South she painted social conditions before and after the dawn of industrial freedom. In Wives and Daughters, her last book, she reached as high a literary standard as in Cranford.

Two years after the death of Charlotte Brontë, Mary Ann Evans, a Warwickshire land agent's daughter, born and brought up in that delightful county before it became industrialized, wrote, under the name of George Eliot, her first book of stories, Scenes from Clerical Life. Thus she began, in the form of tales, a series of descriptions of the people of rural England which remains the supreme study of quality in country character.

HOW GEORGE ELIOT LOST HER WAY IN THE WORLD OF BOOKS

In later years George Eliot wandered in her tales away from the company into which she was born. With that strange longing to write something new and great which spoils so many poets and novelists, she tried to shine in alien surroundings. Her snares were historic Italy and the Hebrew population of London. Laboring hard to compile ambitious studies that would display her versatility, she lost her way as a writer. Her Romola and Daniel Deronda of those formal, heavy days will be forgotten; but her stories of the people she knew from childhood remain a rich literary possession.

The Scenes from Clerical Life, Adam Bede, The Mill on the Floss, Silas Marner, Felix Holt (though marred by an unconvincing plot) and Middlemarch present a wonderful array of thoroughly English character. How faithful and unforced is the character-drawing, how rich and natural the humor, how tender the humanity, how direct the simple parts of the narrative! It is true that as the years went on George Eliot's writings became burdened with intrusive reflections. If, instead of being urged

to show herself a profound philosopher, her pen had been followed by a relentless blue pencil, her tale-telling would have been quickened and lightened. She knew too much and thought too much to be able to empty her mind of reflections on the story page.

A remarkable novelist of a somewhat later period, George Meredith, who had great skill in the analysis of character, made the same mistake in overloading his books with mental display that did not rightly belong to his story. He never won, and will not win, the popularity that his cleverness deserves. The true value of his writing lies too deeply buried for the average reader to dig it up. But his works will always appeal to the literary expert.

THOMAS HARDY AND HIS WORD-PICTURES OF LIFE IN WESTERN ENGLAND

Thomas Hardy is the novelist who, next to George Eliot, has most completely pictured English rural character. He has avoided George Eliot's tendencies and Meredith's cryptic style. No writer has had a greater power of creating, by scenery and surroundings, an atmosphere that suits his story. His sense of the sombre might of fate over human character and destiny makes much of his work depressing. His observation seldom sees much that is altogether admirable, still less heroic, in the common man of the fields and the heath. Indeed, he seems, on the whole, below the normal in human faith. But he has succeeded in creating a little world in a wide district of western England with courageous fidelity to his own view of them all. Great as a novelist, Thomas Hardy is even greater as a poet, and he alone of the men of his generation has reached epical grandeur in his tremendous poem The Dynasts.

Anthony Trollope was another novelist of the period who, by portraying country life, especially in cathedral and county family circles, has preserved for future generations a record of what the England of his day was like. Though his writing was hasty and wanting in polish, he had a fine natural power in story-telling and character-drawing that is likely to give his books permanent value.

At no time has there been such a varied volume of fiction, preserving all aspects of the life of the English people, as during the years when Dickens and Thackeray were the acknowledged masters of the novel, and were surrounded by writers, independent in style, and between them embracing the whole range of national character.

The later years of the Victorian period and the earlier years of Edward VII produced much fiction that has not lost its power.

THE REVIVAL OF SCOTTISH FICTION

In that period came a remarkable revival of Scottish fiction, far surpassing any Scottish record outside of the great days of Scott. It began with George Macdonald (1824–1905), a minister who found greater freedom for a poetic mind and a somewhat mystical fancy in writing books than in the pulpit, though he continued to preach as a layman. In the Sixties, Macdonald's three character novels, David Elginbrod, Alec Forbes, and Robert Falconer, introduced Scottish types afresh to a wide circle of readers, and prepared the English for a new bookish invasion of the Scottish tongue.

It was a feature of the Scottish novelists of this period that most of them had a wider literary range than the novel. More than half of them were poets, and several began life as working journalists. George Macdonald was a notable poet, and a most charming writer of books for children.

William Black, who was born in 1841 and died in 1898, was one of the journalists. After long experience in a London daily-newspaper office he began, in A Daughter of Heth (1871), and A Princess of Thule (1873), to picture Scottish life. His special locality was the west coast and islands, with their scenic atmosphere enthusiastically painted as a background to Gaelic types. Though Black is not read generally to-day, there is no doubt that he helped to popularize western Scotland, as Blackmore, by his fine romance Lorna Doone, has popularized Exmoor.

At a later period—in the Nineties—the mentality of the Gael found expression in a series of tales, poetical in atmosphere, supposed to be written by a woman under the pen name of Fiona Macleod. In 1905 it became known that their author was William Sharp, a man of letters of varied ability, who was known chiefly as a literary critic, but also as a somewhat elusive and mystical poet. Sharp, a man of singularly handsome presence and of charming address, was a puzzle as a

writer. He could, apparently, with equal ease write a matter-of-fact realistic English novel or a shadowy Gaelic tale touched with weirdness. Eighteen years after his death London, which had probably forgotten his name, was flocking to hear and see his poetical musical drama The Immortal Hour—a masterly expression of the Gaelic spirit.

Of Robert Louis Stevenson as an essay-writer, the form of literature in which, with travel descriptions, he first made his mark, we have already read. His success was confirmed and extended by his stories, and they helped to bring back romance into English fiction. Treasure Island, perhaps the most thrilling of all books of adventure for boys, was published in 1883, and Kidnapped in 1886. A large crop of romances followed from many other writers. Catriona, the sequel to Kidnapped, did not appear till 1893. Stevenson was a master of the short story. His long stories are of unequal merit, but he had the air of high romance, with great charm of style; and the story he left as a fragment at his death, Weir of Hermiston, showed that had he lived he would probably have excelled the best of his early stories. He was the centre of the literary world of his day.

THE WORLD OF FANCY IN WHICH PETER PAN IS KING

Three years after Stevenson published Kidnapped another young Scotsman, with an equally delightful personality and style, James Matthew Barrie, issued his Window in Thrums. In that and succeeding books, and even more in exquisitely fanciful plays, he made a niche for himself in English literature where he stands modestly alone. Barrie, born in 1860, was ten years Stevenson's junior. His workmanship is as delicate as Stevenson's, less self-conscious, more tenderly humane, with an even richer humor. Like Stevenson, Barrie is always a poet at heart. By him thousands of people have had their idea of the human soul enriched.

Barrie started life as a journalist in Nottingham, and found his feet as a character-sketcher by describing religious types of rural Scotsmen. One of his most perfect books, Margaret Ogilvy, is a picture of his own mother. His early sketches brought into the field, as distant imitators, two Scottish ministers: the Reverend John Watson (1850–1907), who wrote, under the pen name Ian Maclaren, Beside the Bonnie Brier Bush, and The Days of Auld Lang Syne; and the Reverend Samuel Rutherford Crockett (1860–1919). Ian Maclaren developed the sentimental side of Scottish character, with a strong tendency to pathos.

CROCKETT, MUNRO AND ROBERT BUCHANAN

Crockett quickly turned aside into romance, but failed to sustain the attractions of his early books, The Raiders, and the Lilac Sunbonnet. He overworked himself and ran through his materials to something like an anticlimax. But he could tell a rousing tale, and he gave quite a literary flavor to the Galloway district of Scotland.

A younger novelist, Neil Munro, a journalist by profession, and no mean poet, born in 1864, gained the ear of the world by his fine Highland romance John Splendid, in 1898. His Daft Days represents qualities that will wear, and leave him a lasting position in fiction.

Robert Buchanan (1841–1901), a Scotsman by descent but born in England, was primarily a poet, but he wrote two powerful novels, The Shadow of the Sword, and God and the Man. Buchanan was a man with fine possibilities, but quarrelsome, and with a drift toward unhappiness that marred his life.

These Scottish writers unitedly form a body of Scottish fiction that may be regarded with justifiable national pride.

A GROUP OF ENGLISH WRITERS WHO HAVE WON GREAT REPUTATIONS

It was about 1886, four years after Stevenson's Treasure Island, and the year of Kidnapped, that Rider Haggard, Anthony Hope Hawkins and Arthur Quiller-Couch all broke out into successes in romance. Arthur Conan Doyle followed two years later. Haggard won notice with King Solomon's Mines; Hawkins with the Prisoner of Zenda, Quiller-Couch with The Splendid Spur, Conan Doyle with Micah Clarke. Later, in 1893, Stanley Weyman made his hit with A Gentleman of France, and Maurice Hewlett followed five years after with The Forest Lovers. Each of these fine writers has succeeded since in various veins, but their first considerable encouragement was in romance.

No one would deny to any of them the honors their vigorous writing has brought them. If Rider Haggard worked out his

vein it was well worth working. Anthony Hope made a second reputation by his clever social tales. Quiller-Couch has added to his laurels as a writer those of the most popular lecturing professor at Cambridge. Conan Doyle, after winning his spurs in historical fiction, has beaten all records with his detective stories. Hewlett gained a second reputation as an essayist; and he, Quiller-Couch and Conan Doyle have all written vigorous and tuneful verse; while Stanley Weyman has brought the construction of the novel to its most shapely form.

In the same year that the romanticists were enlivening the reading world with their successes, Hugh Stowell Scott, writing as Seton Merriman, published his fine Russian story, The Sowers, perhaps the best of all English tales with the scene laid in that little-understood country. This writer died comparatively early, at the height of his powers, for his Napoleon story, Barlasch of the Guard, published in the year of his death (1903), was second to none of his earlier volumes.

An earlier success was that of the joint authors Walter Besant and James Rice, with Ready Money Mortiboy and The Golden Butterfly. The division of work between these novel-writing partners has never been explained. The partnership lasted till the death of Rice in 1882. Apparently Rice, who was a sporting man of the world, while Besant was a student, supplied the breezy incident, and the scholar the more polished expression. Afterward Walter Besant, who became Sir Walter, continued to produce sound and gracefully written fiction, such as his Dorothy Forster and All Sorts and Conditions of Men. His studies and descriptions of historic London were also notable.

As far away as 1887 Hall Caine adopted the Isle of Man as the most frequent scene for his stories. Previously he had been on the staff of a Liverpool newspaper. His tales attained a wide popularity.

An instance of success in novel-writing that came late in life was seen in John Inglesant, which appeared in 1881. It was written by a Birmingham manufacturer, Joseph Henry Shorthouse, who was born in 1834. Its setting was historical, its tone that of a subdued piety, and its style graceful and polished.

A more striking late beginning that was amply justified was the publication by

William de Morgan, the well-known decorative artist, of a story called Joseph Vance, when the writer had reached the age of sixty-seven. De Morgan, who revived in some measure the style of Dickens, whom he had known, followed up his belated entry into the field of fiction with several other leisurely stories, of literary interest. He died in 1917.

Mrs. Humphry Ward, a granddaughter of Dr. Arnold of Rugby, made a sensation in 1881 with her story of a religious pervert, Robert Elsmere. Throughout a long and industrious career she succeeded

the Dartmoor region. Eden Phillpotts also takes rank with Hardy and with Sir Arthur Quiller-Couch as one of the most skillful of all English writers of the short story, as witness his Told at the Plough.

The Hebrew race has had its English novelist in Israel Zangwill, a man of many literary gifts in poetry, drama and fiction. Conrad won much admiration by his fine mastery of English, which was not his native language. He was a Pole. That he deserves a seat of honor at the novelists' Round Table is assured.

From the novelists whose best work

Robert Louis Stevenson writes a prayer of good-will and good cheer from his couch in Apia, at the foot of the hill where he sleeps.

in retaining till her death, in 1920, a large share of interest in her work.

The writer most prominent in the public eye during the later part of the period we are considering was Rudyard Kipling, chiefly as a poet and writer of short stories. His fine Indian story, Kim, the longest from his pen, however, amply justified the public view of his literary power. No other story has so satisfactorily painted native life and thought.

Among novelists whose writing has had a distinctly local interest, the next place to that of Thomas Hardy must be taken by Eden Phillpotts for his stories of Devonshire character, more particularly in

belongs to the twentieth century, critical opinion would probably fill the front rank of those who have arrived at the full maturity of their powers, with John Galsworthy, Herbert George Wells, Arnold Bennett and Hugh Walpole. To posterity, however, we must leave the judgment as to where in the development of literature these current authors belong.

Though the fiction of the era following George Meredith and Thomas Hardy has not included much that can lay claim to greatness that endures, it has been skillful in workmanship and stimulating in thought.

THE NEXT STORY OF LITERATURE IS ON PAGE 3999.

Faithful John led the princess, the daughter of the King of the Golden Roof, triumphantly to the ship to view the golden wares, and when the king saw her he thought his heart would leap out of his breast with joy.

THE STORY OF FAITHFUL JOHN

AN old king who was dying summoned his best-loved servant, w h o m he had named Faithful John because he had served him so well.

"Faithful John," said he, "I am about to die, and I wish you to teach my young son all he should know, and be a father to him."

"I will serve him faithfully," was the reply, "even at the cost of my life."

"You must show him the whole palace, all the rooms and treasures; but beware how you show him the room in which hangs the picture of the daughter of the King of the Golden Roof. If he sees it he will fall deeply in love with her and be in great danger."

After the old king's death Faithful John said to his young master: "Come, I will show you your father's palace." Then he showed him all the treasures and all the rooms, except the one wherein hung the picture.

Now, when the young king saw that Faithful John always passed the door of that room, he said: "Why do you not open that door?"

"You would be terrified if I did," replied Faithful John.

"I must know what is in there," cried the king, and tried with all his strength to force the door open.

John held him back, saying: "I promised your father to beware how I

CONTINUED FROM 3837

showed you this room, lest what was within should lead both you and me into great trouble."

"My chief trouble will be not to enter the room," replied the king. "I shall not go away until you show it to me."

With a heavy heart Faithful John opened the door. There was the picture of the princess, and the king stood before it in silent admiration. Then he turned to his servant and asked: "Whose is that beautiful picture?"

"It is the picture of the daughter of the King of the Golden Roof."

But the king said: "My love for her is so great that if all the leaves on the trees were tongues they could not utter it. I will risk my life itself to win her."

Poor Faithful John thought deeply for a long time, and at last said: "All that the princess has about her, the tables, chairs, cups, dishes, all the things in her palace are of pure gold, and she is ever seeking new treasures. Let us order the goldsmiths to work all your gold into beautiful vessels, into birds and wondrous beasts, and let us go disguised as merchants to seek to please her."

So they boarded a ship and sailed away to her country. Then Faithful John bade the king await him, and taking some of the golden vessels, he made his way to the palace.

3901

Now, when the princess saw the wares she was delighted, and said: "They are so lovely that I will buy them all."

But Faithful John said: "I am only the servant of a rich merchant who awaits me in yonder ship, which is full of the most precious golden vessels."

"Let him bring them all here," she replied. "I long to see them."

"They are so numerous that it would take many days," replied John, "and the palace could not contain them."

"Take me to the ship, then," urged the princess.

So Faithful John led her triumphantly to the ship; and when the king saw her he thought his heart would leap out of his breast with joy.

"Come down into the state cabin and view my treasures!" he exclaimed. But Faithful John remained on deck, and ordered the ship to be put off.

"Spread all your sails," he cried, "that she may race over the waves like a bird through the air."

Meanwhile, the king showed the princess all the dishes, cups, and birds, and wonderful beasts, each one singly, and when they returned on deck, and the princess saw that the vessel was far away from her home, she cried aloud: "Alas! I am stolen by a roving trader; I would sooner have died."

"I am no trader," said the young king, taking her hand. "I am a king of as noble birth as yourself. I have taken you away by stealth because of my great love for you." And he told her the whole story. She saw that he was handsome and brave, and she loved him.

Now, while they were sailing home, Faithful John heard three ravens, who had alighted on the ship to rest, talking, for he understood their language.

"There he goes sailing away home with the princess," said one.

"He has her not," said another; "for when he lands a foxy-red horse will spring toward him, and if he mounts it, it will bear him away into the air, so that his bride will never see him more."

"True," said the third; "but if someone quickly kills the horse, the king is saved, but the slayer is turned to stone from the soles of his feet to his knees if he tells of it."

"True," said the second; "but even then the king loses his bride, for the golden bridal robe that lies on the couch

in his palace is really made of brimstone and pitch and will burn him up."

"Alas! Alas! Is there no help?" cried the first raven.

"All will be well if someone throws it quickly into the fire; but if he tells the reason, he will turn to stone from his knees to his heart," replied the second.

"But I know more," added the first raven; "for in the dance after the wedding the young queen will turn pale and swoon, and she will surely die unless someone lifts her up and draws three drops of blood from her. But if he should tell, his whole body will turn to stone from the crown of his head to the tip of his toe." And the ravens flew away, leaving John very sad.

When they came to land, all happened as the ravens had foretold, and Faithful John saved his master three times. But the young king did not know why he had acted so strangely, and condemned him to death.

Then Faithful John exclaimed: "I am wrongfully judged, for I have been ever faithful and true." And he told all that the ravens had said.

"Oh, my most faithful John!" cried the king, "Pardon! Pardon! Set him free." But John had fallen down turned to stone. No doctor could restore life to him. The king grieved bitterly, and ordered the stone figure to be taken to his room.

Some years after, when his two little sons were playing beside him, the king glanced at the statue and sighed: "Oh, that I could bring you back to life, my Faithful John!"

To his surprise, the statue answered: "You can, O king, if you will give up your children."

The king was greatly shocked; but he thought how John had died for his sake, and he said that he would.

The statue came to life at once, saying: "Keep your children, your truth is indeed rewarded."

When he saw the queen coming in, the king hid the children and John in a closet, and tested her in the same way; and she agreed that John must be brought back to life. Rejoicing that his wife thought as he thought, the king opened the closet, and cried: "Behold! Faithful John is indeed ours again, and we have our sons safe too." He told her the whole story, and they all lived happily together.

THE SHEPHERD-MAID AND THE SWEEP

AN old-fashioned oaken-wood cabinet, quite black with age and covered with fine old carving, once stood in a parlor; it was carved from top to bottom— roses, tulips and little stags' heads with long, branching antlers, peering forth from amid the curious scrolls and foliage surrounding them. Moreover, in the centre panel of the cabinet was carved the full-length figure of a man. He was a most ridiculous figure; he had crooked legs, small horns on his forehead, and a long beard. The children of the house called him "the crooked-legged Field-Marshal - Major - General - Corporal - Sergeant."

There he stood, his eyes always fixed upon the table under the pier-glass, for on this table stood a pretty little porcelain Shepherdess, her mantle gathered gracefully round her and fastened with a red rose; her shoes and hat were gilt, her hand held a crook—oh, she was very charming! Close by her stood a little porcelain Chimney-sweep. His face was as fresh and rosy as a girl's, which was certainly a mistake, for it ought to have been black. His ladder in his hand, there he kept his station, close by the little Shepherdess; they had been placed together from the first, and had long ago plighted their troth to each other.

Not far off stood a figure three times as large as the others; it was an old Chinese Mandarin, who could nod his head; he declared that he was grandfather to the little Shepherdess, and when the crooked-legged Field-Marshal-Major-General-Corporal-Sergeant made proposals to the little Shepherdess, he nodded his head in token of his assent.

"Now you will have a husband," said the old Mandarin. "You will be the wife of a Field-Marshal-Major-General-Corporal-Sergeant, of a man who has a whole cabinet full of silver-plate, besides a store of no one knows what in the secret drawers."

"I will not go into that dismal cabinet!" declared the little Shepherdess. "I have heard that eleven porcelain ladies are already imprisoned there."

"Then you shall be the twelfth, and you will be in good company," rejoined the Mandarin. "This very night, when the old cabinet creaks, you shall have a wedding party, as sure as I am a Chinese Mandarin." Whereupon he nodded his head and fell asleep.

But the little Shepherdess wept, and turned to the beloved of her heart, the porcelain Chimney-sweep.

"I believe I must ask you," said she; "to go out with me into the wide world, for here we cannot stay."

"I will do everything you wish," replied the little Chimney-sweep. "Let us go at once. I think I can support you by my profession."

"If we could but get off the table!" sighed she. "I shall never be happy till we are away."

And he comforted her, and showed her how to set her little foot on the carved edges and delicate foliage twining around the leg of the table, till at last they reached the floor. But turning to look at the old cabinet, they saw everything in a great commotion; the old Mandarin had awakened and was rocking himself to and fro with rage.

"Oh, just see the old Mandarin!" cried the little Shepherdess; and down she fell on her porcelain knees in the greatest distress.

"Have you the courage to go with me into the wide world?" asked the Chimney-sweep taking her hand.

"I have," replied she.

And the Chimney-sweep looked keenly at her, then led her to the stove.

"Oh, how black it looks!" sighed the shepherd maid. However, she went on with him, through the flues and the tunnel, where it was pitch-dark.

"Now we are in the chimney," he remarked; "and look, what a lovely star shines above us!"

And there was actually a star in the sky, shining right down upon them as if to show them the way. They crawled and crept till they reached the top of the chimney, where they sat down to rest for a while.

Heaven with all its stars was above them, and the town with all its roofs lay beneath them; the wide, wide world surrounded them. The poor Shepherdess had never imagined all this; she put her little head on the Chimney-sweep's arm and wept so that the gilding broke off from her waistband.

"This I cannot endure!" she exclaimed. "The world is all too large. Oh, that I were once more upon the little table under the pier-glass! I shall never be happy till I am there again. I have followed you out into the wide world, surely you will follow me home again, if you love me."

Then the Chimney-sweep talked very sensibly to her, reminding her of the old Chinese Mandarin and the crooked-legged Field-Marshal-Major-General-Corporal-Sergeant; but she wept so bitterly, and kissed her little Chimney-sweep so fondly, that at last he could not but yield to her request. So with great difficulty

in his neck, then he will be as good as new again."

"Do you really think so?" she asked. And then they climbed up the table to their old places.

No one welcomed them back because the fall of the Mandarin had shocked everyone into silence.

The old Chinese Mandarin was put together; the family had his back glued and his neck riveted; he was as good as new, but he could no longer nod his head.

"You have certainly grown very proud since you broke in pieces," remarked the

THEY REACHED THE TOP OF THE CHIMNEY, WHERE THEY SAT DOWN TO REST

they crawled down the chimney, and at length found themselves once more in the dark stove.

Everything was quite still. They peeped out. Alas! on the ground lay the old Chinese Mandarin; in attempting to follow the runaways, he had fallen down off the table, and had broken into three pieces.

"Oh, how shocking!" exclaimed the little Shepherdess. "Poor old grandfather is broken in pieces, and we are the cause of this dreadful accident."

"He can be put together again," replied the Chimney-sweep. "If they glue his back together, and put a strong rivet

crooked-legged Field-Marshal-Major-General-Corporal-Sergeant, "but I must say, for my part, I am unable to see that there is anything to be proud of. Am I to have her or am I not? Just answer me that!"

And the Chimney-sweep and the little Shepherdess both looked imploringly at the old Mandarin; they were so afraid lest he should nod his head. But nod he could not, and it was disagreeable to him to confess to a stranger that he had a rivet in his neck, so the young porcelain people always remained together. They blessed the grandfather's rivet, and loved each other for the rest of their lives.

THE NEXT STORIES ARE ON PAGE 3981.

EDIBLE AMERICAN MUSHROOMS

1. Beefsteak or Liver Fungus (*Fistulina hepatica*). 2. Meadow Toadstool (*Lactarius distans*).   3. Morel (*Morchella esculenta*).   4. Chantarelle (*Cantharellus*).   5. Coral Fungus (*Clavaria rugosa*).   6. Fairy-ring Mushrooms (*Agaricus*). 7. Cultivated Mushrooms; young and old. 8. Forest Mushroom (*Agaricus silvacola*).   9. Edible Boletus; young.   10. Ochre-gilled Russula (*Russula ochraphylla*).   11. Velvety Clitocybe (*Clitocybe velutipes*).   12. Bear's-head Mushroom (*Hydnum caput-ursi*). 13. Oyster Mushroom (*Agaricus ostreatus*).

POISONOUS AMERICAN FUNGI

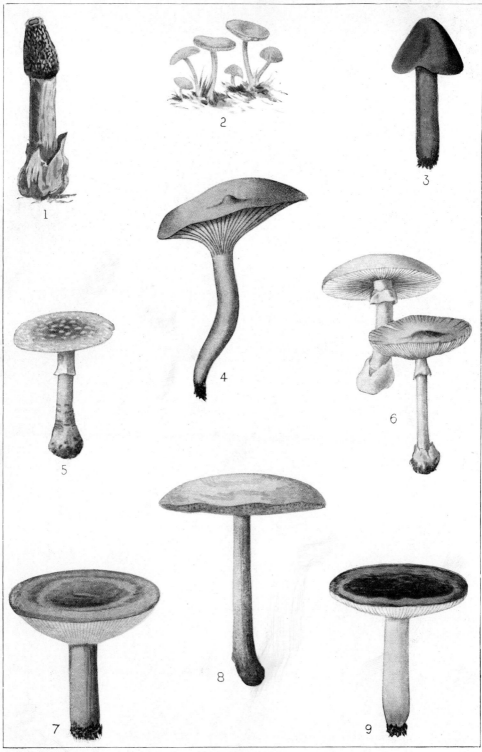

1. Stinkhorn, or Fetid Wood-witch (*Phallus impudicus*).   2. Poisonous Fairy-ring, Agaric (*Marasmius urens*).   3. Red-juice Mushroom (*Hygrophorus conicus*).   4. Deceiving Clytocybe (*Clytocybe illudens*). 5. Fly Mushroom (*Amanita muscaria*).   6. Death-cup, or Spring Mushroom (*Amanita phalloides*); two varieties.   7. Red-milk Mushroom (*Lactarius rufus*).   8. Fiery Boletus (*Boletus piperatus*).   9. Emetic Mushroom (*Russula emetica*).

Where mushrooms may be found in the spring.

MUSHROOMS, EDIBLE AND POISONOUS

VERY often in early summer any one of you can look out over some broad, gently rolling lawn, or else over a close-cropped pasture, and see what at the first glance seem like the ends of tiny eggs peeping through the short grass. A second's thought will tell you what they are, and perhaps your father may tell you of his boyhood in the country, when he roamed the pastures and the fields and saw these same "fairy rings" of "toadstools," with the brighter green circle of the grass surrounding a faded patch within, and he may tell you some stories about them. Only the other day, my boy, an observant lad, called my attention to a beautiful ring on a lawn as we passed quickly by in a car.

Perhaps you have pretended, as children have for centuries, that nimble elves and goblins have danced the night long within the magic ring that so mysteriously has sprung into being overnight, and that they wore the grass out with their pointed slippers. Probably you've called them toadstools and thought them poisonous. If you found them in the open pastures or fields, they are not often harmful. Those that grow in woods are not safe to eat. So be sure not to experiment until you learn more about mushrooms and their habits and appearance.

Many people call all fleshy fungi

CONTINUED FROM 3728

toadstools; but it is not c e r t a i n that toads ever use these queer growths f o r resting-places, and it is quite certain that the right name for them is mushrooms, w h i c h, some think, is derived from two Welsh words meaning "field" and "knob." Others think that the word has something to do with moss. Some mushrooms are edible, and some are very dangerous to eat. One must learn something about them before eating them.

From the first century, and perhaps earlier times, we have records of mushrooms as an article of food, and abundant fossils of mushrooms in the vast coal and peat deposits show that years ago, when this old, old world of ours was a very different place, the gentle pushing of these fragile growths managed, as to-day, to break a way through the ground, even lifting hard clods and pushing aside stones.

Very early historians and writers mention mushrooms. One Roman historian tells of "fine knives and razors of amber and other dishes of silver," which the cooks used in preparing these delicacies for the epicures of his time. Another old writer, however, thought them not at all wholesome. "For every hue they display," he writes, "there is a pain to correspond to it." Possibly those

3905

employed by wicked persons of that age to prepare deadly concoctions used the poisonous mushrooms, and Nero, cruel monarch of Rome, fed a large party of invited guests on mushrooms he knew would cause their death.

Most of the inhabitants of European and Asiatic countries scour the fields and woods for mushrooms, and as many of them seldom have meat, these rapid-growth fungi take its place. China imports mushrooms from Japan and other Pacific islands to supply the demand, and even has officially issued for free distribution "anti-famine" books about mushrooms and their food values. In Southern Europe dogs and pigs are trained to hunt for one sort called truffles, which grow under the fallen leaves of the vast forests; and as the animals, too, like to eat them, the men have to scramble to gather them first as they are uncovered by the sharp little hoofs and claws.

THE "VEGETABLE MEAT" SO PLENTIFUL AND CHEAP

Truffles have not yet been found in the United States, but Americans are beginning to realize that right at their door is a substitute, in many varieties of mushrooms, for the meat that is constantly growing dearer. Since the flavor of different varieties resembles oysters, beefsteak, chicken, sweetbreads and fish, it is no wonder that they are often called "vegetable meat." Of course they have not so much food value, pound for pound, as meat, but when they can be had for nothing they should not be neglected.

The odor of mushrooms sometimes resembles that of other plants or fruit, such as garlic, apricots, radishes, fresh meal or anise. In proportion to the number of varieties, those known as dangerous are no more than among flowering plants. To Dr. M. A. Curtis, of North Carolina, belongs the credit of the first systematic classification and study of mushrooms in North America, and already several hundred varieties are listed as perfectly safe.

MUSHROOMS AND OTHER FUNGI AND HOW THEY GROW

Mushrooms are a division of fungi. Mildew, mold, rust, smut in grain, all are forms of fungi. The fleshy sort that have queer shapes like umbrellas, nests, hoofs, shells, clubs, spheres, hemispheres, cones, bears' heads and ears, although flowerless, are profuse and well known. They spring up overnight from April to late fall, and are the fruit of a running white mold-like growth spreading through dead leaves, earth or decaying wood. After a rain or other favorable conditions a certain point in this mass of fibres suddenly begins to grow. In a few hours it has pushed up out of the ground like an egg, and in another hour or two the outer envelope, or veil, is broken, sometimes leaving remnants on the cap and sometimes showing a ring of itself under the cap on the stem.

THE WONDERFUL SEEDS OF THE MUSHROOMS

Edible fungi are surprisingly different in appearance, ranging from coral-shapes or fluted vases to the usual umbrella form. One has been known to grow to weigh thirty pounds. They have no seeds, but produce "spores," which are as fine as dust and, singly, are invisible to the naked eye. The dust-brown spores of the puff-balls are inside; the spores of the Morel, which is unlike any other fungus and is always edible, are in delicate sacs on the cap which finally burst at the tip; those of the gill-bearing mushrooms shake down from the fan-like drapery attached to the under-side of the cap, and those of the cushioned sort, whose surface is evenly punctured with very numerous little holes as if pricked with a pin, shake themselves out as pepper comes from the shaker.

One can "take a picture" by nature's own developer of any of the last two sorts, in natural colors, too, if he will cut off the stems of several mushrooms close to the cap, and place them, gills or cushion down, upon sheets of white or colored paper. As some of the spores are white, it is well to use both kinds of paper for each specimen until one becomes acquainted with the spores. Cover with a glass dish, or, at least, be sure that no draft of air disturbs mushrooms or papers, and in a few hours, or in the morning if you leave them overnight, you will have an exact reproduction of the mushrooms from their own active spores. Try it; it is one of the most interesting of things to do. Those that have colored spores reproduce each delicate shade, while the white ones are as soft as snow.

Mushrooms have to live on food manufactured by other plants, vegetables or trees, and their spores are quite particular where they shall start their own life as mushrooms. Some baby spores grow only if they alight upon the spines of a dead chestnut burr; others like sawdust, oak leaves, dark coal-mines or decaying animal substance of various kinds. It has been estimated that from one puffball, so aptly called an "elfin teepee" with its thread of invisible spores rising like smoke, come at least ten million spores, and they must fall on exactly the right spot before setting up their own lives. Old-fashioned doctors used these spores to staunch fresh wounds.

FOOD WHICH IS FOUND IN FIELDS AND WOODS

Mushrooms are greedy eaters; they grow rapidly and decay soon. Some sorts respond to artificial culture through "spawn," which is the thread-like substance which goes through muck as yeast does through unbaked bread, and many people make comfortable livings by raising them. But they are so abundant in the United States that almost anyone having access to the open may gather during the summer and fall "an hundred weight of wholesome food rotting under the trees," if he knows the right mushrooms to pick. But, as a whole, they do not bear transplanting, nor respond to cultivation. Instead, they stand on their one leg, quite independent of anyone.

Because some mushrooms are delicious eating and others are extremely poisonous, one must learn a great deal about them before venturing to cook and eat. He must become acquainted with their manner of growth, their color, odor and general appearance. The prejudice against mushrooms is needlessly sweeping, but careful instruction will teach a few, at least, of the edible sorts, and the deadly varieties are easily recognized. Each must be learned as we learn to tell the difference between a blue jay and a robin. However, there is one, and only one, infallible sign that a mushroom is poisonous—the presence of the "cup," or socket, from which the stem grows. It is always below the surface of the ground. Look for it. Any mushroom that turns blue when cut or bruised should be let alone. Mushrooms having worms and those that are decayed have an unpleasant smell, and, again, if you taste a small bit, and the mushroom stings, is bitter or otherwise unpleasant, or exudes a milky juice on being cut or wounded, be sure to let it alone. Some mushrooms which have one or more of these qualities may not be poisonous, but only an expert can decide. Shun as poison a brilliant cap of yellow, orange or even scarlet, studded with white or grayish spots, for this produces the deadly "fly-poison." Czar Alexis died from eating this sort, as did several noted French *savants*.

MUSHROOMS WHICH MAY BE USED AS RAZOR STROPS

Some people say that any mushroom that grows on a tree is poisonous; but those growing *sidewise* from position, with dirty white gills and a light brown or buff top, are safe, according to eminent authorities. From some of these flesh-like growths, however, comes tinder, punk and touchwood, and the phosphorescence that makes old wood gleam in the dark is decaying fungi. One lovely white mushroom springing up overnight contains the most deadly vegetable poison known, and one growing on the birch tree can be used as a razor strop!

Aside from the deaths that occur from careless handling of unknown poisonous mushrooms some people have died because they gathered them when decayed, or they did not cook them *at once*. As mushrooms are so much like animal food, they have the same tendency to decay, and who would think of eating putrid meat? In gathering, be sure to look beneath the surface of the ground for the telltale "cup"; use a sharp knife, cut an inch or two from the cup so no dirt will adhere to the mushroom, and before putting in your basket it is better to wrap each specimen in tissue-paper which you have provided. It keeps them unbruised, and if you have taken one that is not quite safe, it will not hurt the others.

SEVEN KINDS OF MUSHROOMS THAT ARE SAFE EATING

Out of the many mushrooms that are safe we have pictured thirteen to help you to identify some of those you may find; and that you may make no mistake, we also show nine that are either poisonous or unpleasant to eat. Note the difference between the Fairy-ring (number 6 of the edible varieties) mushroom that grows in the open and its wicked counterpart (number 2 of the poisonous) which slinks in the shade as if afraid to come to the light. And be sure not to confuse number 8 (edible) with the most deadly of all poisonous mushrooms, the lovely Amanita, with its death-cup hidden beneath the ground's surface (number 6, poisonous). Look for that cup, always!

Besides the pictures we shall describe six or seven, and after studying the illustrations and text you can gather a good meal outdoors.

The Meadow mushroom is the best known and most widely found. It is smooth or slightly rough, according to its age, and is creamy white or tawny. The color of its gills is most important. If we break away the veil in an unopened specimen we find the gills pallid pink. As the growth advances they· become decidedly pinkish, changing to brownish black, and they are of unequal lengths. The stem is creamy white and solid, and always shows the remains of the veil in a frill or ring under the cap.

The Pasture mushroom is egg-shaped, expanding into a parasol sometimes seven inches across, with the apex raised in a marked degree. It is pale buff, spotted with shaggy patches; gills at first almost white, crowded, finally becoming like the cap in color. The stem is tall, slender, streaked and speckled with brown, encircled with a loose ring, hollow and growing from a fibrous bulb, having no sign of the fatal cup that is a never failing sign of poison. This mushroom has been called the Nut mushroom on account of its flavor, and dries naturally while standing in the pastures. It is also fragrant.

Puffballs are edible, although joyous school children usually think they are made to kick or to pinch so as to make the smoke fly. Yet, in their white stage they make very good eating, but be sure that you are not picking the deadly "cup" sort, for in its earlier stages that dangerous mushroom is apt to look like the innocent puffball. But, remember, the one is below ground, while puffballs are above. Once warned, twice armed! Be sure to open each specimen and be sure to look for the cup before giving your treasures to be cooked.

Green is a rare color among mushrooms, but that of the Green Russula is not the bright green of grass: rather it is a metallic or grayish green. These mushrooms are found in hardwood groves or their edges, and are as sweet as a chestnut. Their cap is slightly hollow and becomes broken at the fluted edge of the gills. The creamy white of the gills has the appearance of network; they are thick, very brittle and of equal length. The stem is solid and creamy white.

This sort also has purple and reddish caps (number 10, edible).

When in late September you come upon what seems a strange nest of goose eggs, their summits spotted with brown, you may know you have found another "safe" mushroom. Nothing else looks like them. As this sort grows in dense masses, you can get a whole dinner for the family right there. These mushrooms are called Shaggy-manes because of a fancied resemblance to a wig, and should be gathered while the concealed, crowded and equal-lengthed gills are either white or pink; otherwise they are unwholesome, and they finally melt away into an inky mass.

The edible Tube mushroom has a cushionlike, moist cap which is light brown or darkish red. The surface of the cap is dull and as smooth as a kid glove, and the stout stem is a pale brown, generally with a fine raised network of pink lines near the cap. The flesh of the light brown ones is white or yellowish and does not change color when broken. When young they are peculiarly nutty to the taste. They can be found during July and August.

One dark red variety closely resembles beefsteak in color, general appearance and flavor. This mushroom can never be mistaken, as it grows with its very short stem on stumps and trunks of oak or chestnut. One has been found weighing thirty pounds, and provided a hearty meal for several men after it was sliced in sections and broiled over live coals. The veins of darker red running through the pinky flesh of the under tube surface, combined with the clammy moistness of the dark red cap, make its name of Beefsteak mushroom most apt. There is also a yellow mushroom, *Polyporus sulphureus*, which grows in the same way. It tastes like lobster and is delicious.

Mushrooms will amply repay ardent study. Look, compare, assort, "photograph" their spores; be careful, and it will not be long before you can add to the family larder by your pleasant rambles through the fields and woods as well as to your fund of knowledge and personal happiness.

Get the illustrated bulletins issued by the Government and choose first those fungi which it is impossible to confuse with any of the dangerous varieties.

THE NEXT STORY OF PLANT LIFE IS ON PAGE 4019.

An ancient Greek coasting vessel.

THE REIGN OF WOODEN SHIPS

EVERY boy who has lived near lake, river or sea has at some time or other cherished a secret longing to be a sailor. Beyond restless water there is always a mystery—something romantic that lures and beckons. Who has ever been content to remain on one side of a lake or stream without wanting to cross over and explore the other side? That is the feeling most of us have to-day, and we can imagine that the same feeling inspired our ancestors in those far-off days before the dawn of history. If we use our imaginations still more we can picture a time still more remote, when man lived entirely on land and regarded a body of water as a treacherous and hungry enemy. If a human being fell into deep water, that was probably the end of him. Rivers and lakes were impassable barriers between tracts of land until someone noticed that a tree would float and in a spirit of daring adventure embarked upon this leafy floater. There must have been many accidents and drownings before it was discovered that a log stripped of its branches could be moved in the water by means of a pole or flattened stick.

It is not hard to see a mind picture of a man braver than his fellows who tried this method of traveling and, caught by adverse tides and winds,

CONTINUED FROM 3800

was carried downstream and out to sea to be lost in the vast unknown. That man was the forerunner of all the gallant sailormen that ever were—of Jason and his Argonauts, of Ulysses and his heroic-hearted comrades, of Leif Ericson, of Columbus and the host of others whose names will live forever on the scroll of sea fame.

The next step was to hollow out the log. This resulted in the dug-out, in which a man could put his family and his simple household belongings. We can be sure that most of the dug-out traveling was done on lakes or rivers, or on sea well within sight of land. But the dug-out and its development have had untold influence upon the civilization of the world. The most advanced nations of all ages were those that brought ships to the highest development of their day. The most backward nations were those that clung to the dug-out almost in its original design.

Probably through chance, not through thought, the use of a sail was discovered, and then a simple form of steering gear was added. Gradually the vessels took a distinct shape which their builders had copied from fishes or the underbody of a duck or swan. These advances we find in the first vessels of which we have any knowledge. They belonged to those Egyptians who lived about 6000 B.C. That is almost eight thousand years ago, but we know something of those early boats because ancient wall-pictures show clearly the types of vessels and rigging. But even more convincing than the pictographs, as the wall-pictures are called, are the little wooden models of boats which have been found in many tombs in Egypt. The dwellers in the valley of the Nile believed that the souls of the dead needed such boats to sail the streams of the other world. The death boats had carved oars, masts and sails.

Until 3000 B.C. the vessels of the Egyptians were sailing boats, not ships. A drawing of the earliest sailing boat shows a low craft with a mast and a square sail set far forward in the bow. Aft is a small cabin for the passenger. A little later the boats were decked in, and masts were lowered to the deck roof when not in use. Paddlers took the place of the dismantled sails. These paddlers were slaves, and plied their oars or paddles at the direction of an overseer with a whip. In some pictures as many as twenty paddlers are seen on one side of a ship.

Someone discovered that rowing gave more power than paddling, so that was the next great change in the means of moving the vessels. For a rudder a huge paddle or oar was mounted on a forked post in the centre of the stern and was worked by means of a leather loop. It is now thought that the hulls of these boats were made of acacia planks.

THE DARING VOYAGES OF EGYPTIAN SAILORS

It seems natural that the eastern end of the Mediterranean should be the region whence ships first came, for to that part of the world we trace the beginnings of our civilization. First on the calm surface of Father Nile and then on the blue Mediterranean the Egyptians tried out their boats. Farther and farther afield did their vessels spread their sails to find new lands and other peoples with whom to trade. With their tiny craft and primitive instruments of navigation these early Egyptian sailors were as bold and as brave as any sailors the world has seen.

Ships by ones or twos had made voyages to such lands, but the first large expedition took place about 1600 B.C., and it was Queen Hatshepsut who was responsible for the ambitious idea. This ruler, who was a wise and fearless woman, felt that the god Amen desired her "to make for him a Punt in Egypt." Punt was a rich and fair land to the southeast of Egypt. Men who have studied the history of the countries in that part of the globe think that Punt was the present Somaliland, but no one really knows. To reach the ancient land the Egyptians sailed down the Nile and into a canal leading through the Wadi Tumilat to the Red Sea. The Suez Canal of to-day is supposed to be constructed at the same place as the ancient waterway.

The expedition was gone three years, and it brought back such cargoes as the Egyptians had never dreamed of before. "Precious woods of the holy land, heaps of incense-resin, gold, tusks of elephants, ebony, silver, frankincense trees, odorous Tepes wood, skins of leopards and living monkeys." In addition, the decks were piled high with shrubs and bushes wherewith "to make a Punt in Egypt." The biggest ships that took part in the voyage to Punt were about 65 feet in length, but were built on the same model as the ordinary Nile boat. They were decked in, had no holds and could carry a total of 50 passengers and crew.

THE PHŒNICIANS BECOME MASTERS OF THE SEA

But Hatshepsut's expedition was the crowning achievement of Egyptian sea plans. Henceforth they "rested on their oars" while the hardy energetic Phœnicians became the rulers of the seas and the captors of the trade of the earth. In the Bible the prophet Ezekiel describes the ships of Tarshish (Phœnicia):

They have made all thy ship boards of fir trees of Senir: they have taken cedars from Lebanon to make masts for thee.

Of the oaks of Bashan have they made thine oars; the company of the Ashurites have made thy benches of ivory.

Fine linen with broidered work from Egypt was that which thou spreadest forth to be thy sail; blue and purple from the isles of Elishah was that which covered thee.

Ezekiel also gives a list of the articles traded in and the peoples with whom the trading was done. Those small merchantmen flitted about from port to port, exchanging gold, silver and other metals, horses and cattle, ivory and ebony, emeralds, coral and agate, purple and fine linen, wheat, honey, oil, balm, wool, wine, spices, and many other treasures.

LITTLE SHIPS OF LONG AGO

Our picture shows a model of a Nile River boat used by the Egyptians about 5000 B.C. A square sail was used when the wind was favorable. Aft was provided a small cabin for passengers. When there was no wind slave paddlers took the place of the dismantled sail. Photo, courtesy Metropolitan Museum of Art.

Photo, George N. Russell; copyright, H. Bloomingdale.

For the tercentenary pageant held at Plymouth, Massachusetts, in 1921, a Norse galley was constructed to represent the episode of the landing of Thorwald and his Vikings in 1000 A.D. The Viking ship which is shown in our photograph was as perfect in detail as men could make her.

HOW THE PHŒNICIANS CARRIED CIVILIZATION TO WESTERN LANDS

But the Phœnicians were adventurers and explorers as well as traders. There is some evidence that one of their number sailed out of the Red Sea and down around Africa. It took more than two years for the Phœnician cockleshell to make the trip around the continent of Africa, but eventually it reached Egypt. This circling of Africa took place six centuries before Christ. Other long voyages were made by these sailors to the British Isles, where a trade in tin was carried on with the inhabitants of Cornwall. Indeed, from the British Isles to India, the bold Phœnician sailors were known in every port. The Eastern and Western peoples of the then-known world obtained knowledge of one another through the visits of these ships. Dr. Botsford, the historian, says that not only were the Phœnicians the greatest commercial people of the ancient world, but they were also the "carriers of civilization." It was their ships that gained for them this deserved reputation.

In appearance the Phœnician ships were an improvement on the Egyptian vessels, from which they were first copied. The bow had become a ram, capable of bumping into a rival vessel. The ships themselves were larger, and were often propelled by two tiers of rowers; then the name "biremes" was given. If three tiers of rowers were used, the ships were called "triremes." Those names describe the ships accurately; *bi* means "two," *tri* means "three," and *remus* means "oar." As the rowers had to sit one above another, the ships were increased in height; also they were long, narrow, straight and flat-bottomed.

THE GREEKS BECOME THE GREATEST SHIPBUILDERS

But the Phœnicians, too, had to give up the mastery of the waves to another nation. The Greeks had copied the manner of building ships from the Phœnician visitors, although in their songs they take all the credit themselves. Charles Kingsley thus describes the building of the far-famed Argo which carried Jason and his heroes in search of the Golden Fleece:

Then they felled the pines on Pelion and shaped them with the axe, and Argus taught them to build a galley, the first long ship which ever sailed the seas. They pierced her for fifty oars, an oar for each hero of the crew, and pitched her with coal-black pitch and painted her bows with vermilion.

Then Jason and Orpheus, the sweet singer, went to the holy oak of Zeus, father of gods and men; and they cut down a bough and nailed it to the beak head of the Argo. But when the heroes tried to launch their vessel, she was too heavy for them to move and her keel sank deep in the sand. Then Orpheus sang his magic song of the sea.

How sweet it is to ride upon the surges and to leap from wave to wave, while the wind sings cheerful in the cordage and the oars flash fast among the foam! How sweet it is to roam across the ocean and see new towns and wondrous lands, and to come home laden with treasure and to win undying fame!

And the good ship Argo heard him [says Kingsley] and longed to be away and out at sea; till she stirred in every timber and heaved from stem to stern, and leaped up from the sand upon the rollers and plunged onward like a gallant horse and the heroes fed her path with pine-trunks, till she rushed into the whispering sea.

So sang the poet Orpheus, and in his heart every man echoed his words; for that is how a sailor must feel or he is not a real son of the sea. Those who go "down to the sea in ships" are attracted by the mystery that lies beyond the visible rim of great waters. Any boy who stands on the shore staring out to sea and wondering what lies beyond the horizon, knows what the feeling is. Orpheus just put the feeling into words.

HOMER DESCRIBES THE APPEARANCE OF A SHIP

Homer, the Greek poet who sang of the siege of Troy and the wanderings of Odysseus, describes a ship which was used by the famed Phœnician seamen. There were fifty-two youths to act as oarsmen. H. B. Cotterill's translation of the Odyssey tells about the embarking thus:

Now when at last they had gotten them down to the sea and the vessel,
Firstly the black-hulled vessel they drew to the deep salt water;
Then, embarking the mast and the sails on the black-hulled vessel,
All of the oars to the tholes they attached with the lashings of leather,
Each in its place, and the white sails hoisting aloft on the yardarm
Anchored her far from the shore. . . .

The Greeks evidently had two types of vessels—the war vessel and the commer-

A PAGE OF OLD-TIME VESSELS

This is a model of a Roman man-of-war. From the ninth to the fifteenth centuries A.D. this type of ship was common in the Mediterranean.

In this Norman vessel of the time of the early Crusades there are resemblances to the Viking ships; for instance, in the shields and sails.

Photos, courtesy H. C. Perleberg, New York.

Here is a model of the ship that discovered a new world—the Santa Maria, in which Christopher Columbus crossed the Atlantic in 1492.

From the fourteenth to the sixteenth centuries the Dutch sailors made themselves feared on the seas. Our picture shows a model of a Dutch ship.

cial vessel. The warship was long and narrow, with three tiers of oars. Sometimes there were 170 oarsmen in a vessel and the sail was used very little. These vessels used their beaks or rams to destroy the enemy. Greek commercial ships were double-ended and flat-bottomed; the bow and stern posts were usually ornamented. These vessels had large square sails on which they depended, rather than on oars. As to their size, reports have come down in history of vessels that carried as many as six hundred people.

The Greeks became the most powerful people in the eastern Mediterranean through their control of the sea. But that high position was not reached without struggles with equally ambitious nations. When Xerxes, the Persian, led an attack against Greece he had 1,200 ships or more to fight 378 Greek triremes. But the Greeks were successful. The Carthaginians, colonists of Phœnicia, also had to acknowledge the superiority of the sailors from the lands bordering on the Ægean Sea. The Greeks discovered means of navigating against such strong tides as those of the Dardanelles; they discovered how to tack, that is sailing against the wind, and how to use an anchor almost modern in appearance.

ROMAN SHIPS WITH FIVE BANKS OF OARS

About 300 B.C., however, the sun of Grecian glory was setting. Rome and Carthage were increasing in power; Rome through her soldiery, and Carthage through her fleet. Rome at last built a fleet, modeling her first vessels on the Grecian triremes. Then ships with five tiers of oars, quinqueremes, were constructed. These were more powerful and much larger than any triremes yet seen in the Mediterranean. To make them even more dangerous for war purposes the Romans invented a sort of drawbridge called a *corvus* (crow). This was a gangway carried on the bow of the ship fastened so that it could be let down with a crash upon an enemy deck. A spike in its end attached this gangway firmly to the deck upon which it fell, and thus a bridge was ready to bear the Roman soldiers from their own ship to the one attacked.

The Romans built huge passenger and commercial ships as well as warships. Kings and rich men had vessels with luxurious deck houses, bronze baths, marbled rooms, libraries decorated with mosaics and wonderful statuary, and covered walks along the deck with vines and trees. Sails were sometimes of silk in the most delicate shades, while some parts of the upper deck were incrusted with jewels. Of course such ships were not common, but they just show what the Romans were able to do. From several galleys which have been found almost intact under the waters of the Lake of Nemi it is known that the Romans sheathed the hulls of their ships with lead fastened on by bronze studs.

Sea-power in the Mediterranean had become more and more dependent upon the size of the vessels and the increased number of oars; sails had become of lesser importance. And for centuries conditions remained the same.

SEA-POWER PASSES TO THE ATLANTIC OCEAN

The next chapter in shipbuilding history leaves the Mediterranean and deals with the Atlantic Ocean and the vessels which dared mountainous waves and mighty storms such as the "inland sea" never knew. It is thought by men who have studied the matter that the adventurous Phœnicians had reached not only Britain but the Scandinavian lands and all that coast which is now France and Germany. The natives had very crude boats, for rock pictures have kept a record of some of them. Certain tribes made more progress than others in the art of shipbuilding. Julius Cæsar in 55 B.C. found that the craft of the Britons were rude coracles, that is frameworks of wicker covered with skins. But the Veneti, a tribe from Gaul, had stout oaken ships quite as seaworthy as the Roman vessels. These Gaulish ships were high in the stern and bow; the sails were of leather, and the oars were used purely for steering.

The Saxons were the next shipbuilders, but their boats were made of skins when they conquered the early Britons. Yet about the beginning of the ninth century they had learned to build large ships of planks. Bow and stern of an old Saxon vessel rose high out of the water to prevent the breaking of the waves on the decks. A single mast carried a square sail, while the steering was done by two oars. The hull was flat-bottomed. Alfred the Great built up a great navy of such ships to defeat the Danes who were

THE HEYDAY OF FRIGATES

Toward the end of the eighteenth century and in the first years of the nineteenth, shipbuilders of the United States excelled in the building of frigates. These were much lighter and faster than English frigates.   Photo, courtesy Metropolitan Museum of Art.

Photo, Ewing Galloway.
The most famous of the American frigates of the nineteenth century was the Constitution. She won a great name for herself and was affectionately called "Old Ironsides." Preserved as an American national relic, she lies in Charlestown Harbor, Massachusetts. A public fund is being raised for necessary repairs.

ravaging the English coast. It is curious that Alfred's ships had sixty oars, and trusted more to them than to sails. A few years later King Edgar had a fleet of eighty ships—the greatest ever known in Atlantic waters.

THE NORSEMEN WHO DARED TO SAIL ANY SEA

The most feared and most skillful sailors who ruled the seas from the seventh to the eleventh centuries were the Vikings, or Norsemen. "From the fury of the Norsemen, Good Lord, deliver us!" was a constant prayer in the churches of England. The very thought of an approach of Vikings struck terror into the hearts of all nations from Gaul to Constantinople. High in the stern and high in the bow with a figurehead terrible to look upon, the ships were built of stout planks. Thirty rowers added their power to that of the wind in the sails, which were of many colors and bore strange designs. Rows of shining shields hung along the rails. The seamen were huge blond heroes who laughed and sang in the teeth of the Atlantic's worst storm, and who never gave nor demanded mercy in battle. The average length of the Viking ships was about seventy-five feet. It was in such vessels that the Norsemen discovered Greenland and even touched the coast of North America.

The peoples of France and England were sorely tried by these hardy Northerners, many of whom landed and settled in their countries. But the result was an improvement in the methods of shipbuilding in both France and England. Probably the presence of these sea masters inspired William the Conqueror when he built a fleet of a thousand ships to invade England.

Very little is known of the changes in shipbuilding for the next couple of centuries, but historians mention the supplies that Richard Cœur de Lion's fleet took to Palestine. Each vessel had 3 span rudders, 13 anchors, 30 oars, 2 sails and 3 sets of ropes.

OTHER NATIONS STRUGGLE TO BUILD BETTER SHIPS

It was this Third Crusade that first brought English sailors into contact with a three-masted tall-sided vessel called a "carack." This was a real ship, and not only a big boat, as the English craft really were. With the passing of unlimited numbers of slaves the galley type of craft had given way to the real sailing vessel on the Mediterranean.

The fourteenth century saw Venetians and Genoese fighting for the control of the waters. Venice won and was hailed as the "Queen of the Seas," with over three thousand ships. But Spain, Portugal and England had improved their ships by additional masts, decks and cabins, as well as sweeter lines. A description of an English ship of the fifteenth century says:

> The stem and stern are very much alike below the upper works. At the forward poop a lofty structure projects considerably over the water. There is a large mainmast, a square mainsail, sometimes one or two smaller masts. Above the main is a large top castle. Latine sails are found on the smaller masts.

The Portuguese and Spanish ships of this period were called "caravels," and were built to make more speed. Columbus had three caravels in his transatlantic voyage. His largest vessel, the Santa Maria, was a decked ship of 100 tons, and her crew numbered fifty-two men. A few years later the French built a four-masted ship, Cordelière, of 700 tons. The Henri Grâce à Dieu, which belonged to Henry VIII of England, had also four masts and two decks, while her tonnage was 1,500 tons.

SHIPS AND SAILORS OF THE ELIZABETHAN AGE

The Elizabethan Age was a period of great activity in shipbuilding, and the galleon, galleasse and pinnace became important types of ships. The length of a galleon was three times her own beam (or width); she was low in the waist (the centre part) with a square forecastle and a high quarter-deck. A galleasse was longer in proportion to her beam, often had level decks, and did not have such high sides or ends as the galleon. A pinnace was a smaller boat which afterward was called a sloop; it belonged to, and served, a mother ship.

Spain was the last of the maritime nations to take the galleon as a model, but when she did she made galleons higher and of heavier material than had yet been tried. But they were hard to manage in any kind of wind, and that fact went greatly against the Spaniards in 1588, when the Spanish Armada was destroyed. Richard Hakluyt says that when the epic fight occurred between the

THE LAST OF WOODEN SHIPS

After the War of 1812 a commercial rivalry began between England and the United States for the control of ocean trade. Competition to build the swiftest ships became acute and resulted in the appearance of the packets. Our picture shows the Liverpool packet Dreadnaught.   © George E. Noyes.

The packets were succeeded by the fastest wooden ships ever known—the clippers. Here we see one of the most famous clippers, the Flying Cloud. The climax in wooden-ship building was reached in these speedy vessels, which reigned on the seas for about twenty years.

Revenge and the Spanish fleet, the Spanish galleon, the great San Philip, of 1,500 tons, was so huge and high that the wind was taken from the sails of the little English ship. The San Philip carried three tiers of guns on a side and eleven cannons in each tier.

It is interesting to trace the changes made in fighting ships from the days of the Armada until the first years of the eighteenth century. Queen Elizabeth had two types of warships in her navy— one with huge sides and "castles" at bow and stern, the other with flat deck and low sides. Both types had one gun deck. But these vessels were clumsy to handle and did not carry guns enough to suit the wishes of naval men. The next century saw the birth of the frigate which was thought to be a vessel which could vanquish the Dutch ships. The Dutch had been warring on the sea for some years, and Dutch shipping and commerce were far advanced.

THE DEVELOPMENT OF SHIPS IN ENGLAND

The seventeenth century saw the trend of shipbuilding toward frigate lines. The founding of "The United Company of Merchant Adventurers of England trading to the East Indies" brought a demand for ships that were fast and seaworthy, and the company patterned its vessels on the frigates of the Royal Navy. Four journeys around the Cape of Good Hope to India were judged all that could be expected of a ship. But the Royal Navy changed its types of frigates from time to time as naval architects designed better vessels, while the East India Company clung to the old style of ship. The frigate was truly a ship of English design, the first being the Constant Warwick, launched in 1647. The French, however, improved the original model, and these improvements were copied by British and American shipwrights. It was from the French frigate that the first American frigates, privateers and later the Baltimore clippers originated.

At the opening of the eighteenth century the British Navy possessed seven first-rate ships having three gun decks each, and each carrying one hundred guns or more. But at this period the French war frigates were of a much better design than those of other nations. English shipbuilders took example from ships captured from the French, and improved the craft of the English fleet. One of the most famous ships of this century was the Royal George. She was over 143 feet long and almost 52 feet wide, and her tonnage was 2,047. She was a gallant ship in her day and was much dreaded by England's foes. But her end was tragic. In 1782, while at anchor in Spithead for repairs, she keeled over and sank, taking to their deaths Admiral Kempenfelt and over eight hundred men. That tragedy was the subject of a poem by Cowper which will be found on page 324.

Toward the end of the century an outstanding improvement was made in the steering gear of a ship. A wheel was used to control the rudder ropes. This was an enormous advance, for the old whipstaff or spar was clumsy to handle. Another step forward was the use of copper plates to protect the hulls of vessels.

In 1765 a ship which was to win fame and glory without end was launched. This was the Victory, Nelson's historic flagship. Her length was 186 feet and her beam 52 feet. She had three gun decks with one hundred guns. It was British skill and bravery that won the battle of Trafalgar, for the French ships were larger, faster and carried more guns.

THE UNITED STATES ALSO BUILDS GOOD SHIPS

The American navy during the Revolution was a makeshift, but in 1794 the construction of six frigates was authorized. The most famous of these, the Constitution and the United States, gave a good account of themselves during the War of 1812. The Chesapeake was captured by the British Shannon, as you know. Later larger ships of war were built.

The American frigates were of much lighter build than were the English vessels and were much faster. After the War of 1812 there began a commercial rivalry between England and the United States for control of the ocean trade. This control could be won only by the possession of faster ships. The competition began with rival packet lines from America to England. These ships had full-bodied able hulls and stout spars, sails and riggings.

The decks were flush, with a galley; the long boat, lashed to the deck, carried the live stock. There were comfortable cabins but not so comfortable quarters for steerage passengers. These vessels plowed the Atlantic with all the speed that the captain could win from the sails, but the voyages usually took from 23 to 40 days. Races took place between packets of rival companies. In 1837 the Columbus, of the Black Ball Line, and the Sheridan, of the Dramatic Line, left New York on February 2. A stake of $10,000 was to go to the packet which first made port. The Columbus won the race in 16 days.

Sails carried by these fast packets were square lower, topmast and top-gallant studding sails, skysails set on sliding gunter masts, with three reefs in the topsails and single reefs in the topgallant sails. On page 4086 these sails are shown. Splendid as the packets were, they were doomed to give front place to the fastest sailing ships that have skimmed the waves—the clippers.

WHERE SPEED MEANS PROFITS

The tea trade with China and India, the wool trade with Australia, the gold rush to California and Australia all called for speedy

Nelson's Flagship Victory.

ships, captained by men who would waste no time between port and port. It was a struggle between British and American ships, for no other nation could compare with these two. American whalers had bred skillful sailors and daring captains. British seamen had centuries of tradition behind them. So it was an interesting struggle upon which the clipper ships entered.

In the tea trade cargoes went to the fastest ships. If there were many ships in a Chinese or Indian port, the slower vessels stood a chance of not getting their holds filled. The tea merchant who first got his tea on the London market made money; so such a man was always

willing to pay more to have his cargo transported on a fast ship. The first American clipper to enter the keen competition of the tea trade was the Oriental. She made the trip from Hongkong to London in 97 days. Her beautiful lines brought every ship-lover in London to the docks to see her. Great was the astonishment when the news went out that she had been paid $30 a ton to take her cargo of tea, while English ships charging $17.50 could not get cargoes. It was her speed that made such a freight rate well worth while.

THE BEAUTY OF THE SWIFT SHIPS

The Sea Witch, built in 1846 and captained by Robert H. Waterman, was the fastest ship on the seas for the first three years of her career. A. H. Clark, in his book The Clipper Ship Era, says she had a speed far in excess of any steamship of that period. She was 890 tons, with a length of 170 feet and a breadth of 33 feet 11 inches.

She carried a cloud of canvas; three standing skysail yards, royal studding sails, ringtail, and water sails. When loaded the Sea Witch lay low on the water; her hull was painted black and her masts had a considerable rake; her figurehead was an aggressive-looking dragon, beautifully carved and gilded. She had the reputation at that time of being the handsomest ship sailing out of New York.

Captain Clark, in writing about a race between clippers, says:

No more beautiful sight can be imagined than a morning at sea, with these magnificent vessels racing in midocean, perhaps two or three of them in sight at once; the sun rising amid golden clouds; the dark blue sea flecked with glistening white caps; long low black hulls clearing a pathway of sparkling foam; towering masts, and yards covered with snowy canvas which bellies to the crisp morning breeze as if sculptured in marble.

THE LIGHTNING WHOSE RECORD FOR SPEED REMAINS UNBROKEN

Of these sea fliers the American-built clipper Lightning wore the crown for many a day. She was one of the sharpest ships ever built and was the perfect clipper. Her length was about 250 feet and her beam 50 feet. Her mainmast was 164 feet in height, and she carried 13,000 yards of canvas. She was built

years later by the British clipper Thermopylæ, which made the trip in 60 days.

The last and best-known of the clippers, the Cutty Sark, was built in 1869 and is still spreading her canvas to the winds. She was in the tea trade for three voyages before she started in the wool trade, flying between Australia and England. When steamships captured the most important trade of the world, she

The Silver Heron, an English frigate of the sixteenth century, was copied in detail by Frank Lloyd for his moving picture The Sea Hawk. Our photograph shows the marvelous replica of the ancient ship spreading sail off the California coast.
Photo, Kadel & Herbert.

by Donald Mackay, a Nova Scotian who had made his home in Boston, and she was owned by the Black Ball Line of Liverpool. Her first commander was Captain "Bully" Forbes, whose name was an everyday word among seamen of the time.

It was on February 18, 1854, that the Lightning sailed on her maiden voyage from Boston to Liverpool, making the trip in less than 14 days. In one day she made 436 miles, the record for any sailing vessel in any age. Her next record run was that from Australia to Liverpool in 64 days. This was beaten some

became a tramp, picking up cargoes wherever she could find them.

Beautiful and speedy though the clippers were, their reign was very short. Iron ships, engine-driven, became common upon the sea lanes. Against the speed of these invaders the wooden sailing ships had to give way; their day was over. For a few years they picked up odd cargoes, but at length those failed. For transoceanic commerce or travel clippers were out of date. Of the vessels which took the place of these canvas-winged birds we can read on page 6397.

THE NEXT STORY OF FAMILIAR THINGS IS ON PAGE 4051.

THE LIGHT THAT EXPLAINS THE STARS TO US

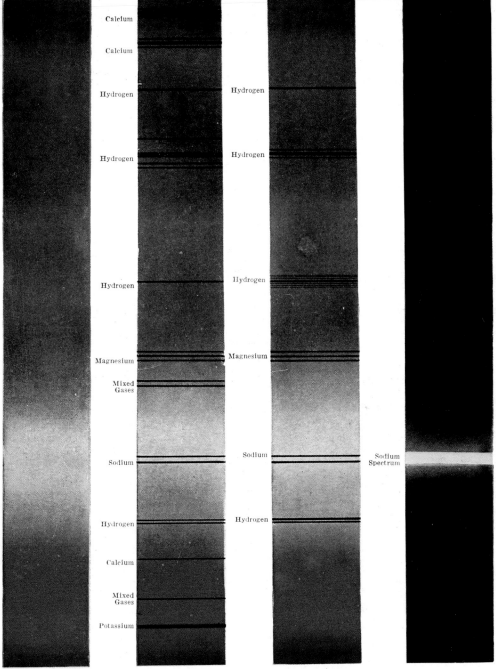

Calcium
Calcium
Hydrogen
Hydrogen
Hydrogen
Magnesium
Mixed Gases
Sodium
Hydrogen
Calcium
Mixed Gases
Potassium

Hydrogen
Hydrogen
Hydrogen
Magnesium
Sodium
Hydrogen

Sodium Spectrum

When pure light, as from a white-hot iron, passes through a glass prism, it is broken up into seven colors, called the spectrum, as shown in the first picture. But light from the sun shows, in addition to the colors, various lines, as seen in the second picture. These lines are caused by some of the different substances that compose the sun. Although here we see only a few lines, the sun's spectrum really shows over 2,000 lines. The third picture is the spectrum of a star, Sirius, and when compared with that of the sun, it shows that the stars are made of the same materials as the sun and earth, because the lines in the spectrum for different substances always appear in the same position in relation to each other, as can be seen by comparing these spectra of the sun and Sirius. Although the spectrum color of the metal sodium is yellow, as in the fourth picture, this appears dark in the sun and star spectra because of the intense light behind it, just as a gas-jet seen in front of the sun's disk appears black; but of course sodium is in the same position in all the spectra.

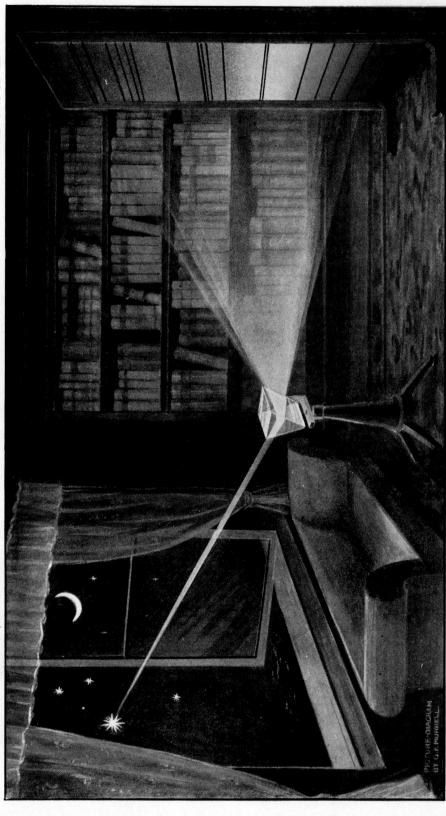

PICTURE-DIAGRAM
BY G.F. MORRELL.

This picture shows us how the spectroscope is used to enable men to catch the light of a star, and by passing it through a glass prism to break up the light into various colors. As different metals give off different colors, we can in this way tell of what the stars are made. This picture does not show the whole spectroscope, but illustrates the principle.

Earth compared with the sun.   The sun compared with Betelgeuse.

How like a speck is the earth if we compare it with the sun. But how
like a speck is the sun if we compare it with another star—Betelgeuse!

WHAT WE KNOW ABOUT THE STARS

COULD we go wandering through endless ages among the giant host of stars, surely we should learn how stars are born, how they grow, how they shrink or decay, how their light fades into darkness till they become dead suns. For among them must be suns in every stage of being: suns formed like our own, and suns altogether different from ours in size, in movement, in history, in fate. Something we might learn, too, of the meaning of the movements of the stars, whither they are going, what their journey, and what their companionship.

Yet, unless we grew in understanding with the ages of our journey, the intricate maze of the movement of the stars would not be easier to thread than it is from our standpoint in this little earth of ours. Even if we should pass to the boundaries of the Milky Way and look on the farthest star, the secret of the path the universe takes would still elude us.

Ours is the humbler hope of learning from our small earthly platform how far distant the stars are, how they move, and whither. We seek to know something also of their history and structure. Then by piecing these bits

CONTINUED FROM 3790

of knowledge together we may learn the shape of the universe to which they belong and a little of the laws that govern it. Two things we most want to know: the history of stars and their distances. The history of the stars would unfold itself as we plunged through space in the strange varieties of suns we encountered. There would be stars of different ages denoted by their colors: Sirius and Vega white and almost bluish white; Capella yellower than the sun; Arcturus, which is orange; Aldebaran, Antares and Betelgeuse all red; and another star redder still, though not very bright, which was called the Garnet Star.

One would naturally think of such stars as being young when they were white, growing yellower when their youth was past, and fading to a red glow in old age. There are no stars that are green or blue, but in the telescope some which are twin companions show all sorts of colors. But from the earth we can learn a great deal about the age of stars, what gives them their colors, and what they are like, though their distance is too great for us to measure. The same instrument that tells us these things will tell

3921

us also whether the stars are moving away from us or toward us. So, although a description of the spectroscope may be a little difficult, it will be worth while to give the explanation.

Light is of many kinds and colors. Coal-gas flame is different from that of calcium light, and both are different from the light given by the carbons of an electric arc, or from the gas mantle, or the osmium filaments of the electric bulb, and all are different from the light of our sun, or from the light which iron would give out when white hot. If a pinch of salt — which contains sodium — were dropped in any of these lights, its color would change again. The stars might be flaming with some or all of the substances which give out such lights; but, appearing only as specks of light, they would not tell the eye of their differences.

THE PRISM THAT BREAKS UP LIGHT INTO A RAINBOW BAND

But there is a way by which they can be told apart. Suppose the light is made to travel through one of the triangular columns of glass which our grandmothers used to hang as "lustres" on their mantelpieces, and which are still to be seen on crystal chandeliers in old houses.

A prism is its proper name. Light of all colors travels at the same speed, but just as there are big waves and little ripples at sea, so light of different colors comes in waves of varying size. When it passes through one side of the triangular prism and comes out at another, it is checked and spread out, like the rolling wave on a beach, so that all the colors appear in a rainbow band. Everyone has seen sunlight spread out like that. All the other lights of hydrogen, carbon, calcium, iron, sodium would be spread out in the same way, and the rainbow bands are different in each case.

If this were all, we still should not be able to identify the glimmer of light from a star; but it is not all. When that rainbow band from the sun is spread out by a very delicate prism into a rainbow band some nine feet across, it presents a very peculiar appearance. It is streaked by perpendicular dark lines. There are more than 5,000 of them and every line has its meaning. The lines are the visiting cards by which hydrogen, carbon, iron, calcium and other elements signify their presence in the flame which has produced the light.

Let us now see what the rainbow band and its lines—which are sometimes bright and sometimes dark—can tell us about the solids and the gases that are in the sun and the stars. We can learn by making experiments with bodies that are heated red hot, white hot, melted, and then heated till they turn into gas, what the rainbow band looks like when it is created by the light coming from such sources. If the light comes from a glowing solid, there is just a plain rainbow band of red, orange, yellow, green, blue, violet, with no lines on it. The bright lines merge into the colors. When the light comes from a glowing gas, there are, instead, a number of bright lines, each standing by itself. If the hot solid body is overlaid with gas cooler than the hot body, then dark lines appear on the band where bright lines would be distinguished if the gas were shining alone.

WHAT THE SPECTROSCOPE CAN TELL US OF THE GASES OF THE SUN

Now let us examine the light coming from the sun, or Sirius, or the Pole Star, or the most distant star that can send a light-message to earth. Take the sun first. There are dark lines there exactly in the places where bright lines would be if iron were heated till it became a gas that gave out light. Therefore there must be iron gas in the sun's atmosphere; though this gas, hot as it is, must be cooler than the sun below. In the same way we can find, and have found, the gases of other metals known on the earth. There are on the sun clouds of calcium, of sodium, of carbon and of several other substances we know.

Again, on earth we can make hydrogen gas glow till it gives out light. That light, on going through the prism, will announce itself where the rainbow band should be by bright lines only. In the band made by light from a heavenly body such as a nebula of gas, bright lines are found in the same places. Therefore, it follows that hydrogen must be glowing in the place the light comes from.

All these five thousand lines in the rainbow band of the sun are carefully mapped, and their exact places are known, so that anything in the sun which causes them can be identified. For a long time there were a number of lines in the sun's band that could not be made by experiment with any substance or gas made to glow on earth.

THE VAST REALM OF STARS THE ASTRONOMERS HAVE FOUND

They were called the helium lines, though what helium gas was, no one knew a generation ago. Then Sir William Ramsay found helium on the earth and proved it by the rainbow band to be the same gas as in the sun.

If we have read this explanation care-fully we shall see how astronomers can say what sort of state a star is in, and with what gases it glows. They have examined the light of about 250,000 stars. Some astronomers have classified this great army, dividing it into nine army corps. Each army corps is believed to have in it stars which are in a particular state of development, so that if the commanding officer were to review the army corps by corps, he would trace the evolution of a star. There are divisions in the army corps which link them with one another, but these we need not trouble about; and, for that matter, the army corps at the beginning and end of the line are also rather more important to experts than to us who are just beginning our inquiries about the stars.

Mizar, the double star in the tail of the Great Bear.

Algol passes its dark companion.

Epsilon Lyræ, two binaries circling round one centre.

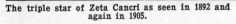

1719   1779   1802   1826   1835   1910

The relative positions at different dates of the two stars of the binary Castor, which take 950 years to revolve around each other.

The triple star of Zeta Cancri as seen in 1892 and again in 1905.

The beautiful multiple star in Orion as seen through a telescope.

Let us therefore review the army, not division by division or even corps by corps, but on a brief survey from left to right. This is supposed to be from the youngest to the oldest. According to these astronomers, the youngest are the hottest, and nothing but blazing helium and hydrogen appear on their uniforms. Then come the helium stars, still very hot, from 14,000 degrees Centigrade to

20,000 degrees, but with something solid under the helium which gives them their name. Rigel, glittering so far away, is one of the tremendous helium stars.

Then come the hydrogen stars, which have lost their helium and are falling to 10,000 degrees. Calcium appears in them, and metals. Sirius is an example of these.

Procyon, a star of about 7,500 degrees, is a captain in the next corps, where the hydrogen is fading out, the calcium and the metals increasing, and the stars becoming like our sun.

Our sun is typical of a large number of stars. The earlier divisions were white, even bluish white, or, as they grew cooler, yellowish white; but the sun is a yellow star, and those which are like it—and, like it, show as much metal as hydrogen, and more calcium—may be only as hot as 5,000 degrees.

THE DULL RED GLOW OF THE COOLING STARS IN SPACE

The other classes which follow are cooling, till the last class of all falls to 2,300 degrees, not so hot as an electric furnace. They become dull and red. They begin to flicker, though at long intervals, as if in their ashes lived their ancient fires. They grow red, the stifling carbon monoxid appears in them, and the poisonous cyanogen. Not many of these stars are near us, but two of the flickering ones are nearer to us than Sirius. They are too faint to be seen except through a telescope.

Thus, though no traveler can ever see the stars closer than now, knowledge and imagination show to him their wonders. His mind's eye can see Betelgeuse, Canopus, Arcturus, Antares, the giant stars which in size may be as great as ninety suns like ours, but which are so largely made up of gas that they may be less than five times our sun's weight. Most astronomers believe that nine-tenths of the number of the naked-eye stars are gaseous. With his telescope and his spectroscope he believes that he can see stars that are waning, and some which have lost their brightness in historic time. He will see ruddy Aldebaran, which, despite its color, is really twenty-three times as bright as our sun; and Sirius with its companion, which, although together less than four times as heavy as the sun, is thirty times as bright, and the brightest star in the constellation of Hercules toward which the sun is winging its way, a star which is double, with one companion orange and the other blue.

HOW WE CAN KNOW WHETHER A STAR IS COMING OR GOING

Among the stars that the eye plainly sees, a great number are double; that is to say, instead of having planets, they are accompanied by another sun, darker usually than themselves. But, before speaking of them, let us say another word about what the spectroscope has to tell us of these doubles, which are usually so far away from us that even a big telescope will not separate them.

When you hear the whistle of a train that is approaching, you notice that the sound becomes shriller as the train comes near. When it has passed and is going away, it falls to a lower note. That is because, as the train is approaching, the sound-waves from its whistle are becoming pushed closer together, and therefore are heard as a higher note. As the train recedes they fall farther apart and so sound lower. The same is true of light-waves. If a star is approaching, the lines on its rainbow band are shifted. They are crowded toward the violet end as the star approaches, and are dragged toward the red end if it is receding.

When the light of a star filters through the astronomer's spectroscope, the lines as they fall tell whether the star is coming or going. But there is more than that to be learned. Of the stars which have been examined thus in the sky, one out of six turns out to be a double star, or binary, as it is called. That is to say, its sun has a companion, not so large or so bright as itself, but still a great body. Our own sun has no such companion; but the earth and its moon furnish a model, on a very small scale, of a binary star.

THE STARS THE SPECTROSCOPE REVEALS AS HEAVENLY TWINS

Some double stars can be seen to be so in a big telescope. Sirius is an example. Mizar, the second star in the handle of the Plow, is a double star, as a small telescope will show; and a very little way from it is Alcor, which to the naked eye seems to belong to Mizar, but is not its true companion. But beyond all these are twins which not even the great telescopes will show to be so. The spectroscope, by the changes of its lines when the light from double stars falls on it, will reveal that a part of the light comes from one fainter

WHAT A LIGHT-YEAR IS

So vast is distance in the universe that miles are hopeless measures for astronomers, and space is measured by the distance light travels in a year. One light-year is six million million miles. How far back in history would a car at fifty miles an hour have to go before it covered the distance covered by a ray of light in a year? The answer is amazing. The car would have to run through all the ages back to the first appearance of man on earth, through the great periods of mastodons and saurians and flying-dragons, back to the days of the iguanodon and the great coal forests.

star moving round the other. Such stars are called "spectroscopic binaries," because the spectroscope alone has told astronomers of their existence and enabled calculation to say how large, how bright, how fast moving, and how far away from one another the twin suns are. There is even more to be learned than this, for the spectroscope will show that some of these far-distant systems of suns are triple. The Pole Star is a good example. Such a discovery is a marvel of man's intellect almost as great as that of the stars themselves. The mind staggers when it tries to picture three huge suns of varied brightness, whirling about one another, raising tides of flame and molten waves thousands of miles high on one another's surfaces. In the constellation of Orion is a multiple star which seems to be a double-treble star of at least six suns.

WHY THE DEMON STAR SEEMS TO TWINKLE

Sometimes the companion sun has faded nearly to darkness. That has happened with Algol, the most famous variable star in the sky, which the Arabian astronomers called the Demon Star, because every three days it winks a malevolent eye. The wink is because its dull companion, which is about the size of our sun, passes between bright Algol and ourselves. The two are only a few million miles apart.

Such stars, double and treble and multiple, are far from exhausting the variety. The heavens disclose others to the instruments that man has made to aid his insufficient vision. The stars like Algol are called "eclipsing variables," because their light is periodically eclipsed by their companions. There are other variable stars of which the light varies, sometimes in a few months, sometimes only over a length of years. The most famous of them is Mira Ceti, the "wonderful star" in the constellation of the Whale, which the astronomer Fabricius found three centuries ago. In these hundreds of years it has punctually waxed and waned every 333 days.

Another variable in Cassiopeia's Chair takes 610 days for changing; and one in the constellation of the Heavenly Twins only 86 days. There is one in the Swan which has been ten thousand times brighter in September than in April. Then there are the short-period ones which vary in a few days.

THE MILLIONS OF STARS IN THE MIGHTY MILKY WAY

Beyond nearly all these lie the stars of the Milky Way. We have said that to the naked eye fewer than ten thousand distinct stars are visible; the Milky Way—that "broad and ample road" of Milton's line, "where dust is gold, and pavement stars"—is calculated to contain 64,000,000 of them, and though Milton spoke of them as dust of gold, the larger number seem to be white stars, and probably therefore the earlier stars. We find it hard to grasp the immensities which lie between us and its ragged scarf and wisps of crowded stars. Close together they seem to us, yet between them lie the same gulfs that separate star from star of those we have described. But between them and us lies a dark abyss of space so overwhelmingly vast that a ray of light takes 3,500 years to cross it.

All of us have seen this light which set out to fall on our eyes about the time the first astronomers of Arabia and Egypt marked the heavens. In summer and autumn it stretches itself over the zenith from horizon to horizon. In one part it flows like a broad river that spreads itself in shallows; in another it narrows and is almost lost. Sometimes the outline seems sharp; sometimes it is fringed by wisps and tassels. Sometimes it is knotted and streaked; dark channels appear in it, and holes of blackness, one of which is famous as the Coal Sack.

THE NEBULA THAT SHUTS OUT THE LIGHT OF A MILLION SUNS

Almost appalling to the mind are these lanes and holes in the Milky Way, but they become less disturbing when closely examined. Then it is seen, when the highest powers of the telescope are turned on them, that some of them are not nearly so dark or so empty as they seemed. They are near to, or connected with, that nebulosity among the stars which coagulates into the objects called the gaseous nebulæ. Moreover, these dark lanes often lead from one nebulosity to another; and it is now more than suspected that they may be masses of dark unlighted nebulæ which have the power of shutting out light. At the Lick Observatory a photograph by a great telescope has, in fact, shown the dark edge of a black nebula. But think of a nebula which can shut out the light of a million suns!

THE NEXT STORY OF THE EARTH IS ON PAGE 4037.

THE POETRY OF SHAKESPEARE

IN this chapter you will find extracts from Shakespeare: some beautiful songs from his plays, some speeches from the same, and some fragments of his verse often quoted for their wisdom. The first is from the play of Hamlet, Prince of Denmark. Hamlet has feigned madness that he may observe his father's murderer. He is, further, a victim of the indecision which often hinders the action of an imaginative man. Ophelia, whom he has previously loved, now has to be given up for revenge. To her Hamlet keeps up the appearance of madness and convinces her. Then Polonius, Ophelia's father, hides behind the arras to spy upon Hamlet and is killed. Fate proves too unkind: Ophelia loses her reason, Laertes, returning from France, finds his father dead and his sister mad.

SPEECHES FROM SHAKESPEARE

HAMLET: To be, or not to be: that is the question:
Whether 'tis nobler in the mind to suffer
The slings and arrows of outrageous fortune,
Or to take arms against a sea of troubles,
And by opposing end them? To die: to sleep;
No more; and by a sleep to say we end
The heart-ache and the thousand natural shocks
That flesh is heir to, 'tis a consummation
Devoutly to be wish'd. To die, to sleep;
To sleep: perchance to dream: ay, there's the rub;
For in that sleep of death what dreams may come
When we have shuffled off this mortal coil,
Must give us pause: there's the respect
That makes calamity of so long life;
For who would bear the whips and scorns of time,
The oppressor's wrong, the proud man's contumely,
The pangs of despised love, the law's delay,
The insolence of office and the spurns
That patient merit of the unworthy takes,
When he himself might his quietus make
With a bare bodkin? who would fardels bear,
To grunt and sweat under a weary life,
But that the dread of something after death,
The undiscover'd country from whose bourn
No traveller returns, puzzles the will
And makes us rather bear those ills we have
Than fly to others that we know not of?
Thus conscience does make cowards of us all;
And thus the native hue of resolution
Is sicklied o'er with the pale cast of thought,
And enterprises of great pitch and moment
With this regard their currents turn awry,
And lose the name of action.
                    —ACT III, *Scene* I

CONTINUED FROM 3743

Laertes: O heat, dry up my brains! tears seven times salt,
    Burn out the sense and virtue of mine eye!
By heaven, thy madness shall be paid with weight,
Till our scale turn the beam. O rose of May!
Dear maid, kind sister, sweet Ophelia!
O heavens! is't possible, a young maid's wits
Should be as mortal as an old man's life?
Nature is fine in love, and where 'tis fine,
It sends some precious instance of itself
After the thing it loves.
  Ophelia (sings):
    They bore him barefaced on the bier:
    Hey non nonny, nonny, hey nonny:
    And in his grave rain'd many a tear:—
Fare you well, my dove!
  Laertes: Hadst thou thy wits, and didst persuade revenge,
It could not move thus.
  Ophelia (sings):
    You must sing a-down a-down,
    An you call him a-down-a,
O, how the wheel becomes it! It is the false steward, that stole his master's daughter.
  Laertes: This nothing's more than matter.
  Ophelia: There's rosemary, that's for remembrance; pray, love, remember: and there is pansies, that's for thoughts.
  Laertes: A document in madness, thoughts and remembrance fitted.
  Ophelia: There's fennel for you, and columbines: there's rue for you; and here's some for me; we may call it herb-grace o' Sundays; O, you must wear your rue with a difference. There's a daisy; I would give you some violets, but they withered all when my father died; they say he made a good end,—
      (Sings):
    For bonny sweet Robin is all my joy.
  Laertes: Thought and affliction, passion, hell itself,
She turns to favour and to prettiness.
                    —ACT IV, *Scene* 5

THE FALL OF CARDINAL WOLSEY

One of the greatest characters in the long roll of English history is Cardinal Wolsey, who was the foremost man in the kingdom during the earlier reign of King Henry VIII. He was a tyrant, unjust in many ways, but a patriot for all that; and when the king dismissed him from his high office, it is thus that Shakespeare, in the play of King Henry VIII, imagines him to have received his crushing blow. The Cromwell mentioned is not Oliver Cromwell, of course, as he lived later, but Wolsey's secretary, Thomas.

WOLSEY: Farewell, a long farewell, to all my greatness!
This is the state of man: to-day he puts forth
The tender leaves of hope; to-morrow blossoms,
And bears his blushing honours thick upon him;
The third day comes a frost, a killing frost;
And—when he thinks, good, easy man, full surely
His greatness is a-ripening—nips his root.
And then he falls, as I do. I have ventured,
Like little wanton boys that swim on bladders,
This many summers in a sea of glory,
But far beyond my depth: my high-blown pride
At length broke under me and now has left me,
Weary and old with service, to the mercy
Of a rude stream, that must for ever hide me.
Vain pomp and glory of this world, I hate ye;
I feel my heart new open'd: O, how wretched
Is that poor man that hangs on princes' favours!
There is, betwixt that smile we would aspire to,
That sweet aspect of princes, and their ruin,
More pangs and fears than wars or women have:
And when he falls, he falls like Lucifer,
Never to hope again.

Enter Cromwell.

Why, how now, Cromwell!

Cromwell: I have no power to speak, sir.

Wolsey: What, amazed
At my misfortunes? Can thy spirit wonder
A great man should decline? Nay, an you weep,
I am fall'n indeed.

Cromwell: How does your grace?

Wolsey: Why, well;
Never so truly happy, my good Cromwell.
I know myself now; and I feel within me
A peace above all earthly dignities,
A still and quiet conscience. The king has cured me,
I humbly thank his grace; and from these shoulders
These ruin'd pillars, out of pity, taken
A load would sink a navy, too much honour;
O, 'tis a burden, Cromwell, 'tis a burden,
Too heavy for a man that hopes for heaven.

. . . .

Go, get thee from me, Cromwell;
I am a poor fall'n man, unworthy now
To be thy lord and master: seek the king;
That sun, I pray, may never set! I have told him

What and how true thou art: he will advance thee;
Some little memory of me will stir him
(I know his noble nature), not to let
Thy hopeful service perish too: good Cromwell,
Neglect him not; make use now, and provide
For thine own future safety.

Cromwell: Oh, my lord,
Must I, then, leave you? Must I needs forego
So good, so noble, and so true a master?
Bear witness, all that have not hearts of iron,
With what a sorrow Cromwell leaves his lord.
The king shall have my service; but my prayers
For ever and ever shall be yours.

Wolsey: Cromwell, I did not think to shed a tear
In all my miseries; but thou hast forced me,
Out of thy honest truth, to play the woman.
Let's dry our eyes: and thus far, hear me, Cromwell;
And—when I am forgotten, as I shall be,
And sleep in dull, cold marble where no mention
Of me more must be heard of—say, I taught thee,
Say, Wolsey—that once trod the ways of glory,
And sounded all the depths and shoals of honour—
Found thee a way, out of his wreck, to rise in;
A sure and safe one, though thy master miss'd it.
Mark but my fall, and that that ruin'd me.
Cromwell, I charge thee, fling away ambition:
By that sin fell the angels; how can man, then,
The image of his Maker, hope to win by 't?
Love thyself last: cherish those hearts that hate thee;
Corruption wins not more than honesty.
Still in thy right hand carry gentle peace,
To silence envious tongues. Be just and fear not:
Let all the ends thou aim'st at be thy country's,
Thy God's and truth's; then if thou fall'st, O Cromwell,
Thou fall'st a blessed martyr. Serve the king;
And,—prithee, lead me in:
There take an inventory of all I have,
To the last penny; 'tis the king's: my robe,
And my integrity to heaven, is all
I dare now call mine own. O Cromwell, Cromwell,
Had I but served my God with half the zeal
I served my king, He would not in mine age
Have left me naked to mine enemies.

THE GREAT SPEECH OF MARK ANTONY

This is one of the most famous speeches written by Shakespeare. It is spoken by Antony, the friend of Julius Cæsar, over the dead body of that Roman ruler who was murdered by Brutus and Cassius and their friends. Antony sought to regain the people who had just been listening to Brutus to the side of Cæsar's friends.

FRIENDS, Romans, countrymen, lend me
   your ears;
I come to bury Cæsar, not to praise him.
The evil that men do lives after them;
The good is oft interred with their bones;
So let it be with Cæsar. The noble Brutus
Hath told you Cæsar was ambitious:
If it were so, it was a grievous fault,
And grievously hath Cæsar answer'd it.
Here, under leave of Brutus, and the rest
(For Brutus is an honourable man;
So are they all, all honourable men),
Come I to speak in Cæsar's funeral.
He was my friend, faithful and just to me:
But Brutus says he was ambitious,
And Brutus is an honourable man.
He hath brought many captives home to
   Rome,
Whose ransoms did the general coffers fill:
Did this in Cæsar seem ambitious?
When that the poor have cried, Cæsar hath
   wept;
Ambition should be made of sterner stuff:

Yet Brutus says he was ambitious,
And Brutus is an honourable man.
You all did see that on the Lupercal,
I thrice presented him a kingly crown,
Which he did thrice refuse: was this am-
   bition?
Yet Brutus says he was ambitious;
And, sure, he is an honourable man.
I speak not to disprove what Brutus spoke,
But here I am to speak what I do know.
You all did love him once, not without cause:
What cause withholds you, then, to mourn
   for him?
O judgment, thou art fled to brutish beasts,
And men have lost their reason! Bear with
   me:
My heart is in the coffin there with Cæsar,
And I must pause, till it come back to me.
  • • • • • • •
But yesterday, the word of Cæsar might
Have stood against the world: now lies he
   there,
And none so poor to do him reverence.

After Julius Cæsar had been killed, the conspirators explained their action to the people. Brutus spoke and the mob was pleased. Then Antony, the friend of Cæsar, praised the murdered ruler and showed his body. The people now turned to Antony's side, and here we see Brutus and Cassius—who wears a helmet —turning away from the angry people. The picture is by the French artist Court, photographed by Neurdein.

O masters, if I were disposed to stir
Your hearts and minds to mutiny and rage,
I should do Brutus wrong, and Cassius wrong,
Who, you all know, are honourable men:
I will not do them wrong; I rather choose
To wrong the dead, to wrong myself and you,
Than I will wrong such honourable men.
But here's a parchment, with the seal of Cæsar,
I found it in his closet, 'tis his will:
Let but the commons hear this testament
(Which, pardon me, I do not mean to read),
And they would go and kiss dead Cæsar's wounds,
And dip their napkins in his sacred blood;
Yea, beg a hair of him for memory,
And, dying, mention it within their wills,
Bequeathing it, as a rich legacy,
Unto their issue.

. . . .

If you have tears, prepare to shed them now.
You all do know this mantle: I remember
The first time ever Cæsar put it on;
'Twas on a summer's evening, in his tent;
That day he overcame the Nervii:
Look! In this place ran Cassius' dagger through:
See what a rent the envious Casca made:
Through this the well-beloved Brutus stabb'd;
And, as he pluck'd his cursed steel away,
Mark how the blood of Cæsar follow'd it;
As rushing out of doors, to be resolved
If Brutus so unkindly knock'd, or no;
For Brutus, as you know, was Cæsar's angel:
Judge, O you gods, how dearly Cæsar loved him!
This was the most unkindest cut of all;
For when the noble Cæsar saw him stab,
Ingratitude, more strong than traitors' arms,
Quite vanquish'd him: then burst his mighty heart;
And, in his mantle muffling up his face,
Even at the base of Pompey's statue,

Which all the while ran blood, great Cæsar fell.
O, what a fall was there, my countrymen!
Then I, and you, and all of us fell down,
Whilst bloody treason flourish'd over us.
O, now you weep; and, I perceive, you feel
The dint of pity: these are gracious drops.
Kind souls, what, weep you, when you but behold
Our Cæsar's vesture wounded? Look you here,
Here is himself, marr'd, as you see, with traitors.

. . . . .

Good friends, sweet friends, let me not stir you up
To such a sudden flood of mutiny.
They that have done this deed are honourable;
What private griefs they have, alas, I know not,
That made them do it; they are wise and honourable,
And will, no doubt, with reasons answer you.
I come not, friends, to steal away your hearts;
I am no orator, as Brutus is:
But, as you know me all, a plain blunt man,
That love my friend; and that they know full well
That gave me public leave to speak of him.
For I have neither wit, nor words, nor worth,
Action, nor utterance, nor the power of speech,
To stir men's blood; I only speak right on;
I tell you that which you yourselves do know;
Show you sweet Cæsar's wounds, poor poor dumb mouths,
And bid them speak for me: but were I Brutus,
And Brutus Antony, there were an Antony
Would ruffle up your spirits, and put a tongue
In every wound of Cæsar, that should move
The stones of Rome to rise and mutiny.

THE SHEPHERD'S HAPPY LIFE

In the play of King Henry VI the king, at the battle of Towton, is supposed to utter these thoughts, and no doubt many a king in time of trouble has envied his humblest subject. Shakespeare displays great insight into the minds of both king and shepherd.

O GOD! methinks it were a happy life,
To be no better than a homely swain;
To sit upon a hill, as I do now,
To carve out dials quaintly, point by point,
Thereby to see the minutes, how they run;
How many make the hour full complete;
How many hours bring about the day;
How many days will finish up the year;
How many years a mortal man may live;
When this is known, then to divide the times;
So many hours must I tend my flock;
So many hours must I take my rest;
So many hours must I contemplate;
So many hours must I sport myself;
So many days my ewes have been with young;
So many weeks ere the poor fools will yean;
So many years ere I shall shear the fleece.
So minutes, hours, days, weeks, months, and years,

Pass'd over to the end they were created,
Would bring white hairs unto a quiet grave.
Ah, what a life were this! how sweet! how lovely!
Gives not the hawthorn-bush a sweeter shade
To shepherds, looking on their silly sheep,
Than doth a rich embroider'd canopy
To kings that fear their subjects' treachery?
O, yes, it doth: a thousand-fold it doth.
And to conclude—the shepherd's homely curds,
His cold, thin drink out of his leather bottle,
His wonted sleep under a fresh tree's shade;
All which secure and sweetly he enjoys,
Is far beyond a prince's delicates,
His viands sparkling in a golden cup,
His body couched in a curious bed,
When care, mistrust, and treason wait on him.

A GREAT DAY FOR ENGLAND

In the play of King Henry V the scene is laid in the English camp at Agincourt, in France, just before the famous battle described in Drayton's poem on page 1885. Some of Henry's generals are discussing the outlook, and the Earl of Westmoreland is wishing they had "but one ten thousand of those men in England, who do no work to-day," to set against the out-numbering French, when the king himself comes up and says:

WHAT's he that wishes so?
My cousin Westmoreland?—No, my fair
  cousin:
If we are mark'd to die, we are enough
To do our country loss; and if to live,
The fewer men, the greater share of honour.
God's will! I pray thee, wish not one man more.
By Jove! I am not covetous for gold;
Nor care I who doth feed upon my cost;
It yearns me not, if men my garments wear;
Such outward things dwell not in my desires;
But, if it be a sin to covet honour,
I am the most offending soul alive.
No, 'faith, my coz, wish not a man from
  England:
God's peace! I would not lose so great an
  honour,
As one man more, methinks, would share
  from me,
For the best hope I have. O, do not wish
  one more!
Rather proclaim it, Westmoreland, through
  my host,
That he who hath no stomach to this fight,
Let him depart; his passport shall be made,
And crowns for convoy put into his purse.
We would not die in that man's company,
That fears his fellowship to die with us.
This day is call'd the feast of Crispian:
He that outlives this day, and comes safe home,
Will stand a-tiptoe when this day is named,
And rouse him at the name of Crispian.
He that shall live this day, and see old age,
Will yearly on the vigil feast his friends,
And say 'To-morrow is Saint Crispian':
Then he will strip his sleeve, and show his
  scars,
And say, 'These wounds I had on Crispian's
  day.'
Old men forget; yet all shall be forgot,
But he'll remember, with advantages,
What feats he did that day! Then shall our
  names
Familiar in their mouths as household words—
Harry the King, Bedford and Exeter,
Warwick and Talbot, Salisbury and Gloster,
Be in their flowing freshly cups remember'd.
This story shall the good man teach his son;
And Crispin Crispian shall ne'er go by,
From this day to the ending of the world,
But we in it shall be remember'd;
We few, we happy few, we band of brothers;
For he, to-day, that sheds his blood with me
Shall be my brother; be he ne'er so vile,
This day shall gentle his condition:
And gentlemen in England, now a-bed,
Shall think themselves accursed, they were
  not here,
And hold their manhood cheap, while any
  speaks,
That fought with us upon Saint Crispian's
  day.

THE NOBLEST ROMAN
From Julius Cæsar

Brutus was persuaded that Cæsar must die for the good of Rome, and so with the other conspirators he killed him. Later Brutus himself died, defeated, and Mark Antony, Cæsar's friend, says of him:

THIS was the noblest Roman of them all:
  All the conspirators, save only he,
Did that they did in envy of great Cæsar;
He, only, in a general honest thought,
And common good to all, made one of them.
His life was gentle, and the elements
So mix'd in him, that Nature might stand up,
And say to all the world, 'This was a man!'

THE LESSON OF THE HONEY
BEES
From King Henry V

So work the honey bees,
Creatures that, by a rule in nature teach
The act of order to a peopled kingdom.
They have a king, and officers of sorts;
Where some, like magistrates, correct at home;
Others, like merchants, venture trade abroad;
Others, like soldiers, armed in their stings,
Make boot upon the summer's velvet buds;
Which pillage they with merry march bring
  home
To the tent-royal of their emperor;
Who, busied in his majesty, surveys
The singing masons building roofs of gold;
The civil citizens kneading up the honey;
The poor mechanic porters crowding in
Their heavy burdens at his narrow gate;
The sad-eyed justice, with his surly hum,
Delivering o'er to executors pale
The lazy, yawning drone.

IN PRAISE OF ENGLAND
From Richard II

THIS royal throne of kings, this scepter'd
  isle,
This earth of majesty, this seat of Mars,
This other Eden, demi-paradise,
This fortress, built by Nature for herself
Against infection and the hand of war,
This happy breed of men, this little world,
This precious stone set in the silver sea,
Which serves it in the office of a wall,
Or as a moat defensive to a house,
Against the envy of less happier lands,
This blessed plot, this earth, this realm, this
  England.

From King John

This England never did, nor never shall,
Lie at the proud foot of a conqueror. . . .
Come the three corners of the world in arms,
And we shall shock them: Nought shall make
  us rue
If England to itself do rest but true.

A FATHER'S ADVICE TO HIS SON
From Hamlet

Polonius, an aged courtier, thus advises his son, the manly and fearless Laertes, how to behave himself in France.

GIVE thy thoughts no tongue,
Nor any unproportion'd thought his act.
Be thou familiar, but by no means vulgar.
Those friends thou hast, and their adoption tried,
Grapple them to thy soul with hoops of steel;
But do not dull thy palm with entertainment
Of each new-hatch'd, unfledged comrade. Beware
Of entrance to a quarrel, but, being in,
Bear't, that the opposer may beware of thee.
Give every man thine ear, but few thy voice;
Take each man's censure, but reserve thy judgment.
Costly thy habit as thy purse can buy,
But not express'd in fancy; rich, not gaudy:
For the apparel oft proclaims the man,
And they in France of the best rank and station
Are most select and generous, chief in that.
Neither a borrower nor a lender be:
For loan oft loses both itself and friend,
And borrowing dulls the edge of husbandry.
This above all—to thine own self be true,
And it must follow, as the night the day,
Thou canst not then be false to any man.

MAN'S GREATEST TREASURE
From King Richard II

THE purest treasure mortal times afford
Is spotless reputation; that away,
Men are but gilded loam, or painted clay.
A jewel in a ten-times-barr'd-up chest
Is a bold spirit in a loyal breast.
Mine honour is my life; both grow in one;
Take honour from me, and my life is done:
Then, dear my liege, mine honour let me try;
In that I live, and for that will I die.

THE WAYWARD DAUGHTER'S FATE
From Two Gentlemen of Verona

NO, trust me; she is peevish, sullen, froward,
Proud, disobedient, stubborn, lacking duty;
Neither regarding that she is my child,
Nor fearing me as if I were her father:
And, may I say to thee, this pride of hers,
Upon advice, hath drawn my love from her;
And where I thought the remnant of mine age
Should have been cherish'd by her child-like duty,
I now am full resolved to take a wife,
And turn her out to who will take her in;
Then let her beauty be her wedding dower;
For me and my possessions she esteems not.

A MAN'S GOOD NAME
From Othello

GOOD name in man and woman, dear my lord,
Is the immediate jewel of their souls;
Who steals my purse steals trash; 'tis something—nothing;
'Twas mine, 'tis his, and has been slave to thousands;
But he that filches from me my good name,
Robs me of that which not enriches him,
And makes me poor indeed.

THE QUALITY OF MERCY
From The Merchant of Venice

Portia, disguised as a young lawyer acting for old Bellario, tries to show Shylock the Jew why he should be merciful and not exact the penalty from Antonio for forfeiting his bond.

THE quality of mercy is not strained;
It droppeth, as the gentle rain from heaven
Upon the place beneath; it is twice bless'd—
It blesseth him that gives, and him that takes.
'Tis mightiest in the mightiest: it becomes
The thronèd monarch better than his crown;
His sceptre shows the force of temporal power,
The attribute to awe and majesty,
Wherein doth sit the dread and fear of kings;
But mercy is above this sceptred sway,
It is enthronèd in the hearts of kings,
It is an attribute to God Himself;
And earthly power doth then show likest God's,
When mercy seasons justice. Therefore, Jew,
Though justice be thy plea, consider this—
That in the course of justice, none of us
Should see salvation: we do pray for mercy;
And that same prayer doth teach us all to render
The deeds of mercy.

FRIENDS AND FLATTERERS
From verses written to music

EVERY one that flatters thee,
Is no friend in misery.
Words are easy, like the wind;
Faithful friends are hard to find.
Every man will be thy friend,
Whilst thou hast wherewith to spend;
But if store of crowns be scant,
No man shall supply thy want.
If that one be prodigal,
Bountiful they will him call:
And with such-like flattering,
"Pity but he were a king."
But if fortune once do frown,
Then farewell his great renown:
They that fawn'd on him before
Use his company no more.
He that is thy friend indeed,
He will help thee in thy need,
If thou sorrow, he will weep;
If thou wake, he cannot sleep:
Thus of every grief in heart
He with thee doth bear a part.
These are certain signs to know
Faithful friend from flattering foe.

THE LIGHT OF OUR VIRTUES
From Measure for Measure

THYSELF and thy belongings
Are not thine own so proper as to waste
Thyself upon thy virtues, they on thee.
Heaven doth with us as we with torches do;
Not light them for themselves; for if our virtues
Did not go forth of us, 'twere all alike
As if we had them not. Spirits are not finely touched
But to fine issues, nor Nature never lends
The smallest scruple of her excellence;
But, like a thrifty goddess, she determines
Herself the glory of a creditor,
Both thanks and use.

THE SEVEN AGES OF MAN

This famous quotation is from As You Like It. Shakespeare places it in the mouth of Jacques, one of the followers of the exiled Duke, and a somewhat gloomy but philosophical sort of man. He is at times very amusing in his reflections on the world in general. A "pard" is a leopard, a "capon" is a tender chicken, and "sans" is the French word for "without," but is sometimes used as an English word.

ALL the world's a stage,
And all the men and women merely players:
They have their exits, and their entrances;
And one man in his time plays many parts,
His acts being seven ages. At first, the infant,
Mewling and puking in the nurse's arms;
And then the whining schoolboy, with his satchel,
And shining morning face, creeping like snail
Unwillingly to school. And then, the lover,
Sighing like furnace, with a woeful ballad
Made to his mistress' eyebrow. Then a soldier,
Full of strange oaths and bearded like the pard,
Jealous in honour, sudden and quick in quarrel,
Seeking the bubble reputation
Even in the cannon's mouth. And then, the justice,
In fair round belly, with good capon lined,
With eyes severe, and beard of formal cut,
Full of wise saws and modern instances,
And so he plays his part. The sixth age shifts
Into the lean and slipper'd pantaloon;
With spectacles on nose, and pouch on side,
His youthful hose, well saved, a world too wide
For his shrunk shank; and his big manly voice,
Turning again toward childish treble, pipes
And whistles in his sound. Last scene of all,
That ends this strange, eventful history,
Is second childishness, and mere oblivion,
Sans teeth, sans eyes, sans taste, sans everything.

WISE SAYINGS FROM SHAKESPEARE

HOW far that little candle throws its beams!
So shines a good deed in a naughty world.
Merchant of Venice

And oftentimes, excusing of a fault
Doth make the fault be worse by the excuse.
King John

O! it is excellent
To have a giant's strength; but it is tyrannous
To use it like a giant.
Measure for Measure

But 'tis a common proof
That lowliness is young ambition's ladder,
Whereto the climber—upward turns his face:
But when he once attains the upmost round,
He then unto the ladder turns his back,
Looks in the clouds, scorning the base degrees
By which he did ascend.
Julius Cæsar

Cowards die many times before their deaths;
The valiant never taste of death but once.
Of all the wonders that I yet have heard,
It seems to me most strange, that men should fear;
Seeing that death, a necessary end,
Will come when it will come.
Julius Cæsar

There is a tide in the affairs of men,
Which, taken at the flood, leads on to fortune;
Omitted, all the voyage of their life
Is bound in shallows, and in miseries.
On such a full sea are we now afloat;
And we must take the current when it serves,
Or lose our ventures.
Julius Cæsar

How oft the sight of means to do ill deeds,
Makes ill deeds done!
King John

I dare do all that may become a man;
Who dares do more, is none.
Macbeth

To be a queen in bondage is more vile
Than is a slave in base servility;
For princes should be free.
King Henry VI

Life every man holds dear; but the brave man
Holds honour far more precious dear than life.
Troilus and Cressida

To gild refined gold, to paint the lily,
To throw a perfume on the violet,
To smooth the ice, or add another hue
Unto the rainbow, or with taper-light
To seek the beauteous eye of heaven to garnish,
Is wasteful, and ridiculous excess.
King John

If all the year were playing holidays,
To sport would be as tedious as to work;
But when they seldom come they wish'd for come,
And nothing pleaseth but rare accidents.
King Henry IV

What stronger breastplate than a heart untainted!
Thrice is he armed that hath his quarrel just;
And he but naked, though lock'd up in steel,
Whose conscience with injustice is corrupted.
King Henry VI

At Christmas I no more desire a rose,
Than wish a snow in May's new-fangled mirth;
But like of each thing that in season grows.
Love's Labour's Lost

Our doubts are traitors,
And make us lose the good we oft might win,
By fearing to attempt.
Measure for Measure

A friend should bear his friend's infirmities.
Julius Cæsar

SONGS FROM SHAKESPEARE

WHO IS SYLVIA?

Words from Two Gentlemen of Verona

Music by Schubert

In moderate time

1. Who is Syl - via, what is she?.... That all our swains com - mend her. Ho - ly, fair,...... and wise is she,...... The heav'ns such grace did lend........ her; That ad - mir - ed
2. Is she kind...... as she's fair?.... For beau - ty lives with kind - ness: Love doth to......... her eyes re - pair,..... To help him of his blind - ness; And, being help'd,
3. Then to Syl - via let us sing,.... That Syl - via is ex - cel - ing; She ex - cels...... each mor - tal thing,.... Up - on the dull earth dwell - ing; Let us gar - lands

pp

A LOVER AND HIS LASS

Words from As You Like It

Music by Thomas Morley

on-ly pret-ty ring time, When birds do sing—hey ding a ding a ding, hey

ding a ding a ding, hey ding a ding a ding, Sweet lov-ers love the Spring.

O, WILLOW, WILLOW

Words from Othello   Traditional Air

Andante

A poor soul sat sigh-ing by a syc-a-more tree, Sing
He sighed in his sigh-ing and...... made a great moan, Sing

wil - low, wil-low, wil - low, With his hand in his bo - som and his head up - on his
wil - low, wil-low, wil - low, I am dead to all plea - sure, my true love she is

knee! } Oh! wil-low, wil-low, wil-low, wil-low! Oh! wil-low, wil-low, wil-low, wil-low my
gone. }

gar - land shall be, Sing all a green wil - low, wil - low, wil-low,

wil - low, Ah! me...... the green wil - low my gar - land must be.

WHAT WE LEARN IN THIS ARTICLE

IN other volumes of our book you learn the history of our land from the beginning, but there was so much to tell that we could not mention every event. Here you are given a list of the presidents of the United States and are told the most important events which occurred during the term or terms of each of them. You will find it a very convenient storehouse of facts, though it is not so interesting as the story of the growth of our country. You will see that during some administrations everything was quiet and very few important events can be named. At other times, many things happened every year.

ADMINISTRATIONS OF THE PRESIDENTS

GEORGE WASHING-TON. First President. Two Terms, 1789-1797.

CONTINUED FROM 3782

With the adoption of the Constitution and the acceptance by a sufficient number of states came the election of the first president of the United States, George Washington. He served two terms—from 1789 to 1793 and from 1793 to 1797—but refused to hold the office a third term. North Carolina and Rhode Island which at first refused to accept the Constitution soon agreed to do so.

His administrations were periods of growth for the new nation, and the wisdom of President Washington enforced peace throughout the land, though there was an uprising known as the Whisky Rebellion in Pennsylvania. Unfriendly Indians were routed by General Wayne. During his first term officers were appointed to carry on the new government, money was somehow found to run it, the national debt was arranged, thus establishing the credit of the new nation, the Bank of the United States was opened, a mint was established, and we adopted the decimal money system of dollars, dimes and cents.

The prosperity of the country was greatly increased by the invention of the cotton gin by Eli Whitney; peace was secured by Jay's treaty with England and by a treaty with Spain. However, the disputes with France made difficulties for the new government. France expected us to help in her war against England, but Washington refused. The number of states in the Union was increased to sixteen by the addition of Vermont (1791), Kentucky (1792) and Tennessee (1796).

JOHN ADAMS. Federalist. Second President. One Term, 1797-1801.

In 1797 John Adams, of Massachusetts, who had been vice-president under Washington, became president of the United States. By this time political parties were developing. They were called Federalist and Republican. During Washington's administration, the French had asked our assistance, and now, in Adams' administration, the corrupt government of France threatened to fight us unless we bribed them with money, "plenty of money." A wave of indignation swept over the United States. We are told that Pinckney, our minister to France at that time, said: "Millions for defense, but not one cent for tribute." Whether he used these words or not, they expressed his sentiments. Soon a short and irregular war opened between our country and France. The United States captured two or three French battleships and several privateers, while our privateers took many French merchant ships. War was not declared, however.

Adams' administration was unfortunate for him, as, owing to the trouble occasioned by foreigners who tried to stir up American citizens to help them in their war against England, Congress passed new laws, called the Alien and Sedition Acts, providing punishment for foreigners who were bent upon mischief, and for all persons who spoke or wrote against the government. These laws were short-lived, and although it was never necessary to put the first into effect, yet they made President Adams very unpopular. The Kentucky and Virginia legislatures adopted resolutions saying that the government had gone beyond its powers.

THOMAS JEFFERSON. Republican. Third President. Two Terms, 1801–1809.

Though President Adams was a candidate for re-election, he was defeated by the candidate of the new Republican party, Thomas Jefferson, of Virginia, who had been vice-president. Jefferson and Aaron Burr received the same number of votes, but the former was chosen by the House of Representatives. According to the Constitution as it was then, Burr became vice-president. Jefferson served for two terms, from 1801 to 1809, but Burr had only one term.

His administration was an eventful one for our country. The pirates of Algiers and Tripoli, who for years had demanded tribute from our vessels, were completely subdued by our warships, so that we were troubled by them only once afterward. In 1803 an immense tract of land, which nearly doubled the area of the United States, was obtained for us from France through the Louisiana Purchase, and was partly explored by Lewis and Clarke in 1804–1806. Louisiana then meant the country west of the Mississippi, which was drained by that river, and from it thirteen states have been made, wholly or in part. The price paid was $15,000,-000. In 1807 the first successful steamship, invented by Robert Fulton, sailed up the Hudson River. Ohio was admitted to the Union in 1803. The vice-president, Aaron Burr, killed Alexander Hamilton in a duel in 1804.

Great Britain was then at war with Napoleon, and each forbade us to send ships to the other. Jefferson had Congress pass the Embargo Act, in 1807, refusing to trade with any foreign country. This caused hard times in this country but did not make either party to the war agree to let our ships alone.

JAMES MADISON. Republican. Fourth President. Two Terms, 1809–1817.

James Madison, also of Virginia, became president in 1809, and served two terms. Trouble with England and with Napoleon continued, and it was seen that war must come. Both had injured us, and some of our citizens wished to declare war on both. England had harmed us most, because she had more ships, and besides had stopped many American ships and taken off sailors, claiming that they were British subjects. Some of them were deserters from British ships, but others were naturalized citizens, or even American born. War was declared against Great Britain on June 19, 1812.

Though the American navy was small, the ships were good, and several British ships were defeated in fair fight, as told on pages 6329–32; but the attempts to invade Canada were not successful, though York (now Toronto) was taken and burned. In revenge the British burned the public buildings in Washington. In a battle fought at New Orleans January 8, 1815, after peace had been declared but before the news had crossed the water, Andrew Jackson, with an army of backwoodsmen, defeated a force of British regulars. The treaty of peace had been signed at Ghent, December 24, 1814, but there were neither cables nor fast steamships then. The first Bank of the United States came to an end in 1811, and another was chartered in 1816. During Madison's administrations, two new states, Louisiana (1812) and Indiana (1816), were added to the Union.

JAMES MONROE. Republican. Fifth President. Two Terms, 1817–1825.

Our fifth president, James Monroe, also from Virginia, had fought in the Revolution and had been sent to France to arrange the purchase of Louisiana. He came into office when the country was recovering from the War of 1812, and in the following years the young republic advanced by leaps and bounds. Florida was purchased from Spain and made a territory of the United States; five new states — Mississippi (1817), Illinois (1818), Alabama (1819), Maine (1820) and Missouri (1821)—were added to the Union; and the people poured over the Alleghenies into the rich bottom lands in the Mississippi Valley. The dispute over admitting Missouri as a slave state was settled by the Missouri Compromise.

The "Monroe Doctrine," forbidding the further colonization of the western hemisphere, or interference with the governments of the republics of South and Central America by European powers, was set forth during this administration.

The Federalist party had opposed the War of 1812, and had almost died out. Party feeling was not so strong, and no candidate opposed Monroe at the election in 1820. It is said that one elector refused to vote for him, saying no man except Washington should receive every vote.

JOHN QUINCY ADAMS. National Republican. Sixth President. One Term, 1825-1829.

At the election of 1824 all four candidates called themselves Republicans, though they differed very much in their ideas. No one received a majority of the electoral votes and so it was the duty of the House of Representatives to elect. John Quincy Adams, a son of the second president, was chosen, though Andrew Jackson had received more electoral votes. While Adams was president the Erie Canal from Albany, on the Hudson River, to Buffalo, on Lake Erie, was completed (1825), making travel to the West far cheaper and easier in every way. It also helped in building up cities and towns in the western part of New York State. President Adams and Congress could not agree and very few important laws were passed during his administration. The Republican party during this period had often been called the Democratic-Republican and now the second part of the name was dropped, and the party has been called Democratic ever since. President Adams was a candidate for re-election, but was beaten by Andrew Jackson.

ANDREW JACKSON. Democrat. Seventh President. Two Terms, 1829-1837.

Andrew Jackson, of Tennessee, was one of the best loved and most hated presidents of the United States. He was elected in 1828 and held office two terms. Not long after his inauguration a newspaper came into existence under the editorship of a young man named William Lloyd Garrison. It was called The Liberator and was in favor of freedom for the slaves in the South. This was thought a wild idea at the time and created a great stir.

About this time South Carolina, under the leadership of John C. Calhoun, objected to a law passed by Congress increasing the tax on all cotton and woolen goods imported from abroad, as the Southerners said they could clothe their slaves much cheaper on imported material than on material sold by manufacturers in the North. The state declared that the law should not be enforced in that state. This was called Nullification. The people became so heated over the matter that war between South Carolina and the Union was prevented only by the firmness of President Jackson and by the wisdom of Henry Clay, who persuaded Congress to make the tax lighter (1832).

The most of the Indians in the East were removed to lands across the Mississippi River, but in some cases resisted by force. President Jackson opposed the United States Bank and helped to destroy it. A new charter was refused. The surplus money in the treasury of the United States was distributed to the states. France paid the money due for damage to United States ships in Napoleon's time. During General Jackson's administration two new states were added to the Union, Arkansas (1836) and Michigan (1837), making twenty-six in all, thus doubling the number of the original states. The first steam railroads began during this administration. The opponents of President Jackson began to call themselves Whigs during his second term.

MARTIN VAN BUREN. Democrat. Eighth President. One Term, 1837-1841.

In the election of 1836 Martin Van Buren, of New York, the vice-president, was chosen president. Shortly after his election the wonderful progress of our young nation was interrupted for a space by hard times and money difficulties throughout the country, but the progress was not stopped long. Steamships began to make regular trips across the Atlantic. Immigrants began to come in from Europe, and the West developed very rapidly as more canals and railroads were built. There was a sharp little war with the Seminole Indians in Florida.

WILLIAM HENRY HARRISON. Whig. Ninth President. JOHN TYLER. Whig. Tenth President. One Term, 1841-1845.

President Van Buren served only one term and was followed by General Harrison, who had won the memorable victory over the Indians at Tippecanoe. His services had not been forgotten by the American people. With shouts and songs of "Tippecanoe and Tyler too," he was elected to the office of chief executive in 1840. But he lived only a few weeks after he took office, and John Tyler, of Virginia, his vice-president, succeeded him in office. The Whigs were not very well united, and Tyler quarreled with many of the leaders of the party. Times once more became prosperous. The first telegraph instrument was invented by Professor Morse and a line was constructed from Washington to Baltimore in 1844. Since then telegraph lines have been constructed over all the known world.

A treaty was made with Great Britain to settle the boundary between Maine and Canada. This was the Webster-Ashburton Treaty. Texas had declared its independence of Mexico and set up as a republic, but asked to be annexed to the United States. During the last months of Tyler's administration a treaty annexing Texas was signed, but it was not admitted as a state until Polk's administration. Florida, however, was admitted the day before Tyler went out of office. The Mormons were driven out of Illinois in 1844. Henry Clay was the Whig candidate at the election in 1844 but was defeated by the Democratic candidate.

JAMES K. POLK. Democrat. Eleventh President. One Term, 1845–1849.

James K. Polk, of Tennessee, who served one term, came to this office in 1845, when the whole country was ringing with the cry "Fifty-four forty or fight." This meant that the northern boundary of the United States was to reach to the southern boundary of Alaska, then a possession of Russia. The region known as the Oregon country was claimed by both Great Britain and the United States. For a while the two nations nearly came to blows over the matter. Finally, in 1846, it was settled by an agreement dividing the Pacific territory between them.

In that same year, 1846, we declared war with Mexico over a strip of land which both that country and the state of Texas claimed to own. Every battle fought in the war we gained, and when the war closed a large tract of land was given up by Mexico, including not only the territory in dispute, but also what is now California, Utah, Nevada and parts of New Mexico, Arizona, Colorado and Wyoming. We paid $15,000,000.

During Polk's administration three new states, Texas (1845), Iowa (1846), and Wisconsin (1848), joined the Union, making thirty states in all. Just before the war with Mexico closed, gold was discovered in California and there was a mad rush to the West, thus rapidly settling that part of the Pacific coast.

ZACHARY TAYLOR. Whig. Twelfth President. MILLARD FILLMORE. Whig. Thirteenth President. One Term, 1849–1853.

In 1848 General Zachary Taylor, of Louisiana, was elected our twelfth president, and not long after his inauguration California asked to come into the Union as a free state. The South, under the leadership of Calhoun, bitterly opposed this, wishing it to enter as a slave state. For some time Congress disputed the matter, but finally, after President Taylor had died, and Fillmore, his vice-president, had succeeded him, a plan of compromise proposed by Henry Clay was accepted, whereby in 1850 California was admitted as a free state, while nothing was said about slavery in the territory taken from Mexico; the slave trade was forbidden in the District of Columbia; also a new Fugitive Slave Law was passed by Congress enabling slave-holders to catch their runaway slaves in the North. The famous book, Uncle Tom's Cabin, was published in 1852. From this time on the dispute about slavery was very bitter. In the election of 1852 the Whig candidate, General Winfield Scott, was defeated by the Democratic candidate. There was a Free-Soil candidate, J. P. Hale, but he got no electoral votes.

FRANKLIN PIERCE. Democrat. Fourteenth President. One Term, 1853–1857.

Our fourteenth president, Franklin Pierce, of New Hampshire, was inaugurated in 1853, and during his term of office the dispute between the North and South upon the slavery question became more bitter than ever. Stephen A. Douglas, the wonderful orator of the West, persuaded Congress to make two territories of Kansas and Nebraska, giving them the right to choose whether they would have slaves or not. Immigrants to Kansas from the North wished to have it free; immigrants from the South determined to own slaves, and the result was that Kansas became a battlefield, with the two parties ready to fly at each other's throats on sight. So long and so disgraceful was the feud that the new territory

THE HOMES OF TWO PRESIDENTS

Photo, by De Cou, from Ewing Galloway.

After he became prosperous Andrew Jackson lived in this house, which he called the Hermitage, near Nashville, Tennessee. After he retired from the presidency in 1837 he lived quietly here, but hundreds of admirers from all parts of the Union called to pay their respects every year until his death in 1845.

When Abraham Lincoln went to live in Springfield, Illinois, he was a poor young lawyer. Later he lived in this house, which was comfortable, though not at all an impressive structure. Here he was living when he was elected to the presidency, and continued to look upon it as his home. The house is still standing, and the picture represents it as it is to-day.

became known as "Bleeding Kansas." Some territory known as the Gadsden Purchase was bought from Mexico for the sum of $10,000,000, and a treaty opening Japan to trade was also an important event.

The men opposed to slavery organized a new party which they called the Republican. This must not be confused with the Republican party of Jefferson, which is now called Democratic. Those opposed to admitting foreigners to the United States organized the American, or Know-Nothing, party. In the election of 1856 the Republican candidate was John C. Fremont, the American was ex-President Fillmore and the Democrats nominated James Buchanan, who was successful.

JAMES BUCHANAN. Democrat. Fifteenth President. One Term, 1857-1861.

With the coming of James Buchanan, of Pennsylvania, to the presidency in 1857, the discussion over slavery became still more bitter. The Dred Scott Decision of the Supreme Court declared that negroes could not become citizens, and that Congress could not keep slavery out of the territories. Many states in the North refused to return runaway slaves, and in fact helped to hide them and to send them to Canada. John Brown, who had been protesting against slavery in Kansas, made a raid upon Harper's Ferry, Virginia, captured the arsenal, and attempted to excite the slaves to rise and kill the whites. He was captured, tried and hanged by the state of Virginia.

The Democratic party split into a northern and a southern branch. The first nominated Stephen A. Douglas, the second John C. Breckinridge. The Constitutional Union party nominated John Bell, while the Republicans nominated Abraham Lincoln. Because of the many candidates Lincoln was elected, though he did not have a majority of the popular vote.

Before President Buchanan's term was over, seven states had seceded from the Union because a Republican president had been elected. President Buchanan did not think that states had a right to secede, but he did not think that he had a right to keep them in by force either.

Three states, Minnesota (1858), Oregon (1859) and Kansas (1861), were admitted to the Union during this administration.

ABRAHAM LINCOLN. Republican. Sixteenth President. ANDREW JOHNSON. Republican. Seventeenth President. Two Terms, 1861-1869.

In November, 1860, Abraham Lincoln, of Illinois, the Republican candidate, was elected the sixteenth president of the United States, and soon South Carolina seceded from the Union. Before Lincoln had been inaugurated, Mississippi, Georgia, Florida, Alabama, Louisiana and Texas had followed her lead. When Lincoln came into office, in 1861, the country was ready for war, and action opened with the capture of Fort Sumter, April 14, 1861, by the Southerners. President Lincoln at once called for 75,000 men, and Virginia, Arkansas, Tennessee and North Carolina seceded, rather than fight against the other southern states.

The story of the war and of the freeing of the slaves is told in the chapter called The Brothers' War. Lincoln was re-elected in 1864 over General George B. McClellan. The war was practically ended by the surrender of the army of General Robert E. Lee at Appomattox, April 9, 1865. A few days later (April 14) all were shocked to hear that the president had been fatally wounded by John Wilkes Booth. West Virginia (1863) and Nevada (1864) became states during Lincoln's term. The Thirteenth Amendment freeing the slaves became a part of the Constitution in 1865.

Vice-President Andrew Johnson, of Tennessee, at once became president. He was not a popular man, and in 1868 a number of the members of Congress attempted to remove him from office, but they did not succeed. After enduring several years of bad government, some of the southern states were received back into the Union and were once more allowed to send members to Congress. The freed negroes also were given the right to vote. Some of the states were not received until the next administration. The Fourteenth Amendment making negroes citizens came into force in 1868. After several failures the Atlantic Cable was at last successfully put into operation in 1866. The Alaskan territory was purchased by us from Russia for $7,200,000, thus adding a vast area to the United States; and in the same year Nebraska entered the Union (1867). The French, who had set up Maximilian as emperor of Mexico, were asked to withdraw, and Maximilian was executed this same year.

ULYSSES S. GRANT. Republican. Eighteenth President. Two Terms, 1869–1877.

When President Johnson's term expired he was replaced in the presidency by the man who had led the Union troops to victory during the Civil War, General Ulysses S. Grant, of Illinois. He was inaugurated in 1869 as the eighteenth president of the United States. During his first term Virginia, Mississippi and Texas resumed their places in the Union. The other eight seceding states had been recognized under Johnson. The Fifteenth Amendment forbidding discrimination because of race, color or previous conditions of servitude was adopted in 1870. While General Grant was president the first railroads running across the continent to the Pacific were completed, in 1869, and thousands traveled over these lines to settle in the great West. Other events of public interest during Grant's administration were serious Indian troubles, including the massacre of General Custer and his men; the panic of 1873, during which many banks stopped payment and many business houses failed; the government's refusal to coin any more silver dollars (1873); trouble with Spain over the Virginius, a ship flying the American flag, which was captured while on the way to Cuba with arms for the rebels; the admission of Colorado to the Union (1876); and the holding of a World's Fair at Philadelphia in 1876 to show the wonderful growth of our young nation during the first hundred years of its existence. This Centennial Exposition was a wonderful success and helped to make the people proud of their country.

RUTHERFORD B. HAYES. Republican. Nineteenth President. One Term, 1877–1881.

The first disputed election for president in our history occurred in 1876. So close was the contest between Samuel J. Tilden, of New York, the Democratic candidate, and Rutherford B. Hayes, of Ohio, that a special body, known as the Electoral Commission, was appointed to settle the matter. It decided in favor of Mr. Hayes.

There were few events of national importance that occurred during the administration of our nineteenth president. The United States troops, which had been kept in the South after the war, were withdrawn. The white people had already gained control in most of the southern states, and after the troops were removed they gained control in all. The Mississippi River was made deeper at its broad mouth. This was of great advantage to the city of New Orleans, as it now enabled vessels to pass in and out of the river without trouble, and thus greatly assisted commerce. The coinage in silver dollars was begun again in 1878, and the government began to give gold and silver in exchange for paper money if anyone wanted to exchange (1879).

JAMES A. GARFIELD. Republican. Twentieth President. CHESTER A. ARTHUR. Twenty-first President. One Term, 1881–1885.

We now come to James A. Garfield, of Ohio, who was elected in 1880 over General Winfield S. Hancock. He had been in office but a few months when a man to whom he had refused to give a position in the government shot him down in the railway station at Washington. Two months later he died, and Vice-President Arthur became our twenty-first president. The terrible death of President Garfield turned the attention of the people to the regulation of government positions, and a law was passed taking many appointments out of the hands of the chief executive and compelling those trying to get government work to pass an examination first, thus protecting the president from private requests for places. President Arthur's administration, coming as it did, some years after the Civil War, was one of great prosperity. Cotton industries, manufactures of all kinds and the opening of great iron-mines throughout the country were among the "signs of the times." An exposition held in New Orleans in 1884 showed the great progress of the South. Postage on letters was reduced from three cents to two cents in 1883. More immigrants than ever before entered the country. In 1884 the Republicans nominated James G. Blaine for president, but he was defeated by the Democratic candidate, Governor Cleveland, of New York.

GROVER CLEVELAND. Democrat. Twenty-second President. One Term, 1885–1889.

Grover Cleveland, of New York, came to the presidency in 1885 as the twenty-second president. Several laws of importance were passed during his administration. One was an act establishing the Interstate Commerce Commission. This body was given the right to study the rates charged by the railroads. Other acts were one regulating the counting of votes in the election of a president, and another providing for the filling of the presidential chair in case of the death of both the president and vice-president. Chinese immigration was forbidden in 1888. An attempt to lower the tariff failed in 1888. The navy was increased. In 1886 the beautiful Statue of Liberty in New York harbor was presented to the country by the French in token of the good will they felt toward our nation. Any night it may be seen, its flaming electric torch on high, guiding vessels coming up the harbor to the great metropolis of the "land of religious and personal freedom." A severe earthquake which did much damage in the South occurred in 1886. President Cleveland was again a candidate in 1888, but was defeated.

BENJAMIN HARRISON. Republican. Twenty-third President. One Term, 1889–1893.

With the administration of Benjamin Harrison, of Indiana, the territory of Oklahoma was opened to white settlers in 1889. During 1889 Montana, Washington, North and South Dakota entered the Union, and Idaho and Wyoming were admitted the next year. It was decided that we should enlarge our navy, so the United States began to build a number of steel warships. Serious labor troubles also caused much loss of life. The tariff rates were raised, and pensions to soldiers of the Civil War were increased. More silver was to be bought and paid for in paper money. A Pan-American Congress was held to consider relations among the republics of the western hemisphere.

GROVER CLEVELAND. Democrat. One Term, 1893–1897.

In 1892 Grover Cleveland was again elected president. Because of the gap between his two administrations he is sometimes called the twenty-second and the twenty-fourth presidents, but this does not seem logical. He is the only president who has served two terms not in succession. There was a great panic in 1893 and much distress. Many people were out of work and prices of farm products were very low. In 1893 a great World's Fair was opened in Chicago to celebrate the discovery of America by Columbus 401 years before. Hard times came in 1893, and there were many business troubles. The tariff was reduced. In 1895, a dispute arose between England and the United States regarding the boundary between Venezuela and British Guiana, and for a time war was threatened. The matter was, however, referred to arbitration; that is, wise men were appointed to decide the matter, and there was no war. Before Cleveland retired from office another state, Utah, was added to the Union in 1896, so that the stars in our flag now numbered forty-five. The farmers and miners continued to demand that all the silver brought to the mint should be coined, and a People's party was organized. In 1896 the Democrats declared for free coinage of silver, and the party divided. The Republican candidate was elected.

WILLIAM McKINLEY. Republican. Twenty-fourth President. THEODORE ROOSEVELT. Republican. Twenty-fifth President. Two Terms, 1897–1905.

William McKinley, of Ohio, was chosen president over William J. Bryan, of Nebraska, at the election of 1896. During his administration the country was again plunged into war. Spain had been treating the people in Cuba in a most heartless way, and in consequence a war broke out between Spain and her possession. So many Cubans died a terrible death from starvation, the United States stepped in and said that Spain should not oppress her colony. We sent the battleship Maine down to Havana to inquire into the conditions. While lying in the harbor of that city she was blown up and many of her officers and sailors were killed. The Spaniards were suspected of the act. President McKinley at once said that the war in Cuba must stop, and Congress declared the people of Cuba free and independent, telling Spain to remove her soldiers from that territory. Spain refused, and war began.

After a few months the war came to an end by Spain's giving Cuba her freedom and selling the Philippines, Porto Rico and another small island to the United States for $20,000,000.

Before the end of the war with Spain we also came into possession of the Hawaiian Islands. The country became prosperous, and plans were made to water the dry lands of the West. But in this time of our growing prosperity President McKinley was assassinated soon after the beginning of his second term, and Vice-President Roosevelt, of New York, became the twenty-fifth president of the United States in 1901.

EXECUTIVES OF THE UNITED STATES

HERBERT CLARK HOOVER, OF CALIFORNIA. Thirtieth President, 1929 — Republican. Born August 10, 1874
©Harris & Ewing

CHARLES CURTIS, OF KANSAS, Vice-President, 1929 — Born January 25, 1860
©Harris & Ewing

CALVIN COOLIDGE, of Massachusetts, 1872 — Twenty-ninth President, 1923-1929. Republican
©Harris & Ewing

THE WHITE HOUSE, HOME OF THE PRESIDENTS

CHARLES GATES DAWES, of Illinois, 1865- Vice-President, 1925-1929.
©Harris & Ewing

ON THIS AND THE FOLLOWING PAGES WILL BE FOUND THE PICTURE OF EVERY MAN WHO HAS SERVED AS PRESIDENT OR VICE-PRESIDENT OF THE UNITED STATES

THE TWENTY-EIGHT PRESIDENTS

THE MEMORIAL TO
ABRAHAM LINCOLN,
IN POTOMAC PARK,
WASHINGTON, D. C.
© Harris & Ewing

ABRAHAM
LINCOLN, OF
ILLINOIS, 1809-1865,
Sixteenth President,
1861-1865. Republican
*From a Photograph by
Brady*

JOHN ADAMS, OF
MASSACHUSETTS,
1735-1826. Second Presi-
dent, 1797-1801. Federalist

THOMAS
JEFFER-
SON, OF
VIRGIN-
IA, 1743-1826. Third Presi-
dent, 1801-1809. Republican

GEO
TON,
1732-

F

ULYSSES S. GRANT, OF
ILLINOIS, 1822-1885. Eigh-
teenth President, 1869-1877.
Republican

JAMES A. GARFIELD, OF OHIO,
1831-1881. Twentieth President, 1881.
Republican

WIL-
LIAM
HENRY
HARRISON
OF OHIO, 1773-
1841. Ninth Pres-
ident, 1841. Whig

CHESTER A. ARTHUR,
OF NEW YORK, 1830-
1886. Twenty-first Presi-
dent, 1881-1885. Re-
publican

JOHN
QUINCY
ADAMS,
OF MASSA-
CHUSETTS,
1767-1848. Sixth
President, 1825-
1829. Republican

GROVER CLEVE-
LAND OF NEW YORK,
1837-1908. Twenty-second
President, 1885-1889 and
1893-1897. Democrat

JOHN TYLER, OF VIR-
GINIA, 1790-1862. Tenth
President, 1841-1845.
Democrat

ANDREW JACKSON
OF TENNESSEE, 1767-
1845. Seventh President,
1829-1837. Democrat

FRANKLIN PIERCE,
OF NEW HAMPSHIRE,
1804-1869. Fourteenth
President, 1853-1857.
Democrat

RUTHERFORD B. HAYES,
OF OHIO, 1822-1893. Nine-
teenth President, 1877-1881.
Republican

NOTE—The following presidents were born in the states named here, not in the states from which they were elected—those given above: Andrew
Jackson, North Carolina; William Henry Harrison, Virginia; James K. Polk, North Carolina; Zachary Taylor, Virginia; Abraham Lincoln, Ken

MOUNT VERNON,
THE ESTATE OF
GEORGE WASHING-
TON IN VIRGINIA
© Harris & Ewing

WOODROW
WILSON, OF
NEW JERSEY, 1856-
1924. Twenty-seventh Presi-
dent, 1913-1921. Democrat
© Harris & Ewing

JAMES MONROE,
OF VIRGINIA, 1758-
1831. Fifth President,
1817-1825. Republican

HING-
RGINIA,
resident,

ng by
art

JAMES
MADISON,
VIRGINIA,
1751-1836. Fourth President,
1809-1817. Republican

WILLIAM McKINLEY, OF OHIO,
1843-1901. Twenty-fourth President,
1897-1901. Republican

WARREN G. HARDING, OF
OHIO, 1865-1923. Twenty-
eighth President, 1921-1923.
Republican
© Harris & Ewing

ZACH-
ARY
TAYLOR,
LOUISIANA,
1784-1850.
Twelfth Pres-
ident, 1849-
1850. Whig

JAMES K. POLK, OF
TENNESSEE, 1795-1849.
Eleventh President, 1845-
1849. Democrat

MARTIN
VAN
BUREN, OF
NEW YORK,
1782-1862, Eighth
President, 1837-
1841. Democrat

RE
LT,
W
358-
nty-
ent,
Re-

WILLIAM H. TAFT, OF
OHIO, 1857-   . Twenty-
sixth President, 1909-1913.
Republican
© Harris & Ewing

MILLARD FILLMORE,
OF NEW YORK, 1800-
1874. Thirteenth Presi-
dent, 1850-1853. Whig

ANDREW JOHNSON,
OF TENNESSEE, 1808-
1875. Seventeenth Presi-
dent, 1865-1869.
Republican

JAMES BUCHANAN, OF
PENNSYLVANIA, 1791-
1868. Fifteenth President,
1857-1861. Democrat

BENJAMIN HARRISON,
OF INDIANA, 1833-1901.
Twenty-third President, 1889-
1893. Republican

ving

tucky; U. S. Grant, Ohio; Chester A. Arthur, Vermont; Grover Cleveland, New Jersey; Andrew Johnson, North Carolina; Benjamin Harrison,
Ohio; Woodrow Wilson, Virginia.
Courtesy New York Evening Post

MEN WHO WERE VICE-PRESIDENTS

The nine Vice-Presidents who became Presidents are shown
on the preceding pages

AARON BURR, of New
York, 1756-1836. Vice-
President for Thomas
Jefferson's first term

GEORGE CLINTON, of.
New York, 1739-1812.
Vice-President during
Jefferson's second term
and part of Madison's
first term

DANIEL D. TOMP-
KINS, of New York,
1774-1825. Vice-Presi-
dent throughout Mon-
roe's two terms

JOHN C. CALHOUN, of
South Carolina, 1782-
1850. Vice-President
during the regime of
John Quincy Adams and
Jackson's first term

RICHARD M. JOHN-
SON, of Kentucky, 1780-
1850. Vice-President for
Martin Van Buren

GEORGE M. DAL
LAS, of Pennsyl-
vania, 1792-1864.
Vice-President under
James K. Polk

ELDRIDGE
GERRY, of Massa-
chusetts, 1744-1814.
Vice-President for
one year of Madison's
second term

The Vice-Presidents of the United States Who Did Not Become President

HENRY WILSON,
of Massachusetts,
1812-1875. Vice-
President during
part of Grant's
second term

WILLIAM A.
WHEELER, of New
York, 1819-1887.
Vice-President dur-
ing the Hayes ad-
ministration

WILLIAM R. KING, of
Alabama, 1786-1853.
Elected to the vice-presi-
dency under Franklin
Pierce, he died before
assuming duties

JOHN C. BRECKIN-
RIDGE, of Kentucky,
1821-1875. Vice-Presi-
dent for Buchanan

HANNIBAL HAMLIN, of
Maine, 1809-1891. Vice-
President during Lincoln's
first administration

SCHUYLER COLFAX,
of Indiana, 1823-1885.
Vice-President for Grant's
first term

THOMAS A. HEND-
RICKS, of Indiana,
1819-1885. Vice-Presi-
dent less than one year
during Cleveland's first
term

CHARLES W. FAIR-
BANKS, of Indiana,
1852-1918. Vice-
President for Roosevelt
©Harris & Ewing

LEVI P. MORTON
of New York, 1824-
1920. Vice-Presi-
dent during Harri-
son's term

GARRET A. HO-
BART, of New
Jersey, 1844-1899.
Vice-President in
McKinley's first
term

JAMES S. SHER-
MAN, of New
York, 1855-1912.
Vice-President dur-
ing part of Taft's
administration

ADLAI E. STEV-
ENSON, of Illinois,
1835-1914. Vice-
President in second
Cleveland term

THOMAS R. MAR-
SHALL, of Indiana,
1854-1925. Vice-Presi-
dent during Wilson's
two terms

After the election of Van Buren in 1836 no other
vice-president was elected president until Roosevelt
was chosen in 1904, and Coolidge in 1924

In President Roosevelt's first administration the United States bought the rights of the French in the Panama Canal, a right for which we paid $40,000,000. The new Republic of Panama was recognized, and a treaty allowing the United States to dig the canal was made. Work was begun to make the Isthmus safe for white men to work in. The great World's Exhibition was opened at St. Louis on April 30, 1904, to celebrate the purchase of the Louisiana Territory.

THEODORE ROOSEVELT. Republican. Twenty-fifth President. One Term, 1905-1909.

President Roosevelt was elected in 1904 over Alton B. Parker, after serving as president for more than three years of the term for which President McKinley had been chosen. During this term great progress was made in the government of our colonial dependencies, and a war against the waste of our natural resources was declared. You will hear a great deal more about the "conservation of natural resources" in the future. A part of the American navy made a voyage around the world and was received with great marks of friendliness. Some progress was made in the control of great combinations of capital.

San Francisco, California, was seriously damaged by an earthquake and the fire which followed in April, 1906. On account of disorder in Cuba the United States took charge of the government until order was restored. Oklahoma was admitted to the Union in 1907. At the end of his term President Roosevelt sailed to Africa and spent over a year shooting big game and collecting specimens for the Smithsonian Institution.

WILLIAM H. TAFT. Republican. Twenty-sixth President. One Term, 1909-1913.

At the election of 1908 William H. Taft, of Ohio, who had been the first governor of the Philippines and had served as Secretary of War in President Roosevelt's Cabinet, was chosen over William J. Bryan, who was the Democratic candidate for the third time (1896, 1900, 1908). On the whole, President Taft's administration was uneventful. Work on the Panama Canal proceeded rapidly, but a revision of the tariff caused great dissatisfaction. New Mexico was admitted as a state in 1911, and the next year Arizona came into the Union. All the territory of the United States proper is now divided into states.

The Sixteenth Amendment to the Constitution making an income tax legal was ratified just before the end of the administration. In 1912 ex-President Roosevelt opposed President Taft for the Republican nomination, and, when defeated, became the candidate of the new Progressive party. The result was a Democratic victory.

WOODROW WILSON. Democrat. Twenty-seventh President. Two Terms, 1913-1921.

At the time of his election President Wilson was governor of New Jersey, and previously had been president of Princeton University. The new administration at once revised the tariff and the currency laws. A great exposition at San Francisco to celebrate the opening of the Panama Canal was held in 1915. The Seventeenth Amendment making United States senators elective by the people instead of by the legislatures became a part of the Constitution in 1913. Trouble with Mexico arose over the ill-treatment of American citizens by bandits, and we came very close to war. There was no regular government in Mexico at the time.

President Wilson was re-elected in 1916 over Charles E. Hughes, who had been governor of New York and a justice of the Supreme Court. In 1917 immigrants who could not read and write some language were forbidden to enter the United States. The World War in Europe affected United States from the first, and the President protested against sinking ships without warning. For a time the practice stopped, but in 1917 it was begun again. The German ambassador was dismissed, and Congress declared war April 6, 1917.

American warships were soon in European waters, and American soldiers were in the trenches before the end of October. Before fighting ended, November 11, 1918, over two million men were in France, and two million more were training on this side. American soldiers fought bravely in some of the hardest battles of the war. After the armistice the soldiers were returned to the United States as rapidly as possible, except a small force which was stationed for a time around Coblenz, on the Rhine, as a part of the Allied army of occupation.

President Wilson attended the Peace Conference at Paris and took part in drawing up the Treaty of Versailles. The Senate refused to ratify the treaty, which included the League of Nations, in 1920.

President Wilson's health failed soon after his return and he was an invalid until his death on February 3, 1924.

Two other amendments to the Constitution were adopted. The Eighteenth (1919) forbade the manufacture or sale of alcoholic liquors as beverages, and the Nineteenth (1920) gave women the right to vote. The latter was ratified by a sufficient number of states after a hard fight. Women voted all over the United States in the elections of 1920. At the time the amendment went into effect, however, women already had full suffrage rights in fourteen states. All of these except Michigan and New York were west of the Mississippi River. In Wyoming women had been voting since the organization of the territory in 1869.

WARREN G. HARDING. Republican. Twenty-eighth President. CALVIN COOLIDGE. Republican. Twenty-ninth President. One Term, 1921-1925.

At the time of his election President Harding was a United States Senator from Ohio. His opponent, James M. Cox, was governor of the same state when he was nominated. Calvin Coolidge, governor of Massachusetts, was elected vice-president over his Democratic opponent, Franklin D. Roosevelt, who had served as Assistant Secretary of the Navy in the preceding administration. In 1921 an act was passed limiting the number of immigrants from any country in a year to three per cent of the number of that nationality living in the United States in 1910. The tariff was raised, a separate peace was made with Germany, and a conference of the leading nations was called at Washington to consider reducing the navies of the world. An agreement was reached, and the number of battleships has been much reduced. An agreement regarding the payment of debt due the United States by Great Britain was also reached in 1923.

While on a trip to visit Alaska and the West President Harding died, August 2, 1923, and was succeeded by Vice-President Coolidge, who finished the unexpired term. An act was passed greatly limiting immigration to the United States in 1924. The percentage of those allowed to enter in any year was fixed at two per cent of the number of that nationality residing in the United States in 1890. After 1927 the whole number allowed to enter is fixed at 150,000, and the number

from any country is to be in proportion to the number of that "national origin" in the Union in 1920. Under the present law members of the yellow races are not allowed to enter or become citizens. However, if born in the United States, members of these races are citizens and have the same rights as anyone else.

President Coolidge announced that the policy of the Government would be one of strict economy. It was found possible to reduce taxes to a considerable extent, and the President gained much popularity.

CALVIN COOLIDGE. Republican. Twenty-ninth President. 1925-1929.

In 1924 President Coolidge was nominated for a full term and was elected by a large majority over John W. Davis, of West Virginia, Democrat, and Robert M. La Follette, of Wisconsin, Independent. President Coolidge was the sixth vice-president to succeed to the office on the death of the president, but the second to be elected afterward for a full term. Mr. Coolidge continued the policy of economy in governmental expenditures, and gained popularity by the reduction of taxes. Italy, Belgium and some of the smaller countries arranged to begin payment of the debt due the United States.

HERBERT HOOVER. Republican. Thirtieth President. 1929-

President Coolidge refused to be a candidate for a second elective term, and Herbert Hoover, Republican, of California, was elected after a stirring campaign over the Democratic candidate, Alfred E. Smith, who had won a nation-wide reputation during his four terms as Governor of New York.

In reading over what has happened during the different administrations you will notice that some questions seem never to be settled, but keep coming up. Though the United States is said to be a peace-loving nation, yet we have been engaged in war a considerable part of the time. Some were very little wars, but others cost much blood and treasure.

You will notice how important the question of slavery seemed for so many years. Fortunately that is settled now, and at present there is no really important question to divide the different sections of our country. As time goes on the different methods of communication will help to make the sections more alike, and we may hope for a time when we shall be truly a united nation.

THE LIVES OF THE PRESIDENTS

HERE we give you in handy form the main facts in the lives of the presidents of the United States, with a great number of dates. While dates are not so important as some teachers think, they really are often of use as pegs upon which to hang our knowledge. The lives are written in compressed form, but you will be able to understand if you will think a moment. Notice that the first figures tell when he lived, then you find where he was born, who his father and mother were, and where he was educated. His wife's maiden name is given, when they were married, and how many children they had. Where the wife was a widow, her maiden name is given in a parenthesis. Then follows his occupation, the church he attended, some facts about his career, when he was president, and when and where he died.

Washington, George (1732–99), born in Westmoreland County, Virginia, February 22, 1732; son of Augustine Washington and Mary Ball; little schooling; married Mrs. Martha (Dandridge) Custis 1759, no children; planter; Episcopalian. He served in the French and Indian War, as commander of the Continental army 1775–83, as president of the convention which drew up the Constitution 1787, and as president 1789–97. Died at Mount Vernon, December 14, 1799. See page 1039 for a longer story.

Adams, John (1735–1826), born at Quincy, Massachusetts, October 30, 1735; son of John Adams and Susanna Boylston; graduated Harvard 1755; married Abigail Smith 1764, five children; lawyer; Unitarian. He served in the state legislature, the Provincial Congress, the Continental Congress, and signed the Declaration of Independence. He was minister to Great Britain 1785–88, vice-president 1789–97, and president 1797–1801. Died at Quincy, July 4, 1826.

Jefferson, Thomas (1743–1826), born at Shadwell, Virginia, April 13, 1743; son of Peter Jefferson and Jane Randolph; attended William and Mary College; married Mrs. Martha (Wayles) Skelton 1772, six children; lawyer, author and planter; not a church member. Served in the state legislature and the Continental Congress, chief author of Declaration of Independence, governor of Virginia, minister to France 1785–89, secretary of state 1789–93, vice-president 1797–1801, president 1801–09; founder of the University of Virginia. Died at Monticello, Virginia, July 4, 1826, the same day as John Adams. See page 1042.

Madison, James (1751–1836), born at Port Conway, Virginia, March 16, 1751; son of James Madison and Nellie Conway; graduated from Princeton 1771; married Mrs. Dolly (Payne) Todd 1794, no children; studied law but practiced very little; planter; Episcopalian. He was in public life almost continuously from his graduation to 1817. He served in the state legislature, in the Continental Congress and later in the Congress of the United States.

He was the most influential member of the convention which formed the Constitution, and drew up the Virginia Resolutions against the Alien and Sedition Laws (1798). He was secretary of state 1801–09, and president 1809–17. Died at Montpelier, Virginia, June 28, 1836.

Monroe, James (1758–1831), born in Westmoreland County, Virginia, April 28, 1758; son of Spence Monroe and Eliza Jones; attended William and Mary College; married Eliza Kortwright 1786, two daughters; public official; Episcopalian. He was a soldier during the Revolution and served in the state legislature and in the Continental Congress; United States senator; minister to France, Great Britain and Spain; twice governor of Virginia, secretary of state 1811–17, president 1817–25, elected without opposition 1821. In 1823 announced Monroe Doctrine in message to Congress. Died in New York, July 4, 1831.

Adams, John Quincy (1767–1848), born at Quincy, Massachusetts, July 11, 1767; son of John Adams (second president), and Abigail Smith; graduated from Harvard 1787; married Louisa Catherine Johnson 1797, four children; lawyer and public official; Unitarian. Before entering college he acted as secretary to the American minister to Russia and to the commissioners to draw up the peace treaty with England. He was minister to Holland and Prussia, and later to Russia and England. He served in the Massachusetts Senate and in the United States Senate; secretary of state 1817–25, and by many is believed to have been the real author of the Monroe Doctrine; president 1825–29. After retiring from the presidency he entered the United States House of Representatives in 1831 and served until his death in Washington, D. C., February 23, 1848.

Jackson, Andrew (1767–1845), born in the Waxhaw Settlement, probably in North Carolina, though possibly in South Carolina; son of Andrew Jackson, a poor immigrant from the north of Ireland, and Elizabeth Hutchison; little schooling; married Mrs. Rachel (Donelson) Robards 1791, no children; lawyer, trader; Presbyterian. He took part in the Revolution, though only a child, and was taken prisoner; moved to Tennessee, where he helped to draw up state constitution. He was elected to the United States House of Representatives, and then to Senate, but resigned to become judge of the supreme court of Tennessee; was prominent during the War of 1812 and won battle of New Orleans; led forces against Seminole Indians and invaded Florida, then a Spanish possession; after purchase of Florida was appointed governor. Again elected to United States Senate in 1823; unsuccessful candidate for president in 1824, but elected four years later, and again in 1832; president 1829–37. Died at his home, the Hermitage, near Nashville, Tennessee, June 8, 1845. See page 1043.

Van Buren, Martin (1782–1862), born at Kinderhook, New York, December 5, 1782; son of Abraham Van Buren and Mary Hoes; academic education; married his cousin, Hannah Hoes 1807, four sons; lawyer; Dutch Reformed Church. He served as state senator and attorney general of New York, United States senator, governor of New York, United States secretary of state, vice-president 1833–37, president 1837–41; he was defeated for re-election in 1840, but was the candidate of the Free Soil party in 1848. Died at Kinderhook, July 24, 1862.

Harrison, William Henry (1773–1841), born at Berkeley, Virginia, February 5, 1773; son of Benjamin Harrison, a signer of the Declaration of Independence, and Elizabeth Bassett; graduated from Hampden-Sidney College and began to study medicine, but soon joined army instead; married Anna Symnes 1795, ten children; soldier and public official; Episcopalian. He served as secretary of the Northwest Territory, delegate to Congress, governor of Indiana Territory, and during the War of 1812 commanded the United States forces in the Northwest. Afterward he was a member of the United States House of Representatives, then United States senator and minister to Colombia. He was an unsuccessful candidate for the presidency in 1836, but was elected in 1840. He caught cold at his inauguration and lived just a month, dying in Washington, April 4, 1841.

Tyler, John (1790–1862), born at Greenway, Virginia, March 20, 1790; son of John Tyler and Mary Armistead; graduated from William and Mary College; married (1) Letitia Christian 1813, and (2) Julia Gardiner 1844; each wife had seven children; lawyer; Episcopalian. He served several times in the state legislature and in the United States House of Representatives, was twice governor of Virginia and twice elected to the United States Senate; elected vice-president 1840 and became president on death of Harrison. In 1861 he presided over peace conference in Washington which attempted to prevent secession. He was a member of the Confederate Congress. Died at Richmond, Virginia, January 17, 1862.

Polk, James Knox (1795–1849), born in Mecklenburg County, North Carolina, November 2, 1795; son of Samuel Polk and Jane Knox; graduated from University of North Carolina; married Sarah Childress 1824, no children; lawyer; Presbyterian. Soon after graduation he removed to Tennessee, and was elected to the state legislature, and was fourteen years in the United States House of Representatives, serving as speaker 1835–39; governor of Tennessee 1839–41, and president 1845–49. Died at Nashville, Tennessee, June 15, 1849.

Taylor, Zachary (1784–1850), born in Orange County, Virginia, November 24, 1784; son of Richard Taylor and Sarah Strother; little schooling; married Margaret Smith 1810, six children; soldier; Episcopalian. He was appointed lieutenant in the United States Army in 1808 and served for forty years. His brilliant record in the Mexican War led to his election to the presidency in 1848, though he took so little interest in politics that it is said he had never voted. He was inaugurated in 1849, and died in the White House sixteen months later, July 9, 1850.

Fillmore, Millard (1800–74), born in Cayuga County, New York, January 7, 1800; son of Nathaniel Fillmore and Phœbe Millard; limited education; married (1) Abigail Powers 1826, two children, and (2) Mrs. Caroline (Carmichael) McIntosh 1858, no children; lawyer; Unitarian. He served in the state legislature and in the United States House of Representatives. He was defeated for governor in 1844, but became comptroller in 1847. He was elected vice-president in 1848, and served as president 1850–53. He was the candidate of the Know Nothing party for the presidency in 1856. Died in Buffalo, New York, March 8, 1874.

Pierce, Franklin (1804–69), born at Hillsborough, New Hampshire, November 23, 1804; son of Benjamin Pierce and Anna Kendrick; graduated from Bowdoin College; married Jane Appleton 1834, three children; lawyer; Episcopalian. He began his career by serving four years in the legislature of his state, was elected to the United States House of Representatives and then to the Senate. He took part in the Mexican War as brigadier-general of volunteers, was elected president in 1852 and served 1853–57. Died at Concord, New Hampshire, October 8, 1869.

Buchanan, James (1791–1868), born near Mercersburg, Pennsylvania, April 23, 1791; son of James Buchanan and Elizabeth Speer; graduated from Dickinson College; never married; lawyer; Presbyterian. He served as a private in War of 1812, served two years in the state legislature and ten years in the United States House of Representatives, was minister to Russia, twice elected to United States Senate, secretary of state 1845–49, minister to England, president 1857–61. Died at Lancaster, Pennsylvania, June 1, 1868.

Lincoln, Abraham (1809–65), born in Hardin County, Kentucky, February 12, 1809; son of Thomas Lincoln and Nancy Hanks; little schooling; married Mary Todd, four sons; lawyer; not a church member. His father moved to Indiana and then to Illinois. The youth worked on the farm and in a store, served a few weeks as captain in the Black Hawk War, and was postmaster at New Salem. He entered public life as a member of the legislature, and was one term in the United States House of Representatives, elected president in 1860 and re-elected in 1864. Shortly after the beginning of his second term he was assassinated by John Wilkes Booth, died April 15, 1865. During almost the whole of his presidency the country was engaged in war. A longer account of his life is found on page 1045.

Johnson, Andrew (1808–75), born at Raleigh, North Carolina, December 29, 1808; son of Jacob Johnson and Mary McDonough; little schooling; married Eliza McArdle 1827, five children; tailor, public official; Methodist. He was apprenticed to a tailor at the age of ten and in 1826 removed to Greeneville, Tennessee. He was in succession alderman, mayor, member of the legislature, of the United States House of Representatives 1843–53, governor of Tennessee 1853–57, United States senator 1857–62, refusing to leave the Senate when Tennessee seceded. He was military governor of that part of the state captured from the Confederates 1862–64, and was nominated for vice-president in 1864. On succeeding to the presidency he quarreled with Congress and was impeached in 1868, but was not convicted. After retiring from the presidency in 1869 he was again elected to the United States Senate, but died near Carter's Station, Tennessee, July 31, 1875, before taking his seat.

Grant, Ulysses Simpson (1822–85), born at Point Pleasant, Ohio, April 27, 1822; son of Jesse Grant and Hannah Simpson; graduated West Point 1843; married Julia Dent 1848, four children; soldier; Methodist. On graduation he entered the army, served in the Mexican War, then resigned in 1854, but re-entered military life in 1861 and became commander of all the armies of the United States. He was president 1869–77. Died near Saratoga, New York, July 23, 1885. See page 1050.

Hayes, Rutherford Birchard (1822–93), born at Delaware, Ohio, October 4, 1822; son of Rutherford Hayes and Sophia Birchard; graduated from Kenyon College and studied law at Harvard; married Lucy Webb 1852, eight children; lawyer, soldier; Methodist. He was a prosperous lawyer at the outbreak of the Civil War, in which he rose to the rank of brigadier-general. He was a member of the United States House of Representatives 1865–67 and three times governor of Ohio. He was the Republican candidate for president in 1876, but the election was so close that the result was decided by the Electoral Commission. Died at Fremont, Ohio, January 17, 1893.

Garfield, James Abram (1831–81), born at Orange, Ohio, November 19, 1831; son of Abraham Garfield and Eliza Ballou; graduated from Williams College 1856; married Lucretia Rudolph 1858, five children; lawyer; Disciple. He taught school while studying law, and served a term in the state senate. In the Civil War he rose to the rank of major-general, but resigned in 1863 to enter the United States House of Representatives, remaining until 1880, when he was nominated for president. When he was inaugurated as president he had already been elected United States senator from Ohio for the term beginning March 4, 1881. On July 2, 1881, he was shot by Charles J. Guiteau, a disappointed office-seeker, and died at Elberon, New Jersey, September 19, 1881.

Arthur, Chester Alan (1830–86), born at Fairfield, Vermont, October 5, 1830; son of William Arthur and Malvina Stone; graduated from Union College 1848; married Ellen Lewis Herndon 1859, three children; lawyer; Episcopalian. During the Civil War he was quartermaster-general of New York, was collector of the Port of New York from 1871 until removed by President Hayes in 1878, elected vice-president 1880, became president on the death of Garfield in 1881 and served until 1885. Died in New York, November 18, 1886.

Cleveland (Stephen) Grover (1837–1908), born at Caldwell, New Jersey, March 18, 1837; the son of Richard F. Cleveland and Anne Neal; academic education; married, while president, Frances Folsom, 1886, four children; lawyer; Presbyterian. The family removed to New York State, and young Cleveland earned his own living after he was sixteen. He studied law in Buffalo, and was in turn assistant district attorney of Erie County, New York, sheriff, mayor of Buffalo 1881–82, governor of New York 1883–85, president of the United States 1885–89 and 1893–97. Died at Princeton, New Jersey, June 24, 1908. See page 7193.

Harrison, Benjamin (1833–1901), born at North Bend, Ohio, August 20, 1833; son of John Scott Harrison (son of President William Henry Harrison) and Elizabeth

F. Irwin; graduated from Miami University 1852; married (1) Caroline Lavinia Scott 1853, two children, and (2) Mrs. Mary Scott (Lord) Dimmick 1896, one child; lawyer; Presbyterian. He began to practice law in Indianapolis, and became reporter of the Supreme Court in 1860. In the Civil War he rose to rank of brigadier-general. He was defeated for governor in 1876, but was United States senator 1881–87; president 1889–93. He returned to the practice of law. Died at Indianapolis, March 13, 1901.

McKinley, William (1843–1901), born at Niles, Ohio, January 29, 1843; son of William McKinley and Nancy Allison; attended Allegheny College; married Ida Saxton 1871, two children who died in infancy; lawyer; Methodist. He entered the Civil War, though only a boy, and rose to the rank of major; then studied law and began to practice at Canton, Ohio; was elected prosecuting attorney in 1869, and was in United States House of Representatives 1877–91; author of McKinley Tariff Bill; governor of Ohio 1891–95, elected president 1896, and again in 1900. On September 6, 1901, while attending the Pan-American Exposition at Buffalo, was shot by an anarchist, Leon Czolgosz, and died September 14.

Roosevelt, Theodore (1858–1919), born in New York, October 27, 1858; son of Theodore Roosevelt and Martha Bullock; graduated from Harvard 1880; married (1) Alice Hathaway Lee 1883, one child, and (2) Edith Kermit Carew 1886, five children; author, office-holder; Dutch Reformed Church. After graduation he began the study of law but did not continue; was a member of New York legislature 1882–84, United States Civil Service Commission 1889–95, New York Police Commission 1895–97, assistant secretary of Navy 1897–98. He organized Rough Riders for Spanish American War, and served as lieutenant-colonel and colonel; governor of New York 1899–1901; vice-president 1901, becoming president on death of McKinley; elected for full term in 1904, retiring in 1909. In 1912 he was again a candidate for the Republican nomination, but was unsuccessful and became candidate of new Progressive party; not elected. He wrote many books and was much interested in natural history. Died at his home at Oyster Bay, New York, January 6, 1919. See page 7193.

Taft, William Howard (1857–   ), born in Cincinnati, Ohio, September 15, 1857; son of Alphonso Taft and Louisa Maria Torrey; graduated from Yale 1878, and Cincinnati Law School 1880; married Helen Herron 1886, three children; lawyer; Unitarian. After filling some minor legal offices he was judge of the Superior Court of Cincinnati 1887–90; solicitor-general of the United States 1890–92, United States circuit judge 1892–1900, president of the Philippine Commission 1900–01, governor of the Philippines 1901–04, United States secretary of war 1904–08, president of the United States 1909–13, professor of law at Yale 1913–21, chief justice United States Supreme Court 1921–   .

Wilson, (Thomas) Woodrow (1856–1924), born in Staunton, Virginia, December 28, 1856, son of the Reverend Joseph R. Wilson and Janet Woodrow; graduated from Princeton 1879, A.M. 1882, studied law at University of Virginia, Ph.D. from Johns Hopkins 1886; married (1) Ellen Louise Axson 1885, three daughters, and (2) Mrs. Edith (Bolling) Galt 1915, no children; teacher, author; Presbyterian. After practicing law for a short time in Atlanta, Georgia, he studied at Johns Hopkins University, and taught at Bryn Mawr College and Wesleyan University; professor at Princeton 1890–1910, president Princeton 1902–10, governor of New Jersey 1911–13, president of the United States 1913–21. Died in Washington, Feb. 3, 1924. See page 7193.

Harding, Warren Gamaliel (1865–1923), born at Corsica, Ohio, November 2, 1865; son of Dr. George Tryon Harding and Phœbe Elizabeth Dickerson; studied at Ohio Central College; married Florence Kling 1891, no children; editor; Baptist. Soon after leaving school he became connected with a newspaper at Marion, Ohio, and for many years was owner and editor; served in Ohio state senate 1900–04, lieutenant-governor 1904–06, United States senator 1915–21, president 1921–23. While on a visit to the West he died at San Francisco, August 2, 1923.

Coolidge, Calvin (1872–   ), born at Plymouth, Vermont, July 4, 1872; son of John C. Coolidge and Victoria J. Moor; graduated from Amherst College 1895; married Grace A. Goodhue 1905, two sons (one died 1924); lawyer; Congregationalist. After beginning practice at Northampton, Massachusetts, he filled several offices in the city government, was a member of the legislature 1907–08; mayor of Northampton 1910–11, state senator 1912–15 (president of Senate 1914–15), lieutenant-governor of Massachusetts 1916–18, governor 1919–20, vice-president of the United States 1921–23, succeeded President Harding, and in 1924 was elected president.

Hoover, Herbert Clark (1874–   ), born West Branch, Ia., Aug. 10, 1874; son of Jesse Hoover and Hulda Minthorn; graduated Stanford Univ. 1895; married Lou Henry 1899, two sons; mining engineer; Quaker; after graduation practiced profession in four continents; organized Belgian Relief (1914); U. S. Food Administrator (1917–19); Sec'y Commerce (1921–28); elected President Nov., 1928.

THE NEXT STORY OF THE UNITED STATES IS ON PAGE 4145.

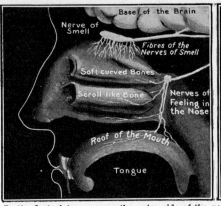
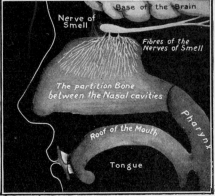

In the first picture we see the outer side of the nose, with the nerves of smell and feeling, and in the second is shown the inner part of the nose, with the dividing plate of bone between the nostrils.

SMELL AND TASTE

CONTINUED FROM 3804

SMELL and taste are two senses which are of small importance compared with hearing and vision, but they are, nevertheless, very interesting. These two senses are often called the chemical senses. Unlike hearing and vision, they do not depend upon waves, whether in the ether or in the air. We smell or taste only when the thing is actually touching the parts of the body which have this power; we see and hear at a distance, so to speak, but we cannot smell or taste at a distance, though we sometimes speak of smelling as "tasting at a distance." When we seem to smell at a distance, particles of the thing we are smelling have been carried through the air to the nose and have come in contact with the membrane lining the nose. The particle may be very small, less than a hundred-thousandth part of an inch, in fact. The fact that smell and taste are so limited in their range makes them inferior to hearing and vision.

Only a very small part of our knowledge of the world in which we live enters by these gateways of knowledge—the senses of taste and smell. We know that these two senses are in great decline among the higher animals, and especially in mankind. The sense of smell, particularly, is much stronger in the lower animals than in man, and these animals get much more of their knowledge from it than we do. On the other hand, some blind persons have so cultivated this sense that they have become able to recognize persons by their odor, just as a dog can.

While the senses of vision and hearing have become more important, the senses of taste and smell have become less so. Though this is true, the memory seems to hold smells very closely. Sometimes an odor will bring back the recollection of events which had apparently been long forgotten. Smell seems to do this much better than taste.

However, these two senses are closely allied, and they very commonly work together. The taste of such a thing as cinnamon is very much like its smell. A very large part of what we usually call taste is really smell. For example, a blindfolded man cannot tell the difference between onion and apple on his tongue if his nose is entirely stopped up. This is true not only of the bouquet, or aroma, of rare wines, but also of ordinary articles of diet. We can prove this for ourselves by noticing how differently our food seems to taste when the nose is thrown out of action by a bad cold.

We do not smell with the whole of our nose. Careful study with the microscope shows us exactly with what part of the nose we do smell. Roughly speaking, we may say that it is the roof of the nose and the upper third of it by which we smell. The rest of the nose is lined with cells which have little projections that wave backward and forward and keep the channel clear; but the smell region of the nose is lined with special smell cells, which correspond to the special cells that we found in the inner ear and in the retina. They are long narrow cells shaped like a cylinder. Each of the smell cells is connected with a tiny nerve-fibre of its own. We find that this tiny nerve-fibre really grows out of the smell cell, which is therefore a nerve-cell that has become changed. This is different from the rods and cones of the retina, or from the special cells in the inner ear, because they are not changed nerve-cells. The difference probably indicates to us how very ancient the sense of smell is.

THE TWO PAIRS OF NERVES IN THE NOSE, AND THEIR BUSINESS

The nose is supplied by two pairs of nerves coming from the brain. These two pairs of nerves are quite different in their duties. One pair has nothing to do with smell at all, but has to do with ordinary feelings in the nose. Anything tickling, or pricking, or hurting the nose affects these nerves; so does a thing like ammonia, which is irritating, besides having a smell. But this pair of nerves is not affected at all by odors that are not irritating.

The other pair of nerves that come to the nose are the nerves of smell. They are known as the first pair of nerves because they come off from the brain in front of any others. These nerves are apt to wear out, so to speak, in old age, so that old people lose, in some degree, their sense of smell, just as they often become deaf.

WHY WE CANNOT SMELL WHEN WE HAVE A COLD

When the ends of these smell cells are covered with mucus, as when we have a cold, the sense of smell is destroyed, or at any rate very much weakened. The cells also easily become tired. A strong smell will prevent us from perceiving other smells. After smelling camphor we may not be able to smell perfume. After we have smelled some strong odor for a little while we may cease to notice it.

As everyone knows, there is an endless number of possible smells. Naturally, we wish to try to group them in the same manner that we group tastes, but it really is very difficult to classify smells in any way that people would agree upon. A very large number of oils found in plants have rather the same sort of smell, though perhaps it is not very easy to recognize any particular resemblance between such smells as turpentine and lavender.

DIFFERENT KINDS OF SMELLS THAT HAVE A FAMILY LIKENESS

Still, on the whole, there is a general family likeness between the smells of plants and flowers; and when we examine the oils that cause these smells, we find that they are related to each other in their chemical build. There are certain other groups of smells, such as the group to which carbolic acid belongs. We can learn enough to see that there is a connection between the chemistry of a compound and its smell, but that is about all we can say. It is interesting to notice that electricity can stimulate our sense of smell as it can stimulate all our senses, and the sensation it causes is rather like the smell of phosphorus. It has also been shown that if we take a series of chemical substances which differ from one another in a regular way, their properties of smell also differ regularly.

For instance, there is a long series of chemical substances beginning with marsh-gas. This has no smell—a very unfortunate fact for miners. The next member of the marsh-gas series has a faint smell, and farther on in the list the smells become very strong. It is also noticed that the things which have the most smell are the things, as a rule, which weigh heaviest.

WHAT SMELL DEPENDS UPON AND WHAT TASTE DOES NOT DEPEND UPON

Late last century Sir William Ramsay, an English scientist, advanced a theory about smell which is probably nearer the truth than anything else we can say. He thought that the power of exciting smell increases with the size of the molecules of a substance, provided, of course, that it is a liquid or a gas, and not a solid.

Hydrogen, oxygen and nitrogen have no smell, probably because their molecules are too small. It is a general rule that a substance must be fifteen times as heavy as hydrogen before it can be smelled.

The first member of the series of alcohols has no smell; the next, which has a larger molecule, has a faint smell; and the still heavier alcohols have very decided smells. All this is very far from fully explaining to us what happens when we smell.

It is interesting to notice that sneezing cannot be excited through the nerves of smell, though it can be excited through the nerves of ordinary feeling in the nose and through the nerves of sight. Lastly, it is noticed in the case of all the senses, more or less, that they are aroused by *differences* outside them, and soon take much less notice, so to speak, of what excited them very much at first if it remains the same. This is more striking perhaps in the case of smell than in that of any other sense. We have all noticed how quickly we cease to be aware of a smell which at first was perhaps felt to be very unpleasant.

It is perhaps rather unfortunate that our sense of smell is becoming less keen. We lose a great deal of pleasure and, perhaps knowledge, because of this fact. On the other hand, people who live in the city or close to unpleasant factories gain by the loss of the ability to perceive odors.

THE SENSE OF TASTE AND WHERE WE FIND IT

The sense of taste resides mainly in the tongue, but does not depend alone on the tongue. The special cells which are concerned with it, corresponding to the special cells found in the organs of the other senses, may be discovered also on the lower surface of the soft palate, and may be scattered over part of the throat in front of the tonsils on each side. A person who has lost his tongue does not entirely lose his sense of taste.

As in other cases, special nerve-fibres run to the cells of taste, called taste buds, or taste bulbs. They are found in the greatest numbers on the back part of the tongue, along the upper part of the edge of the tongue, and at its tip. Taste is generally less acute on the front part of the surface of the tongue, except that sweet tastes are usually more acute at the tip. Sometimes a thing which is sweet on one part of the tongue will be bitter on another. We can notice this especially if we place quinine powder there and then swallow it.

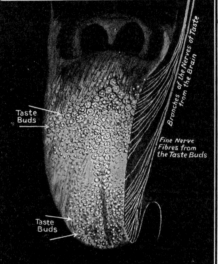

Taste Buds

Branches of the Nerves of Taste from the Brain

Fine Nerve Fibres from the Taste Buds

Taste Buds

In this picture of the tongue the side has been removed to show how nerves run from the sense organs, or buds of taste, to the brain. The taste buds are thickest at the back and tip.

Tastes can be classified much better than smells. Most of them come under the headings of bitter, sweet, acid, alkaline and salt. The last three of these are probably not pure tastes, but mixtures of taste and ordinary feeling, so they can become painful when they are very strong. But bitter and sweet are probably pure tastes, and, however strong, and perhaps unpleasant, they can never cause such pain as the others do. There seem to be different taste cells for bitters, sweets, acids and salines and perhaps others.

If things are to be tasted they must be dissolved in a liquid. We do not taste solids and we do not taste gases unless they are dissolved in water or some other liquid. Things too hot or too cold do not have as much taste as things just under the temperature of the body. Have you not noticed that ice cream seems to be much sweeter after it has melted and become warmer? A glass of lemonade is sweeter after it has become warm.

OTHER INTERESTING FACTS ABOUT THE SENSE OF TASTE

Another interesting fact, which you may have noticed, is that brown sugar seems to be sweeter than white sugar. Some of this feeling is due to the fact that the flavor of brown sugar is stronger because some of the molasses is still in it. The other reason is that. brown sugar is moister and dissolves more quickly, and so we get the taste sooner than we do in the case of white sugar.

With great labor and difficulty the nerve-fibres that have to do with taste have been traced from the tongue, palate and throat to the brain. The curious thing is that there are not separate nerves of taste as there are nerves of smell, vision and hearing; but the special nerve-fibres of taste run along in other nerves which have nothing to do with taste, and they do so in a most extraordinarily complicated way. We do not yet know what the meaning of this is, but it is evident that in the history of the body there must have been a very large number of shiftings and changings in the arrangements that have to do with taste.

THE VALUE OF TASTE AND SMELL AS GUIDES

It is certain that, on the whole, both these chemical senses have great uses, far beyond merely being able to let us distinguish between one thing and another. Nowadays we take it for granted that the food set before us is good to eat. Once the only way of knowing whether food was harmful was by the use of these senses. On the whole, they do indicate what is harmless or good for us, and teach us what we ought to avoid. There is no doubt about this as regards the sense of smell. Much more important, really, is the case of taste, which has so much to do with what we eat and what we refuse to eat. It is probable that the sense of taste of a healthy child rightly brought up is the best guide as to what it should or should not eat.

There are many things which children, or grown-up people if they have not had them before, find unpleasant. We have to make, or acquire, the taste for them, and so we speak of "acquired tastes." It is often true of olives, which few people like naturally. Some of these things seem not to be harmful and the body comes to like them. There are dozens of such things which children almost always dislike, but which grown-ups eat with relish. Generally they have strong flavors of some sort. But it is possible that no taste is worth acquiring, and that most grown-up people would be healthier if their tastes were more nearly what they were in childhood.

CHILDREN ARE NOT ALWAYS THE BEST JUDGES

While it may be a general rule that we should be just as well off if we never learned to eat some things we dislike at first, it is not always true. Children often take foolish prejudices about some articles of food. You may hear a child say that he does not like oatmeal or milk.

Very often these dislikes are due to the mistakes of the parents, who often give children things that are not good for them just because they ask for them. When small children come to the table with the older members of the family it is often hard to refuse to grant their requests, and many parents yield. Children are given desserts, for example, which are too rich for their stomachs, and they grow to have a distaste for plainer food. This is one of the reasons why wiser parents like to give young children their meals at a different time or place from the older members of the family. So, in spite of our rule, it is probably best that children should be required to eat the plain, ordinary foods. If the dislike is imaginary they will soon learn to like them when they find that they cannot get what they think they like better. It is true that some people really cannot eat certain things or take without harm certain medicines that are helpful to most individuals. Some people cannot eat eggs, or strawberries, or take quinine, for example, without being made ill. Such cases, however, are very rare.

THE END OF THE STORY OF THE BODY

We have now come to the end of that part of our subject which deals with the body, and we have finished by discussing certain well-known facts about the body which are also facts about the mind. Let us now, instead of thinking of one sense at a time, think of the senses as a whole, and then we shall find that this place where we have ended the study of the body is the right place for the beginning of the study of the mind.

It has been an interesting story. We have learned many things about our bodies and the various senses by which we get our knowledge of the world outside of ourselves. The feeling we must have is one of awe and wonder. Each one of us can truly echo the words of the Psalmist: "I am fearfully and wonderfully made."

THE NEXT STORY OF OUR OWN LIFE IS ON PAGE 4065.

Representatives of the nations sitting at Vienna to restore order to Europe after Napoleon's fall.

THE BEGINNINGS OF GERMANY

CONTINUED FROM 3828

WHEN we read of Germany in the early annals of the Roman Empire, it was inhabited by a number of restless warlike tribes whom the Celts, and after them the Roman writers, named Germans. They could scarcely be called nomadic, for they cultivated a little of the land, though they lived chiefly on milk and flesh; but they had an unconquerable love of fighting. They had come centuries before from the East, and made their way up the Danube, to the plains in the heart of Europe, pushing the Celts before them as they moved forward on their journey to the west.

The chiefs of their tribes, they thought, were descended from the gods and heroes, and they believed that when they died they joined the heroes in Valhalla, the abode of the gods, where they spent their days in hunting and fighting and their nights in feasting and story-telling.

Round each chief gathered a band of young men—youths who were sworn to his service and fought in the vanguard of his battles. The members of this band of youths, which was called the *comitatus,* as they gained in years grew to be the most trusted counselors of the chiefs. They were called *thegns* in England when the Angles and Saxons founded a nation there.

When the Romans first met the German tribes, they went to battle wearing on their heads the heads of animals, which they afterward changed to helmets; and sheltered themselves from their foes behind tall shields.

They were pagans, worshiping Odin, the father of the gods, and Thor, the god of war. They worshiped their gods in forests and under trees, but when they became Christians they felled the sacred oaks.

The country over which the German or Teuton families chiefly spread is the very heart of Europe, that great middle part stretching from the Alps to the North and Baltic Seas. A relief map shows us plainly what a sharp contrast exists on the face of this middle part of Europe, not unlike that on the face of France.

Mountains and highlands toward the south gradually slope to the sea on the north, so that a vast plain is formed, well watered by rivers which rise in the heights and flow leisurely seaward. The chief of the rivers is the Rhine, which links the Alps with the North Sea and has been a disputed boundary for centuries between France and her neighbor Germany. On the eastern side of the continent were constant changes, as other families of nations, of a different stock from the

Germans, pressed on from Asia behind. One branch of these is called Slavs. In their own language the word means "glorious," but in other tongues it has come to suggest "slaves," because so many men of the race became bondmen.

It was along the Rhine, that great waterway of Europe, that the Romans chiefly came in touch with the German tribes. Julius Cæsar crossed and re-crossed it many times when governor of the neighboring country of Gaul.

For years Roman soldiers and builders pushed steadily up the long Rhine valley, where they left behind to endure to this day fine cities and forts and roads. They tried to conquer the wild German tribes but did not succeed as well as in Gaul and Britain.

On the top of a hill in the great north plain, about a hundred miles from the Rhine, stands a huge statue, over fifty feet high, of one of the first German heroes, Hermann, who, in the autumn days of the ninth year of our Christian Era, in this neighborhood successfully resisted the dreaded Roman army. When the news of its destruction in the woods and marshes reached Augustus Cæsar, he clothed himself in mourning and cried out bitterly: "Give me back my legions."

THE TRIBES THAT FOUGHT IN EUROPE WHILE THE ROMAN EMPIRE FELL

Englishmen can take pride in Hermann's stand for freedom, and trace his bold spirit in the barons who wrung the great charter from King John at Runnymede, and in the leaders who defied the tyranny of the Stuarts. It was from the very region defended by Hermann, the lowlands about the rivers Ems and Weser and Elbe, that their descendants came later to found their new Angle-land across the North Sea.

During those centuries the various tribes and families surged like the waves of the sea over the face of the land, changing their dwelling-places, and fighting with each other and their neighbors. All these years the great Roman Empire was gradually getting weaker and less able to hold her own against oncoming tribes. We remember how the Roman soldiers had to be called home from Britain, then from Gaul. It was a tribe of German stock, the Goths, who appeared at last under the very walls of the city of the Cæsars, and finally carried off its treasures.

The Goths had been pushed on by a terrible host from Asia—the Huns. But this terrible foe soon scattered after the defeat and death of their leader Attila.

We have seen how the Franks pushed into Gaul, and with the Celts, who inhabited the country first, laid the foundations of the kingdom of France. We have seen, too, how other German tribes, the Angles and part of the Saxons, took ship to Britain. The East and West Goths went to Italy and the south of France; and the Longobards, or Lombards, settled in the plain of north Italy.

THE NEW INFLUENCE THAT CAME INTO THE WORLD FROM ROME

About the time of these great changes there came, in place of the old force of the arms and grandeur of Rome, a new influence from the same city. It was the spread of the Christian faith.

We know how it spread to England and to France. Missionaries also went bravely and devotedly to work in the wilds of Central Europe—men who were not afraid to pitch idols into the nearest lake, or to chop down sacred trees with their own hands while the wild heathen stood looking on. Many of these missionaries were eloquent Irishmen, but it was Rome, hitherto famed for the power of the Cæsars, that was now gaining a new power as the seat of the Bishop of Rome, the head of the whole Church, called the pope. Bishops and clergy passed out of Italy over the Alps and the mountains beyond, over the great north plain, down the Rhine valley, to teach Christianity.

THE LITTLE MAN WITH THE GREAT WILL, AND HIS FAMOUS SON CHARLEMAGNE

When Pepin, the leader of the Franks, the little man with the great will, went to keep the Lombards in order out of gratitude to the pope, who had helped him to become king, he took from them the land they owned about Rome, and presented it to the head of the Church. This was the beginning of the pope's claim to rule over an earthly kingdom.

Pepin's great son, the hero Charlemagne, also helped on the influence of the Church in his enormous dominions. These included, besides what is now France, Holland and Belgium, Switzerland, North Italy and part of Spain, as well as nearly all that part of Central Europe we now call Germany. More than that, Charlemagne went in person to the rescue of the

A FOOLISH KING AND A WISE ONE

Henry IV waits in the snow at Canossa to receive the pope's pardon.

Maximilian, the great emperor, receives an ambassador from Venice.—From the painting by Carl Becker.

pope when he was set upon by fierce enemies; we read on page 4408, how the pope crowned him the emperor of the new Roman Empire. Later they called it the Holy Roman Empire.

We shall see at last how a dark shadow was cast over both Germany and Italy by that union, so loudly applauded in St. Peter's on that Christmas Day—a shadow not lifted for a thousand years.

We have seen in the story of France how soon the great empire of Charlemagne fell to pieces, and how France began to take shape under its own line of kings. In Germany it was different. For centuries the tribes were gradually settling down into practically independent states, loosely held together under the tie of the empire. The rulers of the states had different titles and powers, and the chief ones, with the help of three powerful archbishops, elected the emperor of the Holy Roman Empire as need arose.

Looking at the history of these centuries in Germany is like looking into a kaleidoscope, every turn of which, as the years pass, brings fresh combinations and passing changes. Now one state takes the lead, absorbing others or driving them to another part of the country; now another state rises into being as others move about or disappear.

THE GHOST OF AN EMPIRE THAT DISTURBED A THOUSAND YEARS

Within 200 years of the death of Charlemagne there were great changes, too, along the eastern borders. The wild Hungarians, of a quite different race from the German families, spread terror over the land. Later they settled down and became part of the empire, though as independent as the rest.

The French writer Voltaire wittily said that the Holy Roman Empire was neither holy, nor Roman, nor an empire. It has been called a mere ghost of an empire. But it proved strong enough for a thousand years to hinder German kings from looking well after their own country, because it distracted them with the ever enticing vision of power on the other side of the Alps. Their Italian subjects hated them, and quarrels between the emperors and the popes were so constant and so fierce that a just settlement became more and more difficult as the years passed.

Let us see how one of the strongest popes treated one of the weakest em-perors. It was about the time when the Conqueror was in England.

The priest Hildebrand had been so popular, toiling with all his might to set right the wrong things in the Church, and to make it strong and pure, that the people of Rome rushed into the church at the funeral of the pope who had just died, shouting: "St. Peter wills Hildebrand to be pope!"

THE EMPEROR WAITS THREE DAYS IN THE SNOW TO SEE THE POPE

The unwise king of Germany, Henry IV, defied this new pope, who was called Gregory VII, and finally sent out a message to the world declaring Gregory to be pope no longer. Gregory answered with what was then thought to be the terrible punishment of *excommunication*, which meant that the emperor was put out of the Church, and no priest might minister to him.

After a time Henry submitted, and crossing the Alps, went on to Canossa, where Gregory was staying, to beg for pardon. It was the depth of winter, and it is said that Henry had to wait about for three days in deep snow, barefoot and in a miserable thin shirt, shivering, till the pope chose to see him and forgive him.

Of a very different type was the emperor Barbarossa. His strong, pleasant, smiling face seems to stand out across the centuries, and many are the stories of his bravery and endurance.

He tried to make the empire complete and independent. Five times he crossed the Alps, and had many struggles with the popes. But, strong as he was, he, too, had to give way in the end. In that twelfth century there were violent disputes forever going on between the Church and the Christian rulers of Europe.

THE DRAMATIC MEETING THAT MARKED THE END OF AN ANCIENT FEUD

In the story of England we have read of the tragic death of Thomas à Becket at Canterbury, and the penance of the king. Seven years later the long contest between the Bishop of Rome and the Emperor of Rome also ended in victory for the Church. The opponents were persuaded to meet in Venice, the beautiful and independent city at the head of the Adriatic Sea. Three slabs of marble are shown to this day, in the porch of the lovely old church of San Marco, at the spot where the greatest prince of the age,

Barbarossa, knelt to kiss the pope's foot and to receive in return the old man's kiss of peace. It must have been a bitter moment for the emperor.

Barbarossa was drowned while crossing a river in Asia, and he was buried in the sandy desert; but the old German poets have kept his memory green in song and legend, and the hope lived on that the emperor would come again to help his people in time of need.

THE POWERFUL GROUP OF TRADING CITIES KNOWN AS THE HANSEATIC LEAGUE

In the time of the Crusades the power of the nobles in Germany was very great. They held their lands on the same feudal plan as in France and England, and the peasants were very poor and wretched. Fine towns, with strong walls, were raised over the country to resist the foes from without, and by degrees churches and universities, good houses and halls, were built, many of which have survived.

Germany to-day is famed for her splendid old towns. Some of these towns bought privileges and freedom, as did the French towns, and helped to keep alive the spirit of Hermann through the dark years. Eighty cities banded together to form the famous organization for promoting trade which is known in history as the Hanseatic League; the chief ones were Lübeck, Hamburg and Bremen. They had a settlement in London, where they had many special rights which increased their trade and wealth. The trade of the Baltic was in their hands, and they even made war on their own account, being strong enough to withstand not only the nobles, but pirates at sea and robbers on land.

THE KNIGHTS WHO LIVED IN THE HILL-TOP CASTLES OF GERMANY

The robber-knights who lived in the castles still crowning many rocky hills were a terrible hindrance to trade and farming in lawless times. The stories of how they sallied forth, attacking merchants at the fords or bridges, and seizing the newly gathered crops, are most exciting. The knights of the castles were not all robbers, however, for on them depended the keeping of the roads and the tow-paths, and the entertaining of travelers before there were many inns.

One of the emperors who stand out from a time of universal confusion is Rudolph of Hapsburg, who not only ruled the German states, but became the founder of the Austrian House of Hapsburg, in whose family, with some exceptions, the imperial crown remained for about six hundred years.

Austria means the East Land, and the duchy gradually grew and spread, with many a change as the kaleidoscope turned, chiefly along the splendid Danube River, which rises near the Rhine in the Black Forest and flows across Bavaria, Austria and Hungary on its way to the Black Sea. The brave mountaineers of the Alps had to league together against the Hapsburgs, as we learn from the story of Switzerland.

The energetic, intelligent, noble-hearted Maximilian I was also a Hapsburg. It has been said that Maximilian stands as the boundary stone between the old times and the modern. By conquest, treaty and royal marriages the league of the German states had allied within itself Tyrol, the Netherlands and Spain. It was the age of Columbus, the age of expansion and adventure.

THE GREAT PART THAT GERMANY PLAYED IN GREAT WORLD-CHANGES

While the discovery of the compass put into men's hands a guide by which to sail in unknown seas, the invention of printing and the spread of learning made men think and study. Germany had a proud share in this advancement. It was a German who discovered how to make paper out of rags; it was a German who first thought of printing with movable letters; it was a German who set all Europe in a blaze by preaching against the Church.

The emperor at the time was Charles V, the grandson of Maximilian, often called a second Charlemagne from the greatness of his dominions; for by inheritance he added to Germany Spain, the south of Italy and Sicily, and the Netherlands, as well as colonies in the New World discovered by Columbus.

Early in his reign there was a terrible insurrection of the people called the Peasants' War. They burned castles and monasteries, as did the peasants of France about 300 years later, and for much the same reasons: the grievous and unfair taxes, and the bitter oppression under which they suffered. This war was scarcely over when all Germany was roused by Martin Luther's burning publicly the deed of the pope, who excommunicated him for his teaching.

Charles was against Luther, but many of the princes supported him. So they drew up a protest, saying they could not tolerate in their lands the following of a religion which they held to be against God's Word. This gained for them the great and famous title of Protestants, ever since given to all those Christians who reject the authority of the Church of Rome.

The Germans owe the first Protestant translation of the Bible in their native tongue to Luther, as we owe ours to Wyclif. The invention of printing, slowly working from improvement to improvement, made it possible to send it all over the land, in the fine cities, in the beautiful valleys of the hill countries, in the broad north plain.

The story of how religious liberty was won in France and in England is sad enough. In Germany thirty years of war caused unspeakable ruin and misery to the country before people gained the right of following the religion they believed to be the true one. There were the quarrels between Roman Catholics and Protestants, and the quarrels between various kinds of Protestants; and civil war spread gradually all over the land.

For a short time the leader of the staunch Protestants was a man named Frederick, count of a province on the Rhine, who married the daughter of James I of England. Their trials and hairbreadth escapes, and their flight to Holland, are full of interest, and their portraits are in the English National Portrait Gallery. It was through their daughter Sophia, who married the Elector of Hanover, that the princes of Hanover had a claim to the British crown.

THE KING WHO CAME TO THE AID OF THE PROTESTANTS

There came to the help of the German Protestants the famous Swedish king, Gustavus Adolphus, in his leather jerkin, landing his army in Pomerania. The courtiers of the Catholic emperor laughed at the Snow King, as they called him, saying he would melt as he came to the warmer south; but they found that the king's power was truly like a snowball, which gathers as it rolls.

The greatest generals against Gustavus were Tilly and Wallenstein. Tilly could boast that he had won thirty-six battles. The skillful and energetic Swedish king prevented his gaining the thirty-seventh. Gustavus was killed at the battle of Lützen, near Leipzig, in which Wallenstein was defeated.

Wallenstein, an extraordinarily clever and strong man, was a traitor, and was going to tear the crown from the emperor and deliver his troops to the enemy, but he was assassinated. For a long time success was now on one side, now on the other. When the emperor seemed likely to be too powerful, France burned and plundered the beautiful Rhine country.

At last, when the country was quite exhausted, a peace was arranged, the Peace of Westphalia. France took Alsace, Sweden claimed Pomerania, Switzerland and Holland became independent. The greater German princes were left masters in their own states. Catholics and Protestants were to have equal rights and freedom of worship, and the Protestant princes were to keep the Church lands they had taken.

THE BITTERNESS OF A DESOLATE LAND AT THE END OF THE WAR

The number of people in the German states at the beginning of the war was sixteen or seventeen millions; at the end there were not quite four millions. Bitter want was felt in the desolate land; towns and villages were destroyed. Cornfields were trampled down, trade was ruined, and the people were in despair. This peace was made in 1648.

After ten years war broke out again. The German princes, some dissatisfied, some selfish, some greedy, listened to the wily words of Louis XIV of France, who had determined to make the Rhine the eastern boundary of his kingdom. In the struggle that followed, Strasbourg was lost, and the rich province of Lorraine went to France. The treaties that settled the wars of this time were called by the German people the Peaces of Take-away, Tear-away and Unright, because Germany lost something by each one.

A terrible thing happened now to Vienna, the Austrian capital. The Turks who lived beyond Hungary poured through that province and laid siege to the fine city, which, in spite of all their efforts, they could not take. They blew up the walls and sent 87,000 people into slavery. At last John Sobieski, king of Poland, came to the rescue and drove away the Turks. In the tent of the Turkish general were found the letters of Louis XIV stirring them on to attack the Germans. Pursuing his plan of raising

GERMAN HOMES OF LONG AGO

This picture shows what a German village was like two thousand years ago. The people of those times often built their homes on platforms in the middle of lakes, so that enemies could not reach them easily.

The Germans first appeared in history as great warriors and huntsmen, and to make themselves look fierce they decorated their heads with the heads and horns of wild animals. Here we are looking inside a German home of long ago, and we see the men of the family arriving home with a bear. The boy is dressed in an animal's skin. Rough as they were, the German tribes treated their women with great honor.

up enemies in distant parts, to keep the German soldiers away from the Rhine, he also stirred up the Swedes to attack Brandenburg, on the Baltic. The ruler of this province, Frederick William, and Prince Eugene of Savoy, were the chief support of the emperor in these French wars. Prince Eugene was a very little man, with great military ability and a wonderful command over his soldiers.

THE WONDER-HOUSES OF THE GREAT GERMAN NOBLES

When the next great war arose in Europe, about the succession to the throne of Spain, Eugene and the Duke of Marlborough commanded the allied forces of Holland, England and Portugal, which backed the emperor and the rulers of Hanover and Brandenburg. The two great generals beat the French in Germany, in the Netherlands and in Italy. The names of most of these desperate battles are familiar to us all—Blenheim, Ramillies, Oudenarde and Malplaquet.

It has been said by a Belgian traveler in Germany that there was then a fever for building and copying France in every possible way. Because Louis XIV created Versailles out of a sandy waste, one noble built a village on the top of a mountain, another formed a palace in the depths of a forest, another put a fortress where there was nothing to derend. There were about two hundred independent states at this time, and many of them cared little for the good of the country. The peasants, as in France, were ground down to pay for the splendor and luxury of the courts.

THE POWERFUL MAN WHO FOUNDED THE GREATNESS OF PRUSSIA

There was one court, at any rate, where there was no luxury. Brandenburg had absorbed the neighboring state of Prussia, and its rulers were now kings of Prussia. All the money that could be gathered was spent on the army, recruiting the finest men, drilling and training them. When Frederick (called the Great) came to the throne, he spent forty years working hard for his kingdom, rebuilding, draining, making roads and canals, seeing that farmers had grain to sow, adding to his dominions whenever there was a chance. From his time onward it became quite clear that sooner or later Prussia would come to the front and lead the rest of the German states. By his power and perseverance he turned the fortunes of the Seven Years' War against Austria and France.

At this time Austria was under the rule of Maria Theresa, the mother of Marie Antoinette of France. Frederick gained Silesia from her, and she also lost other parts of her dominions. She was a brave and determined woman, and when hard-pressed she had to fly from Vienna to Pressburg, in Hungary. Hungary had been joined to Austria before the Thirty Years' War. There, in Hungarian costume, she appealed to the nobles, holding her baby boy in her arms. In answer they enthusiastically flashed out their swords, shouting together: "We will die for our sovereign, Maria Theresa." The flames of the Seven Years' War spread all over the world, and from this time Prussia became an important power.

HOW A WAR IN AUSTRIA TURNED NAPOLEON FROM ENGLAND

Some thirty years after the treaty which ended the Seven Years' War trouble broke out again. Roused by the terrors of the French Revolution, and to avenge its chief victims, Austria and Prussia advanced against France, to the great rage of the French people. For the next ten years France was defending herself against the attacks of Europe, and the progress of Prussia was stayed for a time by these wars. Austria was first fought in Italy, where Napoleon gained many battles with great rapidity. In 1805 the French army intended for the invasion of England was turned against Austria. The nations had now to defend themselves against the ambition of Napoleon, who, for a time, carried all before him. Thirty thousand Austrians had to surrender at Ulm, Vienna was taken, and the Austrians, with their allies the Russians, were defeated in a famous battle at Austerlitz.

The next year the emperor Francis II, losing heart, laid down the crown of the Holy Roman Empire.

"We must utterly break up Germany," were Napoleon's words and aim all through the years of bewildering, ever changing conditions in Central Europe.

At the most, there were occasional intervals in the war, while he was trying to disunite the German-speaking peoples. These were strong while bound together, like the bundle of sticks in the fable, but easily destroyed when they fell apart. Unhappily, there were many jealousies

TWO FOUNDERS OF GERMAN GREATNESS

The hero-emperor of Germany in the Middle Ages was Frederick Barbarossa, whose name means "red beard." He was elected king at a time of unrest, because he was a strong, brave man; and later the pope crowned him Holy Roman Emperor. The picture shows Barbarossa proclaimed as king of the Germans.

During the Middle Ages the knights who lived in the strong castles of Germany became very powerful, and did just as they liked. When Rudolph of Hapsburg, the ancestor of the former Austrian emperor, was elected emperor of Germany in 1273, he determined to stop the robberies of these knights and to break their power, and here we see him condemning some robber-knights who have been captured.

and divisions among the states from one cause and another, and after the battle of Austerlitz several states joined together in a union supported by the French and leagued against Austria and Prussia. Austria lost her fairest provinces after Austerlitz; Prussia lost half her territory after Jena. When Queen Louise of Prussia begged Napoleon to have some mercy on her unhappy country, the insulting answer sent to her by the vulgar Napoleon was a map of Silesia—the rich province won from Maria Theresa by Frederick the Great—encircled by a golden chain and a pendant heart.

THE VICTORIES OF NAPOLEON AND THE TURNING OF THE TIDE

What a terrible setback it was for the young, rising nation to have its army wiped out, French soldiers occupying the country, Napoleon ruling from Berlin, from where he sent out his Berlin Decrees against the trade of England. None could gainsay this conqueror, who could race about all over Europe—before there were any trains!—without sleep or rest; who could fight five battles on five successive days, and overcome even the snowy Alps. When Napoleon was at the very height of his success, between 1807 and 1809, it could be said that continental Europe was under the power of the two emperors, the Man from Corsica and the Emperor of Russia.

But the tide turned in the bitter Russian campaign, and Central Europe was not slow in seizing the chance. The whole German people rose against the hated yoke, eager to wipe away the dishonor of its defeats.

Prussia was particularly eager to drive out the French garrisons, and people hastily gave money or labor, or volunteered to fight; and nothing was too great or too small to do which might help to recover what had been lost.

SETTING GERMANY FREE FROM NAPOLEON'S GRIP OF IRON

The famous General Blücher, who afterward helped Wellington at Waterloo, earned in one of the first battles at this time the name "Marshal Forwards," from the soldiers who followed the impetuous leader to his thunderous cry of *Vorwärts!* He but expressed the spirit of the time. At the Battle of the Nations, fought near Leipzig through four terrible days, Napoleon was beaten at last, and Germany was set free from the French.

The empire of the successor of Charlemagne, as Napoleon loved to call himself, fell apart even more quickly than it had been formed. It was not an easy task to bring back order in Europe, especially when many of those concerned at the Congress of Vienna proved to be jealous and greedy. But it was accomplished in some fashion at last, in spite of the thrilling interruption of Napoleon's escape from Elba and the startling Hundred Days in which he made a last effort before his final and crushing defeat at Waterloo.

We have seen how Francis II of Austria, forced by Napoleon, laid down the sceptre of Charlemagne and the crown of the thousand-year-old Roman Empire. This empire had kept together in a very loose sort of way these old states of Germany, and many more. After the Congress of Vienna we have a confederation of German states, consisting of many smaller states, including Bavaria, Saxony and Hanover, and two powerful ones, the empire of Austria and the kingdom of Prussia. These were very jealous of each other's powers, and it was soon felt that the arrangement could not last, especially as important changes in every direction were hurrying on all over Europe.

THE GREAT DESIRE FOR FREEDOM THAT CAME TO THE PEOPLES OF EUROPE

It was the emperors, kings and princes who settled matters at Vienna, and their idea was to restore things, as far as they could, to what they were before Napoleon's wars upset the map. But the people could now no longer be forced to pay taxes they had had no voice in settling, to obey laws they had had no share in making or to fight in wars arising out of the quarrels of kings.

The people wanted legislatures, with real representation of all classes; they wanted open courts of law and trial by juries; freedom of the press, freedom in speech, and, above all, freedom in religion. Slowly, through the years that followed the settlement of Europe at Vienna, the friends of freedom gained what they wanted. The revolutions in France during this time, especially the one in 1848, had a great influence in Germany.

Another strong desire, besides the longing for liberty, was working in men's minds through all these years. It was a growing wish for unity, the joining together of German-speaking states, so that

FAMOUS FIGURES IN GERMANY'S STORY

Frederick William, who secured the independence of Prussia from Poland.
From the painting by Wilhelm Camphausen.

The militarist peace—Bismarck concluding the Peace of Versailles in 1871.
From the painting by Carl Wagner.
Some of the pictures on these pages are reproduced by courtesy of the Berlin Photographic Company.

they might show an undivided front to the rest of the world, especially in times of war and trouble. The efforts Napoleon had made to crush what small measure of unity the old Germany possessed had been the means of giving it fresh life, for what draws any family together closer than a common sorrow, or working with a common object in view?

But not only at the Battle of the Nations was there the sympathy of common effort, but the very hardness of the struggle for freedom in each state brought men nearer together.

THE REMOVAL OF THE BARRIERS THAT STAND BETWEEN NATIONS

Changes in the taxes, hitherto set on all goods as they passed the frontiers of each state, were of immense help in opening up intercourse and good-fellowship as well as trade. Now the barriers were done away with, and with them the expense of keeping up guarded frontiers.

Then there were, besides all this, the blessings that came with peace. People were no longer afraid to build factories lest they should be burned or destroyed by an enemy's army. Trade grew as inventions and machinery of all kinds were developed and worked by steam. When the shining steel rails, laid down in state after state, drew distant and out-of-the-way places closer together by making travel easy and quick, people could trade more and know each other better.

In all the growth that was going on in these middle years of the nineteenth century, it was Prussia, the youngest of the German kingdoms, that grew the fastest, and more and more took the lead in the great German family of states.

Both times and men were ripening for the coming change. In the very year of the battle of Waterloo there was born a boy who grew up very clever, determined, far-seeing, through the years of change and growth in Germany. He made his way early into Parliament, and learned much about other countries by being ambassador. Then he became the king's chief minister. This man was Bismarck, who saw plainly from the first how Prussia could rise to greatness, and set his face, like a flint, to make it great.

When the army had been reformed and strengthened, the old king William and Bismarck were ready for the first step. Prussia went to war with Denmark about the two provinces of Holstein and Schleswig, between the Baltic and North Seas, which were claimed by both Denmark and Prussia. Austria joined Prussia in this war, and soon the two giants had their way over smaller Denmark. Then, when Bismarck had settled the dispute as to what should be done with the conquered provinces by taking possession of them for Prussia, he was ready for the second step.

This second step was war with Austria; the long-smoldering jealousy of the two rivals must now be settled by force of arms. General Moltke came to the front, and in seven days the war was finished by the final victory at Sadowa, in Bohemia, and the appearance of the advancing Prussians before Vienna.

There is in Berlin a wide street nearly a mile long, with an avenue of lime and chestnut trees. It is called Unter den Linden, meaning "under the limes." At one end of the avenue is a magnificent gate, looking toward the old province of Brandenburg; at the other is the palace.

THE CHANGES IN GERMANY THAT CAME WITH THE DAYS OF PEACE

Back under that Brandenburg Gate passed the victorious troops, King William welcoming them and leading them up the Unter den Linden, with Bismarck and Moltke, amid the girls scattering flowers, and the waving banners, and the music, and the enthusiastic crowds cheering and shouting to those who "in seven days had sped through Frederick's Seven Years," thus, almost at a blow, settling the leadership of the German people.

The peace that followed this war brought about great changes. New lands were added to Prussia; Austria lost some of hers. The old German Confederation was done away with, and a new one formed of Prussia and the states north of the river Main, which runs into the Rhine at Mainz. A House of Commons, called the Reichstag, was formed of members from all the states that had joined the union, and in this Reichstag were to be discussed all the questions affecting the states as a whole, each state still keeping the government of its own affairs.

Austria, so long the leader and head of the old Roman Empire, was shut out. Then, when the sharp rent between the two rival powers was complete, with the king of Prussia on one side of the mountains of Bohemia and the emperor of Austria on the other, Bismarck was ready

The first king of Prussia, Frederick I, was a good ruler, and so that his subjects should be able to read the Bible, he started thousands of schools in the villages and compelled the children to attend. Here he is examining the children. Frederick I crowned himself king, and Frederick the Great said of this: "It was as though he told his successors, 'I have won for you a title; make yourselves worthy of it.'"

During most of his life Frederick the Great was engaged in wars which threatened to destroy his kingdom, but by brilliant generalship he defeated his enemies and made Prussia great. When not fighting, the king used to travel about his kingdom and talk with the people, encouraging them to make roads and canals and otherwise improve their country. This picture shows subjects giving him a welcome.

and waiting to take the third step in his plan for making Prussia great.

This was the chance of war with France, and it came even sooner than he had dared to hope. The little Napoleon, who was now emperor of France, was disturbed at Germany's growing power, and he wished to make his throne safe by dazzling the nation with military glory.

HOW BISMARCK BROUGHT ABOUT THE WAR WITH FRANCE

But, compared with Bismarck, Napoleon was a very simple man, and he readily fell into a trap when Prussia was ready for war and France was not.

First it was proposed that a Prussian prince should be king of Spain. This was resented by the whole French nation, and while they were in a state of excitement Bismarck contrived that an insulting telegram should be published which would force Napoleon to declare war. The trick succeeded, and war was declared with swift and dramatic results. There have been few more dishonorable tricks played by those who call themselves statesmen than this trick of Bismarck, and the end of it all was that the French army was thoroughly defeated. In the course of a month a large part of the army was driven into a trap, and at Sedan Napoleon wrote to the king of Prussia: "As I have not died at the head of my troops, I hand over my sword to your Majesty." The whole French army surrendered: thousands of men, with officers, generals, marshals, cannon and horses.

When the bitter news reached Paris, Napoleon was deposed and a republic proclaimed, and the new Government insisted on going on with the war. Within a fortnight of Sedan the Germans were besieging Paris. A second French army, larger than the one defeated at Sedan, was now surrounded at Metz; but, in spite of this second disaster, the French gallantly tried to drive the Germans from Paris. Bismarck was now ready for his fourth and last step.

THE GERMAN EMPIRE STARTS ON ITS CAREER AT VERSAILLES

During this time the states of Germany, drawn together in fighting a common foe, their deadliest enemy in the past, took counsel together. They decided that, the arms of Prussia being triumphant beyond all question, the moment had now arrived to put a seal on the unity of feeling that was growing stronger and stronger. So they asked the king of the victorious and leading state to become the German emperor, the head of the confederation of kings and princes.

Thus the German Empire was founded in the Palace of Versailles, where so many schemes for Germany's destruction had been planned in vain. It was on January 18, 1871. By May the peace with France was arranged, and the emperor William I and his great minister Bismarck were free to carry out their plans for the union of Germany under the leadership of Prussia. They had by no means an easy task through the twenty years that followed, for the people in the various provinces had old jealousies and dislikes to overcome. North Germany is chiefly Protestant, and south Germany is chiefly Roman Catholic; while in the Rhine provinces are many of both faiths.

Bismarck, the man of iron, steadfastly kept to his one aim. He had many struggles with various parties, especially with the Reichstag itself when he wanted money to spend on the army. "I hope they will give it," said he once, "or we shall have to take it as we can."

MILLIONS OF FRENCH MONEY THAT HELPED TO MAKE GERMANY GREAT

The enormous sum that France had to pay her after the war ($1,000,000,000) gave Germany much to spend on improvements of every kind. Great efforts were made to find new markets for whatever the country produced, and to open up suitable uses for raw materials obtainable from other countries. Arrangements were made to distribute the workers of some of the poorer and more distant states, placing them where work was to be done. The annoying restrictions existing between the various states were done away with. One kind of money and one kind of weights and measures were introduced all over the empire. The laws of different states were made like each other and a splendid postal and telegraph service was set up. The railways were gradually brought under the control of one central management.

It is not to be wondered at that there were thousands of sorrowful people standing about the Unter den Linden when the old emperor William lay dying. It had been given to him, with Bismarck, to accomplish a wonderful work; and Germany loved him as a father. His son Frederick reigned for only a few months;

GERMANY AFTER THE WAR TREATIES

The new German state is nearly one-seventh smaller than the old, and has lost about one-eighth of the population. As you see, the territory taken from Poland nearly a hundred and fifty years ago has been restored, and Alsace and Lorraine, taken from France after the Franco-Prussian War, have been restored to France. The people of Slesvig (or Schleswig) were given their choice of remaining German or becoming Danish. The inhabitants of the southern part voted to remain German. Belgium received two tiny bits of former German territory. The map does not show every one of the German states. There were twenty-five in the old Germany, but eight make up new Thuringia. There are now eighteen states in the new Germany.

but in that short time he built up a memory for all people and all time in the example of noble courage with which he met suffering and death.

The emperor Frederick was followed by his young son William, whom all the world knew in later years as the Kaiser. During his reign Germany made great strides in prosperity. The mineral wealth of the provinces she tore from France helped her manufactures, and her shipping expanded immensely. Her population rapidly increased, and the Kaiser set his heart on building up an overseas empire. Though that empire never reached more than one-twelfth the extent of the British Empire, Germany hastened to build a navy that would challenge comparison with the British fleet. Her army consisted of the whole manhood of the nation, diligently trained, completely equipped, and ever ready for instant war.

EUROPE IS DIVIDED INTO TWO CAMPS WHICH COME TO WAR

In 1914 the Austrian archduke was murdered at Sarajevo, and Austria determined to crush Serbia, whom she suspected of rebelling against her. This brought in the little Slavic state's elder brother, Russia. Russia was hand in glove with France, and England was committed to alliance with both of them in case of trouble. Italy already had an alliance with Austria and Germany, but this held good only if they suffered the attack and were not the ones to begin the fighting.

Austria persisted in her intention of humbling Serbia, and Russia determined to protect Serbia. Negotiations failed to halt the mobilization of the two countries' forces, and Germany and England followed suit.

England strove to the last to stave off war, but when Germany invaded Belgium in her attack upon France, she was twice committed, for Belgium's neutrality had been guaranteed by the powers.

THE GERMAN EMPIRE ENDS ITS CAREER AT VERSAILLES

Then followed the most fearful war in history, and at the end of four years of unceasing fighting by land and sea, the great force of which the Kaiser was the figurehead was beaten back. Under the strain of defeat, the German, Austrian, Russian and Turkish empires all collapsed. Republics were formed in Germany, Austria and Russia. The Kaiser, who had revealed himself during the war as little more than a toy king playing at soldiers, ran away from his people, hid himself in Holland, and evaded the consequences of his policy. The German navy settled itself at the bottom of the North Sea. German shipping was for the most part handed over to the Allies; the German army was disbanded and disarmed; her fortresses were dismantled; and her colonies were divided among the British Empire, France, Belgium and Japan. The territories she had taken in past years from France, Poland, Denmark and Belgium were handed back to their former owners. History holds no record of a more complete defeat.

The Peace Treaty of Versailles was drawn up in the Hall of Mirrors, which had been the birthplace of the fallen German Empire. Germany was condemned to pay reparations for the damages she had done, and she signed solemnly her willingness to comply with the conditions laid down.

Before long, however, it became clear that, while the Allies themselves were not agreed as to what Germany should pay, Germany was not seeking frankly and promptly to pay at all. Serious trouble arose, until in the end Germany's finances were in ruin and it seemed impossible that the war bill could ever be paid.

THE PROUD NATION THAT LAY HUMBLED IN THE DUST

It is true that her resources had been considerably lessened. Alsace and Lorraine had been returned to France, and the Saar coal-field was held in pawn by the League of Nations because of the willful destruction by the Germans of coal-mines in northern France. Still, Germany appeared not to have the will to discharge her admitted obligations. Under these circumstances France and Belgium proceeded to enforce their claims by occupying the chief German coal-field in the Ruhr valley and the great industrial region from which flowed Germany's lifeblood, against the express wishes of Great Britain. Stagnation followed, and Germany drifted nearer and nearer to national bankruptcy. Finally a settlement known as the Dawes plan was agreed to by Germany, whereby the collection of reparations was taken out of the hands of politicians and given to the leaders of industry.

THE NEXT STORY OF ALL COUNTRIES IS ON PAGE 4161.

WHERE DOES AN APPLE COME FROM?

WE know that when we sow seeds properly they grow, and from a very small seed we may get a very big tree. It may be an apple tree, and it may produce hundreds of apples year after year. Where do they all come from?

CONTINUED FROM 3843

Or, to take another instance, we plant one pound weight of potatoes and get a hundred pounds weight of potatoes. Where does all the difference come from? It almost looks as if the hundred pounds of potatoes were new weight in the world; but the world gets scarcely any heavier, so that cannot be the truth. We are also quite certain that the stuff in the apples or the potatoes is not made out of nothing, but comes from somewhere.

The apple, then, and the potatoes have been made by the wonderful power of the living tree or plant out of the stuff which surrounds them. In the case of the potatoes in the last question, we are quite sure that if we could have weighed the stuff taken as food by the first pound of potatoes it would have weighed 99 pounds. The earth as a whole is not any heavier; merely, in the case of the tree, some of the things that make up the weight of the air, such as oxygen, and the carbon from the carbon dioxid on which the plant feeds, and some of the things that make up the weight of the ground, such as water and many salts, have been built into its body.

It is as if you had a house that could build itself, and make its own bricks into the bargain.

And so it is in the case of the apples or the potatoes—or you. Part of the earth has been built into apples and potatoes, and the builder in this case is the living plant. After a time—and this is true of every living creature—it dies, and the stuff which is taken from the earth and the air for making its body is restored to them, and other living creatures use it in the same way; and so there is a circle or cycle—the cycle of life—through which much of the stuff of the earth and the air goes on passing from age to age.

It might be thought, then, that, as the air gives so much to the apple, the air would be lighter in summer, when the apple grows, than in winter, but we should not like to say that the air is lighter in summer than in winter on this account. In the first place, the weight of the air is so enormous that all the oxygen taken from it for the purposes of life would only be like a drop compared to the ocean; and in the second place, there are many other things happening which might work in the other direction.

For instance, under the influence of the sun, many of the products of past life lying on the surface of the soil are broken up, and the oxygen they contain is given back to the air. For example, animal matter breaks up more rapidly under the influence of heat.

HOW DO FISH LIVE IN A FROZEN POND?

Ordinary ice, we know, is lighter than water, and therefore it floats. So what we call a frozen pond is a pond of which the surface is frozen. Skaters are perfectly aware of this. They want to know how thick the ice is, for they know that there is liquid water underneath it. So when we speak about fish living in a frozen pond, we mean fish living in liquid water that has a layer of frozen water above it.

The really serious part of this for the fish is not, as we might think, the coldness of the water they are in, but the question how that water is to be supplied with enough air for the fish to live. When a pond is not frozen, oxygen from the air above it is passing into the surface of the water as fast as it is being used up by the fish and other living creatures in the water.

When a pond is frozen, this process is very nearly stopped. There may be gaps in the ice here and there—air-holes, such as air-breathing creatures will make in the frozen North—but perhaps there may be none of these. A little oxygen may get through at the edge of the ice, but the best hope for the fish is that there is a supply of new water coming into the pond below the ice from somewhere else, and bringing enough oxygen dissolved in it to keep the fish alive. If the supply of oxygen is kept up in none of these ways, then, when there is no more of it left, the fish will surely die, as must every living creature that is prevented from breathing, whether it be man, mammal, bird, reptile, fish or moss.

WHAT IS THE PRINCIPLE OF AN ESCALATOR?

An escalator is a flight of stairs, always moving, so that it carries us to the top while we stand still. Our great-great-grandfathers would have thought such a thing a miracle, but the escalator—which simply means moving staircase—is becoming quite common to-day. It originated in the United States, but there are many now in other countries.

The escalator developed from the endless band used for conveying goods in factories, and many years ago such a band, placed at an incline, used to carry visitors to the top of a cliff. It was an early form of escalator without steps.

The escalator differs from the moving inclined plane in having stairs which travel up or down, the steps being horizontal all the time. Passengers going up can increase their rate of progress by walking up the moving stairs.

When the steps reach the top they form a horizontal plane and carry the passenger to the stationary landing, where he is left while the steps travel on and, turning round a roller, go upside down underneath the staircase to the bottom again.

The average escalator travels about forty feet a minute, which is not too fast to allow passengers to step on or off with perfect safety. An endless hand-rail of leather on each side moves with the stairs and enables inexperienced people to steady themselves. The great advantage of the escalator over the elevator is that it is always moving and can be used at any time by any number of passengers.

WHY IS A NEEDLE NO HEAVIER WHEN MAGNETIZED?

This question puzzles us because we have not clearly distinguished in our own minds what weight really means and what it does not mean.

We say that weight is a direct consequence of gravitation. Were there no gravitation, there would be no such thing as weight. The power of gravitation entirely depends upon the amount of stuff that is concerned, or the mass of matter that is acted upon. In other words, the weight of a thing depends entirely upon its mass—the amount of matter in it. Everything goes to prove that nothing affects gravitation except this question of the amount of matter present.

If we take a needle and heat it or cool it, magnetize it or unmagnetize it, or do anything else to it, so long as we do not take away any of the matter from it or add any new matter to it, its weight remains the same. When we magnetize it, we endow it with a new power which is very strong and wonderful, and which, for instance, can be brought to bear in such a way that it will overpower the force of gravitation, and will thus enable the needle to lift ten times its own weight. But the weight of the needle itself absolutely depends upon its mass, and upon nothing else. Our bodies weigh just the same whether we hold a weight in our hands or not; the amount of stuff in our bodies is the same in either case. Of course, our bodies and the weight together weigh more than our bodies would alone, but that is a different thing.

WHY ARE THERE MORE STARS SOME NIGHTS THAN OTHERS?

There are not more stars some nights than others, but we see more. What really happens is that the state of the atmosphere differs very much at different times, quite apart from the presence of actual clouds. Even when there are no clouds anywhere, and all over the sky the brighter stars can be seen, the state of the air may be such—whether owing to the presence of a lot of dust high up in it, or to other causes—that the less bright stars cannot be seen. The temperature and the pressure of the air have their own effects in this respect. Much of the recent advance in astronomy has been due to the fact that great new observatories, containing the finest telescopes in the world, have been specially built on the tops of mountains, in parts of the world specially chosen for the clearness of the air; and the higher the telescope, of course, the less the amount of clear air that the light from the stars has to pass through before it reaches the eye of the astronomer or the lens of the camera.

WHAT IS PAPYRUS?

The papyrus is a kind of sedge from eight to ten feet high, found chiefly in Africa. It has been almost as important for the growth of man's mind as wheat for the growth of his body. From its pith was made paper, and for hundreds of years papyrus paper was the chief medium for the record of the thoughts of men. The paper was made of strips of the pith cemented together into sheets, which could be rolled up into scrolls, but later the sheets were bound into pages in book form. Some of the sheets were seven feet long. In Egypt many valuable and interesting scrolls have been found, including previously unknown fragments of Euripides, and a famous but lost work of Aristotle on the constitution of Athens.

DO THINGS WEIGH HEAVIER OR LIGHTER WHEN HOT OR COLD?

This question about gravitation is really extremely interesting, because it so happens that this is one of the very questions on which a great many remarkable experiments have quite lately been made.

There is no doubt about the answer to it, but we must understand what that answer really is. It is that the power of gravitation is not in the slightest degree affected by temperature; in other words, the same thing—if nothing is taken from it or added to it—weighs just the same, whether it is hot or cold.

But we must not be confused. When a thing is heated it swells, as a rule, and as there is no more of it there, but it is occupying more space, it is made lighter in proportion to the space it occupies. Thus hot water will float on the top of cold water; hot air will rise in cold air, and so on. This, however, is not a question of absolute weight, but of the relation between that weight, which is not changed, and the volume of the thing.

DOES A LIGHT-WAVE GO THROUGH GLASS?

Light is not a wave of air, but a wave in the ether, which is everywhere—in the air and in the glass, too. When the light passes through glass, it is a wave in ether all the time, though during part of its journey the kind of matter called air is there, and in another part glass.

This is not to say that matter has no effect on these ether-waves, for we know that it has. All we can say is that some kinds of matter offer no great obstacle to their passage, as, for instance, glass; while other kinds of matter, such as wood or stone, interfere very much with their passage. Sound is a wave of air, and where sound passes through glass, the air-wave on the outside throws the glass into a wave of the same kind, and the wave in the glass starts a new wave in the air on the other side, and so the sound goes on.

HOW CAN WE TELL THE NUMBER OF DAYS IN ANOTHER WORLD'S YEAR?

If we know how long a planet takes to go once round the sun, we know the length of its year. Then, if we can watch the planet, and see how long it takes to spin round once on itself, we know the length of its day. Divide the length of the year by the length of the day, and we have the number of days in the year. But though that is quite easy in some cases, in others it is impossible, and so we cannot yet tell the number of days in a year of every planet.

The trouble is that, though we know how long the planet takes to go round the sun, in some cases—as in the case of Neptune—the planet is so far away that we cannot make out any of the features of its face, and therefore cannot tell at what rate it spins, or even that it spins at all, and we do not know the length of its day, though we do know the length of its year.

CAN A FLY HEAR ORDINARY SOUNDS?

The more we study the senses of different animals, the more do we learn that the sense of hearing ranks high in the scale, and comes late in the history of the progress of life; and thus we find that various creatures, whose powers of touch and of smell and of vision are marvelous, seem to be almost, or entirely, deaf.

There are a few insects that can hear, but the greater number, including flies, cannot hear at all. Every imaginable kind of sound has been tried, and insects, with the exception of very few, take no notice whatever. Lord Avebury thought that perhaps insects might respond to sounds of so high a pitch that our ears cannot hear them, but he could not get them to take any notice.

The highest string of a violin has been scraped an inch away from bees engaged in pillaging flowers, and they have taken no notice whatever. The senses of insects, including flies, are so wonderful, and in some respects so superior to our own, that it is immensely interesting to find that nearly all insects, including not only the flies but the highest insects, such as the bees, ants and wasps, are perfectly deaf.

WHY DO WE NOT LAUGH WHEN WE TICKLE OURSELVES?

This is an exceedingly interesting question, because we cannot think about it without discovering a most important fact about our minds and the way in which they are made for use, for safety and for the purposes of living. If we do not have this mighty key to mind and body, we shall never understand why it is that the same thing should make us laugh and squirm when someone else does it and have no effect at all when we do it ourselves. The whole point and purpose of the feeling in our skins, and of what happens—such as laughing and squirming—when this feeling is aroused in particular ways, is that it gives us information about what is not ourselves.

Our minds have so much power over the way in which our bodies reply to things that when we know the cause of the feeling to be ourselves, and therefore nothing we need concern ourselves about, the body feels no inclination to behave as it does at all other times. The results of tickling are what is called a reflex action, and we learn from this case that a reflex action is a reply to the outside world.

If it is sought to call forth the reply by what we know not to be really the outside world—as when we tickle ourselves—then the body does not trouble. This shows how reflex actions are controlled by and adjusted to the needs of the body.

WHY IS IT THAT THE SEA DOES NOT FREEZE?

Sea-water, like any other kind of water, can freeze, and it does freeze if the conditions are right; but there are some good reasons why the sea does not freeze nearly so easily as a pond or lake, or even a river. The salt in sea-water does not make so much difference as the depth and constant motion of sea-water. Until the whole depth of a quantity of water has been cooled it cannot begin to freeze; for until it has all cooled, the warmer water, being lighter, must always come to the top. Therefore, when water is very deep, it is very difficult to freeze. The great depth of the sea is one reason.

But the sea is also in constant movement under the influence of tides and winds and currents. The motion of water interferes very much with its freezing, though not nearly so much as the depth.

But in the coldest parts of the earth's surface the sea does freeze, as we find in the records of those explorers, like Peary or Shackleton, who attempt to reach the North or the South Pole. The same seems to be the case on our near and wonderful neighbor, the planet Mars, for we can see through our telescopes what looks like the ice or snow-caps at each of its Poles.

WHY DOES STARCH STIFFEN CLOTHES?

Starch is a very curious chemical compound, with its own way of behaving. Like the proteins—white of egg, and so on —it consists of very large molecules, so large that no one knows how many atoms each one contains. It consists of molecules so big that we can scarcely say that it really dissolves, certainly not as sugar and salt, which have small molecules, dissolve. But it forms a sort of solution with water, and when the water evaporates the starch is left behind.

Starch is called one of the substances that are not at all volatile—that is, able to fly off into the air. The big molecules of the starch, left behind in the clothing, form a sort of stiff layer by all holding together. We know how water affects this when we see how our collar gets limp if we perspire.

WHY DOES STEAM PUT A LIGHT OUT?

Of course, it depends upon the kind of light whether steam will or will not put it out, but it is certainly true that a fire or gas light or a lamp may be put out by steam. For this there are at least two reasons. We use the word steam rather loosely, often meaning by it liquid water in the air—the steam that we can see. But sometimes we mean by it water-vapor. Wherever there is steam there is water-vapor—that is to say, water in the air in the form of an invisible gas. Now, this water is already burned; it can neither be burned any more nor can it sustain the burning of anything else.

If the thing which produces the light is supplied with water-vapor in the air instead of oxygen, it is starved and must go out. But the presence of steam means also the presence of liquid water, and liquid water puts a light out because it swallows up the heat which is near it, and makes the burning thing so cold that it cannot burn. Every man who smokes a pipe knows the great difference there is between smoking moist tobacco and dry tobacco.

WHAT IS SMOKE MADE OF?

Smoke is the result of imperfect burning. Most of the things from which we get so much smoke—like coal—if they were properly burned would form nothing but gases, which we could not see, and which would very soon fly away. But in order to burn coal properly some trouble and care are required. When we burn coal in an ordinary fire, we do not supply enough air to it. We put the fresh coal on at the top instead of at the bottom, as we should, and so we partly burn the coal, and small specks of it, unburned, are carried up in the draft, and make smoke. The chief stuff in smoke is simply coal in specks of various sizes. But the trouble is that oily stuff comes out of the coal, and covers the specks of it in smoke, so that these stick to things. The time will come when we shall make our fireplaces differently, so that we can burn our coal in a better way.

At present the smoke makes black fogs in many cities, and cuts off a great quantity of the daylight by which we live, besides making everything dirty, destroying plants and trees, and filling our lungs with dirt which we never get rid of. There are few things about which we are more careless than smoke, and if we had sense enough we should stop making it, even if it were only for the reason that all the stuff in smoke might be burned, and that in making smoke we waste a great deal of fuel.

WHAT MAKES WATER GURGLE WHEN IT COMES OUT OF A BOTTLE?

We know that the air has pressure, and so, if there is an empty space anywhere, the air will press into it. Now, when we pour water out of a bottle which is full, there must be an empty space left behind in the bottle when the liquid comes out, and from moment to moment, as that empty space tends to be formed in the bottle, the air outside is bound to rush in to take its place. If the bottle has a wide mouth, like a tumbler, then, as we pour the liquid out, air can flow in evenly, and there is no gurgling.

But if we take a full ginger-ale bottle, and hold it upside down, then there is a series of fights going on between the liquid which is trying to get out under the pull of gravitation and the air which is trying to push its way past the liquid to fill up the space in the bottle. Sometimes the air pushes back the ginger-ale, and sometimes the ginger-ale pushes back the air. This means that the air is thrown into little disturbances, which we hear as gurgles. We say that water gurgles, but really it is the air that is disturbed by this contest between it and the water, and we call these disturbances "gurgles."

WHY DOES A GLOW-WORM GLOW?

A glow-worm is not a worm at all, but is really a kind of European beetle seen during the summer months up to the end of August on warm banks and hedgerows and in woods and pastures. As soon as the evening's dusk begins, this beautiful insect begins to show a most exquisite yellowish green light, caused by what are called luminous organs placed over the tail end.

The object of this light is not certain, but most of the wise men who study living creatures suppose that the female shows the light for the purpose of attracting males, which do not shine in this way. Whether this is the real reason or not we cannot be quite sure, but the glow-worm is only one of many animals that show light by what is called phosphorescence.

THE NEXT WONDER QUESTIONS ARE ON PAGE 4131.

THE DROLL LITTLE MAN WITH THE UNKNOWN NAME

When the Queen was rejoicing over the birth of her baby, the little old man who had helped her to spin the gold came and threatened to take away her son unless she found out his name within three days. She thought of all the names she could, and she sent messengers all over the country to find out other ones. On the third day came good news. "Yesterday," said the Queen's messenger, "as I was climbing a high hill among the trees of the forest, I saw a little hut, and before the hut burned a fire, and round about the fire danced a funny little man upon one leg, singing, 'Rum-Pel-Stilt-Skin is my name.'"

RUM-PEL-STILT-SKIN

IN a certain kingdom there once lived a poor miller who had a very beautiful daughter. She was, moreover, exceedingly shrewd and clever; and the miller was so vain and proud of her that one day he told the King of the land that his daughter could spin gold out of straw! Now, this King was very fond of money, and when he heard the miller's boast he ordered the girl to be brought before him. Then he led her to a chamber where there was a great quantity of straw, gave her a spinning-wheel, and said: "All this must be spun into gold before morning, as you value your life."

It was in vain that the poor maiden declared she could do no such thing; the chamber was locked, and she was left alone.

She sat down in one corner of the room and began to cry, when the door opened, and a droll-looking little man hobbled in and said: "Good day to you. What are you weeping for?"

"Alas!" answered she, "I must spin this straw into gold, and I know not how."

"What will you give me," said the little man, "to do it for you?"

"My necklace," replied the maiden.

He took her at her word, and set himself down to the wheel. Round about it went merrily, and presently the gold was all spun.

When the King came and saw this he was greatly astonished and pleased;

CONTINUED FROM 3904

but his heart grew still more greedy, and he shut up the poor miller's daughter again with a fresh task. Then she knew not what to do, and sat down once more to weep; but the little man presently opened the door, and said: "What will you give me to do your task?"

"The ring on my finger," she replied. So her little friend took the ring, and began to work at the wheel, till by the morning all was finished again.

The King was vastly delighted to see all this glittering treasure; but he was not satisfied yet, and took the miller's daughter into a still larger room, and said: "All this must be spun to-night; and if you succeed you shall be my Queen."

As soon as she was alone the dwarf came in, and said: "What will you give me to spin gold this third time?"

"I have nothing left," said she.

"Then promise me," said the little man, "your first little child when you are Queen."

"That may never be," thought the miller's daughter; and as she knew no other way to get her task done, she promised him what he asked, and once more he spun the whole heap of gold. The King came in the morning, and, finding all he wanted, married her.

At the birth of her first little child the Queen rejoiced very much, and forgot the little man and her promise; but one day he came into her chamber and reminded her of it. Then she offered

him all the treasures of the kingdom in exchange; but in vain, till at last her tears softened him, and he said: "If in three days you can tell me my name, you shall keep your child."

Now, the Queen lay awake all night, thinking of all the odd names that she had ever heard, and dispatched messengers all over the land to inquire after new ones. The next day the little man came, and she began with Timothy, Benjamin, Jeremiah, and all the names she could remember, but to all of them he said: "That's not my name."

The second day she began with all the comical names she could hear of, Bandylegs, Hunchback, Crookshanks, and so on; but the little gentleman still said to every one: "That's not my name."

The third day came back one of the messengers, and said: "Yesterday, as I was climbing a high hill among the trees of the forest where the fox and the hare bid each other good-night, I saw a little hut, and before the hut burned a fire, and round about the fire danced a funny little man upon one leg, singing:

"'Merrily the feast I'll make,
To-day I'll brew, to-morrow bake;
Merrily I'll dance and sing,
For next day will a stranger bring;
Little does my lady dream
Rum-Pel-Stilt-Skin is my name.'"

Then the Queen jumped for joy, and as soon as her little visitor came she said: "Is your name John?"

"No!"

"Is it Tom?"

"No!"

"Is it Rum-Pel-Stilt-Skin?"

"Some witch told you that!" cried the little man, and in a rage dashed his right foot so deep into the floor that he was forced to lay hold of it with both hands to pull it out. Then he made the best of his way off, while everybody laughed at him for having had all his trouble for nothing.

THE GEESE WHO KEPT GUARD OF ROME

ROME was besieged. An army of tall, fierce warriors, with blue eyes and golden hair, from the land of Gaul, had swooped down upon her and forced their way within the gates of the great city itself.

Fierce battles were fought in the city, and the legions of Rome found themselves driven back again and again. The Gauls were not only strong—they were fearless. They rushed on the Romans with terrible shouts, and tore their ranks asunder.

At last the poor Romans were forced to retire to their last fortress, called the Capitol. They were safe here, for who would dream of climbing up the steep rock to force the mighty walls of the Capitol? But sad and dreadful was it for the Roman soldiers, though they were safe, to look over the walls of their fortress and watch the savage Gauls burning their homes and carrying off all their precious things as booty.

The Romans began to be dreadfully hungry. Many a time they must have looked at the sacred geese which lived in the Temple of Juno, and thought it would be no crime to kill and eat them. But the geese were sacred birds to the Romans. To kill them would be sacrilege.

Now, it chanced one night, as a brave young Roman named Manlius lay sleeping beside his sword near the Temple of Juno, that a strange sound striking across his troubled dreams woke him suddenly out of slumber, and made him grasp his sword and spring to his feet.

He recognized the noise at once. It was the hissing of the sacred geese. What could have roused the birds?

The noise increased; it became a panic of alarm; the whole flock was filling the night with its frightened cries.

Manlius ran to the walls of the fortress and looked down. He came face to face with a Gaul!

The leader of the Gauls had led his men up the pinnacle in a night attack, and he was just about to pull himself over the wall when Manlius appeared. In an instant Manlius seized the straining wrists of the Gaul, and wrenching the fingers free of the parapet, hurled the enemy down the hill.

Louder and louder grew the noisy clamor of the geese. Romans started from their sleep, and snatching their arms, hurried to see what it could be. They found Manlius defending the walls. With a shout of victory they rushed to his rescue, and in a few minutes all the garrison was roused and the Gauls were beaten back and utterly routed.

THE MAGIC BOY FIDDLER OF SICILY

PERO was a merry, simple lad, and he lived in a village in the beautiful island of Sicily. His parents died when he was young, and at the age of fourteen he set out to make his fortune. He wandered about the country, and at last a miserly old farmer engaged him as a goatherd. Pero forgot to arrange about wages, and when, at the end of three years, he asked his master to pay him, the miserly old farmer gave him only threepence. But Pero went away as lighthearted as ever.

and a gun that will never miss, and the gift of speech that nobody can refuse me anything."

The Spirit granted Pero these wishes, and Pero turned back to the farm. Seeing a pheasant fly by, he fired at it to test his magic gun. The bird fell, but before he could pick it up the farmer ran out and seized it."

"Well," said Pero, "you can have it if you like to dance for it."

He played on his violin, and the farmer capered like a madman.

Pero, with his magic fiddle, was traveling in Sicily, and fell among enemies, who resolved to hang him. But just as Pero was going to be hanged he played on the magic violin that made everybody dance, and the magistrate and the hangman and all the spectators danced to his playing. He played till they were weary, and the magistrate promised at last that if Pero would stop playing he should go free.

On the road he met a beggarman, who said: "My son, I am starving. Give me something to buy some bread."

"You can take my wages," said Pero, "and I will go back and serve three years more."

"You are really as kind as you are simple," said the beggarman, and as he spoke he changed into a bright Spirit. "I give you three wishes. Ask and you shall have."

"Well," said Pero, "give me, please, a violin that will make everybody dance,

"Stop, Pero!" he cried at last. "I treated you badly, I know; but stop, and I'll give you a thousand crowns."

Pero received the money, but as soon as his back was turned the farmer ran to the magistrate and denounced him as a robber. There was little mercy for robbers in Sicily in those days. Pero was quickly arrested, tried and condemned. But just as the hangman was putting the rope round his neck he asked the magistrate to let him play one tune on his violin.

"Don't give him the violin!" cried the farmer.

But Pero had the gift of speech, and nobody could refuse him anything. The magistrate gave the violin to him, and Pero played on it, and the magistrate and the farmer and the hangman and the spectators danced to his playing. He played till they were weary; he played till they were worn out; he played till the soles came off their boots, and still he played. And the magistrate at last promised that if he would stop he should go free. Pero then came down from the scaffold, and took his gun and his violin and his thousand crowns, and returned to his native village, and, having the gift of speech, he won the prettiest girl in Sicily as his wife, and settled down contentedly.

THREE NIGHTS IN THE ENCHANTED CASTLE

ONE summer there was a great drought in Spain, and when autumn came there was no harvest. Many peasants wandered about the country in search of work and food, and among them was a good-looking brave lad whose name was Juan Lopez. His mother and father were dead, and his master was ruined, and he had nowhere to go.

One evening Juan came, hungry and homeless, to the town of Granada, and finding no other lodging, he settled down to sleep amid the green ruins of an ancient Moorish castle. But just as he closed his eyes he felt a tap on his shoulder. Looking up, he saw a hand holding a lighted candle. It beckoned to him, and as Juan was desperate with hunger he followed.

The hand led him into a gorgeous hall where a table stood loaded with exquisite delicacies, and there Juan feasted to his heart's content. The hand then beckoned again, and led Juan into another splendid chamber with a bed in it. Juan took off his ragged clothes, and put on a silken nightdress which he found lying on a heap of rich garments, and got into the bed and fell asleep.

When the bells of Granada struck twelve, the hand came and awoke him, and a sweet voice said: "It was very brave of you, Juan, to follow my hand. You are the first who ever dared to do so. Now, will you show yourself braver still, and set an unhappy, helpless maiden free from a wicked spell?"

"What must I do?" said Juan.

"You must stay in this bed for three nights and days," said the voice, "and you must not move or cry out, no matter what is done to you."

"Very well," said Juan, "I will see if I can stand it."

On the first night a troop of spirits came with bludgeons and beat poor Juan until there was not a sound bone in his body. But in the morning the hand appeared and brought refreshment, together with a magic salve which cured him of his wounds and cuts.

On the second night the spirits wounded him again, but he neither moved nor cried out; and the next morning the hand brought him a magic medicine which healed him.

The ordeal of the third night was fearful, and no hand appeared at the break of day. But there came instead a princely maiden, who bathed Juan with magic water that made him hale and whole again.

Juan then put on the rich garments, and went into the hall where the table stood and feasted with the maiden. She was wonderfully lovely, and her loveliness was of a kind which Juan had never seen before. Her skin was of a creamy tint, with a deep rosy color showing beneath the cream; her little mouth was like a scarlet flower; and her dark eyes were large and liquid and tender, like the eyes of a beautiful fawn.

"Surely you are not a Spanish lady?" said Juan.

"No," said the maiden. "I am the daughter of the Sultan of Morocco. And now that the spell is removed I must return at once to my father's palace. Follow and find me."

She vanished, and Juan found himself sitting, ragged and poor, amid the green ruins of the castle.

He bravely set out to follow the Princess, but as he had no money to pay his way, it was a very long time before he reached her palace. The Princess thought he was faithless, and she had promised to marry the King of Arabia; but as she was getting into the wedding coach she saw Juan standing, poor, ragged and sorrowful, by the palace gate.

PRINCE JUAN AND THE CAPTIVE PRINCESS

On the third day of Juan's life in the enchanted castle came a princely maiden, who bathed Juan with a magic water that made him well again. He put on the rich garments and went into the hall where the table stood, and there feasted with the maiden. "I am the daughter of the Sultan of Morocco," she said. Then she vanished, and Juan followed her to her father's palace, where he made the princess his bride.

"Some time ago," she said to the King of Arabia, "I lost the key of my jewel-case, so I took a new one. Now I have found the old key; which shall I use?"

"You should use the old key," said the King of Arabia.

"Here is the old key I meant," then said the Princess, getting out of the coach and taking Juan by the hand. "It was this brave, handsome boy who rescued me from the enchanted palace. So I will marry him, and you, O King, must find another bride."

And marry Juan she did. The King of Arabia, who was really a generous man, realized he had lost the Princess fairly and gave the happy bride and bridegroom a magnificent wedding present, and they lived happily together.

THE FABLES OF ÆSOP THE SLAVE

THE FOWL AND THE JEWEL

A fowl searching for food found a precious stone.

"A great many people would be pleased to have this," he said, "but if I had all the jewels in the world I would willingly give them for one small barley-corn."

He could eat the barley-corn, you see, but the jewel, of course, was useless to him.

The best thing in the world is worth nothing to you if you have no use for it.

THE MAN WHO GAVE UP SINGING

A merry cobbler used to sing at his work from morning till night.

Close by lived a rich man, who for a long time wondered how he could stop the singing, and at last he hit on a plan. He asked the cobbler how much money he earned in a year.

"Oh," said the cobbler, "not more than fifty crowns. But I am quite happy."

"Very well," replied the rich man, "here is a present for you." And he held out a bag containing a hundred crowns.

The cobbler was almost beside himself with delight. All the rest of that day he was wondering what he should do with so much money. Then he began to fear that he might lose it; and soon his alarm became so great that he no longer sang at his work, but became very miserable.

Money does not always bring happiness.

THE DOG AND THE SHADOW

A dog was once walking along a plank over a stream carrying a piece of meat in his mouth. Looking down, he saw his own shadow reflected in the clear water. Thinking it was another dog carrying another piece of meat, he was so greedy that he snatched at it. This caused him to open his mouth, and the meat fell out and sank to the bottom of the stream in the mud.

People who try to get what belongs to others are apt to lose more than they gain.

THE FOX AND THE GRAPES

A hungry fox, who had not killed for two nights, happened to come one day into a vineyard where there were plenty of fine ripe grapes. But these grapes were growing on a trellis so high that, though he leaped his utmost, he was not able to reach them. Still temptingly they hung in the sunlight.

"Oh, well, never mind!" said the fox. "Anyone can have them for all I care. They are sure to be sour."

People very often pretend to dislike things that they are not able to get.

THE NEXT STORIES ARE ON PAGE 4137.

Figures from the Temple of Zeus at Olympia.

THE EARLY DAYS OF GREECE

THE magic of "Once upon a time" clings to all the art of the ancient world, and when we come to the work of the Ægean peoples, though we are drawing nearer, in actual place, to modern European civilization, the magic of long ago strengthens itself. For the islands of the Ægean, centring in Crete and certain towns on the mainland, like Mycenæ and Tiryns, were the cradle of Greek art; and anything that touches Greece spells not only artistic beauty but also the greatest literature we have inherited from the past.

CONTINUED FROM 3880

Just as the art of Egypt, Babylonia and Persia stirs our memories of the Bible, so does the art of Greece, and the work that foreshadowed it, remind us of Homer's tales of heroes and of kings, the voyage of the Argonauts, the unforgettable Trojan War.

We are reminded almost every day of the magic of life and of the fact that mankind is much the same in all ages, when we read in our morning papers how the old walls and columns of buried towns are being brought to light by archæologists. By digging away the covering layers these men and women disclose the very life of the past—not only the buildings and streets, but even the dishes, the toys and the trinkets that belonged to liv-ing, breathing persons like you and me.

In the story beginning on page 447 you have read how Henry Schliemann and Sir Arthur Evans gave back to the world the knowledge of the old Ægean culture. You have seen how, by the discovery of the palace of King Minos at Knossos, we can explain quite reasonably the Greek legend of the Labyrinth and the Minotaur. And no one knows what other legends may be traced to their sources, almost any day.

The art of the Ægean civilization, which was at its best nearly two thousand years before Christ lived, showed here and there slight traces of the Egyptian and Assyrian influences with something added—a freedom of line and thought—that the greater nations did not have. The Ægean sculptors escaped the stiffness and coldness and angularity which marked the reliefs and statuary of their neighbors. They seem to have felt the wish to get "back to Nature"—a doctrine which has been preached ever since civilization has made it more and more impossible for people to be quite natural.

The Ægean artists, turning aside from one old convention, began to chisel nude figures. The absence of the nude from Egyptian and Assyrian sculpture has been explained chiefly on the grounds of religion and custom. When a statue of an Egyptian monarch was set in his tomb to await his coming back to life, it seemed to be a little unfeeling, wanting in reverence, to present this "double" unclothed. Only the meanest slaves went about in a nude, or almost nude, condition. And this convention, which was practically a law, was kept throughout the ages of Egyptian and Babylonian art, even when sculpture was a matter of decoration and had no relation to any living being.

The thoughts and impulses of the Ægean artists ran in another channel. They conceived of unconcealed nature as the most beautiful thing on earth, and wherever possible they introduced natural forms both of plant and of animal life. It seemed to be their ideal to make their work as lifelike as possible, and in the free and voluntary motions of their animal representations, in color and relief, we see something of the greatness of the reindeer-hunter's work. It is quite possible, of course, that some remnant of that work had been found by the earliest Ægean people, and that, though lost to us, it existed sufficiently long to influence their art.

THE SMALL SCALE OF THE WORKS OF THE ÆGEAN SCULPTORS

Generally speaking, the Ægean sculptors worked on a small scale. We have discovered nothing resembling the gigantic statuary or reliefs of Egypt and Assyria. At one period in their art they produced a large number of rather crude little marble statues, but their best work was done on reliefs of precious metal and stone vases. Some of the earliest artists working at Mycenæ hewed a pair of huge lionesses over a gate in the city wall—an almost isolated example of statuary on a large scale.

Probably more than a thousand years before Christ was born the settled civilization of these people in and about the Ægean archipelago was brought to an abrupt end by the breaking-in of some warlike tribes, among them the Dorians, from the hills of Greece lying to the north. The gentle, cultivated Ægeans whose racial strength had been frittered away were helpless before that onslaught which has passed into history as "the descent of the Dorians." They left their islands and towns on the mainland, and scattered east and west. A remnant of them settled in certain islands of the archipelago and in Asia Minor, and there they continued to preserve the elements of their civilization.

THE RICH TREASURE-CITIES THAT LAY BURIED FOR CENTURIES

In the course of time some of their descendants resettled in Greece. They came to be generally known as Ionians, the Ægean archipelago changing its name to the Ionian Isles. The exiled Ægeans had a great deal to do with the rise of Greece to greatness in art. But in the meantime the cities of Mycenæ and Tiryns and Knossos, with all their treasures, were demolished by the invaders and fell to ruin. Other towns rose above or near them, and not till near the end of the nineteenth century, when archæologists set to work upon excavations, was their existence guessed at.

The Dorians and the Ionians formed the two great branches of the Greek peoples; the Dorians centring in Sparta, the Ionians in Athens. It was owing to the Dorians that the term "Hellenes," originating in Hellen, a mythical ancestor of the Dorians, came, at a certain period in their history, to be applied to the Greeks as a whole. The word "Greek" is really an earlier name, and both the terms, Greeks and Hellenes, were originally used only in speaking of a single tribe, afterward becoming general to the nation.

The Dorians and the Ionians gave their names to the chief styles of Greek art. There was a great difference between their thoughts and ideals and character: the Dorians having the hard and stern outlook on life common to mountainous tribes, the Ionians being more ease-loving, pliable and more refined. But from these two influences came in time an art so magnificent as to stand without a peer in history.

It is difficult for us to realize what a wealth of Greek sculpture there was in the golden years of the nation. All the temples and public halls and their precincts were freely adorned with a statuary of whose superb beauty we can only guess from the fragments that remain. When the fall of Greece came there was enough sculpture to make rich the then known world. Much of it was carried away by Roman emperors to decorate their own houses and temples; it went here and there, to Rome, later to Con-

RARE THINGS FROM OLD GREECE

A vase with relief carvings
from Crete.

A beautiful vase of the
Mycenæan period.

A Cretan vase found at
Zakro.

The Shrine of the Snake Goddess, from Crete, as restored by Sir Arthur Evans.

An early Greek vase
from Rhodes.

A store jar from
Crete.

A Cretan jar with reliefs
of the Centaurs.

stantinople; some of it was buried—for pious motives, doubtless. When bronze became valuable, wholesale theft took place; huge quantities of marble sculpture were burned down in kilns for lime. And now a world poorer than it knows by that lamentable loss counts for its chief artistic treasures isolated pieces— nearly all of them buried for centuries— saved from the ruin of Greece.

WHY THE OLD GREEK SCULPTORS WORKED IN MARBLE

Not all this Greek sculpture was pure in the sense of being first hand. There were innumerable original statues, and these were freely copied, often in the workshop of the sculptor; later came work which was merely imitative of the original and the copy.

Wood, stone, metal, marble and terracotta were used by the Greek sculptors. Marble naturally is in the lead, as not only was it a fine sensitive medium to work in, but it was freely quarried on the mainland. And many of the islands, notably Naxos and Paros, were largely composed of marble.

Stone was used to a certain extent, but its unpleasant, rough texture was generally hidden by a coat of paint. In the earliest days statues were painted to look as much like life as possible; as the national taste developed, this practice declined, but for a long time color was made use of to enhance the decorative value of statuary, the nude figure being left unpainted, and the draperies and adornments colored in a striking way.

Even the finest marbles for many generations were given a kind of wash of wax melted in oil and rubbed into the surface, in order, it was supposed, to ease the brilliance, painful to the eye, of naked marble when exposed to the sun's glare. Only in later times did the Greek sculptors, becoming enamored of the lovely texture of the marble itself, allow it to remain exposed to the sun and rain.

It was not often that large statues were made in terra-cotta. This medium seems to have recommended itself for the lovely statuettes and figurines which were made in great numbers and deposited with the dead. Burial places like those at Tanagra, in Greece, and Myrina, in Asia Minor, have yielded a great store. There are fine collections of them in the Louvre, the British Museum and the Metropolitan Museum of Art.

The early work of the Greeks was done in bronze and in wood, and the making of bronze statues and reliefs continued even when the national taste had dictated that marble should be used. Centuries of plunder are responsible for the few existing specimens of this metal work. For the same reason, and also because of natural decay, there are no specimens of the statuary in wood, often inlaid with ivory and gilded, that marked the beginnings of Greek sculpture.

How far the feeling of the natural form of wood influenced the early sculptors it is hard to say; there is certainly a resemblance to the form of a tree-trunk in the broken statue of Hera, the body so beautifully folded in a sheath, now in the Louvre, and in the Artemis of the Athens Museum. These two figures, dating from 600 B.C., are our oldest specimens of Greek sculpture.

RARE FIGURES IN THE ART OF EARLY GREECE

Somewhat similar in feeling is the ancient seated figure of King Chares, now in the British Museum, carved about fifty years later. Single figures like these—"free" statues they were called, statues that could be walked around—were rare in the early days of Greek sculpture. The use of statuary in the first case was to adorn a building, even as the first use of pictures was to adorn the space of a wall. And just as for several centuries pictures were painted on the wall itself as part of its fabric, so the early statuary was part of the body of the temple or public building.

Such free statues as existed were set up apart from a building, being generally placed either on tombs or in the precincts of temples or public buildings. These specimens that we have found, notably the Chares, Hera and Artemis fragments, show that in its first stage Greek art had something of the stillness of the Egyptian.

Generally speaking, the art of a race takes about a thousand years to develop; one of the miracles of Greek art is the speed with which it passed, so to speak, from babyhood to youth. Its entire and stupendous history lies within the compass of six centuries, and of these the first three are of supreme interest.

The first sculptors to break away from the tradition of the rigid sheath-inclosed figures were a family living about 550

Statue of Artemis, from Delos.

"The First Smile in Art," the Nike of Delos.

A statue of Poseidon found at Bœotia.

Carved figures on a tomb in the Acropolis of Xanthos, in Lycia.

The Seated Figure of King Chares.

The Gate of Lions at Mycenæ.

The pictures on these pages are reproduced by courtesy of Messrs. Bruckmann, Mansell, and others.

B.C. on the island of Chios. Four generations of Chian sculptors followed each other, and one of them, Archermos, greatly daring, made a statue of a new kind—a winged goddess with arms lifted and limbs in motion. It was a strange figure, with its attempted chiseled draperies, and such movement as it displayed was stiff. To ourselves, trained to the perfection of the Greeks in their prime, it seems a barbaric and unlovely object. But its appearance was an event of great importance. The new goddess —the Winged Nike, or Victory, it was called—was taken as a Greek type, and it marked the beginning of freedom of action and pose characteristic of Greek statuary.

THE MAN WHO IS SAID TO HAVE INVENTED THE SMILE IN ART

In addition to the novelty of movement, Archermos invented another wonder: he made his goddess smile—the first smile, we are told, in art. It had seemed to be the rule for a stone or granite face to be as serious as Time itself, or, if not definitely serious, vacant and expressionless. Herein in two ways the work of Archermos dimly foreshadowed that liberty which was destined to mark the work of his race.

The Chian sculptors came presently to live in Athens, and their new ideas were adopted by their fellow-artists. Meanwhile another development was taking place: the Grecians were beginning to study drapery and to show the beauty of muscular form in their statues; already they were far removed from the rough-hewn shapes of the earlier years.

The art of a country always serves as a kind of commentary on the thoughts and habits of the nation, and in this development we can see the Greek character asserting itself. The Grecians had a growing passion for athletic strength and beauty. Moreover, Athens was a city of philosophers and poets; her intellectual force, her ideals of freedom and liberty of thought, joined to her instinct for bodily perfection, created an art at once physical and spiritual.

But it was an outside more than an inside force that gave the sudden impetus to Greek art, and brought it to maturity about a hundred years after its beginnings.

For some time there had been trouble between Greece and Persia, and in 490

B.C. the Persian armada, most glorious to behold, sailed up to the mainland and landed near Marathon, about twenty miles northeast of Athens. Darius, king of Persia and overlord of some forty-five nations, thought the small country of Greece might be added very easily to his tale of conquests. But their passion for physical perfection had made the Greeks marvelous athletes, and never since the world began was there a battle of such pageantry and glory as that of Marathon, when the Greek soldiers went into the fight at a run. They covered a mile at this pace without apparently feeling any effort, such was their superb physical condition, and they rushed upon the huge Persian army "with one unwavering line of leveled spears," and defeated it utterly.

Ten years later Xerxes, the son of Darius I, took his revenge and attacked Greece again. And before he was driven away he had sacked Athens the beautiful, burned all her temples and those of many other towns as well.

When the Athenians returned to their beloved city they found that the enemy had not only sacked the Acropolis, the central hilly ground where the chief temple and buildings of Athens stood, but had wantonly thrown down most of the sculpture that adorned it. One or two fine groups Xerxes carried away altogether as spoil to Persia. The citizens repaired some of the statues, and the rest, buried as rubbish, were used as material to bank up the Acropolis terraces again. Toward the end of the nineteenth century these broken statues were dug up by excavators, and to the story of the past another chapter was added.

THE NEW GREECE BUILT UP ON THE RUINS OF THE OLD

These Persian Wars, which have a haunting, epic sound in our ears, as if all the battles had been in a poet's brain, were the cause of a great new birth of Greek poetry and art. Their chief cities scarred and trampled on, the Grecians hastened to restore them and make them still more beautiful. An accident of spoliation by an Eastern tyrant counted for but a moment in the eternal years; presently a new Athens, a new Greece, rose on the ruins of the old.

The defeat of the Persians was more than a mere victorious ending to a campaign of war. It was the triumph of intellect and liberty over tyranny and

SCULPTURES OF EARLY GREECE

Victory, from the
Temple of Zeus.

A fine head of the
Ægina period.

An ancient statue
of Apollo.

Restored figures of a Bowman and a Man with a Lance, from the temple at Ægina.

A Bowman and a Wounded Warrior, from the temple at Ægina.

barbarism; it was all the forces that make men great—religion, philosophy, love of beauty, centred in one small people, altering the story of the world. We dare not think what would have happened had Persia trampled out Greece. If we take away the Greek art and literature that arose after the Persian Wars we take away the loveliest thing in the world.

Of their ultimate destiny—to be the teachers of mankind two thousand years after they were dead—the Greeks, of course, knew nothing; they were thinking of home and country, ideals and independence. And we can imagine with what joy a sculptor chiseled groups showing Greece triumphant over Persia.

THE FINE BRONZE STATUES THAT WERE MADE AT ÆGINA

In Athens centred the finest work and the highest genius, but there were other schools, such as those of Ægina, Olympia, Sparta and Delphi, where great sculptures were made.

The work of the island of Ægina belongs to the earlier history of Greek art. After the fifth century there is no more mention of the Æginetan sculpture. It formed a school of individual and bold work. At Ægina a fine kind of bronze was made, and much of the statuary was cast in that medium. The most famous of the many sculptors who did their work at Ægina were Callon and Onatas. Statues by Onatas, the more important of the two, were found in many towns in Greece.

At Ægina there was a temple dedicated to Aphaia, the goddess of the island, and to the period at the close of the Persian Wars belongs the interesting sculpture on the pediments. It represents a scene in the Trojan War, but really deals with the recent struggle with Darius. Athene herself, goddess of wisdom and patron saint of Athens, stands between the warriors at the apex of the pediment. The figure of the dying warrior falling at the feet of Athene, and the soldier leaning forward to catch him as he falls, make one of the most memorable groups of early Greek sculpture. Remains of these figures, restored by Thorwaldsen, are in Munich. Pictures of some of these and other early sculptures can be seen on pages 1071, 1073, 3993 and 3994.

The construction of the Greek temple had much to do with the growth of composition in decorative statuary. A shallow, triangular space crowned the front part of the building. This space is called the *pediment*—perhaps a corruption of the word pyramid. The shape of the pediment made it necessary to have the central figures tallest, with diminishing figures on either hand. You can understand this better if you look at the pediment of the Theseum, on page 5354. Before the time of the Greek sculptors composition in decorative statuary was unknown. Egyptian and Assyrian sculptors merely placed huge figures where it seemed fitting to them, and ran an endless frieze along a wall, the beauty of the frieze being largely the effect of repetitive lines. But the limits of the pediment made such repetition impossible. The sculpture must be bounded by a triangular shape. The central figures usually are standing; those on either side, seated or kneeling; and the ones at the ends, reclining.

In the statues for the temple at Ægina we can see the early artists working out this problem, and again in the temple to Zeus at Olympia. The two chief sculptors concerned with these pediments were Pæonius and Alcamenes. Excavations have recently been made on the site of the temple, and part of the sculpture discovered is preserved in the museum at Olympia and part in the Louvre. The tallest, or central, figure in one of the pediments was Zeus, in the other Apollo, and the sculpture told the tale of some of the myths of Greece. We shall meet them again and again in sculpture, until they are like old friends.

THE ARTISTS WHO SPREAD BEAUTY THROUGHOUT A FAIR LAND

From the fragments that remain of the Olympian sculptures we can see how Greek art was slowly freeing itself from the too-rigid straightness of the earliest years, but at the same time was keeping that dignity and simplicity which characterized the sculpture of the golden years.

As the Greeks restored their ruined towns their sense of beauty unfolded itself like the petals of a flower. In every city of note were artists on fire with zeal.

Statues that singly would have made any town famous appeared in numbers, east and west; those of Attica, whose chief town, we remember, was Athens, always seeming to be more lovely than the rest.

THE NEXT STORY OF THE FINE ARTS IS ON PAGE 4215.

WHAT THIS STORY TELLS YOU

A SPY in time of war is one who visits in disguise the territory held by the enemy for the purpose of gaining information about their plans. If he wears his uniform he is not a spy, and must be treated as a prisoner of war, but if he wears the uniform of the enemy or ordinary clothes, he is a spy and may be put to death by hanging. Soldiers think such a death disgraceful, and yet the love of their country has always led men to risk their lives to help their commanders gain necessary information, for it is considered fair to send out spies, and every army uses them when needed. Here we tell of two brave men.

TWO SPIES OF THE REVOLUTION

DURING the Revolution many spies were sent out by both sides, but two, one American and one English, have been remembered better than all the others. Both were young officers, well educated and lovable. Both risked their lives, were caught, and suffered disgraceful deaths while the British army held New York. Monuments have been erected to them both, as you can see.

CONTINUED FROM 3852

NATHAN HALE, THE TEACHER AND SOLDIER

Nathan Hale was born in Coventry, Connecticut, June 6, 1755. Though a delicate child, he grew into a strong, handsome boy. When less than sixteen years of age he entered Yale College, and was graduated with honor in 1773, though only eighteen years old. For two years afterward he was a successful teacher, but when the Revolution began, he left his books, joined the army at Boston and was soon made a captain.

When Washington led the army to New York, young Hale went, of course, but we do not know much about what he did until after the American army was defeated at the battle of Long Island. Washington then retreated to the northern part of Manhattan Island. He did not know whether the British were preparing to attack him or to surround him, and called for a volunteer to enter the British camp.

Captain Hale offered to go, though his friends tried to prevent him. It is said that his answer was, "I wish to be useful; and every kind of service necessary for the public good becomes honorable by being necessary." He went to Norwalk, in Connecticut, on September 14, 1776, and easily crossed over to Long Island. Disguised as a traveling schoolmaster seeking employment, he visited the British camps in Brooklyn and New York and gained much information which might have been valuable to Washington.

HOW AN ACCIDENTAL MEETING LED TO CAPTURE

No one seemed to suspect him, and in a few days he returned to the point on the Long Island shore where he had landed. He had given orders that a boat was to meet him there on the morning of September 21 in order to take him back to Norwalk. The night before he spent at a tavern near by, and there he was recognized by a man, who informed the British soldiers who he was. Some say that this man was his cousin, who was a Tory, but it cannot be proved.

Early the next morning he went out to meet the boat which was to take him back. A boat came, but it was a British boat, and took him to a British ship. There he was searched and notes and plans of the camps were found in his shoes. He did not deny who he was or what he had been doing, when taken before General Howe. Though the British general is said to have been much pleased with the be-

havior of the young officer, the case was plain, and he was sentenced to be hanged the next morning.

The officer in charge of the execution is said to have been brutal and cruel. We are told that he refused to send for a clergyman, or to allow the young man a Bible, and that he tore up the letters Hale had written to his mother, his sisters and the young woman he was to marry. When all was ready, the young hero bravely faced death, saying, "I only regret that I have but one life to lose for my country."

A beautiful statue of the young patriot by Frederick MacMonnies stands in City Hall Park and some think is near the spot where he gave his life for his country. It is more probable that he was executed nearer the East River and farther north.

A YOUNG ENGLISHMAN WHO LOST HIS LIFE

Now let us turn to the Englishman who also risked his life and lost it. John André, the son of a Swiss merchant of London, was born in 1751 and was educated at Geneva, in Switzerland. On his father's death he carried on the business for a time, but after a disappointment in love, entered the British army, and in 1774 came to Canada to join his regiment. He was captured in 1775 and kept a prisoner by the Americans for a year. When set free, he was promoted to captain, and during 1778 was with General Howe in Philadelphia.

Under General Sir Henry Clinton he was promoted to major, and made adjutant-general. During 1779 he was with the British forces under Sir Henry Clinton in New York, where he won all hearts by his manners and his talents.

HE MEETS A TRAITOR TO THE AMERICAN CAUSE

Meanwhile General Benedict Arnold had been placed in command of the fort at West Point. Arnold felt that he had been badly treated by Congress. He had enemies who had delayed his promotion, and had attempted to ruin him. While in command at Philadelphia he had married the daughter of a wealthy Loyalist and had gone deeply into debt. Somehow, at some time, the idea of betraying his country came into his mind, and this fact was made known to the British commander.

On September 20, 1780, by order of General Clinton, André went up the Hudson in the Vulture to meet Arnold. He went ashore, wearing his uniform and bearing a flag of truce. The arrangements were not completed when morning came, and they rode to the house of a farmer near by.

It was arranged that Sir Henry Clinton should ascend the river and attack West Point. After pretending to resist, Arnold was to surrender the fort. Possibly Washington, who was then in Connecticut, might also be captured. For his treason Arnold was to be made a British brigadier-general and to receive money for the property he left in America.

ANDRÉ IS CAPTURED WHILE RETURNING TO NEW YORK

The Vulture dropped downstream, and the farmer was unwilling to take André to the ship. He was, therefore, forced to try to reach New York by land. Wearing an old coat given him by the farmer, he set out on horseback. He passed beyond the American lines into what was known as the "neutral ground" because both parties claimed it, though neither was able to hold it. On the morning of Friday, September 23, a party of young men stopped him. André, thinking they were Tories, told them he was a British officer. They would not let him go, though he had a pass signed by Arnold. They searched him and found papers in his stockings which showed him to be a spy, and took him to an American officer, who, not believing that Arnold was a traitor, sent André to him.

THE TRAITOR ESCAPES, BUT THE SPY IS HELD

Before he reached West Point, the officer became suspicious and had him brought back, but a soldier went on to inform Arnold of the capture of the man who, it was thought, had forged his name. Arnold hastily escaped to the Vulture, and reached New York in safety.

When Washington arrived, a military court was assembled, and, after hearing the evidence, condemned the unfortunate young officer to death as a spy, though all regretted to make such a decision. Sir Henry Clinton tried in vain to save his life. On the morning of October 2, 1780, the brave young man was hanged at Tappan, though he begged that he might be shot instead. In 1821 his body was removed to Westminster Abbey and a monument to his memory erected.

THE NEXT STORY OF MEN AND WOMEN IS ON PAGE 4043.

TWO SPIES WHOM ALL ADMIRED

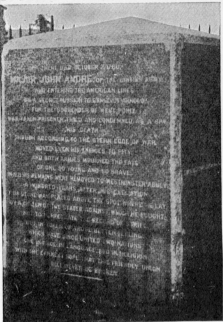

This beautiful statue of Nathan Hale represents him as prisoner. It is by Frederick MacMonnies and stands in City Hall Park in New York City. The brave young officer was hanged as a spy in New York, September 22, 1776.

This monument in memory of Major John André stands on the spot where he died as a spy on October 2, 1780. It was erected by an American admirer. If your eyes are keen perhaps you can read some of the inscription.

The American officers who condemned Major André to death did so with great regret, for his bravery and dignity won the hearts of all, even those of his enemies. Here we see him as his death warrant is being read to him. He begged he might be shot instead of hanged, but his request could not properly be granted.

FRENCH—A LITTLE PICTURE-STORY

First line, French; second line, English word; third line, as we say it in English.

Le taxi—The taxi.

Le taxi arrive à la porte.
The taxi arrives at the door.
The taxi arrives at the door.

Le chauffeur—The driver.

Le chauffeur met les bagages sur le taxi.
The driver puts the luggage on the taxi.
The driver is putting the luggage on the taxi.

Dans le taxi—In the taxi.

Nous sommes six dans le taxi.
We are six in the taxi.
There are six of us in the taxi.

1	2	3
Un	deux	trois
One	*two*	*three*

4	5	6
quatre	cinq	six
four	*five*	*six*

Nous aimons aller en taxi.
We like to go in taxi.
We like riding in a taxi.

En route—On the way.

Le taxi va très bien.
The taxi goes very well.
The taxi goes very well.

La gare—The station.

Nous arriverons bientôt à la gare.
We shall arrive soon at the station.
We shall soon be at the station.

Nous sommes maintenant à la gare.
We are now at the station.
We are now at the station.

L'horloge—The clock.

Il y a une grande horloge à la gare.
There is a big clock at the station.
There is a big clock in the station.

Il est dix heures et demie du matin.
It is ten hours and a half of the morning.
It is half-past ten in the morning.

THE NEXT FRENCH STORY IS ON PAGE 4064.

Lord Bryce.

Lord Morley.

Sir George Trevelyan.

PROSE WRITERS OF OUR TIME

CONTINUED FROM 3899

ANY survey of English literature would be incomplete which did not include a number of prose authors of the later decades of the nineteenth century who have nearly all passed away, but who were busy with writing of value and distinction well within the memory of men active in the literary world to-day.

Many of these writers were men of varied interest and knowledge who cannot be classified satisfactorily in any single group, such as philosophers, historians, essayists or critics. They ranged freely over these and other fields, as the expansion of the range of journalism brought life in all its phases under the notice of the reading public.

Take, as an instance, one of the best-balanced writers of English, John Morley, who lived on through more than twenty years of the twentieth century, and was almost universally acknowledged as the most satisfying prose writer of the age in which he died. Was he a historian, or chiefly a critic, or a biographer, or a philosopher, or a publicist? He was all these, and more; and no one of these classifications sufficiently described him.

Again, Andrew Lang was in some degree a historian, a scientific inquirer, a critic, an essayist, a novelist, a translator of immortal literature, and a poet. Both Morley and Lang were once journalists, and became authors in studious pursuit of knowledge that strongly interested them. They represent a number of men who wrote literature that ranged too widely to be classified under one head in a list.

An earlier writer whose name we should not omit is George Borrow, who died in 1881. Borrow's writings are descriptions, partly in the guise of tales and partly in a loose essay form, of travels in Spain and Wales, and experiences among gipsies, of whom he claimed an intimate knowledge. The circulation of the Bible was the motive of his wanderings in Spain, but the charm of his writing is in his appreciation of the simple romance of travel. Borrow was a wanderer by nature, and no one has appreciated more naturally the sweet things of open-air life.

A literature of travel sprang up during this period. One of the master craftsmen in describing a journey was Robert Louis Stevenson who found by footpath and stream a way to fame. Another writer of great charm when he described country life, whether of men or animals, was Richard Jeffries, a West Country journalist much at home with a gun on a farm. If his

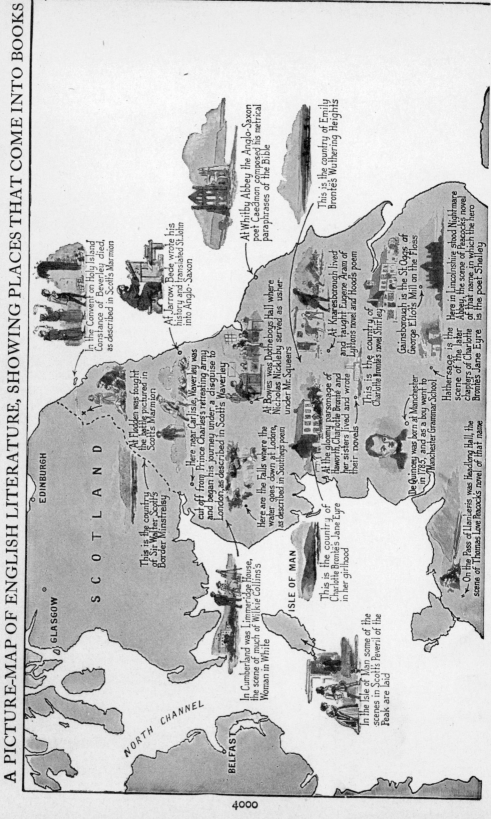

GLASGOW

EDINBURGH

S C O T L A N D

In the Convent on Holy Island Constance of Beverley died, as described in Scott's Marmion

At Jarrow, Bede wrote his history and translated St. John into Anglo-Saxon

At Whitby Abbey the Anglo-Saxon poet Caedmon composed his metrical paraphrases of the Bible

This is the country of Emily Brontë's Wuthering Heights

At Flodden was fought the battle pictured in Scott's Marmion

Here near Carlisle, Waverley was cut off from Prince Charles's retreating army and began his journey under a disguise to London, as described in Scott's Waverley

At Bowes was Dotheboys Hall where Nicholas Nickleby served as usher under Mr. Squeers

At Knaresborough lived and taught Eugene Aram of Lytton's novel and Hood's poem

This is the country of Charlotte Brontë's novel Shirley

Gainsborough is the St. Oggs of George Eliot's Mill on the Floss

Here in Lincolnshire stood Nightmare Abbey, the scene of Peacock's novel of that name, in which the hero is the poet Shelley

This is the country of Sir Walter Scott's Border Minstrelsy

Here are the Falls where the water goes down at Lodore, as described in Southey's poem

At the gloomy parsonage of Haworth, Charlotte Brontë and her sisters lived and wrote their novels

De Quincey was born at Manchester in 1785, and as a boy went to Manchester Grammar School

Hathersage is the scene of the later chapters of Charlotte Brontë's Jane Eyre

In Cumberland was Limmeridge House, the scene of much of Wilkie Collins's Woman in White

ISLE OF MAN

This is the country of Charlotte Brontë's Jane Eyre in her girlhood

On the Pass of Llanberis was Headlong Hall, the scene of Thomas Love Peacock's novel of that name

In the Isle of Man some of the scenes in Scott's Peveril of the Peak are laid

NORTH CHANNEL

BELFAST

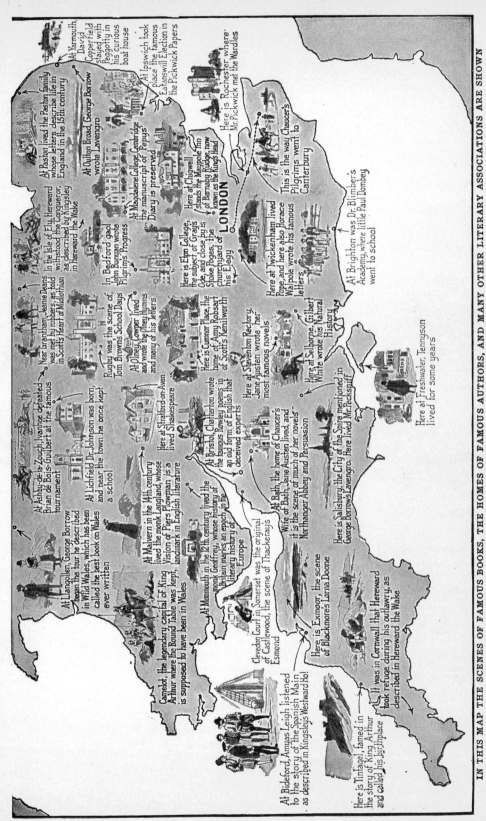

IN THIS MAP THE SCENES OF FAMOUS BOOKS, THE HOMES OF FAMOUS AUTHORS, AND MANY OTHER LITERARY ASSOCIATIONS ARE SHOWN

scene was limited he was liable to make a catalogue of sights, but in such works as Wild Life in a Southern County, where his canvas was broader, he painted with a keen eye, tender heart and finely mastered style.

The most fascinating of all the nature-lovers who transmitted their observations into literature was William Henry Hudson. His schooling in bird life, which remained to the end his favorite study, came to him around the home of his boyhood on the South American pampas. Going to England as a young man, he swiftly acquired a comprehensive knowledge of English birds. No one else has ever shown in books such a sensitiveness to the voices of birds. By a note or two of song or call he could identify any bird, and his memory of sounds never failed him. He finely illustrated the men who, working quietly without public notice or sensation, at last win the world's best judgment by the quality of their work.

THE EARLY STRUGGLES OF A WRITER ON LIFE AT SEA

A writer who made a limited place for himself was Frank Bullen. He described life at sea in the smaller type of sailing vessel, as in the whaling business, with graphic power, his most arresting book being The Cruise of the Cachalot. Bullen was brought up in poverty, and went to sea under the roughest conditions, but educated himself and gained a master's certificate for seamanship. He combined imagination with the power of describing things as they really are. Through life he kept the scars of his early experiences.

The increasing popularity of mountain-climbing brought some additions to permanent literature, the most notable of the writers on the joys of mountaineering being Leslie Stephen and John Tyndall. These both made their mark with other forms of writing. Leslie Stephen's essays on Switzerland as the Playground of Europe remain the best general introduction to mountain influences. Tyndall's Scrambles among the Alps tells fine stories of early Alpine conquests. Stephen's chief lifework as the first editor of the Dictionary of National Biography, and his many literary criticisms in it, have a very substantial value. His special field of study was the eighteenth century.

John Tyndall, an Ulsterman who began life as a teacher and became a most illuminating scientist, had the gifts of clear exposition and picturesque illustration. He rescued science from dullness, and flashed its romance on a surprised world.

HOW PROFESSOR HUXLEY'S PEN SERVED THE CAUSE OF SCIENCE

With him as a popularizer of science was Thomas Henry Huxley, a most trenchant writer and warlike spirit. As real knowledge of the earth's true history grew, religion's first impulse was to intrench itself against science as an enemy. Its chief weapon of defense was misrepresentation of the aims and findings of scientific knowledge. Huxley loved nothing better than storming the forts of such argument, and, wielding a battle-ax of heavy logic spiked with tearing scorn, he battered to pieces the obstructions which timid theologians thrust into the pathway of progressive thought. He would have held a more secure place in the literature of science if his keenness for battle had not been quite so strong, but his essentially honest nature was goaded by the sight of evasion of facts. Huxley remains one of the most skillful and powerful wielders of English prose in controversy and one of the clearest in statement. It is possible that his writings will live historically as a proof of the difficulty with which truth, hampered by custom in thought, emerges into the light of day

It is strange that the age of science did not produce more writers who had the glow of literature. Increasingly throughout the nineteenth century knowledge was making marvelous revelations which changed man's ideas of the universe, and glorified afresh the Divinity that dwells at the heart of all things.

MEN OF KNOWLEDGE WHO WROTE OF THE THINGS THEY KNEW

Not one of the great pioneers of knowledge in the century of its greatest triumphs was a great writer. Tyndall and Huxley came nearest to it. Charles Darwin, Charles Lyell, John Stuart Mill and Herbert Spencer were clear presenters of theories they wished to prove and illustrate. The man who took the widest and highest range, Herbert Spencer, was the dullest of them, and presented his conclusions in what almost amounted to a jargon of his own.

Darwin could write admirably, as in

his Voyage of the Beagle. He marshaled his facts in his more ambitious books, such as The Origin of Species, with clearness and skill and dignity, but they only amounted to a serious argument. They were like gradually filtering light, without heat. Lyell had a gleam of the ampler air. John Stuart Mill was most precise and aptly measured in statement, clear in writing as in thought, but too chilly to convey a spark of the divine fire.

A MASTER OF STYLE WHO WROTE WITH LIGHTNESS AND DIGNITY

The difference between the writing that is, and the writing that is not, true literature is felt at once when we pass from John Stuart Mill to his follower John Morley. In all that Morley wrote, whether it was historical, like his studies of the men who influenced the French Revolution, or philosophy, as in his treatise on Compromise, or biography, in his sketches of Burke, and Cobden and Gladstone, or criticism, in his articles on Wordsworth, Macaulay, George Eliot and other writers, or the delightful memoirs of his closing years, we feel that here is the hand of a master of style. His pen carries full thought with lightness yet dignity, and illustrates the use of our language in its most classically developed form. Indeed John Morley, before he entered into the turmoil of politics as a statesman, and when he was still editing a newspaper, could transform a leading article into literature, and do it without that effort that makes the reader think constantly of style.

CARDINAL NEWMAN, HENRY DRUMMOND, WALTER BAGEHOT AND JAMES BRYCE

This last mistake—writing for style's sake—was the weakness of Walter Pater, the most praised of stylists during his lifetime. But when we look back at it now—as in Marius the Epicurean—it seems affected and elaborately built up.

Some writers of the period under notice could write on almost any subject with the charm and distinction that belong to literature. Cardinal Newman was one. Henry Drummond, who brought religion into line with science in his Ascent of Man, was another. A third, more robust, example was Walter Bagehot, a West Country banker who could make the money market or the British Constitution seem as suitable for literature as the appreciations of poets and historians with which his works are filled.

Among writers of solid books of a historical character that either had a permanent value because of their contents, or a style worth attention, or both these characteristics, was James Bryce, with his American Commonwealth, a comprehensive study of the American Constitution, and other historical works. As a most acceptable ambassador to the United States, Lord Bryce added statesmanship to his substantial literary record.

Sir John Robert Seeley, professor of history at Cambridge, wrote three small books, each of which was lastingly noteworthy—a Life of Stein, the statesman who tried to give Prussia real freedom; Ecce Homo, a study of Jesus as the apostle of "the enthusiasm of humanity"; and The Expansion of England, a book which first made the average English reader realize the part his country has been playing in the world, and its influence as a colonizing power.

MEN WHO LED THE WAY TO THE APPRECIATION OF THE BEST

Sir William Edward Lecky, an Irish professor, by his historical studies of the eighteenth century in England and abroad, his sketches of Irish history, and his essays on life, won universal respect.

We should mention, too, Sir George Trevelyan who wrote admirable studies of Whig statesmanship, and a Life of his uncle, Lord Macaulay, that is one of the most successful biographies in English.

One aspect of English literature which during this period was carried more nearly to completeness than perhaps any other was that of literary criticism. Not much more remains to be written about the great classical writers of English, especially the poets, after the varied criticisms by such writers as Walter Theodore Watts-Dunton, Stopford Brooke, Professor W. J. Courthope, Matthew Arnold, Sir Sidney Lee (on Shakespeare), Sir Sidney Colvin (on Keats), James Russell Lowell, and writers such as Professor George Saintsbury, whose style did not keep pace with his knowledge, and the graceful sufficiency of Edmund Gosse, himself no inconsiderable poet. All these writers led the way toward that appreciation of what is best, which is the true test and defense of writing about books.

THE NEXT STORY OF LITERATURE IS ON PAGE 4227.

THE STORKS AND THEIR COUSINS

The Indian Adjutant.

Common Herons.

The American Jabiru.

The Boatbill.

The Sand Ibis.

The Night Heron.

Great American Egret.

The White Stork.

The Spoonbill.

The Cattle Egret.

The Hammerhead.

The Squacco Heron.

The Whale-headed Stork.

The Trumpeter.

The Great Bustard.

The Bengal Florican.

HERONS, STORKS AND CRANES

CONTINUED FROM 3890

ONE of the disadvantages of our civilization is that too often stress of circumstances places square pegs in round holes in the artificial economy of our lives. A man of splendid frame, who should be exploring the wilds, must sit at a desk; a brain teeming with fine imagination is deadened by routine work in a factory.

Nature never practices such misfit politics. Life and environment fit like a hand into a glove. She obliterates her failures: the quiet bosom of the earth is sown with them. But the successes survive, to make us marvel that Nature is always so efficient where we stumble and halt.

But the tragedies we create for our own kind extend little by little into Nature's province. We are making round holes for her living square pegs. We are growing grain where she grew marsh birds; we are building houses where she set cranes and herons to preside; we are reclaiming fens and moors where her long-beaked beauties once were owners; we raise houses on which storks nest where for a thousand ages storks nested in the wilds.

The old law is still in operation, however, though our lives are too brief to see from the beginning to the end of the chapter. The birds which adapt themselves to the changes effected by man will go on flourishing; the birds which cannot mold their lives to new forms will join the long line of the dead which have left no posterity. Let us be thankful that some of the most interesting birds we have are adapting themselves to conditions which the wisest of humans could never have predicted.

Most people must take the heron very much on trust. This bird has become very rare in Europe. There are high trees where herons nest still in England, but the secret is too precious for publication, lest the birds should be mobbed out of existence, and the last of their eggs stolen to swell a collection.

Time was when herons were protected in England by laws as stern as those which sheltered the king's tall deer. Not mercy but sport was the motive; for herons were fearsome game at which to fly a hawk. For the heron, with its long and powerful beak and the supple, muscular neck which supports and propels it, is dangerous when attacked. If attacked in the air, it strives for the upper position, like a human aviator; when its enemy is above it, it poises its terrific beak and stabs with sufficient force to impale its foe. Once when a hawk battled for half an hour with a European heron the superb tactics of the heron prevailed, and it was the bird of prey which gave up the fight and took refuge in retreat.

THE CROW THAT ATTACKED A HERON AND CONQUERED

Even a stranger sight was noted a few years ago in a great city. There a heron's assailant was an audacious crow. The black brigand soared and manœuvred magnificently, and twice got the advantage of height, and presently he made such a swoop at his quarry that the two birds crashed together into the trees on the side of a park.

The crow did not wish to eat the heron: that was too big a meal. He was simply carrying out in the city the trick of the piratical frigate bird against the booby in the Pacific; it was trying to make the heron disgorge the fish it was carrying home in its crop for its nestlings.

For fish are the mainstay of the heron. See it standing on one leg in the water, eyeing the deeps with anxious gaze. So still it rests that it might be the statue of a heron, and not a living bird. But intense activity suddenly succeeds to immobility. The second leg appears, the great bill flashes into the water faster than a swordsman's weapon, and up comes a fish, speared, as a rule, though the bird will sometimes catch its prey as a flycatcher grasps an insect.

THE VARIED DIET OF THE HERON AND THE SOLUTION OF A MYSTERY

Water-rats, frogs, newts and young birds come acceptably to a heron's appetite. As these are undoubted enemies of trout, herons, for all their hunger in a stream, are really friends of the fisherman. They keep down the coarse fish which devour the eggs and little trout, and it must be only the slowest and least healthy trout that fall to the birds, so they have their value even there.

A charming fact was revealed to the credit of these birds by a great naturalist. It had been a mystery to botanists how certain great water-lilies became distributed from one far isolated lake to another. The seeds are fat and heavy; they could not be wind-borne; they could not travel by water from lakes which have no outlet. It is the herons that achieve the little marvel. They eat the fish which have eaten of the seeds, and, flying from one lake to another, pass the unharmed seeds from their crops into the water, and so

enable these floral beauties of the lakes to be fruitful and multiply.

It is not pleasant to watch parent herons feeding their young—to see rats and eels and fish returned from the adult gullet; but the affectionate fidelity of the elders to the helpless ugly youngsters in the nest is in itself a charming trait.

Then, if we let the eye follow the old birds after they leave the nest, their powerful flight, suddenly accelerated by fear into a majestic upward sweep sheer into the heavens, the unpleasant spectacle of the feeding is forgotten in our delight and admiration at this tremendous upsoaring. To say that no airplane can rise vertically like it is to put the fact in an undertone; for the hawk itself can but sweep round in rising circles, while the heron is mounting like a rocket.

THE HERONS IN DIFFERENT PARTS OF THE WORLD

The largest of the flying waders of Europe is the gray heron. The Night Heron, which hunts when ordinary birds are sleeping, is common in many parts of the New World as well as in Europe, Asia and Africa. It is so bold and so clever that it colonizes the nests of the great eider duck, and makes its nest in the side of that of its host.

The Gray Heron measures about thirty-six inches, but the Goliath of the tribe is half as large again. It is mainly an African species, though known in Ceylon, and sometimes seen in numbers in India. Very weird and fantastic the Goliath Heron looks in its breeding plumage, a living caricature of what we should expect so neat and comely a type of bird to be.

Nuptial plumage is strikingly developed in the Great White Heron of the West Indies and Florida. Its yellow beak turns black during the season in which it desires to seem handsomest in the eyes of its mate. At the same time long filament-like feathers appear on the back, while those on the lower part at the front of the neck become luxuriant. But it is that small group of herons known as White Egrets that are most famous, and sadly famous at that, because of these festival feathers.

The distribution of these birds is so widespread—in Southeastern Europe, many parts of Africa and Asia, and in North and South America—that their place in life should be as well established as that of the starling. But it has received a gift of beauty which is becoming fatal to its continued existence.

THE LITTLE BIRDS THAT ARE STARVED TO DEATH TO MAKE A WOMAN'S HAT

At mating-time the parent egrets are splendid in exquisite, delicate feathers adorning the base of the neck. Heartless women covet these for use in their hats, and hosts of these lovely creatures are slaughtered for fashion's sake. Parenthood should be a bond of tender sympathy throughout all the kingdoms of life, and women should be ashamed to wear these plumes when it is known that to obtain them the parents must be stripped and left to die at the very time when their little ones need their aid.

The sale of these plumes is forbidden, yet the fact that men risk heavy fines to smuggle them in shows that there is still a demand for them. As long as there are cruel people there will be cruelty, and only time, perhaps, will put an end to the shameless fashion which is willing for lovely birds to be extinguished, for thousands of young birds to perish of starvation, for the sake of a woman's hat.

THE VALUE OF THE LITTLE EGRET TO ONE OF OUR GREAT INDUSTRIES

Fortunately commerce is now ranged with humanity against this barbarous fashion. The fact that the egrets are destroyers of insects which spread the deadly sleeping sickness and other diseases in the tropics did not move the creators of fashion, but something has stirred the mind of manufacturers. It has been found that the egret is the natural protector of the cotton plant.

The boll-weevil is threatening all supplies of cotton, and the weevil is food to the birds. So "cotton is king" indeed when it decrees that the little egret must live in order that one of the greatest menaces to prosperity may die. Once more the appeal to the pocket has prevailed.

Other herons found in North America are: the Reddish Egret, the Louisiana Heron, the Little Blue, the Green and Ward's Heron, a large blue heron found in Florida. The Night Heron has two species—the Black-crowned and the Yellow-crowned. Most of these belong to the warmer regions of the continent, though they sometimes straggle northward.

Next we come to the Bitterns, which are clearly akin to the herons. Bitterns nest in solitary fashion, here and there in the marshes, not in colonies like the herons. The American Bittern resembles the Common Bittern of Europe, but is smaller. It is found throughout the continent except in the Far North. The noise it sometimes makes has been compared to the bellowing of a bull, or to the noise made by an old wooden pump. It was formerly believed that the bird struck its bill into the water while booming, but this has been disproved.

Neither the larger nor the smaller bitterns can be said to be common. When attacked they fight viciously, and their sharp beaks may inflict severe wounds. In addition to the larger species we have the Least Bittern and Cory's Least Bittern, both of which breed as far north as Ontario.

The Little Bittern belongs to wilder lands, and the same melancholy fact has to be recorded of the common bittern. This stealthy wonder of bird life, with its marvelous adaptation to the broken lights of reed bed and high-grown marsh, where it matches as famously as the tiger in a jungle setting, was once abundant in our land. But fens feed men where bitterns lurked, and the advance of cultivation is disaster to birds whose shyness makes the approach of mortals terrible.

The American bittern is sometimes over thirty inches in length, and though it is a model of elusiveness in its hiding places, it has not the faculty of the rails and corn crakes for concealment after discovery, but rises, when alarmed out of its attempt to resemble dead rushes and reeds, climbs into the air, and is shot or struck down before it can get out of range.

THE SHY BITTERN THAT HAS BEEN DRIVEN FROM ITS HOME

Bitterns were so persecuted by gunners in England that for many years they were afraid to breed in that country. Of late, however, they have returned and are now to be numbered among the summer birds of Norfolk County.

We have dealt, so far, with birds whose beaks are long, pointed, and ideal implements for the jabbing movement which is fatal to prey—and to human eyes if we approach too near. But now we change to a bird, the Boat-billed Heron, in which the beak attains a striking development in breadth. This is a South American species, frequenting the shores and living chiefly on small shellfish.

The Hammerhead, so called from the shape of its skull and beak, reproduces features of both herons and storks, but is more proficient and cunning than either as a home-maker. Its nest, constructed very strongly of huge domes of sticks, consists of three chambers. The lowest serves as a lookout post; the top story receives the eggs and serves for sleeping-quarters in case of flood; the second houses the young when they are too large to remain in the nursery upstairs.

Beauty, strength, and much that is repulsive to human standards meet in the Storks, which are birds of the Old World. All have great straight pointed beaks of immense power; all are long-legged, with many rough, unkempt feathers; and nearly all enter willingly into partnership with man. The Great White Stork of Europe is a watchdog whose kennel is not in the yard, but up on the roof of the house, with the chimney for foundation, or a box, or even a cart wheel turned on its side, laid there by man. On this the birds rear ambitious structures of sticks and branches, which are renewed year after year.

Tradition enshrines hosts of charming stories about storks, and the birds are received with favor practically everywhere. They are supposed to bring good luck. Probably the superstition arose from .the fact that the great birds are lusty devourers of garbage and carrion. They play the part of jackals in feathers, and their labors to satisfy their appetites must be conducive to the health of the places which they clean up.

THE STRIKING FAITHFULNESS OF THE STORK TO ITS FAMILY

But beyond this there is the fact that the stork is among the most faithful of birds to its kind. Its devotion to its mate and its young has many touching examples, though some of the stories told are pure fancy. Still, when we know that a stork stayed for three winters in succession on a Dutch roof rather than desert its mate, we know that the good nature of the bird is a fact. The explanation of the conduct of this pair was found to be that an injury to the hen prevented her from flying far, so her mate remained all that time with her, denying instinct, refusing the call of the sunny South, for affection's sake.

The best-known storks are the White, which has black about it; the White-bellied, marked not unlike the so-called Black Stork, which is white beneath; and the three big species known as the Jabirus; and the Marabou, or Adjutant, Stork.

The Marabous are the giants of the tribe, and hideous. The strong, thick neck is naked, and in two species this peculiarity is unpleasantly emphasized. The great head is bare or sparsely covered with a woolly-looking, ugly down, and the whole appearance of the adjutant, as the bird is called from its military strut, brings to mind a vulture in caricature. However, some of its feathers are highly prized as trimming.

In tropical Asia and Africa the birds are prized as scavengers. They will eat carrion, they will gulp down live puppies or dead cats, banquet on fish or bird, and enjoy themselves like epicures on the offal that a hyena might suspect.

THE WORK OF THE MARABOU AS A SCAVENGER

The high value of such habits in a bird among people whose practice is to litter the streets with refuse dangerous to health is, of course, easy to understand, and in places the marabou is protected by law. It is the only protection the bird needs, for among vultures and other rivals it pecks its way persistently to victory. The Jabiru, found in tropical America, occasionally ventures into Texas. It is a very large white bird with neck and head bare.

Storks, which hunt in company, often show the cunning of pelicans in combining to round-up shoals of fish, but the habit of the Wood Storks is the most singular. Fish and water reptiles are the food of this species, which belongs to the warmer parts of the Americas. The birds enter the water in company, and, on discovering life in it, set up a prodigious dancing. The effect is to convert the clear stream or lake into a mud-pool and to cause its inhabitants to rise—the fish to clearer water, the young alligators and other reptiles to see and to breathe the open air.

As the swarms appear at the surface, stab, stab, stab! go the beaks of the wood storks. At each blow some living thing is maimed, but not eaten. Not until all the rising life has been thus treated and the whole floats prostrate in sight do the birds begin their feast. When nothing else swims to challenge attention, the storks then return to the floating wounded and gobble.

WHY THE IBIS HAS A LONG CURVED BILL

In some quarters these wood storks are called ibises, but there can be no mistaking the true Ibis, thanks to a peculiarity. The long, down-curving beak is soft for part of its length, though rigid horn at the tip, a feature unknown among the storks. The ibis is a prodder in the mud of lake and river, hence its long curved bill.

There are some thirty species of ibises scattered about the warm countries of the world. That which we call the Sacred Ibis has its counterpart in Africa, in Mad-

ate Spoonbill is a resident of warmer America. It has been unsparingly hunted for its feathers and has become very rare. The Bustards, which follow the spoonbills in the family tree, are birds of the Old World. They run and walk unweariedly, they fly splendidly, they are big and lusty, though their bills are comparatively short. Anything vegetable, from seeds to herbage, anything living, from grasshopper to small lizard, forms their menu. But they needed for their flocks and for their quiet nesting pairs the sanctuary of open moor and plain,

Manchurian Crane.

Balearic Crane.

Cape-crowned Crane.

Australian Cranes.

Asiatic White Crane.

Common Crane.

Great Courlan.

Demoiselle Crane.

agascar, in Australasia and in Asia; but not in Egypt, where for ages and ages, while pharaohs waxed and waned, this bird was an object of worship. Yet not a sacred ibis is to be found in Egypt to-day. Kindly protection of the birds seems to have died with the superstition which made the ibis immune from harm by mortal hand.

Several species of ibis are found on this continent. The outer feathers of the wings of the White Ibis have black tips. This bird lives in flocks and is the common species. The Scarlet Ibis, the Glossy Ibis, which is bright chestnut in color, and the White-faced Glossy Ibis are rare. Nearly allied are the Spoonbills. The White Spoonbill was formerly common in Europe but is becoming rare. Our Rose-

and distances undisturbed like those of the boundless steppes of Asia.

They have vanished from England, except as the rarest of rare visitors during summer days. In fact, they have become uncommon in Europe. Nearly two score species of these fine birds are spread about the Old World, but for ourselves we must seek sight of them alive in zoos, stuffed in museums and private collections.

The sandy heaths of England and Holland still support the Stone Curlews, or Thick-knees, as they are perhaps more properly called. They come next in affinity to the bustards, but are smaller. Their first name is derived from a resemblance in size and plumage to the common curlew, and their second from a curious thickening about the knees, as if the birds suffered from enlargement of the joints. They are birds of great value, working mainly in the dark to clear open spaces of field-mice and reptiles. Their range extends to North Africa and India.

We have to turn to South America for their nearest allies, the Seriemas and Trumpeters. The Seriemas, long-legged, long-necked, rather bittern-like, and very upright in gait, bark like dogs, eat snakes and other reptiles, young rats and mice, and do their hunting in the New World, like the thick-knee of the Old, when darkness sets in.

Following them must come those doubtful birds the Trumpeters, another South American form of grace and notable characteristics. In form they are likened to long-legged guinea-fowl of blackish hue, but in voice they are themselves only, uttering their clarion calls in the night, a full sixty seconds to a single blast. How different from their friends the storks, which have no voice, but talk, if they talk at all, only by snapping together the two halves of their great beaks!

THE GRACEFUL CRANE AS THE FRIEND AND ENEMY OF MAN

The Old World has neither seriemas nor trumpeters, but she has nearly all the Cranes, of which there are nearly twenty species. Here the legs and graceful neck are long, and the beak is big, compared with that of the bustard, but insignificant in contrast with that of the herons and stork. They generally keep to marshes or wide plains, migrate over long distances, and fly with grace and endurance.

The Demoiselle Crane, the Crested Crane, the Manchurian and the Common Crane are superb creatures, and the Manchurian must be specially noted as the bird that figures in much of Japanese art on screens, fans, and a thousand other curious objects. We have three species—the Whooping, or White, Crane; the Sandhill, or Brown; and the Little Brown Crane. The first is the largest bird we have, and has a wide range, while the second is more common in the South, and the third in the West.

Generally the cranes are seed-eaters, though they eat frogs and lizards as well. They must serve us well in the number of injurious growths whose spread is prevented by this destruction of seed. But in districts where cultivation is relatively new, and cranes are one of Nature's ancient institutions, the birds do great damage to crops. They have not abandoned their old haunts to which men have come. They go back, and, finding a new food prepared for them, harvest it in a way not contemplated by the sowers.

A rare heron-like bird is the curious stunted Kagu, notable for the streaming tuft of feathers springing from the back of the head. Its home is New Caledonia; its closest cousin is the South American sun bittern, a beauty of the swamps, delighting to recline with lovely feathers vaingloriously outspread in the sunshine, and looking like some wonderful great butterfly when in flight.

THE PLOVER THAT DOES SO MUCH GOOD IN OUR FIELDS

We march on now into another family of birds, the birds which resemble plovers. The Pratincoles are birds of the Old World. Their tails are forked like those of swallows, and they catch insects in full flight. The swift-running, long-winged desert birds, the Coursers, find their meat in grubs and insects from the sands.

Then there are the birds of the true Plover Family itself. A most admirable family is here, birds which pick up a living anywhere, on the bleak mountain side, in the fields, on the heaths, by the brink of the sounding sea. It is a large family of almost a hundred species, though we have only eight—the Golden Plover, which is found all over the world, the Killdeer, the Piping Plover, the Black-bellied, the Mountain, the Snowy, the Semi-palmated and Wilson's Plover. Some of these feed largely on land and destroy many insects.

Nobody who loves our countryside should hurt a plover, and no true friend of agriculture would ever eat a plover's egg. How well the plovers protect their nestlings, rising into the air from the nursery, fluttering a little way, then running as if with broken wing or leg, simply to lure the fowler from the babies in the little cradle.

THE WRYBILL, AND HOW IT CAPTURES HIDING INSECTS

New Zealand's famous Wrybill is simply a plover with a curious curved beak, an instrument fashioned so that this little wonder may use its bill to pick out the insects which seek to avoid capture by lurking behind stones. Stilts, aptly named from their stilt-like legs, are classed as plovers by some naturalists, as are also the avocets and oyster-catch-

A GROUP OF GOOD BIRD FRIENDS

The Snipe.   The Whimbrel.   The Curlew.

The Knot.   The Ruff.   The Avocet.

The Gray Phalarope.   Black-tailed Godwit.   The Oyster-catcher.

The Ringed Plover.   The Stilted Plover.   The Sandpiper.

The Sanderling.   The Lapwing.   The Woodcock.

The pictures on these pages are by Mrs. M. H. Crawford, Messrs. A. Brook, Coles Finch, E. W. Tayler, and others.

ers, though other students place them in another family. Avocets are beautiful birds of the marsh, lagoon and estuary. The Oyster-catchers live on the shore and work some way up the rivers. They are masters of the art of opening the shells of bivalves which resist all the strength and cunning of a man dependent for success on the use of his hands alone.

Closely related are the Curlews with bill as much arched downward as that of the avocet is curved in the opposite direction. Here is an inland-nesting bird which summers by the sea, but, wherever it is, constitutes itself the guardian of all life around it by raising an alarm at the coming of danger, not only to its own kind, but even swooping down with its piercing anxious cry on sleeping seals to which a dreaded man is seen advancing. A wonderful creature is this solicitous curlew. There are more than fifteen species, of which we have three—the Long-billed, the Hudsonian, which breeds in the Arctic regions, and the Eskimo, likewise a northern bird. It is often found in dry fields.

We find boldness in another form in the Phalaropes. There are three species, all found in North America. The Red Phalarope and the Northern Phalarope are found in Europe also, but Wilson's Phalarope belongs to America. Their boldness reveals itself in the manner in which, when shifts for a living are not well rewarded on the shore, they boldly take to the water and swim for their food.

THE COUSIN OF THE SANDPIPER WITH ITS SHOWY RUFF

Next come the Sandpipers, of which more than a dozen species are found in North America. Some are large, some small. They have little webbing between the toes, but all have web places and both run and fly gracefully. Their colors are gray, brown and yellow. They are brave and lovable little birds.

A bird which might be mistaken for a sandpiper, but which develops at the courting season into a very different plumage, is the sandpiper's cousin the Ruff, common in Europe and occasionally found in America. It is the great showy ruff round the neck of the male which confers the name. The female is always much of sandpiper hue and fashion, but the male, when he is displaying before his lady-love, is one of the show creatures of birddom.

Two related birds, the Godwits and the Turnstones, are among the greatest of travelers. The eastern species of the godwits pass down to Australia for the winter, and the turnstones, which have flown from the Far South to raise their babies on food snatched from hiding beneath the shore stones of the Arctic, pass down again as far as New Zealand when winter storms frown in our hemisphere. Knot, Stint and Sanderling are others of the birds that find rich harvests among the sea-fields that lie between high tide and low.

HOW THE MIGRATING WOODCOCK CARRIES ITS YOUNG

Thoughts of travel suggest that wonderful snipe, the Woodcock, which is devoted to its young. The European species is said to carry off its young to a place of safety. The American Woodcock resembles its European cousin very closely. There are several species of snipe, but none more interesting than the common species whose so-called "drumming" always has been something of a mystery, and so remains. The noise is made only at courting time. Then the males rise into the air in curious circling flight, and suddenly plunge to earth with half-closed vibrating wings. It is this wing motion, so far as can be ascertained, which produces the drumming, a note likened to the bleating of a goat.

Many of the little friends of the plover tribe approach the characteristics of the moorhens, but none so closely as the Jacanas, or Water-pheasants. All ten species are tropical, long-legged, slender, and extraordinarily long-toed. These remarkable feet give the bird its right of way through life, literally on lilies. The jacana upon its widespread long toes, steps daintily from lily-leaf to lily-leaf, secure as a man crossing a bridge. One species comes into the United States from Mexico.

WHY WE MUST ALWAYS BE KIND TO OUR FEATHERED FRIENDS

Nature and the jacana have agreed extremely well, and man has not yet interfered to spoil the little paradise. For the rest, we have broken in on many an idyllic solitude, ringed about many a one-time Eden of birds. Some have vanished like the Arabs of the poem; some have fought like wild things for that of which they have been dispossessed; but others have taken us into their friendship, and, like the storks on the housetops and the adjutants in the villages, have staked their all in partnership with us.

THE NEXT STORY OF ANIMAL LIFE IS ON PAGE 4121.

HOW TO MAKE A USEFUL WORKBENCH

HOW would you like to make a workbench for home use? This useful workbench

CONTINUED FROM 3860

may be made by any boy who is able to use simple woodworking tools and can secure the necessary lumber. The construction of the bench shown in picture 1 will require pine lumber as follows: 26 feet of 2″x4″, 12 feet of 2″x6″, and 23 feet of 1″x6″. Although dry pine lumber is suggested, this bench may be made from any similar wood which is easily worked. The boards come in regular lengths, usually from 10 feet up to 16 or 18 feet. In addition to this lumber needed for the bench, a piece of oak or other hard wood 3″ x 4″ about 34 inches long is required for the bench vise. A screw and handle for the vise may be bought at any hardware store, as can 1 pound of 4-inch nails and 2 square-headed iron bolts, each of which is ½ inch in diameter and 4 inches long. These should be fitted with iron washers and square nuts.

First saw from the 2″ x 4″ lumber four pieces about 33 inches long. These are the legs of the bench, and they are made to stand with their broader faces toward the ends of the bench. Then cut joints in each one of these legs as shown in picture 2. The sides in which the joints are cut must face each other at the ends of the bench. Into these joints is fitted the supporting framework, as may be seen in picture 1. The lower framework is also cut from the 2″ x 4″ lumber. Two pieces 42 inches long and four pieces 19 inches long are needed. Two of the 19-inch pieces should be left plain, while the other two of this size and the two 42-inch pieces should have joints 2 inches by 2 inches cut on both ends from the same edge (see joints on right end of picture 1). These joints, as well as the joints in the legs, are easily cut with a saw, and the wood is quickly split out with a chisel. Next, these four jointed pieces are either

fitted together with screws or are glued and nailed to form the framework. The four legs are then fitted in place and fastened with screws or nails. Then the other two 19-inch pieces are fitted into the top of the uprights across each end and fastened in place.

Four braces for the ends are made from two 16-inch pieces of the 1″ x 6″ stock by resawing these and cutting off the corners 1½ inches in either direction. Each piece is first sawed in two, lengthwise, with a ripsaw. This will give four pieces 20 inches long and 3 inches wide. Then mark the centre joint of each end of each piece. Now measure on both sides, from each end, a distance of 1½ inches. Connect these points with the end points by a line and saw off the corners, leaving on each end a right-angled point. The braces are then fastened in place. This finishes the body part of the bench. Next, cut from the 1″ x 6″ lumber a piece 56 inches long. This is fitted across the front of the frame, just even with the top, and made to project just 7 inches beyond the legs at either end. Then fasten by nailing in position.

For the top of the bench cut from the 2″ x 6″ lumber two pieces 56 inches long. One of these is then placed across the top of the bench at the extreme front, so that it comes even with the wide surface of the front board. This is nailed to the end framework, and the second piece is fastened in position directly back of it. This part of the top is made heavier, for it is near the front, where the main strain of the work will be had. The remainder, or back part, of the top is made of two strips of 1″ x 6″ wood. In order to make this even with the two front strips, which are thicker, it is necessary to put a piece underneath it at each end. Make these two pieces by cutting one piece of 1″ x 6″ board 12 inches

4013

long and ripping it in two. First place these strips along the end frame and place the top boards on them before nailing all of these in place. When this is done the whole top of the bench may be planed smooth. Then cut another strip of 1" x 6" lumber 56 inches long and nail it across the back of the bench, allowing it to project about 3 inches above the top, as shown in the drawing.

The vise as it comes from the hardware store usually consists of a long straight square-headed screw about 1 inch in diameter, which ends in a round iron plate and a T-shaped pipe. The plate is loose, but not removable. Through the T a long wooden handle is fitted. In addition to this there is an elliptical plate holding a threaded pipe in which the screw works. To put it together, first make a piece from the remaining 2" x 6" lumber 6 inches wide and 32 inches long. This piece forms the inner side of the vise and fits just inside of the front piece of the bench. From one end a slot 1¼ inches wide and 4⅛ inches long is cut in the middle of the 6-inch face to form the bottom. It touches the under-side of the top, and is placed outside of the lower framework.

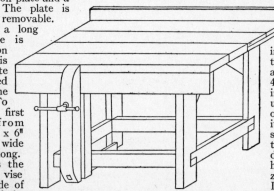

1. A workbench easily made for home use.

pieces are then bolted together. The heads of the bolts and the iron washer fit into the countersunk holes, and the other washer is placed under the nut on the other side. The vise screw is fastened in position through a 1½-inch hole which is bored in the back of the piece that forms the inner side of the vise.

Now you are ready to make this piece of oak into a convenient vise jaw. The piece is first shaped at the ends as shown in picture 3. The outer edges are then rounded. A hole somewhat larger than the vise screw is cut through as shown. Finally a mortise joint is cut through with a chisel and a hammer as shown in the drawing. Into this is fitted one end of a piece of 1-inch wood 4 inches wide and 12 inches long. This is used to keep the jaws of the vise even when it is being used. It should be fitted into the oak piece with a drive fit and should have two rows of holes zigzagged across it. Into these a round 3-inch peg is fitted. This peg is placed in different holes so that the bottom opening of the vise may be adjusted to become parallel with the top opening needed to hold the work. To complete the bench the long screw of the vise is now

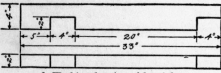

2. Working drawing of bench-leg.

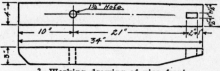

3. Working drawing of vise front.

Its edge should be located 4 inches in from the front leg of the bench. Corresponding holes are made with a bit and brace in this piece and in the front piece of the bench. These are countersunk ½ inch in the front piece through the use of a brace and a special sharp steel bit made for just such a purpose, and the two

slipped through the hole which has been made for it, and the plate is screwed in place.

If you follow these directions you will have a workbench which will prove highly satisfactory for general home use. Later you will doubtless wish to make convenient devices and accessories to be used with this workbench.

ANSWERS TO THE PICTURE PUZZLES ON PAGE 3860

1. The nutcrackers are on the grapes, and the grape-scissors are among the nuts.
2. The handle of the pump is on the left instead of on the right of the spout.
3. The positions of the knife and fork in relation to the plate on the table are reversed.
4. These scissors have no centre screw to join the two parts together and act as a pivot.
5. The handle of this railway carriage door is on the side next to the hinges.
6. The flag is waving against the wind, the direction of which is shown by the driving clouds and the bending trees in the distance.
7. The trigger of the revolver is the wrong way round.
8. The rose is growing on a vine tendril, as is shown by the shape of the leaves.

9. The football player is playing the Rugby game with a round Association ball. In Association, the players are not allowed to handle the ball; the Rugby ball is of an oval shape.
10. The sword which the warrior wears is buckled on to his right side, whence it would be difficult to draw it with his right hand.
11. The train is running past its signal, which is set at danger.
12. The horn of this motor car is out of easy reach of the driver.
13. The hour of four on most watches is indicated by the old sign IIII instead of IV.
14. This motor van has no number at the rear, as required by law.
15. These two trains are running side by side, though there is only a double set of rails.

PREPARING A PICNIC LUNCH BASKET

WHEN we go for a picnic it is best to take things which weigh as little as possible, if we have to carry everything ourselves, for we do not want a heavy load to tire us before we reach the spot decided on for lunch. So we choose a lightly made wicker basket and light cardboard boxes for the eatables. We replace china plates by plates made of paper, linen napkins and tablecloth by paper napkins and a paper tablecloth or doilies which are made especially for picnic parties, a salt-cellar by a paper packet, and so on, taking as few knives and forks as we can possibly do with.

Half the fun of a picnic is the contriving it involves in the absence of table accessories. Little paper cups will do quite well in place of ordinary cups and glasses. As for the eatables, it is well to take things that will not spoil, crush or melt when packed up, so we must avoid juicy, over-ripe fruit, and if it is the strawberry or raspberry season, we take only the dry ones. They carry best between cabbage leaves, on the top of the basket, or in a box covered with leaves. Bananas, plums, greengages, peaches, apricots, apples and oranges are quite easy to carry. Our lunch may be a very simple one, just enough to satisfy the hearty appetites of boys and girls, or something more elaborate to entertain our friends. Suppose we think about a simple lunch first.

We shall find hard-boiled eggs and bread and butter very satisfying, and easy to carry. The eggs are boiled for 5 minutes, and then placed in cold water for 2 or 3 minutes to harden them still more. We wrap each one in white tissue-paper and place them all in a card egg-box at the bottom of the basket, with a paper packet of salt. To eat with the eggs we want slices of bread and butter. The slices should be cut the same size and placed butter sides together in a pile. We may like to put between two slices a little mustard and cress, small sprigs of watercress, shredded lettuce leaves or chopped nuts. The bread and butter or the vegetable sandwiches are then covered with waxed paper, such as confectioners use. The eggs can be cracked, shelled and halved at the time of eating.

For those who do not care for eggs we cut sandwiches of sliced tongue, ham or cold roast beef, using a sandwich loaf of bread for the purpose, and taking care to cut the meat thin, and sprinkle over it a little salt and mustard. Pressing the pile of sandwiches down with the left hand, we take a large sharp carving-knife and cut off the crusts from the four sides of the pile. The sandwiches are then done up in packets of waxed paper, covered with thick white paper.

In preparing sandwiches care should be taken so they will be made with a moist filling rather than one which is too dry. Lettuce spread with mayonnaise dressing will make them moist and fresh. If cold meat is not taken, potted meat is good to use. Boned sardines wet with lemon juice, cream cheese mixed with mayonnaise and stuffed olives or nuts, are all very appetizing. The best plan is to have two kinds of sandwiches, some with fish or meat and others with something green or piquant.

A great deal of fun may be had at a picnic by building a bonfire and toasting bacon in the flames and then placing it between slices of buttered bread. The bacon should be sliced and the bread buttered at home. Then a forked stick does the rest. We shall feel well repaid for the work of building a fire when we taste our appetizing sandwiches.

For dessert we may cut up various kinds of fruits, sweeten to taste, and place in a glass fruit jar, or instead we may put the fruit in a freezer and freeze before starting, remove dasher and pack freezer well with three parts of ice and one part of salt. It is not wise to take layer cake to a picnic. It is better to take small cakes—of sponge mixture—or a plain loaf cake on such occasions. Fresh cookies go well too.

For a plain loaf cake we may try this recipe: Cream ½ cupful of butter, add 1 cupful of sugar, then cream together; add 1 teaspoonful of vanilla and ½ teaspoonful of lemon, and cream all together. Next add yolks of 2 eggs, then add 1½ cupfuls of pastry-flour sifted with 3 level teaspoonfuls of baking-powder alternately with ½ cupful of milk. Stir all of this well. Lastly, fold in the stiffly beaten whites of 2 eggs and bake at 350° Fahrenheit from 40 to 60 minutes. We may frost this cake or not, as we wish.

A few little fancy cakes or biscuits, and fruit in sound condition, will be put on the top of our basket, and we shall hardly need knives and forks, a clasp fruit-knife being alone needed for the fruit. In choosing the spot for lunch we may have in mind a cottage or farm near, where we can get a supply of drinking-water or milk. Failing that, we shall certainly need a bottle of milk and some ginger ale or other tonics. Ice cream is always welcome. It is not a bad plan for the different parties who join the picnic each to contribute provisions for the lunch, thus sharing the expense and dividing the burdens. One may be famed for a special kind of sandwich, another for pie or fancy cakes, another for lemonade. It is well in such a case to have a clear understanding about the contributions, so that provisions do not run short.

Now let us suppose a somewhat more elaborate lunch is to be packed, involving cold chicken, lobster or veal loaf, and requiring knives and forks. Of course we do not take our best knives, and so we cut up the fowl before packing it in waxed paper and wrapping it in a napkin outside that. Shredded lettuce goes well with the chicken, packed between two large outer leaves or cabbage leaves. There is no need to carry home greasy knives and forks. Kind earth cleans them nicely for us, if we just dig them sideways in the turf and wipe them on some of the tissue-paper.

If we are near a wood where sticks can be gathered, it is fun to light a fire and bake a few potatoes with their jackets on, in the ashes, or boil them in a kettle over large stones placed around it. Then, if we care to take a small alcohol lamp and apparatus, we can indulge in tea or coffee. Evaporated milk, which should remain unopened until we are on the spot, makes a very good substitute for cream; and a small pot of jam or marmalade is sure to meet with much appreciation from all.

HOW TO SPEAK BY SIGNS

THE military method of semaphore signaling or flag-wagging, as it is sometimes called, is a splendid way to exchange messages with those who are far beyond shouting distance, but still in sight.

A semaphore message will carry as far as the signaler and the person to whom he or she is signaling are within sight of one another, while the apparatus for signaling is simplicity itself, a pair of semaphoring flags being readily manufactured in a few seconds from two white pocket-handkerchiefs, which may then be pinned on to sticks cut from the nearest hedgerow, or on to any odd bits of wood.

For instance, if you are having a picnic on the beach, and the boys have wandered off while the girls prepare tea, it may be convenient to recall them, and for this purpose no message is more effectual than a series of signals of the ten letters of the alphabet which spell the words "Tea is ready."

Practice on paper might alternate with practice out of doors across a lawn, until the letters come almost mechanically, and after a day or two's practice it will be found possible to send long messages at a fairly even rate of speed.

The letters of the semaphore alphabet are shown in the picture on this page. Imagine the thick lines to represent the body of the person signaling, and the thin lines to represent the flags held in the hands.

The letter A is represented by holding the right-hand flag as if it were pointing midway between the VII and VIII of a clock-dial, assuming the feet of the signaler to be at VI and his head to be at XII. If you look at the picture of the signal A in the message on the page facing, it will be clear.

It is good practice to write the alphabet signals on a piece of paper, beginning by writing out the entire alphabet a few times, and then by writing different letters at random, without consulting the alphabet, thereby testing your memory. Then you can write words, and thus send letters to your friends.

Another way to assist your memory is to study certain circles of flags. Looking at Circle No. 1 on the next page, you see that A, B, C, D, E, F and G are signaled by letting the flag in the left hand hang down in front and by changing the position of the right-hand flag. From Circle No. 2 it will be seen that the letters H, I, K, L, M and N are made by holding the right-hand flag in the position of A, and by moving the left-hand flag to the positions placed opposite the letters. Then Circle No. 3, which illustrates the letters O, P, Q, R and S, shows the right-hand flag at the B position, and

Letters and signs of the flag alphabet.

the left-hand flag moved round as indicated. If you look at the letter R, as shown in the "Tea is ready" message, it is made plain to you.

Circle No. 4 shows the letters T, U, Y and the sign for "cancel," all of which are made by keeping the right-hand flag in the C position and changing only the position of the left-hand flag. Compare this circle with the picture of the letter T, as shown on the opposite page.

Circle No. 5 shows the right-hand flag in the D position, where it is held when indicating the numerical sign, and also for J, or the alphabetical sign, and for V, the position of only the left-hand flag being changed for these different signs.

Circle No. 6 shows that the letters W and X are indicated by holding the right-hand flag in the E position and changing the position of the left-hand flag only.

Probably the meaning of the words "alphabetical sign" and "numerical sign" in the picture need some explanation.

There are no special signals for the numerals, A standing for 1, and other letter signs for other numerals. But in beginning a message, if it is to consist of letters, make the signal for alphabetical signs first, thereby showing that the signs that follow are to be read as letters— A, B, C and so on. Similarly, if, at the beginning, or in the course of a message, the signs that are going to be made are to be read as numerals, and not as letters, make the numerical signal.

The "annul" or "cancel" sign almost explains itself. It means that you wish the previous sign sent to be canceled, perhaps because you find that you have made a mistake in transmitting.

Having seen the meaning of the various signs, you are ready to see how a message is sent. To begin, you stand in the position shown in the first picture on the next page, with the two flags slightly crossed over one another, facing the direction in which the message is to be sent.

Next move both flags to attract the attention of the individual to be signaled to and, when you have succeeded, signal the letter J, which shows that letters, not figures, follow, before returning to the first position.

It has been seen that the letters of the semaphore alphabet are formed by the various angles at which the flags are held to the body, and to send a message, stretch out your arms to their full extent and hold the flags in a straight line with your arms, never allowing them to droop from the hands and never inclining them to the rear. You may, however, turn on the

HOW TO SIGNAL ACROSS A FIELD

Ready to start.   Letters follow.   Numbers follow.   Cancel previous signal.

T   E   A

I   S   R   E

A   D   Y

These pictures show how we can "speak" across great distances. In the top row the first picture shows the signal "Ready to start"; the second means "The signs that follow are to be read as letters"; the third means "The signs that follow are to be read as numbers"; and the fourth means "Cancel previous signal." The other pictures on this page convey the message "Tea is ready," each picture representing a letter. The full alphabet is given on the opposite page.

hips if you are about to form any letter which can be made more easily and seen more distinctly from a distance by doing so. Be careful, when actually signaling, not to make the positions for the letters A and G too close to your body; and remember also, when making the letters T, O and W, and the numerical sign, to keep the two flags well separated from each other.

When signaling, the flags must be kept unfurled, and brought smartly and promptly from one letter position to another, the arms being brought right in to the body between letters, and a pause must be made on the letter itself. A little longer pause should be made—the signaler standing with the flags crossed — between words. The Army regulation speed for sending and receiving semaphore messages is at the rate of eight words a minute.

In order to receive a semaphore message in the correct military manner, two receivers are really required, one to take the actual message and one to write down each letter as it is spoken by the taker. There should be no general conversation between the two signalers while receiving messages.

It is the duty of the writer-down to say "No" should a word fail to make sense, when the

The flag alphabet shown in circles.

receiver of the message will immediately stop the signaler by raising both arms horizontally to their full extent. The signaler will show that he has understood this by signaling back J. The receiver—who should also be armed with two flags—will then send the last word which he received correctly, when the signaler will continue with his message from that word.

To make your knowledge of signaling complete, you should practice sending figures after you have become perfectly proficient in the alphabet.

It is most useful to be able to signal the time, and the signaling instructions say that the numeral sign will be used for the decimal point, and, when sending time, to separate the hours and minutes; thus, for instance, 5:30 will be sent: Numeral sign 5, numeral sign 3, 0, alphabetical sign, the alphabetical sign being used to show that letters, not figures, will follow from this point. If the alphabetical signal is not given, confusion may be the result.

A machine has been made to take the place of the human signaler. It has two movable arms, or vanes, which are worked by a crank. Sometimes the vanes have electric-light installations, so that messages can be sent at night. The method is the same as that used with flags.

THE BOY'S HOME MUSEUM

MOST boys collect things—stamps, birds' eggs, fossils, coins, butterflies, and moths, insects, shells or botanical specimens. The pride of possession is a good thing in its place, but no boy should collect things merely to be able to say that he has them. He should learn as much about the things he collects as he can. If his hobby be the collection of birds' eggs, he should learn not only the names of the birds whose eggs he has, but he should also be able to identify the birds, to know something about their habits, and to recognize their nests. So with insects, shells or any other things collected. The objects and their associations should be studied.

But orderliness should always be a characteristic of the boy who pursues the hobby of making collections. Therefore every boy collector should possess a little museum to hold his collection. A museum is easily made, and every boy who is worth his salt can make one for himself.

A very neat and convenient little museum can be made from a wooden box, which he can probably secure from the grocer. He should line the inside walls with green cartridge wall-paper. Then he should get five or six pieces of board the size of the inside of the box, and nail in a couple of shelves. These shelves are to hold the trays for the collections. The trays can be either the ordinary lacquer trays to be bought in shops, or little wooden trays made out of strips of strong thin wood nailed strongly together. The trays are most necessary, as he will want to draw his collections out without disturbing any of them. In cases where the collection is of some frail or perishable things, such as butterflies and moths, it would be well to cover the tray with a strip of glass cut to fit over it tightly.

Now, this museum is not at all difficult, and every boy could, if he liked, easily make one something like it. Why should he not try? He can have trays for fossils, rocks and odd coins.

THE NEXT THINGS TO MAKE AND TO DO ARE ON PAGE 4079.

HAVE you ever tried to collect and name some of the beautiful wild berries or fruits that you pass in your autumn rambles among the hills and woods? No doubt they seem less precious to you than they are to the birds, who depend upon them for food and time their flights to follow their harvests. But they would repay your interest and love of beauty, and afford you good material for decorating your room. Sprays of Bittersweet make a lovely touch of color when all the flowers are gone; scarlet "hips," as the fruits of the Wild Rose are called, set in among pressed ferns or with dried grasses are most effective. Your Pine Cones will last a long while, and finally when their use for adornment is passed, will make a cheery blaze for story-telling some blustering winter night. Some berries fade very quickly if left without water, but experience will lead you to distinguish. Set your Partridge Berry in a covered glass bowl with a little moisture where it will gaily gleam and draw many an admiring friend to gaze upon its glossy foliage and fruit.

WILD FRUITS OF THE COUNTRYSIDE

NOT all the fruits we show you in the following pages can be found in America, although most of them can. Many of them are immigrants from Europe, some come in as ballast, some are brought by birds, some arrive sticking to the boots of countrymen. They have a hundred ingenious ways of working their passage round the world!

CONTINUED FROM 3908

The Cloudberry is really a species of dwarf raspberry which grows from four to eight inches high in the mountains of Great Britain, in the arctic and sub-arctic regions, and in some localities in Canada and New England. The flowers are large and white. Everybody knows the Crabapple, with its bright red fruit which has such a bitter taste. Originally probably a native of Central Asia, the apple is cultivated now in all temperate regions, in many varieties. It was introduced into America from England by the governor of Massachusetts Bay, and into Canada by the French settlers from Normandy and Brittany.

The Sweet Briar, or Eglantine, native of Asia and Europe, has been brought into Eastern America. It is a tall-stemmed rose, well armed with prickles. It gets its name from the delicious perfume of its leaves, particularly strong in cultivation. The black berries of the Privet succeed its spike of white, somewhat heavily perfumed flowers. Common in the Old World, the privet is planted, and to some extent naturalized, in America. The Strawberry tree is a Southern European plant, common in Mediterranean countries. Its fruit is quite beautiful and agreeable to the taste, and in Spain a popular beverage is made from it. The queer clustered head of the Spurge-laurel does not belong to the true laurel, although its foliage is similar. It grows in England.

All of us know the Acorn, fruit of the oak. In some periods of civilization acorns have been used for food, and indeed are still so used in some countries. We recognize the Barberry by its hanging bunches of yellow flowers which have such a disagreeable odor. The berries are elongated in shape and pleasantly acid in flavor. Although native of Europe, the plant has been naturalized in New England and Canada. We can eat the glaucous black berries of the Whortle, a low bush with numerous angled branches. Common in Europe and Siberia, it grows in America from Colorado to Alaska.

4019

Western Indians mix with their tobacco leaves an herb which they call *kinnikinic*. This is the Bearberry, a trailing evergreen shrub with astringent bitter leaves and bright red drupes. The winged seeds of the Sycamore Maple are queer things that make us almost think of them as vegetable airplanes! In America this maple is not common, although it has been naturalized in eastern United States. The fruit of the small Cranberry shown is not the cranberry that is cultivated and gathered for the market, although it grows on similar sites.

In Europe the Larch is native in the Alps. In England and the United States it is cultivated for its symmetrical shape and durable wood. If we want to sleep well, we should fill our pillows with the dried flowers of the Hop-vine! The blossoms are used to impart a bitter flavor to malt liquors.

There are several species of Wild Gooseberry in North America, but their fruit is rarely eaten, and the cultivated fruit does much better in Northern Europe and Asia. Following the beautiful panoply of white which the Dogwood spreads for us in springtime come its clustered berries in the fall as the leaves are beginning to burn warm crimson in the clear cold November days.

The Hazelnut will reward our search and our appetites if we wait till the hot August sun has done its part toward hardening the shell and ripening the kernel. So, too, with the luscious Dewberry, with its large sweet fruit. A plant with good flavoring properties is the Caper Spurge, or Wild Caper, whose immature capsules are used sometimes as a substitute for real capers.

Though not so juicy and well flavored as the cultivated variety, the Wild Raspberry is a very refreshing and abundant fruit. Beloved of all the birds is the Wild Cherry, first herald of spring, displaying its dainty pearly white blossoms and pale green leaves. The Wild Black Currant will make good jam if enough of its fruit escapes the eager bills of its bird visitors. The Wild Strawberry is ours for the search, and the Beechnut, too. The Hawthorn has been introduced into America, but it is not so widespread as it is in Great Britain.

Open the bright red skins of the fruit of the Field Rose and you will find a number of seeds. Birds devour this cover-ing and liberate the down-fringed seeds. To the plentiful flat white heads of the Elder Blossom succeed the luxuriant spikes of black berries, used by country people in many a good cordial. Jack-in-the-pulpit lays aside his purple spathe and arms himself with knobby scarlet fruits in the autumn. If we are in the North we shall see the Crowberry, and perhaps the Wild Pear, though the latter will disappoint us in the woody texture of its fruit and total lack of flavor. Birds are intensely fond of the Wild Red Currant, which we may see on hillsides and open places in the North.

The lantern-like shape of the European Poppy seed-head, with its millions of little black seeds, we shall seldom find, for authorities in this country have set their faces sternly against this tare among the wheat. Snowberries are native northward in North America. The Oriental Plane tree has more than one ball of fruit dangling from the stem. This tree, introduced into America, has become familiar as a shade tree.

The Bilberry belongs to the Vaccinium Family. Its leaves are small and evergreen, the flowers white, pink and red. One of the Viburnums—the Snowball, or Guelder-rose—is most ornamental in spring, with its fluffy white balls of bloom. The Common Holly shown you in the picture is the European, which has glossier foliage and brighter berries than the American variety to be found south of Massachusetts and west to the Colorado River. The Bog-bean, or Buckbean, belongs to the Gentian Family and is to be found in swamps.

It is easy to see the reason for the term Thorn-apple, as applied to the fruit of one of the Datura. The Black Solanum, or Nightshade, might be called cosmopolitan, so widespread is its distribution. The American Turkey Oak grows chiefly in southeastern United States and is valuable for fuel.

The white berries of the Mistletoe belong to our Christmas gaieties. The plant is a parasite. Common in Europe, the American genus grows only in the South. The Wild Black Cherry of the United States is much visited by birds, and its light, strong and reddish wood is largely used for cabinet-work and finishing. We may find both the American and the European Mountain Ash in our walks.

THE NEXT STORY OF PLANT LIFE IS ON PAGE 4093.

WILD FRUITS OF THE COUNTRYSIDE

1. Cloudberry. 2. Crab Apple. 3. Sweetbriar Fruit. 4. Privet Fruit. 5. Strawberry-tree Fruit (E.).
6. Spurge Laurel (E.). 7. Acorns. 8. Common Barberry. 9. Whortleberry. 10. Butcher's Broom (E.).
Plants marked (E.) are European and are not generally found in America.

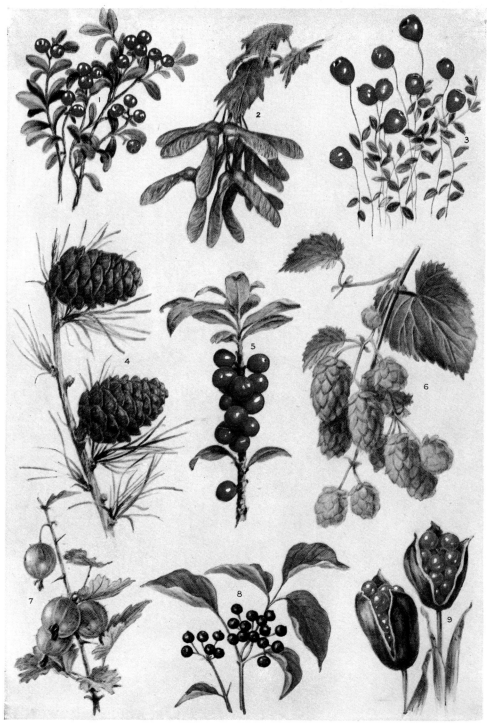

1. Common Bearberry. 2. Maple. 3. Cranberry. 4. Larch. 5. Mezereon (E.). 6. Hops. 7. Gooseberry. 8. Dogwood. 9. Fetid Iris (E.).

4022

1. Hazel. 2. Dewberry. 3. Caper Spurge. 4. Yew (E.). 5. Sea Buckthorn. 6. Wayfaring
Tree (E.). 7. Red Raspberry. 8. Bullace (E.). 9. Wild Red Cherry. 10. Wild Black Currant.

1. Honeysuckle (E.). 2. Laurel (E.). 3. Strawberry. 4. Beechnuts. 5. Medlar (E.). 6. Common Buckthorn. 7. Hawthorn. 8. Tutsan (E.). 9. Fly Honeysuckle (E.).

1. Field Rose. 2. Elder. 3. Jack-in-the-Pulpit. 4. White Bryony (E.). 5. Sweet Chestnut (E.).
6. Crowberry. 7. Alder Buckthorn (E.). 8. Wild Pear. 9. Red Currant.

1. **Common Red Poppy** (E.). 2. Snowberry. 3. Plane Tree. 4. Bilberry. 5. Guelder Rose.
6. Common European Ivy. 7. Black Bryony (E.). 8. Common Holly (E.). 9. English Walnut.
10. Bog-bean.

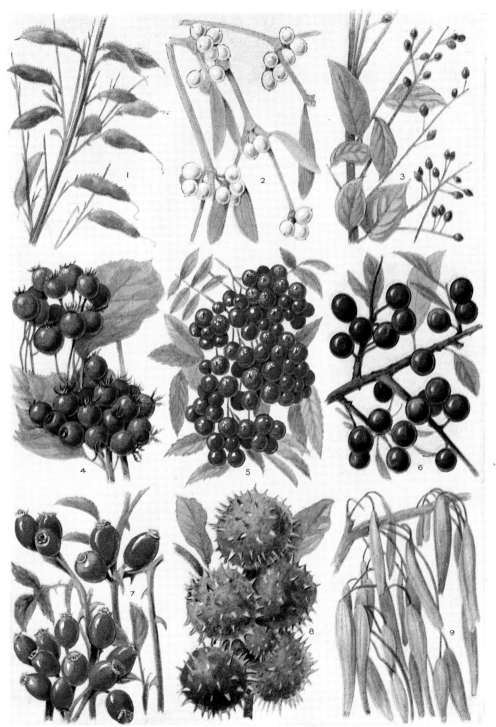

1. Broom (E.). 2. Mistletoe. 3. Wild Cherry. 4. Wild Service Tree (E.). 5. Mountain Ash, or Rowan. 6. Blackthorn, or Sloe (E.). 7. Dog Rose. 8. Horse-chestnut. 9. Common Ash.

1. Blackberry.   2. Scotch Pine.   3. Roebuck-berry, or Stone Bramble (E.).   4. Common Spindle Tree.
5. Thorn Apple.   6. Bitter-sweet.   7. Common English Elm.   8. Black Solanum, or Nightshade.
9. Turkey, or Moss-cupped Oak (E.).   10. Deadly Nightshade, or Dwale (E.).

A POEM ABOUT AN ELIZABETHAN GENTLEMAN

SIR PHILIP SIDNEY, who was born in 1554 and died in 1586 from a wound received while fighting in the Netherlands, was one of the most beautiful characters of his time. Although we know him as one of the finest poets of the Elizabethan period, none of his poems were printed during his lifetime, and the fame which he enjoyed in his own day was due largely to his personal character. Whenever we wish to think of a true hero and a Christian gentleman, the name of Sir Philip Sidney is the one that comes most readily to mind. Sir Fulke-Greville was a fellow-poet and comrade. He wrote the life of his friend, which was printed in 1652. He was also the author of this poem, in which he so beautifully celebrates the virtues of Sidney.

ON SIR PHILIP SIDNEY

CONTINUED FROM 3936

SILENCE augmenteth grief, writing increaseth rage,
Stal'd are my thoughts, which loved and lost, the wonder of our age;
Yet quickened now with fire, though dead with frost ere now,
Enraged I write I know not what; dead quick, I know not how.

Hard-hearted minds relent, and Rigour's tears abound,
And Envy strangely rues his end, in whom no fault she found;
Knowledge his light hath lost, Valour hath slain her knight:
Sidney is dead, dead is my friend, dead is the world's delight.

Place, pensive, wails his fall, whose presence was her pride;
Time crieth out, "My ebb is come, his life was my springtide";
Fame mourns in that she lost, the ground of her reports,
Each living wight laments his lack, and all in sundry sorts.

He was—woe worth that word—to each well-thinking mind,
A spotless friend, a matchless man, whose virtue ever shined,
Declaring in his thoughts, his life, and that he writ,
Highest conceits, longest foresights, and deepest works of wit.

He only like himself, was second unto none,
Where death—though life—we rue, and wrong, and all in vain do moan,
Their loss, not him, wail they that fill the world with cries,
Death slew not him, but he made death his ladder to the skies.

Now sink of sorrow I, who live, the more the wrong,
Who wishing death, whom death denies, whose thread is all too long,
Who tied to wretched life, who look for no relief,
Must spend my ever-dying days in never-ending grief.

Heart's ease and only I, like parallels run on,
Whose equal length, keep equal breadth, and never meet in one,
Yet for not wronging him, my thoughts, my sorrow's cell,
Shall not run out, though leak they will, for liking him so well.

Farewell to you, my hopes, my wonted waking dreams!
Farewell sometime enjoyed joy, eclipsèd are thy beams!
Farewell, self-pleasing thoughts, which quietness brings forth,
And farewell friendship's sacred league uniting minds of worth.

And farewell, merry heart, the gift of guiltless minds,
And all sports, which for life's restore, variety assigns,
Let all that sweet is, void! In me no mirth may dwell,
Philip, the cause of all this woe, my life's content, farewell!

Nor rime, the scourge of rage, which art no kin to skill,
And endless grief which deads my life, yet knows not how to kill,
Go seek that hapless tomb, which if ye hap to find,
Salute the stones, that keep the lines, that held so good a mind.

ONLY A BOY

It cannot truly be said that these lines are poetry. They are poetic in form, they rhyme, but they lack rhythm, or beauty of movement. They give a quick and happy outline of a good healthy type of boyhood.

ONLY a boy, with his noise and fun,
    The veriest mystery under the sun;
As brimful of mischief, and wit and glee,
As ever a human frame can be,
And as hard to manage as—what? ah, me!
        'Tis hard to tell,
        Yet we loved him well.

Only a boy with his fearful tread,
Who cannot be driven, must be led.
Who troubles the neighbor's dogs and cats,
And tears more clothes, and spoils more hats,
Loses more kites, and tops, and bats,
        Than would stock a store
        For a year or more.

Only a boy, with his wild, strange ways,
With his idle hours, or his busy days,
With his queer remarks and his odd replies,
Sometimes foolish and sometimes wise.
Often brilliant for one of his size,
        As a meteor hurled
        From the planet world.

Only a boy, who will be a man,
If Nature goes on with her first great plan—
If intemperance, or some fatal snare,
Conspire not to rob us of this our heir,
Our blessing, our trouble, our rest, our care,
        Our torment, our joy!
        Only a boy.

THE BAILIFF'S DAUGHTER

Here we have a well-known and typical old English ballad. The story it tells is of the simplest, for in the days when ballads were popular people were more simple-minded than they are now. It is a quaint and unlikely story, but its simplicity has a charm for us. It is difficult to imagine that the London apprentice let seven long years go by without seeing his sweetheart at Islington! But we must not expect common-sense views of life from these old ballads.

THERE was a youth, a well-beloved youth,
    And he was a squire's son,
He loved the bailiff's daughter dear
    That lived in Islington.

Yet she was coy and would not believe
    That he did love her so,
No, nor at any time would she
    Any countenance to him show.

But when his friends did understand
    His fond and foolish mind,
They sent him up to fair London
    An apprentice for to bind.

And when he had been seven long years,
    And never his love could see:
Many a tear have I shed for her sake,
    When she little thought of me.

Then all the maids of Islington
    Went forth to sport and play,
All but the bailiff's daughter dear;
    She secretly stole away.

She pulled off her gown of green
    And put on ragged attire,
And to fair London she would go
    Her true love to enquire.

And as she went along the high road,
    The weather being hot and dry,

She sat her down upon a green bank,
    And her true love came riding by.

She started up with a colour so red
    Catching hold of his bridle-rein;
"One penny, one penny, kind sir," she said,
    "Will ease me of much pain."

"Before I give you one penny, sweetheart,
    Pray tell me where you were born."
"At Islington, kind sir," said she,
    "Where I have had many a scorn."

"I prythee, sweetheart, then tell to me,
    O tell me whether you know,
The bailiff's daughter of Islington."
    "She is dead, sir, long ago."

"If she be dead, then take my horse,
    My saddle and bridle also;
For I will unto some far country,
    Where no man shall me know."

"O stay, O stay, thou goodly youth,
    She standeth by thy side;
She is here alive, she is not dead,
    And ready to be thy bride."

"O farewell grief; and welcome joy,
    Ten thousand times therefore;
For now I have found mine own true love,
    Whom I thought I should never see more."

TIME

Sir Walter Scott gives a fine sense of mystery and awe to the grim figure of old Father Time in this little poem. Time is always shown to us an old, old man with an hour-glass and a scythe: the one to suggest the passing of the hours, and the other the reaping of Time's harvest, which means the end of life. *Carle* is an old-fashioned word, still used in Scotland, to denote an elderly and rather rough sort of man.

"WHY sitt'st thou by that ruined hall,
    Thou agèd carle so stern and gray?
Dost thou its former pride recall,
    Or ponder how it passed away?"

"Know'st thou not me?" the Deep Voice cried;
    "So long enjoyed, so oft misused—
Alternate in thy fickle pride,
    Desired, neglected, and accused!

"Before my breath, like blazing flax,
    Man and his marvels pass away!
And changing empires wane and wax,
    Are founded, flourish, and decay.

"Redeem mine hours—the space is brief—
    While in my glass the sand-grains shiver,
And measureless thy joy or grief,
    When Time and thou shalt part for ever!"

ENVOY

An "envoy," from a French word *envoi*, means the verses at the end of a poem in which some general idea of the poem is summed up and emphasized. The "envoy" is thus the "message" which the poem has "carried"—for *envoyer* in French means "to send"—from the poet to the reader. But we often find tiny poems given this title without any preceding verses. In this case it is meant to suggest the last word on a noble life. This poem is by Charlotte Becker.

SAY not, because he did no wondrous deed,
    Amassed no worldly gain,
Wrote no great book, revealed no hidden truth,
    Perchance he lived in vain.

For there was grief within a thousand hearts
    The hour he ceased to live;
He held the love of women, and of men—
    Life has no more to give!

THE BAILIFF'S DAUGHTER OF ISLINGTON

She pulled off her gown of green and put on ragged   And to fair London she would go her true love to
attire,   enquire.

This picture is reproduced, by permission, from the painting by Mr. John Hatherell, R. I.

THE COMING OF SPRING

This charming description of the coming of spring is from
White Rose and Red, a story in verse by Robert Buchanan.

THE swift is wheeling and gleaming,
 The brook is brown in its bed,
Rain from the cloud is streaming,
And the Bow bends overhead;
The charm of the winter is broken!
The last of the spell is said!

The eel in the pond is quickening,
 The grayling leaps in the stream;
What if the clouds are thickening?
See how the meadows gleam!
The spell of the winter is shaken;
The world awakes from a dream.

The fir puts out green fingers,
 The pear tree softly blows,
The rose in her dark bower lingers,
But her curtains will soon unclose,
And the lilac will shake her ringlets
 Over the blush of the rose.

The swift is wheeling and gleaming,
The woods are beginning to ring,
Rain from the cloud is streaming;
There, where the Bow doth cling,
Summer is smiling afar off,
Over the Shoulder of Spring.

A PARABLE

This is a parable by Sir Arthur Conan Doyle for people
who find themselves too busy to make room for the best.

HIGH-BROW HOUSE was furnished well,
 With many a goblet fair;
So when they brought the Holy Grail
 There was never a space to spare.
Simple Cottage was clear and clean,
 With room to store at will;
So there they laid the Holy Grail,
 And there you'll find it still.

SONG OF MARION'S MEN

William Cullen Bryant wrote the following in memory of
Marion and his brave men, who waged guerilla warfare
against the British army during the Revolution.

OUR band is few, but true and tried,
 Our leader frank and bold;
The British soldier trembles
 When Marion's name is told.
Our fortress is the good greenwood,
 Our tent the cypress-tree;
We know the forest round us,
 As seamen know the sea.
We know its walls of thorny vines,
 Its glades of reedy grass,
Its safe and silent islands
 Within the dark morass.

Woe to the English soldiery,
 That little dread us near!
On them shall light at midnight
 A strange and sudden fear:
When, waking to their tents on fire,
 They grasp their arms in vain,
And they who stand to face us
 Are beat to earth again.
And they who fly in terror deem
 A mighty host behind,
And hear the tramp of thousands
 Upon the hollow wind.

Then sweet the hour that brings release
 From danger and from toil;
We talk the battle over,
 And share the battle's spoil.
The woodland rings with laugh and shout,
 As if a hunt were up,
And woodland flowers are gathered
 To crown the soldier's cup.
With merry songs we mock the wind
 That in the pine-top grieves,
And slumber long and sweetly
 On beds of oaken leaves.

Well knows the fair and friendly moon
 The band that Marion leads—
The glitter of their rifles,
 The scampering of their steeds.
'Tis life to guide the fiery barb
 Across the moonlight plain;
'Tis life to feel the night-wind
 That lifts his tossing mane.
A moment in the British camp—
 A moment—and away
Back to the pathless forest,
 Before the peep of day.

Grave men there are by broad Santee,
 Grave men with hoary hairs;
Their hearts are all with Marion,
 For Marion are their prayers.
And lovely ladies greet our band
 With kindliest welcoming,
With smiles like those of summer,
 And tears like those of spring.
For them we wear these trusty arms,
 And lay them down no more
Till we have driven the Briton,
 Forever, from our shore.

CONCORD HYMN

This poem was written by Ralph Waldo Emerson to be
sung at the completion of the Concord monument, April
19, 1836.

BY the rude bridge that arched the flood,
 Their flag to April's breeze unfurled,
Here once the embattled farmers stood,
 And fired the shot heard round the world.

The foe long since in silence slept;
 Alike the conqueror silent sleeps;
And Time the ruined bridge has swept
 Down the dark stream which seaward creeps.

On this green bank, by this soft stream,
 We set to-day a votive stone;
That memory may their deed redeem,
 When, like our sires, our sons are gone.

Spirit, that made those heroes dare
 To die, and leave their children free,
Bid Time and Nature gently spare
 The shaft we raise to them and thee.

A DEDICATION

We do not know many things more touching than these
four lines. They are Janet Begbie's dedication of a volume of poems to her little sister, who had left this world,
and all the desires of it, before the poems were written.

IN vain you asked me for a song:
 My love was idle all too long.
Now you can never ask again;
I bring you all my songs—in vain.

LOVE'S REASONINGS

Charles Mackay, an English poet of some note in the last century, sings here in very simple strains the praise of bird-music, that unfailing source of inspiration to the poets. Every year the birds sing the same song, but it always delights the ear and never grows old, for love lasts always.

WHAT is the meaning of the song,
　　That rings so clear and loud,
Thou nightingale, amid the copse,
　　Thou lark above the cloud?
What says thy song, thou joyous thrush,
　　Up in the walnut-tree?
"I love my love, because I know
　　My love loves me."

What is the meaning of thy thought,
　　O maiden fair and young?
There is such pleasure in thine eyes,
　　Such music on thy tongue;
There is such glory in thy face,
　　What can the meaning be?
"I love my love, because I know
　　My love loves me."

O happy words! at Beauty's feet
　　We sing them ere our prime,
And when the early summers pass,
　　And care comes on with time,
Still be it ours, in Care's despite,
　　To join the chorus free:
"I love my love, because I know
　　My love loves me."

TWO MEN

The point of this little poem is as old as the oldest of lessons which knowledge teaches man. The first thing any man can have realized was that death leveled all worldly distinctions. The writer of the poem is Charles Noble Gregory.

ONE was a king, and wide domain
　　He ruled as his sires had done;
A wooden hovel, a bed of pain
Belonged to the other one.

The king was ill and the world was sad—
　　But the monarch languished, the monarch died;
The beggar was sick unto death, but he had
　　No one to watch at his low bedside.

Then under the minster the king was laid,
　　While o'er him the marbles were piled;
But a shallow grave in the fields was made,
　　By careless hands, for poverty's child.

But now there are those who profoundly declare
If you opened the tomb and the grave,
You could not distinguish, whatever your care,
　　The dust of the king and the slave.

WHY IT WAS COLD IN MAY

This little piece of fanciful verse was written by an American woman named Henrietta Robins Eliot.

THE Year had all the Days in charge,
　　And promised them that they
Should each one see the World in turn,
　　But ten Days ran away!
Ten Days that should have gone abroad
　　Some time in early May;
So when May came, and all was fair,
　　These Days were sent to bed,
And ten *good* Winter Days were sent
　　To see the World instead!

THE POET AND THE BIRD

Elizabeth Barrett Browning, who died in the year 1861, one of the greatest of women poets that the nineteenth century produced, points a moral in this little fable. The natural music of the singing birds is among the rarest delights of our senses, and one of the loveliest things in nature, but the song of the poet springs from the depths of the heart and endures forever, whereas the song of a bird is of the things that perish.

SAID a people to a poet: "Go out from
　　among us straightway!
　While we are thinking earthly things, thou
　　singest of divine.
There's a little, fair, brown nightingale who,
　　sitting in the gateway,
　Makes fitter music to our ear than any song
　　of thine!"

The poet went out weeping—the nightingale
　　ceased chanting:
　"Now, wherefore, oh, thou nightingale, is
　　all thy sweetness done?"
"I cannot sing my earthly things, the heavenly
　　poet wanting,
　Whose highest harmony includes the lowest
　　under sun."

The poet went out weeping, and died abroad,
　　bereft there;
　The bird flew to his grove, and died amid a
　　thousand wails!
Yet when I last came by the place, I swear the
　　music left there
　Was only of the poet's song, and not the
　　nightingale's!

WHAT DOES IT MATTER?

The writer of the following lines voices an eloquent plea for good conduct, and reminds us that it is not by the amount of this world's wealth in money or possessions that we may inherit from others or acquire by our own efforts, not by our seeming success or failure, that we are to be judged, but by what we think and do, and our efforts to lead an upright and useful life.

IT matters little where I was born,
　　Or if my parents were rich or poor,
Whether they shrank from the cold world's
　　scorn
　Or walked in the pride of wealth secure;
But whether I live an honest man,
　　And hold my integrity firm in my clutch,
I tell you, my brother, as plain as I can,
　　　It matters much!

It matters little how long I stay
　　In a world of sorrow, sin, and care;
Whether in youth I am called away,
　　Or live till my bones of flesh are bare;
But whether I do the best I can
　　To soften the weight of adversity's touch
On the faded cheek of my fellow-man,
　　　It matters much!

It matters little where be my grave,
　　If on the land, or in the sea;
By purling brook, 'neath stormy wave,
　　It matters little or nought to me;
But whether the angel of death comes down
　　And marks my brow with a loving touch,
As one that shall wear the victor's crown,
　　　It matters much!

TO A SKYLARK

In the poem To the Skylark, on page 2529, Words-worth expresses, not the general feelings of a poet awakened by the skylark's song, but the emotion of some particular occasion. It is interesting to notice this difference between the poet's addressing "The Skylark" and "A Skylark."

UP with me! up with me into the clouds!
  For thy song, Lark, is strong;
Up with me! up with me into the clouds!
Singing, singing.
With clouds and sky about thee ringing,
Lift me, guide me, till I find
That spot which seems so to thy mind!

I have walked through wildernesses dreary,
And to-day my heart is weary;
  Had I now the wings of a faery,
Up to thee would I fly.
There's madness about thee, and joy divine
In that song of thine;
Lift me, guide me high, and high,
To thy banqueting-place in the sky.

Joyous as morning,
Thou art laughing and scorning;
Thou hast a nest for thy love and thy rest,
And, though little troubled with sloth,
Drunken Lark! thou wouldst be loth
To be such a traveller as I.
Happy, happy liver,
With a soul as strong as a mountain river,
Pouring out praise to the Almighty Giver!
Joy and jollity be with us both!

Alas! My journey, rugged and uneven,
Through prickly moors or dusty ways must
    wind;
But, hearing thee, or others of thy kind,
As full of gladness and as free of heaven,
I, with my fate contented, will plod on,
And hope for higher raptures, when life's day
  is done.

RAIN ON THE ROOF

The author of this familiar poem was Coates Kinney, an American writer, well known in his day, who was born in 1826. The falling of rain while we lie abed in a little country cottage has a soothing effect on the mind, and awakens, in some strange way, the tenderest emotions of the heart.

WHEN the humid shadows hover
  Over all the starry spheres,
And the melancholy darkness
  Gently weeps in rainy tears;
What a joy to press the pillow
  Of a cottage-chamber bed,
And to listen to the patter
  Of the soft rain overhead!

Every tinkle on the shingles
  Has an echo in the heart,
And a thousand dreamy fancies
  Into busy being start;
And a thousand recollections
  Weave their air-threads into woof,
As I listen to the patter
  Of the rain upon the roof.

Now in memory comes my mother,
  As she used in years agone,
To regard the darling dreamers
  Ere she left them till the dawn;
And I feel her fond look on me,
  As I list to this refrain

Which is played upon the shingles
  By the patter of the rain.

Then my little seraph sister,
  With her wings and waving hair,
And her star-eyed cherub brother—
  A serene, angelic pair—
Glide around my wakeful pillow,
  With their praise or mild reproof,
As I listen to the murmur
  Of the soft rain on the roof.

And another comes to thrill me
  With her eyes delicious blue;
And I mind not, musing on her,
  That her heart was all untrue:
I remember but to love her,
  With a passion kin to pain,
And my heart's quick pulses vibrate
  To the patter of the rain.

Art hath nought of tone or cadence
  That can work with such a spell
In the soul's mysterious fountains,
  Whence the tears of rapture well,
As that melody of Nature,
  That subdued, subduing strain,
Which is played upon the shingles
  By the patter of the rain.

NOW THE DAY IS OVER

The Reverend Sabine Baring-Gould was a famous and prolific writer of novels and travel books during the nineteenth and early twentieth centuries. But some of his beautiful hymns may outlive his fine stories. Who has not sung Onward Christian Soldiers? The evening hymn given here has been sung wherever English is spoken.

NOW the day is over,
  Night is drawing nigh;
Shadows of the evening
  Steal across the sky.

Now the darkness gathers,
  Stars begin to peep;
Birds, and beasts, and flowers,
  Soon will be asleep.

Jesu, give the weary
  Calm and sweet repose;
With Thy tenderest blessing
  May our eyelids close.

Grant to little children
  Visions bright of Thee;
Guard the sailors tossing
  On the deep blue sea.

Comfort every sufferer
  Watching late in pain;
Those who plan some evil
  From their sin restrain.

Through the long night-watches,
  May Thine angels spread
Their white wings above me,
  Watching round my bed.

When the morning wakens,
  Then may I arise,
Pure and fresh and sinless,
  In Thy holy eyes.

Glory to the Father,
  Glory to the Son,
And to Thee, Bless'd Spirit,
  While all ages run.

MY LADY WIND

My Lady Wind, my Lady Wind,
Went round about the house to find
A chink to get her foot in;
She tried the keyhole in the door,
She tried the crevice in the floor,
And drove the chimney soot in.

And then, one night when it was dark,
She blew up such a tiny spark,
That all the house was pothered;
From it she raised up such a flame,
As flamed away to Belting Lane,
And White Cross folks were smothered.

And thus when once, my little dears,
A whisper reaches itching ears,
The same will come, you'll find;
Take my advice, restrain the tongue,
Remember what old nurse has sung
Of busy Lady Wind.

TEENY-WEENY

Eugene Field, who wrote this poem and that on the previous page, was an American author and one of the kindest-hearted men that ever lived. He was born in 1850 and died at the end of 1895. His life, which was all too short, was spent chiefly as a writer on Chicago newspapers, but his fame rests on his many poems for and about children.

EVERY evening, after tea,
  Teeny-Weeny comes to me,
And, astride my willing knee,
  Plies his lash and rides away;
Though that palfrey, all too spare,
Finds his burden hard to bear,
Teeny-Weeny doesn't care;
  He commands, and I obey.

First it's trot, and gallop then;
Now it's back to trot again;
Teeny-Weeny likes it when
  He is riding fierce and fast.
Then his dark eyes brighter grow
And his cheeks are all aglow;
"More!" he cries, and never "Whoa!"
  Till the horse breaks down at last.

Oh, the strange and lovely sights
Teeny-Weeny sees of nights,
As he makes those famous flights
  On that wondrous horse of his!
Oftentimes, before he knows,
Weary-like, his eyelids close,
And, still smiling, off he goes
  Where the land of By-low is.

There he sees the folk of fay
Hard at ring-a-rosie play,
And he hears those fairies say:
  "Come, let's chase him to and fro!"
But, with a defiant shout,
Teeny puts that host to rout;
Of this tale I make no doubt,
  Every night he tells it so.

So I feel a tender pride
In my boy who dares to ride
That fierce horse of his astride,
  Off into those misty lands;
And, as on my breast he lies,
Dreaming in that wondrous wise,
I caress his folded eyes,
  Pat his little dimpled hands.

On a time he went away,
Just a little while to stay,
And I'm not ashamed to say
  I was very lonely then;
Life without him was so sad,
You can fancy I was glad
And made merry when I had
  Teeny-Weeny back again.

So of evenings, after tea,
When he toddles up to me
And goes tugging at my knee,
  You should hear his palfrey neigh!
You should see him prance and shy
When, with an exulting cry,
Teeny-Weeny, vaulting high,
  Plies his lash and rides away!

From Poems of Eugene Field, copyright, 1910, by Julia S. Field; published by Charles Scribner's Sons. By permission of the publishers.

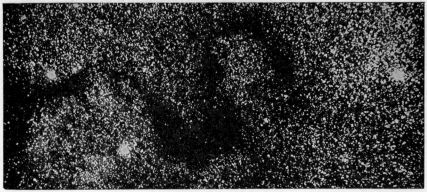

A dark nebula in the heavens.

WHAT IS HAPPENING IN THE SKY?

CONTINUED FROM 3926

BEYOND the stars are the nebulæ, but not all the nebulæ are so far away. Some are tangled with stars on this side of that great assemblage named the Milky Way. The shimmering Pleiades, that group of stars which may be seen on any clear night in the eastern sky, are clothed in a filmy cloud of nebula. In the Milky Way itself are many such clouds, some bright and wispy, some like giant cumulus, and some like black thunder clouds shutting off in some unknown fashion the shine of stars behind them.

It may be that some we do not see are nearer. We must also remember that while we speak of the Milky Way as a distant blaze of stars, we, our sun and our companion stars are all members of that bright galaxy.

It is easy to see how that may be. Suppose you stood on a great prairie in the early morning. You might fancy yourself alone in the world. But if you could see far enough you would soon discover, miles away, companions scattered about you; and the farther you could see, the more you would discover. If your eyes were miraculously sharpened so that you could see hundreds or thousands of miles, then wherever you turned you would see millions of fellow-beings. They would seem to be crowded more and more closely together as your eye took in the more distant ones. Finally they would seem to stand in a broad band of people more numerous than the stars of the Milky Way, all around the horizon.

That would be the effect of perspective; the more distant people, standing behind, or nearly behind, the nearer ones, would fill up the vacant spaces in the ranks, till they appeared like a solid mass. There would be some irregularities, but such would be the general effect; and this general effect would be the same if you had stood in the Sahara Desert or the Australian bush, or in Patagonia.

Thus, also, if you stood on one of the bright stars which seem to be placed in the Milky Way, you would have no impression of being in a crowded area of space. You would still be solitary, seeing with your own eyes no more distinct stars than the few thousand that you behold from the earth. If you had a telescope great enough to find it, the sun which lights the earth would be nothing but a speck in a bright cloud of distant stars—the Milky Way from another angle. This is only a rough sketch of the universe, to which we may add here a few touches because we shall have to refer to the subject again.

To the astronomers the stars seem to be scattered in the shape of a great biscuit, which is 60,000 light-years across and 12,000 light-years thick. The stars are thickly scattered near the central part and thin out toward the edges, though the edges are ragged.

WHY WE SEE THE MILKY WAY AS A GREAT BAND OF STARS

Our sun is fairly near the centre of this great biscuit, perhaps no more than 2,100 light-years away from it. That is what you would have expected, as otherwise one half of the sky would seem much brighter to us than the other. All the bright separate stars we see are at a distance of less than 6,000 light-years, but the stars near the edge of the biscuit are so far removed that they all appear very faint. There is no corresponding collection of faint stars in the *thickness* of the biscuit. Consequently the faint stars appear to be massed in a band which forms a great circle in the sky—the Milky Way.

It now seems that outside this great congregation of the heavenly host there lie a great number of those nebulæ which are called spiral nebulæ. They seem to outnumber the formless nebulæ by six to one. It is thought that there are, besides, a certain number of clusters of stars, which at that vast distance look like balls. They are called globular star-clusters. Remember what has been said about the effect of distance and perspective. You will guess that a great flock of migrating stars, all flying in the same direction like a cloud of silver arrows, would appear crowded together in a bunch. Some of these ball-like clusters are many thousand light-years away. (You remember that a light-year is the distance traveled by light in a year, about *six million million* miles.) The picture drawn of our Universe of Stars is that of a ship sailing on in space to some unknown port, while the clusters come to meet it; and the spiral nebulæ—perhaps—go on ahead.

THE STRANGE BEAUTY OF THE GREEN CONTINENT OF ORION

It is better to think of both the distant globular clusters, and of the spiral nebulæ whose distance we cannot tell, as belonging to our system of stars than to suppose they are separate universes or fragments of them. But all the nebulæ are not spirals. Some are like clouds or wisps of light wrapped about companies of stars great or small. Some are floating by themselves in or out of the Milky Way. The great nebula in Orion is the most dazzling of them all. A peep through

a telescope at the stars is apt to be disappointing. They are reduced to mere pin-pricks of light when seen through the lens; but when the green continent of the Orion nebula swims into the field of the glass it makes one gasp at its strange beauty. There are other famous ones, though none that excites the same awe. We may name the Crab nebula, the America nebula (named for its shape), the Keyhole nebula and the Dumb-bell. When the light from these is tested by that rainbow-band method of which we spoke in dealing with the substance and motions of the stars, nothing but bright lines appear. This indicates that it is no glowing body which produces the light, but merely incandescent gas. Two gases are always there, hydrogen and helium, and we can fancy that they are in the state of the gas which is made to glow in an X-ray tube by electricity; they must be very, very thin, although there are such vast volumes of them. It seems likely that all the "bright-line" messages the light sends to us come from hydrogen or helium in different states.

VAST SUNS THAT HAVE EXPLODED LIKE A SHELL IN SPACE

The same kind of gaseous nebulæ surrounds stars like the Pleiades. They certainly have something to do with the stars they wrap round. There are, besides, what are called planetary nebulæ, which have a bright nucleus, and these are gaseous too. They resemble in appearance the new stars, such as Nova Persei and Nova Aquilæ, when they burst on our sight.

After these new stars had blazed up, the light from them seemed to be lighting up some gaseous nebula into which they had plunged. Nova Aquilæ, the new star which appeared some years ago in the Eagle, is now showing in the great telescopes a sort of expanding disk of gas round where it broke into light. It is therefore thought that the gaseous planetary nebulæ were originally vast suns which burst explosively into destruction like a shell. It is believed that the gaseous rings and curves of light which now are left are the results of the outburst. In the same way the great clouds of brightly lighted gas which surround the Pleiades or other stars do not come there by accident.

They possibly represent some terrific, appalling outburst of the stars them-

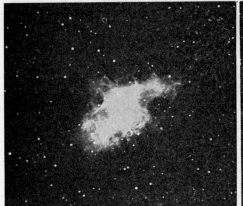

The Crab Nebula in Taurus.

A star-cluster in Canes Venatici.

Spiral Nebula in the Great Bear.

Spiral Nebula in Coma Berenices.

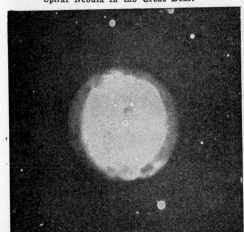

The Owl Nebula in the Great Bear.

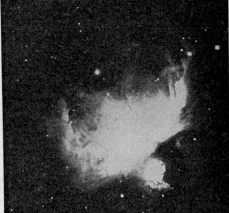

The Great Nebula in Orion.

These pictures are from photographs by Messrs. G. W. Ritchey, W. E. Wilson, and others.

selves. Their atoms have disintegrated and cast these suns into the melting-pot, so that they have swollen to dimensions vaster than a solar system. It used to be thought that the great gaseous nebulæ were assemblages of the first atoms of matter. It was believed fragments of hydrogen or helium in vast ages of time settled down, concentrated, consolidated, to form the elements of suns. It seems now more likely that just the opposite goes on, and that the irregular nebulæ were born when stars exploded. Some of them may now be cold, but the great

lines, but, instead, a band on which dark lines appear. They therefore cannot be gaseous: there must be some solid glowing body to produce their light. For this reason some have supposed that they are not clouds of matter at all, but that they are actual systems of stars, outside our own universe, and perhaps models of it on a small, or even on a large scale. On the whole, most astronomers think that this cannot be.

They suggest, instead, that perhaps the light comes from stars that are in the spiral nebulæ, though we cannot see them.

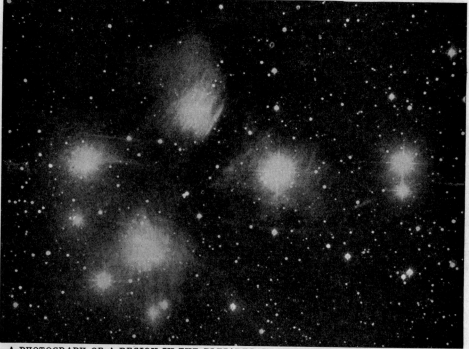

A PHOTOGRAPH OF A REGION IN THE PLEIADES, SHOWING ITS NEBULOUS CHARACTER

Orion nebula is believed to have a temperature of 15,000 degrees Centigrade.

What of the spirals? They are seldom near the Milky Way, although there are thousands of them. They are all, it seems, moving, sometimes at the speed of 600 miles a second. Nothing else in the universe moves like that. Moreover, it seems proved that some of them are spinning—like titanic Catherine wheels. They are full of mystery, but the most inexplicable thing about them is what they are made of.

When their light is tested by the "rainbow band" it does not display bright

It may be that they are collections of the whirling dust of meteors. The first of these ideas has some support from the fact that several apparently new stars have appeared among the folds of the great nebula in Andromeda, the most gorgeous spiral nebula in the skies.

It must be remembered, in speaking of the spiral nebulæ, that we speak with uncertainty and doubt, because we cannot positively say how far away any one of them is, nor what it is made of. One of the most interesting ideas is that from these wonderful spirals we might obtain a hint as to the beginnings of many suns.

This is how many astronomers think our own solar system may have begun.

Suppose two suns sailing through space came close together. What would hap-

till they burst all the bonds that held them, and one or both suns might explode into a mass of flaming gas to which would be given a whirling motion. Giant arms

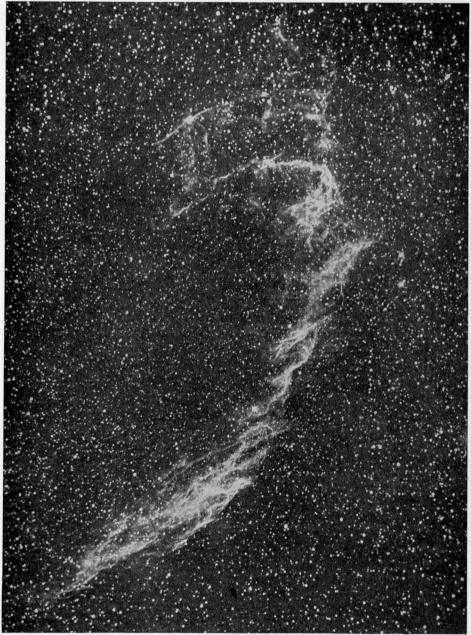

A BEAUTIFUL WISP OF NEBULOUS MATTER IN THE MILKY WAY

pen? As the huge suns approached, the force of attraction would lift up great tides on both. As they came nearer and nearer, the tides of flame would rise higher,

would protrude from it like curved tentacles, and across these the particles would continue to revolve. After many years they might begin to condense again into knots, and a central nucleus. The knots would be the planets of a new system; the largest nucleus would be a new sun to replace the old. One variation of this idea was that out of the explosion a new sun would be born. This would be a kind of third body, after the one sun had passed and left the débris of the other partly scattered, but not wholly broken up.

These ideas have had a great following. The objection to them is that, from what is known of the movements and distances of the stars, collisions must be few—perhaps not one in 15 million years—and the spiral nebulæ are many, and they are very far away from the stars as we know them.

However, it is not necessary that stars come into collision. If they approach within several million miles, their attraction for each other might cause matter to be thrown off.

Nobody can say for certain how suns are born; it is beyond our knowledge. Perhaps they are the sum and substance of the particles ejected from every star that shines, which fly through space and must collect somewhere. Perhaps one star is born of another when, by some inexplicable law, the atoms that compose a star break up under some stress of heat or collision, and explode the fabric of which they are the foundation.

One thing is positive and known. It is that, as one star differs from another in brightness, so do they differ enormously in size and strength and substance. Betelgeuse is 240 million miles across; our sun is a pigmy in comparison with it. But every star has two phases of its history. It expands and expands till it is a giant; it shrinks and shrinks till it is a dwarf. It may be that the expansion is sometimes too great, and that a star disappears, to give birth to fragments that collect and live and grow again—for is it not said that He who made the heavens can restore them, and that old things may pass away, and the scroll of the skies shall be "like a book folded up," till a new heaven and a new earth are re-created?

We have left till the very last the movements of the stars. That is a knowledge which is the slow growth of centuries. They are so far away that in a hundred years some appear not to move at all. That is why great maps of the stars are made. The positions of the stars are marked on them so that they may be compared at long intervals of years. Their movements can then be measured. Hence some vague idea of star-movement is gained. It seemed some years ago as if they might be moving for the most part round the giant disk, taking something like 208 million years for their journeys; but now we think that there are two great streams of migrating stars. Their courses are roughly parallel.

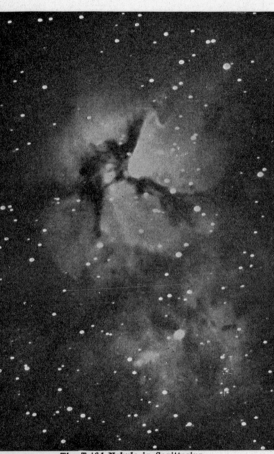

The Trifid Nebula in Sagittarius.
From a photograph taken at the Lick Observatory.

THE NEXT STORY OF THE EARTH IS ON PAGE 4155.

The New Palace at Potsdam, built by Frederick the Great.

THE STORY OF FREDERICK THE GREAT

IT has been said that the history of Prussia is the history of the Hohenzollerns, its ruling family. This is largely true, and of no one is it more true than of Frederick II, whom we know as Frederick the Great. Before his time the possessions of his house were scattered, and the country poor. He added to its wealth by seizing from Austria the rich province of Silesia, and began to link together his scattered territories by taking possession of the part of Poland which divided Brandenburg from Prussia.

Frederick, whose father was Frederick William, the eldest son of Frederick, the first king of Prussia, was born on January 24, 1712. The coming of the little boy was a joyous event in the lives of his father and mother. They had already lost two little sons by death, and had only one child left, a girl named Wilhelmina, who was now five years old. When Frederick was born his grandfather was still alive, but he died the following year. Frederick William, the boy's father, became king, and Frederick himself henceforth was known as the Crown Prince.

Frederick William, who was a gruff soldier, brought his ideas of discipline into his own household, and his chil-

CONTINUED FROM 3997

dren were brought up very simply. For instance, Frederick tells us that his nursery fare included beer, soup and bread, which, to our minds, make strange food for a little child. While he was still very small Frederick was put in charge of Madame de Roucoulles, a gentle, gracious French woman, who taught him carefully and gave him a love of the French language and French people and manners that lasted all his life. He was a bright, affectionate child who loved his gentle teacher, and played and romped about the nurseries with his sister Wilhelmina. A picture that was painted when he was three years old shows him to us as a quaint little figure in a velvet frock beating a drum with one hand while Wilhelmina holds the other. His delight in this drum gave his father the greatest pleasure. He thought it showed that the boy wanted to be a soldier and that was the dearest wish of the king's heart.

The happy days of Frederick's childhood lasted only until he was seven years old. Then the king thought it was high time that his education as a soldier and a king should begin, and he put him in charge of three tutors. From that time on to the end of his life Frederick's days

4043

were filled with work. His father, who did not believe in idleness, laid down very precise rules for every moment of his son's time. His tutors, two soldiers and a Frenchman, were given no freedom about his studies, for the king had very strong opinions about the subjects that a prince ought to study and the time that should be given to each.

WHAT THE FUTURE KING WAS FORCED TO LEARN

Latin the king thought was unnecessary. Therefore the prince was not to learn it. German and French, said the king, were sufficient for his needs, and he was taught no other language. He was to learn arithmetic, mathematics and economy. He was to pay special attention to the history of his family and of the hundred and fifty years before his time; but he was taught only a general knowledge of ancient history. Later on he was to learn the science of fortification and the formation of camps. Above all, said the king, his son's tutors were to impress on his mind the belief that nothing could bring a prince true honor and glory but war, and that if he did not love it, he would be despised by all men. This teaching, as we shall see, bore fruit later on.

At this time the king made up a company of about a hundred boys of Frederick's own age. He and these boys were drilled just as if they were all grown men and soldiers, and a year or two afterward he was put in command of the company. When he was about nine years old an arsenal of tiny guns was set up in one of the halls of the palace, and there, with a few of his friends, he was taught to mount guns and to fire the batteries just as if he were in actual warfare.

This sounds as if it might be very good fun, but it was not fun to Frederick. It was hard work, and the discipline in his little company was just as strict as the discipline in the army. He had to get up at seven o'clock on Sunday and at six o'clock on week days. He was taught to wash and dress himself. To train him to be quick in his movements he was given only fifteen minutes to dress, say his prayers and eat his simple breakfast. Not many boys can move so quickly as all that, and perhaps his father had some reason when he began to find fault with him and call him a dirty boy.

FREDERICK'S UNHAPPY BOYHOOD AND YOUTH

Unhappily, Frederick William had very little patience with his son and found fault with him for many reasons. The king had a very quick temper, and Frederick was afraid of him and shrank from the violence with which he was treated whenever he did anything of which his father did not approve. On the other hand, the father resented the boy's fear of him. He wanted his love and confidence, and resented the affection that was shown by the boy to his mother and sister and his tutors.

As Frederick grew older the differences between him and his father increased. Frederick disliked hunting, which was one of his father's chief pleasures, and said that riding over freshly seeded ground was great waste. He wearied of the perpetual drilling that he had to undergo. He loved music and literature and had visions of being a poet. He was a handsome youth, and as he grew up he developed a love of fine clothes and rebelled against having nothing but his uniform to wear. On the other hand, his father thought that hunting was a manly sport, that time spent on music and literature was wasted, that it was an honor to wear the uniform of his army, and that love of fine clothing was womanish. The truth is that Frederick would have made a very bad poet, and never learned to write well in either French or German. He was a born leader of men, and was of the stuff of which in our day great captains of industry are made. At the same time, his love of music and literature was a great boon to him all his life. If his father had understood that the prince was quite as safe in indulging his love for music as he himself was in making a hobby of creating regiments of very tall, rather useless soldiers who never fought, all might have been well.

But this Frederick William could not see. He loved his country, and had worked hard to make it prosperous and powerful. He feared that his son would grow up to be self-indulgent and useless, and would undo the work of his life. "Fritz," he said, "is a poet, and will spoil all my labor." The queen and the Princess Wilhelmina took the prince's part; the king grew more and more angry. Prince Frederick looked upon his father as a mean, selfish tyrant, and life at the palace was very unhappy.

Unknown to his father, Frederick learned to play the flute, and one of his tutors taught him Latin. But the king found this out. He ordered his son's books to be sold, had the flute put out of the way, and with his own hands burned a handsome coat which the prince had bought.

As the prince grew to manhood, the quarrels between him and his father became more frequent. We have a very

much more of a king. Frederick William always carried a cane, and in his anger and distress did not scruple at all to use it on his son's shoulders. At times he would scarcely speak to the prince. Often he would not help him at dinner, so that the boy had to leave the table hungry. It is said that more than once the king flung plates at the prince's head, and that he even tried to hang him with a heavy window cord. Sometimes he covered him with abuse in the presence of others, and when the prince remained

© Underwood & Underwood, New York.
On this hill stood the castle where the Hohenzollerns lived before they became Burgraves of Nuremberg. The castle was allowed to fall into ruins, but in the nineteenth century was rebuilt by Frederick William IV of Prussia. Nothing of the old castle except the chapel remains, but the new building was designed to look like the fortress of the old counts. The territory which surrounds it belonged to the kings of Prussia, and the castle was sometimes used by the royal family as a summer residence.

pitiful letter written by Frederick when he was about sixteen in which he said that he had not ventured to see his father for a long time, chiefly because he "anticipated a worse reception than usual," and begged his father "to give over the fearful hate which had appeared so plainly in his whole countenance and to which," the poor boy said, "I cannot accustom myself." Much of the trouble, however, was Frederick's own fault. He chose some bad companions, got into debt, and fell into wild ways, which the king, who was a really good man, thought were beneath the dignity of a man, and

silent under his harsh taunts, accused him of cowardice.

At length Frederick felt that he could stay in his home no longer and made an attempt to run away. He was unsuccessful. The king had him arrested and imprisoned in the castle of Cüstrin, and tried by court martial as a deserter from the army. The court was compelled to sentence Frederick to death, and, in spite of the sorrowful prayers of the queen and all his other children, and the indignation of the army and the country, the king threatened to have the sentence carried out. The emperor, however, pleaded for the boy, and this gave the king an excuse to change the punishment. Nevertheless, the friend who had helped the prince in his preparations to escape was by the king's direction sentenced to death, and was executed before the prince's window. "Pardon me, dear Katte," the prince said as his friend was led past. "Oh, that this should be what I have done for you!" And Katte answered: "Death is sweet for a prince I love so well!"

HIS FATHER'S HARSHNESS CHANGES HIS CHARACTER

Frederick, who from the time of his arrest had been very severely treated, did not know for months whether he was to live or die. He was dismissed from the army and his uniform was taken from him, but after he had taken an oath of obedience and written a penitent letter to his father he was released from his prison. He was not allowed, however, to leave the town of Cüstrin except with the permission of the commandant, and then only for a day, and was made to learn the business of governing the province in which he was confined. Then he set himself as he had never done before to gain his father's favor. He worked and studied hard, and made good use of his time, and the reports of his conduct were so good that at the end of a year the king let him go back to Berlin. He was taken back into the army, and after a time was given command of a regiment and made governor of the province of Rüppin. The next year, to please his father, he married a cousin of the empress of Austria, the Princess Elizabeth of Brunswick-Bevern. Unfortunately he never really loved his wife, and though they agreed very well while they were young and gay, they seldom met in their later years.

The shock of Frederick's imprisonment and the death of his friend had been so great that he had become quite changed. He never afterward gave anyone his confidence, and from being an affectionate boy he turned into a cold, hard, selfish and ambitious man. Even his sister Wilhelmina, whom he really loved, complained of his changed manner, and while he was always loving and kind to his mother, she had no really important influence in his life.

Still, the years between his marriage and his father's death were the happiest in his life. He had a beautiful house, at some distance from Berlin, and though he had plenty of work to do, he had freedom to indulge his own tastes. It was in 1836 that he began a correspondence with Voltaire which continued for many years. The king's health grew poor, and as he saw that his son would make him a worthy successor, he learned to depend on him. During these years the king sent an army to the help of the emperor when the king of France invaded Germany. Frederick went with this army, and although he was not in command, his father was much pleased with his conduct in this war.

ON HIS FATHER'S DEATH FREDERICK BEGAN TO REIGN

Frederick William died on May 31, 1740, and the prince succeeded him as Frederick II, king of Prussia, margrave and elector of Brandenburg, and duke of Cleves in Westphalia. Many people had thought that when Frederick ascended the throne he would make the court a scene of splendor, but in this they were disappointed. He contented himself with the simplest ceremonies on his accession to the throne, and spent the first months of his reign in getting the business of administration well in hand. He made no effort to change his father's way of government, and, if anything, he made himself more absolute than his father had ever been. He never had a cabinet. He appointed three ministers, but they had no influence over the affairs of state and simply carried out the instructions that he gave them.

We usually think of Louis XIV as the best modern example of an absolute king, but, as a matter of fact, Frederick II of Prussia, who took counsel with no one, was more absolute than any king of France that ever lived. Nevertheless, he was perhaps as good a king as an absolute ruler could be, and gave a great deal of thought to the welfare of his people. As soon as he began to reign he took measures to relieve the poor of the kingdom. He abolished torture, which up to that time had been used in criminal trials, allowed freedom of the press, and decreed that all the people should be free to worship God in their own way.

THE REGIMENTS OF TALL SOLDIERS ARE DISBANDED

His father had left him a magnificent army, in which there were some regiments of immensely tall men. Frederick at once disbanded these regiments, and the world took this as a sign that he would reduce his army, and hoped that he would treat it as a highly polished weapon to be kept for ornament, not for use. Men said that he would settle down to the ordinary work of government and to the pleasure of his literary pursuits, but Frederick had other ideas. He thirsted for glory, which he had been

Silesia, which slopes gently from the plains of Brandenburg to the crest of the Bohemian Mountains. Frederick wanted to add this rich province to his own possessions, and when he heard of the emperor's death, without losing an instant of time, he laid his plans to invade it. Within a few weeks he had his army ready on the border, and then, setting up an old claim to four small duchies

© Underwood & Underwood, New York.
This is part of the front of Sans Souci Palace at Potsdam, built by Frederick the Great, who also had a part of the fine gardens that surround the palace laid out. Frederick called the palace Sans Souci, which means "without care." He lived here much of the time during the last years of his life. A number of his personal belongings are carefully preserved here. Near by is the large New Palace, which Frederick also built and which was generally used as a residence by later German emperors.

taught to look for in war. Very quietly he raised the army to 100,000 men, drilled and trained it as no army had ever been drilled and trained before, and waited for an opportunity to use it.

The opportunity that he looked for came, a few months after he began to reign, on the death of the Emperor Charles VI. Charles had no son, but, as we have read in the story of Austria, his daughter Maria Theresa succeeded to his dominions. Now in these dominions was included the little country of

in the south, he marched very quickly into the country.

There were only a few thousand Austrian soldiers in Silesia, too few to stop Frederick's army, and in a few weeks the whole country, except a few fortified towns, was in his hands. The next year the Austrians gathered an army together and made Frederick fight to keep his conquest, but they were not able to drive him out.

When peace was made he kept all of Silesia except a small strip of mountainous country which Austria was able to hold, and he also got the little county of Glatz, which lies between Silesia and Bohemia.

While the war for the possession of Silesia was going on, the elector of Bavaria, who claimed the thrones of Austria, Hungary and Bohemia, began another war against Maria Theresa to take her dominions from her. This war, known as the War of the Austrian Succession, was of great assistance to Frederick, and he used his influence to have the elector of Bavaria chosen emperor with the title of Charles VII.

As soon as the treaty was signed which gave him Silesia he set to work to make the country into a Prussian province. In this he was greatly helped by the fact that the people had been more or less oppressed by their Austrian rulers. Frederick had been careful to impose as little hardship as possible upon them during the war. They looked upon him as a champion, and the greater number of the population were glad to change their allegiance. His rule was stern, but it brought prosperity, and the people rejoiced in their new-found peace.

Meantime the War of the Austrian Succession went on, and for two years the armies of Maria Theresa were successful. But Frederick feared that if she were victorious she would try to wrest Silesia from him. Therefore he went to the aid of the emperor, invaded Maria Theresa's kingdom of Bohemia with a large army, and the Second Silesian War began.

This war, like the first, lasted for two years. The king of Saxony joined Maria Theresa, and sometimes it seemed as though Frederick would lose the war. On the whole, however, he was successful. He found out the most secret plans of his enemies, and defeated them, and at the end of the second year peace was made. The treaty was signed on Christmas Day, and when, a week later, Frederick went home to Berlin the people greeted him with cries of "Frederick the Great." He was saddened, however, by the news that one of his old tutors was dying, and it showed his good feeling that he found time to go at once to see this true old friend.

After the Second Silesian War was over, Frederick had ten years of peace. Thanks to his father's training, he was a good man of business and during this time he built up the prosperity of his dominions. He encouraged agriculture, manufactures and commerce. Swamps were drained, and moorlands brought into cultivation. It is strange, however, that with all his love for learning and his interest in the prosperity of the country, Frederick took no pains to see that the great mass of the people were educated.

Meantime the Emperor Charles VII died. Maria Theresa's husband was chosen emperor in his place, and she made peace with Bavaria and France. But, although she had ceded Silesia to Frederick, she never stopped planning to get it back, and before many years had passed he began to suspect that she had made a secret treaty with the Empress Elizabeth of Russia and the king of Saxony to make war against him. His suspicions soon deepened into certainty, and he began the Seven Years' War.

After he began his wars Frederick always wore his uniform, a blue coat with red collar and facings. After the fashion of his time, he wore a short curled wig tied back with ribbon. He always wore a cocked hat of felt.

FREDERICK DURING THE SEVEN YEARS' WAR

It is impossible in a short space to tell of all that Frederick did in these seven years. Austria, Russia, France and, later, Sweden were opposed to him, and his only ally was England. England, who was engaged in America in what we know as the French and Indian War, could not give him men, but she did give him money, without which he could not have carried on the fight. Frederick won many victories, of which the most famous is Rossbach, where with 22,000 men he defeated an army of 50,000. His personal bravery was very great, and he became the idol of his soldiers. But the odds against him were enormous. In one battle he fought so recklessly that an officer asked if he meant to take a battery single-handed. He met many defeats, and once he became so despondent that he was tempted to take his own life. Once he was slightly wounded and narrowly escaped being taken prisoner, and another time his clothing was riddled with shot.

As the years went on it seemed as if the war must end in Frederick's complete overthrow. The climax of his woes was reached when his uncle George II of England died. George III, who cared nothing for Frederick, made peace with France, and Frederick was left without support. The same year, however, the empress of Russia died. Her successor, Peter III, was Frederick's greatest admirer. He at once made peace with Prussia. The Russian armies were ordered home, and Frederick was saved. His only opponent now was Austria, and though the war dragged on for another year, both countries were exhausted and a peace, which left him in possession of Silesia, was signed in 1763.

FREDERICK SHOWED HIS REAL GREATNESS IN TIME OF PEACE

It was now that Frederick showed his real greatness. Few men could have risen as he did to the task of bringing back prosperity to his ruined land. The country had been reduced to penury, but it was not in debt, for there was nowhere that Frederick could borrow. He had somehow got enough money to carry on the war for another year, and this he used to help the people. The army horses were used to cultivate the land, seed was bought and distributed, and by degrees houses were rebuilt, and commerce and industry built up again.

About ten years after the close of the war he shared in the first partition of Poland. This partition completed the ruin of Poland, but brought Polish Prussia, which had hitherto divided Brandenburg from East Prussia, under Frederick's rule and greatly strengthened his position in the empire. Some people have tried to lay the whole blame for the partition on the empress of Russia or on the Emperor Joseph, Maria Theresa's son. There is little doubt, however, that the chief fault was Frederick's. He wanted Polish Prussia. When he saw an opportunity to get it without the cost of a war, he took it, and there can be no justification for his act.

Much suffering has come from the partition of Poland, and the people have always been restless and discontented under the foreign rule to which they have been subjected. In 1919, as one of the results of the World War, Germany was forced to give back this province and other Polish territory besides to the new Polish state.

FREDERICK THE GREAT TRIED TO UNITE NORTH GERMANY

Some years later, when the elector of Bavaria died, another quarrel with Austria was threatened. But Frederick feared to bring on another dreadful war, and the matter was settled by treaty. Then Frederick began to think of making a union of the north German princes to curb the power of Austria. Before he died he partly succeeded, and the League of Princes which he formed was the germ from which grew the idea of the present German Empire.

In his old age his people called him "Father Fritz," a title that was very dear to his lonely heart. He suffered much from gout, but, nevertheless, he continued to work as hard as in his youth. In August, 1785, he held a review at which Lafayette was present. Rain fell heavily, and the king got a chill which brought on the attack of gout. During the next year he gradually lost strength, and died on August 17, 1786, in the seventy-fifth year of his age. Frederick had made Prussia so strong that it was able to attempt to take the leadership in Germany. Because of that he may be called a "maker of history."

THE NEXT STORY OF MEN AND WOMEN IS ON PAGE 4205.

CATCHING FISH NEAR SHORE

This scene off the coast of Florida shows a pound net, which is a long fence of netting supported on stakes starting near shore and ending in an inclosure in which the fish are trapped. It is a modern form of the old weir made of stakes and withes or brush.   Photo, Ewing Galloway, New York.

© J. E. Ford. **Wealth of food taken from the waters.**

HOW FISH AND OYSTERS ARE TAKEN

THOUSANDS and thousands of men, and women, too, all over the world are engaged in getting food from the sea for themselves and others. Many thousands of men, women and children are employed in cleaning and preserving the fish. Thousands more work on shore making and repairing boats, nets and fishing tackle, or preparing boxes and barrels in which the catch may be placed. Thousands of boats, large and small, are employed in the fishing business, and the value of the food brought to shore is many millions of dollars.

CONTINUED FROM 3920

From earliest times men have eaten fish. All savages who live near the water eat fish, and some are very skillful fishermen. In Bible times there were many fishermen who fished both with nets and with hooks, but chiefly with nets. All through history we find stories of fishermen and their work. And in our own time the world still gets a great part of its food from the waters, both salt and fresh.

In proportion to the number of people, the fish industries of Great Britain and Ireland are the most important. These islands are washed by the sea on every side, and some of the best fishing-grounds in the world are within easy reach. The United States comes first in the value of fish caught, and the fisheries of Russia, Canada, France, Norway, Germany and Japan are also important. Every country with a sea-coast has fisheries as a matter of course.

The same kinds of fish do not live in every part of the sea. Some like cold water, which would kill others. Some fish like to go to the warmer waters in winter, but come toward the north in summer. Many fish found in the Atlantic are not caught in the Pacific, and the converse is also true. Even the fish in different parts of the Atlantic are not alike.

Many fish found in European waters are never seen in American waters, and there are others which belong to America alone. Often the fishes called by the same name in Great Britain and North America are not quite alike, though they may belong to the same family. Sometimes a fish can be transferred from one sea to another. The shad belongs to the Atlantic, but the United States Bureau of Fisheries

4051

has set free millions of young shad on the Pacific, and that delicious fish seems to be well established there now. It enters the streams to lay its eggs as far north as Alaska.

Some fish live near the surface; others swim far below. Some will bite at hooks, and can be caught on lines; others must be taken in nets. Then there are oysters, mussels, lobsters and crabs, which are not really fish, of course, though they come from the water and are sold at the fish-market. The index will help you to find the pictures of different kinds.

The simplest way for one person alone to catch fish is to use the hook and line; but this is very slow work unless the fish are plentiful and very hungry. Men fish with hook and line for sport, but those who catch fish for market generally use other methods. One way is to go out in a boat and throw out several lines, which are drawn along behind as the boat moves through the water.

Fishing schooners which go out after cod, often fasten a long line of buoys. To this line are attached hundreds of shorter lines, each with a hook on the end. This is called "setting a trawl." The cod swim along together in great numbers, and sometimes hundreds will be found securely caught when the men go out in a small boat to examine the trawl. They are taken off, and fresh bait is put on the hooks, unless the cod have gone to another place. Then the skipper decides to try his luck elsewhere.

THE FISHERMAN MUST LEARN TO PUT HIMSELF IN A FISH'S PLACE

Sometimes the fish will be plentiful in some region, and then all at once will vanish from that part of the ocean. Masters of fishing schooners learn to guess what the fish are likely to do. When the fish cease to bite, the boats go to the place where it is judged the fish will go. Probably the movements of the fish are affected by their food supply, and this is influenced by currents, temperature and winds.

New England and Nova Scotia are the great deep-sea fishing sections. Gloucester, Massachusetts, and Lunenburg, Nova Scotia, are the great fishing ports. Boston is the greatest market. Sailing vessels are being replaced by steam vessels now, and the business is not so picturesque as it once was, but there are still many fishing schooners to be seen.

THE DIFFERENT KINDS OF NETS WHICH ARE USED

More fish are caught in nets than by lines. There are many kinds of nets, some of them more than a mile long. The pound net is set in shallow water not far from the shore. Poles are driven down into the bottom to form an inclosure, and a net shaped like a huge bag with an opening in one side is set inside. A long net is stretched from the shore to the opening in the net. Fish swimming along come to this "lead," as it is called, and follow its lines, hoping to get around it. Soon they find themselves in the pound and are too stupid to get out. Pound is an old English word meaning "inclosure." The fishermen go out in small boats, pull up the net, and gather in the fish.

NETS WHICH ARE OVER A MILE LONG, AND OTHERS

Other nets, called seines, are long stretches of net with weights on one side and floats on the other. One end is often fastened near the shore, while a boat takes the other out and drops it into the sea. The weights stretch the net toward the bottom, while the floats keep the top from sinking. This makes a wall of net, sometimes more than a mile long. A net as heavy as this cannot be drawn in by a boat. Ropes are attached to the sea end, and are taken to shore and attached to a windlass. The net is now in the shape of a great semicircle, which is drawn to shore, bringing with it whatever fish were swimming within the space over which the net passed. There are other seines which are carried out in boats.

The gill net, or drift net, is often set across a channel or the entrance to a bay. It is like a seine, except that both ends are usually free. Fish try to get through the spaces in the net and become entangled. When it has been set for some time the fishermen go out and take up the net, a little at a time, empty it of fish, and drop it back again to catch other victims which may try to get through spaces too small for them.

There are other kinds of nets used in various parts of North America. The shad net is set in a river in the same way as the lead of a pound net. The shad trying to get up the river to lay their eggs are entangled in the net and held fast. Fyke nets are great bags set at the bottom of the sea. Each has a mouth shaped like a funnel, and the fish, once they have gone inside, are not wise enough to get out.

THE TRAWL IN ENGLAND NOT THE SAME AS IN AMERICA

We have told you that the trawl is a long line to which shorter lines are fastened. In Great Britain the word is used with a different meaning. There it means a great net in the shape of a bag, with a mouth sometimes a hundred feet, or even more, across. This is dragged along the bottom of the sea and gets especially fish living on, or near, the bottom, such as soles and flounders, which are not easily caught in other ways. Many cod and haddock are also caught in trawl nets. Such a net can be used only where the bottom is smooth, for a rough bottom would tear the net. A boat which carries one of these nets is called a trawler. Some such boats are sailing vessels, but the large nets require machinery to draw them in, and so the number of steam trawlers has increased. Recently this method has been introduced on this side of the Atlantic.

FISH OF THE PACIFIC AND OF THE GREAT LAKES

The most important fish on the Pacific coast is the salmon, which is little trouble to take. In fact, this fish almost begs to be caught, as it goes up the rivers to lay its eggs. However, many of them are caught in nets in the bays. The salmon also takes the hook and puts up a game fight, but few men fish for it with hook and line.

The Great Lakes are inland seas in size, even if the water is fresh, and many million pounds of fish are taken from these waters by fishermen from Canada and the United States. The whitefish, the lake herring and the lake trout are the most important varieties. They are taken with gill and pound nets, with seines, and with hooks and lines. More are taken in by Canadian than by American fishermen.

The oyster fisheries of the United States are worth more than those of all the rest of the world. We show you some pictures of them and some of the oyster fisheries of Europe. For a long time oysters could be gathered from their natural beds so easily and so plentifully that no one thought of taking care of them. Chesapeake Bay has given the greatest yield from natural beds. But so many oysters are eaten in the United States and Canada, and so many are destroyed in gathering them, that they have begun to grow scarce in some places. Heavy dredges, dragged over the bottom, bury or break as many oysters as they bring up. The tongs and rakes also do some damage in this way.

HOW OYSTERS ARE RAISED FOR THE MARKET

Men, therefore, are sometimes permitted to mark out a space in the shallow water. There no one else is allowed to fish. If the bottom is very soft mud, they scatter gravel or empty oyster shells over it, and then scatter some full-grown oysters for seed, as they say. Since a large oyster may lay as many as 60,000,-000 eggs, one would think that they should increase very rapidly. Many of the eggs are eaten by fishes, however; many are carried away by the currents; and many never hatch at all. Those that do hatch swim about for a few days and begin to build shells. Then, if they have not been eaten, they sink to the bottom and attach themselves to the old shells or stones. If they do not find such support, they sink into the mud and die.

Such a bed as this may be left until the oysters grow large enough for market, but if it is found that a great many have settled down, some of the stones or shells with the young oysters sticking to them may be raked up and dropped into another bed, where they are allowed to grow. If the men who own the beds are careful and do not take out too many oysters, a bed will last a long time, as countless millions of tiny oysters begin life every year.

In England much the same methods are used; but in France and Holland the tiny oysters are carefully planted on earthenware tiles coated with lime. When the oysters are large enough they are transplanted into cases or into shallow ponds along the shore, where they grow fast, being thinned out from time to time. The Japanese, too, have separate bottoms for the planting and the growing. They use bamboo branches for collectors, and usually transplant their oysters twice—the second time, to fattening beds.

It is said that the Romans, centuries ago, cultivated oysters in their Lake Avernus.

THE NEXT STORY OF FAMILIAR THINGS IS ON PAGE 4185.

CATCHING AND PACKING SPRATS

Sprats are caught in drift nets such as these fishermen are letting out. The nets have pieces of cork along the top to keep them afloat. One end of the net is fastened to the boat, and the fish are caught in the meshes.

The net is hauled in and the boat rowed ashore, where it is pulled up on the beach and the sprats are shaken out of the nets ready to be sorted and packed into boxes for the market.

Here the sprats are being packed into boxes ready to be sent to the cities. After being shaken from the nets, they are carried to the boxes in metal pails, which are used for measuring the catch.

PICKLING A GREAT CATCH OF HERRINGS

Huge quantities of herrings are pickled. The picture shows girls preparing herrings for the pickle.

In this picture we see the herrings being washed before being sent to London and other big cities.

The pickled herrings are packed in barrels, and this work is done mostly by Scottish girls, who follow the herrings down the east coast of Britain, and work for a week or two at a number of ports.

The herring packing is one of the greatest industries of the east coast of England, and the enormous number of barrels used may be estimated from this view taken at Yarmouth during the herring season.

BRINGING IN THE CATCH

Photo, International Newsreel Corporation.
Here you see the steam fishing trawler Surf, after a trip through heavy seas in extreme cold, entering Boston harbor loaded with fish and draped with ice. Such a trip is full of danger and adventure.

A net 65 yards long, containing over half a ton of haddocks and other fish, being hauled to the boat's side on the Dogger Bank, where boats go in all weathers and remain fishing from one to two weeks.

AN OIL FACTORY AT SEA

Some trawlers which catch cod are floating factories where the cod-liver oil is prepared at sea. Here the trawl is being prepared, the wooden rollers enabling the net to run along the bed of the sea.

Even amid such rough surroundings the men do their work with scrupulous cleanliness. Their hands never touch the oil from start to finish of the process. Here a fifteen-ton catch of cod is being hauled on board.

As soon as the catch has been hauled on board and the net emptied, the fish is thoroughly washed.

The oil, pressed out of the livers in these vessels, is put in tins soon after the fish are caught.

This is the Columbia, a fishing schooner of Gloucester, Massachusetts, where lies the chief centre of cod-
and mackerel-fishery interests in the United States. The schooner type of sailing boat is said to have been
designed first in 1713 by Captain Andrew Robinson of Gloucester.   Photo, Wide World Photos.

KEEPING UP THE FISH CENSUS

Photo from the Bureau of Fisheries, Washington, D.C.
To keep the waters stocked the Government protects the lives of fish in various ways, and supports hatcheries where new lives are started under favorable conditions. Of the men shown here—workers in a trout hatchery at White Sulphur Springs, West Virginia—one is measuring trout eggs and the other is placing eggs in hatching troughs. From the hatcheries streams and lakes are replenished with young fish.

This picture, called "Catching fish to save their lives," shows how numbers of fish are taken out of shallow lakes and sloughs before the water dries away in summer's heat, then are transferred to the nearest deep water. This work is done particularly in the Middle West, where millions of fish used to die in dry years. The picture was taken in Iowa.   Photo, Ewing Galloway, New York.

FISH IN RIVER AND BAY IN THE EAST

The shad belongs to the herring family, but is much larger. Every year these fish ascend the rivers to lay their eggs. Once they were very abundant, but the rivers have become dirty from the cities and factories, and so many shad have been caught that they are becoming scarce. Nets attached to poles are placed across the rivers. Here fishermen in the Hudson are taking the catch from the net.

You have seen Cape Cod on the map, even if you have never visited that delightful region. This picture was made at North Truro, not far from the tip of the long arm. The soft beach does not injure the bottom of the boat, which has been pulled up on the sand. Provincetown lies beyond and to the left.

Photos, Brown Bros.

FISHING UPON THE PACIFIC COAST

Photo, Brown Bros.

The fishing industry in the Pacific employs many men. Here we see an old netmaker mending miles of nets upon a wharf on that ocean. A small break soon spreads and makes a net almost worthless. Nets are made of twine, which must be strong and must not rot easily, for a net is quite expensive.

The most important food fish of the Pacific is the salmon. They are easily caught in several ways. Here is one of the methods used on the Pacific coast, where salmon are caught by the ton. The salmon which frequent Puget Sound and the Columbia River are especially prized for their flavor, and millions of pounds are preserved in cans and sent to all parts of the world.

OYSTERS ON THE NEW JERSEY COAST

The United States produces and consumes more oysters than any other country in the world. This boat has been out to the oyster beds off the New Jersey coast and has returned with a heavy load. The boat cannot go into the shallow water inshore, and the oysters, which you see heaped up, are placed in baskets. These are transferred to flat-bottomed scows, one of which is moored beside the boat.

In the oyster bed the oysters often lie in mud. Now they are dumped in the shallow water at the mouth of the creek, which washes them clean as the tide rises and falls. If they are not needed at once they will remain alive here, while they would die and become unfit for food if left long out of water. Soon they will be shipped to the city, either with or without their shells.

COLLECTING OYSTERS AND MUSSELS

In France and other countries oysters are raised most carefully. The spat, or eggs, is placed in cases to hatch. When the oysters are six months old they are planted in oyster beds like that in the picture.

When the oysters have grown to their full size they are collected in baskets from the beds, usually by women who wear trousers like men, as in the picture above. They are then boxed ready for market.

Mussels are largely used as food in Europe, and here we see a big mussel bed in Holland exposed at low tide. These molluscs thrive between the high-water and low-water lines on the coast.

FRENCH—A LITTLE PICTURE-STORY

First line, French; second line, English word; third line, as we say it in English.

Une machine automatique—A slot machine.

Nous voyons une machine automatique.
We see a machine automatic.
We see a slot machine.

J'ai mis un sou dans le trou.
I have put one cent in the hole.
I have put a cent in the slot.

Papa et maman viennent nous chercher.
Papa and Mamma come us to find.
Papa and Mamma are coming for us.

Le train—The train.

La fumée nous entre dans les yeux.
The smoke us enters in the eyes.
The smoke is getting in our eyes.

Le porteur—The porter.

Le porteur met nos malles dans le train.
The porter puts our trunks in the train.
The porter is putting our trunks on the train.

Les locomotives—The engines.

Ils nous montrent les trains.
They us show the trains.
They show us the trains.

J'aime les locomotives.
I like the engines.
I like the engines.

Notre train est en vue. Il entre en gare.
Our train is in sight. It enters in station.
Our train is in sight. It is coming into the station.

Un compartiment—A carriage.

Papa choisit un compartiment.
Papa chooses a carriage.
Papa is choosing a carriage.

THE NEXT FRENCH STORY IS ON PAGE 4276.

THOUGHT AS EXPRESSED BY THREE FAMOUS ARTISTS
The first picture is from Michelangelo's statue of Lorenzo Medici, the second is from a painting by Sir John Millais, and the third is from a statue by Auguste Rodin.

THE REAL MASTER OF THE BODY

WE come now, in our story of our own life, to the most interesting and wonderful thing in the whole world. So far we have read the story of our bodies, the parts of us that we see and know and feel; but our body is a servant, and we are now to read of its master. We take up a pen to write, but the hand acts at the bidding of its master, the Mind.

CONTINUED FROM 3958

What is the Mind? Not all the wisest men that have ever lived have been able to understand the mind of a little child. It is the mind that knows whatever we know at all, yet we know less about the mind itself than about anything the mind knows. Yet one thing we know—that without it we should know nothing.

The first great fact about the mind is that here is something real which cannot be taken hold of. It is not a part of the body. Any part of the body, even the nerves or the highest part of the brain itself, can be seen, touched or cut. The body is a material thing, as material as a solid rock.

Now if we take a rock and examine it we learn all there is to learn about it; but if our bodies were to be examined there would be a tremendously important fact about them missed altogether—the fact of sensation, which does not exist in the rock.

The things we are likely to believe in most are things we see and handle, and it requires an effort of the mind to realize that there are great realities which cannot be seen and handled, and are utterly different from anything that can be seen or handled.

Such a reality is the vision of this page, as we read at this moment. The eye and the brain are not sight; they are the instruments of sight. The eye and the brain might be examined for a thousand years under the microscope, but we should never find sight there, because we have now left the realm of the physical world, made up of matter and ether and motion, and have entered another realm altogether—the world of mind.

The greatest of all follies is to believe that the real world is the world of matter and ether and motion, and that sensation and feeling and thought and will are not real. When we study sensation we are studying something more important, more wonderful, more real, than anything we have studied yet. Indeed, we have only to think for a moment to see that everything we know is known to us through our senses, and it is one of the great discoveries of recent years that the senses which have to do with our own bodies play a great part of their own in the

4065

making of the mind and in the daily lives of our minds.

Feelings of hunger and thirst, feelings derived from the movement of the heart and the lungs and the organs of digestion, feelings from the joints and the muscles, all enter into our minds. In very great measure our happiness or unhappiness depends upon the quality of the feelings that come into our minds from our bodies.

NOTHING IN THE MIND THAT WAS NOT FIRST IN THE SENSES

These sensations from the body are all vague and not well defined. There is a great contrast between these vague feelings and a precise, sharp, definite sensation such as we get from the eye or the ear, and that contrast exists, as a rule, between sensations from within and sensations from without.

Let us suppose it were possible for a human being to grow up without getting any sensations, whether from within or from without. What sort of person would he be? What sort of a mind would he have? What would he think about? What would he know? When we ask ourselves questions like these we see the answer at once. Such a person would have no mind; he would be merely a body, like a cabbage. A man of this kind could know nothing and think nothing. That, then, is what we mean when we say that the mind is built up on sensation.

All this great question was first worked out by an immortal Englishman, John Locke, more than two hundred years ago. He came to the conclusion that nothing is in the mind that was not first in the senses, and that the whole of our knowledge and ideas and beliefs depends on two things: sensation in the first place, and afterward upon reflection on what the senses tell us.

THE CHILD OF NATURE WILLIAM WORDSWORTH DREAMED OF

All real education of the mind must begin by recognizing that the mind is built up on the senses, and that sensation is the very stuff of which the mind is made. These great truths have never been more perfectly expressed than in Wordsworth's noble poem, beginning, "Three years she grew in sun and shower." In it he describes his ideas of the education of a girl. She was to be educated by the clouds and the willow trees, and by the motions of the storm:

The stars of midnight shall be dear
To her; and she shall lean her ear
  In many a secret place
Where rivulets dance their wayward round,
And beauty born of murmuring sound
  Shall pass into her face.

As a rule, when we talk of mind we usually mean the part of the mind that thinks and knows. In other words, we are too apt to suppose that really the whole of the mind is made by the intelligence or the intellect. During the last century a great student of the mind declared that if we are to study the mind of the highest type of man when he is grown up we must try to begin at the beginning. We must study the mind in all its forms; we must even learn all we can of the senses, instincts, habits and doings of the lower animals.

THE SECOND GREAT STEP IN THE BUILDING-UP OF THE MIND

We are not to make the great mistake of supposing that the knowing and reasoning part of the mind is the whole of the mind, and that feeling is not as important as thinking. Let us think for a moment what becomes of our sensations, and how the intelligence and the intellect are built up out of them.

Such a thing as a flash of light or a sudden sound will produce certain results in us, perhaps, but we cannot be said to think: we simply *sense*. Now let us suppose that a little more time is given to us, and that, instead of a mere flash of light, there is light coming from something that has parts and a shape—say, from a tree. Suppose we see this tree very indistinctly from a great distance or in half-darkness, and that we do not expect to see a tree in that place. At first, as we say, we see it, but we do not see what it is. We have all noticed this in a thousand cases. Sometimes in a picture or a photograph we cannot make out what is there. It is not that we are blind; we are *sensing* perfectly, but we have not put together the lines and forms and lights and shadows so as to make a whole of them.

Now, this is the next great stage in the building-up of the mind. The stage of mere seeing yields to the stage of perceiving. The first stage was *sensation*, the second stage is *perception*, and the difference between them is tremendous, because, though mere sensation may have definite effects, yet if seeing never went on to perceiving, intelligence could never possibly be formed.

THE MEMORY THAT COMES BEFORE THE SHADOW OF THE BRAIN

We realize at once the great difference between seeing and perceiving, and we may now consider the memory, without which there could be no real perceiving. It is just because memory makes perceiving and even higher things possible that its importance is so tremendous. If we could not remember, we should be nothing.

Without memory there would be no recognizing, there would be no learning, no knowing. We are so accustomed to use this power of memory that, until we think, we cannot realize what we should be without it. We see something coming along a road, far away, and then we perceive it is a human being; later we can tell that it is a man and not a woman; finally we find that it is someone we know. Here we see that the memory acts even in the simplest kinds of perceiving, and it is worth while to devote some time to the study of it.

THE MEMORY THAT IS A PART OF ALL LIVING MATTER

All living matter is called protoplasm, and it is a fact that memory is a property of all living protoplasm everywhere. No matter how simple creatures are we find that their behavior can be made to change by changing their surroundings. This means that in some degree they remember; they act differently because something has occurred perhaps three times before, and the fourth time it occurs they do not behave exactly as they did the first time. What it is in living matter that enables it to remember we cannot say; neither can we say in advanced cases of memory, as, for example, when we remember an idea.

It is supposed by many people that living matter never forgets. When we say we forget, what we mean is simply that we cannot recall. But the thing we say we forget is still in our mind, and when someone names it we recognize it.

Even where we cannot recall a thing for ourselves, and where we cannot recognize it when it is recalled for us, it by no means follows that we have really forgotten. There are many cases on record where a man appears to have utterly forgotten certain words of some language he learned and spoke as a child; he can-

not recall them, and they mean nothing to him when they are recalled; but he proves that they are still there in his mind when, perhaps, he is suffering from a severe illness. His brain is upset, and these words, which he may not have heard or used for fifty years, come from his lips.

WHAT THE BRAIN DOES WITH THE SENSATIONS THAT RUSH INTO IT

Such cases as these teach us that in all probability living matter does not forget, but, more than that, they show us that what we call memory is far from being a simple thing. In what we call an ordinary act of memory there are three things involved: there is the pure remembering, with which we have not much more to do than a table has to do with remembering a dent made in it; there is the recognizing of what we remember; and there is the power of *recalling*. It is impossible for us to tell what a pure sensation is like because we never feel a pure sensation. Every sensation we get after early babyhood is mixed up with the memories it revives. We must also remember another very important thing. One old wrong view of the mind was that it is like a smooth white sheet of paper on which the outside world comes and prints its marks. According to this view, the mind, like a sheet of paper, is quite passive; it does nothing except receive sensations. We now know that this is far from being the truth. When we hear a piece of music our minds are doing as much in their way as the mind and fingers of the player are doing.

For one thing, if we are paying attention, that in itself is an act, and sometimes a very difficult one, as tiring as hard running or swimming. More than that, many parts of the brain specially concerned with the subject in hand are roused to activity when new sensations come in. The brain is always trying to "make sense out of them," as we say, though the phrase is rather misleading. All the time, though we are often quite unconscious of it, the brain is comparing what has just come in with what has come in on previous occasions—putting two and two together, saying this must be a chair, or that is my brother; or, on a higher plane, declaring that this thing is true because something else we know proves it. The higher and better the brain, the more certainly it is doing these things whenever we read or look or listen. Nothing can be a greater mistake than to suppose that sensation is a passive process, as when a sheet of paper is written on.

Sensation is an active process, and the name of this process is *association*. It is usually called the *association of ideas;* but that is not a good name, because we associate anything and everything.

THE PARTS OF THE BRAIN THAT LINK UP THE SENSATIONS

Sights, sounds, tastes, feelings, and everything else, as well as ideas, are nearly always associated in the mind. We say that one thing reminds us of another. This means that, acting through memory, one thing is associated with another; but association is really going on all the time, in small things as well as in great; faintly, as when we are just noticing things in a general way, or vividly, as when we are thinking with all our might.

All thinking is *relationing,* as it is called, or associating things and ideas. We can understand how it is that the greater part of the human brain consists of association cells and association fibres. They are not directly concerned with any kind of sensation, but are concerned with linking up our sensations, so that it is possible for our minds to pass from baby's first dim appreciation of the difference between light and darkness to the highest ideas which we can have, such as the conception of the nature of light, and the Power whence it springs.

Though association is so wonderful, and lies at the bottom of all thinking, the laws of its working are not difficult to understand. It depends on the memory. We generally associate things when we have seen them at the same time, which would mean an association of place as well as of time; we also associate things because they are like one another, and sometimes, though it sounds curious to say so, one thing suggests another just because that other thing is different. The last two cases we may call association by *likeness* and by *contrast.*

THE THING THAT MAKES UP THE FINE QUALITY OF A MIND

These are all the kinds of association that are usually described; but perhaps there is also a kind of association of cause and effect in the minds of people who are apt to think of causes and effects. Prob-

ably this is so, because we are sure now that there is a kind of memory which goes by causes, as when we remember a thing because we know the reason for it. This is the highest type of memory.

In human beings the power of association varies enormously, and, on the whole, we may say that, beyond a doubt, the greater, the deeper, the wider, the richer, the more varied the power of association in a person, the higher and finer is the mind of that person; but we must particularly add that the *quality* of the associations counts for everything. To one man it may be the mere surface which suggests something else, but to another it is the truth underneath.

THE MIND THAT IS A NOBLE KINGDOM TO A MAN

One of our great duties toward ourselves, therefore, is to fill our mind with things worth having, and worth being reminded of by association in after-years; to avoid foolish books, foolish talk, and things which it is not worth while to have in our minds at all; and to avoid things which are actually wicked or destructive. These may get into the mind by accident before we know what is happening, and at any moment we are liable to be reminded of them. Let us remember that there is no better treasure than a mind well filled with memories of noble things seen, noble sounds heard, noble ideas, great poetry, recollections of friends, and so on. A man with such a mind may say to himself, "My mind to me a kingdom is," or may talk with Wordsworth of "that inward eye which is the bliss of solitude." We cannot express too strongly the importance of filling the mind with good materials for association.

The man who said, "I am never alone when I am by myself" may not have been so conceited as he sounded. He meant, perhaps, that all the fine things he had heard and read came back to him when he was alone and furnished him with food for pleasurable thought. Such company is far better than that of empty-headed fools, and men and women who have filled their minds with the best things need not be lonely if they are without human companionship for a short time. Of course one would not like to live the life of a hermit, but the person who cannot endure being alone usually has little in his head.

THE NEXT STORY OF OUR OWN LIFE IS ON PAGE 4181.

THE TALES OF SIR WALTER SCOTT

THERE is not in English literature any other series of books by one man that can compare in quantity or in quality with the Waverley Novels, written by Sir Walter Scott between the years 1814 and 1831. These wonderful tales of the past would fill about ten thousand closely printed pages, and the period of history covered by them is more than seven hundred years. A complete edition usually contains twenty-five volumes, and there are in all thirty-two stories. We must have some general idea of the whole series, so we shall begin by looking at the whole of this wonderful library before we turn to the particular books. Then we shall give an outline of Waverley: or 'Tis Sixty Years Since. This novel centres in the Jacobite rising of 1745.

THE WAVERLEY NOVELS

ALTHOUGH Sir Walter Scott's novels cover a period of more than seven hundred years of European history, we are not to suppose that he wrote them in the order of time. As a matter of fact, the very first of his stories described the life of only sixty years before his own day. It was called Waverley: or 'Tis Sixty Years Since, and dealt with the Jacobite rising of 1745. The story that goes farthest back into history was one of the last two he wrote in the year 1831. It is called Count Robert of Paris, and deals with the First Crusade of the eleventh century. The scene is laid chiefly in and around the wonderful city of Constantinople.

We must always bear in mind, when we are thinking about the Waverley Novels, that though most of them are founded upon fact, they do not derive their chief interest from being historical. They are told with so much spirit and romantic force that we are enthralled by the swift and straightforward movement of the story, and never stop to ask ourselves whether it is all true history or largely the invention of the wizard story-teller.

In taking a rapid general view of the Waverley Novels we shall think of them, not in the order in which they were written, but rather in what might be called their historical order. That is, we shall arrange them as though they were all chapters in one long tale

CONTINUED FROM 3872

covering seven hundred years of the history of Great Britain.

Count Robert of Paris, as we have already heard, is a tale of the First Crusade, of the year 1098. The story itself, or rather what is called the "plot," is not very remarkable. But the adventures of the count and the other leaders of the Crusade, among whom was the famous Peter the Hermit, are full of healthy excitement, and give us a fine picture of those distant times when men lived only to fight. Most of the Crusaders were even more anxious for the fighting than for the avowed object of the Crusade, which was the delivering of the supposed sepulchre of Christ from the hands of the Mohammedans.

The next novel in point of time is The Betrothed, the scene of which is laid chiefly in Wales about the year 1187. This was the time of the Third Crusade, and indeed the novel was written as one of the Tales of the Crusaders. Its interest, however, centres in Wales, the heroine being Eveline, the daughter of Sir Raymond, a Norman lord. She was "the betrothed," and undertook to wait three long years to become the wife of Sir Hugo de Lacy, who had gone away to fight with the Crusaders. But before he could return, Eveline was captured by a Welsh prince, who had previously sought to marry her but had been defeated by Sir Hugo when attacking Sir Raymond's castle. Sir Hugo's nephew, Sir Damian, rescued her, and was almost killed himself. Eveline nursed him, and they fell in love with each other. When Sir Hugo returned from the Crusade and found that his nephew loved his own bethrothed he generously stood aside and allowed them to marry.

HEROES AND HEROINES OF THE TALISMAN AND IVANHOE

The Talisman, which is one of the finest of Sir Walter's stories, deals with the same period of history and with the battles of the Crusaders in Assyria in the year 1191. The great hero of the story is Richard I, or Richard the Lion-Heart, and his noble enemy is the Sultan Saladin. The "talisman" was just a little red purse which Saladin carried in his bosom, and which, when he came disguised as a physician into the camp of the English king, he used to cure Richard of a fever. There is, of course, a love story in the book as well, and endless adventures. The heroine, the Lady Edith, a kinswoman of Richard, married Sir Kenneth, the heir to the Scottish throne, and Saladin presented her with his talisman.

Ivanhoe is a splendid romance of life in England, just three years later than the period of the previous novel. This is one of the books of which we shall read more farther on.

Next comes Castle Dangerous, which is a romance of The Perilous Castle of Douglas, so called because it was three times taken from the English during 1306 and 1307. This story was the last that the great novelist wrote. At the time he was broken in health and fortune, and had not many more months to live.

THE STORIES OF THE FAIR MAID OF PERTH AND THE BLACK MONK

The Fair Maid of Perth takes us nearly another century onward in history. The period is 1402, though a descendant of the Douglas has an important part to play in the story. Henry IV now ruled in England, and Robert III in Scotland. There are two love stories in the book. The one that interests us most is, of course, that of the "Fair Maid," whose name is Catharine Glover.

On St. Valentine's Day Catharine kissed Henry Smith, the armorer, while he was asleep. Afterward he proposed to marry her, but she refused. In the end, however, and after many adventures,

when Henry might have a knighthood if he cared to accept it, the Fair Maid became the wife of the armorer.

Those were the days when many Scotsmen went abroad to fight for foreign kings and princes in the wars which were always raging on the Continent. Quentin Durward, which is one of the best of the novels, is the tale of a young Scotsman who found his fortune as one of the Scottish guards of Louis XI of France, and ended by marrying a countess in the year 1468.

Just six years later is the period described in Anne of Geierstein, in the scenes of which we travel to Switzerland, Germany and France. We learn much about the secret Tribunal of Westphalia, presided over by the "Black Monk," the father of Anne. Two English gentlemen, the Earl of Oxford and his son, Sir Arthur de Vere, were traveling, disguised as merchants, bearing a letter to the Duke of Burgundy. It would have gone ill with them had it not happened that Anne had met Sir Arthur before and fallen in love with him. So her father acquitted them, and later on Sir Arthur married Anne.

THREE STORIES OF THE DAYS OF THE GREAT REFORMATION

In the story of The Monastery, set in the year 1550, the scene is laid in Melrose, on the Tweed, the neighborhood which Sir Walter loved so much. The Abbot is also a story of Scotland, in the year 1557. Both of these tales are concerned largely with the Reformation, but neither is so interesting as most of the other novels, though Mary Queen of Scots is splendidly described in The Abbot.

Kenilworth is a third story of Reformation times, the period being 1575. It is infinitely more interesting than either of the other two. Nothing could be finer than its animated descriptions of Kenilworth Castle and the fête given there by the Earl of Leicester in honor of Queen Elizabeth, whose character is finely described. Leicester had secretly married Amy, the daughter of Sir Hugh Robsart, but dared not let this be known to the queen. Amy's end was mysterious. The story is full of exciting incidents and characters so well described that we seem to have seen them in real life, and are never likely to forget them.

We arrive at the beginning of the seventeenth century, during the reign of King James I, in The Fortunes of Nigel.

It tells the extraordinary adventures of a young Scottish nobleman who went to London to get the king to restore his estates, and was successful, after many disappointments, in establishing his "fortunes."

In A Legend of Montrose we have passed over forty years, and find ourselves in Scotland during that terrible time when the Civil War was raging in England. The Earl of Montrose was fighting for King Charles in the North against the Covenanters, who were led by the Marquis of Argyll. This story contains one of the novelist's finest characters in the person of Sir Dugald Dalgetty.

IN THE DAYS OF THE MERRY MONARCH AND THE GAY CAVALIERS

King Charles I had been beheaded, and the Commonwealth had been declared by the year 1652, with which Woodstock deals. Though not one of Sir Walter's best works, this is a spirited and entertaining romance. It is concerned chiefly with the adventures of Charles II, ending with the death of Cromwell and the king's entry into London.

Peveril of the Peak carries us forward some twenty years and well into the reign of "the merry monarch," the time being 1678. It is a story of Cavalier and Roundhead, telling how the daughter of Major Bridgenorth, who had been a supporter of the Commonwealth, fell in love with Julian Peveril, a Cavalier, and was married to him. It is a very long story, and contains the enormous number of one hundred and eight characters. The Peak is another name for Derbyshire, in which many of the incidents happen.

THE MOST TRAGIC OF SIR WALTER SCOTT'S STORIES

The time of Old Mortality is the same as that of the previous story, but the scene is changed to Scotland and Holland. The Bride of Lammermoor, perhaps the greatest, and certainly the most tragic, of all the Waverley Novels, comes next in point of time. It tells of the sad fate that befell Lucy Ashton because she yielded to the pressure of her parents and married Hayston of Bucklaw, while her true lover, the last Lord of Ravenswood, was hastening home to her from the wars in the Netherlands.

The Pirate gives us a truly romantic picture of the wild scenery and the primitive life of the Shetland Islands at the beginning of the eighteenth century. The Black Dwarf is a romance of about the same period, the scene being laid in the Lowlands of Scotland. "The Black Dwarf" is a mysterious person consulted by Isabella Vere, the daughter of a Jacobite leader, who would force her to marry his friend Sir Frederick Langley. The Black Dwarf helped her, for he was really Sir Edward Mauley, and had power over the unscrupulous Sir Frederick. He appeared just as the wedding was about to take place and forbade it. Isabella later married her own true love, the young squire Earnscliff.

STIRRING STORIES OF THE WILD SCOTTISH HIGHLANDS

Rob Roy, the splendid story of a Highland chief, brings us to the year 1715. Later on you may read more fully of this story as well as of Waverley, both of which refer again to the first half of the eighteenth century. Next comes Redgauntlet, the story of a conspiracy formed by Sir Edward Hugh Redgauntlet in the year 1763 on behalf of the Young Pretender. Guy Mannering, which introduces us to many memorable characters, though the hero himself is not one of these, brings us to the second half of the eighteenth century. With this period the story of The Surgeon's Daughter is also concerned. This describes the remarkable adventures of Menie Gray in India, and her return to her native country.

The stirring romance of The Antiquary deals with the closing years of the eighteenth century. Last of all there is St. Ronan's Well, which brings us into the earlier years of the nineteenth century. This is not a very successful work compared with some of the other fine stories among the Waverley Novels.

THE STORY OF A HIGHLAND REBELLION
THE ROMANCE OF WAVERLEY

THE Second Jacobite Rebellion was almost confined to the Scottish Highlands. It broke out upon the landing on Scottish soil of Charles Edward Stewart, grandson of James II, of England. By his adherents he was called the "Young Chevalier" and "Bonnie Prince Charlie"; but by the other party, "the Young Pretender." It was the object of the rising to place this young man on the English throne, which was then occupied by George II.

THE YOUNG DAYS OF THE HERO, EDWARD WAVERLEY

Edward Waverley, the hero of Scott's first novel, was the son of Richard Waverley, an ambitious politician who looked to the Whigs, the supporters of the king, for political advancement. He was a nephew and heir of Sir Everard Waverley, of Waverley-Honour, a wealthy bachelor.

Sir Everard had no particular love for the House of Hanover, to which King George belonged. As Edward lived partly with his father, and partly with his uncle—his mother being dead—he came in his early years under the influences of the two great opposing political forces of the time.

Sir Everard and his sister, Mistress Rachel, became somewhat alarmed at their nephew's habits of desultory reading and love of solitude, which his father did nothing to counteract. Mistress Rachel suggested that the boy should travel on the Continent with his tutor.

YOUNG CAPTAIN WAVERLEY'S FATEFUL MISSION TO THE HIGHLANDS

Richard Waverley saw no objection to this plan. But Richard's political friends thought otherwise. The result was that the lad was offered, and accepted, a captaincy in a dragoon regiment, then quartered at Dundee. Thither he set forth, carrying, among other things, a fateful letter of introduction from his uncle to the Baron of Bradwardine at his Perthshire seat of Tully-Veolan, on the borders of the Highlands. The baron was an old friend of Sir Everard's and had borne arms on behalf of the Stuarts.

After being initiated into his military duties at Dundee, young Waverley gained leave of absence for a few weeks. He desired to see the country, but his first object was to visit his uncle's friend at Tully-Veolan, a typical old Scottish manor house. Here he received a cordial welcome from the baron and his daughter Rose, a sweet girl of about Waverley's own age. Her hair was a pale gold shade, and her skin like the snow of her own mountains in whiteness. "Yet she had not a pallid or pensive cast of countenance; her features, as well as her temper, had a lively expression; her complexion,

though not florid, was so pure as to seem transparent, and the slightest emotion sent her whole blood at once to her face and neck. Her form, though under the common size, was remarkably elegant, and her motions were light, easy, and unembarrassed."

It fell to the lot of Rose Bradwardine to perform the duties of hostess and guide combined. Thus the two were constantly in each other's company.

THE ENGLISH GENTLEMAN AND THE HIGHLAND LASS

She rode with him in the vicinity of Tully-Veolan, and listened with delight as he talked of the books he knew and loved. But while those who saw them together so frequently bethought them that the baron was arranging a match between his daughter and the wealthy young Englishman, Rose's father shut his eyes to possibilities in this direction.

If he had thought of an alliance, Edward's indifference would have offered a bar to the project. His mind was still full of the influence of the old romances he had read in the library at Waverley-Honour. His imagination still led him into mental adventures in which female forms of exquisite grace and beauty mingled. Rose Bradwardine, beautiful and amiable though she was, had not precisely the sort of merit or beauty which captivates a romantic imagination in early youth. She was too frank, too confiding, too kind.

"Was it possible to bow, to tremble, and to adore before the timid yet playful little girl, who now asked Edward to mend her pen, now to construe a stanza in Tasso, and now to spell a very, very long word in his version of it?" No; but, for all that, time at Tully-Veolan passed so agreeably that Waverley applied for and obtained an extension of his leave of absence. The permission was accompanied by a hint from his commanding officer, Colonel Gardiner, to the effect that he should not spend too much of his leisure in the company of those who, estimable as they might be in a general sense, were not supposed to be friendly to the Government or the king, to whose service he had been sworn.

About this time it happened that Tully-Veolan was raided by one Donald Bean Lean, a Highland cateran, or robber, who carried off the baron's milch cows. Raids of this kind were of frequent occurrence on the Highland border, and a local chieftain, Fergus MacIvor, Vich Ian Vohr, received from many Lowland gentlemen what was known as "protection money," as a surety against the attention of these robbers. Between this chieftain and the baron there had been a quarrel. Rose's father suddenly discovered that he had unknowingly, through an agent, paid "protection money" to Vich Ian Vohr. Thereupon he had promptly stopped the payment.

HOW WAVERLEY CAME TO THE HAUNT OF THE HIGHLAND ROBBER

But after Donald Bean Lean's escapade, Vich Ian Vohr, who held the baron in great respect, sent to the master of Tully-Veolan, offering aid in the recovery of the missing cattle. This message was brought to Tully-Veolan by a kinsman of the chief's, Evan Dhu MacCombich. From the last-named, Waverley heard accounts of Highland ways and customs that stirred his love of adventure. When, therefore, Evan Dhu offered to conduct him to the stronghold of Donald Bean Lean and the home of Vich Ian Vohr, he decided to accept the invitation.

Waverley's journey in the company of Evan Dhu and the latter's wild-looking companions, through wild mountain scenery, was one well calculated to appeal to his love of the romantic. Particularly was he fascinated by that part of the expedition which took him at nighttime in silence over the waters of an unknown lake to the robber's fastness.

On meeting Donald Bean Lean, Waverley was astonished, even alarmed, to find a person of this description so accurately informed of the strength and composition of the various garrisons and regiments quartered north of the Tay. His feelings were further played upon by the robber's mysterious language. Donald Bean Lean spoke as if Waverley had a secret message for him, and regarded it as a grievance that he was not thought worthy of confidence equally with the Baron of Bradwardine and Vich Ian Vohr.

AMONG THE FOLLOWERS OF "BONNIE PRINCE CHARLIE"

The meaning of all this Waverley was not to learn until later. Meanwhile he was hospitably entertained, and the only disconcerting incident was the disappearance of his seal. This was taken from him while he slept. The outlaw used it as a sign of his authority to the recruits Waverley had taken with him to Dundee from Waverley-Honour. These men Donald Bean Lean urged to desert and to join the forces of Charles Edward, "Bonnie Prince Charlie," whenever they heard of the landing of this personage in Scotland.

After his visit to the secret hold of Donald Bean Lean, Waverley was escorted to Glennaquoich, the home of Vich Ian Vohr. He was received very cordially by this chieftain and his sister Flora. Flora MacIvor bore a striking resemblance to her brother. She had the same antique and regular correctness of profile, the same dark eyes, eyelashes and eyebrows, the same clearness of complexion. But the haughty and somewhat stern regularity of Fergus's features was beautifully softened in those of Flora. Her voice was soft and sweet, yet in urging any favorite topic it possessed the tones which impress awe and conviction.

THE CHARMING HEROINE WHO STOOD FAST FOR THE JACOBITES

Flora MacIvor was most devotedly attached to the exiled Stewarts. To contribute to the restoration of their family to the throne, "she was prepared to do all, to suffer all, to sacrifice all." And Flora was as accomplished as she was beautiful.

At first there was nothing at Glennaquoich to tempt Waverley to take up the cause which Vich Ian Vohr and his sister had at heart. That is to say, he was not directly asked to throw in his lot with the cause. But one day he took part in a hunting expedition. This was organized as a kind of prelude to definite action by the Jacobites. Waverley met with an accident which delayed his return to Dundee. But Donald Bean Lean had gone there. While Waverley was at Glennaquoich, the Jacobite was tempting the men of his regiment to join him, and intercepting letters sent to Waverley by Colonel Gardiner, first of all advising, and then commanding, his return to duty.

HOW AN ENGLISH SOLDIER JOINED THE SCOTTISH REBELS

At last dispatches reached Waverley. They contained matters of very deep interest. His father wrote complaining bitterly of bad treatment at the hands of the Government. There was a long-delayed letter from Colonel Gardiner commanding his return to Dundee within three days. Then his uncle and aunt wrote asking him to resign his commission rather than render himself subject to such treatment as that which had been meted out to his father. From a newspaper put into his hands by Vich Ian Vohr, Waverley next learned that he had been deprived of his commission.

Regarding himself now as a man greatly wronged, one who had been publicly disgraced without a hearing, Waverley threw in his lot with the Highlanders. By this time Vich Ian Vohr had observed, with no little satisfaction, the growing attachment of Waverley to Flora. He saw, indeed, no bar to their union save the relations between Waverley's father and the Government, and his guest's commission in the king's army. These obstacles were now removed.

WAVERLEY MEETS THE PRETENDER TO THE BRITISH THRONE

On her part, if she entertained any feeling other than friendship for Waverley, Flora MacIvor did not show it. And, strongly attached as she was to the cause of the Stewarts, she appreciated the risk involved by the rebels. She bade Waverley consult his reason—not his resentment nor his feelings in regard to herself —before he decided to join them. But the resentment, or the feelings, or both, gained the day.

Thus, it happened that Waverley was introduced by Vich Ian Vohr to the Young Chevalier. And the personal charm of this unfortunate young man completed his conversion. This historic meeting we give in Scott's own words.

BONNIE PRINCE CHARLIE

AS they approached the metropolis of Scotland, through a champaign and cultivated country, the sounds of war began to be heard. The distant, yet distinct report of heavy cannon, fired at intervals, apprized Waverley that the work of destruction was going forward. Even Balmawhapple seemed moved to take some precautions, by sending an advanced party in front of his troop, keeping the main body in tolerable order, and moving steadily forward.

Marching in this manner they speedily reached an eminence, from which they could view Edinburgh stretching along the ridgy hill which slopes eastward from the Castle. The latter, being in a state of siege, or rather of blockade, by the northern insurgents, who had already occupied the town for two or three days, fired at intervals upon such parties of Highlanders as exposed themselves, either on the main street, or elsewhere in the vicinity of the fortress. The morning being calm and fair, the effect of this dropping fire was to invest the Castle in wreaths of smoke, the edges of which dissipated slowly in the air, while the central veil was darkened ever and anon by fresh clouds poured forth from the battlements; the whole giving, by the partial concealment, an appearance of grandeur and gloom, rendered more terrific when Waverley reflected on the cause by which it was produced, and that each explosion might ring some brave man's knell.

Ere they approached the city, the partial cannonade had wholly ceased. Balmawhapple, however, having in his recollection the unfriendly greeting which his troop had received from the battery at Stirling, had apparently no wish to attempt the forbearance of the artillery of the Castle. He therefore left the direct road, and sweeping considerably to the southward, so as to keep out of the range of the cannon, approached the ancient palace of Holyrood, without having entered the walls of the city. He then drew up his men in front of that venerable pile, and delivered Waverley to the custody of a guard of Highlanders, whose officer conducted him into the interior of the building.

A long, low, and ill-proportioned gallery, hung with pictures, affirmed to be the portraits of kings, who, if they ever flourished at all, lived several hundred years before the invention of painting in oil colours, served as a sort of guard chamber, or vestibule, to the apartments which the adventurous Charles Edward now occupied in the palace of his ancestors. Officers, both in the Highland and Lowland garb, passed and repassed in haste, or loitered in the hall, as if waiting for orders. Secretaries were engaged in making out passes, musters, and returns. All seemed busy, and earnestly intent upon something of importance; but Waverley was suffered to remain seated in the recess of a window unnoticed by any one, in anxious reflection upon the crisis of his fate.

While he was deep sunk in his reverie, the rustle of tartans was heard behind him, a friendly arm clasped his shoulders, and a friendly voice exclaimed,

"Said the Highland prophet sooth? Or must second-sight go for nothing?"

Waverley turned, and was warmly embraced by Fergus MacIvor. "A thousand welcomes to Holyrood, once more possessed by her legitimate sovereign! Did I not say we should prosper, and that you would fall into the hands of the Philistines if you parted from us?"

"Dear Fergus!" said Waverley, eagerly returning his greeting. "It is long since I have heard a friend's voice. Where is Flora?"

"Safe, and a triumphant spectator of our success."

"In this place?" said Waverley.

"Ay, in this city at least," answered his friend, "and you shall see her; but first you must meet a friend whom you little think of, who has been frequent in his inquiries after you."

Thus saying, he dragged Waverley by the arm out of the guard chamber, and, ere he knew where he was conducted, Edward found himself in a presence room, fitted up with some attempt at royal state.

A young man, wearing his own fair hair, distinguished by the dignity of his mien and the noble expression of his well-formed and regular features, advanced out of a circle of military gentlemen and Highland chiefs, by whom he was surrounded. In his easy and graceful manners Waverley afterwards thought he could have discovered his high birth and rank, although the star on his breast, and the embroidered garter at his knee, had not appeared at its indications.

"Let me present to your Royal Highness," said Fergus, bowing profoundly—

"The descendant of one of the most ancient and loyal families in England," said the young Chevalier, interrupting him. "I beg your pardon for interrupting you, my dear MacIvor; but no master of ceremonies is necessary to present a Waverley to a Stewart."

Thus saying, he extended his hand to Edward with the utmost courtesy, who could not, had he desired it, have avoided rendering him the homage which seemed due to his rank, and was certainly the right of his birth. "I am sorry to understand, Mr. Waverley, that, owing to circumstances which have been as yet but ill explained, you have suffered some restraint among my followers in Perthshire, and on your march here; but we are in such a situation that we hardly know our friends, and I am even at this moment uncertain whether I can have the pleasure of considering Mr. Waverley as among mine."

He then paused for an instant; but before Edward could adjust a suitable reply, or even arrange his ideas as to its purport, the Prince took out a paper, and then proceeded:—"I should indeed have no doubts upon this subject, if I could trust to this proclamation, set forth by the friends of the Elector of Hanover, in which they rank Mr. Waverley among the nobility and gentry who are menaced with the pains of high-treason for loyalty to their legitimate sovereign. But I desire to gain no adherents save from affection and conviction; and if Mr. Waverley inclines to prosecute his journey to the south, or to join the forces of the Elector, he shall have my passport and free permission to do so; and I can only regret, that my present power will not extend to protect him against the probable consequences of such a measure.—But," continued Charles Edward, after another short pause, "if Mr. Waverley should, like his ancestor, Sir Nigel, determine to embrace a cause which has little to recommend it but its justice, and follow a prince who throws himself upon the affections of his people to recover the throne of his ancestors, or perish in the attempt, I can only say, that among these nobles and gentlemen he will find worthy associates in a gallant enterprise, and will follow a master who may be unfortunate, but, I trust, will never be ungrateful."

The politic Chieftain of the race of Ivor knew his advantage in introducing Waverley to this personal interview with the royal Adventurer. Unaccustomed to the address and manners of a polished court, in which Charles was eminently skillful, his words and his kindness penetrated the heart of our hero, and easily outweighed all prudential motives. To be thus personally solicited for assistance by a Prince, whose form and manners, as well as the spirit which he displayed in this singular enterprise, answered his ideas as a hero of romance; to be courted by him in the ancient halls of his paternal palace, recovered by the sword which he was already bending towards other conquests, gave Edward, in his own eyes, the dignity and importance which he had ceased to consider as his attributes. Rejected, slandered, and threatened upon the one side, he was irresistibly attracted to the cause which the prejudices of education, and the political principles of his family, had already recommended as the most just. These thoughts rushed through his mind like a torrent, sweeping before them every consideration of an opposite tendency,—the time, besides, admitted of no deliberation,—and Waverley, kneeling to Charles Edward, devoted his heart and sword to the vindication of his rights!

The Prince (for, although unfortunate in the faults and follies of his forefathers, we shall here, and elsewhere, give him the title due to his birth) raised Waverley from the ground, and embraced him with an expression of thanks too warm not to be genuine. He also thanked Fergus MacIvor repeatedly for having brought him such an adherent, and presented Waverley to the various noblemen, chieftains, and officers who were about his person, as a young gentleman of the highest hopes and prospects, in whose bold and enthusiastic avowal of his cause they might see an evidence of the sentiments of the English families of rank at this important crisis. Indeed, this was a point much doubted among the adherents of the house of Stewart; and as a well-founded disbelief in the co-operation of the English Jacobites kept many Scottish men of rank from his standard, and diminished the courage of those who had joined it, nothing could be more seasonable for the Chevalier than the open declaration in his favour of the representative of the house of Waverley-Honour, so long known as cavaliers and royalists. This Fergus had foreseen from the beginning. He really loved Waverley, because their feelings and projects never thwarted each other; he hoped to see him united with Flora, and he rejoiced that they were effectually engaged in the same cause. But, as we before hinted, he also exulted as a politician in beholding secured to his party a partisan of such consequence; and he was far from being insensible to the personal importance which he himself gained with the Prince, from having so materially assisted in making the acquisition.

Charles Edward, on his part, seemed eager to show his attendants the value which he attached to his new adherent, by entering immediately, as in confidence, upon the circumstances of his situation. "You have been secluded so much from intelligence, Mr. Waverley, from causes of which I am but indistinctly informed, that I presume you are even yet unacquainted with the important particulars of my present situation. You have, however, heard of my landing in the remote district of Moidart, with only seven attendants, and of the numerous chiefs and clans whose loyal enthusiasm at once placed a solitary adventurer at the head of a gallant army. You must also, I think, have learned, that the commander-in-chief of the Hanoverian Elector, Sir John Cope, marched into the Highlands at the head of a numerous and well-appointed military force, with the intention of giving us battle, but that his courage failed him when we were within three hours' march of each other, so that he fairly gave us the slip, and marched northward to Aberdeen, leaving the Low Country open and undefended. Not to lose so favourable an opportunity, I marched on to this metropolis, driving before me two regiments of horse, Gardiner's and Hamilton's, who had threatened to cut to pieces every Highlander that should venture to pass Stirling; and while discussions were carrying forward among the magistracy and citizens of Edinburgh, whether they should defend themselves or surrender, my good friend Lochiel (laying his hand on the shoulder of that gallant and accomplished chieftain) saved them the trouble of farther deliberation, by entering the gates with five hundred Camerons. Thus far, therefore, we have done well; but, in the meanwhile, this doughty general's nerves being braced by the keen air of Aberdeen, he has taken shipping for Dunbar, and I have just received certain information that he landed there yesterday. His purpose must unquestionably be, to march towards us to recover possession of the capital. Now there are two opinions in my council of war: one, that being inferior probably in numbers, and certainly in discipline and military appointments, not to mention our total want of artillery, and the weakness of our cavalry, it will be safest to fall back towards the mountains, and there protract the war until fresh succours arrive from France, and the whole body of the Highland clans shall have taken arms in our favour. The opposite opinion maintains, that a retrograde movement, in our circumstances, is certain to throw utter discredit on our arms and undertaking; and, far from gaining us new partisans, will be the means of disheartening those who have joined our standard. The officers who use these last arguments, among whom is your friend Fergus MacIvor, maintain, that if the Highlanders are strangers to the usual military discipline of Europe, the soldiers whom they are to encounter are no less strangers to their peculiar and formidable mode of attack; that the attachment and courage of the chiefs and gentlemen are not to be doubted; and that as they will be in the midst of the enemy, their clansmen will as surely follow them; in fine, that having drawn the sword we should throw away the scabbard, and trust our cause to battle and to the God of Battles. Will Mr. Waverley favour us with his opinion in these arduous circumstances?"

Waverley coloured high betwixt pleasure and modesty at the distinction implied in this question, and answered, with equal spirit and readiness, that he could not venture to offer an opinion as derived from military skill, but that the counsel would be far the most acceptable to him which should first afford him an opportunity to evince his zeal in his Royal Highness's service.

"Spoken like a Waverley!" answered Charles Edward; "and that you may hold a rank in some degree corresponding to your name, allow me, instead of the captain's commission which you have lost, to offer you the brevet rank of major in my service, with the advantage of acting as one of my aides-de-camp until you can be attached to a regiment, of which I hope several will be speedily embodied."

"Your Royal Highness will forgive me," answered Waverley, (for his recollection turned to Balmawhapple and his scanty troop,) "if I decline accepting any rank until the time and place where I may have interest enough to raise a sufficient body of men to make my command useful to your Royal Highness's service. In the meanwhile, I hope for your permission to serve as a volunteer under my friend Fergus MacIvor."

"At least," said the Prince, who was obviously pleased with this proposal, "allow me the pleasure of arming you

after the Highland fashion." With these words, he unbuckled the broadsword which he wore, the belt of which was plated with silver, and the steel basket-hilt richly and curiously inlaid. "The blade," said the Prince, "is a genuine Andrea Ferrara; it has been a sort of heir-loom in our family; but I am convinced I put it into better hands than my own, and will add to it pistols of the same workmanship.—Colonel MacIvor, you must have much to say to your friend; I will detain you no longer from your private conversation; but remember, we expect you both to attend us in the evening. It may be perhaps the last night we may enjoy in these halls, and as we go to the field with a clear conscience, we will spend the eve of battle merrily."

Thus licensed, the Chief and Waverley left the presence-chamber.

"How do you like him?" was Fergus's first question, as they descended the large stone staircase.

"A prince to live and die under," was Waverley's enthusiastic answer.

"I knew you would think so when you saw him, and I intended you should have met earlier, but was prevented by your sprain. And yet he has his foibles, or rather he has difficult cards to play, and his Irish officers, who are much about him, are but sorry advisers,—they cannot discriminate among the numerous pretensions that are set up. Would you think it—I have been obliged for the present to suppress an earl's patent, granted for services rendered ten years ago, for fear of exciting the jealousy, forsooth, of C—— and M——. But you were very right, Edward, to refuse the situation of aide-de-camp. There are two vacant, indeed, but Clanronald and Lochiel, and almost all of us, have requested one for young Aberchallader, and the Lowlanders and the Irish party are equally desirous to have the other for the Master of F——. Now, if either of these candidates were to be superseded in your favour, you would make enemies. And then I am surprised that the Prince should have offered you a majority, when he knows very well that nothing short of lieutenant-colonel will satisfy others, who cannot bring one hundred and fifty men to the field. 'But patience, cousin, and shuffle the cards!' It is all very well for the present, and we must have you properly equipped for the evening in your new costume; for, to say truth, your outward man is scarce fit for a court."

"Why," said Waverley, looking at his soiled dress, "my shooting jacket has seen service since we parted; but that, probably, you, my friend, know as well or better than I."

"You do my second-sight too much honour," said Fergus. "We were so busy, first with the scheme of giving battle to Cope, and afterwards with our operations in the Lowlands, that I could only give general directions to such of our people as were left in Perthshire to respect and protect you, should you come in their way. But let me hear the full story of your adventures, for they have reached us in a very partial and mutilated manner."

Waverley then detailed at length the circumstances with which the reader is already acquainted, to which Fergus listened with great attention. By this time they had reached the door of his quarters, which he had taken up in a small paved court, retiring from the street called the Canongate, at the house of a buxom widow of forty, who seemed to smile very graciously upon the handsome young Chief, she being a person with whom good looks and good-humour were sure to secure an interest, whatever might be the party's political opinions. Here Callum Beg received them with a smile of recognition. "Callum," said the Chief, "call Shemus an Snachad (James of the Needle)." This was the heredity tailor of Vich Ian Vohr. "Shemus, Mr. Waverley is to wear the *cath dath* (battle colour, or tartan); his trews must be ready in four hours. You know the measure of a well-made man: two double nails to the small of the leg—"

"Eleven from haunch to heel, seven round the waist—I give your honour leave to hang Shemus, if there's a pair of sheers in the Highlands that has a baulder sneck than her's ain at the *cumadh an truais* (shape of the trews)."

"Get a plaid of MacIvor tartan, and sash," continued the Chieftain, "and a blue bonnet of the Prince's pattern at Mr. Mouat's in the Crames. My short green coat, with silver lace and silver buttons, will fit him exactly, and I have never worn it. Tell Ensign MacCombich to pick out a handsome target from among mine. The Prince has given Mr. Waverley broadsword and pistols, I will furnish him with a dirk and purse; add

but a pair of low-heeled shoes, and then, my dear Edward, (turning to him,) you will be a complete son of Ivor."

. . . .

To continue the tale in our summarized form we find that Flora, ignorant of her own brother's attachment to the baron's daughter, used her influence to make Waverley think more intimately of her friend, Rose Bradwardine. Between love and war Waverley was carried almost breathlessly along in the train of the rebellion. He took part in the victory of the Highlanders at Preston-Pans, and in this battle saved the life of his uncle's friend, Colonel Talbot.

There was another incident of the battle which made a grave impression on Waverley's mind. This was the death of Colonel Gardiner. The colonel, sorely wounded, was maintaining a desperate and unavailing resistance against the Highlanders when Waverley saw him.

"To save this good and brave man became the instant object of his most anxious exertions. But he could only witness his fall. Ere Edward could make his way among the Highlanders, who, furious and eager for spoil, now thronged upon each other, he saw his former commander brought from his horse by the blow of a scythe, and beheld him receive, while on the ground, more wounds than would have let out twenty lives."

After the battle of Preston-Pans, Waverley marched with the rebels into England. He was with them in their enforced return, till the disaster at Clifton, where Vich Ian Vohr was taken prisoner. Then he was separated from them. Unflinchingly loyal to the cause he had espoused, Vich Ian Vohr met his death within the grim walls of Carlisle Castle. Broken at last in spirit, Flora MacIvor, lamenting that she had urged her brother on to his terrible end, sought refuge in the convent of the Scottish Benedictine nuns in Paris. Waverley was pardoned, and his life was saved largely through the affectionate devotion of Rose Bradwardine. Her kindness to the outlaw's daughter was the means of bringing to light Donald Bean Lean's treacherous use of Waverley's letters.

A wiser and an infinitely stronger man for his adventures, Waverley married Rose Bradwardine, and became master of Waverley-Honour.

THE NEXT STORY OF FAMOUS BOOKS IS ON PAGE 4235.

HOW TO PREVENT NAILS AND SCREWS FROM RUSTING QUICKLY

IT is a well-known fact that iron, during the process of rusting, tends to destroy CONTINUED FROM 4018 any vegetable fibre with which it may remain in contact. This explains, to a certain extent, the rapid destruction of the wood that surrounds the nails used in outdoor work, whereby the nail is soon left in a hole much larger than itself and all power of adhesion is lost. Part of this effect is, no doubt, due to the action of water and air which creep along the surface of the nail by capillary attraction and tend to produce rottenness in the wood, as well as oxidation in the iron. But when we compare an old nail-hole with a similar hole that has been exposed during an equal time, but is filled with a wooden pin instead of an iron nail, we find that the wood surrounding the wooden pin has suffered least; and therefore we may fairly attribute the destructive action to the rusting of the iron.

It might be supposed that as the oxid of iron is more bulky than the pure iron, the hole would be filled more tightly and the nail held more firmly in its place. Although this effect is produced in the first instance, the destruction of the woody fibre and the pulverization of the oxid soon overbalance it, and the nail becomes loose. Of course the iron itself being also destroyed, its strength is diminished; and we have therefore a double incentive for preventing or diminishing the action that we have described. The only way to prevent this action is to cover the nail with some substance that will prevent oxidation. This might be done by tinning, as is common with carpet tacks, which are now extensively tinned for the purpose of preventing them from rusting, and thus rotting holes in the carpets. Coating them with oil or tallow would be efficient if the act of driving did not remove the protecting matter entirely from a large portion of the surface. But, even then, it will be found that the oil or fat is stripped off the point and gathered about the head in such a way as to prevent the entrance of air and moisture into the hole.

The most efficient way to coat nails with grease is to heat them to a point sufficient to cause the grease to smoke, and then pour the grease over them, stirring them about in a kettle or pan. When the nails are hot, the melted grease will attach itself to them more firmly than it would have done if they were cold; indeed, so firmly that it will require actual abrasion of the metal to separate it. In erecting fences, laying plank or board sidewalks and the like, it becomes an important matter to secure the nails against the influences that we have mentioned, and yet the work must be done rapidly and cheaply. Nails may be readily prepared as described, or they may simply be dipped in oil or paint at the moment when they are driven in. It has been found by experiment that in cases where it is not advisable to paint the whole fence, it is, nevertheless, a good plan to go over the work and touch the head of every nail with a brush dipped in oil or paint prepared so as to be of the same color as the old wood. Of course it is obvious that nails may be more easily driven into hard wood by first touching the small ends in grease.

To draw a rusty nail that sticks tight, first hit it a blow with a hammer sufficiently hard to drive it in a little, which breaks the rusted connection. The nail then can be easily drawn out.

There are poor as well as good screws. A good screw should have sound and well-cut heads, no breaks or flaws in the thread part, and good gimlet points. If they are warmed and dipped in raw linseed oil or tallow, it will prevent their rusting. They can then be unscrewed easily.

When the work in which they are used is

4079

exposed to much wetting and drying, screws are of little use. They soon rust, rot the wood around them, and draw out, having the appearance of screws without threads. Dipping them in thick paint or tallow before driving helps to protect them. When they are to be used in inside work and in soft wood, they may be dipped in glue. This makes them hold well, and when thus treated they are more easily driven. But the best plan is to heat them with oil or tallow in a pan. The grease then adheres more strongly, and the protection is more complete. This plan is the easiest and cheapest, as well as the best.

It is a common thing, when a screw or staple becomes loose, to draw it out, plug up the hole or holes with wood, and then reinsert it. But screws and staples so secured soon come out again. It has been found that a much better way is to fill up the holes tightly with cork. Screws and iron so secured will remain perfectly tight just about as long as when put into new wood.

Few things are more annoying than obstinate screws which refuse to move, much less to be drawn out, and in the struggle against the screwdriver power possibly suffer the loss of their heads. If the screw is turned into iron and is not very rusty, it is only necessary to clear the head with the wedge of the driver and let a few drops of oil penetrate to the threads. However, if you find that excessive heat or rust has seemed to fix the screw so it will not turn, then heat, either by placing a piece of hot iron upon it or by directing a flame upon the head, and, after applying a little oil, turn out gently. In this case care must be taken not to let the tool slip so as to damage the notch. If, however, the screw refuses to come out, try to force it back with a blunt chisel by carefully tapping with a light hammer; but if even this does not dislodge the screw, it is best to cut the head away and drill it out. When an obstinate screw happens to be in wood, merely give it a few taps on the head; but, if this fails, heat it with a piece of hot iron, which may be readily done with a red-hot kitchen poker. Then it may be easily turned.

THE COIN AND THE HANDKERCHIEF

THE young wizard will find this a trick after his own heart. It is completely deceptive. It may be exhibited offhand with any penny and with any handkerchief. Lastly, it is very easy of execution. Its only drawback is that the necessary movements are a little bit difficult to explain in writing.

The performer begins by borrowing a penny and a handkerchief. A conjurer should always borrow when he can, because anything of his own always lies open to the suspicion, however unfounded, of being in some way specially prepared. Besides, the lenders of the articles used in a trick feel a sort of personal interest in it. In the present case the performer may also borrow a short piece of string, though there is no objection to his providing this for himself.

Taking the penny in his left hand, and holding it upright between the forefinger and thumb, he throws the handkerchief over it, letting the four corners hang gracefully down around it. "Let us settle it comfortably," he remarks. So saying, he nips the coin, through the handkerchief, between the first and second fingers of the right hand, held palm upward, as shown in the picture, and tilts it over toward the left.

The forefinger and thumb of the left hand release the coin for a moment, and nip it again by its opposite edge, through the handkerchief. The upright hand is then removed.

"Now," says the performer, "you would hardly suppose that this simple movement has already caused the coin to vanish. You are quite right, for here it is still." As if to prove the words that he has just uttered—though nobody in the audience doubts them—he lifts with the right hand the hanging portion of the handkerchief and shows the coin.

How to hold the penny.

"Once more we will cover it over." He lets the handkerchief fall around it on all sides. "To make the coin still safer," he says, "I will ask somebody to tie this piece of string round the handkerchief." This is done at a distance of about six inches from the coin.

"And now," he continues, "I want the assistance of the strongest gentleman in the company." Someone having volunteered, he says: "Now, sir, I want you to take hold of this handkerchief"—he gives him the hanging portion—"and hold it as tightly as you can. 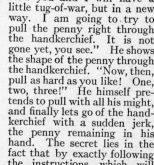 Now you and I will have a little tug-of-war, but in a new way. I am going to try to pull the penny right through the handkerchief. It is not gone yet, you see." He shows the shape of the penny through the handkerchief. "Now, then, pull as hard as you like! One, two, three!" He himself pretends to pull with all his might, and finally lets go of the handkerchief with a sudden jerk, the penny remaining in his hand. The secret lies in the fact that by exactly following the instructions, which will be found in practice perfectly simple, complicated as they may look in print, the coin is left, after it has been shown for the second time and the handkerchief let fall around it, in an outside fold, whence, under the pretense of pulling, it is an easy matter to work it out into the palm of the hand. The "strongest gentleman in the company" will look rather foolish as he holds the empty handkerchief.

It is hardly necessary to remark that the trick may of course be worked with a half-dollar, dime or quarter, just as well as with a cent. Two or three coins may be pulled through the handkerchief at the same time as easily as one, when once we have grasped the method to be employed.

DOLLS OF MANY NATIONS
The colored plate showing the dolls is opposite page 3510.

LOTUS BLOSSOM—THE LITTLE JAPANESE DOLL

ON pages 3510 and 3627 some dolls' dresses are described. Here are some more dolls of other nations we can dress. The costume worn by the little Japanese girl is one of the most beautiful in the world. The Japanese are great artists; they are wonderful at making exquisite objects out of simple, cheap material. They excel in this point, and we find the idea carried out in their garments. They have, too, a great love of color, and, by some instinct, they seem to know how to blend colors in a most wonderful way. So, we shall find their clothes simple in shape, made from almost straight pieces of material—and not much of it. We shall also find the colors very beautiful and well arranged.

Now we shall find out how to make the costume shown in the picture for Lotus Blossom, which is the English translation of a real Japanese girl's name. The Japanese are passionately fond of flowers; they give the children flower names, and a large number of their dresses are made in material with flowers upon it. It is quite easy to buy Japanese printed cotton at any large dry-goods store. We must be sure that it is real, and not an imitation, for there is a great deal of difference.

Perhaps at the same shop we shall be able to buy a Japanese doll with almond eyes and black hair.

The shape of the dress is very simple—very much like our dressing-gowns, though the sleeves are different. They are long and straight in shape, and have deep pockets in the end which hangs down.

Let us suppose that we have bought a pale green material with branches of flowers, pink, purple and gray trailing across it, and here and there lines of black and gold.

A little fold of purple silk a slightly deeper shade than the flowers, will just show where the gown crosses at the neck. For the sash we must get a piece of stiffer material—Japanese brocade or gold tissue.

The Japanese girl thinks a great deal of her sash and is very particular about the way it is tied behind. It should be very wide in front, folded at the back with one loop going up and another going down, threaded through a crossway piece.

Lotus Blossom wears wooden shoes with detachable short stilts that fit into holes in the bottom. She fixes in these stilts during rainy weather to keep her feet off the wet ground.

To dress the hair of a fashionable girl generally takes about two hours—never less, and often longer; it is not surprising, therefore, that the hair-dressing is expected to last for two or three days.

A great variety of combs is used, and plenty of pomade to form the hair into shapes before it is finally fixed. A Japanese girl does not wear a hat in the street—she carries a paper sunshade. We can buy one (doll's size) at a toy shop.

CHANDI—THE LITTLE INDIAN DOLL

IN our collection of dolls we must certainly have one to represent India. Among the natives of that country we find a great many different kinds of costumes. The class distinctions are very great, and the costumes of each class vary more or less. In our picture we see a nurse-girl, or *ayah* as she is called. Her name is Chandi. We see that she has bare feet. She would not wear shoes in the house—that would be considered very rude to her mistress. Just in the same way that an Englishman lifts his hat, an Indian removes his shoes before entering a house. When in the street Chandi would wear a pair of loose, heelless slippers made of goat-hide, with turn-up toes and no fastening.

The dress is made of woven cotton material, yellowish in tint and soft in texture. The bodice is like a tunic in shape; it hangs outside the skirt and comes three or four inches below the waist-line. It is plain in shape, buttoning up in front with three sets of small buttons, each set containing two buttons.

On the hips at each side the bodice is cut up a little way, and a small piece of the material is inserted to make the garment fuller. The sleeves are plain and fit tightly to the arm, coming only to the elbow. A piping of scarlet cotton edges the neck, the sleeve and the bottom of the bodice. The Indian woman is exceedingly fond of decorating her costume with a piping of bright color.

The skirt is made of the same material. It is cut very full and pleated into the waist.

The rest of the costume is composed of a strip of material bordered with a band of scarlet. This piece is draped round the figure and over the head, taking the place of a cloak and hat. To arrange the drapery we must start by tucking one end in at the waist in front; then we must twist it round over the back of the head, and bring the other end over the left shoulder. The ayah holds this in position with her hand as she walks.

She wears many metal bracelets, and on each foot is a metal anklet, one inch wide; they clank together as she walks. A similar piece of jewelry clasps her neck—fastened as old-fashioned bracelets were, with a hinge and a snap at opposite sides of the circle. Her next piece of jewelry is quite easy to make. It consists of very large earrings, made of clay or mud, which, while soft, has had stuck into it a number of brightly colored beads, carefully arranged in a pattern composed of either circles or diamond shapes. These earrings are so heavy that they are supported by a chain which goes right round the ear.

Chandi's hair is black and very shiny, and is quite straight. It is parted in front and brushed down behind the ears, to be fastened, without hairpins, in a tight knob at the nape of the neck. Her complexion is deep brown all over, and her eyes are dark.

WHAT TO DO IN TROUBLE

DUST OR GRIT IN THE EYE

WHEN a little speck of grit or dust gets into the eye and no one is at hand to take it out for us, there are several things we can do. If we feel that the speck is moving about, we can first try shutting the eye a minute. Sometimes the speck will come out with the tears. We might take hold of the upper lid with the thumb and forefinger and work it gently over the eye toward the nose. If the speck gets fixed on the surface of the eyeball we can dislodge it in this way, or by passing a moistened fine camel's-hair brush or the corner of a handkerchief over the surface of the eye, using a looking-glass, of course. Bathing the eye with cold water, and opening it in cold water will take down the inflammation; so will a cold-water compress. A solution of boracic acid is also a good remedy. If a spark from a cigar or a piece of hot ash enters the eye, a drop of olive or castor oil will ease the pain. It is bad to rub the eye.

SOMETHING IN THE EAR

When by accident an insect flies into the ear we should try to coax it out by turning the ear toward a bright light. If a bead or hard substance gets in, we risk destroying the drum by poking the bead against it. If we pour water in to try to wash a pea or other seed out, we might simply make it swell in the ear. The proper thing to do is to hold the ear downward and gently pull at the lobe. If that fails we must go to a doctor.

TO STOP NOSE BLEEDING

If the bleeding is slight we can sniff cold water up the nose, apply a handkerchief dipped in cold water to the root of the nose, sit in a chair with the head back, and place a key or a piece of steel at the back of the neck. We should not bend down over a basin. If the bleeding is in a constant stream we should apply ice, lie flat, and pack the nostril with cotton, until a doctor comes. The collar should be loosened, the hands held above the head, fresh air breathed, and a hot-water bottle applied to the feet.

HOW TO TREAT BRUISES

A blow or a tumble may cause a painful and unsightly bruise, which hurts much at the time and turns purple, black, greenish and yellow, due to bleeding underneath the skin. One remedy is to apply something cold, whether it be ice, the blade of a table-knife, or a cold-water bandage. Sometimes bathing with very hot water for 10 or 15 minutes will give relief. A bruised limb should be rested. Arnica and water—1 teaspoonful of arnica to 1 teacupful of water—are soothing when the skin is unbroken. When it is broken, witch-hazel may be applied, but the surface must first be washed with an antiseptic solution free from dust or gravel. Should it be much grazed, it must be bound with a clean handkerchief to exclude the air. If the wound is severe, the surface should be cleansed with equal parts of hydrogen peroxid and water, and zinc oxid ointment on a piece of sterilized gauze applied.

STRAINS AND SPRAINS

We "strain" the wrist when we overstretch its tendons or muscles. We "sprain" the ankle when we stretch or tear the ligaments of the joints in that part of the foot.

Hot fomentations should be applied to cure a strain or sprain—that is, we lay on the part a cloth dipped in water as hot as we can stand; then we apply a cold-water compress covered with oil-silk and bandaged with gauze, and rest it.

WHEN A BONE IS BROKEN

If the bone of a limb is broken, the limb is powerless. Should this happen to the leg, we must not try to move it, but wait till someone comes to lift us on to a stretcher or something hard and flat, such as a door. In doing this a rug or sheet should be carefully passed under the legs and these raised and lowered on to it. The injured limb can be lightly tied to a stick or umbrella which may be at hand, to give it support and prevent the broken bone from piercing the skin. When the arm is broken a sling should be made for it.

BITES AND STINGS

If an unhealthy cat, dog or any other animal bites us, its saliva may poison our blood, especially if the bite is taken on a part unprotected by clothing. If the finger is bitten, we must at once bind it tightly higher up toward the hand, then suck the bite and spit out the saliva. As soon as we can get warm water we wash the wound; if it bleeds, all the better. Then we get it cauterized; a burning fuse has done duty when proper cauterizing was impossible. The bites of insects are relieved by applying liquid ammonia or rubbing with a lump of moistened washing-soda.

The sting of the bee can be removed by squeezing the part.

THORNS IN THE FINGERS

If we cannot seize the splinter or thorn with the thumb and finger of the other hand or with a pair of tweezers, we must get a fine needle, which we should first sterilize by holding over a lighted match, and tear open the skin in the direction the thorn entered. Then we stroke it along with the needle toward the opening, squeezing the finger toward the same point now and then, and also sucking it to draw out the thorn.

FALLING INTO WATER

If we tumble into a river, lake or sea, the worst thing we can do is to throw up our arms, try to breathe under water, and struggle and scream away all our strength. If we cannot swim, we can at least keep our presence of mind and remember that water will float us if we lie quietly on our backs. So we lie flat with the hands down and call for help. If a rope is thrown or a stick held out to us, we seize that and are drawn to shore; but if someone swims to the rescue, we must be careful not to grip that person round the neck, shoulders or waist, and drag him down under water.

A FLEET OF LITTLE BOATS

BIG boats and small boats, heavy boats and little fairy boats we can make from fruits, nuts, and treasures of the garden and wood. Nimble fingers will soon build our little fleet; and in a bathtub filled with water we can set the boats afloat.

First we will make a gondola out of a banana-skin, choosing a perfect fruit, well turned up and flat between the ends. We cut down along the middle of the flat part, and through the opening cut the pulp into sections, which can be drawn out on the point of a penknife, leaving the skin perfect. Then we curve a piece of thin card, insert it toward the pointed end, and put a match for a seat toward the stalk end. We may have to put a coin in the bottom of the boat to steady it in the water. The result is seen in picture 5.

We can make another boat out of half a lemon or a small orange cut lengthwise. We remove the pulp, and trim the edges with scissors, insert strips of card for seats, and put the coracle-shaped boat in the oven to dry

secure the mast to the bottom of the boat. Picture 4 shows us what it is like. The walnut is easy to halve, but not so an eggshell; yet this makes a pretty white boat if we can manage to secure a sound half. Perhaps the best way is first to crack an egg in the middle and from that hole remove the shell in small pieces before carefully taking out the contents. It is better to leave an irregular edge to the shell, as in picture 1, than to risk cracking our boat.

As to the sail for this boat, it can be made of thin white paper fastened to a mast of very stiff paper folded in halves, with one end bent at right angles, so that the bent part can be stuck down to the inside of the boat with sealing wax, while the edge of the sail is gummed into the folded paper that forms the mast. Being fragile, the eggshell boat may easily be injured in a collision. As shipwrecks do sometimes occur, it is just as well to have a lifeboat or a raft on our miniature sea. A raft might be made of match-sticks or pieces

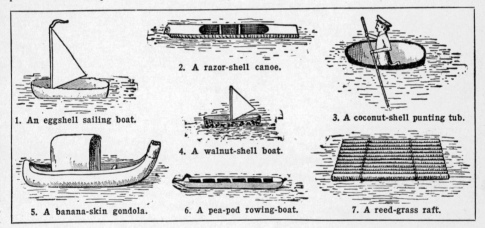

1. An eggshell sailing boat.

2. A razor-shell canoe.

3. A coconut-shell punting tub.

4. A walnut-shell boat.

5. A banana-skin gondola.

6. A pea-pod rowing-boat.

7. A reed-grass raft.

and harden. Little wooden dolls to represent ancient sailors, with pieces of wood for oars, can be seated in the coracle.

For a rowboat we can use the half of a very large pea-pod with the stalk cut away. Small strips of card will do for the seats, as we see in picture 6, and if we are skilled in cutting out, we can shape little card rowers with two oars each, made of card or of blades of grass.

We know, of course, that coconuts float. So out of the sawn half of one we can make a round punting tub, and in it place a small wooden doll, with a stick for a punting pole, as in picture 3.

All these things make fairly large boats; but there are many things from which we can make dainty little ones. There is, for instance, the half of a walnut-shell. We divide the walnut carefully with a knife, taking pains not to crack the shell, remove the nut, and scrape the inside of the shell clean. As this is suitable for a sailing boat, we get a piece of stiff white paper, gum one side round a piece of match-stick, and with a little sealing wax

of reed-grass roped together with coarse white cotton, as in picture 7. Small strips of cork cut lengthwise from the corks of bottles will answer the purpose of a raft, and refuse to sink. Failing any other material, the raft can be shaped from a large flat leaf, such as the plane or ivy.

During the acorn season we probably gathered some acorns with their cups; if so, we have nice little punting tubs ready to be floated at once. An acorn in a cup can serve the purpose of a buoy, if we secure a thread to the stalk and a weight to the other end of the thread, which must, of course, be long enough to reach the bottom of our sea. The acorn can be cut in halves lengthwise, the nut removed, and the shell used for a small boat, the flat end forming the stern and the pointed end the bow.

The petals of flowers float easily on water, so that from them alone we can get dainty small boats of many colors. Red, pink, yellow and white roses will give us variety. As a rose petal is very fragile, a sail, if we want one, would have to be made of tissue-paper, say pink for a pink boat. To form the mast we can roll the paper down one side. A drop of gum or paste will be all that is necessary to keep it in its proper position.

In autumn the halved outer coats of horse-chestnuts and walnuts make strong little boats. Then, if we get a large piece of cork or a small block of wood, we can shape it into a modern warship, and even use monkey-nuts, acorns or filberts for torpedoes. A fireship is made from a lump of camphor set alight.

Some shells make admirable boats and float well. The long-shaped razor-shell answers for a canoe, as in picture 2. Paper can be pasted over the two ends, and an uncovered space left in the middle. As such a boat is comparatively large, it can be launched near the gondola shaped from a banana. Mussel-shells also make good boats; and small black closed ones will suggest to us not only dangerous torpedoes, but porpoises floating on the surface of the water. Small empty tin cans with tight covers can be made into oil tankers by using sealing wax to put on masts.

For all these things we must use our imagination and inventiveness; and we shall be surprised to find how interesting boat-making can be when we go to Nature's wonderful storehouse for materials wherewith to build them.

HOW TO KEEP FRUIT FRESH

UNFORTUNATELY for boys and girls, and for grown-ups too, fruit becomes ripe only in the autumn, so that at one season of the year we may have more fruit than we can eat with comfort to ourselves, and at other times, when we would like to have certain fruits, we cannot have them, either because the season of that fruit has passed or has not yet come. But in this age of great inventions and progress we are far more fortunate than our grandparents were, and even than our parents were when they were as old as we are now.

We get large supplies of fruit from California and from Florida, to say nothing of the great quantity of tropical and subtropical fruit shipped from the West Indies.

Thanks to the quickness with which railway trains and modern steamships can carry fruit, and to the modern methods of keeping fruit while it is being carried on the ocean, we have two seasons a year for many kinds of fruit. But, in spite of that, it is as well to know how to keep fruit longer than we can do by letting it lie about without any special measures being taken to prolong its life. So we shall learn how to do it in this article.

First, we must know what causes fruit to spoil. The decomposition of fruit, as we call it, is caused by the attacks of microbes, which are the very tiny little living things that we read something about on page 437. Once the microbes have begun to settle on fruit, it gets bad ever so much more quickly. Thus the effort to keep fruit fresh is really a fight between the microbes and ourselves. It seems ridiculous to talk about a fight between men and creatures so tiny that we can see them only with the help of a strong microscope. But, in spite of that, if we are not very careful the microbes will win the battle and our fruit will spoil very soon. The microbes are bound to win eventually; we cannot help that. The most we can do is to beat them off for a time, to keep the fruit a few weeks or months longer than otherwise. We cannot make its freshness indefinite. If we know what conditions favor the growth of microbes, then we know that by avoiding or preventing these conditions we can make fruit remain fresh a little longer. Microbes thrive and multiply in damp and stagnant air; therefore our fruit should be kept in a place that is cool and shady yet airy and dry. Fruit that is intended to be kept should be gathered when not fully ripe. Care should be taken not to break the skin, and any bruised fruit should be put aside to be eaten first. A dry, dark attic or cellar with plenty of ventilation makes a good place for keeping fruit. The fruit should not be heaped up. Each apple, pear or other fruit should lie by itself, not touching its neighbor, and every few days each one should be examined to see if it has begun to decay. If it has, it should be removed so that it may not contaminate the rest. Wrapping each one in paper separately is a good plan, and if this is done, the fruit need not be examined at such frequent intervals as when it is stored unwrapped. If these hints are followed, apples may be kept fresh for many months. Indeed, some fruits, such as winter pears, need to be kept for some time to get thoroughly ripe, as they do not ripen on the tree.

Nowadays fruit-preserving has become quite a domestic art. The fruit is pared, cored, and put into glass jars, which are then filled with a hot, thin syrup, and firmly sealed. The syrup is made by dissolving sugar in water and boiling it slowly for a few minutes after the sugar is dissolved. The solution must not be stirred after it has started to boil.

The spoiling of a can of peaches or other fruit is due to the development within it of great numbers of small forms of plant life, the germs of which are present in the fruit or the can before or during the process of canning. To prevent the fruit from spoiling, it is necessary to sterilize both the fruit and the jar. Sterilization consists in raising the temperature to such a point as will insure that all the germs are killed. The fruit should be put into cans or jars as soon as possible after it is pared; otherwise the surfaces turn dark.

On board ship, in hotels, and elsewhere, fruit is often kept in cold storage; that is to say, the temperature of the room or box in which the fruit is stored is kept down to a temperature of about 32° Fahrenheit, which is freezing-point, by means of ice or refrigerating machinery. But this involves the use of expensive machinery or other apparatus, and is not suitable for an ordinary person who merely wishes to enjoy the lusciousness of fresh fruit a few weeks longer than he would otherwise be able to do.

A LITTLE TOY CANNON

THE idea of loading a cannon with a seidlitz powder seems funny. Of course our cannon will not be a real cannon; it will be an ordinary pint or quart bottle. And we need not be afraid that we shall shoot ourselves or anybody else when we discharge it, for it is really quite harmless.

First we take a bottle and put sufficient water into it so that when it is turned on its side none of the water will run out. This means that the bottle will be about one-third full. Into the bottle we put the powder that we shall find in the blue paper of a seidlitz powder, and we shake the bottle so that the powder will dissolve properly. Now we take a piece of paper, and by rolling it round a lead pencil make a paper tube from 2 to 3 inches long. We close the tube at one end, either by plugging it with a cork or with another small piece of paper, or simply by folding the end over a little and fastening it with a small pin.

The seidlitz-powder cannon. The lower picture shows how the powder is fixed.

Then we take a cork that fits the bottle tightly, and having tied a thread to the upper, or open, end of the paper tube, we fix the other end of the thread into the under-side of the cork by using a pin. The thread should be of such a length that when the cork is put into the bottle, the tube will be about halfway down the bottle inside and just floating above the surface of the water in the bottle.

We now put into the paper tube the contents of the white paper in a seidlitz powder, and put the paper tube into the bottle, and then push the cork in tightly. All that we need to do now is to lay the bottle on its side on a table or chair. Presently our cannon will fire itself. As the water gets into the tube with its powder it will fizz, and the force of this will send out the cork with a bang. The experiment is perfectly safe, but we must stand to the side and not in front of the bottle. It is well to perform this trick out of doors.

A WHISTLE THAT A BOY CAN MAKE

WHEN we are in the woods in springtime or early summer we can make a good whistle easily and quickly. All we need is a knife and a thin piece of green sycamore or willow that we can cut from a bush or tree. The method of manufacture is simple. First we cut off the wood, selecting a piece with nice smooth bark and as nearly round as possible. It should be 4 or 5 inches long. Cut it straight across one end, and then at the same end cut a slanting piece off, as seen in picture 1. That makes the lip of the whistle. Now we make a notch at the top side of the lip, as seen in picture 2. We then cut a ring around the bark only, down near the other end. Now we take it and moisten the bark all around, either in a stream or pool or in the mouth. Using the knife like a tiny hammer, we beat the bark all around and up and down with the handle of the knife, moistening the bark several times as we do so. We should beat it gently with the knife, and not hard enough to injure the bark. When we have done this, we shall find that the bark can be slipped off in one piece right from the ring that we made to the point of the stick where the lip is. The surface of the stick, when we have removed the bark in this way, will be smooth, with a transparent and somewhat sticky fluid adhering to it. That fluid is the sap of the tree; and if it were not for this sap flowing up the tree under the bark as the tree grows, it would

die. We wipe off the sap, and then with the knife we enlarge the notch that we have made by cutting away a piece of the wood lower down, as seen in picture 3, which shows the piece we should cut away. Now we cut a very thin strip from off the top of the stick between the notch and the pointed end, or lip. Our whistle is now made. All we have to do is to replace the bark that we took off in one piece, as we see in picture 4. The whistle should now work perfectly, giving a clear, shrill note when we blow into it. If it does not quite work well, we may discover that the notch was not enlarged sufficiently, or that we did not cut away enough of the

1. First stage.

2. Second stage.

3. Third stage.

4. The completed whistle.

top of the mouthpiece. Let us remedy these defects if they exist, and see if the result is better.

If we are entirely successful, we may become more ambitious, and try to make a whistle giving several notes on the scale, thereby making a musical instrument that can play simple tunes. For this larger instrument we need a little longer twig, say about 9 inches long, and before loosening the bark we must cut several round holes that extend farther down the stick. Then, when we have removed the bark, we must extend the notch right down past all the finger-holes. We must handle the larger instrument very gently indeed, for it is easily broken. The different notes are made by placing fingers over the holes when we blow into the mouthpiece.

HOW TO KNOW SAILING SHIPS

To hear men talk about sailing ships is sometimes very confusing. Many boys, and even men, who live by the sea and see ships sail along the coast and come into harbor, do not know the names of the various kinds of ships, and cannot distinguish one kind of ship from another. They may hear sailors and other people talk about a schooner and a brig and yawl, but they cannot tell one of these things if they see one. There may be an excuse for this sort of ignorance if we have never had the opportunity of learning what the different kinds of ships are like, but there will be no excuse for *us* if we do not know them, because this article and the pictures in it have been specially prepared in order that we may learn many things worth knowing about the ship masts and sails and ropes and spars.

It is necessary to begin by understanding something about masts and sails. A mast is a long pole sticking upright, or nearly upright, in the ship and made to carry a sail, or several sails. The masts stick up through the deck. A mast is always tapered, its lower end is very securely fixed to the bottom part of the ship, and a rope, usually a wire rope—and sometimes more than one rope—has one end attached to the mast near the top, and the other end attached to the sides of the deck or to another mast. If there is only one mast in a ship, it is called simply *the mast*. If there are two masts, the front one is called the *foremast* and the second one is the *mainmast*. If there are three masts, the third is called the *mizzen-mast;* and if there is a fourth mast, it is called the *jigger-mast* if it has no yards, and the *after-mizzen-mast* if it has yards. We shall see what yards are presently. Masts for large ships are made in more than

1. Yards.

2. Trysail.

3. Cutter or sloop.

4. Yawl.

5. English ketch.

6. English schooner.

7. Four-and-aft schooner.

one piece, and these are fastened together as shown in picture 1.

Every sailing ship has a *bowsprit,* that is, a spar sticking out in front in a horizontal, or almost a horizontal, position.

The sails could not spread out on the masts alone; there must be spars attached to the masts to assist in carrying the sails. There are three kinds of such spars, and they are called *yards,* as shown in picture 1, and *booms* and *gaffs,* as shown in picture 2. The yard is a spar that goes across the mast; from it and in front of the mast the sail hangs downward. In its normal position the length of the yard is across the ship, but of course it can be moved around to any angle so as to catch the wind. The boom is a horizontal spar, and it stretches backward from the mast toward the stern, or back, of the ship. It also can be moved around so as to spread the sail to catch the wind from any quarter. The gaff is something like a boom, and it holds at the top the sail which the boom holds below. Its position is not horizontal; it slopes upward toward its point. The spars on the masts are called by the names of yards. The foreyard is the yard on the foremast, the mainboom is the boom on the mainmast, the mizzen-gaff is the gaff on the mizzen-mast, and so on. The sail between a boom and a gaff is called a *try-sail,* or a *spanker,* and is illustrated in picture 2. A mast cannot have more than one boom and one gaff, but it may have several yards. The bottom yard, which is well shown in the first picture, is called the *lower yard,* or by the name of its mast, as *foreyard, mainyard,* etc. The one above it is the *topsail yard* and if the topsail is in two parts, the two parts are called the *lower topsail yard* and

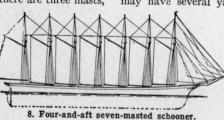

8. Four-and-aft seven-masted schooner.

9. Brigantine.

the *upper topsail yard*, respectively. Above the topsail is the *topgallant yard*, or if the topgallant sail is in two parts, the two parts are called the *lower topgallant yard* and the *upper topgallant yard*, respectively. T h e yard above the topgallant yard is called the *royal yard*, and if there is one higher still, it is known as the *skysail yard*. Now, if we remember these points about masts and sails we are ready to consider the *rigs* of various ships. The name given to the sails and their disposition on the various masts and spars is the *rig*.

Small sailing ships and yachts have what is called the *cutter* rig, which is seen in picture 3; there is only one mast, and the mainsail is stretched between a boom and a gaff. In the United States this boat is often called a sloop also. Once there was some difference, but now both words are used to describe the same thing.

The *yawl* is very much like a cutter, but has a small jigger-mast at the stern, as seen in picture 4. The yawl is generally a little

10. Brig.

sail, but a trysail instead of a lower yardsail, and on the rear, or mainmast there is a trysail and topsail. The fore-and-aft schooner rig, which is most common on this side of the Atlantic, has no yardsails but only trysails, which are generally uniform on all the masts. In picture 7 we see a two-masted schooner with fore-and-aft sails, and in picture 8 is shown a seven-masted schooner with fore-and-aft rig. A schooner may have as many masts as may be found convenient, and still be a schooner. Some very large schooners have been built in the United States. If a schooner of the first-mentioned type has more than two masts, the foremast only has yards, the remaining masts having trysails only.

The rig of the *brig* is a rare type in these days. It is found only on two-masted ships, and, as seen in picture 10, it has a main, or rear, mast

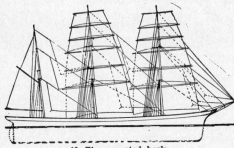

11. Barkantine.

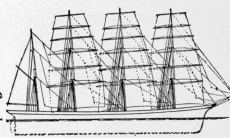

12. Three-masted bark.

13. Four-masted bark.

larger than a cutter. The *ketch* is like the yawl, but the rear mast is generally larger and farther forward. It is seen in picture 5. The rig of the *schooner* is the most common on sailing vessels to-day, especially those which sail up and down the coast. Although steamers may not have sails at all, if they have sails these are the schooner rig. There are two kinds of schooner rig: the ordinary schooner rig, and the fore-and-aft schooner rig. The ordinary schooner rig, which is seen in picture 6, has a foremast with a topsail and topgallant

with yardsails and one trysail, and a foremast with yardsails only.

The *brigantine* and the *barkantine* are much alike. The brigantine has a foremast with yards and a mainmast with a fore-and-aft sail like a schooner. The barkantine is seen sometimes in three-masted sailing ships. It is as seen in picture 11, which shows that it is like the brigantine with a mizzen-mast added to it.

The most popular rig for modern sailing ships is the *bark*. It requires not fewer than three masts. The mast near-

14. A Full-rigged ship.

est the stern has a trysail, but the other masts have yards and yardsails. Picture 12 shows a three-masted bark, and picture 13 shows a four-masted bark.

For very large ships barks are sometimes made with five masts, in which case the front four are rigged alike with yardsails, and only the fifth mast has a trysail.

Finally, there is a *full-rigged ship*, which must have not fewer than three masts, and has sometimes four masts. Only a few full-rigged ships with five masts have been built. All the masts on the full-rigged ship have yards and yardsails, and the mast nearest the stern has a trysail as well. A full-rigged ship with three masts is illustrated in picture 14. In spite of the fact that steamships are quicker, the sailing vessel has not yet disappeared from the seas.

ICES MADE WITHOUT A FREEZER

IN hot summer weather few things are more cooling and refreshing than ices. They cost but little, and can be quite well made at home. If we all knew how easily a delicious ice could be made without an elaborate freezer, we should more often want to make one. Let us see what we can contrive, even if we have no freezer.

First, we shall need a round can with a lid that shuts down tight. A coffee can or a syrup can would do. Then we need a large square tin cracker box or a wooden pail. This is to hold the freezing mixture, with the syrup or coffee can in which we are going to make our ices in the middle of it. Before doing so we must see how and why the ice is formed inside the smaller can.

We know that water freezes below a certain temperature, but if we chop up a little ice and pour on it a little water and sprinkle it with coarse salt, we get a very low degree of cold indeed, because the salt acts on the ice and increases its power to freeze. So any liquid will freeze when buried in the freezing mixture if it is left there long enough. It would turn into a block of ice if it were not hindered from doing so. How can we prevent it? The liquid will freeze first around the inside of the can, and to stop that we must stir it and scrape the can just as, but for a different reason, we stir the milk in a saucepan.

The box or pail has a layer of chopped ice and the salt placed at the bottom; the can is placed on that, and ice and salt are piled around it up to the brim. The ice should be just double the weight of the salt. The mixture for the ice is placed in the can, the lid put on, and a blanket wrapped round the outside of the whole. It is then allowed to stand for some time. Removing the lid, we take our wooden stirrer and scrape it round and round the inside of the can to prevent the mixture from freezing solid; and then we replace the lid. We must be careful not to let the salt and ice get into the can, or our ice cream will be spoiled.

And now what kind of ice shall we make? We can choose a water-ice, made with water, or an ice cream, made with cream. An ice cream is nicer, but costs more. We may like to make both kinds, or custard can form a substitute for the cream, and fresh fruit or jam can be added.

Water-ices can be made by mixing some syrup—sugar boiled in water in the proportion of 1 pound to 1 pint—with a fruit-juice from pressed strawberries or raspberries. There should be about twice as much syrup as fruit-juice. An ice cream without cream is made from a custard in which are 1 tablespoonful of condensed milk, $\frac{1}{2}$ pint of milk, the yolks of 2 eggs, and sugar. This may be flavored with vanilla or almond extract, and put into the freezer. Or we can take $\frac{1}{2}$ pint of the custard, add to it $\frac{1}{4}$ pound of jam, and if this contains seeds, rub it through a sieve and then freeze it. Coloring-paste will make the ice a deeper red.

HOW TO APPLY PAINT TO WOOD

PAINT is usually applied to wood surfaces which are exposed to the weather. However, paint should also add to the appearance of the window-box, bird-house, toy or building, as well as to protect the object from the weather. Of course, when exposed to the weather, paint will wear off in a few years. Sometimes it cracks and peels off soon after it is applied, either because of the poor quality of the paint or because of failure to prepare the surface properly before painting. In any case, the bare wood surface should not be exposed to the weather for any length of time.

In applying paint to new wood it is advisable to shellac all knots first. Then add a thin coat of boiled linseed oil and white lead to prime the wood. This coat is brushed carefully in order that all of the surface may be covered. After this has dried for about a day, be sure to putty all nail-holes and the like. Now apply the first coat of paint or color, which should be properly thinned. This will require two days for drying before applying the second coat of color, which is not thinned. A third coat may be added if a first-class job is required.

If you are applying paint on wood which has been previously painted you should first clean the surfaces with a stiff brush to remove any loose paint. If knots are exposed, these should next be shellacked. For this work the first coat of paint is thinned with oil. After this has dried for about two days, all defects should be puttied before the second coat is applied. As before, a third coat of paint may be applied if desired. Unpainted wood which has been exposed to the weather becomes porous, so a coat, or perhaps several coats, of filler should be applied before an attempt is made to paint it. Sometimes blistering of the painted surface occurs. When this happens it is due usually to the mistake of painting upon a wet surface or upon unseasoned wood. Coats of water paint and oil color prevent this.

THE NEXT THINGS TO MAKE AND TO DO ARE ON PAGE 4261.

THE GIRL WHO HELD THE FORT

MANY of us have heard or read of the dangers and hardships that our ancestors had to face as they tried to make a home or hold a settlement in this new country, then only a wilderness. Hunger and loneliness, hard toil and anxious waiting were among the least of their ills. Danger from Indians or wild beasts was an ever present trouble. The same is true of the early French settlers in Canada.

CONTINUED FROM 3811

Over two hundred years ago a log fort stood on the St. Lawrence River about twenty miles from Montreal. The land near the fort was cleared so that there should be no cover for attacking enemies, and the open space served as pasture land for the cattle, and fields for the garrison. Around the fort itself was built a strong palisade made from the trunks of trees stuck upright in the ground and set so closely together that not even a bullet could penetrate the wall. In front of the fort and joined to it by a covered alley was a blockhouse where guns and ammunition were kept.

The commander of the fort was M. de Verchères. His family consisted of his wife, his two little sons of ten and twelve, and his daughter Madeline, a girl of fourteen. The fort was not heavily garrisoned, for distances were great and there were but few soldiers in those early days. M. de Verchères' company consisted of only twenty men who with their wives and families lived within the palisade. Besides keeping the defenses in order, and occasionally making exploring or relief expeditions, the soldiers had to cultivate the fields, and get fish from the river and game from the forest, to support the settlement. In harvest time nearly everyone left the fort to work in the fields, for in the long hard winters food was very scarce, and often the boats from France failed to arrive.

It happened one day in harvest time that M. de Verchères and all the soldiers, except two on guard at the fort, were out in the fields. Though he appeared quite calm, the commander was uneasy and anxious on that beautiful day. Everything around seemed peaceful enough. The forest shone gorgeous in scarlet, green and gold, and the river rippled lazily in the warm air. But a fur-trapper going north had stopped at the fort the night before and had spoken beside the watch-fire of a rumor that the Iroquois were on the war-path. The man's words had been vague and it was unlikely that the Indians would dare to come so near to Montreal. Nevertheless, M. de Verchères' thoughts dwelt on the dark possibility, and he made up

4089

his mind to hurry the harvesting that he might keep watch within the fort.

He had hardly formed this determination when a scream pierced the summer stillness. One of the soldiers sprang high in the air and fell transfixed by an arrow. "The Iroquois! To the fort!" shouted M. de Verchères, but it was too late. In a long line that swiftly formed itself into a circle the yelling savages enveloped the harvesters. The unequal fight was soon over, the Frenchmen quickly overcome, and the thirsting savages turned toward the forest to take counsel before they attacked the fort.

Madeline had been standing by the river when she heard her father's cry. She alone of all the harvesters had time to obey, and she alone escaped. Besides herself there remained in the fort only the two soldiers, who had been on guard duty, an old man of eighty, some women and children and Madeline's two young brothers.

At the first sign of danger the soldiers fled to hiding. As the Indians delayed their attack, Madeline went round to inspect the defenses. She ordered the gaps in the stockade to be filled in and then ran down the covered alley-way to the blockhouse to look at the ammunition. There she found the two soldiers preparing to set light to the gunpowder and blow up the fort, rather than risk falling into the hands of the Indians. Her courage shamed them and they set themselves to defend the place. They and Madeline's two little brothers, who had been taught to shoot, opened fire from the loopholes.

"Crack! Crack! Crack!" the muskets rang out in quick succession. Through a loophole they could see the astonished savages scurrying back to the cover of the woods. Three forms lay still on the ground.

"The cannon," cried Madeline, and when it was loaded she fired it as a signal of distress. It frightened the savages, for they did not know that it was an appeal for help, which would be repeated from post to post till it reached the city of Montreal. How long would it be till help came? Could they deceive the Indians until that hour?

Hour after hour passed and there was not a sign of the Indians in the woodland beyond. All kept anxious watch, and once Madeline thought she saw the

leaves of a low bush part and a coppery face look out; but she was not certain.

Late in the afternoon the watchers in the fort saw a canoe coming around the bend of the river.

"Here come La Fontaine, the settler down the river, and his family," cried one of the children.

Madeline frowned anxiously.

"We can't let them be killed," she said. She clutched her gun. "I will go out and meet them."

Slipping through the gate, she marched boldly, her musket on her shoulder, down to the wharf. There was no sign of movement on the edge of the forest. The Indians evidently believed that she was trying to lead them into some kind of ambush.

"Welcome, M. de la Fontaine," said Madeline. "The Iroquois are in the wood! March up behind me to the fort and do not hurry."

The little procession reached the stockade in safety. Night came on, and had the Indians attacked them in the darkness, all would have been lost. Madeline ordered her elder brother and the soldiers to guard the women and children in the blockhouse, while she posted her young brother, the old man and herself as sentinels. All night long the sentries posted around the palisade cried at intervals: "All's well!" and the man in charge of the blockhouse answered: "All's well!" In this way they led the Iroquois to believe that there was a strong force in command of the fort and no attack was attempted. Once during the night Madeline's quick ears caught a soft sound of rubbing against the gates, and her heart began to beat faster.

"It sounds like the cattle come in from the field, Ma'm'selle," whispered old Gaston, who in his time had been a cowherd.

"I don't know," said Madeline doubtfully, "the Indians are full of tricks. They may be trying to fire the stockade. They might even be among the cows hidden in skins. Stay where you are. I will find out."

She crept around to the gate, and, opening it a little way, slipped out her hand. A cool, moist nose nuzzled into her palm. Reassured, she opened the gate a little wider, so that one cow at a time could slip in. "Bossy, bossy," she called softly, and the big animals lurched eagerly through the opening. As they passed her she touched the moist nose of each one with her hand to satisfy herself that there were no Indians hidden among them. They entered quietly, the soft pad-pad of their hoofs not distinguishable from the lapping of the waves, and noiselessly she closed and barred the gate behind them.

Day after day went by, until a whole week had passed. The Indians could now and then be seen watching the fort, but the place seemed too well guarded to attack, and they dared not venture out in the open to reconnoitre more closely. Big Eagle had done this on the second day, and that night Big Eagle's body had to be drawn back under cover of dark. So they watched and waited. The time seemed endless in the fort. All day and all night for seven horrible, anxious days, the watchers never left their posts. They snatched a little food as they stood at their posts, but as they ate it seemed to choke them.

On the seventh day, when they felt as though their powers of endurance could hold out no longer, help came. It was night when the succor arrived. Madeline sat in the living-room of the fort, her head on the table, fast asleep. Her gun lay across her arms. One of the sentinels called her.

"Ma'm'selle," he said, "I hear a noise down at the landing. Frenchmen or Indians are moving up the river."

"Which is it?" cried Madeline, springing to her feet, and hurrying out to the stockade.

Just then a loud knocking broke through the night sounds of the wilderness.

"Who goes there?" cried the sentinel.

"Who goes there?" cried Madeline.

"Frenchmen," was the response. "We bring you help."

Quickly the household gathered around and opened the gates. A young lieutenant marched in at the head of his company of soldiers. The relief was accomplished; the Indians had fled. The watchers in the fort could now rest secure. Madeline stepped forward, musket in hand, head high.

"Monsieur," she said formally, "I deliver the fort into your care. You have not arrived a moment too soon. My men are all worn out."

Then suddenly the strain of those awful seven days was too much for her.

She forgot that she had been the stern commander of a garrison, and remembered only that she was a little girl and very tired. With a weary movement, she put her head down in her hands, and began to cry. The lieutenant lifted her up in his arms and carried her into the house.

"You poor, brave, wonderful little girl!" he said. "It is time for you to go to bed."

That night M. de la Monnerie discovered traces of the Indians back in the forest, and he decided to dash out and surprise them.

Accordingly, as the cold gray dawn broke over the river and forest the soldiers issued from the fort at a run, firing and reloading to fire again as they advanced. The Indians were not prepared, for they had planned to begin the attack and, believing that they had no chance, they hurriedly retreated, carrying off with them about twenty prisoners. The little French force could not follow them into the wilderness, but shortly after their departure a band of friendly Indians visited the fort, and learning of the attack, hastened after the retreating foe and surprised them on the shores of Lake Champlain.

In the battle that followed many of the Iroquois were slain and the rest put to flight. The French prisoners were recovered and restored by the friendly Indians to their own people, who had given up all hopes of ever seeing them again.

The news of Madeline's bravery spread far and wide through Canada, for M. de la Monnerie wrote an elaborate report of it to the Governor of Montreal. The Viceroy himself wrote her a letter, and her heroism was rewarded by a pension. She grew into a brave woman, and later had yet another adventure with the Iroquois, for her father's seigniory was directly in the way of the Iroquois when they marched against the settlers, and for that reason the fort was called Castle Dangerous. This time Madeline, rifle in hand, saved the life of Monsieur de la Perade, and later she married the man whom she had so gallantly rescued.

In Canadian history she is still remembered as the heroine of Castle Dangerous. In the wigwams of the Iroquois, the squaws tell the little Indian boys of the white maiden who with an army of three men had kept the fort for seven days against the whole tribe.

THE MAN WHO SAVED ST. HELIER

THE people in the Isle of Jersey, one of the islands in the English Channel off the coast of France, were celebrating the anniversary of the coronation of King George III on June 4, 1804. Everybody was rejoicing, and all the morning royal salutes had been fired from the big guns in the forts. One of these was the New Fort, which stood above St. Helier, the town shown in the picture below.

The guns were fired by means of long pieces of stick which had been dipped in brimstone, and looked something like giant matches. When the saluting was over, the unused "matches" were taken back to the great magazine, where hundreds of barrels of gunpowder were stored. The magazine was then locked up by the firing-party, and the keys were taken away by Captain Salmon, the artillery officer.

Nothing more was thought about it till the evening, when the sentries, going their rounds, noticed smoke coming out under the door. They at once ran to give the alarm, shouting: "Fire!" The signal officer, whose name was Lys, ran down from his station at the watch-house on the hill, and found that smoke was already pouring from both ends of the powder magazine.

Two carpenters named Edward and Thomas Touzel were with the signal officer, and Thomas was asked to carry the news at once to the Commander-in-Chief, and to bring back the keys of the magazine as quickly as possible.

As he was starting, he urged his brother Edward to go with him, or at the very least to keep out of danger; but Edward replied: "We have all got to die some day, and I mean to save the magazine if I can."

He then called to some soldiers to lend a hand, and one of them named Ponteney answered: "I am ready to take the risk."

Touzel then seized a strong iron bar, wrenched open the iron railings fixed round the magazine, and after great efforts succeeded in forcing open the door of the building, from which dense clouds of smoke came rolling forth. Great piles of the sulphur matches and many of the ammunition cases had caught fire, and the flames were already curling round the great barrels in which the gunpowder was stored. It seemed that every moment a tremendous explosion must take place and that everyone standing near would probably be blown to pieces.

But Edward Touzel, though he fully realized the danger, was not the man to draw back. Rushing in, he caught up great armfuls of the burning matches and began to throw them to Lys and Ponteney, who in their turn threw them farther away from the entrance.

Touzel continued doing this till the skin of his face and hands had been badly burned, and he was almost choked by the dense smoke. By this time soldiers were running from all directions bringing pails of water, and the fire was at last conquered. If Touzel had waited until the keys had been brought from the governor's house, the magazine would have blown up, wrecking the town. This would have been a shocking end for the celebration.

THE NEXT STORY OF GOLDEN DEEDS IS ON PAGE 4223.

St. Helier, the principal town on the island of Jersey in the English Channel, is a very old town. Part of its church was built in the fourteenth century, and an ancient chapel, or cell, in the ninth or tenth. Two forts, Fort Regent and Elizabeth Castle, guard the harbor. At Elizabeth Castle, in 1649, Prince Charles, who was then living there, was proclaimed Charles II of England.

The miracle of spring.

THE LIFE OF A TREE

CONTINUED FROM 4028

THE crowning glory of the plant world is the tree. Although there is really nothing different in kind between the little plants in our flower beds and the majestic trees of the forest, we cannot help regarding the tree with a respect we do not give to the smaller plant that we can tread underfoot.

The majesty of the spreading oak and chestnut, the dainty loveliness of the lilac and laburnum, the sombre dignity of the cedar and yew, seem to place these trees above the common run of flowering plants. In fact, their story is the story of the daisy or the dandelion once again.

A little seed is planted in the ground and soon begins to throw out roots downward and a stem upward. The stem grows, and branches appear bearing leaves and flowers and fruits. When the fruits containing the seeds fall on the ground they also germinate, and once again the whole process is repeated.

For convenience it is common to speak of herbs, shrubs and trees, but there is no sharp distinction dividing one class from the others. Shrubs differ from trees only in their size; or in having several stems which proceed from the ground, or near it; or in having much-forked stems.

Although it is generally true that trees have usually stout main trunks from which smaller and more slender branches spread out, the main stem of a tree is sometimes short, with branches longer than itself. A shrub may really be described as a miniature tree. On the other hand, trees which in favorable circumstances grow to towering heights often become mere shrubs when found in the Far North or high on mountain slopes. On high mountains, for instance, the mountain-ash, which in the lowlands may become a really fine tree, is reduced to a low creeping shrub only a few inches high.

Many a man walks through a wood or up a fine avenue of tall trees without giving a thought to the giant plants around him. If he does think of them at all, he does not think of them as things which are as truly alive as himself. Yet a tree is a living and breathing creature. It has a real circulation, digests and assimilates its food, rears a family as truly and beautifully as any other form of life. It has also the power of adapting itself to its surroundings in a wonderful way. It may lack will-power and intelligence, a nervous system and the power of locomotion, but in all the other elements that make up a living being the tree performs vital acts as truly as the body of a man. This may seem surprising, but it is nevertheless a fact.

The tree, like other plants, takes in air through its leaves. It enters through tiny openings on the under-

sides of the leaves. Once inside the leaf, the elements that make up the air are separated from one another.

The carbon dioxid is used in sunlight in the manufacture of solid substance, while the unused oxygen is given off again to the air. This process is called photosynthesis, because it is a union, or synthesis, of material in light. The oxygen taken in is used by the leaves, as by every living cell in all parts of the plant, in respiration, and the unused carbon dioxid is given back to the air. The process of respiration is the same in plants as in animals—the union of oxygen with oxidizable materials. Respiration and photosynthesis take place together *in sunlight,* but photosynthesis is the more vigorous; it does not take place at all in the dark.

The tree has a circulation as truly as man himself. While it does not move so fast as ours and does not go round and round as the result of pumping by a heart, the circulation system of the tree operates from the tiniest root-hair to the most distant leaf, and back again. On the upward flow the circulation goes on through the sapwood, traveling from cell to cell, from the small roots to the larger ones, then into the trunk and branches and leaves. From the leaf, where it is transformed into tree food, the circulation travels down once more through the cells of the inner bark on the way to the smallest roots, building up layers of cells all the time.

HOW SUNLIGHT HELPS A TREE TO DIGEST ITS FOOD

Like all other living beings, the tree produces young trees to carry on the race. It arranges that its young shall have as good a start in life as possible. In some cases, as in the sycamore and maple, the seeds are given wings to carry them far enough from the parent tree to find sustenance in the soil. In other cases, as in the coconut, the seed containing the embryo tree is carefully protected from danger and from enemies of all kinds by being wrapped up in armor. In some cases the male and female flowers are found on the same tree. At other times the two parents are on separate trees.

The way in which the tree adapts itself to its surroundings is just as wonderful as the way in which man adapts himself to varying conditions. If water is scarce, the roots go down deeper

and deeper; if nourishment is poor, the roots stretch out farther and farther, traveling backward and forward, above and below and around obstacles, in their search for what will be good for the tree. If the trees are crowded together, they reach higher and higher, and their branches, instead of growing outward, rise almost perpendicularly to reach the sunshine. If several trees are grouped together, they grow on one side much more than on the other, in order to accommodate themselves to their fellows. If the situation is windy, the tree takes firmer hold of the ground with its roots.

THE BATTLE OF LIFE WHICH EVERY TREE MUST FIGHT

It is good for us that the tree is such a sturdy fighter in the battle of life. It can meet and defeat most of its enemies, except man. It may bend before the wind, but it rarely breaks; snow and frost it can keep out; animals and birds it can often resist; and in the tougher fight against its own relatives—like the ivy which tries to strangle it—it puts up a good fight and sometimes wins. Man can beat the tree every time, but even man, in destroying trees on a large scale, does so at his own peril.

Most of the forests of the world are self-planted. In Europe there are miles and miles of trees planted in rows, but the area is small compared with the natural forests. In North America there are a few planted forests, and in the remainder of the world almost nothing has been done. Man has cut down forests again and again, and in some countries has brought ruin and disaster upon himself, for the forests have been the very life of certain areas.

The trees of the forest shield the soil from the hot rays of the sun which would otherwise dry up the pastures so that no herbage could grow. They also preserve the springs in the earth. Once the Mediterranean lands were far more fertile than they are now, and there were far more springs; but man came with his ax, which he laid to the root of the tree and cut down the forests.

THE FORESTS THAT HELPED TO MAKE THE LAND FERTILE

Wherever these large and majestic forests stood on the upper slopes of the mountains they prevented waste of water, protected the soil, warded off the chilly blasts, and made rich cultivation possible on the lower slopes. When the trees were removed, the icy blasts swept over the fields, the water dried up, the soil was blown or washed away by the storms. In many areas cultivation became impossible. What had been a garden became as bare and silent as the desert.

At one time the mountain slopes of India were covered with magnificent forests, but the trees were cut down. Little did the people realize the evils that would follow such a course; they thought only of present profit. Those idle-looking trees were, in fact, the most useful servants of India. In the rainy season they stored up millions and millions of drops of water to refresh the earth in the dry season. Now, when the rain falls, there are few forests to catch and store it; the water evaporates or runs away rapidly to the sea, and many large areas are, as a consequence, dry and barren.

WHY THE TREES ARE AMONG THE BEST FRIENDS OF MAN

Only in recent times has man begun to realize what true friends the trees are. It is true that without trees it would be difficult for civilization to exist. What would life be without wood for our floors, doors, furniture, carts, railway carriages, pencils, mallets, rules, boxes and telegraph poles? Where should we be without paper for our newspapers, magazines, books, parcels and letters? The chair in which we sit, the table at which we write, the floor on which we stand, the paper on the walls of the room, are all the product of the tree. Gas is now made from wood, and tanning materials are obtained from the bark.

What a story the doors of many an old building in Europe could tell of the days when they grew in a forest—a tale of birds that nested in their branches long before the Thirty Years' War, of the woodpecker that tapped at their bark long before Shakespeare walked to London.

THE FALLEN TREE THAT RISES INTO NEW LIFE

No tree ever dies, in the sense that it is done with. When certain oaks were cut down in the old days they rose into new life as fighting ships. Many a fallen giant lives again in a cathedral or a palace. Even if a tree is struck by lightning, and lies rotting on the ground, its work is not done, for it goes on feeding the soil from which will rise its children in new glory to take its place.

We have a bookshelf many, many years old. It is not impossible that it may once have been a tiny seed carried by a bird that was fed by St. Francis of Assisi. We have a chair that was once an acorn which may have fallen from its branch and struck Robin Hood. Only the other day the writer of these words was eating mulberries from a tree planted by Milton. Shakespeare and Dante and Goethe wrote their masterpieces at tables made from trees. Even the leaves that fall in autumn do not cease to exist; they continue their usefulness, giving fresh life to the soil and helping the tree from which they have come to increase in health and vigor.

How thrilling would be the story of the trees if they could only speak! Think of the giant sequoias of California, with their thousands of years of life! Some of them may have been well grown when Christ was born. When the first Londoner built his hut on the banks of the Thames they were old. Or think of the venerable catalpa tree in Gray's Inn Gardens, London, which, according to the old tradition of the Inn, was brought from the West Indies by Sir Walter Raleigh and planted where it is by Francis Bacon.

THE MANY TREES THAT MUST DIE SO THAT OTHERS MAY LIVE

The life-and-death struggle among the trees is as fierce as among the animals, and is constantly going on. One of the greatest authorities in the United States forestry service states that a forest at maturity contains scarcely five per cent of all the trees that have started life there. Yet the death of the other ninety-five per cent is a necessary condition to the development of the survivors. In some natural pine forests, during the age between twenty and eighty years, over four thousand trees on an acre die, whereas at the age between eighty and a hundred years only three hundred trees an acre die. With some trees this natural dying-out with age proceeds faster than with others. Thus in pine, birch, aspen, and all other species which demand a great deal of light, the death-rate is enormous. With spruce, beech, fir, and species which are satisfied with less light, the process is less rapid.

The growth of a tree is very wonderful. Except in the buds, leaves, fruit, and twigs less than a year old, the new material that results from growth is deposited in a thin coat over the whole tree between the wood and the bark. There are two layers in this coat, separated by a third one called the cambium, in which the actual making of the new substance goes on. The inner side of the cambium layer forms new wood, and the outer layer new bark. In addition to the true cambium, which forms both wood and bark, there is another cambium which makes the corky outer bark and nothing else. This cork cambium may encircle the whole tree like the true cambium, or may form little separate films in the bark. In both cases it dies from time to time, and is re-formed nearer the wood.

THE WONDERFUL LIFE AND POWER OF A GROWING TREE

Wood is chiefly made of small tubes or cells of various kinds which have special uses in the life of the tree. Some cells convey water from the roots to the crown, others store away digested food, and others strengthen the structure of the wood and hold it together. Not all trees, of course, are alike in structure; the wood of the coniferous, or cone-bearing, trees is much simpler than that of trees like the oak and maple. There are fewer kinds of cells, but in each case some of the cells have thick walls and small openings, while others have wide openings and thin walls.

In climates which have regularly a season of growth and a season of rest each year, the cells of the new wood formed at the inner surface of the cambium are arranged in a definite way. In the spring, when growth begins and fresh leaves and twigs are put out, much water is needed in the crown of the tree to supply these new moist green parts. Water rises in most trees through the new layers of the wood, and especially through the last ring. The result is that the tree at first makes thin-walled cells with wide openings, so that the water can rise rapidly; but later, when there is less demand for water, and there is an abundance of digested food available to supply the necessary building material, the cells formed are thick-walled and have small openings. That explains why the summer wood in each year's growth is heavier and stronger than the spring wood. In some trees this difference is quite easy to see.

It is a wonderful thing to think that water rises to the top of the tallest trees, even in the giants of California and Australia; but exactly how this happens is still something of a mystery to science.

The rings of growth in the trunk of a tree are spoken of as annual rings, for, so long as the tree goes on living healthily, a fresh ring will be formed each year. Sometimes, for some reason or other, the growth of a tree is interrupted and begins again during the same season, and then two false rings appear; but they are not hard to detect and to distinguish from ordinary annual rings, for they are much thinner and do not always extend right round the tree. A drought or a big attack by caterpillars may lead to interrupted growth and give rise to the false rings.

WHY A HOLLOW TREE CAN STILL GO ON LIVING

An annual layer once formed does not change in size or position during the remaining life of the tree, though it becomes covered by younger layers. Thus, if a nail is driven into the trunk, say, nine feet from the ground, it will remain at that height, though in the course of years it may have become overgrown by a score or two of layers of annual growth. In most trees, however, the wood gets darker and harder as time goes on. The cell openings become choked, and sap can no longer run through them. The wood is then no longer living sapwood, but dead heartwood, for it has nothing to do with growth. It is still useful to the tree, however, for it forms a strong framework which helps to support the living parts of the tree. That explains why a hollow tree can still go on living and produce many leaves, though the trunk is a mere shell.

WHAT IT IS THAT HAPPENS WHEN A PIECE OF WOOD IS BURNED

The wood is made up chiefly of carbon, oxygen and hydrogen; and when perfectly dry, about half its weight is carbon, and half oxygen and hydrogen, in almost the same proportions as in water. It contains also about one part in a hundred by weight of earthy matter, and a similar proportion of nitrogen. When the wood is burned, all these disappear into the air except the earthy matter.

In the old days a man who planted a tree was looked on as a benefactor of his fellows, and he is still a true benefactor of future generations.

THE NEXT STORY OF PLANT LIFE IS ON PAGE 4245.

THE TREE THAT IS GROWN FOR AN INSECT

The heart-shaped leaves of the mulberry, which do not appear till May, provide food for silkworms.

Mulberry flowers grow in short, irregular catkins, and are not attractive, but the fruit is pleasant.

This mulberry is not a native American tree, but has been introduced from the Far East. In the south of France large plantations of mulberry trees are grown to provide food for silkworms. The silkworm does not like the leaves of our native mulberry trees.

THE POPLAR THAT GROWS LIKE A GIANT

A Lombardy poplar covered with leaves is a fine sight as it sways in the breeze like a plume.

The flowers are in the form of catkins, but produce no seeds. Only staminate flowers grow here.

Although the Lombardy poplar was brought to Western Europe and thence to America from Lombardy, Italy, and so received its name, it is really a native of the Himalaya Mountains. It grows very rapidly, and a man who plants a cutting may live to see it become 125 feet high.

THE WHITE POPLAR WITH SILVERY LEAVES

The purple catkins of the white poplar grow several inches long.

The leaves are very light on the under-side, owing to a kind of down that covers them and makes the tree look silvery white.

The leaves of the white poplar, where they join the stalks, are flattened at the sides instead of top and bottom, and when the wind catches the tree it blows the leaves from side to side, instead of up and down as in other trees. The wood of the white poplar does not burn easily.

THE SYCAMORE MAPLE

The sycamore maple is called "the false plane," from the shape of its leaves. A sugary juice comes from them, and sugar has been made from the sap. The flowers are yellowish green.

This maple has been introduced from Europe, where it is called the sycamore. It will flourish even on the seacoast, where the gales and salt air kill other trees. The sycamore of the Bible is really a fig tree, and the tree we usually call the sycamore is the plane tree, or buttonwood.

THE SAD AND SORROWFUL WILLOW TREE

The leaves of the common willow, like those of most of its relatives, are long and lance-shaped.

At the top are flowers of the white willow, or golden osier; below is the sallow, or goat-willow.

A great botanist has called the willows the "troublesome family," because the different kinds are so difficult to distinguish. But most of them, like the white willow shown here, are graceful trees or shrubs. One of the family, which originally came from Asia, is called the "weeping willow."

THE ALDER, THE TREE OF THE RIVERSIDE

The leaves of the alder are rather sticky to the touch and are dark green in color. The long hanging catkins are yellow, and are followed in the autumn by cone-like fruit.

The best charcoal for gunpowder is obtained from alder wood. This wood is also valuable for use where it is to remain under water, as in piers; and for this reason the French make their sabots of alder. Alders flourish in moist places, such as river-banks. Dyed black, alder wood is an excellent imitation of ebony. This is the European black alder, often found in our parks.

THE LINDEN, THE TREE OF THE BEE

The heart-shaped leaves of the linden are among the first leaves to fall. Cattle are fond of them.

Clusters of flowers appear when the tree is covered with leaves. Swarms of bees visit them.

The linden tree, which is frequently seen in parks and gardens, was brought from Europe, where it is quite common. The American linden, better known as the basswood, is also a tall handsome tree. The leaves are almost the same in shape, but our tree is taller and heavier.

The "rosy plumelets" of the larch, as Tennyson calls the flowers, vary in color from pink to purple, though they are usually reddish purple. The leaves grow in tufts; but, unlike other trees that bear cones, the larch loses its leaves in winter.

The larch is a mountain tree. In the Alps, forests of larch grow 6,000 feet above the sea. The European larch, shown here, also grows in this country. The tamarack is our best-known native larch. The tree becomes a fine green pyramid a hundred feet high, and the wood is used for telegraph poles.

THE CEDAR, "THE GLORY OF LEBANON"

The leaves of the cedar grow in tufts like those of the larch, and remain upon the tree four or five years. These leaves are about an inch long.

The flowers grow at the ends of short branchlets, and the brown cones are shaped like bananas. They remain on the tree for several years.

All kinds of superstitions have grown up round the cedar, "the glory of Lebanon," as Isaiah calls it. One is that the Cross was made of cedar wood, but there is no evidence of this. The name cedar means "power," and refers to the strength of the wood. Our common "red cedar" is a juniper.

THE NATIONAL TREE OF SCOTLAND

The slender leaves of the Scotch pine remain on the tree for two years. The first year they are a light bluish green, which gradually changes to dark green. The fallen leaves kill other plants.

This sturdy tree, known as the Scotch pine, is common in Scotland. Its pollen falls in large quantities and looks like sulphur. When, in 1902, people found the pollen lying thick on the ground, they wrote to newspapers that sulphur from the volcanic eruption at St. Vincent had fallen in England.

THE YEW TREE OF THE CHURCHYARD

The leathery leaves of the yew are poisonous to cattle and human beings, although the berries are not harmful. When a yew hedge has been cut, and the leaves thrown aside, cattle have been found dead, from eating the leaves. This picture shows the leaves and the small staminate flowers.

The yew tree may grow to a large size and live to a great age. The famous yew tree in the cloister of Muckross Abbey, on the Killarney Lakes, was planted when the abbey was built in the fifteenth century, and there is a tree in Perthshire, Scotland, which is nearly two thousand years old.

A CATHEDRAL AISLE OF TREES

You can learn much of Gothic architecture in our book and can see many examples of the pointed arch, which is one of the marks by which we recognize this style. Someone said long ago that men got the idea from the arches made by the branches of trees.

HENRY HUDSON'S LAST VOYAGE

IS anything in all the history of the sea sadder than the story of Henry Hudson turned adrift by his cruel crew with his little boy and two faithful men? Here a splendid American, Dr. Henry van Dyke, imagines Hudson talking in his boat on Hudson Bay on that last day that history heard of him, June 22, 1611. We seem to catch the throb in Henry Hudson's voice as he says, "My little shipmate, come and lean your head against my knee." Hudson's name is written on the map of the world—in Hudson Bay, Hudson River, Hudson Island and Hudson Bay Territories.

ONE sail in sight upon the lonely sea,
And only one! For never ship but mine
Has dared these waters. We were first,
My men, to battle in between the bergs
And floes to these wide waves.
This gulf is mine!
I name it! and that flying sail is mine!
And there, hull-down below that flying sail,
The ship that staggers home is mine, mine, mine!
My ship Discoverie!

       The sullen dogs
Of mutineers, the bitches' whelps that snatched
Their food and bit the hand that nourished them,
Have stolen her. You ingrate Henry Greene,
I picked you from the gutter of Houndsditch,
And paid your debts, and kept you in my house,
And brought you here to make a man of you!
You, Robert Juet, ancient, crafty man,
Toothless and tremulous, how many times
Have I employed you as a master's mate
To give you bread? And you, Abacuck Prickett,
You sailor-clerk, you salted Puritan,
You knew the plot and silently agreed,
Salving your conscience with a pious lie!

CONTINUED FROM 4036

Yes, all of you—
hounds, rebels, thieves! Bring back
My ship!

Too late—I rave—they cannot hear
My voice: and, if they heard, a drunken laugh
Would be their answer; for their minds have caught
The fatal firmness of the fool's resolve,
That looks like courage, but is only fear.
They'll blunder on, and lose my ship, and drown,
Or blunder home to England and be hanged.
Their skeletons will rattle in the chains
Of some tall gibbet on the Channel cliffs,
While passing mariners look up and say:
"Those are the rotten bones of Hudson's men
Who left their captain in the frozen North!"

O God of justice, why hast thou ordained
Plans of the wise and actions of the brave
Dependent on the aid of fools and cowards?

Look—there she goes—her topsails in the sun
Gleam from the ragged ocean edge, and drop
Clean out of sight! So let the traitors go
Clean out of mind! We'll think of braver things!

Come closer in the boat, my friends. John
    King,
You take the tiller, keep her head nor'west.
You, Philip Staffe, the only one who chose
Freely to share our little shallop's fate
Rather than travel in the hell-bound ship—
Too good an English sailor to desert
Your crippled comrades—try to make them
    rest
More easy on the thwarts. And John, my son,
My little shipmate, come and lean your head
Against my knee. Do you remember still
The April morn in Ethelburga's church,
Five years ago, when side by side we kneeled
To take the Sacrament with all our men
Before the Hopewell left St. Catherine's Docks
On our first voyage? It was then I vowed
My sailor-soul and yours to search the sea
Until we found the water-path that leads
From Europe into Asia.

                    I believe
That God has poured the ocean round His
    world,
Not to divide, but to unite the lands.
And all the English captains that have dared
In little ships to plough uncharted waves—
Davis and Drake, Hawkins and Frobisher,
Raleigh and Gilbert—all the other names—
Are written in the chivalry of God
As men who served His purpose. I would
    claim
A place among that knighthood of the sea;
And I have earned it, though my quest should
    fail,
For, mark me well, the honour of our life
Derives from this: to have a certain aim
Before us always, which our will must seek
Amid the peril of uncertain ways.
Then, though we miss the goal, our search is
    crowned
With courage, and we find along our path
A rich reward of unexpected things.
Press towards the aim: take fortune as it
    fares!

I know not why, but something in my heart
Has always whispered: "Westward seek your
    goal!"
Three times they sent me east, but still I
    turned
The bowsprit west, and felt along the floes
Of ruttling ice along the Greenland coast,
And down the rugged shore of Newfound-
    land,
And past the rocky capes and wooded bays
Where Gosnold sailed—like one who feels his
    way
With outstretched hands across a darkened
    room,
I groped among the inlets and the isles
To find the passage to the Land of Spice.
I have not found it yet—but I have found
Things worth the finding!

                    Son, have you forgot
Those mellow autumn days, two years ago,
When first we sent our little ship Half Moon—
The flag of Holland floating at her peak—
Across a sandy bar, and sounded in
Among the channels to a goodly bay

Where all the navies of the world could ride?
A fertile island that the red man called
Manhattan lay above the bay: the land
Around was beautiful and friendly fair.
But never land was fair enough to hold
The seaman from the calling of the sea.
And so we bore to westward of the isle,
Along a mighty inlet, where the tide
Was troubled by a downward-flowing flood
That seemed to come from far away—perhaps
From some mysterious gulf of Tartary?
Inland we held our course; by palisades
Of naked rock; by rolling hills adorned
With forests rich in timber for great ships;
Through narrows where the mountains shut
    us in
With frowning cliffs that seemed to bar the
    stream;
And then through open reaches where the
    banks
Sloped to the water gently, with their fields
Of corn and lentils smiling in the sun.
Ten days we voyaged through that placid land,
Until we came to shoals, and sent a boat
Upstream to find—what I already knew—
We travelled on a river, not a strait.

But what a river! God has never poured
A stream more royal through a land more rich.
Even now I see it flowing in my dream,
While coming ages people it with men
Of manhood equal to the river's pride.
I see the wigwams of the red men changed
To ample houses, and the tiny plots
Of maize and green tobacco broadened out
To prosperous farms, that spread o'er hill and
    dale
The many-coloured mantle of their crops.
I see the terraced vineyard on the slope
Where now the fox-grape loops its tangled
    vine,
And cattle feeding where the red deer roam,
And wild bees gathered into busy hives
To store the silver comb with golden sweet;
And all the promised land begins to flow
With milk and honey. Stately manors rise
Along the banks, and castles top the hills,
And little villages grow populous with trade,
Until the river runs as proudly as the Rhine,
The thread that links a hundred towns and
    towers!

Now, looking deeper in my dreams, I see
A mighty city covering the isle
They call Manhattan, equal in her state
To all the older capitals of earth—
The gateway city of a golden world—
A city girt with masts, and crowned with
    spires,
And swarming with a million busy men,
While to her open door across the bay
The ships of all the nations flock like doves.
My name will be remembered there, the world
Will say, "This river and this isle were found
By Henry Hudson, on his way to seek
The North-West Passage."

                    Yes, I seek it still—
My great adventure and my guiding star!
For look ye, friends, our voyage is not done;
We hold by hope as long as life endures!

Somewhere among these floating fields of ice,
Somewhere along this westward widening bay,
Somewhere beneath this luminous northern
night,
The channel opens to the Farthest East—
I know it—and some day a little ship
Will push her bowsprit in, and battle through!
And why not ours—to-morrow—who can tell?
The lucky chance awaits the fearless heart!
These are the longest days of all the year;
The world is round and God is everywhere,
And while our shallop floats we still can steer.
So point her up, John King, nor'west by north,
We'll keep the honour of a certain aim
Amid the peril of uncertain ways,
And sail ahead, and leave the rest to God.

THE FLY-AWAY HORSE*

OH, a wonderful horse is the Fly-Away
    Horse,
    Perhaps you have seen him before;
Perhaps while you slept his shadow has swept
    Through the moonlight that floats on the
        floor.
For it's only at night, when the stars twinkle
        bright,
    That the Fly-Away Horse, with a neigh
And a pull at his rein and a toss of his mane,
    Is up on his heels and away!
        The moon in the sky,
        As he gallopeth by,
    Cries: "Oh! what a marvellous sight!"
        And the stars in dismay
        Hide their faces away
    In the lap of old Grandmother Night.

It is yonder, out yonder, the Fly-Away Horse
    Speedeth ever and ever away—
Over meadows and lanes, over mountains and
        plains,
    Over streamlets that sing at their play;
And over the sea like a ghost sweepeth he,
    While the ships they go sailing below,
And he speedeth so fast that the men at the
        mast
    Adjudge him some portent of woe.
        "What ho there!" they cry,
        As he flourishes by
    With a whisk of his beautiful tail;
        And the fish in the sea
        Are as scared as can be,
    From the nautilus up to the whale!

And the Fly-Away Horse seeks those far-
        away lands
    You little folk dream of at night—
Where candy-trees grow, and honey brooks
        flow,
    And corn-fields with popcorn are white;
And the beasts in the wood are ever so good
    To children who visit them there—
What glory astride of a lion to ride,
    Or to wrestle around with a bear!

* From Poems of Eugene Field, copyright, 1910, by
Julia S. Field; published by Charles Scribner's Sons. By
permission of the publishers.

The monkeys, they say:
    "Come on, let us play,"
And they frisk in the coconut trees;
    While the parrots that cling
    To the peanut vines sing
Or converse with comparative ease!

Off scamper to bed—you shall ride him to-
        night,
    For as soon as you've fallen asleep,
With a jubilant neigh he will bear you away
    Over forest and hillside and deep!
But tell us, my dear, all you see and you hear
    In those beautiful lands over there,
Where the Fly-Away Horse wings his far-
        away course
    With the wee one consigned to his care.
        Then grandma will cry
        In amazement: "Oh, my!"
    And she'll think it could never be so;
        And only we two
        Shall know it is true—
    You and I, little precious, shall know!

SLAVE AND EMPEROR

When the Flag of the Free flew over Nazareth after the
World War, Alfred Noyes, one of the most famous of the
young English poets, put his solemn thoughts in stately
verse. He calls his poem Slave and Emperor because he
remembers that the war-makers of Germany called Christianity a creed for slaves, and his poem begins by telling
how the Emperor "mocked at Nazareth in his almighty
hour." Finely contrasted with the Emperor's pride is
the humility of Christ, whom Mr. Noyes pictures as the
slave. The three following verses are taken from the
poem.

I HEAR a shout that moves the earth, a cry
        that wakes the dead.
    Will no one tell me whence they come?
    For all my messengers are dumb.
What power is this that comes to birth, and
        breaks my power? he said.

Then all around his foundering guns, though
        dawn was now not far,
    The darkness filled with a living fear,
    That whispered at the Emperor's ear,
"The armies of the dead draw near, beneath
        an Eastern star."

The trumpet blows in Nazareth, the slave is
        risen again,
    Across the bitter wastes of death
    The horsemen ride from Nazareth,
And the power we mocked as wasted breath
        returns in power to reign,
Rides on in white through Nazareth to save
        His world again.

FOOT SOLDIERS

'TIS all the way to Toe-town,
    Beyond the Knee-high hill,
That Baby has to travel down
    To see the soldiers drill.

One, two, three, four, five, a-row—
    A captain and his men—
And on the other side, you know,
    Are six, seven, eight, nine, ten.
                    —JOHN BANISTER TABB.

THE DOUGLAS TRAGEDY

This is an old ballad dating from very early times. It is known in Denmark and in other European countries, and the Scotch have localized it as happening in Black-House on Douglas Burn.

"RISE up, rise up, now, Lord Douglas," she says,
  "And put on your armor so bright;
Let it never be said, that a daughter of thine
  Was married to a lord under night.

"Rise up, rise up, my seven bold sons,
  And put on your armor so bright,
And take better care of your youngest sister,
  For your eldest's awa the last night."

He's mounted her on a milk-white steed,
  And himself on a dapple gray,
With a bugelet horn hung down by his side,
  And lightly they rode away.

Lord William lookit o'er his left shoulder,
  To see what he could see,
And there he spied her seven brethren bold,
  Come riding over the lea.

"Light down, light down, Lady Marg'ret," he said,
  "And hold my steed in your hand,
Until that against your seven brothers bold,
  And your father, I mak' a stand."

She held his steed in her milk-white hand,
  And never shed one tear,
Until that she saw her seven brethren fa',
  And her father hard fighting, who loved her so dear.

"O hold your hand, Lord William!" she said,
  "For your strokes they are wond'rous sair;
True lovers I can get many a ane,
  But a father I can never get mair."

O she ta'en out her handkerchief,
  It was o' the holland sae fine,
And aye she dight her father's bloody wounds,
  That were redder than the wine.

"O chuse, O chuse, Lady Marg'ret," he said,
  "O whether will ye gang or bide?"
"I'll gang, I'll gang, Lord William," she said,
  "For ye have left me no other guide."

He's lifted her on a milk-white steed
  And himself on a dapple gray,
With a bugelet horn hung down by his side,
  And slowly they baith rade away.

O they rade on, and on they rade,
  And a' by the light of the moon,
Until they came to youn wan water,
  And there they lighted down.

They lighted down to tak a drink
  Of the spring that ran sae clear;
And down the stream ran his gude heart's blood,
  And sair she gan to fear.

"Hold up, hold up, Lord William," she says,
  "For I fear that you are slain!"
"'Tis naething but the shadow of my scarlet cloak,
  That shines in the water sae plain."

O they rade on, and on they rade,
  And a' by the light of the moon,
Until they cam' to his mother's ha' door,
  And there they lighted down.

"Get up, get up, lady mother," he says,
  "Get up, and let me in!—
Get up, get up, lady mother," he says,
  "For this night my fair ladye I've win.

"O mak my bed, lady mother," he says,
  "O mak it braid and deep!
And lay Lady Marg'ret close at my back,
  And the sounder I will sleep."

Lord William was dead lang ere midnight,
  Lady Marg'ret lang ere day—
And all true lovers that go thegither,
  May they have mair luck than they!

Lord William was buried in St. Mary's kirk,
  Lady Marg'ret in Mary's quire;
Out o' the lady's grave grew a bonny red rose,
  And out o' the knight's a brier.

And they twa met, and they twa plat',
  And fain they wad be near;
And a' the warld might ken right weel,
  They were twa lovers dear.

And bye and rade the Black Douglas,
  And wow but he was rough!
For he pull'd up the bonny brier,
  And flanged in St. Mary's loch.

LA BELLE DAME SANS MERCI

Some young readers may have seen Rossetti's picture of Keats's Belle Dame accompanied by the young knight whom, by her fatal charms, she has lured from honor and duty, and left to a strange, sad fate.

AH, what can ail thee, wretched wight,
  Alone and palely loitering:
The sedge is wither'd from the lake,
  And no birds sing.

Ah, what can ail thee, wretched wight,
  So haggard and so woe-begone?
The squirrel's granary is full,
  And the harvest's done.

I see a lily on thy brow,
  With anguish moist and fever dew;
And on thy cheek a fading rose
  Fast withereth too.

I met a lady in the meads,
  Full beautiful, a faery's child;
Her hair was long, her foot was light,
  And her eyes were wild.

I set her on my pacing steed,
  And nothing else saw all day long,
For sideways would she lean, and sing
  A faery's song.

I made a garland for her head,
  And bracelets too, and fragrant zone;
She look'd at me as she did love,
  And made sweet moan.

She found me roots of relish sweet,
  And honey wild, and manna dew,
And sure in language strange she said,
  "I love thee true."

She took me to her elfin grot,
  And there she gazed and sighed deep;
And there I shut her wild wild eyes—
  So kiss'd to sleep.

And there we slumber'd on the moss,
  And there I dream'd—Ah! woe betide!
And latest dream I ever dream'd,
  On the cold hill side.

I saw pale kings, and princes too,
  Pale warriors, death-pale were they all;
Who cried—"La Belle Dame sans Merci
  Hath thee in thrall!"

I saw their starved lips in the gloam,
  With horrid warning gapèd wide,
And I awoke, and found me here
  On the cold hill side.

And this is why I sojourn here,
  Alone and palely loitering,
Though the sedge is wither'd from the lake,
  And no birds sing.

ODE TO THE WEST WIND

This is a very fine example of a lyric—that is, a poem which expresses the poet's own thoughts and feelings with spontaneity and unreserve. Shelley's sensitive spirit was depressed by some cause or other, and he appeals to the West Wind, who will upbear a dead leaf, a swift cloud or a wave, to lift him, too, above the thorns of life and scatter his thoughts abroad like the sound of a great trumpet blowing.

O WILD West Wind, thou breath of Autumn's being,
Thou, from whose unseen presence the leaves dead
Are driven, like ghosts from an enchanter fleeing,

Yellow, and black, and pale, and hectic red,
Pestilence-stricken multitudes: O thou,
Who chariotest to their dark wintry bed

The wingèd seeds, where they lie cold and low,
Each like a corpse within its grave, until
Thine azure sister of the Spring shall blow

Her clarion o'er the dreaming earth, and fill
(Driving sweet buds like flocks to feed in air)
With living hues and odors plain and hill:

Wild Spirit, which art moving everywhere;
Destroyer and preserver; hear, oh, hear!

Thou on whose stream, 'mid the steep sky's commotion,
Loose clouds like earth's decaying leaves are shed,
Shook from the tangled boughs of Heaven and Ocean,

Angels of rain and lightning; there are spread
On the blue surface of thine airy surge,
Like the bright hair uplifted from the head

Of some fierce Mænad, even from the dim verge
Of the horizon to the zenith's height—
The locks of the approaching storm. Thou dirge

Of the dying year, to which this closing night
Will be the dome of a vast sepulchre,
Vaulted with all thy congregated might

Of vapors, from whose solid atmosphere
Black rain, and fire, and hail will burst: oh hear!

Thou who didst waken from his summer dreams
The blue Mediterranean, where he lay,
Lulled by the coil of his crystalline streams,

Beside a pumice isle in Baiae's bay,
And saw in sleep old palaces and towers
Quivering within the wave's intenser day,

All overgrown with azure moss, and flowers
So sweet the sense faints picturing them! Thou
For whose path the Atlantic's level powers

Cleave themselves into chasms, while far below
The sea-blooms and the oozy woods which wear
The sapless foliage of the ocean, know

Thy voice, and suddenly grow gray with fear,
And tremble and despoil themselves; oh, hear!

If I were a dead leaf thou mightest fear;
If I were a swift cloud to fly with thee;
A wave to pant beneath thy power, and share

The impulse of thy strength, only less free
Than thou, O uncontrollable! If even
I were as in my boyhood, and could be

The comrade of thy wanderings over heaven,
As then, when to outstrip thy skyey speed
Scarce seemed a vision, I would ne'er have striven

As thus with thee in prayer in my sore need.
Oh, lift me as a wave, a leaf, a cloud!
I fall upon the thorns of life! I bleed!

A heavy weight of hours has chained and bowed
One too like thee: tameless, and swift, and proud.

Make me thy lyre, even as the forest is:
What if my leaves are falling like its own!
The tumult of thy mighty harmonies

Will take from both a deep, autumnal tone,
Sweet though in sadness. Be thou, Spirit fierce,
My spirit! Be thou me, impetuous one!

Drive my dead thoughts over the universe
Like withered leaves to quicken a new birth;
And, by the incantation of this verse,

Scatter, as from an unextinguished hearth
Ashes and sparks, my words among mankind!
Be through my lips to unawakened earth

The trumpet of a prophecy! O wind,
If Winter comes, can Spring be far behind?

ON THE ROAD

Charles G. D. Roberts, who as a novelist and a poet has brought fame to Canada, in this poem compares the years of a person's life to a road. The journey leads the traveler up and down until, at the end, a supreme faith brings a contented anticipation of what lies beyond the road.

EVER just over the top of the next brown
  rise
I expect some wonderful thing to flatter my
  eyes.
"What's yonder?" I ask of the first wayfarer
  I meet.
"Nothing!" he answers, and looks at my
  travel-worn feet.

"Only more hills and more hills, like the many
  you've passed,
With rough country between, and a poor
  enough inn at the last."
But already I am a-move, for I see he is
  blind,
And I hate that old grumble I've listened to
  time out of mind.

I've tramped it too long not to know there is
  truth in it still,
That lure of the turn of the road, of the crest
  of the hill.
So I breast me the rise with full hope, well
  assured I shall see
Some new prospect of joy, some brave venture a tip-toe for me.

For I have come far, and confronted the calm
  and the strife.
I have fared wide, and bit deep in the apple
  of life.
It is sweet at the rind, but oh, sweeter still at
  the core;
And whatever be gained, yet the reach of the
  morrow is more.

At the crest of the hill I shall hail the new
  summits to climb,
The demand of my vision shall beggar the
  largess of time.
For I know that the higher I press, the wider
  I view,
The more's to be ventured and visioned, in
  worlds that are new.

So when my feet, failing, shall stumble in
  ultimate dark,
And faint eyes no more the high lift of the
  pathway shall mark,
There under the dew I'll lie down with my
  dreams, for I know
What bright hill-tops the morning will show
  me, all red in the glow.

AT TWILIGHT*

In this poem William Carman Roberts portrays under-standingly and tenderly a fisherman's home in a New Brunswick fishing village on a stormy evening.

OUT of the dusk, wind-blown and thin,
  The shadowy woodboats gather in,
And twilight hushes the harbour's din,—
  Sleep, little head, on my shoulder.
  * By permission of Small, Maynard & Co.

The gold lights wake through the evening grey
In the little village beside the bay,
And a few cold stars gleam far away,—
  Sleep, little head, on my shoulder.

The sailor turns his face once more
Where his sweetheart waits at the open door.
The lone light washes the wave-swept shore,—
  Sleep, little head, on my shoulder.

Here where the dancing shadows swarm
Our driftwood fire is bright and warm;
Beyond our window wakes the storm.
  Then sleep, little head, on my shoulder.

RENCONTRE†

Was there ever a happier setting in verse of the meeting of Age and Youth? The poet Henry van Dyke was not quite so old as he suggests when he wrote this; but then the lady whom he greets was no doubt quite young. Only in verse could such a delicate greeting be properly penned.

OH, was I born too soon, my dear, or were
  you born too late,
That I am going out the door while you come
  in the gate?
For you the garden blooms galore, the castle
  is en fête;
You are the coming guest, my dear; for me
  the horses wait.

I know the mansion well, my dear, its rooms
  so rich and wide;
If you had only come before I might have
  been your guide,
And hand-in-hand with you explore the treasures that they hide;
But you have come to stay, my dear, and I
  prepare to ride.

Then walk with me an hour, my dear, and
  pluck the reddest rose
Amid the white and crimson store with which
  your garden glows.
A single rose—I ask no more of what your
  love bestows;
It is enough to give, my dear—a flower to him
  who goes.

The House of Life is yours, my dear, for
  many and many a day;
But I must ride the lonely shore, the Road to
  Far Away.
So bring the stirrup-cup and pour a brimming
  draught, I pray;
And when you take the road, my dear, I'll
  meet you on the way.

IN ABSENCE

ALL that thou art not makes not up the sum
  Of what thou art, belovèd, unto me;
All other voices, wanting thine, are dumb;
  All vision, in thy absence, vacancy.
          —JOHN BANISTER TABB.

† From Poems of Henry van Dyke, copyright, 1911, 1920, by Charles Scribner's Sons. By permission of the publishers.

FIDELITY

Among the numberless poems in which the fidelity of the dog is celebrated, this, by William Wordsworth, takes a high place. There are many instances of dogs that have shown as great fidelity to their masters as the shepherd's dog here described, and they are all worthy of the poet's praise.

A BARKING sound the shepherd hears,
   A cry as of a dog or fox;
He halts, and searches with his eye
Among the scattered rocks;
And now at distance can discern
A stirring in a brake of fern;
And instantly a dog is seen,
Glancing through that covert green.

The dog is not of mountain breed;
Its motions, too, are wild and shy;
With something, as the shepherd thinks,
Unusual in its cry:
Nor is there anyone in sight
All round, in hollow or on height;
Nor shout, nor whistle strikes his ear:
What is the creature doing here?

It was a cove, a huge recess,
That keeps, till June, December's snow;
A lofty precipice in front,
A silent tarn below;
Far in the bosom of Helvellyn,
Remote from public road or dwelling,
Pathway, or cultivated land;
From trace of human foot or hand.

There, sometimes, doth a leaping fish
Send through the tarn a lonely cheer;
The crags repeat the raven's croak,
In symphony austere;
Thither the rainbow comes, the cloud—
And mists that spread the flying shroud
And sunbeams; and the sounding blast,
That if it could would hurry past;
But that enormous barrier holds it fast.

Not free from boding thoughts, a while
The shepherd stood; then makes his way
O'er rocks and stones, following the dog
As quickly as he may;
Nor far had gone before he found
A human skeleton on the ground:
The appalled discoverer with a sigh
Looks round to learn the history.
From those abrupt and perilous rocks
The man had fallen, that place of fear!
At length upon the shepherd's mind
It breaks, and all is clear:
He instantly recalled the name,
And who he was, and whence he came;
Remembered, too, the very day
On which the traveller passed that way.

But hear a wonder for whose sake
This lamentable tale I tell!
A lasting monument of words
This wonder merits well.
The dog, which still was hovering nigh,
Repeating the same timid cry,
This dog had been through three months' space
A dweller in that savage place.

Yes, proof was plain that since the day
When this ill-fated traveller died,
The dog had watched about the spot,
Or by his master's side:
How nourished there through that long time,
He knows who gave that love sublime;
And gave that strength of feeling great,
Above all human estimate.

SHE IS FAR FROM THE LAND

Thomas Moore, the celebrated Irish poet, is likely to be remembered in time to come chiefly for his exquisite songs, of which The Minstrel Boy, on page 484, is one of the best examples. The following is another of his tuneful lyrics. "The island of sorrow" referred to in the last line is, of course, the poet's native land of Ireland.

SHE is far from the land where her young
   hero sleeps,
   And lovers are round her, sighing;
But coldly she turns from their gaze, and
   weeps,
   For her heart in his grave is lying.

She sings the wild songs of her dear native
   plains,
   Every note which he loved awaking;—
Ah, little they think who delight in her strains
   How the heart of the minstrel is breaking.

He had lived for his love, for his country he
   died,
   They were all that to life had entwined
   him;
Nor soon shall the tears of his country be
   dried,
   Nor long will his love stay behind him.

Oh, make her a grave where the sunbeams rest,
   When they promise a glorious morrow;
They'll shine o'er her sleep like a smile from
   the West,
   From her own loved island of sorrow.

THE OLD FAMILIAR FACES

Charles Lamb is one of the most attractive characters in the whole history of English literature. His fame rests chiefly on his charming essays, as he gained no great distinction in poetry. Together with his sister Mary, he wrote a number of poems for children, several of which appear in our pages, though the following lines in blank verse cannot be described as juvenile poetry. The sentiment which they convey, however, is so human and so universal—the pathos of looking in vain for "the old familiar faces" when one has lived through the long years, lingering after one's friends have all departed—that they really appeal to "children of all ages."

I HAVE had playmates, I have had companions,
In my days of childhood, in my joyful schooldays—
All, all are gone, the old familiar faces.

I have been laughing, I have been carousing,
Drinking late, sitting late, with my bosom
   cronies—
All, all are gone, the old familiar faces.

I loved a love once, fairest among women,
Closed are her doors on me, I must not see
   her—
All, all are gone, the old familiar faces.

I have a friend, a kinder friend has no man.
Like an ingrate, I left my friend abruptly;
Left him, to muse on the old familiar faces.

Ghost-like, I paced round the haunts of my
   childhood.
Earth seemed a desert I was bound to traverse,
Seeking to find the old familiar faces.

Friend of my bosom, thou more than a brother,
Why wert not thou born in my father's dwelling?
So might we talk of the old familiar faces.

How some they have died, and some they
   have left me,
And some are taken from me; all are departed;
All, all are gone, the old familiar faces.

CUDDLE DOON

One of the finest poems of childhood, Cuddle Doon, derives not a little of its beauty from the quaint Scots tongue in which it is written. It is just a simple picture of what happens every night in millions of homes. Many of the words are peculiar to Scotland and the north of England. *Muckle faught* means much noise or disturbance; *waukrife* means wakeful; *hap* is to cover up; *kittlin* is the Scots for tickling; to *steek* the door is to shut and bolt it; to *straik each croon* is to stroke each head or crown; *quaten doon* is to quiet down; *ilka ane* means each one, and *pow* is, of course, a head, or, more correctly, the top of the head. Alexander Anderson, whose fame rests almost entirely on this one gem of Scottish poetry, was a workingman employed on the railway in Scotland, and his verses were written over the signature of "Surfaceman." Born at Kirkconnel, Dumfriesshire, on April 30, 1845, he eventually became, thanks to his poetic gifts and his self-application to literary studies, librarian to Edinburgh University, where he remained until his death, in 1909.

THE bairnies cuddle doon at nicht
　Wi' muckle faught an' din;
"Oh, try and sleep, ye waukrife rogues,
　Your faither's comin' in."
They never heed a word I speak;
　I try to gie a froon;
But aye I hap them up an' cry,
　"Oh, bairnies, cuddle doon!"

Wee Jamie wi' the curly heid—
　He aye sleeps next the wa'—
Bangs up an' cries, "I want a piece,"
　The rascal starts them a'.
I rin an' fetch them pieces, drinks,
　They stop awee the soun',
Then draw the blankets up an' cry,
　"Noo, weanies, cuddle doon!"

But ere five minutes gang, wee Rab
　Cries out, frae 'neath the claes,
"Mither, mak' Tam gie ower at ance,
　He's kittlin' wi' his taes."
The mischief's in that Tam for tricks,
　He'd bother half the toon;
But aye I hap them up an' cry,
　"Oh, bairnies, cuddle doon!"

At length they hear their faither's fit,
　An', as he steeks the door,
They turn their faces to the wa',
　While Tam pretends to snore.
"Hae a' the weans been gude?" he asks,
　As he pits aff his shoon;
"The bairnies, John, are in their beds,
　An' lang since cuddled doon."

An' just afore we bed oorsel's,
　We look at our wee lambs,
Tam has his airm roun' wee Rab's neck,
　And Rab his airm roun' Tam's.
I lift wee Jamie up the bed,
　An' as I straik each croon,
I whisper, till my heart fills up,
　"Oh, bairnies, cuddle doon!"

The bairnies cuddle doon at nicht,
　Wi' mirth that's dear to me;
But soon the big warl's cark an' care
　Will quaten doon their glee.
Yet, come what will to ilka ane,
　May He who rules aboon,
Aye whisper, though their pows be bald,
　"Oh, bairnies, cuddle doon!"

COMMON NATURES

Aaron Hill, the writer of these lines, was born in 1685, and died in 1750. He was famous in his day as a poet and playwright but has since been forgotten except for such quotations from his writings as this little poem.

TENDER-HANDED stroke a nettle,
　And it stings you for your pains;
Grasp it like a man of mettle
　And it soft as silk remains.
'Tis the same with common natures:
　Use them kindly, they rebel;
But be rough as nutmeg-graters,
　And the rogues obey you well.

DISPUTE BETWEEN NOSE AND EYES

William Cowper in this quaint little poem would seem to be having a sly dig at the lawyers, for there can be no doubt that the decision of Baron Ear is distinctly absurd, being based on the arguments of Lawyer Tongue, who, having used all his skill in pleading the case of Nose, had, unfortunately, left himself without a good case for Eyes.

BETWEEN Nose and Eyes a strange contest arose,
　The spectacles set them unhappily wrong;
The point in dispute was, as all the world knows,
　To which the said spectacles ought to belong.

So Tongue was the lawyer, and argued the cause
　With a great deal of skill, and a wig full of learning,
While chief Baron Ear sat to balance the laws,
　So famed for his talent in nicely discerning.

"In behalf of the Nose, it will quickly appear,
　And your lordship," he said, "will undoubtedly find
That the Nose has had spectacles always in wear,
　Which amounts to possession—time out of mind."

Then holding the spectacles up to the court—
　"Your lordship observes they are made with a straddle,
As wide as the ridge of the Nose is—in short,
　Designed to sit close to it, just like a saddle.

"Again, would your lordship a moment suppose
　('Tis a case that has happened, and may be again),
That the visage or countenance had not a Nose,
　Pray who would, or who could, wear spectacles then?

"On the whole it appears, and my argument shows,
　With a reasoning the court will never condemn,
That the spectacles plainly were made for the Nose,
　And the Nose was as plainly intended for them."

Then shifting his side (as a lawyer knows how),
　He pleaded again in behalf of the Eyes;
But what were his arguments few people know,
　For the court did not think they were equally wise.

So his lordship decreed with a grave, solemn tone,
　Decisive and clear, without one "if" or "but,"
That, whenever the Nose put his spectacles on,
　By daylight, or candle-light, Eyes should be shut.

"Pus-sy-cat, pus-sy-cat, where have you been?" "I've been to Lon-don to

vis-it the Queen." "Pus-sy-cat, pus-sy-cat, What did you there?"

"I caught a lit-tle mouse un-der the chair."

OLD KING COLE

Old King Cole was a mer-ry old soul, And a mer-ry old soul was he. He called for his pipe, and he called for his bowl, And he called for his fid-dlers three. Now ev'-ry fid-dler

had a fine fid-dle, and a ver-ry fine fid-dle had he. Twee-dle

dee, twee-dle dee, twee-dle dee, twee-dle dee, Twee-dle dee, twee-dle dee went the fid-dlers three, Other's

none so fair as can com-pare with King Cole and his fid-dler's three.

Black-headed gulls alighting.

SEA BIRDS AND THEIR INLAND KIN

THE Drakes and Raleighs of the bird world are the Terns. As those sturdy adventurers "roamed the world about," fearless and free, but were drawn back after long wanderings by the lure of home in the land that sent them forth, so these seafaring birds make light of journeys wide as the world.

It is believed that the Arctic Tern may sometimes travel upward of 22,000 miles in a year. There is nothing of witchcraft, nothing of spells or charms, in the enterprises of the bird. Its brain and its stout little heart bear it north as far as it can find land for nesting in the Arctic spring, and carry it south as far as it can find open water for feeding in the Antarctic summer, though most individuals winter north of the Equator.

That seems, if one considers, the most heroic endeavor in nature, for the bird is so small. In spite of its long swallow-like tail and the spread of its pearly wings, its body is insignificant in bulk. It is amazing that so small a mass of tissue can provide the sustained energy necessary for this tremendous flight.

One part of the secret is that the bird is a fish-eater; and, with open ocean always beneath it for the great

CONTINUED FROM 4012

flight, it has an unending dinner-table spread, beckoning it to food whenever appetite grows urgent. Still, we must marvel at a system of adjustment and accommodation which enables this bird to pass from the home of lasting ice and snow through the heat of the tropics unharmed and unwearied.

Not all of the more than fifty species of tern fly the same distance as this species. The Common Tern, to be distinguished from the all-red-beaked Arctic Tern by the black tip to its crimson bill, has its northernmost nesting limit at the most southerly boundary of the Arctic bird's range, and is commoner to the South than to the North; whereas the Arctic Tern is thinly represented south of the Arctic Circle, but swarms beyond it.

Some of the terns avoid the seacoast for nesting, and like the marsh terns, of which there are three European species, cradle their eggs on tussocks of grass or among floating vegetation in marshes. Our Black Tern has the same habit. For the most part, however, the terns, when undisturbed by the presence of man, have their nurseries by the sea, in receptacles scooped out among the pebbles, which the eggs themselves resemble.

4121

North America has about fifteen species of terns, though some, like the Common, the Gull-billed, the Caspian, the Arctic, the Roseate, the Royal and the Sandwich, also inhabit the Old World. On the other hand, we have a little beauty, the Least Tern, which is not over nine inches long. It is sometimes called the Silvery Tern.

So swift and shifting are their aerial movements that we call them sea-swallows. Much of the beauty of the family is lavished on the terns, and their splendid flight, their magnificent dives from the wing into the water for fish, the affectionate sympathy they show in collecting round a wounded comrade, make them among the best-loved birds of our shores.

THE AMAZING SKILL OF THE NODDIES IN FINDING THEIR WAY AT SEA

Warm islands of the Atlantic and Pacific shelter a related, but slightly larger, form in the Noddies, birds not so adventurous in flight as the terns, though amazingly skilled in finding their way home over hundreds of miles of unknown sea, across which they have been carried in the darkness of captivity. They have had so little experience of men in the past that they tolerate our near approach to their nests and permit themselves to be caught when they alight on ships. So travelers who knew the ways of sailors with birds called these trustful ones what they seem—noddies or noodles.

From the same family stock as these there has arisen a notable example of specialization in the beak of the Skimmers, birds known to American, Indian and Red Sea waters. Our species is called the Black Skimmer, though it is white underneath. The bird in general outline is a large tern, but the upper part of the beak is much shorter than the lower.

The purpose of this great development of the lower mandible is seen as the bird, with splendid power of wing, skims just above the surface with the under half of the bill scooping the water, or the oozy bed of the sea at low tide on the shore, and even the muddy shallows of the Nile estuary. The beak picks up food as the tube of an express engine picks up water from the long trough between the rails as the train speeds on its way. This bird, which is also called the Cut-water and the Scissorbill, is now seldom seen farther north than the coast of New Jersey.

THE BEAK OF THE GULL THAT CAN TEAR LIKE AN EAGLE'S

The Gulls have no such peculiarity. They are superbly competent birds, and the fact that the arrangement of the beak with them is the reverse of that in the skimmer is an asset. The gull bill is longer in the upper than the lower half; only a little, but sufficient to furnish a hook to the superior half—and that hook can rip as fiercely as an eagle's.

They are scattered round the shores of all the seas, and till the fuel oil from our modern ships began to pollute our waters, whoever saw the gull tribe saw a tribe most prosperous. The gull is as adaptable to widely differing conditions as a rat or a sparrow; as clever and as ruthless.

Cliffs, rocks, lone marshy moors and trees are safe abiding places for the nests in which gull eggs turn to squawking babies. Fifty species and more there are of the better-known sorts, in addition to exotic types found only in restricted areas. We have about fifteen of them, but can glance at only a few.

One of the most fascinating is the Glaucous Gull, a giant nearly a yard long, coming down to rest with us for a breathing space as he wings his way south from the wild Arctic, where he has reared his babes. The Black-headed, or Laughing, Gull is common in Europe as well as in America. It is white-headed in winter and assumes its rich ebony mantle only in the spring, when love summons it to its finest apparel.

SOME OF THE OTHER SPECIES OF GULLS

Another that we see often in the fields is that pearly-bodied, yellow-billed fisher of the shallow seas, the Herring Gull, which finds, however, an increasing harvest in our fields, to our very great advantage. The European form is smaller than ours. Then there are the Great Black-backed Gull, thirty inches long, and that wonder of plumage, the Ivory Gull, whose feathers, in their creamy purity and enamel-like sheen, make it one of the most beautiful of a beautiful family of birds. We must not omit the Kittiwake, with white head and neck, gray mouth and white-tipped wings. It is also found in Europe. Then, too, there is Bonaparte's Gull, only a little larger than the Least Gull of Europe. Franklin's Gull is a resident of the interior plains.

THE GRACEFUL GULLS AND THEIR COUSINS

The Herring Gull.

The Great Black-backed Gull.

Parasitic Jaeger.

The Arctic Tern alights at its nest.   The Black-headed Gull guards its eggs.

McCormick's Antarctic Skua.

The Kittiwake.

The Common Gull.

THE GOOD WORK THE GULLS DO FOR US ALL

In our ports the gulls earn their keep as a delightful free aviary; in the country and by the sea they take their keep and merit it for services unacknowledged, though the fishermen cry out that gulls rob them of their fish, and farmers complain that gulls take their grain. So far from depleting our fishermen's earnings, they call the fleet to the herring shoals, and the fish they take can well be spared. They are the flying beacons to summon us to the fish, they are the unpaid guardians of our sailors in little boats drifting, but for the warning cries of the gulls, on to lee shores in fog.

What of the grain-eating? There is some truth in it, but tests extending over seven months failed to discover proof, while finding that the birds ate enormous numbers of insect enemies of our crops. Examination of gull crops shows that these birds devour the enemy wholesale. Careful calculations proved that the gulls each eat at the rate of twenty-eight thousand insects a week, to say nothing of the myriads of eggs from the perfect insects also taken. And, as hundreds of the birds work together in the hunt, the total must be colossal.

THE DEVOTION OF THE BLACK-BACKED GULL TO ITS YOUNG

The Great Black-backed Gull has an evil reputation for snapping up eggs, young birds and rabbits, and has been known to kill weakly lambs. But much must be forgiven this bird for its splendid devotion as a parent. An evidence of the kind was unexpectedly afforded a naturalist who was fishing recently on the Isle of Skye. Seeing a full-sized young black-backed gull not quite able to fly, he took it home as a pet and put it for safety for the night in a hen coop. The youngster raised its voice in piteous appeal, and lo, an echo answered from the sky, where two great creatures, giving call for call, were seen flying in lower circles, seeking their offspring.

All that night the young gull clamored for deliverance, so in the morning its kindly captor let the bird out of its coop. Hardly had he done so when there was a flash of wings and a great black-back swooped from the air, seized the young one, carried it off, and deposited it in the sea. There the two were presently joined by a third, and all swam away.

THE TERRIBLE WEAPONS OF A PIRATE OF THE AIR

All these gulls are dependent for part of their career on the sea, yet not to the same extent as the pretty and nimble Kittiwake, which covets no aid from man, but swims the inshore waters for its food and finds its lodging on the edges of cliffs nearest the sea.

The creature gulls most 'fear is, next to man, the Skua, or Jaeger Gull, and the reason is sufficient when skuas are plentiful, which is not now the case. For this sea bird, which attains a length of well over two feet in the great skua, is one of the fiercest of all fliers. It has the powerful hooked beak of a bird of prey; its talons are strong and sharp and viciously used in gripping the prey it tears. It is a pirate wherever it is found.

Superb on the wing, it can overtake the tern and make it disgorge its food. It can kill and devour birds of great size. In defense of its nest it will attack a man, swooping like a hawk at his head, perhaps to use that mighty beak, certainly to attack his eyes with whip-like lashes from the tips of its tremendous wings. One species actually nests as far south as the Antarctic mainland.

Antarctica is a foodless land, yet the skuas find plenty there. They prey on the nesting penguins, steal their eggs, carry off nestlings far heavier than the heaviest skuas, and pick their bones bare. They are as dependent for life on the penguins as a sheep on grass.

A skua's power of offense and defense, its tigerish courage and wanton aggressiveness, render it immune from all bird attacks. How, then, is it that it does not outnumber other birds and become a world-wide scourge? Nature herself supplies the check.

HOW NATURE KEEPS DOWN THE NUMBERS OF THE SKUA

Ferocity is born with the breath of life in a baby skua. The nestlings fight to the death in their cradles. The victorious little murderer survives, triumphant over its slaughtered brothers and sisters. By that process of elimination skua numbers are kept down, and only the most efficient little ruffian emerges from the cradle to carry on the species.

Many a meal in northern latitudes comes to the skuas from the next family, the Auks, which includes the Auks proper, Murres, Guillemots and Puffins.

QUAINT AND BEAUTIFUL BIRDS OF THE SEA

The beautiful Albatross in flight over the sea.

Giant Petrels.

The Razor-bill.

A group of Puffins.

Guillemots on a rocky crag.

The Manx Shearwater.

The Stormy Petrel.

The Fulmar Petrel.

The pictures on these pages are by Messrs. Mortimer Batten, Berridge, Brook, Chislett, King, Kirk, Lodge, Herbert G. Ponting, Roberts, Seth-Smith, and others.

The Razor-billed Auk interests us as the closest surviving link with the great auk, once enormously numerous, but which has been exterminated in modern times by brutal seagoers, who mowed it down on its island homes as gardeners mow down the grass of a lawn.

The razor-bills will survive because they have fine wing power. They and the guillemots keep the sea, save for nesting times, and fish for herring and other small fish. The Little Auks dwell in the north, as we have noted, and well they fare there.

THE LITTLE AUKS THAT PEARY'S MEN CAUGHT IN THE ARCTIC

When Peary was making his successful journey to the North Pole some of his men sat wrapped in furs, hour after hour, on one of Greenland's icy mountains, netting little auks as they streamed home, thousands and thousands strong, from their fishing. The white men let their little victims go, but the Eskimos, counting on the birds for food, net them at night like butterflies as they fly.

There is a memorable picture, too, of a rather earlier day of the little auks in a Spitzbergen bay. They extended across the water in an unbroken line more than three miles long. A calculation made at the time showed that there must have been over four million little auks. Yet the little auk lays but one egg a year, in place of the ten or twenty of the partridge. We know from this that little auks can take care of themselves, and that they are very long-lived birds.

Another auk, and the strangest, is the Puffin, or Sea-parrot, a grotesque little bird which, in the nesting season, wears a huge many-colored beak. The outer sheath is shed in winter. Probably the development is related to the unique habit of the puffin when foraging for its young. It catches little fishes, one after another, and arranges all in symmetrical order in its beak. How it can keep number nine in place when it is catching number ten we cannot guess. But there are more wonders in bird structure and method than we have yet solved; one has heard a blackbird whistle cheerily to its nesting mate when its mouth was stuffed with worms! On the Pacific coast we find the Tufted Puffin, which is similar except for two tufts of yellow feathers above the eyes. The Large-billed Puffin breeds only in the Far North.

THE WONDER OF THE SILENT FLIGHT OF THE ALBATROSS

Our next step leads us to a family of birds in which another unique feature is a guide to classification: the nostrils take the form of tubes lying along the surface of the beak. They are great fliers all, sea birds in the truest sense, dependent on land only for nesting sites.

Chief of the family is the Albatross, the wonder bird of the ocean; light of body, narrow of wing, but with those great living sails, or propellers ten or twelve feet, or even more, from tip to tip. The ocean is their kingdom. They fly unweariedly day after day, night after night, hundreds and hundreds of miles with the fastest steamer, sailing round and round her with such marvelous skill of wing that for ages the secret of their flight has been debated.

Many watchers have believed that the sailing is effected with stationary wings on unperceived currents of favoring air. But the truth is that the albatross adjusts its great wings to match its needs in the air, just as an airman contrives his balance in an airplane. The camera will settle the problem for all time one of these days, but already we know that a flicker, a swift rise or down beat are among the bird's master strokes in aviation. The flight of these birds seems effortless; the truth is Nature has given the albatross a mastery of the art of conserving energy, and its flight is the marvel and despair of every man who contrives to rise by artificial method into the air. Though this bird is found chiefly in the southern ocean, occasional specimens are seen in northern waters.

Another great flier is the Giant Petrel, a thirty-two-inch bird which plays the vulture at sea, gorging itself on carrion till it can no longer rise from the water, but must swim itself back to efficiency. The Fulmar Petrel is a related species, smaller, but equally notable on the wing.

A BIRD OF THE SEA THAT MAKES A BURROW ON LAND

As devoted children of the ocean are the Shearwaters, so called from their habit of skimming just above the surface in quest of food. When they come to land they turn cave-dwellers, but their caves are of their own making, burrows neatly excavated in the soil.

They seem, as they skim the water with feet paddling the waves, to be running

THE FLIGHTLESS BIRDS OF THE SOUTH

The Emperor Penguin.

An Adelie Penguin and young.

The Rockhopper Penguin.

Adelie Penguins sunning themselves at Cape Royds, in Antarctica.

A King Penguin and a Gentu Penguin.

A group of Black-footed Penguins.

actually on the surface, so they and the group to which they belong are all called Petrels, in allusion to St. Peter's walking on the Sea of Galilee. Most famous of the petrels is the Stormy Petrel, a delightful little mariner which seems happiest when great billows rage and storm winds blow. The presumption is that the churning seas bring up the food it seeks. The wash created by a steamer has the same effect, and so lures these dainty beauties on long, unflagging pursuit of the vessels which carry men and merchandise across the ocean. They are sometimes called Mother Carey's Chickens.

And now, as in a transformation scene, we pass suddenly from power of navigation in air and water to a strange assembly of birds that do not fly at all, yet are master mariners and landsmen of the first magnitude. The Penguins, of course, are the birds in question, birds which once had wings and flew.

WINGLESS BIRDS OF THE SOUTH THAT LIVE AMID SNOW AND ICE

About fifteen species of penguins exist to-day, all in the southern half of the world, in parts of South America, Australia and New Zealand, and on many islands of the south Pacific. The Emperor Penguin, largest of all, lands for the winter on the Antarctic ice, while the Adelie Penguin spends the summer there, but sails north with the ice pack before darkness and winter cover the tragic land.

All penguins have an upright gait on land, except when, to relieve the strain on nerve and muscle, they bring their breasts flat on smooth ice or snow, and toboggan, kicking themselves along with their stout little webbed feet, like boys pushing sledges before them.

At sea they swim superbly, as much under the water as on it. They work down to the bottom in search of fish and crustaceans, and sometimes bring up stones and pieces of coral in sport. But another method is known as porpoising. With flippers used as oars they make a dash beneath the water, then rise suddenly and leap into the air, with bodies bent forward, and progress in a series of rapid curves, first in and through the water, then up and above its surface, all at top speed, so that they are mistaken for small examples of the mammals they imitate so perfectly.

In most places they march out of the sea on land, like two-legged animals, and the black volcanic rock of the Falkland Island coast is deeply scored where for ages and ages millions of penguins have climbed their way inland. One species uses the tips of its flippers as legs and runs along on all fours, like a mammal. But the most wonderful method of getting to land is that of the Adelie penguins as they go ashore for their summer nesting.

HOW THE ADELIE PENGUIN LEAPS FROM SEA TO SHORE

They have an ice-foot to scale, for there are only certain parts of the continent to which they can go. These are the bleakest parts, swept bare of snow by the gales, so that they may have clear spaces for their nests. They survey the position from the sea and mark a landing-place unerringly.

Then they dive down beneath the surface, get a tremendous kick-off in the sea, and rise from it like a cork popping out of a bottle. With such a leap they clear the water and jump ten feet forward and four or five feet straight up on to the ice, all done in a second, after one momentary glance at the landing-place chosen.

Hundreds of thousands of penguins assemble in Antarctica in this way, arriving singly, in couples, in droves. They make nests by building up stones, and lay their eggs there, one or two, without any other protection than that afforded by their own bodies. And the marvel is that the birds, with the tremendous tax on their strength implied by egg-laying and brooding of the eggs, fast for a full month and more—an amazing exception to the rule that birds must eat often and heartily.

At the end of a month one bird will go down to the sea to feed, and then he will return and relieve his mate, who in turn will be absent for a fortnight while the male takes duty. When the chicks are hatched, the parent birds go in turn to feed, and return bulging with food so that they can barely walk and have to balance their protruding little stomachs by carrying the head far back.

All is simple so long as the nestlings are helpless, but when they can run, they do, popping off at a moment's notice. So, as both birds now have to go together to bring back food, nestlings from a number of nests are gathered together under the joint protection of many penguins, and apparently the parents returning to this communal nursery identify and feed their own babes.

The Adelie penguins go back to sea with their babes full-fledged when summer is ending, first teaching the reluctant and cowardly youngsters the main business of their lives, to swim. As the Adelies go out the Emperors come in. Theirs is the strangest existence in all the world.

They have the most desolate, cold, appalling nursery ever imagined. The young ones take many months to attain feathers and maturity; therefore they must have the full summer before them for the process, so their parents have to endure the agony and horror of nesting through the long winter night.

The parent birds establish themselves on the ice with a temperature of perhaps 100° and more of frost. One egg is laid, and, there being no nesting material, it is balanced on the upper side of the bird's

The birds seem almost human in some of their instincts. They have the most courtly way of bowing to each other and of holding what seem to be animated conversations. They bow and talk to men in the same way, and when not understood go through the same performance of gesture and speech again, as if in sad contempt for our ignorance.

Among themselves they play like boys. They fight tremendously during the breeding season, but before and after that they are fast friends. At the water-side they romp like children, doing their best to push one another into the water. Once in, they sport with delight, call to those on shore and show the keenest perception of fun. When ice-floes come sailing by on the racing tide they board them and ride in ecstasy to the end of the bay, then

The Black-throated Diver.   The Coot.   The Great Crested Grebe.

feet and pressed there by a fold of skin on the lower part of the body. So great is the parental passion of these extraordinary birds that they fight for each other's eggs; they take up stones and pieces of ice and seek to incubate these; and when the chick is born scores scramble to nurse it. The greater part of the emperor chicks are killed by kindness, being trampled to death by eager competitors for the honor of keeping it alive.

Examinations of emperor rookeries have shown that three-fourths of the little ones perish in the same way. So emperor penguins are never abundant, yet never in danger of dying out, so remote is their breeding-place. They attain considerable size, forty-two inches in height and with a weight of ninety pounds. Many an Antarctic explorer has owed his life to flesh obtained from their plump bodies. Nevertheless, no man of feeling likes to kill a penguin.

slip off, swim back, and go for another happy journey in the same way.

Certain features ally the penguins with the Divers, or Loons, and Grebes—birds which in past days had other flightless kindred in the famous old hesperornis whose remains we find in the earth. Their modern representatives are smaller, but fly, swim and dive with power.

Chief of the group is the Common Loon, or Great Northern Diver, whose cousins are the Black-throated and the Red-throated Loons. They generally resort to inland lakes for nesting, but afterward they return to purely oceanic habits. Here they are in their true element. They swim like corks; they dive in a manner unexcelled; and such is the development of their breathing system that they are known to remain under water for eight minutes at a stretch.

These birds are, of course, web-footed, but their kin, the Grebes, have the feet lobed, with broad flat nails—a modification associated with their habit of keeping more to inland waters and frequenting the land. There are over twenty species, of which we know best the Western Grebe, one of the largest; Holbœll's Grebe, one of the commonest; the Horned Grebe, which has a wonderful growth of feathers about its head in the breeding season; and the beautiful Pied-bill Grebe, or Dabchick. The Great Crested Grebe belongs to the Old World. Its plumage is much sought for millinery purposes.

Finally, we have the Rails, an immense family comprising nearly two hundred species, many with a penguin-like tendency toward loss of flight. One, the Weka Rail of New Zealand, seems equally doomed, for though big wings are there, ability to fly has departed owing to long disuse.

THE CRY OFTEN HEARD OF THE BIRD SELDOM SEEN

The Corncrake is common in Europe, but seldom seen in America. It is a fast runner, but it flies away in autumn to warmer winter lands. The Virginia Rail is very much like the Water Rail of Europe, but is smaller. It is wholly confined to fresh-water marshes and never visits the borders of the sea, and accordingly its haunts are in the interior. Though it migrates to the shores of the St. Lawrence, it is unknown in the far countries of the North, and retires at the first touch of frost to the southern states. The Sora Rail of the southern states is much like the Dotterel of Europe.

Next we must mention the closely related Gallinules. The Common Gallinule of Europe is often called the Moorhen. At the coming of danger it submerges silently in the water, and one sees apparently a little autumn-tinted leaf floating where a big bird was a moment before. That leaf is really the bill of the moorhen, its periscope, through which it breathes, generally undetected. The Florida Gallinule occasionally nests as far north as southern Canada. It is a slate-colored bird, with yellow legs, long toes and red bill. In South America it extends over a great portion of the continent, frequenting pools, lagoons and streams. It makes its clumsy bed of reeds in a swamp or marsh on a dry knoll, or occasionally hanging in flags or rushes over water. You would find no music in its voice, although it is deep. Shy and retiring in its habits, it leaves its marshy haunts only when it is time to migrate, and then it steals off under cover of darkness. On the wing it looks very awkward, but when walking or swimming it is noticeably graceful! The Purple Gallinule is similar, except in color, but prefers the warmer regions. It is a beautiful bird; its back a bright olive, its wings deeper green shading off to blue, and its head, neck and breast purple. When in the southern states the purple gallinule lives in rice-fields and fresh-water pools. In its native marshes of the North it is shy and vigilant and can be flushed only with the help of a dog. If irritated, this bird will bite hard; it can run swiftly, and holds on to objects very firmly with its long, spread toes. Its favorite food is a mixture of water-snails and plantains.

The Coot, which is larger and plumper, with a white patch, instead of a red, over the base of the beak, keeps more to the water than its cousins, and is a treasure of quiet overgrown streams and marshy waters. It deserves honorable mention in any list of clever birds, for when attacked by a bird of prey Master Coot collects all his family and friends, and by means of wings and feet they all set up such a shower of water that the enemy is drenched and in danger of falling helpless into the stream and drowning. So victory rests with the weaker, wiser little coot.

THE SHY LITTLE FINFOOT THAT GROWLS LIKE A FIERCE WILD BEAST

The coot's foot is grebe-like as regards the lobe of the toes. The toes of the Finfeet are clad with broad scalloped webs, and have claws sharp enough to make the hand that catches them bleed smartly for its daring. The finfeet are shy birds, peculiar to tropical South America and parts of Africa and southeast Asia. Perched like kingfishers on rock or bough above a stream, they launch themselves in a lightning dive into the water on any living thing which moves below in such a manner as to suggest a meal.

The finfoot has a habit of filling himself with air and then exhaling it so noisily that he sounds like a fierce animal growling. In that he has the ostrich for a master, a bird whose roar deceives even experienced hunters into mistaking him for a lion. Doubtless the finfoot would like to be mistaken for such a beast.

THE NEXT STORY OF ANIMAL LIFE IS ON PAGE 4283.

Dance of the Seasons to the music of Time.—From the painting by Nicolas Poussin.

WHO ARRANGED THE DAYS?

CONTINUED FROM 3979

THE division of time into days and weeks and months and years is partly natural and partly artificial. An era is a period of years reckoned from a given point of time, and the Christian Era begins with the birth of Jesus.

All Christian countries reckon time from the supposed date of the birth of Jesus. Things occurring before that time are said to have taken place in such a year B.C., or Before Christ; and things happening since then are spoken of as occurring in such and such a year A.D., or Anno Domini—"in the Year of our Lord."

The Mohammedans reckon their dates from the Hegira, or flight of Mohammed from Mecca to Medina in 622 A.D., and speak of events as occurring in such and such a year A.H., or Anno Hegiræ. The year 1925 A.D., for instance, is 1343 A.H.—the Mohammedan year not being quite the same length as ours.

The Jews speak of any date as A.M., or Anno Mundi—"in the Year of the World"—dating everything from the supposed time when the world was created. That is why in the Jewish Calendar A.D. 1925 is A.M. 5686. The Romans reckoned their dates as A.U.C., or Anno Urbis Conditæ, which really means "from the Year of the building of the City," or the founding of Rome. During the first five centuries after the birth of Christ Christians recorded time in the same way as the people among whom they lived; but in 532 A.D., when their numbers had increased considerably, Dionysius Exiguus, a monk of Scythia, proposed that Christians should date all events as from the birth of Christ.

He looked into the matter, and came to the conclusion that Jesus was born on December 25 in the year 753 after the founding of Rome. But as the Roman year began with January, it was considered too inconvenient to have the Christian year beginning on a different date, and so it was later decided that the beginning of the Christian Era should be reckoned as January 1, 754 A.U.C., which to Christians henceforth became A.D. 1. Therefore, the first year of the Christian Era is not the year of the birth of Jesus, but the year after.

Another curious thing in connection with the beginning of this era is that later researches have shown that Jesus was probably born, not in 753 A.U.C., but about four years earlier, for Herod died in 750 A.U.C., and Jesus was certainly born before that. We have, therefore, the strange contradiction that Jesus was born in 4 B.C.!

Stupid people often argue as to whether the years ending in hundreds—1800, 1900, and so on—are the last year of one century or the first of the next. Of course they are the last years of a century, because the first century ran from January 1, A.D. 1, to December 31, A.D. 100. The beginning of the second century was, therefore, January 1, A.D. 101.

There are only three natural divisions of time—the day, the month and the year; and of these, the day and the year are more suitable for reckoning than the month. A day is the interval of time which elapses between two successive appearances of the sun at the same point in the heavens, and there is no doubt that this, being the easiest to observe, was the very first fact by which man reckoned time.

A year is the time occupied by the earth in making a complete revolution round the sun. This period was in the very earliest times noticed by observant men, and so time was reckoned in years as well as days. Then it was seen that the moon waxed and waned in regular periods of roughly four weeks, and these were called *moonths*.

These natural divisions of time date back to the days before history was written. The divisions into weeks, hours, minutes and seconds are purely artificial and came into use later.

HAS THE DAY ALWAYS BEEN DIVIDED INTO TWENTY-FOUR EQUAL HOURS?

The division of the day into twenty-four hours is very ancient, and its origin is lost in the mists of time. No one can say why twenty-four was chosen. In Egyptian and Greek times the daily period of light and the period of darkness were each divided into twelve hours, and as the periods of light and dark vary at different times of the year, the length of an hour varied, which must have been very inconvenient in reckoning. At one season there would be something like sixteen hours of light and only eight of darkness, and the light hours and the dark hours would be of different lengths.

So awkward was an arrangement like this that in the thirteenth century Abul Hassan, an Arabian mathematician, introduced equal hours all the year round, based on a twelfth part of the daylight at the equinoxes, when day and night are of equal length. It was not till some centuries later, however, that the modern hour was adopted generally.

The reason for the division of the hour into sixty minutes, and of the minute into sixty seconds is also unknown. It is a very ancient arrangement and may have been due to the fact that in their first rough attempts at measuring time the Egyptians gave a year 360 days divided into twelve equal months of thirty days. This is supposed to be the origin of the division of the circle into 360 degrees, and may have led to the use of the number 12 in dividing the day, hour and minute. The lunar month of twenty-eight days has no exact proportion to the day or year, and so to make a certain number of months fit into the year the length of the months has been varied from time to time, and even the number of months in the year has not always been twelve. The week of seven days originated in Eastern lands, but no definite explanation of it is found, except in the story of the creation of the world in six days, with a day of rest following, as found in the Bible.

WHY DOES THE WHISTLE CHANGE AS THE TRAIN COMES NEARER?

If we are standing in a station, and an engine approaches us blowing its whistle, we hear the pitch of the note rise as the train approaches us and fall as the train leaves us. The effect is like a shriek, first rising in shrillness, and then falling again.

The explanation of this lies in the fact that the pitch of a note varies with the number of waves which beat on the drum of our ears in a given time. For example, the middle treble C—the C on the third space of the treble staff—as arranged in pitch on our ordinary pianos, has 522 vibrations to the second.

Now we can understand what happens to the railway whistle on the approaching train. It is giving out a certain steady note, but the locomotive is rushing toward us, and, therefore, in a second we receive more vibrations than the whistle is actually giving out in a second; that is to say, fresh vibrations come before others have died away. So, although to the engine-driver the pitch of the whistle remains steady, the note rises for us as the train rushes toward where we are standing. Similarly, as the locomotive leaves us behind, the number of vibrations per second which reach our ears from its whistle is smaller than actually leaves the whistle, and, therefore, the pitch of the note falls.

HOW FAR DOES RAIN SINK INTO THE EARTH?

This depends chiefly on the slope, nature and temperature of the soil and on the character of the rainfall. On sloping, hilly soil the rain will drain away into streams and rivers before it has had time to penetrate very far, whereas on a broad plateau or sunken plain the rain will form marshes and lakes and pools, and usually sink much deeper. The nature of the soil will also determine the depth to which rain will sink. If the soil or subsoil happens to be clay, it will act like a vessel of clay and retain the water. Most of our wells owe their water to a bed of clay. Again, under the soil may be rock, and the rock may be very hard or very porous. Or there may be loose gravel extending to great depths, allowing water to trickle down. The distance the rain penetrates into the ground depends on all these things, and also, of course, on the volume and rapidity of the rainfall. It is possible that in some cases it may sink until the heat in the depths of the earth's crust converts it into steam; and some people think the steam from volcanoes comes from subterranean water which has sunk into the crust from seas and lakes.

WHERE IS THERE A MONUMENT TO AN APPLE?

In a field in Madison County, Iowa, there stands a monument to the parent tree of the variety known as the Delicious apple. More than fifty years ago a young Quaker farmer called Hiatt planted an orchard in Iowa and started to grow apples. In the spring of 1852 a shoot issued from the root of a dead apple-tree trunk, and when it grew to a tree it produced apples of quite a new variety—big red apples with a special flavor and aroma. Hiatt named the apple "Hawkeye," and for twenty years the tree bore its crop without attracting much notice. But when he sent the apples to a big show in 1893, the judge, biting into one, exclaimed "Delicious! Delicious!" And from that day the variety has become famous the world over. The original tree, now more than half a century old, is still standing, protected by a fence, and beside it is a granite monument with an inscription in its honor.

Certainly the Delicious apple deserves to be immortalized, for it has been a tremendous gift to the world. Its offspring has now been numbered at seven or eight million trees, and it has been calculated that the annual market value of the Delicious apple must be at least twenty million dollars. In Australia and New Zealand, there are about two hundred thousand trees; in China and Japan, about one hundred thousand; in Korea, ten thousand; in Africa, fifty thousand; in Mexico and Brazil, five hundred thousand; in Argentina, three hundred thousand; in Canada, nearly four hundred thousand. There are also hundreds of thousands of trees in Europe. Well might a monument be raised to this old apple tree!

WHY IS IT DIFFICULT TO WRITE ON GLASS?

Writing depends on the transfer of some colored material to the writing surface; and the colored material and the surface must both be suitable for the transfer. When, for instance, we write with ink on paper, the ink flows off the pen on to the paper and is, to a slight extent, absorbed. If the paper be too glossy and shiny, the ink flows too widely, and if, on the other hand, the paper is too absorbent, the ink spreads and blots. So, in the case of a lead pencil, the paper must have a certain amount of roughness to rub the particles of lead off the point of the pencil.

Now, glass is suitable for neither ink, pen nor pencil, because it is quite smooth and non-absorbent. The ink runs over it, and the lead pencil transfers no lead to it. If we wish to write on glass we must use ink or lead prepared specially to make them sticky.

WHY DOES A FLAME RISE TO A THING HELD ABOVE IT?

The direction of a flame, and its height, depend chiefly on the fact that its heated gases and incandescent particles rise through the cooler air, helped in their rise by the cool air rushing in to take their place. Any object held above the flame becomes heated, and its heat causes a slight additional upward draft of hot air which hastens and increases the ascent of the gases and incandescent particles of the flame. The flame is not attracted in the normal sense; it is drawn in the direction of the heated body by the upward draft the heated body creates. On this principle depends the value of the practice of standing a poker across a fire to make it "draw." The poker's presence does actually help the fire to burn.

CAN A FLY SEE ALL WAYS AT THE SAME TIME?

A fly cannot see in all directions at once, because, whatever the shape of its eyes, one part of them, at any rate, must lie against the fly's head, and in that direction, at least, the fly cannot see. But it is true that the eyes of flies, and of many other insects, can see in far more directions at once than ours can. This is especially the case where the eyes are not flat, but very much rounded and bulging.

We must not suppose that this means clear vision at the same time in all directions; but it does mean that, while looking in one direction, the insect can get a hint of movement much farther round the corner than we can. The proper way of saying this is that their field of vision is very large, even though it does not quite amount to seeing "all ways at once."

In order that the eye may receive light from so many different directions, it is made somewhat like a precious stone that has been cut into many little faces, or facets. The number of these tiny facets on the eyes of insects is extraordinary. A male ant, for instance, may have twelve hundred facets on each eye, and the number on the eye of the dragon-fly has been reckoned as high as seventeen thousand.

ARE NEW CLOUDS ALWAYS BEING MADE?

Clouds are always being made and unmade. No cloud lasts for more than a short time, and the surface of a cloud is constantly changing. The making and unmaking of clouds depend upon a great many different conditions in the air; for instance, the temperature of the air, the amount of moisture it contains, the nature and temperature of winds, the amount of dust in the air, and state of the electricity in the air at the time.

These things are changing from moment to moment; indeed, it is not possible that they can all remain the same for two moments together. The earth never ceases to spin, and this means that different parts of the air are being brought under the rays of the sun or out of them. Even though the sun is shining on parts of the air for many hours at a time, the spinning of the earth makes it shine at a different angle, which alters the force of its rays. As the sun shines it warms the air, and so increases the amount of water which it can hold in the form of transparent water-vapor rather than in the form of clouds. So clouds are always being made and melted, as no one needs telling who has watched the face of the sky steadily and carefully for even a short period.

WHY DOES THE KETTLE SING?

Everything that sings sings really for the same reason: because it is set vibrating. That difficult word simply means "trembling." When you sing or speak, you make the little cords in your throat tremble, and when a kettle sings, we may be sure that something is vibrating somewhere. This sets the air round it vibrating, and if it vibrates quickly enough, we can hear it sing. If you had a stick in your hand and could turn it quickly enough in the air, you could make the stick sing.

Now, kettles do not always sing quite the same tune, and that depends upon a number of things; but at any rate we can understand that, as the water gets hot and begins to boil, it is turned into water-gas, or water-vapor, and it has to force its way out through the spout and past the lid of the kettle. As it does this it sets various parts of the kettle trembling, and so the air is made to tremble, and so the drum-head, or window, in your ear is made to tremble, and somehow your brain feels this, and you therefore say the kettle is singing.

It is the pressure of the gas coming out that sets the kettle trembling. When you speak or sing, you nearly close your throat and then squeeze the air in your lungs through the small opening; and it is the pressure of the gas that sets your vocal cords trembling. So the kettle sings just as you do.

WHAT ARE THE GROOVES ROUND A COIN FOR?

Pennies and nickels have smooth edges, but silver and gold coins are "milled," as we say, round the edge. The reason is that people used to pare the edges of coins, especially gold coins, and then sell the precious metal. This is, of course, a form of theft from the nation's money, and the best way of stopping it was found to be to "mill" the edges of the more valuable coins, so that no one could pare them without letting it be seen at once.

Copper and nickel coins are not milled because it would not be worth while to pare them.

HOW DOES FROST HELP THE FARMER?

Frost is one of the most valuable aids to the farmer, unless it happens too late or too early. The freezing of the ground and the subsequent thaw amount to a most useful cultivation of the soil. When soil freezes it is not the earth itself that becomes solid, but the water lying between the lumps and particles of earth. When the frost comes, therefore, we have a condition in which the particles of water lying in and around the pieces of soil, large and small, are changed into explosive bombs. That is because water, when it freezes into ice, increases in size. Imagine all the water in and between the bits of earth becoming larger as it changes into ice. The pieces of earth are thrust apart, and when the thaw comes the soil is more finely pulverized than before the frost. A natural cultivation has been at work on behalf of the farmer, helping him in the winter to make ready for the spring. This is important, because seed will grow only in a good seed-bed of well pulverized ground. The wise farmer helps the frost by plowing up his land so that the frost can get at it.

WHO IS THE SPEAKER OF THE HOUSE OF COMMONS?

The Speaker is the Chairman of the House of Commons. He sits, wearing silk robes and a full-bottomed wig, in a raised and canopied seat called the Chair. He is elected to preside over the House, to keep order, to conduct debate, and to safeguard the rights and privileges of the Commons. Great confidence is placed in him, and upon his tact, judgment and fairness the efficiency of Parliament largely depends.

The Speaker is elected by a vote of the House of Commons itself from among its own members. He is chosen for non-political reasons, and very often does not belong to the political party in power when he is elected. When the Members of Parliament go to the House of Lords to hear the King open Parliament, he walks at their head. He has a fine palace, which is part of the Houses of Parliament, in order to enable him to devote the whole of his time to his office.

The Speaker decides who shall speak in debates by calling on such members as he chooses, and his endeavor is to give all sides a fair hearing. It is very comical to see a dozen members all rise together in the hope of being called upon. The Speaker calls one of them and the others then sit down. That process is called "catching the Speaker's eye."

Curiously, the House of Lords has a different custom. Its Chairman is the Lord Chancellor, who is a member of the Government, and, unlike the Speaker, he can and does make party speeches. On these occasions he rises and steps aside from his seat, which is called the Woolsack. Curiously, too, he does not decide who shall speak in the debate, as the Speaker does in the House of Commons. What happens is that one of the lords gets up and speaks without being called upon, and if two lords rise together to speak one gives way to the other.

DO ANY PEOPLE HAVE BLUE BLOOD?

In the old days many people had the belief that there were two sorts of human beings, the aristocrats and the common people. With this belief went another, that the aristocrats had a superior kind of blood—blue blood. Even in our own time this curious expression still lingers. The truth is, of course, that the blood of a healthy aristocrat is exactly the same as the blood of a healthy and obscure man. More important still it is to know that every human being has both red blood and blue blood. The red blood is in our arteries, while the blue, or more accurately the purplish, is in our veins.

Here is the thing that every boy and girl should know. The heart receives from the body, through the little tubes called veins, blood which has lost oxygen and become charged with carbon dioxid, and is therefore purplish. The heart then pumps this purplish blood into the lungs, and, as we breathe, the purplish blood loses its carbon dioxid, gains oxygen, and becomes bright red. This bright red blood then goes back to the heart, and is pumped all over the body, not through the veins, but through other little tubes called arteries. The blood passes in waves with each pumping, and that is why, when we put our finger on our wrists or our temple, we feel the wave which we call a pulse. That is why we must always breathe plenty of fresh air, so that our lungs may change blue blood into red.

THE NEXT WONDER QUESTIONS ARE ON PAGE 4277.

After traveling for some hours, they reached the place, and Princess Maybloom pulled off her stockings and dipped her feet into the fountain. The moment her feet touched the water they grew smaller.

THE STORY OF FAIRYFOOT

CONTINUED FROM 3986

ONCE upon a time there stood far away in the West Country a town called Stumpinghame. Stumpinghame had a king of its own, and his name was Stiffstep; his family was very ancient and large-footed. Great feet had been the fashion there from time immemorial, and the higher the family the larger were they. His queen, Hammerheel, was the greatest beauty in Stumpinghame. Her Majesty's shoe was not much smaller than a fishing-boat; and their six children promised to be quite as handsome, and all went well with them till the birth of their seventh son, when it was whispered throughout the city that the queen's seventh child had been born with such miserably small feet that they resembled nothing ever seen or heard of in Stumpinghame, except the feet of the fairies.

The king and queen were so ashamed of him that the young prince was sent secretly out to the pasture lands, to be brought up by the shepherds. The chief man there was called Fleecefold, and people came from all quarters to see the young prince.

The king and queen had given him fourteen names, beginning with Augustus; but the honest country people could not remember so many; besides, his feet were the most remarkable thing about the child, so with one accord they called him Fairyfoot.

He was a handsome boy, but the news of the court traveled to the shepherds, and Fairyfoot was despised among them. Fleecefold was ashamed to have him in his cottage, and as soon as he was old enough, Fairyfoot was sent every day to watch some sickly sheep that grazed on a wild, weedy pasture, near the forest.

Poor Fairyfoot, who was often lonely and sorrowful, was lying in the shadow of a mossy rock one warm summer noon, when a robin, pursued by a great hawk, flew into the old velvet cap which lay on the ground beside him. Fairyfoot covered it up, and the hawk, frightened by his shout, flew away.

"Now you may go, poor robin!" he said, opening his cap; but instead of the bird, out sprang a little man dressed in russet brown, looking as if he were a hundred years old. Fairyfoot could not speak for astonishment, but the little man said:

"Thank you for your shelter, and be sure I will do as much for you. Call on me if you ever want help; my name is Robin Goodfellow." And, darting off, he would have been out of sight in an instant had not Fairyfoot jumped up and called him back.

"What is it?" said the little man.

"I am very lonely, and no one will play with me, because my feet are not large enough," said Fairyfoot sadly.

4137

"Come, then, and play with us," said the little man. "We lead the merriest lives in the world, and care for nobody's feet; but there are two things you must mind—first, do as you see the rest doing; and, secondly, never speak of anything you may hear or see."

"I will do that, and anything more you like," said Fairyfoot. Then the little man, taking his hand, led him over the pasture into the forest, and along a mossy path among old trees wreathed with ivy, till they heard the sound of music, and came upon a meadow where the moon shone as bright as day, and all the flowers of the year bloomed together in the thick grass. There was a crowd of little men and women, some clad in russet color, but far more in green, dancing round a little well as clear as crystal. And under great rose-trees, which grew here and there in the meadow, companies were sitting round low tables covered with cups of milk, dishes of honey, and carved wooden flagons filled with clear red wine.

The little man led Fairyfoot to the nearest table and bade him drink. Immediately the red wine touched his lips, all his troubles seemed to leave him, and the little people about the well cried: "Welcome! welcome!" and everyone said: "Come and dance with me!" So Fairyfoot was as happy as a prince, and drank milk and ate honey till the moon was low in the sky; then the little man took him by the hand and led him back to his own bed of straw in the cottage corner.

Next morning Fairyfoot was not tired for all his dancing. Nobody in the cottage had missed him, and he went out with the sheep as usual; but every night all that summer, when the shepherds were safe in bed, the little man came and took him away to dance in the forest.

The wonder was that he was never tired or sleepy, as people are apt to be who dance all night; but before the summer was ended, Fairyfoot found out the reason. One night, when the moon was full, Robin Goodfellow came for him as usual, and away they went to the flowery green. The fun there was high, and Robin was in haste. So he only pointed to the carved cup from which Fairyfoot every night drank the clear red wine.

"I am not thirsty, and there is no use losing time," thought the boy, and he joined the dance; but never in all his life did Fairyfoot find it such hard work to keep pace with the company. Fairyfoot did his best, but at length he was glad to steal away and sit down behind a mossy oak, where his eyes closed for very weariness. When he awoke, the dance was nearly over, but two little ladies clad in green talked close beside him.

"What a beautiful boy!" said one of them. "What handsome feet he has!"

"Yes," said the other, "they are just like the feet Princess Maybloom had before she washed them in the Growing Well, which has now dried up. Nothing in this world can make them small again, you know."

When they were gone, Fairyfoot could sleep no more for astonishment. It amazed him that Princess Maybloom's father was troubled at her feet growing large. Besides, he wished to see that princess and her country. All that day he was so weary that he got into sad disgrace with the shepherd for neglecting his sheep. The old man beat him so cruelly that he determined to run away.

So on and on he ran, far into the forest, until at last, utterly exhausted, he sank down at the foot of a tree and fell fast asleep. When he awoke, he heard voices.

"What boy is this?" said a nightingale on a branch above him. "He cannot have come from Stumpinghame with such small and handsome feet."

"No," said another; "he has come from the West Country. How in the world did he find the way?"

"How simple you are!" said a third nightingale. "What had he to do but follow the ground-ivy which grows over height and hollow, bank and bush, from the lowest gate of the king's kitchen-garden to the root of this rose-tree?"

Fairyfoot was greatly astonished at this conversation, and thought it might be as well for him to follow the ground-ivy, and see Princess Maybloom. It was a long journey, but he found the gate at last, and walked through the garden, till a white fawn came frisking by, and he heard a voice saying sorrowfully:

"Come back, come back, my fawn! I cannot run and play with you now, my feet have grown so heavy." And, looking around, he saw the loveliest young princess in the world, dressed in snow-white, and wearing a wreath of roses on her golden hair. At once he guessed that

THE BOOK OF STORIES

this must be the Princess Maybloom, and made her a very humble bow.

"Royal princess, I have heard of your trouble because your feet have grown large, and I know of a certain fountain in my country that will make them smaller and finer than ever they were," said he.

When the princess heard that, she danced for joy in spite of her large feet, and she and her six maids brought Fairyfoot before the king, who consented to allow the princess to accompany Fairyfoot to the marvelous fountain.

After traveling for some hours, they reached the place, and, sitting down, Princess Maybloom pulled off her stockings and dipped her feet into the fountain. The moment her feet touched the water they grew smaller, and when she had washed and dried them three times, they were as small and finely shaped as Fairyfoot's. There was great joy among the company, and the princess thanked Fairyfoot again and again.

Just at that moment they heard a sound of music, and Fairyfoot knew it was the fairies going to their dancing-ground. Rising quickly, he took the Princess Maybloom by the hand, and all followed the music through the forest. At last they came to the flowery green. Robin Goodfellow welcomed the company for Fairyfoot's sake, and gave everyone a drink of the fairies' wine. So they danced there from sunset till the gray morning; but, before the lark sang, Robin Goodfellow took them all safe home.

There was great joy that day in the palace because Princess Maybloom's feet were made small again. The king gave Fairyfoot all manner of fine clothes and rich jewels; and when they heard his wonderful story, he and the queen asked him to live with them and be their son.

In the course of time Fairyfoot and Princess Maybloom were married, and they both lived happily ever after.

THE DOG THAT KNEW HIS MASTER
A TRUE TALE OF A SCOTTISH COLLIE

GOILA was a Scottish collie, born on a sheep-farm near the picturesque banks of Loch Goil. Hence the name which, by a child's happy freak, was his. His parents were of high degree on both sides, and had won prizes on the show-bench and in the trial-field.

When full grown, Goila was a perfect type of animal grace. The head was poised on a long, arched neck; the back broad, with an upward curve in the loins; the quarters muscular; the shoulders well set back and powerful; the legs rather high and never tiring; the body, except the deep chest, which boasted a snow-white "shirt-front," was covered with the glossiest blue-black coat, which one could feel was impenetrable to the sharpest cold; and the tail was large and bushy—a true flag-signal in frolic, peace or war.

But it was the head itself which won love and admiration: the broad skull was flanked by small, forward-drooping ears when quiet, but instantly erect when alert; the muzzle was smooth, fine and tapering, and a white line ran down the forehead; the eyes were full, bright, expressive, spirited and intelligent. Goila grew up more than a pet. With the children he was a comrade in fun and play; with the head of the household he was a

friend and companion in the best sense of the term.

Early in puppyhood Goila showed musical tastes. In the parlor was an upright piano, and it was noticed that Goila, if he possibly could get access to the room, lay beside the pedal just below the keyboard.

By and by, as his musical education progressed, so did his likes and dislikes in harmonies.

When some compositions were being played he became almost frantic, running round the room, barking angrily. Others seemed to please him, and he would crouch down on the carpet and emit a prolonged cry, which rose and fell with a distinct cadence. He was a loyalist: he invariably joined in with fervor, and not out of tune, when the children sang God Save the King.

One day, when it was known that there was no one in the parlor, notes were heard coming from the piano as if someone were striking the keys at random. When the door was opened, Goila was found standing on his hind legs, with his two fore-paws pressing here and there on the keys, the response from which was evidently to his intense delight. The hint was enough.

The children taught him, with assistance, of course, to pick out Haydn's Hymn not at all badly. He was a religious doggie, as he never ventured to utter a note during the Sunday evening hymn. But the greatest fun was when a German band came round to the street. The moment Goila heard the toot-toot he ran to the band with the keenest enjoyment. He jumped round the somewhat resentful musicians, howled and pranced approval or otherwise, and if, perchance, which was often the case, an inexpert or careless instrumentalist played a wrong note, Goila rushed at his heels. In fact, he became so unwelcome a critic that the band very soon ceased to come to the street.

He had social instincts. His most curious friendship was that with a tortoise. When the tortoise became accustomed to the dog, it put out its head from its shell, and allowed Goila to lick it. There was a step leading from the kitchen to the scullery, and another from the scullery to the

The dog stopped and pricked his ears.

back garden. When the tortoise wished to take its walks abroad, Goila would carefully assist it down the steps, and watch it with curious interest searching for and eating lettuce. But Goila's love for his mailed friend was the undoing of the latter. When autumn came, the tortoise dug a hole in the garden soil in which to sleep through the winter. Goila smelt him out, and excitedly rescued his friend from premature burial. From cold and want of his winter sleep the tortoise died.

Goila was a wonderful retriever both of children's boats and caps on the lake, as well as of articles artfully hidden in holes or beneath stones. He had cunning distinctions as to what was fair game. Early in the morning after a first day's stay in the schoolhouse of a Highland village, Goila was found to have brought to the kitchen door a rabbit and a partridge. We wished to live at peace with the gamekeeper, and solemnly admonished Goila never to bring in another

bird; we soothed our conscience by telling the dog that rabbits were vermin. Never another bird was found on the doorstep; but, truth to tell, there was occasionally rabbit-pie for dinner.

How long does a dog's memory remain fresh? It is hard to say. The writer had occasion to go abroad. Although Goila was supposed to be locked up when he left home to take the train for London, the dog came tearing along the departure platform as the guard gave the signal for the start, and was last seen galloping at a great speed and howling furiously as the train disappeared in the darkness of the night. Some days afterward he returned home, footsore and with a ragged coat. The dog was disconsolate; he lost all interest in his old home and its inmates, and after a few weeks disappeared. Seven years elapsed, and the writer returned to Scotland. One afternoon, a month afterward, in the southern district of his own town—Edinburgh —he saw Goila trotting at the tail of a butcher's cart. Merely on the off chance of a recognition, he called out: "Goila!" The dog stopped, pricked up his ears, gave a wild yelp of delight, circled round and round, leaped up with his fore-paws on the shoulders, and licked the dearly loved face of his old master.

When he was taken home his recognition of the children—so grown and so changed in the long interval—was immediate and most joyful. Indeed, he knew each one as individually as of old, and when old tricks were not called for would remind us of them. To the new members of the family, a small boy and a girl, he exhibited at first great curiosity which soon changed into kindly protection and almost monopoly.

But the new joy was very short-lived. Before many months had gone Goila had again disappeared, as if it had all been a dream; and, despite every inquiry by advertisement and otherwise, he was, to our great sorrow, heard of no more.

UNDINE, THE STORY OF A WATER NYMPH

ONCE upon a time, many years ago, there lived an old fisherman and his wife. They were lonely people, for their bit of land lay upon the edge of a large lake, while back of it stretched an enchanted forest through which lay the road to the market where the old man sold his fish. To their great joy, it came to pass that a child was born to them, a beautiful little girl. One day as the mother sat by the edge of the lake, her baby in her arms, the child, attracted by some beautiful thing in its clear depths, leaped forward into the water, sank instantly below its surface and was gone. That same evening, while the parents were mourning the loss of their child, a tap came at the cottage door and a lovely little girl about three or four years of age stood upon the threshold.

The fisherman and his wife took her in gladly and brought her up as their own daughter. When the girl was about eighteen years old, there came through the enchanted forest to the old fisherman's hut a wonderful knight named Huldbrand. He had made his way through the gloom and mysteries of the forest with great difficulty. Horrible little dwarfs had tried to frighten him away; a great tall man, with flowing robes, had continually blocked his path.

Hardly had the knight reached the shelter of the cottage when a great storm came up which lasted several days. The water of the lake rose to such an extent that the little promontory where the old couple and their foster-daughter lived became an island and all passage out into the world beyond was cut off. During this time the lovely Undine and the handsome knight were very much together, and became very fond of each other.

One night while the storm was still raging, a priest, who had been driven to their shore by the fury of the waves, sought the protection and shelter of the little cottage. The good father soon became aware of the attachment of the young couple, and before the evening was over it was arranged, much to the joy of her foster-parents, that Undine and the knight should be joined in holy wedlock.

Now it happens, as perhaps you've heard, that the air and elements among which we live are inhabited by beings as wonderful as ourselves, and far more beautiful. Especially are the seas and rivers, and even the little brooks, full of these lovely beings, so like us but with this great difference, that they have no souls. Therefore, when they die they vanish into dust, leaving no trace behind, and have no hope of a more beautiful after-life. To find a soul it is necessary for one of these lovely creatures to become united to one of our race, and it was for this purpose that Undine's father, a great prince of the Mediterranean Sea, had sent his little daughter to the fisherman's cottage that night so long ago.

When Huldbrand became aware of this fact he was at first dismayed, but Undine was so lovely, and indeed since the night of the wedding so changed, so gentle, so biddable, that he dismissed his fears, and clasping her to him, vowed eternal love and protection. The morning after the wedding found the sun shining gloriously and the waters so far receded that there was no longer need of delay. So, accompanied by Father Heilmann—Undine mounted upon the knight's horse, Huldbrand walking at her side—they started back through the enchanted forest.

The sudden departure and long disappearance of the young knight Huldbrand had caused great consternation among his friends in the royal city, and great, therefore, was the rejoicing at the return of the knight, accompanied by his beautiful bride. There was one, however, who could not rejoice. This was Bertalda, foster-child of the Duke and the Duchess of the imperial city; for she it was who had sent the knight into the enchanted forest as a test of his love for her. So there was, as you can see, nothing but jealousy in her heart for the young bride who had won his love at the other end of the dark forest. For Bertalda, however, Undine soon felt the greatest affection, and when she discovered from her uncle Kühleborn, a powerful water sprite, who inhabited the waters of that region and with whom she had frequent intercourse, that Bertalda was no other than the lost daughter of the old fisherman and his wife, her joy knew no bounds.

Thinking in her innocent heart to give a delightful surprise, she planned a dinner, at the end of which the secret of Bertalda's birth, which up to that time had remained a mystery, was to be revealed. At the appointed time the old fisherman and his wife were led into the dining hall, and Undine, with every mark of affection and delight at giving so much happiness, proclaimed them Bertalda's long-lost parents. Bertalda, however, who never for an instant had dreamed but that some lady of high rank would claim her as her child, was enraged at what she considered an attempt to humble her in the eyes of Huldbrand and all his guests. She treated the poor old couple so discourteously that the Duke and Duchess withdrew their protection, and her own parents refused to accept her as their child until she should show a change of heart, and in habit befitting her lowly birth come to them alone through the enchanted forest as proof of her regard.

Feeling that the disastrous results of her plan must have made the city forever distasteful to Undine, Huldbrand decided to start the next morning for Castle Ringstetten, situated near the source of the Danube River. As they drove out of the city they encountered Bertalda in the costume of a fishermaiden, forsaken by everyone, trying to sell her fish as means of a livelihood.

At sight of Bertalda's misfortune Undine was full of sympathy, and would hear of nothing but that Bertalda should accompany them on their journey and that they should share all things as sisters in love and affection. For a time all went well at Castle Ringstetten, but gradually Bertalda lost her suddenly acquired humility; she became again the proud and haughty lady, and encouraged by the admiration which Huldbrand no longer strove to conceal, she frequently assumed the position which Undine as rightful lady of the castle should have held. Kühleborn, ever watchful for the welfare of his niece, became aware of her unhappiness, and by his frequent visits and sudden appearances in the castle frightened Bertalda and added to the knight's growing aversion to his gentle wife. At last, in order to prevent the reappearance of her mysterious relative, Undine ordered the great fountain in the courtyard of the castle to be sealed up. For a time again all went well, Huldbrand felt a return of affection for his trusting wife, and secure in their newfound happiness, Undine suggested a

much-talked-of trip down the Danube as far as Vienna. Bertalda of course was to accompany them, and they began to plan their journey with great delight.

Undine had often warned her husband against showing any trace of anger or displeasure toward her while on the water, but no sooner had they entered the domain of the watchful Kühleborn than they were tormented by his impish tricks. Undine had constantly to rebuke him for his insolence, and their pleasure was completely spoiled. Kühleborn's mischievous pranks became more and more violent, until in a flash of rage Huldbrand commanded his trembling wife to return to her mysterious kindred of the sea and trouble him no more. In the greatest distress Undine began to weep. "Alas," said she, "farewell. They shall do you no harm, only remain true so that I may be able to keep them from you. I must, alas, go away! Oh, woe, woe, what have you done! Oh, woe, woe!" She vanished over the side of the vessel and disappeared from sight, but it seemed as if the little waves kept saying: "Oh, woe, woe; remain true; woe, woe!"

The Lord of Ringstetten and Bertalda returned alone to the castle and for some time lived in mourning and great sorrow, thinking only of their love for Undine and forgetting entirely their feeling for each other. But as often happens, gradually the knight's sorrow grew less. He thought less often of Undine and more often and with still greater fondness of Bertalda. At last the nuptial day was set, and Father Heilmann was summoned to perform the ceremony. Upon receiving the summons, the priest immediately set out for the castle, not indeed to perform the marriage rite, but if possible to prevent it, for Undine had appeared to him in a dream imploring him to prevent the marriage, and thus to save Huldbrand's life, for she was still alive. In spite of Father Heilmann's advice, preparations for the coming festival went on according to arrangement, and indeed, all might have been well had not Bertalda bemoaned the fact that the fountain, from which such healing waters used to flow, had been sealed up. One of her maidens, hoping to please her new mistress, hastened to summon attendants to lift the stone from the fountain. The task proved an easy one, for scarcely had they touched it when, as if impelled by some hidden power, the giant stone rolled away, and from the opening of the fountain rose a female figure draped in white. Weeping bitterly and wringing her slender hands, the sorrowful figure glided silently through the courtyard and up the stairs to the knight's own room, where he stood lost in gloomy melancholy.

He was pondering in his heart the meaning of a dream he had had the previous night. It seemed to him a dream, but his spirit had in reality been translated to the Mediterranean Sea, where Undine now dwelt. He could see her sitting beneath a crystal arch weeping bitterly. Presently her uncle Kühleborn approached her and, as if to warn her anew, they talked of the danger he would incur by leaving his castle or opening the fountain, should he indeed marry Bertalda. "But," said Undine, "I have prevented that, for he is now in spirit hovering over the sea, listening to our conversation, and he will remain true to me." And ever and anon through his dream floated the exquisite music of the Swan Song, symbol of death.

But now, in spite of all warning, he had broken his vow of faith and love, and Undine had been sent to perform her mournful task. "They have opened the spring and you must die," she said very gently. Paralyzed with terror and the certainty that his end had come, Huldbrand nevertheless felt his breast swell once more with love for this beautiful creature, for raising her veil, Undine appeared before him fair as when he had wooed her beyond the enchanted forest.

Drawing him to the couch, she laid her head against his breast, and encircling him with her arms, she wept and wept until he, too, began to weep, and finally, exhausted, sank back upon the pillows dead. "I have wept him to death," she said to a group of maidens as she passed.

They buried him in a little country churchyard near the castle. In the funeral procession was a white-robed figure that wept unceasingly. When the mourners knelt, it knelt too, but when the rest arose, the white figure had vanished and in its place gushed forth a little silver streamlet that gradually encircled the knight's grave and continues to do so to this very day.

LA PLUS SAGE FILLE DU WESSEX

THE ENGLISH VERSION OF THIS STORY IS GIVEN ON PAGE 5441.

IL y avait autrefois un Roi de Wessex appelé Ina. Il était grand, brave et beau, mais avait un grand défaut. La moindre des choses le vexait et le mettait dans une colère terrible. Le sachant, il décida d'épouser une fille sage qui pourrait le calmer et le diriger. Une après-midi, il quitta Winchester et alla dans la grande forêt, à cheval. Ayant soif, il s'arrêta à la cabane d'un bûcheron pour boire du lait. La jolie fille du bûcheron lui apporta du lait et quand il lui rendit le gobelet, il lui dit:

"Je suis le Roi de Wessex, Ina. Videz toutes les mers du monde avec ce gobelet et je vous ferai ma Reine."

Edith entra dans la cabane, en ressortit avec une poignée d'étoupe et la tendant au Roi Ina, elle s'écria gaiement:

"Barrez toutes les rivières avec cette étoupe et j'obéirai à votre désir."

"Vous êtes celle que j'ai cherchée," dit le Roi Ina.

Et il la mit sur son cheval et la conduisit à son palais de Winchester.

Mais juste avant le mariage, Edith lui dit:

"Vous savez que vous avez l'humeur ombrageuse. Promettez-moi donc, si vous vous fâchez avec moi et me chassez du palais, de me laisser emporter un cadeau d'adieu."

Le Roi Ina y consentit, naturellement. Comme ils étaient à souper, un soir, Ina fut offensé par un bon conseil que sa femme lui donna, et s'écria:

"Vous vous mêlez trop de mes affaires. Demain vous retournerez avec votre père à votre cabane."

Quand son mari eut le dos tourné, elle versa une potion dans son breuvage, ce qui le fit s'endormir. Ensuite, elle le fit transporter doucement à la cabane dans la forêt.

"Qui m'a conduit ici?" cria-t-il en s'éveillant le lendemain matin.

"C'est moi, chéri," dit la Reine Edith. "Vous êtes mon cadeau d'adieu."

"Ah!" dit le Roi Ina en l'embrassant, "j'ai eu raison d'épouser la plus jolie fille du Wessex, et aussi la plus sage!"

THE FABLES OF ÆSOP THE SLAVE

THE PEACOCK AND JUNO

A PEACOCK, feeling one day quite discontented, said to the goddess Juno:

"Why did you not give me such a good voice as the nightingale? Everyone is pleased to hear its voice, whereas I am laughed at for the ugly, screaming noise I make."

Juno, who was very much concerned at the discontent of her favorite bird, replied:

"True, the nightingale has a fine voice, but you have the advantage in your beauty and elegance."

"But what is the use of my silent beauty when I have such a poor voice?" demanded the peacock.

Juno dismissed him, saying:

"Each creature has some of the good things of nature. This one has beauty, that one a glorious voice, another strength, and so on, and each should be content with its particular quality."

Be content with what you have.

THE FOX AND THE FROG

A FROG one day told the animals in the forest that he was able to cure all kinds of illness. He spoke in a hoarse croak that was little understood, and the animals therefore admired his learning, and believed what he said. A fox, however, who happened to be passing at the time, said, with indignation:

"How can you have the impudence to offer to cure others when you have such an ugly spotted body and horrible croaking voice?"

People should cure their own faults before finding faults in others.

THE HEN AND THE FOX

A HUNGRY fox went into a fowlhouse in search of something to satisfy his appetite. He saw, sitting on a perch, a fat hen; but, try as he would, he was unable to reach her. At last he thought of trying to make her descend from her position.

"Cousin hen," said he, "I heard that you were ill, and so I have come to inquire how you are now. Come down, and I will feel your pulse, and tell you what to do to get better."

"True, I am not feeling very well," answered the hen; "but I am sure that I should catch my death if I happened to come down from this cozy perch."

Flattery is the last resort of fools.

LE ROI, LE NOBLE ET LE PAYSAN

THE ENGLISH VERSION OF THIS STORY IS GIVEN ON PAGE 857.

LOUIS XII de France apprit un jour qu'un certain noble avait très brutalement châtié un paysan. Comme le Roi était appelé le "Père du Peuple," et était vraiment adoré de tous ses sujets à cause de sa bonté de cœur, on peut s'imaginer combien il dut être irrité et désolé. Il résolut de donner au noble une leçon sur la façon de traiter ceux qui étaient moins fortunés que lui, mais il ne révéla pas son plan. Pendant plusieurs semaines il réfléchit et à la fin il trouva un plan qui, selon lui, devait être excellent.

Un jour il invita le noble à son palais et le garda à dîner. Il ne dîna pas avec son hôte, mais fit servir au seigneur un banquet magnifique. Tout ce qu'on peut imaginer de meilleur à manger fut servi, excepté du pain, car le Roi avait donné l'ordre absolu que l'on ne serve pas de pain. Le noble fut naturellement surpris par cette omission, mais, par courtoisie, n'osa pas demander une chose aussi petite et commune, en présence de tant de mets rares et délicats. Mais de plus en plus il sentit le manque de pain, tant que vers la fin du repas, il était presque enragé par l'absence d'une chose aussi nécessaire.

A ce moment le Roi entra.

"Monsieur," dit le Roi à son hôte, "vous a-t-on servi un bon repas?"

"Sire," répondit le noble, "on m'a servi un festin superbe, un festin de Roi. Et cependant, pour dire à Votre Majesté toute la vérité, il me semble que je n'ai pas bien dîné; car, pour vivre, le pain est nécessaire, et il n'y avait pas de pain à ce banquet."

"Allez," dit Louis XII, sévèrement; "et comprenez bien la leçon que j'ai désiré vous donner. Puisque vous avez besoin de pain pour vous satisfaire, apprenez à traiter plus humainement ceux qui travaillent pour le faire pousser, afin qu'on vous le serve."

THE NEXT STORIES ARE ON PAGE 4193.